The History of Government and Public Law in China

Xin Nie

The History of Government and Public Law in China

商務印書館
创于1897
The Commercial Press

Springer

Xin Nie
Law School
Tsinghua University
Beijing, China

ISBN 978-981-97-6062-6 ISBN 978-981-97-6063-3 (eBook)
https://doi.org/10.1007/978-981-97-6063-3

Jointly published with The Commercial Press, Ltd.
The print edition is not for sale in China (Mainland). Customers from China (Mainland) please order the print book from: The Commercial Press, Ltd.

This work is supported by the Chinese Fund for the Humanities and Social Sciences

This Springer imprint is published by the registered company Springer Nature Singapore Pte Ltd.
The registered company address is: 152 Beach Road, #21-01/04 Gateway East, Singapore 189721, Singapore

Preface

Traditionally, Chinese legal historians focused on criminal law, and their teaching and textbook compilations revolved around the history of criminal law, which might be attributed to the tradition of criminal law that "unified all laws without distinguishing civil and criminal matters". In recent years, overseas scholars have directed much domestic research to traditional customary law, civil contracts and adjudication, but scant attention has been paid to the history of traditional politics and law (history of political systems and public law) in the field of teaching and research. Personally, I think that the ancient Chinese legal tradition has had a particularly profound impact not on today's criminal law or civil customary law because they (together with their studies) have been fully modernized ("Westernized"), but on public law where it is clear to see traces of traditional institutions and thoughts with the modern Chinese supervision system as typically a new leaf growing out of an old tree. In traditional China of centralized power and a highly developed bureaucracy, even private law and norms in the Western sense were both public and private in nature, and even more public than private. For example, the land system used to be an important issue in public law and politics in traditional China.

A Japanese scholar proposed a "train model for a country with a large population", comparing the living environment there as a crowded train at peak hours. In the packed carriages, a wide variety of passengers cannot take up the average space so that they have to restrain themselves, both defending their minimum space and making moderate concessions and adjustments toward others. "The silent mutual shoving and compromise helps to seek an equilibrium that satisfies (or can be tolerated by) all passengers on board". The crowded train concept of society "repudiated individual claims on interests, or more precisely, restricted pursuit of them as 'selfish', fostering a logical world view based on creation of group order". "This type of power structure inevitably transcended a world of innumerable competing private interests", "seeking and giving authority to public entities that aimed to promote peaceful coexistence of concerned parties". The government emphasized "self-restraint" of the people, preaching "the fault with pursuit of private interest" and confronting a litigious society with "an aversion to litigation". "Through the rhetoric of public versus private and group versus individual, the authorities in fact deprived the individual of any absolute justification for private claims, and subtly installed public power as representative of the general interest" (Hiroaki, 2012, pp. 415–421). This might explain the fact that public power was so dominant in ancient China that people liked "appealing to the government" in all circumstances and even somewhat relied on it (e.g., for disaster relief).

In modern China, nomology was largely viewed as "Western learning" and legal modernization was equated with Westernization. Social Darwinists thought that "complete Westernization" was the only way to save the nation from ruin, but questions arose as to "what survival meant" and "who we would be without national quintessence" (Pusey, 1983/2009, p. 104). The more national is said to be the more international in English language. Culture exists because of its uniqueness. "A nation cannot erase the past culture of its own, and it is impossible to do so". "A nation should have her dignity, and would hate to say its inferiority to others in every way" (Wang, 2012, p. 62). "Complete Westernization" caused many problems such as inadaptability of law to national circumstances, loss of self-confidence on the part of national psychology, and restrained national spirit. China's legal modernization is still difficult and one of the major reasons is that it has not been able to coordinate with the traditions in the course. The modernization drive has failed to make full use of local resources and obtain assistance from tradition by opposing itself to tradition, ending up "partially profound". Modern Chinese legal civilization should be created with Chinese people as the main body, China's reality as the raw material, and foreign materials and methods as the references (Cai, 2005, p. 18). The legacy of traditional political system and culture must, of course, play a role in developing and innovating modern Chinese public law.

My research interests include legal history, comparative jurisprudence and constitutional law with the history of public law and comparative constitutional law as my specialization. In 2008, I came to work at Tsinghua University and, in the next spring, proposed to teach postgraduates a new course, "History of Chinese Politics and Law", covering the history of Chinese public law (constitutional law and administrative law), specifically the official system, finance, economics, talent selection, justice and supervision in ancient China, and the major issues of constitution making, law revision, national assembly, justice and supervision in modern China, because such a course had been rarely offered in Chinese universities. Although Ch'ien Tuan-sheng, a renowned scholar during the period of the Republic of China (hereafter ROC), compiled *History of Political Institution in the Republic of China* and delivered lectures on Chinese government and politics at Harvard University in the 1940s, but both his book and lectures focused merely on the Republican period and ignored ancient China. Given the inconsistency of ancient Chinese legal system with modern constitution and administrative law in terms of concepts and connotations, I named the course "History of Chinese Politics and Law" instead of "History of Chinese Public Law". I declined some senior professors' suggestion to name the course "History of Chinese Political Institutions" because the students were from the law school and my research path was not situated in the field of the traditional political history. Methodologically, this course is related to jurisprudence, history and political science, and specifically to constitutional administrative law, legal history, comparative law, and government organization with the purpose of empowering students with relevant knowledge, interdisciplinary research skills, and a deeper understanding of the sporadic resurfacing of the traditional political and legal system and its culture in China's modernization drive. Since 2009, I had been teaching postgraduates "History of Chinese Politics and Law"; ten years later, I offered the course to undergraduates, and the enrollment was large, which prompted me to prepare the course handouts for publication. I decided to title the book *The History of Government and Public Law in China* by dispelling doubts "whether ancient and modern legal concepts can match up" and "whether there was public law in ancient China". Personally, this might be called a resolution.

This book is sort of a "reading journal".[1] As a textbook of a general history of the legal system, it contains some discussions that are not within the author's area of interest, but "occasional observations" after "a little learning". "Ancient learning is quite general whereas modern learning is highly specialized". The academic research in contemporary China is increasingly specialized so that it is unthinkable to "keep the whole history in mind" as Qian Mu did. Knowledge explosion confined academics to exploration of a single area or several minor areas and publication of thematically concentrated papers as the primary indicator of academic performance assessment. Reading for pleasure is a luxury for scholars who "have taken research as their profession" because, generally speaking, we "read materials" merely for writing papers, which is not true reading. However, humanities research needs to be supported by the pleasure in academic devotion, and satisfaction gained from a wide and impractical reading delighted me so much as to carry me away from worries and the stark reality of "publish or perish".

Beijing, China Xin Nie

References

1. Cai, S. (2005). *Zhongguo fali zijue de fazhan* [Self-conscious development of Chinese nomology]. Tsinghua University Press.
2. Hiroaki, T. (2012). *Quanyi yu yuanyi: Sitianhaoming zhongguo fashi lunji* [Rights and injustice: Collected essays on Chinese legal history] (Y. Wang, et al. Trans). Tsinghua University Press. (Original work published 1953).
3. Pusey, J. (2009). *Zhongguo yu Daerwen* China and Charles Darwin (Y. Zhong, Trans.). Jiangsu People's Press. (Original work published 1983).
4. Wang, B. (2012). *Zhongguo lishi tonglun* [A general history of China]. SDX Joint Publishing Company.

[1] The lazy author here does not use "book journal" in the literal sense that keeps record of the reader's observations, but means it to be those notes on the margins and slips of note in the books.

Contents

About the Author

Xin Nie is a scholar of Chinese law and legal history at Tsinghua University. He is a member of the 14th National Committee of the Chinese People's Political Consultative Conference (CPPCC). His research fields include legal history, comparative law, constitutional law and legal education.

His scholarly work includes over 40 papers published in both Chinese and English academic journals. His books include *Experiments and Improvements in Representation* (The Commercial Press, 2021), *The History of Chinese Public Law* (The Commercial Press, 2020), *The Judiciary in Modern China* (The Commercial Press, 2019), *Studies on the Constitution of the Republic of China* (City University of Hong Kong Press, 2017), *Between China and the West: Legal modernization in historical and comparative perspective* (Law Press China, 2015), and *Lectures on the History of Chinese Legal System* (Peking University Press, 2014). He is the translator of the book *Goodbye, Montesquieu: The New Separation of Powers* (China University of Political Science & Law Press, 2016).

Professor Nie was recognized as one of the Top Ten Outstanding Young Jurists in 2020. He is also a leading talent in philosophy and social sciences under the "National Talents Program". He is the Executive Director of the Chinese Legal History Research Association and the Secretary-General of the Basic Law Research Association. He was ever been the Deputy Director of the Trial Management Office at the Supreme People's Court.

Professor Nie is a graduate of Nanjing University (B.A.), Peking University (LL.B.), and Renmin University of China (Ph.D.). He has also been a visiting scholar at Harvard Law School. He teaches "Comparative Law", "Chinese Legal History" and "The History of Chinese Public Law" to graduates and undergraduates respectively at Tsinghua.

About the Translators

Xiao Lin is an Associate Professor at the School of Foreign Languages, Jiangxi University of Finance and Economics. She holds a Ph.D. in Literature from Peking University (2016) and was a visiting scholar at the State University of New York (2014–2015). Her research focuses on language and identity, translation competence development, and medical translation.

Li Chunchang is a Professor at the School of Foreign Languages, Jiangxi University of Finance and Economics. He holds a Ph.D. in Literature from Sun Yat-sen University (2006) and was a Visiting Scholar at the University of Cambridge, UK (2013–2014) and the University of Florida, USA (2019–2020). His primary research focuses on British and American literature and translation studies.

Lu Ying is a Lecturer at the School of Foreign Languages, Renmin University of China. She holds a Ph.D. in culture studies from Tilburg University (2020). Her main focus in research and teaching is on sociolinguistics, online culture and cultural diversity, English public speaking and society and culture in the context of globalization.

Chapter 1
Chinese Feudal Society and System of Rites

1.1 The Shang-Zhou Revolution

Historical records of the Xia Dynasty are scanty, the Shang Dynasty may be a tribal alliance, and "it is still unknown if the Zhou was a region in the Shang or an independent country having close ties to the Shang." Although the Zhou seemed to be formally the Shang's vassal after Wuding's conquest, there are still many inconsistencies in name and events (Zhang, 2013, pp. 165–166). This chapter focuses on the Zhou Dynasty and unfolds with a comparison of the Shang and the Zhou Dynasties. "The Zhou was old, but its mission was new", and the transformation from the Shang to the Zhou was historically known as the "Shang-Zhou Revolution" led by the Duke of Zhou (Ji Dan). "The Zhou, a tiny and weak country in contrast with the Shang, overpowered the Shang in a single battle in Muye. On the one hand, the Zhou people believed the military feat to be a miracle that only the mandate of heaven could explain. On the other, God exclusive to the Shang people no longer blessed the Shang so that the Zhou's campaign was ordained by God instead of blood and tribal relations. The Zhou was chosen to receive the Mandate of Heaven because the Shang had failed morally and the Zhou had done the otherwise" (Hsu, 2012, p. 117). Having seized the power, the Zhou had to design rites and compose music to be politically and governmentally innovative so that their regime could be legitimatized.

1.1.1 Political View from Looking-Up to Looking-Down

i. The transcendental concept of "Heaven"

The Shang people were superstitious, believing in ghosts and divination, such that they entrusted their national destiny to the gods of the unknown world and to the ancestor-like gods, while the Zhou's Mandate of Heaven was universal. Similar to such ancient culture as Egypt, the Shang people had a theocratic tradition and paid

X. Nie, *The History of Government and Public Law in China*,
https://doi.org/10.1007/978-981-97-6063-3_1

special attention to religious affairs. It was recorded in the oracle bone scripts that a king of the Shang sacrificed hundreds of animals for peace merely because of his tinnitus. King Zhou of the Shang, ignoring the boiling public discontent, believed that the national destiny depended on God's favor instead of the hearts of the people. The king represented the supreme authority among his subjects; "On the king's part, he demanded that the people 'obey the words I have spoken to you'; otherwise, he 'will put your children to death with you' and 'you will find no forgiveness'" (The Speech of King Tang, *Book of Documents*) (Chang, 1980, p. 200). In terms of religion, "the Chinese 'Heaven', unlike the Egyptian or the Mesopotamian concepts, replaced the Shang 'God' as the highest deity in the Zhou Dynasty, embodying natural phenomena. It ...was both God and a transcendental concept and the latter made it universal ... The Mandate of Heaven was changeable, helping only moral people, so that the two transcendental concepts of universality and morality were consequently united into one. This breakthrough established ancient China as one of the pivotal human civilizations along with the Jewish and Greek civilizations" (Hsu, 1998, p. 376).

ii. The emphasis on "morality"

Both the Shang and the Zhou appear to have believed in theocracy and the supreme power of Heaven, and to have accepted the king as the agent of Heaven on earth. Kings of the Zhou assumed themselves to be "Sons of Heaven". Although the Zhou derived the "Mandate of Heaven" from the Shang and claimed to have received a "divine order", they created the "rule of morality" to amend the "Mandate of Heaven", proposing that "Heaven was just and blessed only the moral", "Only the worthy deserved the Mandate of Heaven", and "Morality should be promoted and punishment, prudent". In this way, "the transition from the Xia and the Shang was made to celebrate morality, and neglect of morality led to their downfall". There was no such a word as "morality" in the Shang records. "Man had been powerless with an all-powerful Heaven, but he began to take on responsibilities for himself upon the establishment of the Zhou Dynasty. Heaven blessed when man did well, and struck otherwise so that Heaven had to follow man" (Gu, 2015, pp. 51–52). The Zhou people conclusively attributed their replacement of the Shang Dynasty to its immorality, attributing this moral assessment to social reality based on the people's support. The Duke of Zhou cautioned the people and encouraged them to know that it was back-breaking to establish a country which they should protect with intense devotion. The "Shang people" (traders) came to be a synonym for the merchants' profession. Even now, under no circumstance will a Chinese say he has no morals.

1.1.2 A Comparison of the Shang and Zhou

Shang	Zhou
worship spirits	worship Heaven and emphasize man's initiative
advanced handicrafts and trade	advanced agriculture, promoted agriculture and downplayed trade
writing (oracle bone scripts)	writing (bronze inscriptions)
a variety of eastern tribal lives: chaos	a typically western tribal life: order
communication in commerce	a political mode required by an agriculture empire
loosely knit coalition government of tribal nations	closely knit feudal government

It is noteworthy that the Zhou and Shang were not diametrical opposites although they had different cultures and institutions. "When establishing their government on the Shang's land, the Zhou respected and even absorbed indigenous systems on the condition that their rule was not threatened". "They brought their own institutions and customs to the newly established eastern colony, but they were not bigoted in following their old ancestral systems. Such vassal states as Lu and Teng were well-known in ancient literature as 'fundamentalists' in practicing the Zhou culture, but they respected the old systems of the Shang and even invited the Shang people to assist them in making laws and running the country" (Wang, 2018, p. 13).

1.1.3 Questions

i. What happened during the transition from the Shang to the Zhou?

   (1) Divination declined.
   (2) Heaven-man relations went from indirect to direct.
   (3) Materially, bronze ware with inscriptions was invented in middle Western Zhou Dynasty.
   (4) The society was dominated by an agricultural mindset in terms of commerce.

ii. The power structure the Zhou Dynasty had built dominated the majority of the Chinese history, but was it the only native political path for China? The Shang's political mode might point to an alternative that had been annihilated.

Of course, the Shang might be more productive than the Zhou, but it was clearly less developed than the latter in terms of culture and politics because the institutions of the Zhou were said to be "splendidly diverse" (Confucius). Next is a detailed discussion of the Zhou's institutions.

1.2 System of Rites

1.2.1 Origin and Development of Rites

As a code of conduct, the earliest rites originated from the sacrificial customs in the era of family clans. When classes were clearly defined and countries came into being, some spiritual principles reflecting hierarchical differences and autocratic requirements were gradually abstracted and summarized from the concrete rituals, forming a series of principles and norms regulating the social life in the class society, i.e., the abstract principles of rites. The symbolic rituals continued to function institutionally. Historical records show that "rites" existed as rules of conduct during the Xia and Shang Dynasties. Confucius once said, "It is knowable that the Shang Dynasty adopted and modified the rites of the Xia Dynasty; so is it that the Zhou did the same to the rites of the Shang", which shows a close relationship among the Xia, Shang, and Western Zhou in terms of the rite system. Especially in the early years of the Western Zhou after the Duke of Zhou instituted the rites, the rites of the Zhou evolved into an enormous system playing a regulatory role in all aspects of national and social life.

i. Customs, rites, national law

> A nation has laws as a region has customs. (*Guanzi*)
> Rites should comply with folk customs while government should be subject to the top. (*Shenzi*)
> Rites are based on customs while ceremonies are contingent upon human nature. (The Treatise on Rites, *Records of the Grand Historian*)

The rite system originated from folk customs, an ancient source. The rite of the Zhou Dynasty was not quite the same as the folk customs because the feudal Zhou, no more a small or elementary community based on regional or blood ties, had a well-developed political system with considerable public administration and political power. The rite system, unlike the legal system, did not separate itself totally from politics (administration) so that the latter could not have an independent role and purpose. Furthermore, it resorted to native interpersonal relations—"Humans-initiated rites need to comply with customs"—so as to restore and keep good human nature.

ii. Rites and criminal code

Rites hailed from sacrifice with a special emphasis on ceremonies so that rites and ceremonies were usually used together and we Chinese regularly call China a country of rites and ceremonies. "Rites are different among different levels of society" so that different classes of people needed to "know their own place". Even today, politeness actually means "addressing different people in their different ways". For example, elders and children, teachers and students all have their own place like the difference between the addresses "will you" and "would you". "All are equal before the law", but there is relative inequality and uneven distribution in reality so that it is usually the weak in the imbalanced relations that make complaints. Ancient Chinese said that "Violations of rites shall be held criminally liable" and that "Any conduct inconsistent with rites incurs a penalty". Anyone who breached rites ran the risk of a penalty. The two norms, rites and criminal code, when put together in the Western Zhou period, are approximately equal to the laws of modern countries.

1.2.2 Classification of Rites

Generally speaking, rites largely include abstract spiritual principles (substance) and concrete forms.

i. Substance

Abstract spiritual principles such as loyalty, filial piety, continence, righteousness, benevolence and empathy are all fundamentals of rites with the nearness of the kinship and respect for the superiors at the core, emphasizing hierarchical place and difference.

ii. Form

Formally, rites are usually said to be five, six and nine types. The "five types" refer to auspicious, inauspicious, hosting, military, and congratulatory rites.

1.2.3 Culture of Rites and Music

Similarity and union are the aim of music; difference and distinction, that of ceremony. From union comes mutual affection; from difference, mutual respect.

Music is (an echo of) the harmony between heaven and earth; ceremonies reflect the orderly distinctions (in the operations of) heaven and earth.

> From that harmony all things receive their being; to those orderly distinctions they owe the differences between them.
>
> (Music Rites from the *Book of Rites*)
>
> The rise and fall of previous dynasties depend on music … pleasure comes from the harmonious hearts instead of the tune.
>
> (*Essentials of Politics under the Reign of Emperor Taizong in the Tang Dynasty*)

In a broad sense, rites included rites themselves and music so that a principle for interpersonal relationship was "harmony in diversity". Music played a significant role not only in religion, politics, education and military, but also in social integration, i.e., achieving harmonious joy with the people by collective singing and dancing (carnival) (Yan, 1996, p. 482). Today, programs like "The Same Song", "The Festive Gala" still air on Chinese media to aim at universal happiness.

1.2.4 Universal Application of the Rites of Zhou

In the Western Zhou Dynasty, rites regulated all aspects of life including public administration, justice, military, religion, education, and even ethics, morality, and family life. "The course (of duty), virtue, benevolence, and righteousness cannot be fully carried out without the rules of propriety; nor are training and oral lessons for the rectification of manners complete; nor can the clearing up of quarrels and discriminating in disputes be accomplished; nor can (the duties between) ruler and minister, high and low, father and son, elder brother and younger, be determined; nor can students for office and (other) learners, in serving their masters, have an attachment for them; nor can majesty and dignity be shown in assigning the different places at court, in the government of the armies, and in discharging the duties of office so as to secure the operation of the laws; nor can there be the (proper) sincerity and gravity in presenting the offerings to spiritual Beings on occasions of supplication, thanksgiving, and the various sacrifices." (*Book of Rites*)[1]

1.3 Feudalism

"In the Chinese context, 'feudalism' refers to the practice that the monarch enfeoffed or recognized vassal states and granted hereditary title to their rulers; conversely, an empire might be divided into commanderies and counties respectively administered for a certain term by governors and magistrates the central government had appointed. In short, the former was a federal union of vassal states, and the latter, a centralized empire" (Yang, 2015, p. 95). The Zhou king divided the land and population among the vassals or feudal lords so that vassal states were founded; those lords did the same to their ministers (*qing*, 卿) and grand masters (*dafu*, 大夫) so that aristocratic families came into being. Consequently, a pyramid shaped feudal system was formed from the Son of Heaven down to feudal lords, ministers, grand masters, servicemen and commoners. Feudalism was closely connected with the patriarchal clan system (*zongfa*, 宗法) when coming to the House of Ji including the Son of Heaven (king of Zhou) and some feudal lords. The king of Zhou was both the political ruler and the major clan (*dazong*, 大宗) of the House of Ji in the country, a combination of political leadership and kinship which was the essence of feudalism. In the transformation from feudalism to monarchy, the lords annexed land by various means, but they kept it to themselves by suspending or delaying its feoffment to anyone else. This is how the "county" originated because "suspending" (*xuan*, 悬) and "county" (*xian*, 县) were the same characters and had the same pronunciation in classical Chinese. To use Hsu's metaphor, the Son of Heaven (king) wholesaled the power to the feudal lords in a feudal country whereas the emperor retailed it to officials in an absolute monarchy (Hsu, 1998, pp. 47–48).

[1] Translations are James Legge's. (The Li Ki, 1885, p. 64). (Notes by translators)

1.3.1 Enfeoffment of the Western Zhou Dynasty

"The Zhou conquered the world and partitioned it into 71 vassal states of which 53 rulers or lords descended from the same House of Ji as the royal" and had their land located on the fertile soil around the capital. Those non-cognate lords were granted power and land out of necessity. Some of them descended from ancient sages and kings with the offspring of Shennong (Emperor of the Five Grains), Huangdi (Yellow Emperor), Emperor Yao, Emperor Shun, Yu the Great, and the royal family of the Shang Dynasty enfeoffed respectively in the kingdoms of Jiao, Zhu, Ji, Chen, Qi, and Song while those ministers known for their meritorious service in the conquest of the country also had to be granted feoffs. However, the non-cognate lords were usually enfeoffed with borderlands and even with an unconquered land like a blank check which they were instructed to write by themselves. For example, the Duke of Qi, when enfeoffed, was granted "the power to subjugate any other nobles" (Airs of Qi, the *Book of Songs*). And later when the Zhou people were hounded by an ethnic group called Quanrong and had to move east, King Ping of Zhou told Duke Xiang of Qin that "the Quanrong ruthlessly seized Qi, Feng and other regions of my country and you will have the land if you are able to expel them", and they reached an agreement under oath and had the Duke created (the Qin Dynasty, *Records of the Grand Historian*). Soon after, Duke Wen of Qin, having ousted the Quanrong, "took charge of the remaining people of Zhou, extended the Qin's territory to Qi, and restituted the land to the east of Qi to the Zhou Dynasty". Those non-cognate lords all developed into mighty powers by themselves. Some other non-cognate lords, such as the rulers of Chu and Yue, had their own states with such formidable might that the Zhou Dynasty could do nothing but grant them titles and land (Ch'ü, 2003, pp. 30–31).

Qian Mu said that, "in terms of feudalism, the Western Zhou Dynasty, built upon an aggressive armed migration and military occupation, was military colonization by a farming nation, quite different from the later unified governments where political regions were separated from the regime". Faced with the political situation of numerous independent states after the Shang Dynasty collapsed, the king of Zhou learned from the isolation and ruin of the Shang and enfeoffed "all the subdued states and unclaimed land" to his brothers and in-laws who founded vassal states across the country "to defend the Zhou". Those "military-backed" vassal states, "were newly established colonies that were artificially wedged among original states like sand mixing" (Wang, 2012, p. 56).

In addition, both land and population (ethnic groups) were essential elements of enfeoffment. "The enfeoffment of the Western Zhou involved both the colonialists' occupation of different eastern lands and regrouping of the population. Each created lord was enfeoffed with land and more importantly with different groups of people." In the early years of the Zhou, enfeoffment meant more "population grant" than "land grant" because the states migrated frequently, showing that "the lords did not have a strong sense of nativeness". The Zhou Dynasty integrated and assimilated other peoples in the vassal states so that "enfeoffment meant the overlapping relations between the ruling ethnic group and the indigenous populations of different regions" (Hsu, 2012, pp. 163, 167).

Some scholars believe that there are fundamental differences between the enfeoffment of the Western Zhou and that of the medieval Europe. Firstly, there were actually two parallel codes in the early years of the Zhou with one for regulating the political relationship between the king of Zhou and the eastern vassal states, and the other for the capital region directly under the king. Enfeoffment applied chiefly to the eastern states. Secondly, enfeoffment in the Western Zhou which included both "the granting of regional states" and "the grant of people" was very different from the "fiefs" of medieval Europe, "which were essentially land 'stipends' with no political and legal authority but with specifically defined obligations in the form of military service" (Li, 2006, pp. 111–112). Thirdly, "... the relationship between the Zhou king and the regional rulers as his subjects was much closer and more dictatorial than the contracted ties between the 'lord' and his 'vassal' under the "feudo-vassalic" institution of medieval Europe" (Li, 2006, p. 112). "The regional rulers, though equipped with full authority over civil, economic, and military affairs within their states, were not left completely free to rule" (Li, 2006, p. 115), which will be discussed in the next part, "The Relationships between Feudal Lords and the Son of Heaven".

1.3.2 Relationships Between Feudal Lords and the Son of Heaven[2]

i. Tribute. The regional lords paid tribute of locally produced goods to the Son of Heaven (the king of Zhou) and would do their utmost to provide relief when natural hazards befell the royal family and the capital region. It was the lords' obligation to pay tribute, but the Son of Heaven should not make a request for it because the Son wanted nothing, and a request was not in accord with propriety. For example, it was considered inappropriate in the *Spring and Autumn Annals* when the King asked the state of Lu for carts.
ii. The lords' dispatched service to the Son of Heaven
    1. Labour such as city building
    2. Military service such as guarding the borders, suppressing the royal rebels, and subjugating the non-compliant lords to the king.
iii. Inspection tour made by the king to the vassal states.
iv. Regular performance report to the king either by the lords themselves (audience) or their ministers or grand masters (substitute audience).
v. The central government appointed some of the ministers and grand masters and could even institute hereditary supervisors in the vassal states. "In the Spring and Autumn Period, the king's orders were ignored, but the king still ceremonially appointed the senior ministers of the vassal states, who were

[2] Refer to Ch'ü (2003, pp. 60–72) for more details.

called 'Appointed Minister' or 'King's Guardian'. It seems that the Western Zhou practiced this system because "The Son of Heaven designated a minister", that is, Minister of War of the feudal lords. Of the three ministers of War, Education, and Works, the Minister of War commanding troops was pivotal and needed to be appointed by the king of Zhou to facilitate military maneuvers and expeditions" (Yang, 2016, pp. 375–376).

vi. The feudal lords needed to attend the king conducting sacrifices.
vii. The king might bestow sacrificial meat, clothing, ware, land, and titles upon the lords.
viii. The king and lords attended each other's weddings and funerals.
ix. The lords were the king's ministers.
x. Marriages might be arranged between the royal House of Ji and the lords' families, for example, the Jiang family.

1.3.3 Patriarchal Clan System and Feudalism

When the ancient countries were in the making in China, the kinship and the national political system were long entangled so that a prolonged feudalism featuring a patriarchal clan system ensued upon the ending of the tribal society. The patriarchal clan system defended feudalism such that "the family pedigree in the ancestral temple meant political place". "The hereditary states hailed from enfeoffment; the aristocratic families, the patriarchal clan system" (Chen, 2001, p. 7).

"Feudalism was based on the patriarchal clan system" and "it was an enormous network of blood relationship from the king to the lords, grand masters and servicemen". "The relationship between the feudal and the patriarchal clan system went like this: the King designated his eldest son of the primary consort to be next king and had his other sons created lords; the lord designated his eldest son of the primary consort to be next lord and had his other sons created grand masters; the grand master designated his eldest son of the primary consort to be next grand master and had his other sons created serviceman. The serviceman was the minor clan compared with the grand master who was the major clan; the grand master was the minor clan compared with the lord who was the major clan; the lord was the minor clan compared with the king who was the major clan. In general, a blood relationship or kinship existed between the king of Zhou and the lords, the lords and the grand masters, and the grand masters and the servicemen, which constituted the patriarchal clan system. The feudalism was a geographical relationship while the patriarchal clan system was a blood relationship, and they were two sides of a coin with the geographical relationship supporting the blood relationship." (Zhou, 2014, p. 12)

i. The patriarchal clan system

1. Primary primogeniture and the difference between the primary lineage and the secondary lineage

In ancient China, nobles usually hoped to have many sons and grandsons to empower their own families, but succession disputes might arise among the sons, and the conflicts therein could even cost a family or a country. The archaeological discoveries show that the order of succession to the throne was too complicated in the Shang Dynasty to be generalized into succession by the son upon the death of the father or by the younger brother upon the death of the elder one. Scholars even proposed "alternate succession" by two lines of royal descents because the lineage of the Shang kings was obscure (Chang, 1980, p. 179). In order to permanently solve the problem of succession, the Zhou Dynasty adopted primary primogeniture by which the firstborn son of the primary consort inherited not only fiefs and titles but also the hosting position of sacrificial rituals in the ancestral temple. The nobles of Zhou practiced monogamy with concubines so that the sons, depending on their birth mothers, might be primary or secondary, and the sons from the same woman were also different due to their birth order. The firstborn son that inherited the ancestral temple was called "son of the major clan" (*zongzi*, 宗子); his wife, "daughter-in-law of the major clan" (*zongfu*, 宗妇); and his brothers, "separate sons" (*biezi*, 别子). The eldest sons of the Zhou kings all were the "major clan" while those separate sons were the "minor clan". The minor clan had the obligation to serve the major one which, together with the ancestral temple, was located in the capital.

2. Sacrifice

The Son of Heaven had seven fanes in the ancestral temple; a lord, five; a grand master, three; a serviceman, two; a commoner, none. "A country could not have two monarchs as a temple could not have two masters of sacrificial ceremonies." "The major clan took precedence over the minor one". Only the family of the major clan could offer sacrifices to the earliest ancestors. The firstborn son of the primary consort was the son of the major clan who would inherit the ancestral temple (*zongshi*, 宗室). The first monarchs, as the major clan and common forefathers of all offspring, would stay eternally in the ancestral temple whereas the later ones, as the minor clan, would have to be moved into the temple of distant ancestors after five generations because they were distant kin, which was usually called "moving in the earliest ancestors and moving out the later ones". The fanes in the ancestral temple were built in a crosswise with three on the left, three on the right and one for the earliest in the middle to show the line of succession.

ii. The impact of the patriarchal clan system and filial piety

1. Political extension of the patriarchal inheritance system

The patriarchal inheritance system, including the primary primogeniture and the eternal major clan system, determined the stability of the royal lineage and the Confucian "orthodoxy" so that scholar-bureaucrats defended it throughout history. Emperors regularly refused to designate the firstborn son as heir apparent, but the primary primogeniture was still the Confucian orthodoxy. For example, Emperor Wanli of the Ming Dynasty, displacing the eldest son in favor of the younger one as his successor, brought him into a serious confrontation with the scholar-bureaucrats, and eventually had to submit to Confucian ideas even though he was the supreme ruler. However, his grandfather, Emperor Jiajing, was the son of a regional prince instead of an immediate relative of the preceding Emperor Zhengde. After coronation, Emperor Jiajing pitted the Great Rites Controversy against the staunch Confucian officialdom over the posthumous honors of his natural father and the imperial title of his living mother.[3] All this was centered on the fundamental problem: legitimate succession in the dynastic line and succession by family descent or adoption. Nearly 200 court officials were punished by the imperial power for confronting Emperor Jiajing head-on, but they were undaunted, priding themselves on death (Geiss, 1998).

2. "The rule of filial piety", "removal of fanes of distant ancestors" and the Controversy over Costume[4]

Foreign conquerors, such as Emperor Xiaowen of the Northern Wei Dynasty, the Jin Dynasty, the Yuan Dynasty and the Qing Dynasty, highly esteemed the *Book on Filial Piety* in order to relate filial piety (to parents) to loyalty (to monarchs). With their regime built upon trickery and plundering, the Wei and Jin Dynasties "ruled the country by filiality" instead of loyalty and attacked political enemies on the charge of unfulfilled filial piety. On the basis of filiality, Emperor Xiaowen introduced all the Han institutions of family (including surnames and clans) and ancestor worship (ancestral temples, ancestral halls, and dress codes). He changed his father's temple name from Daowu into Taizu (grand progenitor) and adopted the dress code of five mourning costumes indicating nearness of relations to exclude distant relatives from the royal family clan. As a result of Emperor Xiaowu's reform of the dress code, "titles and wealth were totally open to the firstborn son of the primary consort, but totally closed to the sideline siblings". After the emperor's death, the reform triggered a backlash from the nobles who had been deprived of their privileges due to their identity as sidelines.

---

[3] With the patriarchal inheritance system in mind, the scholar-bureaucrats insisted that Emperor Jiajing be an adopted son of his deceased emperor uncle and treat his natal father, a regional prince, as uncle. However, the emperor conferred royal titles on his biological father and mother on account of filial responsibilities.

[4] Refer to Kang (2005) for more details.

1.3.4 Retainers

In the Western Zhou Dynasty and the Spring and Autumn Period, the ministers and grand masters in the states were very important aristocrats. "They enjoyed their hereditary titles, land and fiefs, dynastically holding pre-eminent positions and controlling the military and political power. In the fiefs, they set up their clan temples, cities, armies, and clan-centered ruling institutions called 'Clan', 'House' and 'Family'". As the head of a "House", the firstborn son of the primary consort (*zongzi*, 宗子) ruled with the assistance of clansmen and retainers or domestic servants so that the retainer institution came into being. "In the Spring and Autumn Period, those retainers also had different ranks and the senior ones were titled 'Grand Master of the House'"; "Certain powerful retainers even had their clans and fiefs with servants". The relationship between the head of the House and his retainers, similar to that between the monarch and the lords, needed to be officially instituted. Retainer must pay homage to their masters. "As long as they must be loyal to the House, there was nothing of the state but House on their mind" (Yang, 2016, pp. 476, 479).

1.4 Ruin of the Feudal Rite System

1.4.1 Regional Rulers' Threat to Feudalism

The regional rulers were the rank between the king and the feudal lords. As major lords in certain regions, they represented the king politically and had the power to mount military expeditions. The king usually reluctantly created regional rulers because they enjoyed considerable acclamation from the lords, which was similar to how the king came to power. With growing strength and authority, those regional rulers posed a threat to the king as the Shang Dynasty had fallen to a regional ruler (Lord of the West).

The integration of political power and lineage might seem rock solid, but it was not true. The king of Zhou granted the lords land and population to "create states", and the lords did the same to the ministers and grand masters to set up their Houses so that there was an opposition between the country and the house among the servicemen and commoners who, calling their clan "House", were solely loyal to the "House" rather than the country. This centrifugal force was a fatal weakness of feudalism, resulting in separatist regimes opposed to the central government as the Spring and Autumn and the Warring States Periods fully proved.

1.4.2 Decline of the Zhou Dynasty, "Ruin of Rites and Music", and "Law Tripods"

The rites and music declined after the Zhou Dynasty moved its capital to the east. Hierarchical rites were ignored among the king, lords and grand masters, the lords looted crops in the royal fields, and three grand masters from different clans even carved up the state of Jin into three states in the Warring States Period. During those political upheavals, numerous schools of thought (Confucianism, Legalism, Mohism, Taoism, Yin-yang, Names…) contended with each other. Confucius emerged as a saint. He traveled through different states, advising the lords to "restrain themselves and return to rites", but the latter all "restrained him instead of themselves". It is said that Confucius composed the *Spring and Autumn Annals* in a terse style to "strike terror into the hearts of those rebellious ministers and villainous sons" so that "Spring and Autumn" came to be a name for the early Eastern Zhou Dynasty. The "Warring States" was derived from the *Stratagems of the Warring States*. There had been no such term as the "Eastern Zhou Dynasty" except the "Western Zhou Dynasty", the "Spring and Autumn Period" and the "Warring States" before the publication of the *Romance of the Eastern Zhou Dynasty* in the Qing Dynasty. In order to consolidate their position, the new nobles courted the new landlords and merchants to reassure them. "Impromptu consideration of punishment" was replaced by promulgation of written law that was also binding on the nobles. When law was inscribed on the tripods, the nobles would no longer "make irresponsible remarks".

Here are some of the relatively well-known publications of written law: (1) Zichan, Prime Minister of the state of Zheng had law cast onto tripods in 536 BC, and it was historically known as "Cast Code"; (2) soon after, Dengxi, Grand Master of Zheng and a renowned legal expert, privately compiled laws and inscribed them onto bamboo slips, which were called "Bamboo Code" in history; the then Prime Minister of Zheng killed him on the charge of private writing of laws, but adopted his text as official law; (3) in 513 BC, Zhao Yang, a powerful minister of the state of Jin, cast "Law Tripods" with Fan Xuanzi's law on them. The "Cast Code" and "Law Tripods" courted criticism from Shuxiang and Confucius who adhered to the traditional rites. The two men deemed that the written law would inflict substantial damage on the rite system of "early kings' deliberation of punishment based on seriousness without making law", disrupt the normal order of nobles and commoners, and give rise to political and social chaos. However, the lawmakers stood firm. Zichan even defended himself on the grounds of "setting the time right" and "adapting to the changing situation".

Unlike the Warring States Period, the Spring and Autumn Period witnessed numerous conflicts among the royal family, lords, and grand masters. However, blood is thicker than water. When discords arose within the clan or in-laws, it was always easy to have them reconciled and there was always room for mediation. Self-restraint in due consideration of old kinship, coupled with hesitation to over-offend in fear of one's place, distinguished the Spring and Autumn Period from the Warring States, preventing China from falling into a jungle during the three hundred years after the Zhou Dynasty moved to the east (Over sixty states were destroyed in the Spring and Autumn Period, but most of them fell to the barbarians or the other way around. Rarely did the states under the Zhou government annex each other, and more rarely did feudal lords from the House of Ji subjugate one another). Clanship and kinship thinned out after a number of generations. The hierarchical order among monarchs and lords was no more binding and was found faulty when the power that had created it declined or went away. The more problems were found with it, the less awe it commanded. Consequently, the feudalism built on kinship and a hierarchy could not live long (Zhang, 2003, pp. 65–66).

In the Spring and Autumn Period, hegemony was achieved under the "just" slogan of "venerating the royal", "expelling foreigners", and "prohibiting usurpation, regicide, and annexation"; However, after the state of Jin was partitioned into three states, and the ruler of Qin was replaced, the royal Houses of Ji and Jiang came to an end and there was no more hegemony.

1.4.3 Division of the Country into Commanderies and Counties

The country was divided into commanderies and counties and the feudalism collapsed firstly because the "the privileges granted to the lord's clansmen were abolished across the state" (which began in the state of Jin) and the ruler could appoint officials to administer confiscated fiefs instead of enfeoffing it, and secondly because the ruler also appointed officials to govern the annexed land.

i. Counties

The Chinese character "县" (*xian*, county) originated in the Western Zhou dynasty, meaning "suspended" or "uninstitutionalized". Ancient Chinese also interpreted it as "pending". For example, as one of the regions suspended from enfeoffment in the early Zhou, Tang was of such strategic importance due to its proximity to the capital that no one was found to be fit as its lord at that time and suspense proved to be a better choice. It was until King Cheng ascended the throne that it was granted to Shuyu, Cheng's brother. During the interval, the central government had to designate an official to administer Tang to prevent it from falling into anarchy. This was the origin of "county" (suspended). The suspense was merely temporary in the early Zhou because any region had to be enfeoffed eventually. However, it became a rule later so that the "county" referred to the first tier of local government. In the Spring and Autumn Period, the powerful states frequently annexed the small ones, but they were reluctant to remit the annexed land to the now powerless king for enfeoffment so that they appointed their own governing officials over the land by "suspending" its enfeoffment after the Tang precedent. Those officials were called "county governor", "county magistrate", "county duke" or "county grand master". Prolonged suspense made the county a regular institution. Statistics show that there were at least 40 counties in the state of Jin in the late Spring and Autumn Period. "An examination of the historical records of Qin, Chun, and Jin reveals that the counties used to be capitals of small neighboring states or nobles and fell under the direct administration of the powerful states after their conquest and confiscation." (Du, 1990, p. 122)

ii. Commanderies

Commandery (*jun*, 郡) and county had been different and totally unrelated administrative units before the first emperor of Qin united China. Explained as "city and pronounced '*jun*'" in the *Analytic Dictionary of Characters*, "郡" is a pictophonetic character that seems to have been invented specially for political areas or timely needs. "At the end of the Spring and Autumn Period, commanderies were less important than counties in the state of Jin because the former were desolate and the latter, prosperous"; "The usage accepted by subsequent generations might have started in the state of Wei in the early Warring States Period" where "commanderies, mostly set up in the military border regions at the beginning, might be large special county cities with mighty troops and a large population" (Du, 1990, p. 123). They all seem to have been connected with military and national defense before the Qin Dynasty. "The Wei state instituted Shang Commandery to the West of the Yellow River along the border with the Rong ethnic group;" "The Qin had Rongxi, Beidi and Shang Commandery where the Great Wall was erected against the Hu people" (Biographies of the Barbarians, *Records of the Grand Historian*). In the Warring States Period, wars were more frequently waged so that military officers naturally enjoyed higher status and commanderies came to take priority over counties. In its wars of unification, the state of Qin constantly set up commanderies. The border commanderies kept expanding and the inland counties kept diminishing as the annexing wars continued. When the country was finally unified, the first emperor of Qin divided it into 36 commanderies, specifying counties to be subordinate to commanderies, which naturally evolved into two tiers of local government.

1.4.4 Transformation of Economic and Social Systems[5]

i. The well-field system based on the opposition between the city and the countryside and land distribution according household registration under the private land ownership

Under the feudal system, there was an opposition between the city and the countryside in both the crown land and the states. The capitals and their surrounding areas were mainly inhabited by big and petty nobles called "townspeople" who, being political and military pillars of the country, enjoyed political and economic rights. The vast rural areas were the "countryside" inhabited by farmers called "plebs" or "commoners". "Before the middle of the Spring and Autumn Period, the vast rural areas had retained village communes whose land system had been adopted by different ranks of

[5] Refer to Yang (2016, pp. 162–177) for more details.

nobles to 'divide land and regulate allowances', resulting the well-field system". The late Western Zhou Dynasty saw the preliminary disintegration of that system because the "public fields lay waste" on the one hand, and private farmland burgeoned with land increasingly going private on the other. Some small farmers reclaimed land for themselves in the outskirts of the well field in the Spring and Autumn Period while the "townspeople" privatized their land first. By the end of the period, most of the "townspeople" were yeomen in the states. In the Warring States Period, the Wei, Qin and other states all allocated land according to household registration, and to seek hegemony, they competed to reward military successes with titles and farmland. The Qin "promoted Shang Yang's reform to modify the imperial system, abolish the well-field system, and allow trade among the people" (Treatise on Food and Commodities, *Book of Han*). The merit land system established by Shang Yang's reform did not specify "free trade among owners", but "land trading was publicly possible when bestowed land was confirmed to be private under the owner's name and hereditary". The disintegration of the well-field system increasingly blurred the differences between "plebs" (commoners) and "townspeople" (petty nobles) in terms of wealth and status (Yang, 2016).

ii. From city family clans to universal household registration[6]

Household registration was to register the family residence (listed in the national registers). In the feudal society, the registration was considered ominous so that only a member per household was recorded for conscription, land registration and hunting. In the imperial era, censuses were conducted regularly for household registration including all the members of each family, intended partly to expand conscription and practice military administration. Universal household registration meant everybody to be equal before law, or merely administratively and legally equal because not all enjoyed the same social and economic status and there were numerous inequalities in equality. Aristocrats from different strata (dukes, marquises, earls, viscounts and barons) enjoyed different titles and advantages from those of commoners, but the middle and late Spring and Autumn Period witnessed the fading distinction between diverse groups of people in the city-states. First of all, there was no difference between the townspeople and the plebs, and then the nobles were gradually plebeianized, which can be seen from the following aspects:

1. Military organizations transformed from warriors riding chariots (nobility) to infantry (commoners).
2. Local administration developed into tightly organized communities of citizens including soldiers and farmers; the mutually independent political and social units such as crown land, states, and fiefs were replaced by the subordinate system of commanderies, counties, townships, and villages.
3. A mutual surveillance and accountability system of fives and tens was adopted with a family as the smallest unit, moving up to groups of five families, villages of 50 families, aggregations of 500 families and districts of 5000 families.

[6] Refer to Du (2005) for more details.

4. Land ownership went from state-owned to private (Granted land would not be returned).
5. A legal system was practiced to protect the lives and property of citizens on household registration.
6. Settlement communities replaced blood and geographical relations.
7. The Qin Dynasty implemented a system of twenty ranks, ending hereditary posts and emoluments.

1.4.5 The Changing Relations Between the Ruler and Ministers: Changes and Controversies

i. The pre-Qin feudalism: ruler-minister relationships based on rituals, territorialism, and moral consensus

When Confucius said that "The ruler should rule, the minister should minister, the father should be a father, and the son should behave like a son", he emphasized the relative obligations and rights of the ruler and his subjects who needed to know their own place. Mencius said it more frankly: "When the prince regards his ministers as his hands and feet, his ministers regard their prince as their belly and heart; when he regards them as his dogs and horses, they regard him as another man; when he regards them as the ground or as grass, they regard him as a robber and an enemy".[7]

ii. The imperial system since the Qin and Han: Ruler-minister relationships based on nature, imperial cosmopolitanism and favor.

Most of the Confucian classics were completed and targeted at the political situation in the Warring States Period. It was totally impossible for them to include what would happen to the Qin politics after unification so that they could not serve as a blueprint for the imperial system of the Qin and Han Dynasties. Therefore, to establish a "Confucian state", the Confucians of the Western Han must reinterpret the classics. In due course, controversies arose over the changing relationships between the monarch and his ministers.

1. "Dual ruler-minister relationships" and "mourning for the late ruler"[8]

In the feudal hierarchy of the king, lords, ministers, grand masters and servicemen, officials usually swore loyalty first of all to their immediate superiors instead of the king of Zhou so that multiple levels of ruler-minister relationships (loyalty) were formed in the hierarchy. When the Qin and Han Dynasties adopted the imperial system, that tradition was not immediately discontinued, forging dual ruler-minister relationship in the three-rank pecking order of the emperor, ministers, and common people wherein the subordinate official must be loyal foremost to his senior in preference to the emperor. The supervisor-subordinate relationship was lifelong. When

---

[7] Translations are James Legge's (Mencius, 1970, p. 39). (Notes by translators)

[8] Refer to Kan (2005) for more details.

the leader passed away, his former subordinates would go into mourning, which was called "mourning for the late ruler". Under the imperial system that sought "absolutely centralized power", the emperor certainly could not brook the tendency to "set up separate central governments among small groups" and he hoped to reduce the three-rank pecking order to a two-rank hierarchy of the emperor and ministers/common people in terms of loyalty so that all subjects were merely loyal to him. The Eastern Han Dynasty instituted special laws against "mourning for the late ruler", but the scholar-bureaucrats took the risk, which reflected the contradiction between the mandatory norms of the scholar-bureaucrats and the bureaucratic system.

2. Issues with the ceremonies ("investiture")

The "investiture" refers to ceremonies by which the candidates were granted titles by the king of Zhou and "invested as ministers", affirming the subordination of the ministers to the ruler. Once invested, the ministers would "die before switching their allegiance". The rites of Zhou stressed the ritual acceptance of gifts on both sides so that most of the bronze inscriptions were records of investiture (Hsu, 2012). In the feudal era, the symbolic investiture was necessary in establishing the relationship between a ruler and his minister whereas the imperial era seldom witnessed such "close contact" between the emperor and his officials, giving rise to the distinction between "close ministers" (those who was appointed by the emperor in person) and "distant ministers". However, it was impossible for the two types of officials to have different duties of allegiance to the emperor in an absolute monarchy.

3. From morality to favor

The ruler's favor to the ministers was compared politically to the paternal love for the sons in the imperial era so that the ruler-minister relationship switched from relative moral consensus to absolute subordination, leaving no room to the ministers for negotiation. "Imperial cosmopolitanism settled all human beings into a single family" where any minister, after offending the emperor, would find it impossible to escape from one state to another like they used to in the Spring and Autumn and Warring States Periods. When Emperor Taizong of the Tang Dynasty was in power, the duty of allegiance went totally from relative to absolute. He meted out severe penalties to the turncoat ministers of the Sui Dynasty and honored the loyal ones, claiming that "the ruler may not rule, but the minister has to minister". "They rejected the revolution of King Tang of Shang and King Wu of Zhou for loyalty to the monarch by citing Bi Gan's death from his blunt remonstration with the king" (Sa, 1993, pp. 337–338).

1.5 The Chinese Rite System After the Zhou Dynasty

1.5.1 Feudalism and "A Country with Multiple Systems"

Feudalism and centralized administration (the *junxian* system) were "considered in traditional academia to be exact opposites, and their merits and demerits were debated enthusiastically without referring to any definition. However, it was inadvisable to see the two government institutions as incompatible. Given the entire history of political institutions, it seems more meaningful to consider them as opposite ends of a broad spectrum" (Yang, 2015, p. 95).

Due to the enfeoffment of the Western Zhou, the relationship between the king of Zhou and the lords was similar to the European feudal relationship because enfeoffment was somewhat division of sovereignty. The *Book of Songs* reads that "Under the wide heaven, all is the king's land; within the sea-boundaries of the land, all are the king's servants",[9] but "that merely represents an ideal government or a centralized country instead of the real decentralized society of the Western Zhou". In his *On Feudalism*, Liu Zongyuan of the Tang Dynasty spoke the truth that "Feudalism had been adopted not out of the sages' intention, but out of sheer necessity". The monarchs did not intend to practice feudalism, but "they had no choice" (Zhou, 2014, p. 13).

Feudalism after the Zhou Dynasty might be seen in the following cases. Firstly, the Western Han and Western Jin Dynasties practiced enfeoffment. Secondly, at the beginning of many dynasties after the Western Jin, royal family members and meritorious generals were enfeoffed with lands, especially with the borderlands. For example, Emperor Taizu of the Ming Dynasty granted the northern border areas to several princes, and Yunnan province to Mu Ying and his descendants; The Yuan and Qing Dynasties enfeoffed generals of the Han ethnic group who surrendered with lands such as the three border provinces in the early Qing Dynasty. Thirdly, scholars noticed a long history of "one country with multiple systems" in China due to ethnic, religious, and regional problems. Take for example, the suzerain-vassal state relationship between the dynasties in the central region and the states of ethnic minorities in the borderlands, and the native chieftain system of the Ming and Qing. "Interestingly, one of the ways to control chieftains in the Ming was to send officials to work as chieftains' subordinates, especially clerks, who were similar to the counselor-delegates dispatched to oversee those princedoms in the Han Dynasty" (Yang, 2015, p. 97).

"A flexible China allowed multi-dimensional and multi-level expressions and practices, including both the 'one' that united numerous ethnic groups and the 'many' that retained relative independence." (Wei, 2019, p. 8) Take the Qing Dynasty as an example. The constitutional system of the Ming continued in the 18 provinces in the central region while Manchus, Mongols, and Tibetans had their own institutions, with the emperor of the Qing as the only node in the network. "In terms of the world

[9] Translations are James Legge's (The She King, 1960, p. 360). (Notes by translators)

history and international law, Manchuria and Mongolia resembled Flanders, Kosovo, and 16 counties of Yan and Yun." (Liu, 2015, pp. 314–315) The Western theory of "personal union", in spite of certain limitations, is undeniably true in that different systems of governance can be adopted within a country. In the Qing, it was the Court of Colonial Affairs instead of the six ministries that handled Mongolian and Tibetan affairs. The Republic of China established the "Committee on Mongolian and Tibetan Affairs" in addition to various ministries. Today, the United Front Work Department of Communist Party of China Central Committee, together with its affiliate, the National Ethnic Affairs Commission, plays an important role in regional affairs of ethnic minorities in the People's Republic of China. Traditionally, "the central government of China in the central region always practiced different systems in the borderlands and regions of ethnic minorities from those in the agricultural areas where the Han people lived. As long as effective control was maintained, the central government agreed to keep the original native institution, allowed ethnic autonomy, respected religious beliefs, and provided economic assistance. When successfully implemented, this policy of 'one country, multiple systems' necessarily maintained and consolidated a unified regime." (Ge, 2013, p. 221)

Thinkers from different dynasties disagreed with each other about the merits of feudalism and centralized administrative. For example, Cao Tong, a member from the royal House of Cao in the Wei Dynasty, proposed to restore feudalism in his *On the Six Dynasties*; Lu Ji of the Jin Dynasty also considered feudalism to be more desirable than administrative division. In his *On Feudalism*, Liu Zongyuan of the Tang Dynasty vehemently attacked feudalism featuring hereditary aristocracy; Huang Zongxi and Gu Yanwu, enlightenment thinkers in the late Ming and early Qing, recommended their reconciliation: "Feudalism failed due to its autocracy at the regional level, and administrative division, at the central level". It was advisable to "blend feudalism into administrative division" to limit the excessive centralization of power in the hands of the monarch, "which would solve the bimillennial problem and revive the society" (Yang, 2015, pp. 98–105).

A federal state resulting from enfeoffment occurred occasionally after the Zhou Dynasty and was always associated with "separatism" and "secession", but "In imperial China, it [the term of *fengjian*] had developed a historically critical role as a check on absolutist power" (Duara, 1995, p. 200). At the end of the nineteenth century, autocracy was attacked again in the name of feudalism; the Movement of United Autonomous Provinces even partially fulfilled the decentralization of power in the early years of the ROC. Soon after, however, "feudalism" came to be associated with divisive warlords and turmoil, and became a totally derogatory term so that it was spurned ideologically and politically, and a centralized nation-state tended to be the only appeal at that time (Duara, 1995).

1.5.2 The Rite System and Political Legacy of the Zhou Dynasty

The rite system (rule of rites), "a Confucian political and cultural model in the first place, cannot be equated with actual politics in ancient China and has grown into a 'distant echo' in modern China". However, having transcended the feudal society in the temporal dimension, it had a profound influence on the political thought, system planning and political action of ancient China in the several thousand years of history, and put down roots deep into the Chinese national psyche. Unlike legalists' single-minded pursuit of prosperity and strength, Confucians would make further inquiries into what the ultimate goal of the country was after prosperity and strength have been achieved. Does the government have a more appealing long-term mission in addition to Zichan's "setting the time right"? The Confucian rite system is centered on "harmony" and "people" instead of "development" and "business"; its idea of "governance" "goes beyond the purely political goals and order" toward attainment of a higher and greater cultural ideal, "accordingly entrusting cultural groups and educational institutions with special political and social responsibilities". Given the traditional Chinese culture of rites and music and the spirit of "harmony in diversity", can we find something in the same vein today that can inspire cultural creativity? (Yan, 1996, pp. 505–508)

"As the last of the early royal dynasties in China, the Western Zhou state left its clear imprint on later Chinese history", and "... had left behind it the core of the ancient Chinese Classics" (Li, 2006, p. 279), such as the *Book of Songs*, the *Book of Documents*, and the *Book of Changes* which, through the able agent of Confucianism, exerted a huge impact on the political culture of succeeding generations, including political ethics, political philosophy, governmental practice, and the scholar-officials' outlook on life. "The Western Zhou state left to China not only an ethnic core, but also a cultural base that was crucial for the continued prosperity of the Chinese civilization during the next centuries and millennia under empire. To claim a connection between the Western Zhou state and the Qin and Han Empires entails a gap of more than 500 years. But cultural elements can survive such a long period. It is in the cultural and ethnic assimilation achieved under the Western Zhou state that we should look for the origins of China's great empires, and in the homogeneous cultural elements that the Western Zhou state had installed in every corner of the Zhou world that we should look for the foundation of China's later unification" (Li, 2006, p. 296).

References

Ch'ü, T. (2003). *Zhonguo fengjian shehui* [*The Chinese feudal society*]. Shanghai People's Publishing House.

Chang, K. (1980). *Shang civilization*. Yale University Press.

Chang, K. (2013). *Zhongguo qingtong shidai* [The Chinese Bronze Age]. SDX Joint Publishing Company.

Chen, Y. (2001). *Suitang zhidu yuanyuan luelun gao* [Draft essays on the origins of Sui and Tang institution· Draft outline of Tang political history]. SDX Joint Publishing Company.
Du, Z. (1990). *Bianhuqimin: chuantong zhengzhi shehui jiegou zhi xingcheng* [Household registration: The formation of traditional political social structure]. Linking Publishing Co., Ltd.
Du, Z. (2005). *Bianhuqimin lun de pouxi* [An analysis of household registration]. In J. Wang (Ed.), *Zhengli yu quanli* [Politics and Power] (pp. 14–41). Encyclopedia of China Publishing House.
Ge, J. (2013). *Tongyi yu fenlie—Zhongguo lishi de qishi* [Unity and secession—Lessons from Chinese history]. The Commercial Press.
Geiss, J. (1998). The Chia-ching reign, 1522-1566. In F. Mote & D. Twitchett (Eds.), The Cambridge history of China: The Ming Dynasty, 1368–1644, Part I. (Vol. 7, pp. 440–510). Cambridge University Press.
Gu, J. (2015). *Guoshi jianghua: shanggu* [Lectures on history of China: Ancient times]. Shanghai People's Publishing House.
Hsu, C. (1998). *Lishi Fenguang jing* [A spectroscope on history]. Shanghai Literature & Art Publishing House.
Hsu, C. (2012). *Xizhou shi* [History of the Western Zhou Dynasty]. SDX Joint Publishing Company.
Kan, H. (2005). *"Jiujun" de jingdian quanshi—Hantangjian de sangfu li yu zhengzhi zhixu* [Classical interpretation of the "former ruler": Mourning gowns and political order from the Han to the Tang Dynasty]. In J. Wang (Ed.), *Zhengzhi yu quanli* [Politics and Power] (pp.305–336). Encyclopedia of China Publishing House.
Kang, L. (2005). *Xiaodao yu Beiwei zhengzhi* [Filial Piety and the Politics of the Northern Wei Dynasty]. In Y. Xing & L. Lin (Eds.), *Shehui bianqian* [Social evolution] (pp. 186–216). Encyclopedia of China Publishing House.
Li, F. (2006). *Xizhou de miewang: Zhongguo zaoqi guojia de dili he zhengzhi weiji* [Landscape and power in early China: The crisis and fall of the Western Zhou 1045-771 BC]. Cambridge University Press.
Mencius. (1970). *The Works of Mencius* (J. Legge Trans.). Dover Publications.
Sa, M. (1993). *Zhongguo zhengzhi sixiang* [A new theory on the constitution of the Republic of China]. San Min Book Co., Ltd.
The She King. (1960). In J. Legge (Trans.), *Chinese classics* (Vol. 4). Hong Kong University Press.
The Li Ki. (1885). (J. Legge Trans.). In F. M. Muller (Ed.), *The sacred books of the east by various oriental scholars* (Vol. 28). The Clarendon Press.
Wang, B. (2005). *Jindai falv sichao yu Zhongguo guyou wenhua* [Legal thoughts in modern China and traditional Chinese culture]. Tsinghua University Press.
Wang, J. (2012). *A general history of China*. SDX Joint Publishing Company.
Wang, P. (2018). *Xingshu yu daoshu: dabianjuxia de zaoqi Zhongguo fa* [Criminal code and Taoism: Early Chinese laws amid great revolutions]. Law Press.
Yan, B. (1996). *Shidafu zhengzhi yansheng shigao* [Draft history of scholar-gentry governance]. Peking University Press.
Yang, L. (2015). *Guoshi tanwei: hongguan shiyexia de weiguan kaocha [Exploration of national history: A micro-examination in the macro-perspective]*. Citic Press Group.
Yang, K. (2016). *Xizhou shi* [History of the Western Zhou Dynasty]. Shanghai People's Publishing House.
Zhang, Y. (2003). *Zhongguo shigang* [An outline of Chinese history]. The Commercial Press.
Zhou, Z. (2014). *Zhongguo defang xingzheng zhidu shi* [A history of China's local administrative institutions]. Shanghai People's Publishing House.

Chapter 2
Government Organization of Ancient China

2.1 Organization of the Central Government

The traditional Chinese official system of the central government was rather precocious. In the Western Zhou Dynasty, court officials were classified into the two levels of lords and ministers. The former consisted of the Grand Guardian (*taibao*, 太保), the Grand Preceptor (*taishi*, 太师) and the Grand Astrologer (*taishi*, 太史) in the early period, but only the Grand Preceptor and the Grand Astrologer later, with the position of the Grand Preceptor possibly occupied by two officials simultaneously. "The latter (similar to the Six Ministries and Nine Ministers of later dynasties) included initially Overseer of the Masses (*situ*, 司徒), Overseer of Mounts (*sima*, 司马), Supervisor of Constructions (*sigong*, 司工), Overseer of Bandits (*sikou*, 司寇), Grand Steward (*taizai*, 太宰) and Overseer of Ducal Lineages (*gongzu*, 公族). Since the middle Western Zhou period, there were only five ministers left as the Overseer of Bandits was reduced in rank." (Yang, 2016, p. 385) The present section focuses mainly on the official system of the central government of the imperial era.

2.1.1 *The Central Government*

i. Transition of Private Officials of the Emperor into Court Officials of the State[1]

The official system of the central government of our country was in a process of constant changes since the Qin and Han periods. The essence of this process was the change of the private officials of the emperor (called "officials of the Inner Court" in the Han Dynasty) into court officials of the state. Fearful that his power might be undermined or his Mandate of Heaven usurped by a court official, the emperor intended to take the powers of court officials into his own hands and often sought to suppress the court officials with his own private officials. In the course of time, the emperor's private officials would grab the powers

[1] Refer to Sa (1975a, pp. 107–111).

X. Nie, *The History of Government and Public Law in China*,
https://doi.org/10.1007/978-981-97-6063-3_2

> of the court officials, whereas the court officials had to take a back seat. Once the private officials had evolved into court officials, the emperor would try to strip them of their powers and place trust in his private officials once again. As this process of evolution from private officials into court officials went on, the official system of the central government of our country became increasingly complicated.
>
> —Sa Mengwu

For example, the top-level officials of the central government of the Qin and Han Dynasties, i.e., the Prime Minister (*chengxiang*, 丞相), the Defender-in-chief (*taiwei*, 太尉) and Censor-in-chief (*yushi dafu*, 御史大夫), all originated from positions of the Inner Court. The system of the three administrative departments (the Secretariat, the Chancellery and the Department of State Affairs) also emerged in the process of evolution from the emperor's private officials to state officials.

1. The Prime Minister: The Prime Minister used to be an official in charge of protocols when the feudal lords paid a visit to the royal court or met to form an alliance. In the Warring States Period, the feudal lords gradually rose in power while the aristocrats declined. As a feudal lord employed scholars around him to weaken the power of the nobility, the power of the Prime Minister steadily increased. Eventually the Prime Minister became the top administrator in essence as well as in name. The Chinese name 丞相 (pronounced as *chengxiang*) for the Prime Minister first appeared in the Qin.
2. The Defender-in-chief: In the feudal era, aristocrats served as ministers in charge of civil affairs in times of peace and as commanders in charge of military affairs in times of war. However, in the Warring States Period when chariot battles gave way to cavalry and infantry battles as the prevailing form of combat, aristocrats fell out of power in the military realm and were supplanted by military officials of commoner origin, such as Sun Wu (general of the Wu State) and Wu Qi (general of the Wei State). Initially, they were no more than attendants and advisors of the feudal lords. Inside the palace, they waited on their feudal lords, and outside the palace, they led the troops in battle. Over time, they evolved from attendants into military officials of the state. The top-level military official was the Defender-in-chief.
3. The Censor-in-chief: Censors were initially officials responsible for clerical work. They followed their lord and noted down the words and acts of the officials. Thus, they could play a role in rectifying the disciplines of officialdom. In charge of the receipt and dispatch of all the official documents, they could keep themselves informed of all the administrative affairs of the state. In the course of time, they began to serve as informants for their master and oversaw officials both inside and outside the imperial palace. In the Qin State, the Censor-in-chief was set up to head the Censors.

In the official system of the Han Dynasty (202 BC–AD 220), there were several Chinese characters shared by the names of multiple different official positions. These characters did not indicate the rank of the position but convey other information such as the nature of the functions of the position. A typical example was the character 丞 (*cheng*), which indicated a deputy position irrespective of the rank.

For another example, "the character 史 (*shi*) denoted a civil official position, especially a scribe". Within the same organ (such as the office of the Prime Minister), there were *shi* officials of different ranks (such as *chengxiang-shi*, 丞相史, a Clerk of the Prime Minister, and *chengxiang shao-shi*, 丞相少史, a Junior Clerk of the Prime Minister). Among low-ranking officials with an annual salary of one hundred *dan* (石 = 28.8 m^3) of grain, there were *ling-shi* (令史), *wei-shi* (尉史) and *zu-shi* (卒史), all subordinate or clerical positions. Among senior officials, there were *yu-shi* (御史, Censor), *ci-shi* (刺史, Regional Inspector) and *zhang-shi* (长史, an Aide in the Prime Minister's office). "It can be seen that *shi* does not indicate the rank, but the responsibility of the position." An additional example was the character 尉 (*wei*), which meant a military official. The top military commander was called *tai-wei* (太尉, Defender-in-chief). In the central government, there was *wei-wei* (卫尉, Commander of Bodyguards), *zhong-wei* (中尉, Commander-in-ordinary) and *shuiheng du-wei* (水衡都尉, Commander of Waterways). At the local level, there was *du-wei* (都尉, Prefecture Commander), *xiao-wei* (校尉, Commander of a remote area) and *xian-wei* (县尉, County Commander). An exception seemed to be *ting-wei* (廷尉, the Chamberlains for Law Enforcement), the top judiciary official of the civil bureaucracy. According to Ying Shao, a historian of the Eastern Han Dynasty, this mismatch had resulted from the custom of arranging military and judiciary positions under the same category according to the ancient thinking of unity between military and judicial affairs (Osamu, 1882/2017, pp. 19–20) (Fig. 2.1).

ii. Evolution of the Three Departments

1. The Imperial Secretariat

The Imperial Secretariat (*shangshutai*, 尚书台) with its Imperial Secretaries (*shangshu*, 尚书, literally "secretaries of documents") originated in a secretarial apparatus subordinate to the Palace Administrator of Finance of the Qin, in charge of organizing the paperwork. ("In the Qin, the Imperial Secretaries were set up within the imperial palace to take care of issuing imperial edicts and decrees, with a staff of four.") Emperor Wu of the Han once appointed eunuchs to this position, and they were called Director of the Central Secretariat (or Director of the Central Secretariat and Chief Receptionist because an Imperial Secretary often concurrently held the post of Receptionist). Later, Emperor Cheng of the Han reverted to the old practice of entrusting this position to regular state officials and revived the old name of "Imperial Secretary". Therefore, Director of the Central Secretariat and Imperial Secretary were merely different names for the same position, depending on whether the position was occupied by a eunuch or a regular state official, and there were times when the two names co-existed. This differentiation had nothing to do with the distinction between the Imperial Secretariat (or the Department of State Affairs) and the Palace Secretariat (or simply the Secretariat) in later dynasties (Lin, 1976, p. 167).

In the Western Han Dynasty, a number of sections were set up under the Imperial Secretaries. The Imperial Secretariat had one Director (*shangshu ling*, 尚书令), one Deputy Director (*puye*, 仆射), and four Imperial Secretaries, with each Imperial Secretary heading a separate section. In the reign of Emperor Cheng, the number

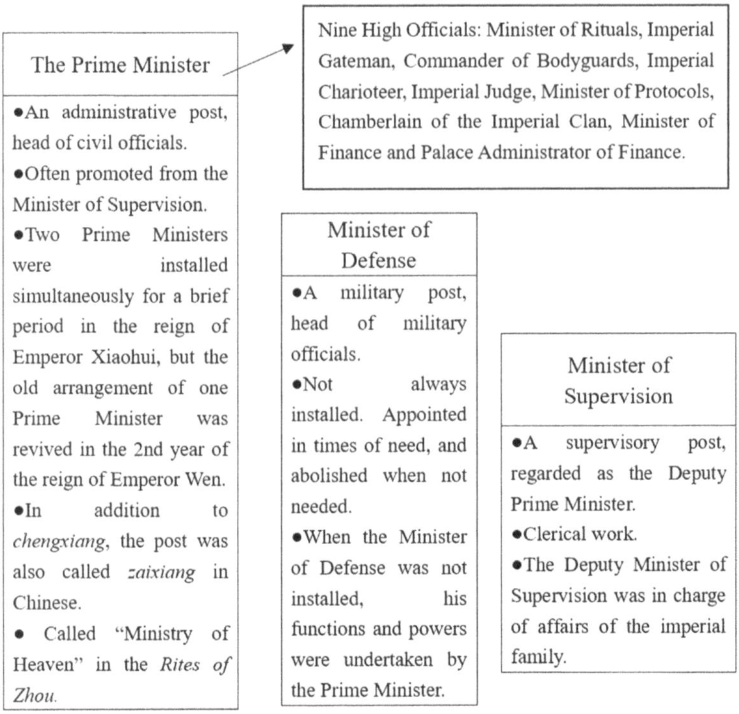

Fig. 2.1 Government organization of the Han Dynasty[2]

of Imperial Secretaries was increased to five. The Imperial Secretaries were entitled to read reports to the throne and draft imperial edicts and decrees. Thus, the clerks who used to handle the paperwork became the mouthpiece of the emperor. The Prime Minister and the Censor-in-chief had to look up to the Director of the Imperial Secretariat. In Emperor Guangwu's reign of the Eastern Han, the Three Dukes were rendered sinecure positions and high responsibilities were entrusted to the Imperial Secretariat. The Imperial Secretariat eventually grew from a group of scribes to a complex institution even weightier than the Three Dukes. In the Wei Dynasty, the Imperial Secretariat emancipated itself from the Palace Administrator of Finance to become an independent organization. Thus, the original subordinate to the Palace Administrator of Finance evolved into a multi-tiered organ comprising officials of different ranks, including the Director, Left Deputy Director, Right Deputy Director, Left Aide (*zuocheng*, 左丞), Right Aide (*youcheng*, 右丞), Imperial Secretaries, Attendant Gentlemen (*shangshu lang*, 尚书郎) and Clerks (*lingshi*, 令史).

The Imperial Secretariat was the predecessor of the Department of State Affairs in the later dynasties (Fig. 2.2).

[2] This chart has been made by Bian Ge, a student of Tsinghua University.

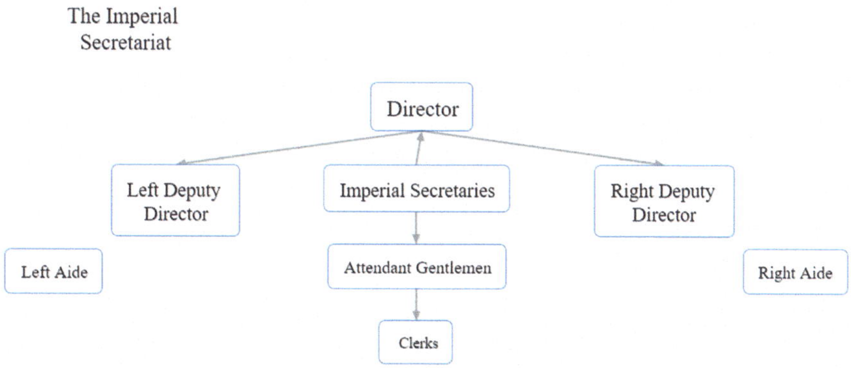

Fig. 2.2 The Imperial Secretariat[3]

2. The Palace Secretariat[4]

As the Imperial Secretariat was institutionalized into a government organ of the Outer Court with administrative responsibilities, the emperor created a new secretarial post called the "Director of the Archives Secretariat" (*mishu ling*, 秘书令). Emperor Wen of the Wei changed its name to the "Palace Secretariat" (*zhongshu*, 中书). The Palace Secretariat (abbreviated as the Secretariat) was headed a Supervisor (*zhongshu jian*, 中书监) and a Director (*zhongshu ling*, 中书令), who were in turn assisted by four Deputy Directors (*zhongshu shilang*, 中书侍郎) and several Subordinate Secretaries (Receptionists). Over time, the original functions of the Imperial Secretariat were shifted to the Palace Secretariat. The division of power between the Palace Secretariat and the Imperial Secretariat was as follows: The Palace Secretariat was responsible for drafting edicts and decrees, and thus involved itself in the process of decision making and acquired the Prime Ministerial status. The Imperial Secretariat was an executive organ responsible for implementing the imperial edicts and decrees. Across the Wei, Jin and Southern Dynasties, the Palace Secretariat became increasingly powerful, especially in the Liang and Chen Dynasties. Therefore, it was said: "A high official wishing to take part in deciding major state affairs must concurrently hold the position of Supervisor or Director of the Palace Secretariat, which was a vital source of administrative power." The Imperial Secretariat, on the other hand, "simply obeyed and executed the orders". In the Wei Dynasty, the Subordinate Secretaries (*zhongshu sheren*, 中书舍人) were called Receptionists (*tongshi*, 通事) and later renamed Receptionist-Secretaries. Since the Song and Qi of the Southern Dynasties, the functions and powers of the Palace Secretariat were increasingly concentrated in the hands of the Deputy Directors, whereas the Supervisor and the Director were reduced to sinecure positions. "The imperial edicts and decrees were drafted exclusively by the Deputy Directors, rather than the Supervisor or the Director". This could be attributed to two factors. In the first place, people of

[3] This chart has been made by Bian Ge, a student of Tsinghua University.

[4] Refer to Sa (2007, pp. 414–416).

the Southern Dynasties tended to pursue the abstract and metaphysical, to the neglect of "worldly affairs". Secondly, the royal princes of the Southern Dynasties served as local administrators from quite a young age and entrusted all administrative affairs to their document clerks. Upon ascending the throne, they often appointed their document clerks to the position of Deputy Directors, resulting in their manipulation of power.

3. The Chancellery[5]

The Jin Dynasty replicated the official system of the Wei, except that the Palace Attendant (*shizhong*, 侍中) became weightier in status and the Chancellery headed by the Palace Attendant was instituted. The Chancellery, together with the Imperial Secretariat and the Palace Secretariat constituted the embryonic form of the three central ministries of later dynasties. Since the Han Dynasty, the Palace Attendant was entrusted with enormous responsibilities thanks to his easy access to the emperor and proximity to the center of power. In the Wei Dynasty, the Palace Attendant took care of a wide range of administrative affairs, and in the Jin Dynasty, his functions and powers became even greater.

An examination of China's history reveals that the private officials of the emperor often turned into court officials. Once a private official evolved into a court official, a new post would be instituted inside the palace to fill the vacancy. The transformation of officials of the Inner Court into officials of the Outer Court, from officials close to the emperor to those distant from him was one characteristic of the evolution of China's official system. The Three Dukes, the Imperial Secretariat and the Palace Secretariat were all manifestations of this pattern of evolution. Although the Palace Attendant, in this process of evolution, gradually turned into an official of the Outer Court, he still retained the nature of an official of the Inner Court in that he continued to wait on the emperor as an attendant in spite of his enormous power. At first, the Palace Attendant only passively provided advice to the emperor regarding the edicts drawn up by the Palace Secretariat so as to correct the emperor's errors in the administration. However, as the Palace Secretariat attached more and more weight to his opinions, the Palace Attendant was able to play a more assertive role. In this way, the Palace Attendant became the Director of the Chancellery and was deemed to have the Prime Ministerial status. The Deputy Director of the Chancellery was known as the Minor Prime Minister.

In the Southern Dynasties, the position of the Director of the Chancellery was often assumed by members of prominent families, especially of the Wang and Xie clans. In the selection of candidates, "good looks took precedence over talent". The Southern Dynasties were similar to the Wei and Jin Dynasties in terms of configuration of the official system, and no position was regarded as the indisputable Prime Minister. Even if an official assumed the functions and powers of the Prime Minister, his tenure would not last long without external support. In the Northern Wei, the Deputy Director of the Chancellery was regarded by many as the Minor Prime Minister.

[5] Refer to Sa (2007, pp. 419–421).

4. Innovations in the Sui Dynasty[6]

Prior to the Sui period, one or two institutions, such as the Imperial Secretariat of the Han and the Palace Secretariat and the Chancellery of the Wei and Jin, ran the government and acted as the Prime Minister. In the Sui Dynasty, the three departments (*sansheng*, 三省), i.e., the Department of State Affairs, the Secretariat and the Chancellery, were joint and parallel organizations. They mutually checked one another and each took charge of one aspect of the administration. The heads of the three departments jointly discussed major state affairs. The Department of State Affairs, which headed the Six Ministries (*liubu*, 六部), processed all administrative affairs, the Secretariat was responsible for issuing orders, and the Chancellery was entitled to refute orders. The three departments constituted the central administrative organization of the Sui Dynasty.

5. The Three Departments and the Administration Hall System of the Tang Dynasty

The Tang Dynasty perpetuated the official system of the Sui, with some changes to the specific Chinese names of the three departments and their officials. The heads of the three departments held joint meetings at the Administration Hall to work on edicts. This arrangement had something of the spirit of the Cabinet in modern political history. The division of power among the three central ministries was as follows: (1) The Secretariat was responsible for drafting edicts and formulating policies on behalf of the emperor and was headed by two Directors. (2) When the the Chancellery received the government orders and policies, they would re-examine them. This ministry was headed by two Directors. (3) The Department of State Affairs was an executive organ, responsible for the implementation of orders and policies. This department used to be headed by the Director. However, since Emperor Taizong had served as the Executive Minister before he ascended the throne, no official dared to take that position thereafter. There were two deputies, Left Deputy Director and Right Deputy Director, who actually headed the department. In the eyes of the Tang people, only the Directors of the Secretariat and the Chancellery were the real Prime Ministers. The Department of State Affairs was no more than an executive organ. Only when the Left Deputy Director and Right Deputy Director concurrently held the position of Para-Secretary-Reviewer (*tong zhongshu menxia pingzhangshi*, 同中书门下平章事) or Administrative Consultant (*canzhi jiwu*, 参知机务) were they true Prime Ministers and entitled to attend Administration Hall meetings. Besides heads of the three departments, some lower-level officials who were concurrently appointed as Administrative Consultants, Para-Third-Ranking Officials or Para-Secretary-Reviewer were also eligible to attend the Administration Hall meetings. As other officials participated in the deliberation of court policies, the power of the Secretariat came to be eroded, and the responsibility of drafting edicts gradually shifted to the Hanlin Scholars (Qian, 2005, p. 37; Lin, 1976, p. 168).

[6] Refer to Lin (1976, pp. 167–168).

6. Collapse of the System of the Three Departments in the Song Dynasty

(1) Evolution from division of power among three departments to sharing of power by two departments and to monopoly of power by a single department

In the Song Dynasty, the Prime Minister did not have the final say in major state affairs, but drafted decrees or handled administrative documents based on what the emperor had to say. When the emperor was lazy or ignorant, the Prime Minister would make the decision on major administrative and military affairs. The Hanlin Scholars were drafters of proclamations. They were often around the emperor, could contribute their opinions when necessary and were often promoted to the position of the Prime Minister. Given the exalted status of the Directors of the three departments in the Song Dynasty, these positions were not filled when they became vacant, or were concurrently held by other officials as honorary titles. In the early Song period, the Para-Secretaries-Reviewers were real Prime Ministers, like in the Tang, and this title was often held by the Deputy Directors of the Secretariat and the Chancellery. The number of Prime Ministers was not large in the Song Dynasty (generally two or three), and was no more than four or five with the Administrative Consultants counted. When there were two Prime Ministers, one would be the Grand Scholar of the Zhaowen Pavilion and the Director for Compilation of the National History, and the other would be the Grand Scholar of the Jixian Hall. If there were three Prime Ministers, they would be respectively the Grand Scholar of the Zhaowen Pavilion, the Director for Compilation of the National History and the Grand Scholar of the Jixian Hall.

In the Song Dynasty, power was initially divided among the three departments of the Secretariat (receiving orders), the Chancellery (re-examining orders) and the Department of State Affairs (implementing orders), but this arrangement became distorted not long after its implementation. The fundamental cause lay in the fact that only the Secretariat could directly receive decrees from the emperor. Thanks to its easy access to the emperor, the Secretariat enjoyed more exclusive opportunities and steadily rose in power and status as compared with the two other ministries, resulting in the monopoly of power by a single ministry (autocratic rule by one department) (Lin, 1976, p. 168). In the early Song period, the heads of the Department of State Affairs, the Secretariat and the Chancellery jointly ran the government. After the bureaucratic reform of the Yuanfeng reign, the Left and Right Deputy Directors of the Department of State Affairs served as the Prime Ministers. Furthermore, the Left Deputy Director of the Department of State Affairs concurrently held the position of the Deputy Director of the Secretariat, and the Right Deputy Director of the Department of State Affairs the position of the Deputy Director of the Chancellery. Now that leaders of the executive organ also headed the other two departments, the system whereby the three departments mutually checked each other's powers was destroyed. After retreating to Southern China, the Song government no longer kept the Chancellery. Emperor Gaozong bestowed the title of Para-Secretary-Reviewer on the Left and Right Deputy Directors of the Department of State Affairs so that they no longer needed to be Deputy Directors of the other two departments. The Deputy Directors of the Chancellery and the Secretariat were changed into Administrative Consultants.[7] Emperor Xiaozong set up the Left and Right Prime Ministers to substitute for the Deputy Directors of the Chancellery and the Secretariat, abolished the Deputy Director of the Department of State Affairs, and appointed Administrative Consultants to take the place of the Deputy Directors of the Chancellery and the Secretariat. The Secretariat and the Chancellery became no more than empty names, and "the powers of the three departments were concentrated in a single entity". (Sa, 1975b, p. 114)

(2) Separation of administrative, military and financial powers[8]

Now that the system of the three departments fell apart in the Song, central power came to be divided among the Secretariat (in charge of administrative affairs), the Bureau of Military Affairs (in charge of military affairs) and the Three Divisions (in charge of financial affairs). Carrying forward an arrangement of the Five Dynasties, the Song government set up the Three Divisions, namely, Household, Salt and Iron, and Accounting, to take care of financial affairs. The Three Divisions gradually rose in power and were collectively referred to as the "Department of Finance". The directors of the Three Divisions, nicknamed the "Ministers of Finance", had a status second only to the Prime Minister. After the bureaucratic reform of the Yuanfeng reign, the Three Divisions were put under the Ministry of Revenue, and the Secretariat came to have an equal status with the Bureau of Military Affairs.

The Palace Secretary used to be a position occupied by the Prime Minister. In the late Tang period, the emperor favored his closest eunuchs so much as to entrust this position to them. In the Five Dynasties period, this post was often held by a military official, with a huge power comparable to that of the Prime Minister. Carrying forward this arrangement of the Tang and Five Dynasties, the Song government established the Bureau of Military Affairs (*shumi yuan*, 枢密院) to take care of military matters of the country, including troop organization, border defense and provisions. The head of this ministry, a position concurrently held by the Prime Minister, was responsible for transmitting confidential decrees and assisting the emperor in running the armed forces. After the bureaucratic reform of the Yuanfeng reign, the Prime Minister no longer concurrently headed the Bureau of Military Affairs. In the Southern Song Dynasty, the Prime Minister sometimes held this position and sometimes did not. Constant conflicts between the Secretariat and the Bureau of Military Affairs gave rise to the opinion that "administrative and military affairs should not be split up". During restructuring of the official system in the Yuanfeng reign, Wang Anshi, Prime Minister to Emperor Shenzong, proposed to abolish the Bureau of Military Affairs. However, adhering to the admonitions of earlier Song rulers, Emperor Shenzong did not wish to concentrate both administrative and military powers in one government

[7] Administrative Consultant, which was not the name of an official position at first, later became "the Deputy Prime Minister".

[8] Refer to Sa (1975b, pp. 148–153).

organ, but instead would like to divide the powers between two ministries, which could check on each other's power. Owing to frequent warfare in the Southern Song Dynasty, the emperor came to realize the inseparability of administrative and military powers, and Emperor Gaozong often instructed the Prime Minister to concurrently head the Bureau of Military Affairs. The situation fluctuated from time to time until the Kaixi reign, when it became an established practice for the Prime Minister to head the Bureau of Military Affairs.

7. The one-department system of the Yuan Dynasty

Emperor Shizu of the Yuan established a system which retained only one of the three central departments, similar to the system of the Qin (or Han) Dynasty. The Secretariat was in charge of administrative affairs, the Bureau of Military Affairs took care of military matters, and the Censor-in-chief oversaw the entire political machinery. The Secretariat was headed by the Director. The position of the Director, assumed by the Crown Prince, had a rank above all the officials but was of a nominal nature. Below the Director were the Right and Left Prime Ministers (the Mongols esteemed right over left), who were the real Prime Ministers. The Prime Ministers were assisted by Managers of Governmental Affairs (*pingzhang zhengshi*, 平章政事), each of which had a Right Aide and a Left Aide, and Administrative Consultants. These officials ran the central government and handled major military and state matters.

8. The Imperial Cabinet as the central administrative organization of the Ming Dynasty

In its early years, the Ming regime kept the official system of the Yuan Dynasty. The Secretariat was retained with its Left and Right Prime Ministers. In the 13th year of the Hongwu reign (1380), Prime Minister Hu Weiyong was executed for manipulation of power. The enraged emperor abolished the Secretariat and the Prime Ministerial position and shifted their powers to the Six Ministries. Since then, the Ministers of the Six Ministries took care of government affairs. In addition, Grand Scholars were installed at the Zhongji, Jianji, Wenhua, and Wuying Halls, and the Wenyuan and East Studios, with two Grand Scholars for each hall or studio. Although the Grand Scholars ranked above the Six Ministries, they only served as advisers to the emperor. As the Grand Scholars attended upon the emperor inside the imperial palace, they were referred to as the "Cabinet", to avoid using the term "Prime Minister". In terms of the political system, the Grand Scholars were not real Prime Ministers, but merely private secretaries of the emperor. Emperor Chengzu started the precedence of permitting the Cabinet Scholars to participate in state governance. Since then, the Six Ministries in practice gradually became subordinate organizations under the Cabinet and handled administrative affairs based on the intentions of the Cabinet. In this way, the Grand Scholars virtually evolved into "real Prime Ministers".

9. The Grand Council of the Qing Dynasty

At the central-government level, the Qing Dynasty followed the Ming practice in the structure of the Cabinet as the central secretariat and the Six Ministries responsible for specific tasks within defined spheres of administration. The Cabinet was staffed by six Grand Scholars, with two Manchu and two Han Grand Scholars appointed by the emperor through special decrees as well as one Manchu and one Han Assistant Grand Scholars concurrently held by high officials such as Ministers or General Governors (*zongdu*, 总督). Grand Ministers of the Deliberative Council (*yizheng-wang dachen*, 议政王大臣) were responsible for deliberating and reporting military affairs. The Hanlin Academy served as counselors to the emperor as it was charged with drafting the edicts, and shared, to a limited extent, the power of the Cabinet. Because of wars waged in the northwest in the Yongzheng reign, the emperor set up the Grand Council (*junjichu*, 军机处) within the imperial palace, so that military secrecy could be maintained. Sealed Envelope Decrees did not pass through the Cabinet, and their content was not made known to the Six Ministries. Instead, such a decree was drafted by the Grand Council. The emperor would review the decree, seal it in an envelope, and stamp the envelope. The stamp carried the words: Office for Military Affairs. A Sealed Envelope Decree, carrying the stamp of the Grand Council, was passed on to the Minister of War, whose sole role was to put the sealed decree inside another envelope and dispatch the package to the recipient. The Grand Council handled only military affairs at the beginning, but later gradually encroached upon the functions and powers of the Cabinet, so that "all major issues both inside and outside the imperial palace were processed by the Grand Council" and the Cabinet was reduced to an empty name. The Grand Council was staffed by 4–6 State Councilors, selected by the emperor from among both Manchu and Han high officials. The State Councilors were assisted by 16 Manchu and 16 Han secretaries. Under the "New Policies" Reforms in the reign of the Guangxu Emperor, the Supervisory Bureau of Government Affairs (*duban zhengwu chu*, 督办政务处) was established, which had considerable power comparable to the Grand Council. In the 3rd year of the Xuantong reign (1911 AD), the Grand Council was abolished upon promulgation of the new cabinet system (Chen, 1977, p. 106).

iii. The emperor's power and the Prime Ministerial power

1. Functions and powers of the Prime Minister in the early Han period[9]

In the Qin period, the Prime Minister was set up to head the officials of the government and take charge of all administrative affairs. The Han Dynasty continued the system of the Qin and installed the Prime Minister to be in charge of all administrative affairs. The Prime Minister both wielded weighty powers and commanded a high position.

(1) Functions and powers of the Prime Minister

First, the Prime Minister was entitled to be treated with great courtesy by the emperor: "When the Prime Minister meets with the emperor, the emperor should rise from his seat or alight from his coach." (*Book of Han*)

Second, he has the power to make decisions on fundamental state policies.

[9] Refer to Sa (1975a, pp. 242–250).

Third, he has the power to mete out awards and punishments. He could have a high official executed before reporting the case to the throne, or even without reporting it to the throne.

Fourth, "if the emperor does not personally attend to government affairs, the Prime Minister should do it on his behalf". (*Book of Han*)

Fifth, the emperor must approve a request made by the Prime Minister, whereas a proposal made by the emperor was invalid if disapproved by the Prime Minister. In some cases, the Prime Minister could even refute an imperial edict.

(2) Why the Prime Minister commanded an exalted status and weighty powers in the early Han

In terms of the philosophy on government, according to Huang-lao thought (a school of thought named after the legendary Yellow Emperor and the ancient philosopher Laozi), the lord rules by non-action, hence the lamentation by a Tang poet that "the ruler asked questions about gods, but no questions about the people". The emperor must be assisted by someone in handling the specific matters of government. This someone was no other than the Prime Minister. Prior to the reign of Emperor Wu of the Han, the position of Prime Minister was assigned only to a marquis (someone ennobled because of merit in founding the dynasty). This meritorious group was a potent force on the political arena. It supported Liu Bang in his bid to the throne, removed all of Empress Lü's family members from their positions of power, and installed Emperor Wen on the throne. In the early Han period, the Prime Minister constituted a check on the autocracy of the emperor on behalf of the meritorious group.

(3) The Censor-in-chief as the Deputy Prime Minister in the Qin and Western Han

In the Qin and Western Han periods, the Censor-in-chief was called the Deputy Prime Minister, and the offices of the Prime Minister and the Censor-in-chief were known as the two Prime Ministerial offices. "The Censor-in-chief is the Deputy Prime Minister, above the Nine Ministers." (*Book of Han*) Censor-in-chief was comparable to the Prime Minister in functions and powers and often contended with the Prime Minister for power. Sometimes the former commanded even greater power than the latter. "As the Censor-in-chief, Chao Cuo wielded greater power than the Prime Minister; Zhang Tang served as the Censor-in-chief … The Prime Minister was merely a sinecure position, and Zhang Tang had the final say in all matters under heaven. As the Censor-in-chief, Xiao Wangzhi did not hold the Prime Minister in esteem." (*Rongzhai Suibi*, a collection of essays by the Southern Song scholar Hong Mai) In the Eastern Han Dynasty, the Censor-in-chief was abolished, and the Deputy Censor-in-chief headed the Ministry of Supervision, which was an exclusively supervisory organ. In later dynasties, the Ministry of Supervision was headed by either the reinstated Censor-in-chief or the Deputy Censor-in-chief, but neither concurrently held the position of the Deputy Prime Minister.

(4) The system of court deliberations

Under the Han system, court deliberations were frequently held on major issues, such as the enfeoffment of kings, judgement of conspiracy cases, revision of laws, decisions on new policies (on salt and iron trade, for example). "When such an issue arose, the customary practice was for the emperor to consult the courtiers and instruct the Prime Minister to preside over the court discussion. Unless initiated by the emperor, the Prime Minister was not entitled to hold a court deliberation. Once instructed by the emperor to do so, the Prime Minister must be responsible for reporting the conclusion of the court discussion." The scope of officials participating in the court discussion varied depending upon the nature of the issue to be discussed. A discussion in which officials pertinent to the deliberated issue participated was called a "miscellaneous discussion" (Osamu, 1982/2017, p. 34).

2. Rise of the Inner Court and weakening of the Prime Minister's power[10]

In the early Han Dynasty, the emperor reigned with his arms folded, in a posture of ease. In case of a problem to deal with, the emperor consulted the Prime Minister, not other courtiers who were the Prime Minister's subordinates. The Prime Minister was in general charge of state government, whereas the Nine Ministers took care of specific aspects of administration. Prior to the reign of Emperor Wu, there was no other force standing between the emperor and the Prime Minister, thus no place for the so-called "Inner Court". As an ambitious ruler bent on taking the initiative, Emperor Wu delegated heavy responsibilities to his private secretaries and rendered the Prime Minister powerless. At that time, most Prime Ministers of the Outer Court, such as Dou Ying and Tian Fen, ended with a tragic fate, and others like Gongsun Hong filled the position merely for his cultured and refined manners. Crucial government matters no longer passed through the hands of the Prime Minister. The private officials of the emperor (officials of the Inner Court) steadily rose in status and encroached upon the power of the Prime Minister. From then on, the Nine Ministers took orders directly from the emperor and his Inner Court. In this way, the central administrative power of the Han Dynasty shifted from the Prime Minister to another group of officials, namely, the Inner Court. The Inner Court might have emerged because the disposal of military affairs at a time of military confrontation was beyond the capability of a Prime Minister with cultured and refined manners. However, once the distinction between the Inner Court and the Outer Court was drawn, infringement upon the Prime Minister's power by the emperor's private officials began to occur in times of peace as well. As a result, the Prime Minister was reduced into a mere executive organ.

[10] Refer to Lao (2005).

3. Alternation between the Three Dukes and the Prime Minister

It is said that in the official systems of the Shang and Zhou Dynasties, the Three Dukes referred to the Grand Preceptor, the Grand Mentor and the Grand Guardian, who were the tutors and protectors of the Crown Prince. Below the Three Dukes were the Six Ministers, who were practicing officials responsible for specific administrative areas. In the Qin Dynasty, the Three Dukes were executive officials including the Prime Minister, Defender-in-chief and the Censor-in-chief. The Han Dynasty perpetuated this arrangement of the Qin: The Prime Minister was the chief of civil officials. Although the Defender-in-chief was at the same level as the Prime Minister, this position was not always filled, and even if appointed, he did not necessarily have military power. The Censor-in-chief assisted the Prime Minister in running the government and was known as the Deputy Prime Minister. Emperor Wu abolished the Defender-in-chief and installed the Grand Commander (*dasima*, 大司马), who was also the leader of the Inner Court. Acting on the advice of He Wu, Emperor Cheng concentrated all the powers of the Three Dukes on the Prime Minister. When the Prime Minister proved incapable of such a burden, the Censor-in-chief was renamed the Grand Minister of Works (*dasikong*, 大司空) and the Grand Commander was installed to take powers from the Prime Minister. Thus, the Three Dukes became the Prime Minister, the Grand Commander and the Grand Minister of Works. During Emperor Ai's reign, the post of the Prime Minister was changed to the Grand Minister over the Masses (*dasitu*, 大司徒), and the Grand Commander and the Grand Minister of Works also had their respective areas of responsibility. Thus, the Three Dukes were restored as the top administrators of the central government. After usurping the throne, Wang Mang maintained this arrangement without any modification.

Emperor Guangwu initially replicated this arrangement of the Three Dukes, but later made some slight modifications in nomenclature, and the titles of the Three Dukes became the Defender-in-chief, Minister over the Masses and Minister of Works. The Three Dukes were equal in status and mutually checked each other's powers, but the real power of the central government was vested in the Imperial Secretariat, in charge of receiving and publicizing the emperor's orders. "Learning from the lessons of previous reigns of the Han Dynasty when the emperor's power was lost or the Mandate of Heaven was usurped by a court official, Emperor Guangwu overcorrected and took all powers into his own hands. Even though the Three Dukes were installed, real power fell into the hands of the Imperial Secretary." (biography of Zhong Changtong in Chap. 49 of *Book of Later Han*) (Zhang, 2003, pp. 233–235)[11]

[11] When Emperor Guangwu went to study in the imperial capital as a young man, his professed aspiration was "to be appointed to the position of Superintendent of the Capital (similar to chief of the police bureau of the capital) and marry Yin Lihua (beautiful girl of a wealthy family in his ancestral place)". After ascending the throne, his chief political concern was to strengthen his power and perpetuate the rule of his imperial family. All his limited reforms were geared toward this purpose: (1) In terms of the central bureaucracy, he deleted the word "Grand" from the titles of the "Grand Minister over the Masses" and "Grand Minister of Works", and changed the Grand Commander into the Defender-in-chief, which was no longer concurrently held by the General-in-chief. The functions and powers of the Three Dukes were shifted to the Imperial Secretariat. Thus, offices with high ranks did not possess real power, and offices with real power were not given high

Emperor Ming (r. AD 57–75) of the Eastern Han created the title of Intendant of the Imperial Secretariat. The Three Dukes, unless they were given the intendantship of the Imperial Secretariat, were not entitled to involvement in government affairs. Thus, the Imperial Secretariat evolved from a minor clerical office into the central administrative organ that took comprehensive charge of state affairs, whereas the Three Dukes took a back seat. Towards the end of Emperor Ling's reign of, the two posts of the Grand Commander and the Defender-in-chief co-existed. In the Jian'an reign of Emperor Xian, the Minister over the Masses was changed back into the Prime Minister, and the Minister of Works into the Censor-in-chief. This was because at that time, Cao Cao seized power of the Eastern Han Dynasty. He had the early Han official configuration whereby the Prime Minister, assisted by the Censor-in-chief (Deputy Prime Minister), ran the government revived. Nevertheless, the Wei Dynasty reverted to the arrangement of the Eastern Han after supplanting the Han regime.

When the Prime Minister fell out of power in the Western and Eastern Han Dynasties, imperial relatives and eunuchs, who were the closest to the emperor, constantly manipulated power and fought against each other.

4. The Administration Hall and countersigning of the emperor's edict by the Prime Minister in the Tang Dynasty

The Administration Hall was the place for a joint meeting between the Secretariat and the the Chancellery. The emperor's signed edicts must also bear the chops of the Secretariat and the Chancellery, i.e., formally passed at the Administration Hall, before being issued to the Department of State Affairs for implementation. Imperial edicts not countersigned by the two ministries were regarded as illegal and were therefore not recognized by lower government departments. Empress Wu Zetian abused her power by issuing orders directly without going through the Administration Hall. Consequently, there was the criticism "how could an imperial edict come about without passing through the Phoenix Pavilions?" The "Phoenix Pavilions" referred to the Secretariat and the Chancellery during Empress Wu Zetian's reign. Emperor Zhongzong, who ruled after the Empress from 705 to 710 AD, also appointed officials without bothering the Secretariat and the Chancellery. These edicts were ridiculed as "slanted edicts in black ink", indicating they had not gone through the Secretariat and the Chancellery. This system of countersigning the emperor's edict by the Prime Minister persisted all the way until the Song Dynasty. In the Song period, the founding Emperor Taizu wanted to appoint Zhao Pu as the new Prime Minister when the position was left vacant following three consecutive resignations. Under normal circumstances, his edict had to be countersigned by the Prime Minister. Given the

---

ranks, so as to prevent an official from abusing his power. (2) In terms of the local bureaucracy, he changed the Regional Governor back into the Regional Inspector and increased his annual salary from six hundred *dan* to two thousand *dan*. The Regional Inspector had a fixed seat locally and sent someone to make a report at the imperial capital at the end of the year. His impeachments went directly to the emperor without going through the Three Dukes. (3) In terms of the military system, he cancelled local military training to weaken the local military forces, which rendered the troops of prefectures and subordinate kingdoms useless. In case of wars on the frontiers, he relied on hired barbarian soldiers (Zhang, 2003, pp. 233–235).

absence of a Prime Minister, however, the emperor could not get his edict validated for execution. Eventually, the "Ganlu Incident" (in 835 AD) was cited to enable another official to stamp the edict on the Prime Minister's behalf (Qian, 2005, pp. 36–39).

In the early years of the Kaiyuan reign, Emperor Xuanzong of the Tang set up the Hanlin Academy, initially as the office for Scholars Awaiting Orders (officials who helped the emperor read memorials and gave him advice thereon). Later, the Hanlin Academy began to get involved in the central decision-making system and took over the responsibilities of the Secretaries. During the Zhide reign, which was a period of turmoil and warfare, the Hanlin Scholars served as both attendants and advisors for the emperor thanks to their easy access to the throne and came to be known as the Inner Prime Ministers. Thus, the central administrative organization shifted from the Prime Minister to the Hanlin Academy (Sa, 1975c, p. 303).

5. Division of the Prime Minister's power and strengthening of the emperor's power

The Song Prime Minister's power was rather limited compared with his Tang counterpart. Of the three departments, only the Secretariat was based inside the imperial palace to receive decrees directly from the emperor. The Secretariat was also called the Administration Hall. The Bureau of Military Affairs was in charge of military matters. Financial power was divided among three divisions, namely Household, Salt and Iron, and Accounting. The power for appointing government officials was shifted from the Ministry of Personnel under the Department of State Affairs led by the Prime Minister to a newly established Assessment Department (later renamed the Auditing Department). The Assessment Department was further divided into two parts: the East Part for selecting civil officials and the West Part military officers. In this way, the Prime Minister lost the power for appointing and promoting government officials. According to an ancient practice, the Three Dukes discussing matters of importance had the privilege of being seated. In the early Song period, however, the Prime Minister insisted on standing in a self-effacing manner at court in an attempt to restore the emperor's Power lost during the Five Dynasties period. In the drafting of imperial decrees by the Prime Minister on behalf of the emperor, in the Tang Dynasty, the imperial edicts prepared by the Secretariat were called Ready Drafts, to be submitted to the emperor for approval. In the Song Dynasty, the Prime Minister only drafted the outline of a decree, with several suggestions or proposals for the reference of the emperor. Therefore, the emperor's power was greatly strengthened. Nevertheless, the centralization of power on the emperor in the Song Dynasty was carried out only institutionally, not in personnel arrangement. None of the emperors of the Northern Song were known to be cruel or autocratic (Qian, 2005, pp. 67–69).

Another domain in which the emperor's power expanded in the Song Dynasty was the administration of justice (including re-legislation). The official law code was rarely applied in judicial practice and was substituted by the emperor's decrees, precedents, injunctions and their compilations. As the compilations of the emperor's decrees and precedents grew too voluminous and cumbersome, the officials were at a loss in their application. Therefore, since the late Northern Song period, officials began to shift the problems to their superior and sought the emperor's intervention on special cases that they were handling. This middle course of resorting to the emperor for the final decision (with the judgement becoming a precedent) was only one indication of the progression of the Song Dynasty towards autocracy (McKnight, 2004, p. 332).

6. The Cabinet system and monopoly of power by the emperor in the Ming Dynasty

The Yuan Dynasty conquered the Central Plains as a minority ethnic group. In comparison with the Song Dynasty, the Prime Ministerial power expanded and the emperor's power was restricted to some extent in the Yuan, a fact that was ridiculed by Emperor Taizu of the Ming as "not following the ancient practice". Because the Prime Minister Hu Weiyong allegedly attempted a coup, Emperor Taizu abolished the Secretariat and the Chancellery, eliminated the position of the Prime Minister, and threatened to impose the death penalty on anyone requesting to re-appoint the Prime Minister. Since then, no Director was placed to head the Department of State Affairs, and the Six Ministries under the Department of State Affairs had six Ministers, instead of one Director. As none of the Ministers of the Six Ministries were subordinate to one another, the Department of State Affairs was in effect turned into a multi-headed entity.

Emperor Taizu did not just abolish the system of the Prime Minister. In fact, he dismantled all the top-level (executive, military and supervisory) organs of the central government and concentrated power securely in his own hands. He acted as the First Grand-Secretary and the top military commander, and directly led more than a hundred Investigating Censors. In addition to dismantling the Secretariat, Emperor Taizu also fragmented the Chief Military Commission (*dadudu fu*, 大都督府, the top military organ of the central government) into five Military Regions with the directional prefixes Central, Left, Right, Front, and Rear. Thus, there was not a single general who was able to gain control over the military establishment. In the meantime, Emperor Taizu eliminated the Censorate and swept away all its senior executive posts. He only retained the leaderless Bureau of Supervision as the office site for the numerous co-equal Investigating Censors. In 1382 and 1383, Emperor Taizu made attempts to rectify this chaotic situation by organizing the Investigating Censors into a number of agencies called Regions and establishing a new executive superstructure comprised of three tiers including the Censor-in-chief (*duyushi*, 都御使) on top of the Regions. The reunified supervisory body was given a new name: the Chief Surveillance Bureau. Nevertheless, the supervisory organ was unified only for internal personnel and administrative purposes. There was not a single appointee in the central government who could possibly gain control over the surveillance establishment, and the emperor was now "the sole coordinator for … more than a hundred censors" (Hucker, 2008, pp. 74–76).

Cabinet Scholars acted as consultants to the emperor and occupied only the fifth-level rank. Later as the emperors slacked off and allowed the Cabinet to handle state affairs, The Cabinet became a power organization. The position of Cabinet Scholars was usually held concurrently by the court teachers for the emperor and the princes and the heads of the Six Ministries of the Department of State Affairs. Thus, the post of Cabinet Scholars became respectful. Nevertheless, according to the Ming system, political power rested with the emperor, from whom all the imperial edicts and decrees came from, and the Cabinet Scholars were no more than private secretaries of the emperor. The Six Ministries under the Department of State Affairs were the top administrators of the government, and they only obeyed orders from the emperor, not the Cabinet. The Cabinet was not the same as the Prime Minister. If a Cabinet Scholar took powers into his own hands, he would be deemed as a power-grabbing or treacherous official. Zhang Juzheng, the "able" First Grand Cabinet Scholar, was a typical example. He was not the government leader according to the Ming system, but overstepped his authority in order to exercise power and interfered with the affairs of government departments.[12] Thus, he was regarded by some as a power-grabbing or treacherous official.

Besides the Cabinet, another group that struggled to control the decisions of government throughout Ming times was the eunuchs, with their institutional base in the bulky eunuch offices headed by the Rituals Supervisor (*sili jian*, 司礼监). The eunuch group also had control over the secret service agency. The Cabinet and the eunuch group were "two sets of imperial advisors", sometimes collaborating with and sometimes struggling against each other. "Under the Ming system, after the abolition of the prime ministership in 1380, neither of these groups had a clear, constitutional basis for exercising advisory functions. Both were of the inner court, both were close personal attendants of the emperor, and both gained their authority from their relationship to him." The fundamental reason for the rising eunuch power in the Ming Dynasty lay in the fragmentation of the central administrative system after Emperor Taizu abolished the prime ministership. Consequently, the emperors had to resort to their eunuch attendants in handling important documents, particularly in consideration of the fact that the Ming Dynasty had few intelligent and diligent rulers besides Hongwu and Yongle. "Eunuch assistance to the throne was one inevitable makeshift response to the destruction of the leadership in the outer court that had provided rulers in earlier dynasties with responsible executive assistance." The Ming regularization of a vast eunuch administrative establishment really had no parallel even in those eunuch-plagued Han and Tang Dynasties (Mote, 2008, pp. 362–365).

After the fall of the Ming Dynasty, Huang Zongxi (a great Chinese historian) pointed out in his *Critique on Past Dynasties* that it was a grave mistake to abolish the Prime Ministerial position. He believed that the Prime Minister must be established in his proper title and capacity. The government must be headed by the Prime Minister, not by the emperor himself (Qian, 2005, pp. 97–103).

7. The Grand Council and autocracy by the emperor in the Qing Dynasty

Although the institution of the Prime Minister was dispensed with in the Ming Dynasty, autonomy of the Outer Court headed by the Cabinet Scholars gradually emerged when many of the do-nothing emperors failed to play a strong leading role at the helm of the government. "By the end of the Ming much of the ordinary business of government had come to be managed in the outer court at a distance from

[12] For stance, he issued orders directly without the emperor's approval. He required all the government departments to prepare duplicates of reports to the throne, with one set bypassing the Supervising Secretaries of the Six Ministries and going directly to the Cabinet.

the emperor and without constant recourse to him for guidance." The Inner Court in the Kangxi Emperor's reign included the Imperial Household Department and the Deliberative Council, whose top posts were monopolized by Manchus and Mongols, and the South Studio staffed by Han Chinese scholars. The Yongzheng Emperor did not use the established dignitaries of the factions of his father's day. Instead, he downgraded his father's Inner-Court organizations, created new Inner-Court structures and brought in his own men. At the top level, he abandoned the ethnic division of his father's Inner Court and assigned Chinese to work alongside Manchus. He set up Superintendents above the Ministers of the Six Ministries to strengthen the Inner Court. These measures paved the way for the founding of the Grand Council in the following reign of the Qianlong Emperor (Bartlett, 1991, pp. 30–31).

(1) The South Studio

The South Studio was established in the 16th year of the Kangxi reign (1677 AD). The Kangxi Emperor selected some members of the Hanlin Academy "with superior literary attainment and high moral integrity" to work in the South Studio, titled "Special Aides of the South Studio". The appointees mainly accompanied the emperor in the composition of poetry, calligraphy and painting and drafted edicts based on the comments dictated by the emperor. As a vital agency that received orders directly from the emperor and could issue edicts and decrees at any time, the South Studio grew increasingly weightier in power. When the Kangxi Emperor took over the reins of government, major state matters should be discussed on the meetings of the Deliberative Council attended by the Manchu nobility, and the Cabinet was nominally still the top administrative body of the Outer Court. The Deliberative Council and the Cabinet exercised a certain check on the emperor's power. In order to secure state power in his own hands, the Kangxi Emperor decided to put the South Studio at the core to weaken the power of the Deliberative Council and in the meantime shift certain functions of the Cabinet of the Outer Court to the Inner Court. Even so, the South Studio was only a secretariat in the political system. It did not replace the Cabinet and institutionalize into a central administrative organ in the technical sense of the term.

(2) The Grand Council

As mentioned previously, the Grand Council was set up so that military secrecy could be maintained. This agency used to be called "High Officials in Charge of Military Finance". Later on, the scope of its power extended gradually from the military domain to routine administration in general. "The so-called Council of State was not an innovation of the Qing Dynasty. It was essentially one variant of the Cabinet, adapted by the Qing rulers to suit the circumstances of their times. Later, it took over the powers of the Cabinet and became the sole top administrative organ of the government." After the demise of the Yongzheng Emperor, the Inner Court was quickly enlarged, the Grand Council experienced a drastic increase in its responsibilities, and the Interim Council was established in the Grand Council. The Grand Council directly controlled by the monarch, was the top organ for deliberating state policies, and the emperor came here on a daily basis to handle state affairs. The

Grand Council paid particular attention to the keeping of secrecy in the handling of military and other important matters. To avoid arousing suspicion, State Councilors generally did not receive local officials and rarely had personal associations with officials of the central government (Oda, 2003, pp. 165–171). Under the Qing system, the Cabinet was the central administrative organ of the Outer Court, and the Grand Council was only a set of imperial advisors of the emperor's Inner Court. Prior to the Jiaqing reign, it was not even listed in the *Da-Qing Huidian* (*The Code of the Qing Dynasty*). However, the Grand Council was the de facto top central administrative organ owning to the imperial power behind it. The Qing emperors were particularly diligent, and rarely did a day pass without the emperor meeting with his Grand Councilors. As major administrative matters and military deployments were handled by the Grand Councilors based on the emperor's orders, the imperial autocracy of the Qing Dynasty reached its apex.

iv. Outranking (sinecure) posts in history

In the early Western Zhou period, the central government was headed by the Grand Guardian and the Grand Preceptor, "who held the military and political power and acted as regents for the young King". "This political institution of guardianship by elders had evolved from the ritual system of child nursery and guardianship in aristocratic families." "Since the middle Western Zhou period, there were no longer records on the Grand Guardian serving as a high-ranking administrative official", but the Grand Preceptor was still head of the Ministerial Department (*qingshiliao*, 卿事寮) of the central government. As head of the Department of the Grand Astrologer (*taishiliao*, 太史寮), which was on a par with the Ministerial Department, the Grand Astrologer became an administrative official second only to the Grand Preceptor, "charged with immense powers in administration and appointment of officials". (Yang, 2016, pp. 337, 356–358) Since the Western Han Dynasty, the most honorable posts of the Western Zhou, such as the Grand Preceptor and the Grand Guardian, became outranking titles (namely, titles above the official rank system) for those who enjoyed an exalted status but held no real power. These titles are listed in detail as follows:

In the Western Han, the Grand Preceptor, the Grand Mentor and the Grand Guardian were honored as the Superior Dukes. In the Eastern Han, the Grand Mentor was esteemed as the Superior Duke.

In the Wei Dynasty, Superior Dukes included the State Chancellor, Grand Mentor, Grand Guardian, Grand Preceptor, General-in-chief, Defender-in-chief, Minister over the Masses and the Minister of Works, all of which were of the first rank.

The Jin Dynasty had the Specially Appointed Dukes (*teren gong*, 特任公) and the Eight Dukes. The former included the Prime Minister and the State Chancellor. The latter included the Great Steward, the Grand Mentor, the Grand Guardian, the Grand Commander, the General-in-chief, the Defender-in-chief, the Minister over the Masses and the Minister of Works. The first five of the Eight Dukes were outranking positions, while the last three were first-rank positions. The Northern and Southern Dynasties basically maintained the official system of the Jin, except that some of the above positions were left vacant or not always filled, such as the State Chancellor and the Prime Minister.

The Sui Dynasty had the Three Preceptors and the Three Dukes. The former were outranking posts, including the Grand Preceptor, the Grand Mentor and the Grand Guardian. The latter were first-rank posts, including the Defender-in-chief the Minister over the Masses and the Minister of Works.

The Tang Dynasty continued the official system of the Sui, except that the Three Preceptors and the Three Dukes were all of the upper first rank (hereafter referred to as 1a). The Three Preceptors were tutoring positions without specific responsibilities. The Three Dukes were officials engaged in the discussion of government matters, with all-embracing responsibilities in assisting the emperor in running the country.

The Song Dynasty had the Three Preceptors and the Three Solitaries, all of which were of the rank of 1a.

The Yuan Dynasty had the Three Dukes, i.e., the Grand Preceptor, the Grand Mentor and the Grand Guardian, which had the rank of 1a.

The Ming Dynasty had the Three Dukes and the Three Solitaries. The former were the Grand Preceptor, the Grand Mentor and the Grand Guardian, with the rank 1a. The latter were the Junior Preceptor, the Junior Mentor and the Junior Guardian, with the lower first rank (hereafter referred to as 1b).

The Qing Dynasty did not have a fixed system for these positions, but Hong Chengchou (a Chinese official who served under the Ming and Qing Dynasties) was once conferred with the title of Grand Preceptor of the Crown Prince, and quite a few other high officials were honored with the title of Grand Guardian of the Crown Prince either in their lifetime or posthumously.

2.1.2 *Functional Departments of the Central Government: The Six Ministries and Nine Ministers*

i. Evolution of the Nine Ministers[13]

According to legend, the Zhou Dynasty set up the Nine Ministers (*jiuqing*, 九卿), namely, the Junior Preceptor, Junior Mentor, Junior Guardian, Minister of State, Overseer of the Masses, Overseer of Ritual Affairs, Overseer of Mounts, Overseer of Bandits, and the Minister of Works. In the Qin Dynasty, the Prime Minister was in comprehensive charge of the administration, and the Nine Ministers were tasked to oversee specific aspects of the administration. The Superintendent of Rituals (*fengchang*, 奉常) was in charge of the rituals for offering sacrifices. The Imperial Gateman (*langzhong*, 郎中) guarded the gates to the imperial palace. The Commander of Bodyguards (*weiwei*, 卫尉) was in charge of security of the Imperial Palace. The Superintendent of the Imperial Clan (*zongzheng*, 宗正) took care of affairs of the emperor's family members. The Superintendent of Finance (*zhisu neishi*,

[13] Refer to Yang and Ou (2005, pp. 121–123) and Lin (1976, p. 171).

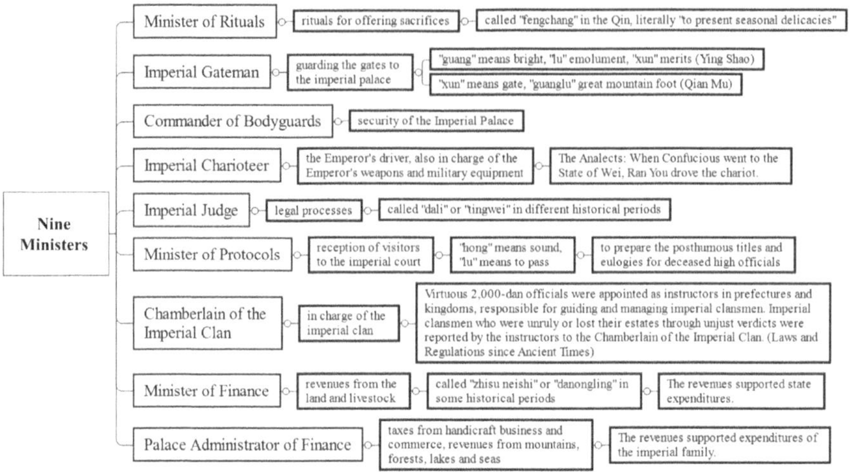

Fig. 2.3 Nine Ministers of the Han Dynasty[14]

治粟内史) was in charge of collecting the land tax and the storage of grains. The Chamberlain for Law Enforcement (*tingwei*, 廷尉) was in charge of legal processes. The Superintendent of Protocols (*dianke*, 典客) was responsible for receiving visitors to the imperial court. The Imperial Charioteer (*taipu*, 太仆) was in charge of the imperial coaches and horses. The Palace Administrator of Finance (*shaofu*, 少府) collected taxes on the produce of hills and lakes. The Han Dynasty replicated this system of the Qin with some modifications in nomenclature (fengchang into taichang, 太常; langzhong into guangluxun, 光禄勋; zhisu neishi into dasinong, 大司农) and placed the Nine Ministers directly under the jurisdiction of the Prime Minister (or the Grand Minister over the Masses). The offices of the Nine Ministers were called "Courts". When Emperor Cheng of the Han set up sections under the Imperial Secretaries, political power was shifted to the Imperial Secretaries and the Nine Ministers gradually lost their importance. However, as the Imperial Secretaries were still low in status, they were only able to take over part, but not all of the functions and powers of the Nine Ministers. In the Eastern Han Dynasty, the Nine Ministers were subordinated to the Three Dukes, with the Superintendent of Rituals and Imperial Gateman under the Defender-in-chief, the Imperial Charioteer, Commander of Bodyguards and Superintendent of Protocols under the Minister over the Masses, the Superintendent of the Imperial Clan, Superintendent of Finance and Palace Administrator of Finance under the Minister of Works. In the Jin Dynasty, several new posts were added to the original Nine Ministers, and subordinates and clerks were provided to each official (Fig. 2.3).

Emperor Wu of the Liang Dynasty adjusted the Nine Ministers. A Superintendent of the Imperial Treasury was split from the Palace Administrator of Finance, the Court Architect was changed into the Superintendent of Palace Buildings, and the

[14] This chart has been made by Bian Ge, a student of Tsinghua University.

Commissioner of Waterways was changed into the Superintendent of Waterways. This resulted in a total of Twelve Ministers, divided into four categories named after the four seasons, with three ministers under each season. The Twelve Ministers all had deputies and subordinates in charge of personnel evaluation and the preparation of records and accounts. Even though the Nine Ministers (*jiu qing*, 九卿) existed in the Han Dynasty, their Chinese titles did not contain the character 卿. This suffix was added to the official titles in the reign of Emperor Wu of the Liang, and this designation was continued in later dynasties.

In the Northern Wei Dynasty, there were still Nine Ministers, and a deputy was established for each of the Nine Ministers. In the Northern Qi Dynasty, the Chamberlain for Law Enforcement was changed into the Court of Judicial Review (*dali si*, 大理寺), and the Palace Administrator of Finance was changed into the Superintendent of the Imperial Treasury (*taifu*, 太府). As the offices of the Nine Ministers were called "courts", the Nine Officials came to be known as "the Nine Courts" (*jiusi*, 九寺). The Sui Dynasty maintained the Northern Qi's system of the Nine Courts and in the meantime set up Five Directorates (*wujian*, 五监) for Education, Imperial Manufactories, Armaments, Palace Buildings and Waterways respectively. The Tang Dynasty copied the system of the Sui, except for the addition of the Directorate of Astronomy. The Song Dynasty inherited the system of the Tang, but after the Song imperial court relocated to the south (and became the Southern Song Dynasty), some of the Nine Courts and Five Directorates were abolished, leaving only Five Courts and Three Directorates. The Ming Dynasty had Five Courts, Three Directorates, Three Offices and Two Administrations, such as the Office of Transmission, the Court of the Imperial Clan and Household Administration of the Heir Apparent. The Qing Dynasty had Five Courts, for rituals, management of banquets, judicial review, ethnic and religious affairs, and management of horses and animal husbandry respectively, as well as the Directorate of Astronomy, the Court of the Imperial Clan, the Imperial Household Department, and the Office of Transmission. Later, the Office of Transmission was abolished, the Court for Rituals, Court for Managing Banquets, and Court for Ethnic and Religious Affairs were merged into the Department of Rituals, and the Court for Managing Horses and Animal Husbandry was merged into the Division of the Armies.

Among the Nine Ministers half were responsible for handling affairs of the imperial family for the emperor, hence the saying that "officials in the imperial palace and in the Prime Minister's office are inseparable". As can be seen, "the Prime Minister and the Censor-in-chief both evolved from the learned private officials of the emperor, and the Nine Ministers also developed from the emperor's servants." In the Qing Dynasty, with the exception of the Court of Judicial Review, all the other courts became agencies that exclusively served the imperial family. A clear distinction was drawn between agencies for the imperial family and departments of the government, so that the claim "officials in the imperial palace and in the Prime Minister's office are inseparable" was no longer valid.

ii. Evolution of the Six Ministries

1. The Imperial Secretariat branching into sections[15]

In the reign of Emperor Cheng of the Han, four Imperial Secretaries were installed below the Deputy Director of the Imperial Secretariat, each heading a separate section. The four sections and their functions are as follows: (1) The Section for Regular Attendants (*changshi cao*, 常侍曹) handled all correspondence with the Three Dukes and the Nine Ministers. (2) The Section for Commandery Governors (lit., Section for 2000-bushel officials) (*erqiandan cao*, 二千石曹) was in charge of correspondence with Regional Inspectors and Prefecture Governors. (3) The Section for the Civil Population (*mincao*, 民曹) received memorials to the throne from officials and people. (4) The Section for Receptions (*kecao*, 客曹) was responsible for receiving and communicating with foreign dignitaries and tribal leaders. Later in the reign of Emperor Cheng, the Section for the Three Dukes (*sangong cao*, 三公曹) was added to manage judicial correspondence. Thus, the number of sections under the Imperial Secretariat increased to five.

Emperor Guangwu of the Eastern Han established six sections: (1) The Section for the Three Dukes was in charge of the annual evaluation of the performance of Prefecture Governors. (2) The Section of Regular Attendants was changed into the Section of Personnel (*licao*, 吏曹), in charge of the selection of officials and offering of sacrifices. (3) The Section for the Civil Population was concurrently responsible for repairs, manufactories, ponds and parks. (4) The Section for Receptions was responsible for security of the emperor and reception of foreign emissaries. (5) The Section for Senior Officials was in charge of legal processes. (6) The Section for General Administration (*zhongduguan cao*, 中都官曹) was responsible for handling such matters as floods, fire as well as cases of robbery and theft. The Six Sections, plus the two Deputy Directors, were collectively called the "Eight Executives" (*bazuo*, 八座). They were the embryonic form of the system of the Six Ministries in later dynasties.

In the Wei Dynasty, there were five Imperial Secretaries, heading respectively the Section of Personnel, Section of Census, Section for Reception, Section of the Five Troops and Section for General Accounts. The Jin Dynasty instituted six sections: the Section of Personnel, Section for the Three Dukes Section for Reception, Section for Equipment, Section for State Farms and Section for General Accounts. Both the Wei and Jin Dynasties also had the Section for Sacrifices, held concurrently by the Right Deputy Director of the Imperial Secretariat. This is why in historical sources, the number of sections of the Imperial Secretariat was said to be either five or six. In the Wei and Jin periods, not only were the Imperial Secretaries divided into sections, but the Attendant Gentlemen were segregated into divisions as well, which pioneered the practice of setting up divisions under the Six Ministries.

[15] Refer to Lin (1976, pp. 172–173).

2. The Six Ministries under the Department of State Affairs

In the Northern Qi Dynasty, there were Six Ministries under the Department of State Affairs (the former Imperial Secretariat), i.e., the Ministry of Personnel, Ministry for Palace Affairs, Ministry for Sacrifices, Ministry of the Five Troops, Ministry for Criminal Administration, and Ministry for General Accounts. The Sui Dynasty initially copied this arrangement of the Northern Qi, but later made modifications to all the ministries except for the Ministry of Personnel. The Ministry for General Accounts was changed into the Ministry of Revenue, the Ministry for Sacrifices into the Ministry for Rituals, the Ministry of the Five Troops into the Ministry of War, the Ministry for Criminal Administration into the Ministry of Justice, and the Ministry for Palace Affairs into the Ministry for Works. Each of the Six Ministries had four divisions under it. The Tang Dynasty maintained this arrangement, and the Six Ministries became an established institution. After the Rebellion of An Lushan and Shi Siming from 755 to 763 AD, the central government lost control over the Military Zones (*fanzhen*, 藩镇) supervised by the Central Commissioners, and eunuchs seized the military power in the central government. Consequently, the Ministry of War gradually fell out of power. The Ministry of Revenue lost its power to three Commissioners for Salt and Iron, Accounting, and Finance. The power of checking the performance of officials of the Personnel Ministry was grabbed by the emperor and the Prime Minister in the central government and by the various Supervisors and Commissioners at the local level. This also weakened the power of the Ministry of Justice (Yan, 2006).

In the Song Dynasty, the Six Ministries functioned separately and were not subordinated to the Prime Minister. With the exception of the Ministry of Personnel, none of the Six Ministries was headed by a Minister, but instead had one or two Supervisors (*panbushi*, 判部事). Later, in imitation of an arrangement in the Five Dynasties, the Song government set up Three Divisions, namely Household, Salt and Iron, and Accounting. The Three Divisions took control of the financial power of the state and grew increasingly weightier in their responsibilities. After the bureaucratic reform of the Yuanfeng reign, the Three Divisions were merged into the Ministry of Revenue. In the Yuan Dynasty, the Six Ministries were placed under the Secretariat. Each Ministry was headed by three Ministers, which had no sections under them. In the Ming Dynasty, the Secretariat was dismantled, and the Six Ministries became independent organizations. Each Ministry was headed by one Minister, assisted by a Left Deputy Minister and a Right Deputy Minister. The Qing Dynasty followed the Ming practice, except that each Ministry had two Ministers (one Manchu plus one Han Chinese) and four deputies (two Manchus plus two Han Chinese).

iii. Relationship between the Courts, Directorates and the Six Ministries

In the Qin and Han Dynasties, the Prime Minister was the central administrative organ in charge of issuing orders, whereas the Nine Ministers were the executive organs. Since the late Han and Wei periods, the Imperial Secretariat (which later evolved into the Department of State Affairs) involved itself directly in state affairs by wresting much power from the Prime Minister and taking over some functions of the Nine Ministers. In the Sui and early Tang Dynasties, the Director and the Deputy Directors were the Prime Ministers, and the Six Ministries, each of which branched into a number of sections, were responsible for implementing state policies. Therefore, the Department of State Affairs was both the Prime Ministerial organ and the executive machinery. Since the Shenlong reign, the Deputy Executive Ministers were removed from the central administrative system. Nevertheless, the Department of State Affairs, which served as the crucial hub that passed the orders of the emperor and the Prime Minister down to the specific offices, fell nothing short of being the top administrative organ of the state. Although since the late Han period, the Imperial Secretariat (or the Department of State Affairs) participated in running the government and encroached upon the powers of the Nine Ministers, the Nine Ministers still survived and functioned alongside with the Imperial Secretariat (the Department of State Affairs) as administrative organs. Consequently, there would necessarily be some degree of overlap in their functions and powers, giving rise to confusion in the division of their responsibilities. For example, similar and overlapping duties existed between the Ministry of Revenue and the two Courts for Finance and the Imperial Treasury, between the Department for Rituals and the three Courts for Rituals, the Imperial Gateman and Protocols, between the the Ministry of War and the two Courts for the Imperial Charioteer and Commander of Bodyguards, between the Ministry of Justice and the Court for Judicial Review, as well as between the Department for Works and the two Directorates for Imperial Manufactories and Palace Buildings. Some scholars have concluded on this basis that the Nine Ministers ran the risk of being reduced to redundant offices, and suggested that "the Nine Courts (Ministers) could be merged under the Department of State Affairs". Upon an examination of historical facts, it becomes clear that the Department of State Affairs and the Six Ministries had an extremely simple structure with a staff of only 150-odd officials and over 1100 clerks, which fell far short of handling all the major matters of the country. The Nine Ministers, on the other hand, was a vast and far more complicated apparatus, with a staff of not less than 10,000. All the chiefs of this enormous apparatus were on a par with the Ministers of the Six Ministries in rank. Seen in this light, it is rather irrational to claim that the Nine Ministers were redundant offices. In fact, the relationship between the Six Ministries and the Nine Ministers essentially boiled down to a division of power. The former were in charge of formulating government orders based on the decisions of the emperor and the Prime Minister while the latter were responsible for implementation of the orders. The Six Ministers were superior organs in charge of administration, and therefore had a limited number of officials. The Courts and Directorates were subordinate organizations responsible for specific affairs, and therefore had a vast network of offices. The Ministers of the Six Ministries were administrative officials with an exalted status, whereas the chiefs of the Courts and Directorates were practicing officials who commanded much inferior powers (Yan, 2009).

2.1.3 *Organs of Supervision*

The supervisory system has a long history in China. Back in the era of the legendary emperors of Yao and Shun, there was a system of aristocratic democratic supervision, which was in some aspects similar to the ancient system of aristocratic democracy in the West. However, the traditional system of supervision with Chinese characteristics was the system of Censors and remonstrating officials, which sprouted in the Xia, Shang and Zhou Dynasties, came into shape in the Qin and Han Dynasties, and persisted through later dynasties (Tao, 1978, pp. 11–12).

i. From the Censorate to the Chief Surveillance Bureau

1. The Qin and Han Dynasties

In the Zhou Dynasty, the Junior Steward (*xiaozai*, 小宰, undertaken by two Ordinary Grand Masters) was in charge of supervision. In addition, Royal Scribe (*yushi*, 御史) as an official historian concurrently performed the function of supervision. In spite of his low position, an official historian had a high reputation and enormous responsibilities. In the Qin Dynasty, the Royal Scribe changed from an official historian into a supervising official with a high position. The Censor-in-chief, one of the Three Dukes that ran the government (the other two being the Prime Minister and the Defender-in-chief), was mainly in charge of supervision and punishments. The Han Dynasty maintained this arrangement of the Qin, except that supervising officials of the Qin were similar to today's procurators, while those of the Han were pure supervisors (Tao, 1978, pp. 13–15). The central organ of the supervising officials, called the Censorate (*yushi tai*, 御史台), was charged with supervising both the imperial court and the government as well as reporting on the wrongdoings of all officials. The Ministry was headed by the Censor-in-chief, who also served as the Deputy Prime Minister.[16] The Censor-in-chief was assisted by two deputies, i.e., the Palace Aide to the Censor-in-chief (*yushi zhongcheng*, 御史中丞) and the Aide to the Censor-in-chief (*yushi cheng*, 御史丞). The Ministry had 45 censors, including 15 Palace Censors who worked in the imperial court and 30 others who worked in the Censorate. At the local level, Emperor Wu of the Han divided the country into a number of regions for the purpose of supervision and dispatched Regional Inspectors (*cishi*, 刺史) to inspect the work of prefectures. One Regional Inspector was sent to each Region. The immediate director of Regional Inspectors was the Palace Aide to the Censor-in-chief. According to China's past traditions, supervising officials were entitled to exercise their functions and powers independently. Although a subordinate under the Censor-in-chief, the Palace Aide to the Censor-in-chief, who internally led the Palace Censors and externally directed the

[16] In the Eastern Han Dynasty, the Censor-in-chief was changed into the Minister of Works, and the Deputy Censor-in-chief became the head of the Censorate.

Regional Inspectors, was able to contend with the Censor-in-chief. In case the latter had any wrongdoing, the Palace Aide to the Censor-in-chief was entitled to investigate and report it (Sa, 1975a, pp. 253–259, 291). "As administrative officials were not trustworthy, Censors were installed to supervise them, but how could Censors be deeply trusted?" This led to the question of who should be employed to supervise the Censors. Therefore, in the Han system, the power of supervision did not reside entirely in the Censorate. The post of Director of Uprightness (*sizhi*, 司直) was set up in the Prime Minister's office to assist the Prime Minister in impeaching lawbreakers. Furthermore, the independent Metropolitan Commandant (*sili xiaowei*, 司隶校尉) was instituted to supervise all the officials. As an extremely powerful official, the Metropolitan Commandant could impeach the Prime Minister and the Censor-in-chief, and even investigate the Empress Dowager and imperial clansmen. In order to prevent abuse of power, the Metropolitan Commandant (*sili xiaowei*, 司隶校尉) was ranked below the Director of Uprightness under the Prime Minister. This led to a system of supervision featuring the parallel operation of the Censorate, the Director of Uprightness to the Prime Minister and the Metropolitan Commandant, with the three supervising all the officials and mutually supervising each other. This arrangement could help preclude the possibility of the Censors abusing their power and disrupting the operation of the government (Sa, 1975a, pp. 321–323).

The ranks and emoluments of supervising officials in the Han Dynasty may be characterized as "humble position, enormous power and heavy rewards". Such an arrangement was out of the following consideration: No supervising officials below the Palace Aide to the Censor-in-chief had a high position. The Palace Aide to the Censor-in-chief had a salary of 1000 *dan* of grain. Palace Censors and Regional Inspectors were only junior officials with a salary of 600 *dan*, but they had to supervise ranking ministers of the central government, Prefecture Governors, and senior officials of subordinate kingdoms. However, they also enjoyed ample opportunities of promotion for doing an excellent job.[17] Their low rank spurred them to aim high, and the enormous power enabled them to accomplish what they set out to achieve. It was precisely because of their junior position that supervising officials did not refrain from speaking out for fear of losing their post. This was why supervising officials without exception were characterized by a humble status and immense power in later dynasties. Rational as this institutional arrangement may seem (to some extent), there have also been people who viewed it with suspicion or even took it as one of the deficiencies of the system of supervision of ancient China (Qiu, 1992, p. 138). We might as well look at this matter from another perspective: The supervising officials were "the bird of ill omen and watch dog for the emperor" (Tao, 1978, p. 15). As the imperial falcons and hounds, they were not entitled to an exalted status enjoyed by the ranking ministers assisting the emperor in ruling the country. This may have been one of the reasons underlying the low status of supervising officials. A Censor was a ruthless post charged with investigating and impeaching lawbreakers. Therefore, in

[17] A six-hundred-*dan* Regional Inspector with merits could be promoted to a Prefecture Governor or the chancellor of a subordinate kingdom with an annual salary of two thousand *dan*. (See the biography of Zhubo in Chap. 83 of *Book of Han*.)

the Han Dynasty, this post was often filled by someone resolute and intrepid with a thorough knowledge of the law (Sa, 1975a, p. 256).

Censors (the Director of Uprightness to the Prime Minister and the Metropolitan Commandant included) monitored two aspects of the officialdom: dereliction of duty and breaking of the law. With respect to the former, officials were punished for failure to perform their duties, so as to enforce official disciplines; with respect to the latter, officials were penalized for abuse of their power, so as to maintain the social order. "In our country, a clear distinction was not drawn between these two aspects. Therefore, the supervisory body maintained surveillance on not only breach of the law by officials, but also their negligence of duty." (Sa, 1975a, p. 320) Under the Han system, the supervising organ was responsible for reporting on the wrongdoings of officials, but it was the Chamberlain for Law Enforcement (the top judiciary organ in the Han Dynasty) that was in charge of judging the cases of law-breaking officials. Cases deemed of particular importance would be jointly examined by five 2000-*bushel* officials designated by the emperor. When an official was impeached for dereliction of duty, the case would also be verified by three officials dispatched by the Three Dukes. This arrangement demonstrates that the power of trial and the power of impeachment were in principle separated from each other. Nevertheless, the emperor had the final say in all matters in an era of autocratic monarchy (Sa, 1975a, pp. 323–324).

2. The (Sui) Tang Dynasty

In the Tang Dynasty, the Censorate[18] was led by one Censor-in-chief, with the rank of 3a, and two deputies, with the rank of a lower 4b (hereafter written as "4b2"). Under the Censorate were three bureaus: the Headquarters Bureau (*taiyuan*, 台院), Palace Bureau (*dianyuan*, 殿院) and Investigation Bureau (*chayuan*, 察院). The Headquarters Bureau, with four Attendant Censors (shiyushi, 侍御史) at the rank of 6b2, kept a watchful eye on all officials to expose their wrongdoings. The Palace Bureau, with six Palace Censors (*dianzhong shiyushi*, 殿中侍御史) at the rank of 7b2, was responsible for impeaching wayward officials of the two imperial capitals, examining palace ceremonies and rectifying palace procedures. The Investigation Bureau, with a number of Investigating Censors (jiancha yushi, 监察御史) at the rank of 8a1, made inspection tours across the country and supervised local governments (Na, 2004, pp. 45–46). The Investigating Censors also maintained surveillance over the Six Ministries under the Department of State Affairs, i.e., Personnel, Revenue, Rituals, War, Justice, and Works. At the local level, the country was divided into ten Regions, each under the surveillance of an Investigating Censors to supervise local administration (Chang, 1979, p. 14). After the Zhide reign of Emperor Suzong, the commissioners of the various Regions were concurrently given the title of Censors, and thus were called the "Outer Bureau" of the Censorate. "Although in the Qin and Han periods, the Censorate had some power of judicial supervision, it did not have the adjudicative power. In the Tang Dynasty, the Censorate was granted partial adjudicative power ... Censors of all the

[18] Empress Wuzetian in 684 AD renamed the Censorate as the *Suzheng* Bureau (肃政台).

three bureaus could hear and investigate legal cases. It was just through hearing legal cases (often acting on an imperial order) and deciding on verdicts that the Censorate secured partial adjudicative power." (Qiu, 1992, pp. 249–250) The Censorate was authorized to build its own prisons, one called the East Prison and the other the West Prison. Hearing legal cases was an auxiliary function of the Censorate in addition to its primary function of supervision. The Censorate could hear legal cases either independently or jointly with other judicial offices. Hearing of major legal cases was generally conducted collectively by the chiefs of the Censorate, the Ministry of Justice and the Court of Judicial Review.

The (Sui) Tang Dynasty "was a turning point in the history of development of China's supervision system, inheriting the legacies of the system of Censors from the Wei and Jin Dynasties and blazing the trail for the system of three function-specific bureaus under the Censorate" (Chang, 1979, p. 10). "Not only did the division of supervision into central supervision (supervision of the imperial central government) and local supervision (supervision of local administration) originate in the Tang, but also such practices as independent impeachment by supervising officials, impeachment based on rumors, and right of the Palace Aide to the Censor-in-chief to reject an illegitimate imperial edict reached their zenith in the Tang." (Chen, 1977, pp. 133–134) A Censor was even entitled not to comply with an illegitimate order from the emperor, which was quite rare in the Chinese history. The far-reaching influences of the Tang system of supervision on later dynasties may be roughly summed up as follows: First, the system of the three bureaus under the Censorate was maintained by the Song Dynasty, and the *Suzheng* Bureau (name of the Censorate during the reign of Empress Wuzetian) was the origin of the name *Suzheng Ting*, a department in charge of administrative supervision and procuratorial work in the early Republic period. Second, the Outer Bureau of the Censorate was the precursor of the Branch Censorate of the Yuan Dynasty, which in turn was the precursor of the system of General Governors and Regional Supervisors (*xunfu*, 巡抚) in the Ming Dynasty. Third, the practice of surveillance of the Six Ministries under the Department of State Affairs by the Investigating Censors evolved into the arrangement of surveillance of the various government departments and courts by the Investigating Censors appointed for the fifteen Regions. Fourth, the system of Touring Supervising Inspectors, one for each of the ten Regions, was the precedent for the Investigating Censors in the Qing Dynasty (Chang, 1979, p. 16).

3. The Song and Yuan Dynasties

In the Song Dynasty, the position of the Censor-in-chief was not filled, and the Censorate was headed by the Palace Aid to the Censor-in-chief. This arrangement essentially lowered the status of the Censorate. In the meantime, the position of the Palace Aid to the Censor-in-chief was often held concurrently by another official, even a subordinate of the Prime Minister. Therefore, while outwardly, the Song Dynasty maintained the supervisory system of the Tang, in reality, the Censors could hardly function independently, even to the point that their impeachment power became merely a dead letter.

The system of supervision implemented in the Yuan Dynasty was structured after that of the Liao and Jurchen-led Jin Dynasties. However, appointees of the Censorate were promoted to an unprecedentedly high rank and increased significantly in number. The Censorate was headed by the Censor-in-chief, of the rank 1b. The Censor-in-chief was assisted by two deputies, of the rank 2a. Among the staff, there were two Palace Censors, of the rank 4a, and thirty-two Investigating Censors, of the rank 7a. Among the three bureaus under the Censorate, an arrangement instituted in the Tang and Song Dynasties, only two Bureaus were now left, i.e., the Palace Bureau and Investigation Bureau. Furthermore, the Palace Bureau had only a staff of two Palace Censors, a number proportionally insignificant as compared with that of the Investigation Bureau. The arrangement of three bureaus under the Censorate was approaching its end. A salient feature of the Yuan system of supervision was the establishment of the Branch Censorate (*xing yushitai*, 行御史台) as the top local supervisory body, with Surveillance Commissions under it for the various Regions. At that time, the whole country was divided into three major districts for the purpose of territorial surveillance, each under the jurisdiction of one of the following Branch Censorates: the Inner Censorate (i.e. the Censorate), overseeing eight circuits (Surveillance Commissions), the Branch Censorate of Jiangnan, overseeing ten circuits, and the Branch Censorate of Shaanxi, overseeing four circuits. Altogether there were three Branch Censorates, maintaining surveillance over 22 circuits (Editorial Committee of the Veritable Record of the Control Yuan, 1981, p. 4).

4. The Ming and Qing Dynasties

The Ming Dynasty discontinued the arrangement of the Censorate branching into three bureaus (the Headquarters Bureau, Palace Bureau and Investigation Bureau) since the Tang Dynasty, and consolidated the supervisory machinery into the Chief Surveillance Bureau (*ducha yuan*, 都察院). All the duties of impeaching officials for misconduct, checking court ceremonies and procedures, and making territorial inspections resided with the Investigating Censors. The superstructure of the Chief Surveillance Bureau included two Censors-in-chief, of the rank 3a, two Vice Censors-in-chief (*fu duyushi*, 副都御史), of the rank 3b, and four Assistant Censors-in-chief (*qian duyushi*, 佥都御史), of the rank 4a, all differentiated as being the left and the right. The Left and Right Censors-in-chief took care of the affairs of the Chief Surveillance Bureau, responsible for inspecting local affairs of the various circuits, impeaching officials for misconduct, as well as participating in Court Investigation (into major cases), Court Recommendation (of high officials) and Court Discussion (about important matters). The Vice Censors-in-chief and Assistant Censors-in-chief assisted the Censors-in-chief in the work of supervision, but were also frequently dispatched to make touring inspections. The Chief Surveillance Bureau also had 110 Investigating Censors, of the rank 7a, for thirteen Regions. Although subordinated to the Chief Surveillance Bureau, the Investigating Censors enjoyed a high degree of autonomy. Their main objects of supervision included local officials and medium-and lower-level central officials. Specifically speaking, they were responsible for impeaching officials for misconduct, making territorial inspections, participating in Court Recommendation and Court Discussion, checking court ceremonies and procedures, as well as undertaking various kinds of specific tasks and temporary assignments (Pi et al., 1991, pp. 181–182). In the Qing Dynasty, the Chief Surveillance Bureau was higher in rank and powers than its Ming counterpart. The Censors-in-chief of the Chief Surveillance Bureau, of the rank 1b, were on a par with the Ministers of the Six Ministries under the Department of State Affairs. In addition to managing the affairs of the Chief Surveillance Bureau, they were also entitled to involve themselves in state affairs. The Chief Surveillance Bureau had two Left Censors-in-chief, one Manchu and one Han Chinese, four Left Vice Censors-in-chief, two Manchus and two Han Chinese, but no Assistant Censors-in-chief. The titles of Right Censor-in-chief and Right Vice Censors-in-chief were held concurrently by General Governors and Regional Supervisors respectively.[19] As for the local Investigating Censors, the number of circuits that they inspected was changed from thirteen to fifteen.

ii. From parallel operations of supervision and remonstration to their integration

In the Han Dynasty, it was the Grand Masters (*dafu*, 大夫) who were in charge of making comments to criticize court policies.[20] The Grand Masters included the Superior Grand Master of the Palace (*taizhong dafu*, with an annual salary of one thousand *dan* of grain), Grand Master of the Palace (*zhong dafu*, renamed Guanglu Grand Master in the first year of the Taichu reign of the Western Han, with an annual salary of two thousand *bushels*) and the Grand Master of Remonstrance (*jiandafu*, 谏大夫 or *jianyi dafu*, 谏议大夫, eight hundred *dan*). "In later dynasties, Grand Masters were mostly prestige titles (titles awarded solely to some long-serving former or meritorious officials to highlight their seniority, but bearing no relation to their actual duties) or prestige ranks. The only exception was the post of Grand Master of Remonstrance, which was instituted alongside with the Censor-in-chief. The former was responsible for criticizing court policies, whereas the latter impeached officials for misconduct." "In history, Grand Masters were mostly selected from erudite and cultivated people, for only erudite people could tell the merits and deficiencies of the policies and only cultivated people could refrain from engaging in factionalism." (Sa, 1975a, p. 262) A comparison of remonstrating and supervising officials reveals that the former enjoyed higher ranks and were selected according to a more stringent set of standards. Remonstrating officials must be learned and cultivated, while supervising officials only had to be upright. In the traditional Chinese culture, the study of the law was not a prestigious discipline, and as far as learning was concerned, to be well versed in the law was by far inferior to being erudite. While to be upright was undoubtedly a virtue, there was still a world of differences between being upright and being cultivated, similar to the distinction between the courageous and the wise.

[19] This is why when we visit the headquarters of the General Governor of Zhili in Baoding, we can see a plaque bearing the inscription "Gate to the Department of Supervision".

[20] See "Table of nobility ranks and government offices", Chap. 19 of the *Book of Han*.

Censors focused on legal issues, whereas Remonstrators concentrated on political problems, that is, correcting errors in governance. This latter may be likened to the modern parliamentary system of the West, in spite of their crucial differences in nature (Sa, 1975c, pp. 291–293). In the Han Dynasty, remonstrating officials had not emancipated themselves from the Inner Court of the emperor. Therefore, the system of remonstration was still in its preliminary stage of formation (Pi et al., 1991, pp. 69–70).

Learning from the lessons of the fall of the Sui Dynasty, early Tang rulers attached great importance to the building of institutions. Emperor Taizong, in particular, regarded remonstrating officials as his mentors, friends and a mirror. Quite a number of remonstrating posts were set up in the Secretariat and the Chancellery. The Grand Masters of Remonstrance and the Supervising Secretaries (*jishizhong*, 给事中) belonged to the Chancellery. The Cavalier Attendants-in-ordinary (*sanqi changshi*, 散骑常侍), Reminders (*shiyi*, 拾遗) and Rectifiers (*buque*, 补阙) were differentiated as being the left and the right. The left ones belonged to the Chancellery, while the right ones were under the Palace Secretariat. The Chancellery and the Imperial Secretariat, which had a large number of remonstrating officials, were already known as the "Remonstrance Bureau". The remonstrating officials could independently exercise their power of remonstrance, and could follow the Prime Minister to the "Cabinet", thus involving themselves in state affairs. A major development in the system of remonstration in the Tang Dynasty was the remonstrating officials' power to refute the emperor's edict. For a major military or state issue, the Secretaries would prepare a draft edict, which was passed on to the Chancellery for re-examination. The edict would be refuted if it was found to be inappropriate. The Supervising Secretaries would write their comments on the edict and return it to the Secretariat. This was called "comment and return". Th Chancellery could write a comment on a yellow piece of paper and attach it to the draft edict (Qiu, 1992, pp. 229–233).

Into the Song Dynasty, the posts of Reminders and Rectifiers were abolished, and Remonstrators (*sijian*, 司谏) and Exhorters (*zhengyan*, 正言) were instituted. The latter two, plus the Cavalier Attendants-in-ordinary and the Grand Masters of Remonstrance were all differentiated as being the left and the right. The left ones belonged to the Chancellery, while their right counterparts belonged to the Imperial Secretariat. The Secretariat had four Secretaries, who directed six offices, and the Chancellery had four Supervising Secretaries, who also directed six offices. In case a government order or the appointment or dismissal of an official was improper, a remonstrating official was entitled to report and rectify it. Censors and remonstrating officials, Secretaries and Supervising Secretaries, the four were often put together and referred to as the same category of offices. In the Southern Song Dynasty, the Chancellery was abolished. Although the posts of remonstrating officials were still prefixed by "Left" and "Right", they no longer belonged to two different departments, but to a single newly created organization. The Secretaries and Supervising Secretaries, who only recorded the emperor's words and acts, were no longer remonstrating officials.

In the Song Dynasty, there were already instances of Remonstrators encroaching upon the power of impeachment of Censors, to the neglect of their own duty of remonstration. "Remonstrating officials often played the role of supervision, but neglected their own duty of admonishing the emperor." (Sa, 1993, pp. 464–465) This was due in part to the fact that there was some degree of overlap between supervision and remonstration, and there was not a clear-cut line between misconduct of officials (the jurisdiction of Censors) and problematic governance (the jurisdiction of Remonstrators). But more importantly, impeachment was directed against ordinary officials, while remonstration targeted the emperor and central administrative organs. Remonstrating officials were prone to evading the difficult task (of correcting the emperor) and focusing on the easy one (impeaching undisciplined officials). This paved the way for the integration of supervision and remonstration in later dynasties. In the Yuan Dynasty, remonstrating officials were not instituted. The Censorate, in addition to overseeing the officialdom, was charged with judging and rectifying the deficiencies in governance.

In the Ming Dynasty remonstrating posts were abolished. The power of remonstration was shifted to Six Offices of Scrutiny (*liuke jishizhong*, 六科给事中), which were created as an independent set of supervising agencies under the direct control of the emperor. Each of the Six Offices (i.e., Personnel, Revenue, Rituals, War, Justice, and Works) had one Chief Supervising Secretary (*du jishizhong*, 都给事中), of the rank 7a, one Left and one Right Supervising Secretaries, of the rank 7b, and some Supervising Secretaries (their actual number depending on the amount of work of each Office), of the rank 7b. Specifically speaking, the Supervising Secretaries of the Six Offices were responsible for admonishing the emperor, refuting edicts, overseeing the Six Ministries, and impeaching central officials for misconduct. In the Ming Dynasty, Censors and Supervising Secretaries became homogeneous in their functions and powers, or in other words, the functions of censure and remonstration were integrated, but in terms of the bureaucratic structure, the Censorate and the Six Offices of Scrutiny were still separate entities. In the first year of his reign (1723 AD), the Yongzheng Emperor of the Qing Dynasty prevailed over all dissenting views and placed the Six Offices of Scrutiny under the jurisdiction of the Chief Surveillance Bureau and subjected the Supervising Secretaries to the appraisal of the Censors-in-chief of the Chief Surveillance Bureau. Thus, the Six Offices of Scrutiny became a supervisory body within the Chief Surveillance Bureau, parallel to the fifteen circuits of Investigating Censors, and one more step forward was taken in the unification between supervision and remonstration. This measure, in effect, also put an end to the practice of refuting an edict by Supervising Secretaries, which could have functioned as a check on the power of an autocratic emperor (Pi et al., 1991, pp. 182–183, 196–197).

iii. Advantages and disadvantages of the supervisory system in ancient China

It is said that half of the responsibility for the downfall of the Ming Dynasty rested on Censors and Supervising Secretaries. In the Ming Dynasty, remonstrating officials were superseded by Supervising Secretaries, who used to have different functions and powers from Censors. Under the Ming system, Supervising Secretaries were officials whose job was to speak on government matters, and they were selected only among the sons of ranking ministers. In addition to raising comments on the merits and demerits of court policies, they were also entitled to report on the wrongdoings of officials. Gradually, the distinction between Censors and Supervising Secretaries became blurred, which gave rise to conflicts between them. Both Censors and Supervising Secretaries had access to court discussions. With little knowledge of the actual situation, they often made a point of contradicting others to gain greater fame. "In the discussion of state affairs, the only thing that they were concerned with was their fame ... They were willing to dwell on an extremely trivial issue endlessly and submit a lengthy memorial of impeachment." "Supervising Secretaries took part in court discussions and made impeachments to impose charges on their opponents. Censors also involved themselves in state affairs by way of making impeachments and effected changes to established policies. Censors and Supervising Secretaries became increasingly powerful. They followed no principle and made comments without taking any responsibility, so that right and wrong, the virtuous and the treacherous all got confused. Officials were in a frenzy to attack each other and could not calm down to attend to their own official duties." Yan Song, Zhang Juzheng and Wei Zhongxian all employed Censors and Supervising Secretaries as a tool for removing their adversaries in the government. "Therefore, Censors and Supervising Secretaries should be held partially accountable for the demise of the Ming Dynasty." (Sa, 1975c, p. 440)

The system of supervision in ancient China was unique in the world. The censors impeached officials for misconduct, whereas remonstrators corrected the emperor. This arrangement to a certain extent substituted the function of the congress in supervising the government in the West since the modern era. It is a shining point of the imperial system over the past two thousand years. However, along with the gradual concentration of power of the emperor and integration of supervision and remonstration, Censors often only targeted petty officials and left powerful ones untouched, let alone incurring the wrath of the Son of Heaven. Thus, they were reduced to a tool of the emperor and a weapon in political struggles. This constituted a degradation of the system of supervision.

2.2 Centralization of Power and Arrangement of the Local Government

2.2.1 Relationship Between the Central Government and Local Governments: Centralization and Division of Power

i. "Grand unification" and "division of power" in imperial China

> Speaking of "unification", tribal states like the Xia, Shang and even earlier legendary regimes were already united under what were called "Emperors" so as to avoid fragmentation. In the early Zhou period, a feudal system was established, but the Zhou court was strong enough to command the obedience of its vassals, and the country moved in the direction of unification. The Zhou court declined in the Spring and Autumn Period, but the hegemons (especially powerful feudal lords) still upheld the banner of "respecting and supporting the Zhou king". In the Warring States Period when the feudal lords contended with one another for supremacy, Mencius still placed his hope on unification. As the Qin Dynasty unified China, the feudal system came to an end. The Han Dynasty tried the feudal system on a much smaller scale, and ended up with the Rebellion of Seven Kingdoms. The Jin Dynasty tried it again, resulting in the Upheaval of the Eight Princes. The early Qing rulers followed their example slightly, and the empire was shaken by the Revolt of the Three Feudatories. Nevertheless, the vassal states were still under the jurisdiction of the central government, except that feudal lords secured the military power. The presence of a unified country, which persisted throughout the past two millennia, has come to be accepted as a perfectly justified pattern of existence. Thus, the concepts of orthodoxy and usurpation came into being. Orthodoxy was the token of the country's unification, while usurpation ran contrary to unification. The former was what it was supposed to be, whereas the latter was irregular. *De facto* separate rule of the country was not valid proof that China was not a unified country. With the downfall of the Han Dynasty, Three Kingdoms were established. Chen Shou (author of the *Records of the Three Kingdoms*) regarded the Wei as the orthodox regime, while Zhu Xi (a scholar of the Song Dynasty) placed orthodoxy on the Kingdom of Shu. Whatever their arguments, neither of them believed that fragmentation of the country was a normal phenomenon, and they both harbored the belief of a unified country. Although driven to a corner of the country, the Eastern Jin and the Southern Song were still regarded as the orthodoxy, something their contemporary regimes, like the Wei, Qi, Zhou as well as the Liao, Jin and Xia, were not entitled to share ... Furthermore, the establishment of émigré prefectures was also the indication of a unified country. (Chen, 2006, p. 524)

Under the feudal system of the Western Zhou, the nobility at various levels, such as regional lords and grand masters, were granted hereditary fiefs. For the relationships between the Son of Heaven, regions lords, grand masters and other estate holders, please refer to Chap. 1 "China's Feudal Society and the System of Rites". In the Spring and Autumn and Warring States Periods, when a regional state seized the territory of another state, the land was no longer granted to the aristocrats, but was often turned into commanderies and counties directly under the control of the regional lord. After the First Emperor of the Qin unified China, he divided the country into thirty-six commanderies (subsequently expanded to forty), each of which had jurisdiction over a number of counties. This gave rise to a two-tier local government comprising commanderies and counties. Both Commandery governors and County magistrates were centrally appointed so that power was concentrated in the central government and local governments became isolated from each other. Learning from the lessons of the downfall of the Qin, the Han rulers enfeoffed princes and meritorious officials and implemented the commandery-county system at the same time. Over time, the enfeoffed subordinate kingdoms became powerful. When Chao Cuo proposed reducing the size of the subordinate kingdoms, the disaffected kings of seven kingdoms revolted. After suppression of the rebellion, Emperor Jing prohibited noblemen from going to their own fiefdoms and only allowed them to collect the taxes and rents. As a result, the system of commanderies and counties prevailed. Emperor Wu further dispatched Regional Inspectors to inspect the work of local officials and monitor powerful local families. In the late Han Dynasty, Emperor Ling sent out high officials of the central government to serve as Regional Governors (zhoumu, 州牧). As a result, the country fell to the separatist rule by various regional powers. Emperor Wu of the Jin enfeoffed the imperial clansmen and planted the seeds for disaster, first the Upheaval of the Eight Princes and eventually the invasion of alien enemies.

According to some scholars, enfeoffment in the Western Han and Western Jin was done out of necessity, not purely for the sake of following a time-honored tradition. Although replacement of the Qin by the Han was regarded as a "commoner revolution", the group of aristocratic warriors (such as "the fathers and brothers east of the river" that supported Xiang Yu) was a primary force of the revolution as well. This was why a "commoner revolution" did not bring about "commoner politics". When the Western Han had just been established, the autocracy of the Qin emperors was widely resented by the people. Besides, it was the adherents of the former six regional states that overthrew the Qin Dynasty. The feudal system was the best arrangement that the contemporaries could think of. Under such circumstances, it was theoretically and politically inevitable for Emperor Gaozu to enfeoff meritorious officials and members of the imperial family. "Although Emperor Gaozu defeated Xiang Ji (Xiang Yu) in the struggle for supremacy, it would not have been sanctioned by the people at that time for one man to monopolize all the power of the country. This was also beyond the fondest expectation of Emperor Gaozu as well. What he wished for at that time was to secure as large a share of the country's territory as possible for himself so that he could become powerful enough to keep the subordinate kingdoms under control. In the meantime, he tried to enfeoff as many members of the imperial family as possible so that they could assist each other in times of need." "Monopoly of the power of the whole country was not feasible in the early Han Dynasty." (Lü, 2005, pp. 556–557) "The fall of the Wei Dynasty within fifty years after its establishment aroused new concerns of the royal family of the Western Jin and led them to believe that the feudal system was a magic formula for maintaining long-term stability. Coupled with the fact that Sima Yan (Emperor of the Jin) wanted to reward his relatives by enfeoffing them as kings", enfeoffment was carried out once again as soon as the Western Jin was established. Compared with the practice of the early Han Dynasty, the enfeoffment of the Western Jin had serious flaws: In the first place, Emperor Wu of the Jin (Sima Yan) enfeoffed 27 kings in the Taishi reign, but none of them was a prince. These kings were mostly rather distant relatives and could not play an effective role in defending the royal family. Second, in order to secure the goodwill of these clansmen, the estates granted were significantly larger than those in the Western Han, and all the subordinate kingdoms were authorized to establish their own armies. "When the various kings, who already commanded an exalted political status, laid their hands on military power, a formidable force was formed that was strong enough to contend with the central government". Third, not long before his death, Sima Yan elevated the power and status of his princes to counteract the influences of those kings enfeoffed from distant branches of the royal family. This measure ended up producing a new clique capable of challenging the central authority (Zhou, 2014, pp. 53–55). Nevertheless, for all its disastrous consequences, the enfeoffment of the Western Jin was done out of realistic political considerations. Faced with the political reality of domination of various regions by prominent and powerful families, the Sima emperors had to enfeoff their relatives to expand the scope of their power to shield the central authority. Appointment of imperial princes to key strategic locations (such as Jingzhou) in the Southern Dynasties was a continuation of this tradition, except that it was not called enfeoffment of vassal kingdoms.

Besides, below the surface of a unified system of commanderies and counties, there also lurked the issue of "division of power" between the central and local governments, and there were occasionally cases of fragmentation and separatist rule. Grand unification itself also entailed an inherent paradox. On the one hand, power was concentrated in the central government, while local governments lacked an independent will and merely executed orders from the central government in a rigid manner. On the other hand, the administrative machinery of the state was only able to reach the county level. Coupled with the fact that "China was a vast country with tremendous regional differences, the surveillance of the court over local governments, though not uniform across various regions (roughly in reverse proportion to the distance from the imperial capital), was generally far weaker than that in monarchical states of Europe … In fact, 'unification' also had its limitation, and it was often essentially one country with multiple systems". More importantly, the power system of the state to some extent ran detached from the system of social life, and operation of the civilian society and economy often followed its own natural rules. "The hard shell of unification wrapped a motley of diversified, loosely-connected blocks. Forced integration was both fake and fragile, and under certain circumstances, could degenerate into a mere formality or even a state of separatist rule" (Wang, 2012, p. 11).

Conversely speaking, "fragmentation and division are presumably the normal state in the development of a civilization." Then, how did historical China "manage to deviate from the normal state to remain a country 'with a vast territory and a large population'? This to a large extent was closely related to the compatibility of the notion of a unified world as well as its elasticity in practice, and it is a unique set of Chinese experience" (Wei, 2019, p. 1). It should be pointed out that "division is not the same as 'separation' or 'secession', and 'division' in its broad sense should include decentralized rule, self-government, power division and various other forms of dispersion. In this sense, unification and division are intertwined with each other." Due to the existence of multiple systems within the same country as well as the general pattern of gradual expansion with occasional contractions of the Central

Plains dynasties in ancient China, autonomous regimes or self-governed regions survived for prolonged periods of time within China's territorial scope. For example, "prior to the Yuan Dynasty, the Qinghai-Tibet Plateau had featured self-government or been ruled by the autonomous regime established by the Tubo people and their ancestors. Before the Qing Dynasty, no regime on the Chinese mainland had ever extended its jurisdiction to Taiwan, which was either governed by the aborigines or controlled by Chinese immigrants or foreign invaders. Of course, these situations cannot be treated as separation or split. Instead, they are merely self-government or decentralized rule" (Ge, 2013, pp. 218, 280).

ii. Measures for power centralization in the Han Dynasty

1. Laws of the Western Han for preserving centralization of power

In the early Han period, members of the meritorious group shared the political power with the throne, but their descendants witnessed the end of their period of power in the reign of Emperor Wu. "(T)he Han imperial system had to secure direct control of the individual subject and the government would not tolerate other social forces standing between the ruler and the ruled. Thus, almost all the meritorious marquises were stripped of their domains and titles by the last two years of Emperor Wu's reign. Verdicts were often based on extremely trivial accusations." (Hsu, 1980, pp. 45–46)

The laws of the Han Dynasty prescribed quite a number of crimes for undermining the authority of the central government as well as their respective punishments. The following are some examples. The first was the so-called "*zuoguan*" crime. In the reign of Emperor Wu of the Han, regional kings were prohibited from selecting and appointing their own officials. Anyone who held an official post in a kingdom without authorization from the central government would be liable for the *zuoguan* crime, therefore punishable under the *zuoguan* statute. The second was the crime for collusion with a regional king. If the officials of a regional kingdom formed a clique with their king and failed to report on the king's wrongdoings, or if officials entered into a secret alliance with a regional king and plotted against the imperial power, they were considered guilty of this crime and subject to severe punishments under the statute on collusion with a regional king. The third was the crime for overstepping the kingdom boundary. A regional king would be guilty of this crime if he went beyond the boundary of his kingdom without approval. A minor offense could be punished by labor service, and a serious one might lead to execution.

In addition to imposing criminal punishments on regional kings undermining the authority of the central government, the *tui'en ling* (推恩令), or edict for extending favor, was enacted to weaken local powers. With this edict, a king would divide his territory equally among all his sons, instead of just the eldest one. In the meantime, the Son of Heaven often degraded or abolished the fiefs of regional kings on the pretext of the liquor-gold crime. (When participating in the sacrifices to the imperial ancestors, the regional kings must contribute liquor and gold of superior quality. If the liquor or gold was found to be of inferior quality, the regional kings would be guilty of the liquor-gold crime, their fiefs would be reduced in size or revoked according to the liquor-gold statute.)

2. Struggle between the central authority and local powers[21]

(1) Check of the emperor's power by the meritorious group

Prior to Emperor Wu's reign, the position of the Prime Minister had been monopolized by the meritorious group. The immensely powerful Prime Minister exercised a certain check on the power of the emperor on behalf of the meritorious group. After eliminating meritorious officials such as Peng Yue, Ying Bu (also called Qing Bu) and Chen Xi, Emperor Gaozu had firmly established himself as the top leader of the empire. Nevertheless, the meritorious group still shared the power of the emperor, and the Prime Minister must be selected from among the meritorious officials. Only when the meritorious officials had gradually aged and perished was it possible for Shentu Jia, who used to be a middle-ranking officer, to be promoted to the post of the Prime Minister. In addition to enfeoffing regional kings, Emperor Gaozu also appointed quite a number of meritorious officials to be Commandery Governors. "With the narrow perspective of a small clique, people of the metropolitan region (Guanzhong) did not trust people of the eastern regions (Guandong), and the passes between the capital area and the eastern regions were carefully guarded. The regional kings were always eyed with suspicion until the reigns of Emperor Wen and Emperor Jing. They were treated like foreigners and could not cross the passes without special passports." Before subduing the autonomous kingdoms of the eastern section, the imperial government only had effective jurisdiction over the metropolitan area around the imperial capital. At that time, special discriminatory policies were in place in the metropolitan area against people of the regional kingdoms. For example, people from the regional kingdoms were prohibited from serving as imperial court attendants or taking office in the imperial capital. Emperor Wu forbade officials to associate with regional kings. The celebrated general, Li Guang, never got promoted to a marquisate despite his merit in pacifying the Rebellion of the Seven Kingdoms, on the ground that he accepted a general's seal from the king of Liang.

"In fact, the only structural check of the central government of the early Western Han on the autonomous kingdoms was the installing of governors in commanderies and the enfeoffment of immediate members of the imperial family, scattered around and between the autonomous kingdoms." As the primary duty of Commandery Governors was to act as imperial watch-dogs, these posts were mostly held by military men. On the other hand, although Commandery Governors and County Magistrates were not hereditary like the regional kings, but appointed by the central government, they nevertheless had a somewhat free rein within their own respective jurisdictive areas. This sometimes led to conflicts between the imperial decrees from the central government and the regulations of the Commandery Governors in the legal system at that time.

[21] Refer to Hsu (2005, pp. 157–176).

(2) Powerful elements in a homogenized society: strained relationship between the centralized state and the local elites and magnates:

Against the backdrop of a homogenized populace under the prefectural system in the imperial era, local elites and magnates still existed at the local level. They played a vital role in shaping the social order of a locality, and commanded an influence even greater than that of local officials appointed by the central government. In an effort to strengthen the power of the central government, Emperor Wu of the Han took a series of measures to curtail the influence of these local elites and magnates.

First, he moved compulsorily wealthy people, the local elite and former ranking officials from the commanderies and kingdoms to Maoling, the tomb county of the capital area, to uproot the leaders, or potential leaders, of the local communities by means of relocation.

Second, he employed cruel officials, who were the personification of the royal power, to slay or massacre the local elites and magnates that were allowed to remain in their native places.

Third, he instituted Regional Inspectors, which constituted the institutionalized royal power, to watch over Commandery Governors and their relatives and prevent them from colluding with the local elites and magnates.

Fourth, economically, he undercut wealthy merchants by such policies as salt and iron monopolies, state management of intra-regional trade, and heavy taxation on merchants.

Fifth, the early Han society inherited from the Qin the law on the segmentation of households, which prohibited father and adult sons from living under the same roof. This measure in effect restricted the potential power of prominent families.

(3) Revival of the local elites

First, after the reigns of Emperor Zhao and Emperor Xuan, the regulation that a Commandery Governor and County Magistrate had to avoid serving in his native place became strictly observed, but most staff positions in the local administration were still reserved for the local elites. Thus, the general trend of centralization of power since the reign of Emperor Wu was reversed.

Second, the local gentry, the local administrative staff and those recommended to enter the central officialdom formed a sort of power trinity.

Third, powerful families began to form and expand at the local level, and thus a pattern gradually emerged whereby "the gentry shared the power of the empire with the ruler".

Fourth, Emperor Yuan, Emperor Cheng and Emperor Ai were no longer able to relocate the local elites to the capital area.

3. From Regional Inspector to Regional Governor: from centralization of power to separatist rule

In the Qin Dynasty, a Supervisory Imperial Clerk (*jianyushi*, 监御史) was installed in each commandery to keep watch on the administrator. In the early Han period, a Clerk of the Prime Minister (sent out by the Prime Minister) was charged with the supervision of several commanderies. In order to strengthen control over local governments, Emperor Wu abolished the post of the Clerk of the Prime Minister in the 5th year of the Yuanfeng reign (106 BC) and divided the country into thirteen Regions for the purpose of supervision. One Regional Inspector was assigned to each Region to inspect the work of the local government (the Region where the imperial capital was located was taken care of by the Metropolitan Commandant). Thus, the Regional Inspector became the regular supervisory organ, "with a humble status but weighty powers". In addition, the Local Inspector (*duyou*, 督邮), a clerk of the prefectural government, was charged with the supervision of officials of subordinate counties. The Regional Inspector checked the work of the commanderies of his respective Region against the following six articles: (1) whether the land and houses of powerful families had exceeded the proper limit; whether the strong were oppressing the weak or those with many retainers were bullying individuals; (2) whether the Commandery Governors (who were 2000-*bushel* officials) were observing the bureaucratic rules, working for the benefits of the public, or oppressing the people for their own interests; (3) whether they judged difficult cases in a fair and objective manner, or allowed their personal emotions to sway the judgement, therefore victimizing the people and incurring their resentment; (4) whether they hired competent personnel or merely their favorites and relatives, thus keeping back worthy men while promoting stupid ones; (5) whether their sons and relatives had taken advantage of their position and made undue demands on the people under their jurisdiction; (6) whether they attached themselves to powerful local interests, accepting bribes and gifts and so injuring the conduct of the government. All these six articles targeted the top local administrators (as well as their sons and relatives) and the local elites. "Regional Inspectors shouldered a weighty responsibility, for officials recommended by them could rank above the Nine Ministers while those they reported against faced immediate dismissal". The underlying principle for a 600-*dan* Regional Inspector to supervise the top local officials was that "the top local administrators were prone to get out of control owing to their immense power, the grand masters could not abuse their power because of their humble status, and this arrangement could help strike a balance between senior and junior officials as well as between central authority and local power". The local supervisory system of such a design could "spur the Regional Inspectors to fulfill their duties diligently while preventing them from encroaching upon the powers of the local administrators."

In Emperor Cheng's reign, Prime Minister Zhai Fangjin and Grand Minister of Works He Wu memorialized: "The practice of junior officials reporting on senior officials contradicts the tradition of the ancients. The Regional Inspector, who is only a junior grand master, supervises 2000-*bushel* officials. This arrangement leads to a confusion in the hierarchy of power and ranks. Therefore, it is hereby proposed that the Regional Inspector should be abolished and the Regional Governor be instituted to align with ancient traditions." Emperor Cheng acted upon this proposal and reformed the system of local supervision. Later, as the Regional Governor only sought to consolidate his own power and failed to fulfill his function of supervision, Emperor Ai abolished this post and reverted to Emperor Wu's system of Regional

Inspectors. However, Regional Inspectors rose in status as a result of their enormous power and became permanently settled locally. In Emperor Guangwu's reign of the Eastern Han, the Regional Inspector rose in rank to become a 2000-*bushel* official and had a fixed office in his respective Region. During Emperor Ling's reign, the Regional Inspector was renamed "Regional Governor" (for shepherding the people). This marked the beginning of an era of powerful Regional Governors. The central government gradually lost control over the Regional Governors, who had evolved from "grand masters" to "local administrators" and became essentially autonomous regional lords (Lü, 2002, pp. 527–528). Although Regional Inspectors were changed into Regional Governors in the reign of Emperor Cheng of the Western Han, it was only an elevation of their rank (salary), and Regional Governors were still supervisory officials, not administrative officials. The change made in the reign of Emperor Ling was quite different from that in the reign of Emperor Cheng. "Charged with both military and civilian duties, the Regional Governor was fully an administrative official. Thus, the two-tier system of local government comprising the prefecture and the county became a three-level system featuring the Region, the prefecture and the county by the time the warlord Dong Zhuo seized power. Backed by vast territories and large populations, Regional Governors were difficult to control when they rose against the central government. The change of Regional Inspectors into Regional Governors, which led to a weak central government and powerful local governments, was a process whereby an empire with its power centralized in the imperial government disintegrated into a host of regions ruled by warlords." (Sa, 1975a, p. 468)

iii. Centralization and division of power since the Sui Dynasty[22]

Following the fragmentation during the periods of the Sixteen Kingdoms and of the Northern and Southern Dynasties, China was united under the Sui Dynasty. However, the Sui repeated the fate of the Qin Dynasty and fell as a result of over-centralization of power. The Sui followed the official system of the Northern Qi, and the Ministry of Personnel of the central government stripped the local officials of the power to select and appoint their own subordinate officials. The Tang Dynasty preserved the official system of the Sui, and the central government dispatched Local Supervisors (xuncha shi, 巡查使) to oversee local administration, thus weakening the power of local officials. After the Rebellion of An Lushan and Shi Siming from AD 755 to 763, the central government lost control over the Military Zones supervised by the Central Commissioners (*jiedushi*, 节度使), who as military officials handled civilian affairs. The Central Commissioners turned against and eventually toppled the Tang government.

The chaos resulting from the powerful Military Zones grew even more severe in the Five Dynasties period. After his enthronement, Emperor Taizu of the Song strove to weaken the local governments and concentrate power in the central government, so that "his imperial edicts and decrees would be executed to the letter without any impediments". Three measures were taken to achieve this purpose. First, the

[22] Refer to Lin (1976, pp. 175–176).

administrative affairs of a Region were divided among four regional posts, generally called Supervisors, to weaken the powers of the local governments. The four Supervisors included the Financial Supervisor, the Judicial Supervisor, the Relief Supervisor and the Military Supervisor. Second, military generals were persuaded at banquets to renounce their military power, and the Central Commissioners and Regional Inspectors were retained in the imperial capital, where they remotely administered their respective prefectures. The top administrator of the prefecture was not always appointed, and the central government would send a civil official to govern, with the title of Managing Prefect. Furthermore, one or two Controllers-general (*tongpan*, 通判) were sent by the central government to each prefecture. The Controller-general was on the same footing with the Managing Prefect. Over military, civil, financial, judicial, and various other affairs, no document issued by the Managing Prefect was considered valid without being countersigned by the Controller-general. Third, the local elite troops were organized into the imperial army and stationed at the imperial capital. Under the Song system, officials were categorized into officials of nominal ranks (*guan*, 官), officials of nominal titles (*zhi*, 职) and officials on provisional assignments (*chaiqian*, 差遣). The real tasks were only undertaken by officials on provisional assignments. The early Song Dynasty pursued the policy of a strong central government with weak local governments. This led to scattered administrative powers of the local governments, a gradual decline in the overall strength of the country, and rising external threats. In the Southern Song Dynasty, the Financial Supervisor, Judicial Supervisor, Relief Supervisor and the Military Supervisor were regional administrators. The Military Supervisor, who had a particularly weighty status and commanded greater powers than the other three Supervisors, was the top administrator of a Region. Sometimes several Regions were combined to form a Supra-region, and Pacification Commissioners (*xuanfu shi*, 宣抚使) and Supervisory Commissioners (*zhizhi shi*, 制置使) were appointed to take charge of the Supra-regions. Thus, the local governments became steadily more powerful. At the legislative and judiciary levels, the early Song Dynasty was known for settling local issues through (the emperor's) imperial decrees on a large scale in order to achieve centralization of power. The overuse of extensive "decrees for handling petty issues" and the emperor's verdicts for individual cases led to confusion in judicial application, "but they were also a reflection and token of the emperor's authoritative status" (McKnight, 2004, p. 332).

The Yuan Dynasty was keen on centralization of power and established the Branch Secretariat,[23] which was an office dispatched by the Secretariat to a local place. Later as Branch Secretariats became too powerful, the central government was unable to have its policies implemented. A post called *darugachi* (达鲁花赤) was set up at each administrative subdivision, including the Region, the commandery and the county. *Darugachi* held the official seal and was mostly undertaken by a Mongol. The

[23] This marked the first time when "*sheng*" (province or Branch Secretariat) denoted the office of the top tier of the local government. Prior to the Yuan Dynasty, *sheng* had been used in the names of organs of the central government, such as *zhongshu-sheng* (中书省, the Imperial Secretariat), *menxia-sheng* (门下省, the Chancellery) and *shangshu-sheng* (the Department of State Affairs).

chiefs of Regions, Prefects and county Magistrates, undertaken by Han Chinese, were only deputies of the local government. The Han Chinese, who had administrative experience, were charged with running the local governments, but they were not trusted. Therefore, *darugachi* were sent to oversee the work of the Han Chinese. All local policies and orders had to be stamped by the *darugachi* before they could be issued. This constituted a check on the powers of the Han Chinese local officials (Sa, 1975b, pp. 300–301).

In the 9th year of the Hongwu reign (1376), Emperor Taizu of the Ming scrapped the Branch Secretariats that had grown too powerful, and set up Three Commissions to take over some of the administrative powers of the local governments. The first was the Regional Administrative Commission (*chengxuan buzhengshi si*, 承宣布政使司), in charge of administrative and fiscal affairs; the second was the Regional Judiciary Commission (*tixing anchashi si*, 提刑按察使司), in charge of the judgement of criminal cases of a Region; the third was the Regional Military Commission (*du zhihuishi si*, 都指挥使司), in charge of the military affairs of a Region. "Later in case of military campaigns, Ministers of the Six Ministries could be dispatched in the name of General Governors, and Deputy Ministers could be dispatched in the name of Regional Supervisors. General Governors originally oversaw military affairs, and Regional Supervisors were only appointed in times of need. Their duties were no more than to supervise and impeach the subordinate officials. These two posts did not become an established institution throughout the Ming period."

The Qing Dynasty continued the arrangement of the Ming, but General Governors and Regional Supervisors became regular official positions. After the Taiping Rebellion broke out in 1850, Han-Chinese officials such as Zeng Guofan, Zuo Zongtang and Li Hongzhang commanded armies in the capacity of General Governors and Regional Supervisors to revive the Qing Dynasty and gradually became powerful. When the Empress Dowager Cixi issued an imperial decree declaring war on the invading powers in 1911, General Governors and Regional Supervisors including Li Hongzhang, Zhang Zhidong, Liu Kunyi and Yuan Shih-k'ai entered into the *Mutual Defense Pact of the Southeastern Provinces*. They refused to carry out the imperial decree promulgated by the Qing imperial court to declare war on the foreign powers, and the Qing imperial court could do nothing about them.

2.2.2 Local Government—Administrative Division and Setup

i. Evolution of the local government system

The local government of the Qin Dynasty had a two-tier structure comprising the commandery and the county, and this arrangement was continued in the early Han Dynasty. In Emperor Jing's reign, noblemen were prohibited from going to their own fiefdoms and Chancellors and Defenders were centrally appointed to take care of the administration of the subordinate kingdoms. In Emperor Wu's reign, the country was divided into thirteen Regions for the purpose of supervision. In the late Eastern

Han period, the Regional Inspector was changed into the Regional Governor, who became essentially the top local administrator in charge of both civil and military affairs of a Region. Thus, the local government evolved from a two-tier structure to a three-tier structure comprising the Region, the prefecture and the county.

The Jin Dynasty maintained the three-tier structure of the local government. Learning from the lesson of powerful and uncontrollable Regional Governors in the late Han period, the Jin regime divided the functions and powers of the Regional Governor between the Regional Inspector and the Commander-in-chief. "The Commander-in-chief was in charge of military affairs, while the Regional Inspector took care of civil affairs" (*Comprehensive Statutes* by Du You of the Tang Dynasty), which effected a separation of civil and military administration. However, the position of Regional Inspector was often held concurrently by the Commander-in-chief. A Regional Inspector having the title of a general was in comprehensive charge of the administration with military authority and was called the "Regional General". Essentially, this was the Commander-in-chief serving concurrently as the Regional Inspector, but his primary task was still to handle the military matters of the Region. A Regional Inspector not having the title of a general had no military authority and was only in charge of civil matters. Such a Regional Inspector, called a "Restricted Regional Inspector" (*danche cishi*, 单车刺史), was purely a civil local administrator. Into the Eastern Jin Dynasty, the Regional Inspectors, with the exception of Restricted Regional Inspectors, commanded both civil and military powers, thus undermining the political stability of the empire (Sa, 2007, p. 265).

In Emperor Wen's reign of the Sui, as the Regions increased in number and did not differ significantly from commanderies, the commanderies were abolished and counties were placed under the jurisdiction of Regions. Emperor Yang of the Sui changed the name of Region into commandery and, following the old system of Emperor Wu of the Han, appointed Inspectors to inspect the work of commanderies. The local government had the two-tier structure of commandery and county. In the early Tang Dynasty, the name of commandery was changed back into Region.[24] Depending on the number of households, prefectures were classified into three grades (upper, medium and lower), and an Inspector was appointed for each prefecture. A command was established in a strategically important prefecture, and the Inspector of the prefecture where the command was located served concurrently as the Commander-in-chief to oversee several prefectures. In the Zhenguan reign (AD 627–649) of Emperor Taizong of the Tang, the country was divided into ten Regions for the purpose of supervision. Officials from the Censorate were dispatched to inspect the work of the various prefectures. The number of Regions was subsequently increased to fifteen, and the Local Supervisor was installed in each Region. The Local Supervisor also served concurrently as the Inspector of the prefecture where the Local Supervisor was stationed. The Local Supervisor took comprehensive charge of the military, civil, judicial and fiscal matters of the whole Region. When Local Supervisors stayed on in

[24] For the purpose of simplicity and uniformity, the name prefecture will still be used for the administrative level above the county, and Region will be reserved for the name of a supervisory unit hereafter in this book. (Translator's notes)

frontier regions, they became Central Commissioners, who were given full power by the central government to deal with contingencies. After the Rebellion of An Lushan and Shi Siming from AD 755 to 763, the empire was divided into over forty Regions, and the areas under the supervision of the Central Commissioners evolved into Military Zones. "Military Zones were set up one after another, with the larger one having jurisdiction over a dozen prefectures and smaller ones over two or three prefectures." But nominally, the Central Commissioners were still commissioners appointed by the central government. The Song Dynasty copied this arrangement of the Tang, but established four Supervisors in each Region, namely, the Financial Supervisor, the Judicial Supervisor, the Relief Supervisor and the Military Supervisor. Of the four Supervisors, the Military Supervisor, who was in charge of both civil and military matters of a Region, was especially powerful. In order to monitor the Military Supervisor, the central government established the Mounted Courier (*zouma chengshou*, 走马承受) to report to the court annually on the work of the Military Supervisor. The office of the Mounted Courier was a continuation of the practice from the Tang Dynasty whereby eunuchs were employed to monitor the armies. While this post was normally held by regular officials, there were still instances when eunuchs were indeed appointed. In principle, one Mounted Courier was sent out to each Region, but there were also cases of two Regions sharing one Mounted Courier or one Region having two Mounted Courier. Therefore, the local government of the Song Dynasty actually had a three-tier structure comprising the Region, the commandery and the county, even though the Region was not purely a local administrative level, but a supervisory area defined by the central government that took comprehensive charge of both military and civil administration. In the Tang Dynasty, the prefecture was headed by a governor and a deputy. In the Song Dynasty, the positions of the governor and the deputy of the prefecture were not always filled, and only Managing Prefects were appointed. After the Zhidao reign, the official title of the Managing Prefect was always prefixed by "Provisionary" to indicate its acting and temporary nature (Lin, 1976, p. 178).

The local administrative organization of the Yuan Dynasty was quite complicated. In addition to the prefecture and the county, there was also the route. A uniform arrangement did not exist between the route and the prefecture. The route was sometimes above the prefecture and sometimes on the same footing with the prefecture. Besides, there was also the Branch Secretariat. Though nominally an office dispatched by the Secretariat to a local place, the Branch Secretariat was essentially the top administrative organ of the local government. Thus, the local government had either a three-tier structure (Branch Secretariat, prefecture and county), or a four-tier structure where the route was placed above the prefecture. Furthermore, the Secretariat of the central government had direct jurisdiction over the so-called "hinterland" encompassing Shanxi and Hebei. Then several Branch Secretariats were combined into a Region, and there was the Branch Bureau of Military Affairs to take care of military matters and the Branch Censorate to watch over the officials. Each Branch Secretariat also had the Pacification Commission, the Placation Commission, and the Cooption Commission for undertaking military inspection, the Surveillance Commission for inspecting the judgement of cases, the Supervisor of Confucian

Schools to oversee education, and the Salt Taxes Supervisor to administer the salt trade.

The Ming Dynasty continued the institution of Branch Secretariats (or called provinces) of the Yuan. Each province had the Three Regional Administrative Departments, in charge of fiscal, military and judicial matters respectively. The local administrative division featured co-existence of the four-tier structure and the three-tier structure. The former comprised the province, the prefecture (*fu*, 府), the sub-prefecture (*zhou*, 州) and the county, while the latter did not have the level of prefecture. Sub-prefectures were divided into two types: independent sub-prefectures (*zhili zhou*, 直隶州) and department sub-prefectures (*shuzhou*, 属州). An independent sub-prefecture had the same status as a prefecture, and a department sub-prefecture had the same status as a county. Garrisons were established at the various prefectures to lead troops. In frontier areas, prefectures and counties were not set up, and the garrisons, which concurrently took care of civil matters, became essentially a special form of administrative units. General Governors and Regional Supervisors were established since the middle Ming period. The Regional Supervisor was the gradually localized Supervisor sent out by the central government, with one installed in each province. The Regional Supervisor eventually became the top administrator of the Three Regional Administrative Departments of each province. The four-level or three-level structure of the Ming local government may have been instituted out of fiscal considerations:

> Counties comprised the basic tax collecting unit, prefectures the basic tax assessment unit, and the provinces, the revenue transit unit. Sub-prefectures either broke large prefectures into administratively manageable units or covered territories which had an intermediate level of revenue, but were in areas that were remote or difficult of access. Created to adjust this imbalance, the sub-prefectures had no distinctive administrative features of its own. When the sub-prefecture was subordinate to a prefecture, it functioned as a branch office of the prefect. If it was immediately subordinate to a province, it functioned as a prefecture of a minor order. When a level of government became unnecessary in the chain of command, it was eliminated. Since all the prefectures of the two metropolitan areas were close to administrative offices of the northern and southern capitals, provincial organs were considered superfluous. (Huang, 2008, pp. 119–120)

ii. Changes in concepts

1. Changes in the names of county officials

In the Qin Dynasty, a large county was headed by a *xianling* (县令, magistrate), and a small one by a *xianzhang* (县长, County Chief). This arrangement was followed by the two Han, Wei, Jin and Northern and Southern Dynasties. In the Sui and Tang Dynasties, a county Magistrate was called *xianling*, and the designation of *xianzhang* was not used. The name of *zhixian* (literally "presiding over the county affairs") first appeared in the 3rd year of the Jianlong reign of the Song Dynasty (962 AD). In the Yuan Dynasty, the county was headed by a darugachi assisted by a deputy. The Ming and Qing Dynasties followed the arrangement of the Song, and a *zhixian* was installed for each county.

2. Fluctuations in the status of *zhou*

In the early Han Dynasty, *zhou* (Region) was a unit of supervision and inspection, and the Regional Inspector had a rank below that of the Prefecture Governor. In Emperor Cheng's reign, the Regional Inspector was changed into the Regional Governor, who ranked above the Prefecture Governor. It was not until Emperor Ling's reign of the Eastern Han, when ranking ministers were appointed as Regional Governors, that *zhou* became the top tier of the local government. In the early Sui Dynasty, as *zhou* increased in number and did not differ significantly from prefectures, the prefectures were abolished and counties were placed under the jurisdiction of *zhou*. Since then, *zhou* lost its elevated status. In the Tang and Song Dynasties, *zhou* were classified into seven grades, but there were no categorical differences among them. Thus, *zhou* was reduced to an intermediary level of the local government between the Region and the county. In the Yuan Dynasty, *zhou* were not only graded as upper, medium or lower, but also were classified into the following four categories: *zhou* subordinate to the province, *zhou* subordinate to the route, *zhou* subordinate to the prefecture, and *zhou* subordinate to larger *zhou*. Into the Ming and Qing Dynasties, *zhou* were no longer graded, and they were only divided into two types: independent *zhou* and department *zhou*. The former had the same status as the prefecture, and the latter was on the same footing with the county. Thus, department *zhou* became the lowest level of the local government on a par with the county (Yang & Ou, 2005, pp. 345–353).

3. Decline in the status of *fu*[25]

In the Qin (221–206 BC) and Han (202 BC–9 AD, AD 25–220) Dynasties, *fu* denoted the office of an organ of the central government, such as *chengxiang fu* (丞相府, the Prime Minister's office), *yushi fu* (御史府, the Censorate), *shaofu* and *taifu* (少府、太府, the Palace Administrator of Finance). Since the Tang Dynasty (AD 618–907), *fu* became somewhat synonymous with *zhou* (prefecture). "Prior to the Yuan Dynasty, *fu* and *zhou* had a similar meaning; since the Ming Dynasty, *fu* superseded *zhou* as the name of the prefecture." "Transformation of *fu* from the name of an office to a geographical name was identical to that of the province (Branch Secretariat)."

The use of *fu* as the name of a geographical unit started in the Tang Dynasty. It was used to refer to prefectures of the two metropolitan areas. In the Song Dynasty, the use of *fu* was expanded to include other vital prefectures, such as *Daming Fu* of Beijing. *Fu* in the Song Dynasty were divided into the two grades of capital prefectures and superior prefectures. The capital prefectures included *Kaifeng Fu*, *Lin'an Fu* and *Yingtian Fu*. In the Yuan Dynasty, *fu* were not graded but had different types. One type was the independent *fu*, which was directly under the jurisdiction of the province,

---

[25] Refer to Yang & Ou (2005, pp. 361–366).

while the other type was subordinate *fu*, which was indirectly under the jurisdiction of a larger *fu* via the route. Since the Ming Dynasty, *fu* increased drastically in number. It became the generic term for the intermediary level of the local government between the province and the county and lost its earlier elevated status. In the Ming Dynasty, there were three categories of *fu*: 14 military-civil *fu*, established in Sichuan, Guangxi, Yunnan and Guizhou, two tribal *fu*, established in Yunnan, and regular *fu*. In terms of their ranks, out of the 160 fu of the Ming Dynasty, only Shuntian and Yingtian, which were located at the two metropolitan areas, enjoyed an exalted status, with their top administrators ranked at 3a. All the other 158 *fu* had an identical status, with their top administrators ranked at 4a. In the 6th year of the Hongwu reign (AD 1373), an attempt was made to grade *fu* into three levels, i.e., upper, medium and lower, based on the amount of tax grains, but this differentiation was discarded before long. In the Ming Dynasty, "most prefectures supervised only a handful of subprefectures and counties, usually less than ten. But there were exceptional cases. Kaifeng prefecture of Honan had four subprefectures and thirty counties. Tsi-nan prefecture of Shantung had four subprefectures and twenty-six counties." (Huang, 1974, p. 27) The Qing Dynasty copied this arrangement of the Ming, "except that *fu* had become a regular unit of the local administrative system, with no differentiation whatsoever either in grade or in type."

2.2.3 Local Government of the Qing Dynasty

i. Local government setup and local administrative units

According to the *Daqing Huidian* (*The Code of the Qing Dynasty*), "the General Governor and Regional Supervisor had jurisdiction over the Regional Administrative Commission, the Regional Surveillance Commission as well as their subdepartments. The Regional Administrative Commissioner and the Regional Surveillance Commissioner had jurisdiction over the prefectures, independent departments and independent sub-prefectures. The prefecture was above the departments (*ting*), the sub-prefectures and the counties. The independent department and independent sub-prefecture had jurisdiction over a number of counties." The Regional Supervisor was usually the top administrator of a province. Two or three provinces were sometimes combined to form a larger administrative area, and a General Governor was installed to govern this area. The Regional Administrative Commissioner was the top civil official of a province, in charge of fiscal matters. The Regional Surveillance Commissioner was in charge of judiciary matters only. The Regional Administrative Commissioner and the Regional Surveillance Commissioner had their respective sub-departments in lower-level localities, and their heads were respectively titled Sub-regional Administrative Commissioner and Sub-regional Surveillance Commissioner. Prefectures, sub-prefectures, departments and counties were all headed by their respective local officials. Under the Qing system, in localities where bannermen were stationed, the Judicial Assistant Prefect (*lishi tongzhi*, 理事同知) and Judicial

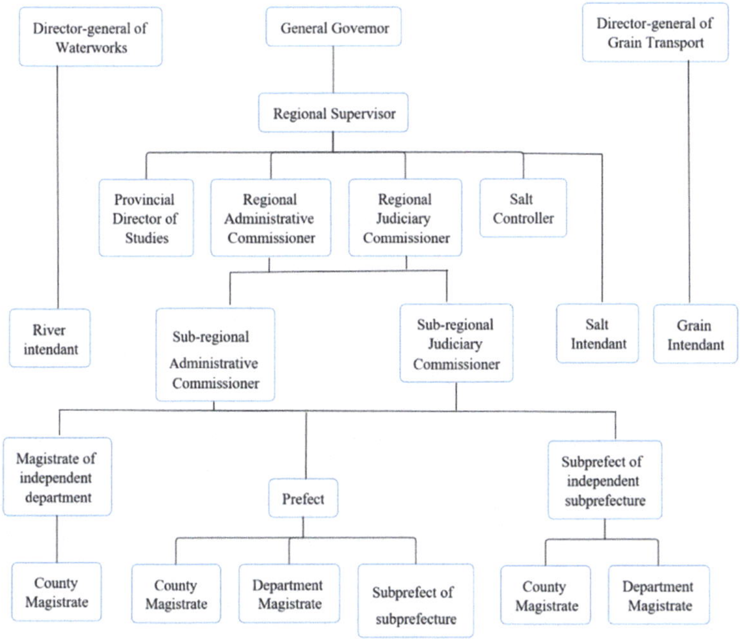

Fig. 2.4 Local government of the Qing Dynasty (Ch'ü, 1988, p. 5)

Departmental Administrator lishi tongzhi, 理事同知 were set up as deputies to the Prefects to investigate cases involving bannermen. The local government had a three-level (or four-level)[26] structure: province → (circuit) → prefecture/independent department/independent sub-prefecture → department/sub-prefecture/county.

In addition to the above General Governor, Regional Supervisor, Regional Administrative Commissioner and Regional Surveillance Commissioner, the local government of the Qing Dynasty also included offices for education, waterworks, grain transport, salt trade, and customs duty. Among these, the Provincial Education Commissioner inspected the work of Confucian studies of the province; the Director-general of Waterworks took charge of water conservancy projects; the Director-general of Grain Transport was responsible for the transport of tax grains and had under him the Grain Intendant; the Salt Administrator was the top local official for handling salt-related affairs and had under him the Salt Controller and Salt Intendant; the Customs Office was headed by the Overseer or the Customs Intendant (Zhang, 2008, p. 225) (Fig. 2.4).

[26] Whether the local government had a three- or four-level structure depends on whether the Circuit is regarded as a level of the local government.

ii. Unique features

1. Establishment of local offices for handling ethnic affairs

"In order to rule the Mongols, Hui (Chinese Moslems) and Tibetans, the Qing Dynasty, in addition to establishing the Department for Ethnic Affairs for overall administration, also sent out Generals, Commanders-in-chief, Vice Commanders-in-chief and Grand Ministers to various regions such as Inner and Outer Mongolia, Qinghai, Xinjiang and Tibet for direct administration. These were the top military and administrative officials for ruling these regions. Furthermore, the minority peoples were organized into a number of Banners. Each Banner was directed by a Banner Head (filled by a member of the nobility of the minority race), subject to the supervision of the Grand Minister in charge of inspecting the Banner. Besides, aboriginal officials (both military and civil) were installed in all regions inhabited by ethnic minorities to handle ethnic affairs (indigenous people presiding over indigenous affairs). These aboriginal officials were under the jurisdiction of the Ministry of Personnel and the Ministry of War respectively and directly administered by the General Governor, Regional Supervisor, General or Grand Minister of the respective province." (Zhang, 2008, p. 247)

2. Allowances for heterogeneity in the Qing official system (local government setup)

One of the most noteworthy aspects of the Qing official system was sufficient allowances for heterogeneity within the bounds of general uniformity based on local characteristics. This was reflected in the following points[27]:

(1) The central government had Six Ministries, but Fengtian, one of the three northeastern provinces, only had five Sub-ministries, without the Personnel Sub-ministry. The Six Ministries of the central government were headed by Ministers, whereas the Sub-ministries of Fengtian were headed only by Vice Ministers. The underlying reason was that as the former imperial capital of the Qing government, the significance of the setup of Fengtian's local government was more symbolical than practical.
(2) With respect to General Governors, some administered one province (Zhili), some administered two provinces (Guangdong & Guangxi, Fujian & Zhejiang), and still others administered three provinces (Jiangsu, Anhui & Jiangxi). Some provinces had both the General Governor and the Regional Supervisor, some had the General Governor serving concurrently as the Regional Supervisor (Zhili, Sichuan, Fujian and Gansu), and some had only the Regional Supervisor without the General Governor (Shandong, Shanxi, Henan and Xinjiang). For an important province, both the General Governor and the Regional Supervisor were

[27] Refer to Oda (2003, pp. 223–229).

installed "in case the Regional Supervisor alone would be unable to fulfill all the duties".

(3) Generally, each province had one Regional Administrative Commissioner, but Jiangsu, because of its vastness and great wealth, could not be managed by one Regional Administrative Commissioner. Therefore, two Regional Administrative Commissioners were appointed, one based in Jiangning (the seat of government of Jiangsu, Jiangxi and Anhui) and one based in Suzhou (provincial capital of Jiangsu).

(4) Each province had one Regional Surveillance Commissioner to handle judiciary affairs, but Xinjiang only had a Sub-regional Surveillance Commissioner, who concurrently held the title of the Regional Surveillance Commissioner.

(5) Of all the Sub-regional Commissioners and Intendants, some had jurisdiction over an entire province (the Grain Intendant, the Salt Intendant), while others had jurisdiction over an area smaller than the province (Sub-regional Surveillance Commissioner). Their offices varied in complexity according to the local conditions.

(6) Among the sub-prefectures and counties, some had deputies to the Sub-prefects and county Magistrates, while some did not.

(7) Shuntian Prefecture, the local government of the metropolitan area, differed in status from other prefectures. Its top official was the Governor (*fuyin*, 府尹), who had somewhat different powers and status from regular Prefects. Sometimes, the Governor could submit a memorial jointly with the General Governor of Zhili; on some other occasions, he could make decisions directly, not subject to interference from the General Governor. Shuntian Prefecture had under it four sub-divisions, which directed the sub-prefectures and counties in handling their affairs.

3. Functional overlap of the General Governor and Regional Supervisor with offices of the provincial government

The Qing Dynasty perpetuated the arrangement of the Ming in designating the province as the highest level of the local government. The whole country was divided into eighteen provinces, and the number increased to twenty-two in the Guangxu reign. Within the province, the Regional Supervisor had jurisdiction over the Regional Administrative Commissioner and the Regional Surveillance Commissioner. In addition, the General Governor was instituted, who ruled one to three provinces. The position of the General Governor having jurisdiction over one province was as a rule held concurrently by the Regional Supervisor, but this arrangement was not uniform throughout the country. The General Governor was originally a military official, but could check on the powers of the Regional Supervisor. The Regional Supervisor originally administered in civilian terms, but also supervised over military affairs. "The General Governor and the Regional Supervisor did not differ much in their functions, and neither did they have a superior-subordinate relationship as both were directly answerable to the emperor. This overlapping and mutually opposing arrangement could naturally play a role in checking each other's powers. Neither the General

Governor nor the Regional Supervisor was a standalone official, but was instead assisted by six offices and his own personal staff. The six offices, which somewhat resembled the Six Ministries of the central government, were clerical posts. The personal staff, hired by the General Governor or the Regional Supervisor himself, were in charge of specific matters, such as judicial and fiscal affairs and the preparation of reports and memorials to the throne. As such, they got themselves involved in the administration like advisors or secretaries to the General Governor or the Regional Supervisor." (Guo, 2012, p. 5)

Where the seats of the General Governor and the Regional Supervisor were collocated in the same city, conflicts often arose between the two due to the overlap in their functions and powers. To solve this problem, the General Governor was subsequently designated as the top local administrator. Nevertheless, as both the General Governor and the Regional Inspector carried the affiliated title of (Vice) Censor-in-chief (head of the Chief Surveillance Bureau), each was entitled to independently memorialize and impeach the other. Since the Regional Supervisor became a local administrator, the Regional Administrative Commissioner lost his power. When the General Governor was designated as the top local administrator, the Regional Supervisor, in turn, lost his power as well, leaving only a redundant layer of office in the chain of transmission of official documents. In the late Guangxu reign, the Regional Supervisor was abolished where the General Governor and the Regional Supervisor were based in the same city; otherwise, the General Governor was the top local administrator as of old, "but official documents still passed through the Regional Supervisor as a formality". It was explicitly stipulated that the General Governor and the Regional Supervisor were the supreme provincial administrators, having jurisdiction over the Three Commissioners (the Regional Administrative Commissioner, Regional Educational Commissioner, and Regional Surveillance Commissioner) and two intendants (the Industrial Intendant and the Police Intendant). All the commissioners and intendants had their respective offices and sub-divisions. This actually marked the beginning of the present-day system of provinces (Lin, 1976, p. 179).

iii. The sub-prefecture, the county and local administration

1. "One-man government" of the sub-prefect and magistrate

In the formal imperial bureaucratic system, the sub-prefect and county magistrate constituted the extremely small number of officials directly in touch with the people. Hence, they were referred to as "officials close to the people" (officials administering the people, or officials handling practical affairs). They were officials truly in charge of local administration. Their superiors above the sub-prefectural level, on the other hand, were all supervisory officials, or officials in charge of officials. Under this arrangement, the sub-prefect and magistrate played a vital role in local administration in spite of their low ranks: The Regional Surveillance Commissioner, Regional Administrative Commissioner, their sub-departments, and prefects "are able to talk about but unable to act on the desirable things that should be done and the undesirable things that should be removed." Even the General Governor and the Regional Supervisor "rely mainly on empty words." Only the sub-prefect and magistrate "can be seen in real action." The local administration of the empire was in the hands of the sub-prefects and magistrates. "Without them, it would have been at a standstill." The sub-prefect or magistrate "had a 'one-man government' because all the functions of the sub-prefectural and county government rested on him alone." In spite of the subordinate officials and clerks that assisted in the administration, the sub-prefect or magistrate himself was the sole entrustee and responsible person for all the local affairs. All tasks, including tax collection, judiciary matters, local policing, education, public welfare and public works, ultimately rested on him alone (Ch'ü, 1988/2003, pp. 29–64, translator's introduction, pp. 7–8).

2. Subordinate officials and educational officers of the sub-prefecture and county[28]

(1) Assistant Sub-prefect and Magistrate: These included the Vice Magistrate (first-class assistant) (*zhoutong*, 州同), the Assistant Department Magistrate (second-class assistant) (*zhoupan*, 州判), the Assistant County Magistrate (known as the Deputy County Magistrate) and the Registrar (known as the Second Deputy County Magistrate). Not all sub-prefectures and counties had assistants. Even if assistants were appointed, they were often referred to as "idle officials" or "superfluous officials". Most were mot recruited from the successful candidates in the civil service examinations and had very little power in the local government.
(2) Chief officers: Both the sub-prefecture and the county had a jail warden, also known as *youtang* (右堂, official presiding in the right hall). As the jail warden was also in charge of police duties, his office was also known as the police bureau.
(3) Miscellaneous officials: These included sub-district magistrate (*xunjian*, 巡检), the postmaster, the tax collector and the granary supervisor.
(4) Educational officers: In each sub-prefecture or county, there were two educational officers: the Director of Studies (*xuezheng*, 学正 or *jiaoyu*, 教谕) and the Assistant Director of Studies (*xundao*, 训导). They were not the subordinate officials of the sub-prefecture or the county, but were under the Regional Educational Commissioner, concerned with the supervision and direction of the students in the sub-prefectural and county schools. However, they also occasionally participated in the administrative and judicial affairs of the sub-prefecture and the county. The educational officer had to hear cases together with the sub-prefect or the magistrate in which the chastisement of a student was called for, since the sub-prefect or the magistrate was not allowed to administer punishment to a student. He had to make sure that students who had failed to pay a tax made the payment. Sometimes, they were also entrusted with some administrative duties, such as opening the wrappings of silver that came from the taxpayers.

3. Aides of a sub-prefect or magistrate

Of the four groups of aides in a Sub-prefect or Magistrate's *yamen*, the clerks and the government runners were natives of the province where they served, while the

[28] Refer to Ch'ü (1988, pp. 8–13).

private secretaries and personal servants were the private staff of the sub-prefect or magistrate. As the sub-prefect or magistrate was legally prohibited from serving in his own native place, he was often appointed to a locality where he was not familiar with the local situation and problems and might not even understand the local dialect. To a large extent, he needed to rely on his private secretaries and personal servants to direct and supervise the native clerks and government runners.

(1) Clerks

As to be discussed in the chapter on "Scholar-bureaucratic Politics and Civil Service System", since the Western and Eastern Han Dynasties, there gradually emerged the distinction between the scholar-officials and clerks in the government, with marked differences in their status. As the political and cultural elite, scholar-officials were not familiar with and had no particular interest in the routine office work. Furthermore, the criminal laws, past cases and precedents indispensable for hearing cases were not the necessary knowledge for passing the civil service examinations, and fiscal matters were especially shunned away by scholar-officials who "valued righteousness above material gains". Consequently, the enormous amounts of documents and registers had to be taken care of by the clerks. Engaged in the clerical work one generation after another, the clerks were extremely well versed in all kinds of government regulations and precedents. In accordance with the traditional division of official business in the Chinese government, the clerks of the sub-prefectural and county *yamen* were organized into six offices, namely, personnel, revenue, rituals, military, justice and works.

Clerks were deemed to be morally deficient and they were prone to manipulation of power and embezzlement of funds. They were the necessary evil that had to be relied upon under gentry politics. In extreme cases, the clerks would secure a tight grip on the administrative affairs, engage in all sorts of malpractices, and deceive their superiors, but the officials could not do much about them owing to their lack of understanding of the inner workings of the official business. In the 1st year of the Kangxi reign (1662 AD), the central government issued an illogical order to eliminate the pay for clerks altogether out of a deep resentment for their corruption. However, clerks still remained highly contended posts. In order to prevent a clerk from controlling the administrative affairs of a locality for a prolonged period of time, the government placed a limit on a clerk's term of office. Nevertheless, many clerks still remained on their posts after their terms had expired, often by changing their names. The post of a clerk was so lucrative that when the term of a clerk expired, a sum (called *quedi*, 缺底) had to be paid to the retiring clerk by the successor for the post. This malpractice persisted in spite of the severe punishments prescribed by laws enacted by the imperial government.

(2) Government runners[29]

As the name suggests, government runners were people who served the local government in various menial capacities. They had a greedy and despicable character for two

[29] Refer to Na (2006, pp. 34–37).

reasons: First, runners had an inferior social status and were mostly recruited from among "the scoundrels on the street". Sometimes, they were even prohibited from marrying people of good standing, and their offspring for three generations were not allowed to take the civil service examinations and were thus prevented from entering officialdom. Second, they only had a meagre pay, which was insufficient for supporting either their parents or their wife and children. They served as government runners for two purposes: First, they could evade rendering labor service. Therefore, some people even paid a sum of money to be nominal runners (*guaming chaiyi*, 挂名差役), who were listed as government runners without actually serving. Second, they could extort money from the people. Thus, some people were willing to work as extra runners (*baiyi*, 白役), that is, runners whose names were not listed in the government record. They worked under the command of regular runners to exact personal gains.

(3) Private secretaries[30]

Private secretaries (*muyou*, 幕友 or *shiye*, 师爷) were administrative experts employed by local officials. The use of private secretaries to assist in the administration was a time-honored tradition, and this practice was especially prevalent in the Qing Dynasty. All local officials, from the provincial authorities down to the Sub-prefect and county Magistrate, hired private secretaries as their aides. Their emergence as a group was the outcome of functional necessity instead of a legal requirement. According to a saying at that time, there was no *yamen* without private secretaries. Private secretaries gradually formed a professional group, and the requisite skills of a private secretary were passed down by apprenticeship. The private secretary of a superior official often recommended a secretary to a lower-level official so that the secretaries of the superior official and the subordinate official were often on intimate terms, even with kinship, professional or regional ties. As far as their native place was concerned, private secretaries from Shaoxing were the most famous.

Private secretaries were administrative experts. As private advisors, they were the guests, not subordinates, of the official. They were hired and entrusted with important duties by the official. Their pay was called *shuxiu* (束修), which means tuition. They performed two primary functions: providing assistance to the official and supervising the other staff. As a proverb went: "An honest and upright official could hardly escape the fate of being deceived by his wily staff." Clerks were the first target that a local official should guard against, and this important task fell on the private secretaries. A local official would hire a certain number of private secretaries of different categories. Depending on the complexity of the administration, the size of his staff of secretaries could range from two or three to more than a dozen. Among these, the secretary of law and the secretary of taxation were indispensable, as the local official had to rely on them in hearing cases and handling fiscal matters. "If his secretaries were honest, diligent and highly competent, the Sub-prefect or county Magistrate could of course govern through inaction." However, the trustworthiness

---

[30] Refer to Na (2006, pp. 18–22).

of private secretaries was extremely precarious. Private secretaries of different *yamen* often took advantage of their relationships as a professional group to ally with one another to control the administration. They could even collude with the runners and clerks in malpractice to deceive the official and prey on the innocent people.

(4) Personal servants[31]

Since personal servants were hired and paid by the sub-prefect or magistrate himself, they had a personal tie with him, and perhaps even a sense of loyalty to him. They were the official's family servants, confidential aides, as well as his eyes and ears. Servants were chiefly responsible for supervising and coordinating the work of the various offices and personnel within the *yamen*, especially the work of runners and clerks (the so-called "wicked clerks") whom the sub-prefect or magistrate did not trust. As such, they were in a relationship of both rivalry and cooperation with the clerks and runners. Personal servants had an inferior legal status, and were even classified as "mean" people. Personal servants were indispensable to a sub-prefect or magistrate who was interested in practicing corruption, and they acted as go-betweens in the negotiation for bribes. While servants were considered confidants of the Sub-prefect or Magistrate, they could still deceive their master, abuse their authority to extort fees or bribes, or even cooperate closely in corruption with clerks and runners.

4. Functions of sub-prefecture and county governments

(1) Administration of justice. Administration of justice was an important and even the primary function that the Sub-prefect or Magistrate performed. In fact, our first impression of a local official in ancient China is someone presiding over a trial, seated under a plaque hanging above, inscribed with the phrase *mingjing gaoxuan* (明镜高悬, "a bright mirror hung high"), denoting a just trial by an honest official. Therefore, it is said that local officials in ancient China were not so much administrative officials concurrently handling judiciary affairs as judicial officials concurrently handling administrative affairs.
(2) Taxation. Taxes were the fundamental source of revenue that financed the operation of the governments at various levels. Since sub-prefectures and counties were the basic tax collecting unit, the sub-prefects and magistrates shouldered a vital fiscal responsibility. They were subject to punishment if they failed to collect the proper quota of taxes, and therefore failed to accomplish their fiscal duty. On the other hand, if they collected too heavy taxes irrespective of means, it could lead to large-scale evasion of taxation, or even public grievances or revolts.
(3) Security. The sub-prefects and magistrates must be responsible for local security. Widespread thefts and robbery or failure to do a good job in arresting the thieves and robbers would inflict disastrous damages on the career prospects of local officials. Local security was closely intertwined with the *baojia* (保甲) system.

[31] Refer to Ch'ü (1988, pp. 74–92).

(4) Other aspects of local administration. These included population registration, courier service, public works, public welfare, educational, cultural, religious, ceremonial, and other functions.

5. Fees collected by the local government: customary fee and illegitimate fees

In times of peace of imperial China, the statutory tax quotas set by the government were not high, resulting in very limited fiscal revenues. Not much surplus was left after covering the enormous daily expenditures of the central government. In case of wars in the frontiers or massive construction projects, it would be difficult to make ends meet. Under the Ming and Qing fiscal systems, all tax revenues were submitted to the central government, and local governments did not have the power of independent disposal of the taxes. In the process of levying and transiting the taxes, the central government did not set aside a rational portion of the taxes for the local governments to cover their office expenses, and local governments were expected to raise their own funds. With a low pay themselves, local officials had to pay the private secretaries and personal servants out of their own purse, undertake financial burdens apportioned by the superior officials (to cover deficits of the superior *yamen*), accommodate visiting or en-route officials, and even pay for the stationery and wages of subordinate officials… With meagre remunerations, the officials of imperial China often had trouble making ends meet. This led officials of superior *yamen* (capital officials included) to expect local officials to offer gift money to them during festivals or near the Spring Festival. They hoped to make up their deficits in the form of customary fees (such as *bingjing*, 冰敬, or fees for cooling in the summer, *tanjing*, 炭敬, or fees for heating in the winter). Under such circumstances, even an honest and upright local official had to levy some fees under various pretexts to cover the official expenses. As for clerks and runners, they went even further to regard the extra fees as part of their regular wages and fabricated even more excuses for extorting money.

(1) Legitimate fee: meltage fee

A definite amount was collected by the local government under the name of "meltage fee" (*huohao*, 火耗, or silver lost in the process of melting). This item was collected as a kind of customary fee and kept by the Sub-prefect or Magistrate to cover various official and personal expenses. In 1724, with the emperor's permission, the collection of this fee was legitimatized and the money thus collected became part of the tax known as *haoxian* (耗羡, surplus). It was not submitted to the Ministry of Revenue of the central government, but was used exclusively for the supplementary salaries (*yanglian yin*, 养廉银) of officials in the province and for certain types of office expenses in the various *yamen*. According to the customary practice, the Sub-prefects and Magistrates would draw from it their supplementary salaries as well as the payment for government runners before delivering the remainder to the Regional Administrative Commission (Ch'ü, 1988, p. 132).

(2) Illegitimate fees

As a proverb goes, the *yamen* gate is wide open, yet with only right on your side but no money, do not go inside. In addition to the exaction of bribes by the various personnel in charge in the *yamen*, the common people had to pay a lot of extra fees (shady in nature) collected at various links of the office work in order to purchase public services of the local government (such as the hearing of a case). As for defendants and witnesses, they were compelled to pay the fees passively. Fees extorted by the clerks included the fee for stamping a document, the fee for transmitting a document, the fee for purchasing approval of a request (in case it was not approved for several days), the fee for commencing a trial (in case the trial had been delayed for several days), the fee for providing service in a trial, and the fee for settling the case. Fees exacted by runners included on-site inspection fee for a criminal case, land surveying fee for a property dispute, shoes and socks money, transport and food expenses for summoning witnesses and parties to a case, fee for unlocking the chains or untying the ropes upon bringing a prisoner to the court, fee for being present in a trial, prison fee for staying in jail, as well as fee for mediating or quelling a litigation (Na, 2006, pp. 28, 35). Pressed by the needs for a livelihood of his staff and financial necessity, even an honest and upright official could only limit, but not entirely eliminate, customary fees. For example, when sending runners to deliver a subpoena or summon an accused person, a benevolent and experienced official would specifically indicate on the subpoena the names of the runners and their assignment and clearly prohibit others from going along so as to reduce the chances and number of personnel extorting the fees and thus lighten the burden on the common people.

"Fees under various pretexts, from … *jiaoqian* (脚钱, fee for transporting a tax commodity) in the Northern and Southern Song Dynasties to *huohao* in the Ming and Qing Dynasties, can all be regarded as the precursor of present-day arbitrary charges. The justification put up for these fees was also practically identical to that of today, namely, to make up for the insufficiency of government funds. From the perspective of the common people in history, the motive behind these extra fees was also strikingly similar, i.e., to fill up the pockets of the government personnel." (Zhao, 2001, p. 216)

2.3 Communications Across Different Levels of the Government

2.3.1 Routine Memorials and Palace Memorials

In ancient China, the reports and recommendations (memorials) submitted by officials to the throne took various forms. Two most important ones were routine memorials (*tiben*, 题本) and personal memorials (*zouben*, 奏本). A routine memorial was submitted in the name of a government agency on an official matter, while a personal memorial was submitted in the name of an individual official, thus of a somewhat personal nature. A routine memorial was stamped with the official seal, but a personal memorial was not. The early Qing Dynasty copied the Ming arrangement in allowing the use of both routine memorials and personal memorials. Since the Kangxi reign, the emperor authorized a small number of trusted officials to report to him through secret memorials. Secret memorials became widely used in the reign of the Yongzheng Emperor as classified documents. They came to be called "palace memorials" and became an established institution. Their use may have been associated with the establishment of the Grand Council. In 1784, the Qianlong Emperor put an end to the use of personal memorials and substituted them with palace memorials. Since then, routine memorials and palace memorials became the two major types of memorials with equal importance (Zhang, 2011, pp. 10–11).

In fact, most imperial edicts were quite concise, written directly on a routine memorial or palace memorial, instead of in the formal format of "The Emperor, by the Grace of Heaven, hereby decrees…"

i. Routine memorials

The procedure for the transmission of routine memorials was as follows. After being prepared by the local official, a routine memorial was sent to the Office of Transmission via the courier stations. A routine memorial prepared in Chinese was translated into Manchu script at the Office of Transmission before being submitted in both Chinese and Manchu languages to the Cabinet. There it was reviewed by the Cabinet Scholars and a rescript slip was attached to the memorial to serve as reference for the emperor when he made the final decision. The emperor would review the routine memorial. Then it was passed down to the Chief Surveillance Bureau, where it would be examined by the Censors and Supervising Secretaries. It was also sent to the Cabinet. The Chief Surveillance Bureau would forward the routine memorial to the pertinent government agencies for deliberation. The response given on the memorial (called "red rescript") was written by a Cabinet Scholar based on the comment dictated by the emperor. The routine system of communications was abolished in the Guangxu reign owing to its inefficiency, lack of secrecy and being too formalistic (with telegrams already available at that time). When a censor made an impeachment, he did not necessarily use a palace memorial and was more likely to use a routine memorial, so as to build up pressure of public opinion at court through this public channel of communications.

ii. Palace memorials

In addition to deficiencies in efficiency and secrecy, the routine system that had evolved from the Outer Court (Cabinet) of the Ming Dynasty was especially unfavorable to the autocratic rule of the emperor. "The chief difficulty with the routine system inherited from the Ming was that it had favored the outer-court bureaucracy's control over central-government decision making and reduced the emperor's opportunities for taking the initiative. Most central-government policies were framed in response to the routine memorials by specialists who worked in various outer-court agencies. The purpose of sending their proposed responses, known as 'draft rescripts' (*nipiao* 票拟, *piaoni* 拟票 or *piaoqian* 票签), to the emperor was not so much to obtain inner-court advice and opinion as to secure the imperial authorization (in the form of a vermilion circle on the draft rescript) for official promulgation of their own proposals." "In most cases the outer-court recommendations went through without change." "(O)nce an approved proposal was returned to the outer court it had to run the gamut of obstructionism at both the central and the provincial government levels." "Thus, while in theory the inner court checked and balanced the outer court, in fact the routine communications system allowed the inner court a very weak role in both decision making and implementation." (Bartlett, 1991, pp. 28–30) In order to strictly control the Outer Court through the Inner Court and bypass the Outer Court on key administrative issues, the institution of palace memorials (*zouzhe*) emerged and functioned in collaboration with the Grand Council. The use of palace memorials was in principle confined to high officials such as General Governors and Regional Supervisors. These officials personally prepared the palace memorials and submitted them to the emperor in the form of personal letters. Palace memorials did not pass through the courier stations, but were carried via a private channel of transmission with en-route offices in various provinces. They were submitted directly to the emperor, who wrote his replies (red rescripts) on them. Then the memorials with the red rescripts were sent back to the memorializing General Governors and Regional Supervisors. Palace memorials and red (or vermillion) rescripts became an institution peculiar to the Qing Dynasty.

2.3.2 Courier Superintendents and Government Gazettes of the Qing Dynasty[32]

In the Qing Dynasty, the central government established the post of Courier Superintendents (*titang guan*, 提塘官) with a staff of sixteen. They were stationed in Beijing and placed under the jurisdiction of the Ministry of War, since the postal relay system (courier horses) were administered by the Ministry of War. The Courier Superintendents were responsible for: (1) transmission of official documents and correspondence back and forth between the central government and local government agencies; (2) escorting the official seal to local officials; (3) printing and publishing released official documents.

All the Courier Superintendents had reporting offices in charge of publishing capital gazettes (*jingbao*, 京报). The memorials, imperial edicts and rescripts in the capital gazettes were copied by the Courier Superintendents personally from the Six Offices of Scrutiny under the Chief Surveillance Bureau. After printing, the capital gazettes were sent to the provincial agencies. If a memorial presented by a central agency, whether it had been approved or passed down for re-examination, was to be published, the central agency concerned should deliver a copied version of the memorial to the Courier Superintendent on duty. The Courier Superintendent printed and published such documents on a daily basis. The Courier Superintendent should

[32] Refer to Oda (2003, pp. 71–73).

not print and publish official documents whose disclosure was prohibited. Copied versions of official documents containing confidential information should be held up for ten days after reaching the relevant government departments before they could be published as manuscripts by the Courier Superintendent. The Courier Superintendent would be impeached if he published documents that had not reached the relevant departments, copied and published petty matters, or disclosed confidential information. "Official gazettes in China date back to as early as the Tang Dynasty", and in the Qing Dynasty, there were capital gazettes, capital manuscripts, court gazettes and court manuscripts.

Sources of information for capital gazettes: A clerk of the Cabinet went to the imperial palace on a daily basis. He had access to the imperial edicts and rescripts coming out of the Grand Council, took the opportunity to record the information, and sent it to the Cabinet. The Cabinet, in turn, forwarded the information to the pertinent government agencies. This was the formal procedure of information transmission. In reality, officials of the various ministries and other central agencies could go directly to the Cabinet to copy the imperial edicts and rescripts so as to bypass the intermediary links and save time.

Capital gazettes had the following format and contents: They were printed with movable wood type. Each gazette contained 10–12 pages with yellow covers. The two Chinese characters "京报" (*jingbao*, capital gazette) appeared at a left corner of the front cover. The first main section of the capital gazette was palace notes, followed by imperial edicts and rescripts, followed by selected memorials. (The income derived from publishing the capital gazettes went to the Courier Superintendents.)

Besides capital gazettes, there were still two other media through which official documents could be published. The first was the manuscript edition (*chaoben*, 抄本), a handwritten form of official documents. As a semi-official and semi-private undertaking, the manuscript edition was more expeditious in supplying information, usually several days ahead of capital gazettes, but they also came at a higher subscription fee. The second was the long edition (*changben*, 长本), so called because of its greater length. The long edition was published by the Courier Superintendents. It was rather coarse in terms of both style of writing and printing and served as a reference for those who wished to learn the official documents in greater detail.

Local dissemination of the capital gazettes: Local agencies would instruct their gazette offices to reprint the capital gazettes and disseminate them locally. The local gazette office would also keep a close eye on any moves of the General Governor and the Regional Supervisor, compile such information into a provincial supplement (*yuanmen bao*, 辕门报) for printing and publication.

2.3.3 *The Lijia System: The Government's Administration of the Grassroots Society*[33]

The *lijia* system, also called *xiangli*, *baojia* or *shiwu* system, refers to a grassroots administrative system below the county in ancient China. The system constituted an extension of the power of the government, but it also had some elements of local self-governance. On the one hand, the state attempted to divide the local population into small units so as to better control them. On the other hand, the state also sought to edify the people through various social forces, such as *sanlao* (three local dignitaries), elders and the village lecture system (*xiangyue*).

> [In the interior districts] Five households should be made a *bi* (比) so that they can protect each other; five *bi* should be made a *lü* (闾) so that they can benefit from each other; four *lü* should be made a *zu* (族) so that they can help with the burial when someone dies; five *zu* should be made a *dang* (党) so that they can rescue each other in the event of an emergency; five *dang* should be made a *zhou* (州) to make them amicable towards each other; five *zhou* should be made a *xiang* (乡) to make them hospitable to each other … [In the outlying districts] Five households form a *lin* (邻), five *lin* form a *li* (里), four *li* form a *zan* (酂), five *zan* form a *bi* (鄙), five *bi* form a *xian* (县), and five *xian* form a *sui* (遂). ("Ministry of Earth" of the *Rites of Zhou*)

i. A multitude of local offices in the pre-Qin period

According to "Ministry of Earth: Overseer of the Masses" of the *Rites of Zhou*, in the interior districts, "each *xiang* has an administrator, undertaken by a man with the rank of Minister (*qing*); each *zhou* has a head, undertaken by an Ordinary Grand Master (*zhong dafu*); a *dang* has a head, undertaken by a Junior Grand Master (*xia dafu*); a *zu* is headed by a master, undertaken by an Upper Serviceman (*shangshi*); a *lü* is headed by a village assistant (*lüxu*), undertaken by a Middle Serviceman (*zhongshi*); a *bi* (比) has a headman, undertaken a Junior Serviceman (*xiashi*)". In the outlying districts, "each *sui* had an administrator, undertaken by an Ordinary Grand Master; each *xian* has a head, undertaken by a Junior Grand Master; each *bi* (鄙) has a head, undertaken by an Upper Serviceman; a *zan* has a head, undertaken by a middle serviceman; a *li* has a head, undertaken a Junior Serviceman; each *lin* has a headman, with one appointed for every five households." "Discourses of Qi" of *Discourses of the States* (Guoyu) has recorded the following local offices that existed during the reform by Guan Zhong (statesman of the Qi): in the interior districts there was the *gui* (made up of five households) headman, the *li* (consisting of ten *gui*) captain, the *lian* (consisting of four *li*) head, and the *xiang* (consisting of ten *lian*) master; in the outlying districts, there was the *yi* (thirty households) captain, *zu* (ten *yi*) commander and *xian* (thirty *zu*) commander. The local officials in the *Zuo's Commentary of the Spring and Autumn Annals* (Zuozhuan) included *li* headman, *sui* leader and *xiang* master for the State of Song, the *sui* leader for the State of Lu, and *xian* grand master, *xian* overseer and *yuwei* (a military officer) for the State of Jin. The local offices recorded in *Mozi* included *xiang* administrator, *li* headman and the three local dignitaries (*sanlao*). The

---

33 Refer to Zhao (1998).

largest number of local offices could be found in *Guanzi*: "Rectifications of the Lord, Third Register" mentions *gui* headman, *li* captain, *lian* head, *xiang* master and *xiang* administrator for the interior districts and *gui* headman, *yi* captain, *zu* commander and *xiang* master for the outlying districts. "On Appraising the Terrain" mentions the three local dignitaries, *li* captain and squad (consisting of five men) leader. "On the Cultivation of Political Power" mentions the *xiang* master. "The Lord and his Ministers (Part One)" mentions *sefu* (Landlord). "Outer Congeries of Sayings" of *Hanfeizi* mentions *li* headman and the squad leader. "On the Regulations of a King" of *Xunzi* mentions *xiang* master. Shuihudi Qin bamboo texts contain *li-dian* (里典 village chief) and *sanlao* (三老).

ii. Changes in organizational levels of the *lijia* (里甲) system of the imperial period

In the Qin period, the *lijia* system consisted of *xiang*, *ting* and *li*. Shang Yang (statesman, chancellor and reformer of the State of Qin) created the system of *shiwu lianzuo* (什伍连坐), whereby the population were organized into units of five and ten, and members of the same unit were held mutually accountable in criminal affairs. The penalty for not reporting a fellow member who had engaged in treason was the waist chop (*yaozhan*, 腰斩). The reward for reporting such a traitor was the same as that for killing an enemy in battle.

In the Han Dynasty, the system consisted of *xiang* (乡), *ting* (亭) and *li* (里). Ten households formed a *shi* (什), and five households formed a *wu* (五). One hundred households constituted a *li*, ten *li* made up a *ting*, and ten *ting* comprised a *xiang*.

In the Three Kingdoms, Wei, Jin, Northern and Southern Dynasties period, the Three Kingdoms, Jin and Song followed the arrangement of the Qin and Han and established *xiang*, *ting* and *li*. The Northern Wei, Eastern Wei, Northern Qi and Northern Zhou set up a three-tier system (with slight variations in the names of specific tiers) based on the *Rites of Zhou*. Among these, the Northern Wei had *lin* (邻), *li* and *dang*, the Northern Qi had *dang*, *lü* and *linli*, and the Northern Zhou had *dang*, *lü* and *li*.

In the Sui Dynasty (AD 581-618), the *lijia* system originally had the three levels of *zu*, *lü* and *bao*, without the level of *xiang*. Later it was changed into a two-level system made up of *xiang* and *li*.

In the Tang Dynasty, the *lijia* system had the three levels of *xiang*, *li* and *fang*/*cun*. One hundred households made up a *li*, and five *li* made up a *xiang*. The third level was called *fang* within the walled city (of the two imperial capitals, prefectures and counties), but *cun* in the countryside. Four households were organized into a *lin*, and five *lin* into a *bao*. A *bao* had a headman, who was responsible for maintaining social order through mutual surveillance.

In the Song Dynasty, the *lijia* system had the three levels of *pai*, *jia* and *bao*. The *baojia* system emerged out of the reforms introduced by Wang Anshi (Prime Minister of the Song Dynasty). Under the *baojia* (保甲) system, five households made up a *bao*, five *bao* made up a great *bao*, and ten great *bao* made up a superior *bao*. Each household with more than two adult males was to provide one security guard (*baoding*, 保丁). Each great *bao* always had five men on duty in charge of local policing. Twenty to thirty neighboring households formed a *jia* and took turns to serve as the *jia* headman, responsible for supervising the payment of taxes and performance of labor services.

The Yuan Dynasty implemented the *xiangli* system (with the two levels of *xiang* and *li*) and the *she* system. Fifty households were organized into a *she*, and an elderly and experienced man was selected as its headman.

In the Ming Dynasty, some localities had a three-level system consisting of the *xiang*, *du* and *tu*, or *xiang*, *du* and *li*, while other localities had a four-level system consisting of the *xiang*, *bao*, *cun* and *li*, or *xiang*, *bao*, *qu* and *tu*. Some regions had the *she* and *jia* organizations as well.

In the Qing Dynasty, most localities preserved the arrangement of the Ming and had a three-level system of *xiang*, *du*, and *tu* (or *li* or *cun* instead of tu). Some localities adopted a two-level system, with the two levels called *bao* and *li*, or *li* and *jia*, or *zhen* and *bao*. In the early Qing Dynasty, it was decreed that in the rural areas, every ten households should have a *jia* headman, and one hundred households should have a *zongjia* chief. Cases of thefts, other crimes as well as escaped criminals should be reported to the *jia* headman, who should relay the message to the *zongjia* chief, who should in turn make a report to the corresponding sub-prefecture or county government. In case one household committed a crime, the other nine households as well as the *jia* headman and the *zongjia* chief would be held accountable and punished accordingly if they failed to report the case to the government. Since the Qianlong reign, ten households were organized into a *pai*, which had a *pai* headman. Ten *pai* were organized into a *jia*, which had a *jia* headman. Ten *jia* were organized into a *bao*, which had a *bao* headman. *Baojia* bureau and sub-bureaus were established in every province to take comprehensive charge of the *baojia* apparatus. All mining sites, Buddhist and Daoist monasteries, shops and marine vessels were incorporated into the *baojia* scheme.

iii. Changes in the functions of the *lijia* system

Ever since the pre-Qin period, local officials at the grassroots level performed four major functions: organizing production; registering the population and allocating labor services; presiding over litigations, mediating disputes and ensure local security; oversee the work of education. "Table of Nobility Ranks and Government Offices" of the *Book of Han* says: "Generally speaking, ten *li* made up a *ting*, which had a head. Ten *ting* made up a *xiang*. Each xiang had the *sanlao*, *youzhi*, *sefu* and *youjiao*. *Sanlao* (three local dignitaries) oversaw education of the masses, *sefu* (Landlord) was in charge hearing cases and collecting taxes. *Youjiao* (游徼, Police Head) was in charge of eradicating thefts and robbery." Since the mid-Tang period, the offices in the *lijia* system underwent significant changes. The posts began to be filled by rotation instead of by selection. There was also a shift in the focus of the *lijia* system: "from mutual assistance to mutual surveillance, and from benefiting the common people to levying taxes and labor services". Emperor Taizu (r. 1636–1912 AD) of the Ming, who rose to power from the bottom of society, revived the *lijia* system to a certain extent. In the 27th year of the Hongwu reign (1394 AD), Zhu Yuanzhang (Emperor Taizu) set up the system of elders: "The competent authorities of the government are hereby ordered to select just and able village elders from the folks to handle the litigations of their respective localities. ...People would be considered guilty of breaching the regular procedure of litigation if they bypass the elders and bring their cases directly to the prefecture or county government." The village elders had the following functions: edifying the people (encouraging them to do good deeds), voicing their opinions on government policies, recommendation and surveillance, encouraging people to engage in agriculture, and handling litigations.

The Qing emperors paid considerable attention to the village lecture system (*xiangyue*). "The term *xiangyue* in Song and Ming times had referred to a local community organization within which social harmony was to be promoted through proper instruction and material aid...the early and mid-Qing rulers gave the term new meaning as a kind of public lecture system". "(E)ighteenth-century rulers intended the village lecture system to be a vertically integrated system that specialized in moral indoctrination." Apart from these, the Qing government mounted a considerable effort to implement the *baojia* system "to provide for mutual surveillance and security". Through these institutions, a centralized state could organize local social order (Wong, 1997, pp. 117–118).

References

Bartlett, B. S. (1991). *Monarchs, ministers: The Grand Council in mid-Ch'ing China, 1723–1820*. University of California Press.

Ch'ü, T. (1988). *Local government in China under the Ch'ing*. Harvard University Press.

Ch'ü, T. (2003). Qingdai defang zhengfu [Local government in China under the Ch'ing] (Z. Fan et al., Trans.) Law Press China. (Original work published 1988).

Chang, Z. (1979). Zhongguo xiandai jiancha zhidu [The supervisory system in modern China]. The Commercial Press.

Chen, G. (1977). Zhongguo fazhi shi gaiyao [An overview of China's legal history]. San Min Book Co., Ltd.

Chen, G. (2006). Zhongguo wenhua yu zhongguo faxi—Chen Guyuan falü shi lunji [Chinese culture and China's legal system—Collection of Chen Guyuan's essays on legal history]. China University of Political Science and Law Press.

Editorial Committee of the Veritable Record of the Control Yuan. (1981). Guomin zhengfu jianchayuan shilu [A veritable record of the Control Yuan of the National Government] (Vol. 1). Secretariat of the Control Yuan.

Ge, J. (2013). Tongyi yu fenlie—zhongguo lishi d qishi [Unity and secession—Lessons from Chinese history]. The Commercial Press.

Guo, T. (2012). Jindai zhongguo shigang [Modern Chinese history]. Truth & Wisdom Press, Shanghai People's Publishing House.

Hsu, C. (1980). *Han agriculture: The formation of early Chinese agrarian economy (206 B.C.–A.D. 220)*. University of Washington Press.

Hsu, C. (2005). Xihan zhengquan yu shehui shili de jioahu zuoyong [Interactions between the Western Han Regime and social forces]. In J. Wang (Ed.), *Politics and power*. Encyclopedia of China Publishing House.

Huang, R. (1974). Shiliu shiji mingdai zhongguo zhi caizheng yu shuishou [Taxation and governmental finance in sixteenth-century Ming China]. Cambridge University Press.

Huang, R. (2008). The Ming fiscal administration. In D. Twitchett & J. K. Fairbank (Eds.), *The Cambridge history of China: The Ming Dynasty 1368–1644* (Vol. 8, Part 2, pp. 106–171). Cambridge University Press.

Hucker, C. O. (2008). Ming government. In D. Twitchett & J. K. Fairbank (Eds.), *The Cambridge history of China: The Ming Dynasty 1368–1644* (Vol. 8, Part 2, pp. 9–105). Cambridge University Press.

Lao, G. (2005). Lun handai de neichao yu waichao [On the Inner Court and Outer Court of the Han Dynasty]. In Q. Huang (Ed.), Zhidu yu guojia [Institutions and the state] (pp. 40–82). Encyclopedia of China Publishing House.

Lin, Y. (1976). Zhongguo fashi shi [A legal history of China]. For internal circulation.

Lü, S. (2002). Zhongguo zhidu shi [A history of China's institutions]. Shanghai Education Publishing House.

Lü, S. (2005). Qin han shi [History of Qin and Han Dynasties]. Shanghai Chinese Classics Publishing House.

McKnight, B. E. (2004). Cong Lü dao li: songdai falü jiqi yanbian jianlun [From statute to precedent: An introduction to the Song law and its transformation]. In G. Turner, H. Gao, & W. He (Eds.), Meiguo xuezhe lun zhongguo falü chuantong [Recent American academic writings on traditional Chinese law] (pp. 310–333). (pp. 缺起始页码). Tsinghua University Press.

Mote, F. W. (2008). The Ch'eng-hua and Hung-chih reigns, 1465–1505. In F. W. Mote & J. K. Fairbank (Eds.), *The Cambridge history of China: The Ming Dynasty 1368–1644* (Vol. 7, Part 1, pp. 343-402). Cambridge University Press.

Na, S. (2004). Zhongguo shenpan zhidu shi [History of Chinese trial system]. Zhengdian Publishing Co., Ltd.

Na, S. (2006). Qingdai zhou xian yamen shenpan zhidu [The trial system of the sub-prefecture and county governments in the Qing Dynasty]. China University of Political Science and Law Press.

Oda, Y. (2003). *Administrative law of the Qing Dynasty*. China University of Political Science and Law Press.

Osamu, Ō. (2017). Qin han fazhi shi yanjiu [Studies on the history of Qin and Han legal systems] (S. Xu, Trans.). Sōbunsha; Zhongxi Book Company. (Original work published 1982).

Pi, C., Pan, H., & Wang, F. (Eds.). (1991). Zhongwai jiancha zhidu jianzhi [A brief history of Chinese and foreign supervisory systems]. Zhongzhou Ancient Books Publishing House.

Qian, M. (2005). Zhongguo lidai zhengzhi deshi [Merits and demerits of political systems in dynastic China]. SDX Joint Publishing.

Qiu, Y. (1992). Zhongguo jiancha zhidu shi [A history of China's supervision system]. East China Normal University Press.

Sa, M. (1975a). Zhongguo shehui zhengzhi shi [A socio-political history of China] (Vol. 1). San Min Book Co., Ltd.

Sa, M. (1975b). Zhongguo shehui zhengzhi shi [A socio-political history of China] (Vol. 4). San Min Book Co., Ltd.

Sa, M. (1975c). Zhongguo shehui zhengzhi shi [A socio-political history of China] (Vol. 3). San Min Book Co., Ltd.

Sa, M. (1993). Zhongguo xianfa xinlun [A new theory on the constitution of the Republic of China]. San Min Book Co., Ltd.

Sa, M. (2007). Zhongguo shehui zhengzhi shi [A socio-political history of China] (Vol. 2). San Min Book Co., Ltd.

Tao, B. (1978). Bijiao jiancha zhidu [Comparative supervisory systems]. San Min Book Co., Ltd.

Wang, J. (2012). Zhongguo lishi tong lun [A survey of Chinese history]. SDX Joint Publishing.

Wei, B. (2019). Wanzheng de tianxia jingyan: Song liao xia jin yuan zhijian de hudong [The experience of a holistic country: Interactions between the Song, Liao, Xia and Jin]. Beijing Normal University Press.

Wong, R. B. (1997). *China transformed: Historical change and the limits of European experience*. Cornell University Press.

Yan, G. (2009). Lun tangdai shangshusheng zhi zhiquan yu diwei [On the powers and status of the Department of State Affairs]. In G. Yan, Yan Gengwang shixue lunwen ji [Collection of Yan Gengwang's essays on historical studies] (Vol. 1, pp. 261–338). Shanghai Classic Publishing House. Zhonghua Book Company.

Yang, H., & Ou, Y. (2005). Zhongguo zhengzhi shi [History of Chinese political institutions]. Wuhan University Press.

Yang, K. (2016). Xizhou shi [History of the Western Zhou Dynasty] (Vol. 1). Shanghai People's Publishing House.

Zhang, D. (2008). Qingdai guojia jiguan kaolüe [An investigation and outline of offices in the Qing Dynasty]. Xueyuan Press.

Zhang, Q. (2011). Shangzou yu zhaodui: Zhongguo gudai juece he chengxu yanjiu [Memorials and interviews with the emperor: Studies on rules and procedures of decision making in ancient China]. Shanghai People's Publishing House.

Zhang, Y. (2003). Zhongguo shi gang [Outline of Chinese history]. The Commercial Press.

Zhao, X. (1998). Zhongguo xiangli zhidu [China's xiangli system]. Social Sciences Literature Press.

Zhao, X. (2001). Songdai guanshang jiqi falü tiaozheng [Official merchants and legal adjustments in the Song Dynasty]. China Renmin University Press.

Zhou, Z. (2014). Zhongguo difang xingzheng zhidu shi [History of China's local administrative institutions]. Shanghai People's Publishing House.

Chapter 3
Scholar-Bureaucratic Politics and Civil Service System

3.1 Scholar-Bureaucratic Politics

3.1.1 Dual-Role of Scholar-Bureaucrats (Bureaucratic and Literati)[1]

The Chinese term *shidafu* (士大夫) has been translated in a variety of ways. Translations such as scholar-official, scholar-bureaucrat, literati, and officialdom all attempt to capture the multifaceted nature of *shidafu* as individuals who combined both bureaucratic and scholarly roles. These designations imply that *shidafu* occupied a unique position in society, embodying the union of intellectual pursuit and administrative responsibility. The scholar-bureaucrats held a position of paramount importance in imperial China, "symbolizing the highest cultural values and wielding significant social power". This dominance was established as the influence of aristocratic politics gradually waned, allowing the scholar-bureaucrats to emerge as the central figures in imperial China's bureaucratic politics—an arena known as elite politics. Although dynastic rulers took into consideration popular support and public opinion, the political system they upheld differed fundamentally from modern democracies. As described by Wen Yanbo, a prominent figure from the Song Dynasty, it was the scholar-bureaucrats, rather than the common people, who governed the world under the emperor's guidance.

Max Weber once referenced the quote "The gentleman is not a utensil" to illustrate the traditional "lack of expert politics in China". Certain scholars have employed the term "amateur" to encapsulate the "dual-role" of scholar-bureaucrats, stating that they are "amateurs in the realm of government due to their scholarly background in art, while their amateurish passion for art arises from their governmental duties". However, the presence of specialized administration does not automatically constitute an ideal political system with inherent social adaptability. The effectiveness of

[1] Refer to the first section of Chap. 1 in Yan (1996).

X. Nie, *The History of Government and Public Law in China*,
https://doi.org/10.1007/978-981-97-6063-3_3

such a system also relies on political and cultural traditions, as well as the sociopolitical context. Despite the perceived absence of specialization, Chinese scholar-bureaucratic politics has thrived for over two millennia, demonstrating its intricate and nuanced nature as a delicate mechanism.

In addition to their involvement in administrative affairs and cultural activities, the ancient Chinese scholar-bureaucrats were vital embodiments of the Confucian orthodox ideology. Confucianism, as a comprehensive belief system, provided a systematic interpretation and organization of the intricate connections between heaven, earth, and humanity. It aimed to address a wide range of issues encompassing life, family, education, culture, governance at both national and global scales, and even the existential question of the universe. Through the application of this all-encompassing system, scholar-bureaucrats sought to exert their influence over imperial politics.

The comprehensive nature of Confucian ideology and the dual-role status of scholar-bureaucrats are inherently interconnected, representing two complementary aspects of the same concept. These aspects mutually reinforce each other, leading to the seamless integration of scholarly pursuits and administrative responsibilities within the scholar-bureaucrat class.

The traditional Chinese imperial examination system and scholar-bureaucratic politics are intricately intertwined and mutually supportive. Firstly, the imperial examination system utilized poetry, rhythm-prose, and eight-legged essay questions as a means to evaluate and select talented individuals, aligning with the cultural interests and knowledge structure of the intellectual community. Secondly, the examination encompassed policy questions that assessed candidates' understanding of state affairs and their ability to analyze and propose solutions. Thirdly, the interpretation of the classics within the examination served as a crucial mechanism for upholding the orthodox status of Confucianism. Additionally, the aesthetic requirements in the poetry and essays evaluated during the examinations endowed the entire social institution with cultural charisma.

3.1.2 Rite and Law

The "ritual system" represents an idealized cultural framework that integrates various aspects of societal order, including political, kinship, and cultural dimensions. At its core, it establishes a trinity consisting of the emperor, kinship ties, and the teacher. This trinity operates through the reciprocal support of kinship relations, the observance of respect, and the embodiment of sageliness. Furthermore, it involves a complementary relationship among different paths, namely the way of the emperor (officialdom), the way of the father, and the way of the teacher complementing each other. The term 'law' in this context extends beyond a mere reference to punitive measures. Instead, it encompasses the rational administrative principles and norms employed within an authoritarian bureaucracy. The "legal system", on the other hand, solely emphasizes the political order in which the state asserts dominance over society and traditional rites and customs, with a particular focus on the way of officialdom (the way of the emperor). From a legalist perspective, the "legal system" is characterized by a centralized authority structure, hierarchical distribution of functions and resources, and the utilization of impersonal, procedural, calculable, and utilitarian written regulations as the foundation for administration. This perspective sets it apart from the "ritual system" (Yan, 1996, p. 470). Additionally, it has been noted that a fundamental distinction between legalism and other schools of thought lies in the fact that "legalism is inherently geared toward serving the monarch" (Zhang, 2003, p. 147).

There are four factors that contributed to the "discontinuation" of legalism. Firstly, the fall of the Qin Dynasty was largely attributed to the perceived shortcomings of legalistic governance. As a result, when Emperor Xiaowu of the Han Dynasty assumed power, he actively promoted the Six Classics of Confucianism and suppressed non-Confucian schools of thought. This shift in endorsement diminished the influence of legalist theory as people became apprehensive and refrained from praising legalism. Secondly, during the period following the Qin and Han Dynasties, China experienced a prolonged period of unified rule, resulting in reduced competition among vassals for power and hegemony. Consequently, even though some scholars may have held legalist ambitions during the Warring States era, they lacked opportunities to advocate for legalism to vassals and were reluctant to voice legalist arguments. Thirdly, the Han Dynasty actively propagated Confucianism as its ethical philosophy. This choice was driven by the alignment of Confucianism with the interests of the royal family and its compatibility with the Chinese agrarian society based on a natural economy. Consequently, Confucianism became deeply ingrained in the collective consciousness of the populace. Lastly, legalism's emphasis on the supremacy of the law and formalistic approaches could not compete with the Confucian emphasis on natural principles of justice and human emotions, which encompassed a more ritualistic perspective. Despite legalism's decline, its spirit continued to influence subsequent generations. Figures such as Cao Cao and Zhuge Liang during the Three Kingdoms era, Wang Anshi of the Northern Song Dynasty, and Zhang Juzheng of the Ming Dynasty can be considered "legalists in their own right". However, due to the prevailing influence and societal pressure of the Confucian tradition, these individuals refrained from openly acknowledging their affiliation with legalism (Xu, 1976, pp. 9–10).

3.1.3 Mencius and Xunzi[2]

i. A singled-minded pursuit of "rule by rites" by (Confucius) Mencius

Mencius, following in the footsteps of Confucius, emphasized the importance of "rites" and the pursuit of "rule by rites", which can be viewed as an extension of the

[2] Refer to Yan (1996, pp. 180–211).

cultural practices of "ritual music" and "ritual education" prevalent during their time. These cultural traditions were closely tied to the role of "music teachers" who played a significant part in their development. "Music", according to Confucius and Mencius, was regarded as "the harmonious union of heaven and earth", and the concept of "harmony" held canonical significance in two main ways. Firstly, it involved advocating love and fostering harmonious interpersonal relationships. Secondly, "harmony" also encompassed the harmonious adjustment between diverse and heterogeneous factors. The virtue of "benevolence", or love for others, and the state of "Great Harmony" represented the highest ideal within the Confucian ethical framework. Confucians excelled in the system for the dissemination of Confucian orthodoxy, focusing more on the ideological system rather than the political framework. Mencius, in particular, "showed proficiency in the *Book of Poetry and the Book of History*", yet "his expertise did not extend to the *Book of Rites*" and "the administration of the empire". Conversely, Xunzi "demonstrated a higher level of proficiency in institutional knowledge and had a preference towards the importance of rites over the Book of Poetry and the Book of History." (quotes from Zhang Taiyan).

ii. "Synthesizing rites and law" by Xunzi

When examining the concept of autocratic bureaucracy, Mencius consistently adopted a lofty and discerning position, whereas Xunzi veered towards practical and tangible approaches. Although they shared an appreciation for "rule by rites", Mencius prominently endorsed the way of teachers, whereas Xunzi retained a commitment to "the way of officials". Furthermore, their perspectives diverged when it came to the importance placed on rites. The specific contributions of Xunzi can be delineated as follows.

First, from the perspective of the "transmission of scriptures", Xunzi was the foremost Confucian scholar during the concluding period of the Warring States. His profound insights laid the conceptual groundwork for the subsequent "Great Unity" of imperial politics, which ensued during the Qin and Han dynasties. The *Book of Rites*, with the exception of *The Doctrine of the Mean*, substantially fostered the development and propagation of Xunzi's philosophical doctrines. Consequently, scholars assert that the sociopolitical and ideological traditions that permeated imperial China can be perceived as "an amalgamation of Confucian values and legal principles". It has even been posited that "the quintessential essence of two millennia's worth of erudition bore the imprint of Xunzi's doctrines".

The second significant contribution of Xunzi lies in his response to the divergence and potential disintegration of the Zhou Dynasty's political and cultural traditions during the Spring and Autumn Period and the Warring States Period. At that time "the system of the Dao was about to be torn in fragments all under the sky", engendering instability and discord across the realm. In contrast to his contemporaries, Xunzi demonstrated a judicious and comprehensive approach, transcending any paranoiac sentiment. He embarked upon a transformative endeavor to reconceptualize and revitalize the ritualistic governance model, encompassing the interplay between the realms of politics, kinship, and culture. Consequently, this intellectual and practical reimagining laid a solid theoretical foundation for the continued prominence and advancement of the ancient Chinese scholar-bureaucratic political tradition[3].

Another noteworthy aspect of Xunzi's contributions pertains to his distinctive approach in the sphere of governance. He championed a model known as "scholar-gentlemen—officials and functionaries", which not only upheld the principles of gentry politics prevalent during the enfeoffment era but also played a pioneering role in shaping the subsequent mode of "scholar-bureaucrat—clerks" within the imperial era.

3.1.4 Music Teachers and Historians, Scholar-Masters and Clerical Officials

Musician officials and historiographical officials held prominent roles in preserving and transmitting ancient cultural practices. The former, responsible for ritual and educational matters, fostered the emergence of the "Way of the Teacher", while the latter, tasked with historical documentation and legal affairs, contributed to the advancement of the "Way of the Official". The evolution of historiographical officials during the Zhou Dynasty serves as the foundational framework for the subsequent development of scholar-officials. Notably, the pioneering efforts of historiographers in "recording historical events and codifying legal principles played an instrumental role in the standardization, systematization, archival documentation, and institutionalization of administrative practices". Musician officials primarily focused on instructing scholars and carrying out ritualistic duties, thereby being less directly involved in the specific administration of "warfare, legal penalties, financial matters, and food distribution" (Yan, 2001). In contrast with scholar-bureaucratic, clerical officials possessed distinct characteristics. These traits encompassed specialized training in administrative skills, strict adherence to laws and regulations, and an occupation primarily centered on paperwork. Furthermore, these officials endured advancements in their careers based on their abilities, merits, and years of service. The emergence of the dual-role scholar-bureaucratic governance system did not materialize until the Han Dynasty. The dynamic relationship between scholar-masters and administrative clerks underwent several stages characterized by periods of separation, opposition, integration, and division.

i. Separation and opposition: differentiation of "scholars" and "clerical officials" and the clerical-official politics in the Qin[4]

1. Separation

During the latter stages of the Spring and Autumn Period and the Warring States Period, a notable entity known as the "scholar class" occupied a significant role in

[3] Translations are James Legge's. https://ctext.org/zhuangzi/tian-xia/ens. (Notes fromtranslators).

[4] Refer to the sixth chapter in Yan (1996).

political affairs. This class encompassed various subgroups, such as scholar-masters (specialists), strategists (coalition advisors), necromancers, alchemists, and retainers. Notably, the comprehensive reform movement that unfolded during the Warring States Period can be construed as an extensive sociopolitical transformation towards autocratic bureaucracy. In this transformative era, the State of Qin surfaced as a quintessential example of a bureaucratic empire, characterized by the establishment and operation of a professional bureaucratic cadre known as "clerical officials". These officials were distinct from the scholar-masters, marking a clear separation of roles and functions within the bureaucracy.

2. Opposition

The Qin Dynasty adhered to legalist ideologies, which emphasized the paramountcy of law, the importance of "learning from clerical officials" and the "non-confucianism". It manifested a disdain for cultural traditions, perceiving scholar-masters as "undesirables", "burning books, and burying Confucian scholars". The Qin Dynasty can be characterized by its adoption of a model of cultural autocracy, wherein the promotion of law and administrative control took precedence. This legalistic perspective fostered an environment where "moral excellence, cultural development, and academic deliberations held little value". "The bureaucracy operated as a rigid machine, with officials merely functioning as impersonal gears, while the common people were reduced to mere objects of taxation and servitude, devoid of intrinsic worth beyond their assigned roles and numerical contributions" (Yan, 1996, p. 175). In retrospect, it can be argued that the philosophical underpinnings of legalism, coupled with the limitations inherent in the prevailing system of official politics, ultimately played a significant role in the downfall of the Qin Empire.

ii. Integration: combination and integration of Confucian scholars and clerical officials in the Han Dynasty

In the Han Dynasty, scholar-masters and clerical officials, previously perceived as separate entities, underwent a process of amalgamation, resulting in the emergence of the scholar-bureaucrat class. This transformation occurred during the selection process for officials, wherein candidates were primarily chosen from among the existing pool of clerical officials at the commandery and district levels. Confucian scholars often relied on beginning their official careers as "government clerks", enabling them to ascend the bureaucratic ladder. Consequently, it can be asserted that "Confucian scholars became fully integrated into the bureaucracy, while in general, all officials were clerks". Notably, the Ministry of Personnel, despite its label, held jurisdiction over all officials, highlighting the dominance of the bureaucratic system. During the Han Dynasty, candidates for state offices were selected based on their aptitude in virtue, knowledge of Classics, understanding of the law, and proficiency in political affairs. Selection was contingent upon candidates' moral integrity if they were Confucian students or based on their working abilities if they belonged to the clerical officials. The commandery quota system, designed to recruit officials known for their "filial piety and incorruptibility", adhered to the principles of the "ritual rule" wherein talent selection was based on virtue. The Eastern Han Dynasty rectified the deficiencies of Wang Mang's "New Deal" in AD 8 by adopting an evaluation system that assessed officials for their "political competence, achievements, and capability", in addition to their "filial piety and incorruptibility". This approach significantly facilitated the integration of Confucian scholars and clerical officials within the system (Yan, 1996, pp. 13–15).

iii. Division

In the historical context, a clear distinction existed between Confucian scholars and clerks in the perception of the populace. "Clerks were regarded as proficient in executing routine tasks, yet lacking in devotion. In contrast, Confucian scholars were esteemed for their moral integrity but were considered inadequate in handling practical matters. Both groups possessed their own strengths and weaknesses, as well as specific job suitability ... The recruitment of Confucian scholars centered on evaluating their morality and virtue, while clerks were assessed based on their aptitude for office work ... Confucian education imparted the principles known as the Way (*dao*, 道) to its students, whereas clerks were instructed in the practical handling of specific affairs ... The responsibilities of Confucian scholars encompassed fundamental aspects, while clerks focused on the intricacies and details. Consequently, a comparison between the fundamental principles and detailed specifics manifests a clear distinction in the selection of talent" (*Discursive Weighing · Weighing of Talents*). During the reign of Emperor Xiaoshun in the Eastern Han Dynasty, the focus on promoting individuals possessing filial piety and incorruptibility shifted towards emphasizing "literary competence". This emphasis endured throughout the Wei, Jin, Northern and Southern Dynasties, evolving eventually into the imperial examination system during the Sui and Tang Dynasties. In this system, maintaining the political and cultural sphere became the responsibility of the gentry class, while clerical officials took charge of technical and administrative matters (Yan, 1996, pp. 15–16).

"There was already a big difference between officials and clerks in the Tang Dynasty, but the two were not categorically divided." It was during the Ming Dynasty that this categorical differentiation in rank and grade between officials and clerks became firmly established. The root causes of this differentiation can be traced back to the Yuan Dynasty, where the Mongols were appointed as officials while the Han people were relegated to the position of clerks. Emperor Chengzu of the Ming implemented policies that barred clerks from assuming supervisory positions and prohibited them from taking the *jinshi* (进士) examination, the highest-level recruitment examination. Consequently, clerks were comprised of individuals who had failed the imperial examinations or those who passed the lowest-level examination but were not assigned corresponding positions. "A clerk would always remain a clerk, regardless of his virtue or talent. Consequently, the clerks had no self-respect, no ambition for advancement. But at the same time, they handled all the documents, records, and cases, manipulating opportunities to restrict the officials above them." (Ch'ien, 2005/2019, pp. 96-98).

3.1.5 Confucians in the Han Dynasty and Benevolent Officials[5]

> The men of former times in the matters of ceremonies and music were rustics, it is said, while the men of these latter times, in ceremonies and music, are accomplished gentlemen. If I have occasion to use those things, I follow the men of former times. (*The Analects*)[6].
>
> Based on extensive observation, it can be surmised that a universal fondness for singing and attending operas exists, underscoring a natural inclination towards poetry and music. Likewise, a pervasive engagement with novels and storytelling can be observed, highlighting a fundamental affinity towards books and historical narratives. Furthermore, a widespread belief in divination and the practice of offering sacrifices to gods and spirits can be discerned, indicative of an innate predisposition towards the contemplation of cosmic changes and adherence to ceremonial rituals. These inherent inclinations form the basis for the transmission of knowledge through the teachings of the Six Classics of Confucianism, which are rooted in the fundamental nature of humanity. (*Guangyang zaji*)
>
> Learning from the collective wisdom makes him a saint.
>
> —Zhang Xuecheng

Since the mid-20th century, there has been a shift among anthropologists and historians in their perception of culture as a homogenized entity, leading to the emergence of a dichotomous view that segregates culture into distinct categories such as Great tradition and Little tradition, Elite culture and Popular culture, and elegant literature and popular literature. In this regard, imperial China stood out as a unique case wherein the interaction between the Great and Little traditions exhibited a greater degree of fluidity, particularly during the early imperial period. Notably, the Han Confucian scholars, who assumed the role of "benevolent officials", played an irreplaceable role in facilitating the amalgamation and communication between these two cultural traditions.

From a philosophical standpoint, the Han Confucians may not have introduced "groundbreaking concepts". However, their significance lies in their ability to "influence and transform societal norms and practices". Their efforts led to the widespread adoption of values such as filial piety and fraternal duty, ingraining these ideals in the collective consciousness. In contrast to the intricate philosophical arguments of Pre-Qin Confucianism, the Han Confucians resorted to popular concepts such as Yin, Yang, and Five Elements to convey their teachings. By embracing the beliefs prevalent in popular culture, Confucianism broke through the confines of elite culture and resonated with the general public. As Confucius himself noted, he sought to elucidate his "insights on human affairs through concrete examples, rather than relying solely on theoretical discourse". During the Han Dynasty, the influence of Confucianism primarily extended to the realm of human morality and everyday life, which fall within the sphere of modern understanding of culture and society. However, it is important to note that Confucianism did not solely dictate the political landscape during the Han Dynasty. Confucianization was a subtle process, relying more on

[5] Refer to Yu (2005).

[6] Translations are from Legge (1960, p. 237). (Notes by translators).

the general public than on the imperial court, and more on societal customs than on institutional mechanisms. In this context, the benevolent officials, who were "close to the civilian population", played a pivotal role that surpassed that of ministers and scripture teachers.

The benevolent officials, such as Wen Dang, Ni Kuan, and Han Yanshou, achieved notable progress in three key areas.

1. Enrichment. These officials focused on enhancing agricultural productivity by implementing irrigation projects to improve farmland conditions. Additionally, they actively promoted commerce and trade, contributing to the economic development of the region.
2. Education: Building schools and changing customs. One significant achievement was the establishment of schools, particularly exemplified by Wen Dang's initiation of government schools in Shu—an important milestone in the evolution of local public education within China. During the early Han period, social issues such as the abandonment of the elderly were prevalent, and in border areas instable gender relations were highly common. The benevolent officials, drawing on Han-Confucian principles, sought to transform these traditions and customs through the simplification and localization of rituals. Guided by the belief that "the rites of weddings, funeral, and sacrifice should be done to a certain extent, but not excessively in the ancient manner", they "directed school masters and students to dress up and prepare ceremonial vessels to perform funeral and wedding ceremonies, thereby enabling the public to learn and emulate proper conduct."
3. Handling litigation and withdrawing lawsuit to achieve "no litigation". Han Yanshou's approach to handling litigation and promoting the withdrawal of lawsuits demonstrates his commitment to "strict self-discipline while maintaining an attitude of tolerance towards others". Historical records highlight a specific incident during his tenure where two brothers engaged in a dispute over land property. Han Yanshou, as an official responsible for "providing moral guidance", recognized the conflict as his "failure in adequately fostering moral education within the county". He secluded himself indoors to engage in deep introspection and reflection on his shortcomings. Meanwhile, Han Yanshou's subordinates anxiously awaited their punishment for perceived negligence in preventing the dispute. This period of introspection and self-punishment extended until the moment the contentious brothers expressed remorse and voluntarily withdrew their lawsuit. It was with this acknowledgment and act of contrition that Han Yanshou resumed his duties as an official.

3.1.6 "Wei-Jin Style" and Great-Family Politics[7]

The concept of "great-family politics" refers to a dynamic wherein political power was shared between prominent gentry families and the emperor. This phenomenon was exemplified by the well-known expression, "The families of Wang and (Si) Ma share the power." During the Eastern Jin period, the incomplete execution of imperial duties by the emperor, the ascent of influential families to power, and the influx of refugees collectively contributed to the perpetuation of great-family politics. This was "a deviation from the ideal of imperial politics", characterized by three distinct conditions: the existence of a mature and influential social class known as *shizu* (士族, referring to influential and privileged families of scholar-officials), a weakened royal family with residual appeal, and significant ethnic tensions.However, it is important to note that great-family politics was a temporary and transitional phenomenon. Firstly, it was challenging for exiled eminent families from the north to establish a secure foothold in the south of the Yangtze River, and even more difficult for them to consolidate their influence in the region. Secondly, the gentry families, while in command of the army, seldom participated in battlefield activities. As a result, their "ability to effectively wield military power was constrained", leading to a gradual weakening of their influence. Lastly, the declining talent within gentry clans could be attributed, in part, to limited intermarriage, which contributed to a degradation of their gene pool. Although the emperors of the Southern Dynasties eventually restored their authority, the great families continued to maintain their social standing, political influence, and "distinguishable air of refinement". Consequently, the selection of officials by the emperors became closely intertwined with these influential families, often seeking to consolidate their ties through strategic marital alliances.

The cultural boom [8]during the Wei and Jin Dynasties could be attributed to three key factors. Firstly, following a period of chaos, scholars experienced spiritual turmoil and reacted by turning towards metaphysics and profound conversations, departing from the Confucian orthodoxy of the Han Dynasty. Secondly, the decline of power among the rulers of the Southern Dynasties created an environment where scholar-bureaucrats could enjoy relative freedom in their pursuits without concerns about basic necessities. They were able to prioritize their intellectual and cultural pursuits, as expressed in the famous quote, "retaining their dignity instead of succumbing to five decalitres of rice, a modest remuneration of a county magistrate's official salary," "While picking asters' neath the Eastern fence, My gaze upon the Southern mountain rests". Thirdly, the Sima family, known for their affiliation with Confucianism, gained prominence in politics rather than as ideological scholars. During the Jin Dynasty, Confucian families needed to align with the philosophical current of *xuanxue* (玄学, the school of mystery or neo-Taoism) to produce renowned scholars and maintain their status as gentry families. However, it is notable that few individuals within the *xuanxue* school completely rejected Confucianism, highlighting the

[7] Refer to Tian (2005).

[8] Active intellectual and cultural life often presents itself during the disintegration of an old system, not during the period of great unification.

interconnectedness of Taoism and Confucianism. The transition "from Confucianism to the school of mystery" became a necessary path for the formation of the gentry class during this period. "The formation of the gentry class being related to a philosophical trend in the Wei and Jin Dynasties was because the gentry families were composed of scholars who were cultural aristocrats" (Yan, 2017, p. 22). At that time, prominent figures in the great-family politics such as Wang Dao, Yu Liang, Xie An, and Heng Wen "demonstrated the symbiotic relationship between Confucian principles and Taoism". "Wang Rong asked Ruan Zhan, 'Confucius valued rites while Laozi and Zhuangzi taught nature. What are the similarities and differences between them?' Zhan said, 'There is no similarity.'" In the view of the then famous scholars involved in politics, nature in Taoism and rites in Confucianism were intertwined with each other, because "Confucianism was originally established based on the law of nature", with "nature as substance, and rites for application" (Chen, 2012, pp. 45, 50). It is worth mentioning that the philosophical conversations during the Wei and Jin Dynasties can be categorized into two distinct phases. The early stage, occurring during the late Wei Dynasty and Western Jin Dynasty, revolved around practical political issues. Scholars employed profound discourse to express their opinions and defend their positions within the bureaucratic system. In the later stage, particularly during the Eastern Jin Dynasty, these conversations became detached from politics, reduced to mere abstract and mysterious utterances used by renowned scholars to embellish their identities[9].

3.1.7 Changes in the Status of Confucian Scholars

The establishment of the elevated social status of Confucian scholars could be traced back to Emperor Xiaowu of the Western Han Dynasty. During this period, Han Confucians successfully adapted Confucianism to wield influence over politics and to educate the population. However, from the late Eastern Han Dynasty to the Tang Dynasty, the social status of Confucian scholars experienced significant decline. Buddhism and Taoism gained prominence ideologically, while politically, great families attained political power. It was not until the Song Dynasty that the status of Confucian scholars was genuinely solidified (Fu, 2005). The Song Dynasty witnessed the "full blossoming" of three fundamental elements of Chinese culture: national consciousness, Confucianism, and the imperial examination system. Ideologically, Confucianism evolved into a more inclusive, all-encompassing philosophy, synonymous with "learning" itself. Politically, the Song emperors emphasized the importance of intellectual pursuits, restraining martial arts in favor of scholarly endeavors. Economically, emerging landlord and urban middle-class families provided the necessary economic support and fertile ground for the scholar-bureaucrats. In the Southern Song Dynasty, Zhu Xi, a renowned scholar, even took

[9] Translations are from Yang and Yang (2005). (Notes by translators).

the initiative to "establish his own orthodox Confucianism", exerting influence to limit the "political legitimacy" of imperial power.

The disparity between the Han and Song Confucians is noteworthy and can be further analyzed. The former actively advocated Xunzi's teachings and placed significant emphasis on the principles of righteousness elucidated in the *Spring and Autumn Annals*. Additionally, they prioritized efficient management of state affairs, the maintenance of order within the country, as well as the distinction between China and barbarian civilizations. However, the Han Confucians did not impose excessive requirements on the private lives of emperors. 'In contrast, during the Tang Dynasty, Han Yu showed admiration for Mencius, while Zhu Xi of the Song Dynasty held the *Four Books* in high regard. As a result, the Song Confucians placed particular emphasis on self-cultivation and ardently sought to rectify the mistaken ideologies of the reigning emperors. Yan Fu, a influencial translator and writer in modern China, observed that the compilation of the *Spring and Autumn Annals* had not deterred traitors and usurpers, whereas the flourishing of neo-Confucianism (*daoxue*, 道学, literally the learning of the Way) during the Song Dynasty truly terrified them. Subsequent downfall of dynastic China was more frequently ascribed to foreign nations. It is crucial to note that, Ye Shi, a neo-Confucian of the Song Dynasty, recognized the shortcomings of the Song Confucians, stating, "Those who endlessly discuss human nature and the purpose of life fail to recognize the significance of day-to-day affairs. Likewise, those who engage in speculative and fallacious notions of destiny neglect the distinction between Cathay and barbarian cultures." In response to such criticisms, Zhu Xi, a philosopher and politician during the Song Dynasty, asserted, "Why should we perceive matters in this manner? As long as the country remains united, with all vassals and lords pledging their allegiance to the emperor, and with all legal disputes impartially resolved, then the path followed is considered orthodox."

The prevailing notion regarding the status of Confucians during the Yuan Dynasty was that they occupied a considerably low position in society. According to the ten-caste system of the time, the three lowest castes were derogatorily labeled as "prostitutes, Confucians, and beggars," hence attributing to Confucians the pejorative epithet of "Stinky Old Ninth". However, this assertion was somewhat exaggerated. In reality, Confucian students in the Yuan Dynasty were classified as members of the "literati households" and were accorded certain economic privileges. What truly transpired was a reclassification of Confucianism from being the sole "Way" to becoming one of various "schools" of thought. Consequently, Confucians were relegated to a status comparable to that of Taoist priests and monks (Xiao, 2005).

3.1.8 Political Legitimacy and Cultural Legitimacy[10]

i. Separation between political legitimacy and cultural legitimacy, and the superiority of the latter

The concept of *daotong* (道统), which refers to the orthodox transmission of cultural legitimacy, should not be confused with *wangtong* (王统), the transmission of imperial legitimacy or *zhitong* (治统), the transmission of political legitimacy. Confucius held in high regard sage rulers such as Yao, Shun, Yu, and the Duke of Zhou, rather than figures like Qi (son of Yu and founder of the Xia Dynasty), Tang (founder of the Shang Dynasty), King Wen of Zhou, and King Wu of Zhou. Similarly, Mencius revered Yao, Shun, Yu, and Confucius, not the Five Hegemons of the Spring and Autumn Period or the Seven Heroes of the Warring States Period. Han Yu, a prominent philosopher and politician of the Tang Dynasty, also revered Yao, Shun, Confucius, and Mencius, rather than Qin Shi Huang, the first emperor of a unified China, or Emperor Xiaowu of the Han Dynasty. Respecting cultural legitimacy does not equate to loyalty to the emperor. Mencius aptly stated, "Yao and Shun were what they were by nature; Tang and Wu were so by returning to natural virtue." This implied that if emperors possessed cultural legitimacy, they could maintain their power, whereas lacking cultural legitimacy would result in their loss of power. The theory of cultural legitimacy originated from Han Yu's *Original Confucianism*, and was further developed by Zhu Xi, a philosopher of Neo-Confucianism during the Southern Song Dynasty. The legitimate succession of the Way resembles the orthodoxy in political legitimacy. An illustrative example of the unification of three generations of governance and cultural legitimacy (dual-role of ruler and teacher) can be found in the Duke of Zhou. However, over time, the feudal rites collapsed, music spoilt, and the two became disjointed. The Southern Song Dynasty even "established its own cultural legitimacy". "Sages who show the Way" held greater significance compared to "those who take the Way." This is because practical application is transient, but teaching and perpetuating knowledge are considered eternal. Within the ideology of scholar-bureaucrats, the concept of "cultural legitimacy" embodied by Confucius held greater weight than the "political legitimacy" conferred by emperors. For instance, Emperor Xiaozhang of the Han Dynasty visited the Confucius Temple, and Kong Xi, a descendant of Confucius, conveyed to the emperor that the visit would not enhance the glory of the Confucian family, but rather, the emperor needed the visit to enhance his own charisma. Similarly, Emperor Taizu of the Ming Dynasty attempted to diminish the status of Confucianism and belittle Mencius. However, this plan backfired, leading to the "martyrdom of Confucians for their beliefs" and ultimately forcing the Ming court to abandon their endeavors[11].

---

[10] Refer to Huang. J (2005).

[11] Translations are from Legge (1970, p. 495). (Notes by translators).

ii. Paradox of unification of political legitimacy and cultural legitimacy, and sage emperor ("philosopher king")

The process of reunifying political legitimacy and cultural legitimacy commenced during the reign of the Kangxi Emperor of the Qing Dynasty and continued under the leadership of the Yongzheng Emperor and the Qianlong Emperor, ultimately resulting in the amalgamation of political authority and cultural authority. The Qing Dynasty witnessed the emergence of many wise emperors, with Kangxi epitomizing the archetype of a "sage emperor". He strongly emphasized "the significance of learning as the foundation of all endeavors" and maintained that "the Five Classics provided the most comprehensive guidance for governing the country, while histories offered extensive insights into matters of state." Confronted with the complex relationship between political legitimacy and cultural legitimacy, the Qing Dynasty departed from Emperor Taizu's confrontational policies and instead sought to achieve unity between the two domains. The emperor took control of cultural legitimacy, assuming the roles of both ruler and teacher. During this era, unprecedented honors were conferred upon Confucius, the Confucius Temple, and the Confucian family. For instance, the Kangxi Emperor performed the grand salute of three kowtows and nine prostrations before the statue of Confucius, while the Qianlong Emperor arranged a marital union between his daughter and a member of the Confucian family. Confucianism was recognized as a unifying force within traditional society and was deemed "particularly beneficial to the emperors", as attested by the Yongzheng Emperor of the Qing.

Notwithstanding the accolades bestowed upon Confucianism, the Qing court retained the authority to scrutinize and regulate its influence. Despite the Kangxi Emperor's visit to the Confucius Temple, Kong Shangren, a descendant of Confucius in the 64th generation during the Qing Dynasty, no longer harbored the ambitions of his predecessor, Kong Xi. The Yongzheng Emperor responded to Zeng Jing, a minor official who attempted to incite rebellion against the Qing government in the 18th century, by asserting that although Confucius and Mencius were esteemed sages, they were "not suited for the role of emperor". This solidified the finalization of the ruler-official relationship between the emperors and Confucians. The Qing court did not have a prime minister position, thus the highest attainable status for Confucians carried neither actual political power nor political commitment, nor even an official title. A prominent scholar of the Qing Dynasty, Zhang Xuecheng, opined that "the Duke of Zhou was superior to Confucius" , which was a product of both the enduring influence of tradition and the prevailing trends of the time.

This phenomenon exemplified the inner dilemma of Confucians. They aspired for the emergence of "sage emperors. Paradoxically, the attainment of such ideal rulers would come at a great expense for Confucians themselves, as it would render the pursuit of cultural legitimacy unnecessary. Consequently, this would undermine the very foundation upon which Confucians based their criticism of political authorities.

3.1.9 The Gentry and Local Administration—"Imperial Power and Gentry Power"[12]

i. Gentry-literati (local elite)

"The gentry were local elites who shared with the government the control of local affairs." They were "the only group that could legitimately represent the local community in discussing local affairs with officials and in participating in the governing process." Local officials always treated them with courtesy. (Ch'ü, 1988, p. 168).

"In the sense that the gentry and the officials belong to the same group as either members or potential members of the bureaucracy, their power was derived from the political order … The same group of men were officials in their public capacity and gentry in their private capacity" (Ch'ü, 1988, p. 169). According to Ch'ien Mu (a historian, philosopher and writer of modern China), "entering into officialdom" was almost a religion for scholars, for being an official was "the most efficient way to benefit mankind" and to realize the ideals and ambitions of a literatus. "If they could not become an official, the second-best choice was to a teacher, or to write books, with the hope that their disciples or readers would materialize their beliefs or ambitions in politics in the future." (Ch'ien, 2002, p. 127) Membership in the gentry did not derive from wealth, but from "the attainment of bureaucratic status or of the qualification for such status" (passing the imperial examinations, or with official ranks) (Ch'ü, 1988, p. 171). Wealth did not translate directly to gentry status until when official ranks or academic titles could be purchased from the government, but the official ranks and academic titles that could be bought were of a low level and not considered the "regular path".

The gentry, composed of official-gentry and scholar-gentry, were collectively referred to as "scholar-officials living in their home town" (Ch'ü, 1988, p. 172). The official-gentry encompassed active, retired, or dismissed officials, including those who obtained their official titles and ranks through purchase. In observance of the regulations barring officials from serving in their native province, they held a dual status: that of an official in their current locality and that of an "absentee gentry member" in their native province. On the other hand, the scholar-gentry, distinguished by their official ranks or academic titles, encompassed civil and military palace graduates (*jinshi*, 进士), civil and military provincial graduates (*juren*, 举人), tribute students (*gongsheng*, 贡生) (students selected from local government schools for the Directorate of Education, including those who purchased this title), national university students (*jiansheng*, 监生) (students of the Directorate of Education, including those who purchased this title), civil and military licentiates (*shengyuan*, 生员; that is, candidates licensed to participate in high-level imperial examinations) ("cultivated talent", *xiucai*, 秀才).

Unlike local officials, who were "nonnatives", the gentry had a natural sense of responsibility to guard and promote the welfare of their own communities.

[12] Refer to the tenth chapter of Ch'ü (2003).

ii. Privileges of the gentry class and differentiated treatment of different gentry members

1. Courteous reception during interaction with local officials (depending on their status within the gentry stratum).
2. Social (clothing, residence, rite, etc.) and economic (taxation) privileges.
3. Legal privileges and special protection. The official-gentry class held a position of authority which granted them immunity from local jurisdiction, while the scholar-gentry enjoyed preferential treatment within the judicial system when compared to the commoners. It is worth noting that the gentry class was absolved from minor penalties, such as the option of monetary redemption in lieu of physical punishment, such as caning. In disputes between the gentry and the commoners over marriage and landed property, they were "permitted by law to send a family member or servant to act as their representatives at a trial. A commoner who injured an official, whether the active retired, was punished more severely than if the injured man had been his equal" (Ch'ü, 1988, p. 174).

iii. Channels for the gentry to exert influence

1. As community leaders of commoners.
2. To exert influence on local officials. The influence of the gentry is relevant to prominence of their reputation and the local situation. For instance, in regions such as Jiangsu and Zhejiang, characterized by a substantial population of degree holders, provincial graduates would find their impact considerably diminished. Conversely, in areas where individuals possessing degrees were few and far between, even a modest level of educational attainment could potentially bestow significant influence. It is worth noting that the "official-gentry" who held privileged positions could even directly petition the emperor.
3. The affiliation between the gentry and positions of authority, as well as the interpersonal networks fostered by the imperial examination system, played a significant role in facilitating the exertion of influence by the gentry class. These affiliations were observed among three key groups closely associated with the examination process, namely the teachers (comprising examiners-in-chief and examiners), the disciples (retainers), and the individuals who successfully passed the same examination in the same year (fellow degree-holders).

Licentiates were outside the power hierarchy and occupied a position of minimal influence within the gentry class. Individually, their impact was negligible, with their power and authority primarily stemming from collective action and solidarity as a group. Examples of such collective action included joint petitions, mass refusal to participate in examinations, and rioting in the yamen. Prior to engaging in such actions, licentiates often congregated at a Confucius Temple, which served as both a Civilian Temple and a school location. Here, they would conduct the ceremony known as "Weeping to the Confucius Temple" (Chen, 2005). The complete ritual consisted of various components, including the offering of sacrifices to Confucius, burning of the Confucian costume and tearing of student costume to a rejection of officialdom, making a renunciation gesture to symbolize a desire to relinquish their scholarly pursuits), as well as beating drums and ringing bells to attract public attention and expand social influence. A prominent example of this ceremonial practice occurred in the 18th year of the Shunzhi Emperor's reign during the Qing dynasty (AD 1661), when over a thousand licentiates participated in the Weeping ceremony as a response to corrupt officials levying excessive taxes in Suzhou, an event famously known as the "Weeping Incident". Another occurrence took place in Suzhou during the 26th year of the Kangxi Emperor's reign in the Qing dynasty (AD 1687), following rumors of cheating by senior officials in the Jiangnan provincial examination. Apart from the Weeping ceremony at the Confucius Temple, licentiates employed another form of protest: holding a wooden statue spirit tablet of Confucius in front of the target's door, thereby subjecting them to public embarrassment. Subsequent to the reign of the Yongzheng Emperor in the Qing dynasty, some licentiates even regarded the statue of Confucius as a talisman in their acts of resistance, "carrying the wooden statue of Confucius and the spirit tablets of all the Confucian sages while engaging in physical altercations with others" (Wu, 2005).

iv. Gentry families

1. Prestige and privileges of the gentry could be extended to their families

The transfer of an official's status to family members could be observed through the practice of bestowal and inheritance. This system entailed the conferral of an honorary official title upon both deceased and living ancestors, as well as the spouse of the official, ultimately resulting in the succession of this title by subsequent generations. "Technically, the law treated holders of honorary titles (known as [*fengzeng guan*], bestowed officials) in the same way as regular officials" (Ch'ü, 1988, pp. 177-178), which was even extended to an official's family members not yet granted such honorary titles. Not only did the fathers and close relatives of gentry members possess greater influence than commoners, but their influence was nearly on par with that of the gentry member themselves. It is worth noting that family members of "official-gentry" occupying significant positions often wielded even greater influence compared to low-ranking official-gentry or scholar-gentry.

2. The words and behavior of the gentry were significantly influenced and regulated by their family—the fundamental unit in Chinese society.

"One's ability to protect one's self and one's family depended primarily on one's position in the bureaucratic hierarchy. It followed that each family or clan looked upon the gentry member within it as its protector. He in turn accepted this responsibility" (Ch'ü, 1988, p. 180).

v. Status and role of the gentry in local administration

1. The gentry's active involvement in local administration was driven by their pursuit of fostering local social stability. Primarily, as captured by the adage, "officials come and go, but the office remains". Unlike "officials" who, due to the

constraints of the institution of avoidance, were prohibited from serving in their hometowns, the gentry held a distinct advantage of possessing long-standing ties and commitments to their respective communities. Moreover, in contrast to commoners, the gentry enjoyed specific privileges, enhancing the significance they placed on upholding the established social order.

2. The gentry played a crucial role as intermediaries between the common populace and governmental authorities. They acted as vital conduits of communication, facilitating a crucial connection between the ruling administration and the general public. On one hand, the gentry effectively relayed the decrees and regulations enacted by the local government to the populace. On the other hand, they safeguarded the commoners from the undue encroachments of local officials, while simultaneously collecting and transmitting public sentiment and viewpoints for official deliberation and consideration.
3. The gentry served an advisory role to local officials, providing counsel and recommendations attuned to regional conditions. "While regional differences existed in the vast territory of the empire, the administrative code was extremely rigid and contained few provisions for dealing with these differences" (Ch'ü, 1988, p. 180). Compared to subofficial functionaries within the bureaucracy like bailiffs and clerks, members of the gentry were considered more educated, both intellectually and culturally, as well as more virtuous. Additionally, the gentry possessed intimate knowledge of their local regions that imperial officials, appointed from outside the locality, often lacked. Thus, the gentry were well-positioned to offer advice that accounted for on-the-ground realities. The administrative experience accumulated by the "official-gentry" made their input particularly useful for complex local issues like public works and defense. "The advice of the local gentry was not only frequently sought by the magistrates voluntarily but at times was required by his superior officials" (Ch'ü, 1988, p. 181).
4. To engage in local governance, encompassing initiatives such as public works, public welfare, educational endeavors, and the management of communal self-defense and local militia. An exemplary instance of this could be seen in Zeng Guofan's leadership during the late Qing Dynasty, when he established the "Xiang Army" in his native province of Hunan while temporarily stepping away from the central government to mourn the passing of his father.

vi. Cooperation and conflict between magistrate and gentry

"In general, conflict of interests occurred between the magistrate and individual members of the gentry rather than the local gentry as a whole" (Ch'ü, 1988, pp. 190–191). As the two parties "belonged to the same privileged class, they depended on each other for the *status quo*, with the result that they remained entrenched in their perpetuation of their common interests" (Ch'ü, 1988, p. 192). The advancement and reputation of local officials were significantly contingent upon the support and endorsement of the gentry, who, in turn, depended on these officials to uphold their privileges and exert influence within the local community. However, the cooperation "between the gentry and the magistrate was reversed whenever there was a clash of interests between the two–for example, when the magistrate insisted on enforcing laws that the gentry customarily violated, or when he prevented them from seeking personal gain" (Ch'ü, 1988, p. 191). Consequently, local officials frequently found themselves vulnerable to fault-finding, intimidation, slander, and malicious accusations from the gentry. Similarly, the gentry, particularly the scholar-gentry whose societal position held less security, confronted pressures and strains originating from these officials.

3.2 Talent Selection and Recommendation and Imperial Examination

3.2.1 Talent Selection and Recommendation

i. The commandery quota system[13]

During the Han Dynasty, the selection and appointment of officials were mainly carried out through two primary methods: elevation based on recommendations and imperial recruitment. These approaches were further complemented by the utilization of examinations and inheritance processes.

The commandery quota system, known as *chaju* (察举) in Chinese, originated during the Han Dynasty under Emperor Gaozu's reign in 196 BC. This system was established through imperial edicts issued by subsequent emperors such as Emperor Xiaohui and Emperor Xiaowen, who sought to recruit individuals displaying "filial piety and fraternal duty," "wisdom and virtue, uprightness and correctness," or those who were "frank and unflinching in admonishing the emperor". Early in Emperor Xiaowu's reign, commanderies and princedoms were mandated to recommend one individual annually who exemplified filiality-incorruptibility. Filial piety, an essential aspect of governance in ancient times, was often associated with imperial posthumous titles, which frequently incorporated the Chinese character "xiao" (孝), meaning "filial piety". As the Han Dynasty progressed, commanderies and districts were ordered to select talented individuals with exceptional abilities from clerks and commoners who demonstrated potential as military generals or envoys to distant regions. During the Eastern Han Dynasty, the term "*xiucai*" (秀才), which denoted cultivated talent, was later renamed as "*maocai*" (茂才) to avoid the taboo associated with the character "xiu" in Emperor Guangwu's name, Liu Xiu (刘秀).

The primary pathway for literati in the Han Dynasty to enter officialdom was through recommendations based on their reputation for wisdom, virtue, uprightness and correctness, or filiality-incorruptibility. A less prominent means of entry was through the title of "xiucai". These selections were predominantly made from "individuals residing in villages and hamlets". Supplementary examinations, such as *shece* (射策), which required candidates to provide quick and accurate responses

---

[13] Refer to Yan (1997).

akin to arrows, or *duice* (对策), which involved participating in political discussions, were also utilized. Distinguished figures such as Jia Yi, a renowned political commentator in the early Western Han Dynasty, Gongsun Hong, a prime minister in the Western Han Dynasty, and Dong Zhongshu, a philosopher and erudite during the Western Han Dynasty, gained imperial favor after being recommended due to their impressive performances in political discussions. Overall, talent selection during this period followed three main methods: recommendations by commanderies and princedoms, dispatching central government officials to "select talents after examination", or high-ranking ministers providing recommendations.

The practice of internal recommendation, originating in the Western Han Dynasty and prevailing during the Eastern Han Dynasty, differed from the village and hamlet-based recommendations, as it allowed candidates to bypass the traditional progression and ascend beyond their designated qualifications or ranks. In the recruitment and appointment process conducted by imperial order (*zheng*, 征), the emperor personally extended invitations to individuals showcasing remarkable talent. However, it should be noted that not all invitees would ultimately receive appointments. Within the framework of elevation or appointment by the emperor (*bi*, 辟), talented individuals were chosen to serve in administrative institutions, prefectures, and counties. Their behaviors and capabilities were assessed during their tenure, and subsequent promotions or appointments were made as vacancies arose. In some cases, these candidates were even granted access to high-ranking positions equivalent to 2000 bushels (a measurement of grain storage) (Sa, 1975, pp. 306–307).

During the Wei, Jin, Southern, and Northern Dynasties, a system known as the "Nine-rank Selection Method" was implemented. This approach aimed to address the issues that had emerged during the Han Dynasty when the responsibility of talent recommendation gradually shifted from local officials to retired scholar-bureaucrats. As a result, malpractices arose, leading to instances where "cultivated talents lacked knowledge of the *Four Books* or filial and incorrupt talents neglected their familial obligations". To prevent such deficiencies, the Wei and Jin Dynasties introduced the "Nine-rank Selection Method". During the tumultuous end of the Han Dynasty when Cao Cao seized power, the nine-rank system was established within the military to evaluate the quality of talents. Under the reign of Emperor Wen of the Wei Dynasty, the "nine-rank officials" method was used to allocate senior and junior rectifiers (*zhongzheng*, 中正) in provinces and commanderies. Their role was to identify and assign talents to corresponding ranks based on their abilities. Initially, junior rectifiers at the commandery and county levels reported their selections to senior rectifiers at the prefecture level. The senior rectifiers reviewed the lists and reported to the Minister of Education in the central government. The final decision on appointments was made by the grand ministers.

The purpose of the nine-rank system was to overcome the flaws of the recommendation system. However, it began to exhibit its own shortcomings during the Southern Dynasty. Firstly, the detrimental practice of exerting personal influence exceeded the negative aspects of seeking fame in the recommendation system. Additionally, there were no established criteria for ranking. During this period, the power of influential gentry families increased, and a candidate's social standing, rather than their capabilities, determined their appointment rank. Consequently, a common critique emerged, stating that "individuals from humble backgrounds seldom achieved high-ranking positions, while those from esteemed families rarely held lowly posts". With the advent of Emperor Wen's reign in the Sui Dynasty, "the tradition of talent recommendation by prefectures, commanderies, and counties was abolished. Instead, the Ministry of Personnel assumed responsibility for official appointments." Thus, the recommendation system was officially abolished during this period.

ii. Special examinations in later dynasties[14]

Following the Sui and Tang Dynasties, the system of imperial examination experienced significant growth and prominence. However, alongside the regular examination process, there were parallel special or irregular examinations that took place. These special examinations involved the emperor directly issuing edicts to recruit talented individuals.

During the early years of Emperor Yang's reign in the Sui Dynasty, a significant change occurred in the talent selection process. The emperor issued a decree ordering officials above the fifth rank to recommend candidates from various categories. These categories included individuals renowned for their filial piety and fraternal duty, commitment to honesty and sincerity, their persistence in law enforcement, remarkable academic achievements, literary talents, or exceptional abilities to serve as effective military generals, among others. As a result, while the Sui Dynasty abolished the previous recommendation system, it introduced the institution of special examinations, which would have a lasting impact on subsequent dynasties.

Building on the talent selection practices introduced during the Sui Dynasty, the Tang Dynasty incorporated special examinations as a complementary system to the regular imperial examinations and recruited people of capabilities and integrity with a straight tongue, learned experts in ancient classics capable of educating the people, and men of extraordinary military talent to serve as generals, etc.

In the Song Dynasty, apart from the examinations administered to palace graduates, additional components were introduced. These included the fearless and candid admonition of the emperor, the demonstration of extensive and profound knowledge, and the renowned "*dake*" (大科) or grand examination, where the emperor personally evaluated candidates to identify individuals of exceptional

During the inception of the Yuan Dynasty, the implementation of the imperial examination system was notably absent, as the ruling power relied primarily on a recommendation-based system to garner the allegiance of the literati belonging to the Han ethnicity. The responsibility for talent recruitment was entrusted to the Academy of Scholarly Worthies, with the presentation of a comprehensive roster of capable individuals falling within the purview of the Surveillance Commission.

Following the successful conquest of Jinling, the historical capital of the Southern Song Dynasty, the Ming Dynasty undertook a deliberate effort to employ distinguished senior Confucian scholars within the bureaucracy. To facilitate this process,

---

[14] Refer to Chen (1977, pp. 147–150).

the administration established the Worthies Reception Institute and introduced specialized examinations aimed at assessing whether candidates were of intelligence and integrity; whether they were capable and good persons who were four-square and upright; and whether they were of filial piety and diligence, etc. All recommended talents were invited to the capital and appointed to offices. Subsequently an increasing importance was placed on the imperial examination system for the purpose of talent recruitment in the Ming Dynasty.

Within the Qing Dynasty, the governing authorities implemented specialized examinations as per imperial decree, encompassing diverse subjects such as "broad learning and extensive words" in the 17th year of the Kangxi Emperor's reign (1678 AD) and the inaugural year of the Qianlong Emperor's reign (1736 AD). Additionally, an examination focusing on the art of "statecraft" was conducted during the 22nd year of the Guangxu Emperor's rule in 1896.

iii. Guaranteed recommendation[15]

In order to compensate for the limitations of the assessment system, high-ranking officials possessed the authority to recommend their capable and deserving subordinates for advancements. This arrangement effectively curtailed the influence of the Ministry of Personnel. In the Han Dynasty, this process of recommendation and appointment was referred to as *biju* (辟举). It involved the Three Dukes, commanderies, and counties, who held the prerogative to endorse talented individuals and subject them to a period of probation within lower offices. Candidates were then appointed or promoted based on their demonstrated competence and conduct, with some even ascending to positions of great prominence, such as the high-ranking posts of 2000 bushels. However, during the Northern Qi period, the Ministry of Personnel usurped the power of high officials to recommend their own subordinates.

The practice of guaranteed recommendation, which gained prominence during the Ming and Qing Dynasties, had its origins in the 17th year of the Hongwu era (1384 AD) in the Ming Dynasty. This marked a significant moment when court officials were instructed to propose competent and morally upright individuals for positions of authority. In the Yongle era of the Ming Dynasty, measures such as collective punishment were introduced to hold recommenders accountable for any misconduct displayed by their recommended candidates. Over time, the guaranteed recommendation system became susceptible to widespread corruption. Some officials exploited their positions to grant undue favors to individuals from their hometowns, relatives, or subordinates. Concurrently, other officials faced significant delays in their career advancements due to the absence of influential recommenders.

In the middle period of the Qing Dynasty, the practice of guaranteed recommendation was introduced when the empire was faced with internal unrest and external threats. At that time though "it was possible to save the dynasty from collapse", "imperial examination system was not suitable for selecting virtuous heroes who can safeguard the empire." It was in such a context that the guaranteed recommendation was employed, and it sustained till the fall of the empire. Consequently, subordinates

[15] Refer to Chen (1977, pp. 150–151).

and private secretaries with exceptional abilities and virtuous qualities were often identified and appointed based on the recommendations of their superiors. A notable example of the influence wielded by recommenders can be observed during Zeng Guofan's suppression of the Taiping Rebellion. Among his private secretaries, there existed a wealth of talented individuals who rose to high positions through Zeng's personal recommendations. Notable figures such as Zuo Zongtang, Li Hongzhang, Peng Yuli, and others garnered prominence and achieved remarkable success due to their association with Zeng.

3.2.2 Imperial Examination

Strictly speaking, the imperial examination system should be categorized into two distinct components: the civil examination and the military examination. The military examination, which emerged during the second year of the Chang'an era (AD 702) under the administration of the Empress Regnant of the Tang Dynasty, persisted for an impressive span of 1,200 years before its abolition in the 27th year of the Guangxu Emperor's reign of the Qing Dynasty in 1901. Although the examination procedure shared similarities with the civil examination, it diverged in terms of content and duration of testing. Throughout the Tang Dynasty and beyond, both civil and military imperial examinations were utilized as means to select officials. However, due to the perceived significance ascribed to civil examinations, they consistently held a position of prominence in the imperial examination system. Consequently, the documentation available on military examinations is limited, primarily due to their relatively restricted influence.

i. An overview of the imperial examination system across dynasties

1. The Sui and Tang Dynasties

During the reign of Emperor Wen of the Sui Dynasty, the examination category known as "cultivated talent" was established. Under this category, each prefecture was tasked with selecting three candidates annually to participate in the examination. The candidates who achieved the highest scores were conferred the esteemed degree of "cultivated talent". It is worth noting that, during Emperor Wen's lifetime, the number of cultivated talents did not exceed ten. Emperor Yang of the Sui Dynasty further expanded the examination system by introducing the category of "palace graduates". This particular examination, which assessed candidates' proficiency in poetry and rhythm-prose, served as a prototype for the imperial examinations of subsequent dynasties. The Tang Dynasty inherited and refined the examination system established by the Sui Dynasty, culminating in Emperor Taizong's assertion that "all the country's heroes are under my command."

Within the imperial examination system, two noteworthy categories were the *shengtu* (生徒, disciples) from dynastic schools, such as the Guangwen School and Hongwen School in the capital, and the *xianggong* (乡贡, lit., local tributes), who were prefectural nominees. These candidates underwent annual examinations based on predetermined themes. The prefectural nominees included self-taught literati who voluntarily presented themselves for examination in their home provinces. Following district banquets hosted by local chief officials, the selected nominees were then sent to the capital for examinations administered by the Ministry of Rites under the Department of State Affairs, and thus the name "department examination".

Among the numerous examination categories documented in history—totaling over 50—the most prominent ones included cultivated talents, classicists, palace graduates, experts in law, experts in arithmetic, and more. Of these, the two most noteworthy categories were classicists and palace graduates. In the classicist examinations, the initial session involved questions relating to stripe texts (*tiejing*, 帖经), wherein the candidate was required to either transcribe the entire text from memory or fill in the missing characters on tags placed over the text. This was followed by an oral examination comprising ten questions on the interpretation of the *Classics*, as well as three policy questions pertaining to practical statecraft.

The palace graduate examinations commenced with poetry and rhythm-prose questions in the first session. If successful, candidates proceeded to be assessed on policy questions related to practical statecraft and stripe texts extracted from one of the "greater" *Classics*, which included works such as *Liji* (礼记, *Book of Rites*) and *Chunqiu-Zuozhuan* (春秋左传, The Commentary of Zuo). However, this system faced criticism for its shortcomings. "Classicists focused solely on the *Classics*, while palace graduates demonstrated limited familiarity with the *Classics* and history."

During the late Tianbao era of the Tang Dynasty, literary competence gained increasing significance in the selection of officials. However, the tested contents of the examination became misaligned with the requirements of the governmental positions, resulting in the predominance of ostentatious and empty responses.

Two examples illustrated the disadvantages of this system. Firstly, the issue of cheating in the imperial examination sparked conflict between two political factions led by Niu Sengru and Li Deyu within the central government. Secondly, Huang Chao's failure in the palace graduate examination ultimately led to his rebellion against the Tang Dynasty (Chen, 1977, pp. 155–156).

2. The Song, Jin and Yuan Dynasties

The Song Dynasty adopted and refined the examination system established during the Tang Dynasty, making substantial developments that influenced subsequent generations. Emperor Taizu of Song played a pivotal role in the evolution of the examination system by introducing the palace examination, building upon the foundations of the department examination. During the reigns of Taizu and Taizong, the practice of categorizing palace graduates into three tiers was already in place. In the eighth year of the Taiping Xingguo era (AD 983), the formal selection of palace graduates from the top three ranks was established. Following Emperor Yingzong's reign, the imperial examination took place every three years, a practice that endured in later dynasties. During the Song Dynasty, the institution of sealing and copying was implemented, gradually resulting in a more stringent examination system. However, "[b]eing circumspect in designing a system, such as putting too much emphasis on preventing fraud, may sometimes lead to diversion from the main purpose … The stricter system thus might result in missing out on truly talented candidates" (Ch'ien, 2019, p. 69). Among the various examination categories, palace graduates held the highest esteem and consequently attracted the most candidates. In his political reforms, Wang Anshi, a prominent chancellor and reformist during the Song Dynasty, made significant changes to the examination system. He abolished examination questions on poetry, rhythm-prose, and the clarification of the *Classics*, opting instead to assess candidates' interpretation of the *Classics* and their ability to compose political essays. Wang Anshi even published a commentary entitled *New Meanings of the Three Classics*, which was distributed to educational officials. However, when Sima Guang assumed the position of chancellor, he abolished *New Meanings of the Three Classics*, but retained the interpretation of the *Classics* and political essays. Additionally, during the Song Dynasty, an examination category specifically for "experts in law" existed. This examination assessed candidates' knowledge of administrative and penal codes, as well as their interpretation of the penal law system. Candidates who demonstrated competence in settling lawsuits were granted admission (Fu, 2005).

Emperor Shizong of the Jin Dynasty inherited the Song system and classified the imperial examination into four levels: prefectural, provincial, metropolitan and palace examinations, whence the "department examination" in the Tang and Song was changed to "metropolitan examination".

During the Yuan Dynasty, under the reign of Emperor Renzong, a comprehensive imperial examination system was instituted. This system provided individuals who successfully passed the prefectural examination with the opportunity to partake in the metropolitan examination. Graduates of the metropolitan examination, in turn, gained eligibility to engage in the palace examination. Significantly, candidates were segregated into two groups based on their regional and ethnic backgrounds—Mongols and Semu, Northern Chinese and Southern Chinese, and they were subjected to varying sets of questions. Poetry and rhythm-prose were no longer included in the examination content. Instead, emphasis was placed on classical studies. Additionally, a policy question and a practical essay were added to the examination.

3. The Ming Dynasty

In the Ming Dynasty, the examination system borrowed categories from the Tang and Song Dynasties, although it imposed certain limitations on the question content, confining it to the realm of the *Four Books and Five Classics*. Specifically, the essay component of the examination bore resemblance to classical essays from the Song Dynasty, requiring candidates to adopt the persona of ancient writers and employ parallel prose writing. These essays were referred to as "eight-legged essays", commonly known as "crafted essays" (*zhiyi*, 制义).

Examinations were conducted triennially, with candidates initially participating in provincial examinations, held in their respective home provinces. Successful candidates from the provincial examinations would then advance to metropolitan and palace examinations. Graduates of the palace examinations were categorized into three tiers. Provincial examinations took place in August and metropolitan examinations in February, both commencing on the nineth day of their respective months, both comprising of three sessions, and each session lasting three days.

The testing papers in black ink, known as *mojuan* (墨卷), were transcribed in red ink on vermillion papers, referred to as *zhujuan* (朱卷). The examination compound, known as the *gongyuan* (贡院), contained designated cells for the candidates, referred to as *haofang* (号房, literally numbered cells). The examination rooms were closely supervised by guards known as *haojun* (号军, literally soldiers guarding the numbered cells). Once the examiners entered the examination compound, both the internal and external doors were secured.

The examination process involved the presence of education commissioners and presiding examiners outside the examination hall, known as outer aids (*wailianguan*, 外帘官, officials outside the curtain). Inside the examination hall, the examiners responsible for overseeing the examination hall were referred to as inner examiners (*neilianguan*, 内帘官, officials inside the curtain). The grading of examination papers of palace examinations was entrusted to academicians of the Hanlin Academy and high-ranking officials well-versed in the *Classics*. The final rankings were then reported to the emperor for ultimate decision. The emperor had the discretion to accept the rankings as presented or make adjustments accordingly (Lin, 1976, pp. 195–196).

ii. The imperial examination system in the Qing Dynasty[16]

1. Licensing examinations and qualifying examination

Provincial education commissioners established examination sites for candidates to take "examinations in separate sheds" across all prefectures and independent departments. These examinations included a licensing examination (*suikao*, 岁考) and a qualifying examination (*kekao*, 科考) held every three years for students from all prefectures, subprefectures and counties. The purpose of the licensing examination was to select and admit "apprentice students" (*tongsheng*, 童生) and "government student" (*jinxue*, 进学), while also assessing the diligence of the admitted licentiates. Candidates participating in the licensing examinations needed to meet certain criteria. They were required to have local registration, possess a clean familial background for at least three generations, and not originate from families associated with prostitution, slavery, yamen runners, or debased servants. Additionally, they were not allowed to be in mourning for their deceased parents. Five fellow candidates would join together, with a salaried student from the same district serving as their guarantor. If any candidate was found to have a forged family origin or name, or came from a debased family background, the guarantor would face charges for the same offense. The examination process consisted of three stages: a preliminary test known as the ("county examination", followed by a repeat test called the "prefectural examination", and finally the "commission examination", i.e., the licensing examination or qualifying examination. Candidates would face elimination in each of the three

[16] Refer to Xu (1976, pp. 111–116).

sessions of the examination. The admission quota for each licensing examination in each department and district varied from 20 to 40, depending on the population.

Apprentice students who successfully passed the licensing examination were referred to as “appended students” (*fusheng*, 附生, short for fuxue *shengyuan*, 附学生员), which marked their entry into the learning process known as *jinxue* (进学, literally entering school). Appended students, unless they had been licentiates for 30 years or had reached the age of 70, were required to take the licensing examination whenever it was held. Those who demonstrated exceptional performance in the licensing examination would be promoted to to “additional students” (*zengsheng*, 增生) and “salaried students” (*linsheng*, 廪生). On the other hand, those who did not fare well would be downgraded from salaried students to additional students or supplementary students, or in more severe cases, would face corporal punishment or demotion to the status of “commoners”. Salaried students were entitled to receive a monthly “nourishment pay” of four taels, and there were specific quotas for salaried and additional students in each department and district. In cases where there were no available positions, additional students “qualified for promotion to salaried students” were referred to as “salaried candidates” (*houlin*, 候廪), while appended students qualifyied for promotion to additional students would remain appended students.

On the other hand, those who did not fare well would be downgraded from salaried students to additional students or supplementary students, or in more severe cases, would face corporal punishment or demotion to the status of “commoners”. Salaried students were entitled to receive a monthly “nourishment pay” of four taels, and there were specific quotas for salaried and additional students in each department and district. In cases where there were no available positions, additional students “qualified for promotion to salaried students” were referred to as “salaried candidates” (*houlin*, 候廪), while appended students qualifyied for promotion to additional students would remain appended students.

Qualifying examinations were conducted to identify candidates for the upcoming “provincial examinations”. Examinees who achieved the top two tiers were selected by the provincial education commissioner to participate in the provincial examinations. Licentiates who were unable to take the qualifying examinations due to various reasons were given an opportunity to retest before the provincial examinations, a process known as “*luyi*” (录遗), meaning admitting the left-out.

Salaried students, additional students, and supplementary students, collectively referred to as “cultivated talents”, all obtained the licentiate status. Enjoying a higher social standing than commoners, they were permitted to wear hat buttons reserved for state officials of the ninth rank and were exempt from labor taxes. Furthermore, they were exempted from kneeling in court, and local officials were not allowed to physically punish them without the consent of educational authorities. In cases involving minor violations of laws and regulations, local officials communicated with the respective local educational officials (instructors at prefectural, departmental, or county levels) to administer appropriate punishments. However, in instances of more severe infractions, punishments could only be imposed upon them after being deposed by the education commissioners on the requirement of local officials.

Tribute students (*gongsheng*, 贡生) were nominally "tributed" to the Dynastic School, and were divided into "five classes of tributes": tribute students by imperial grace, tribute students for preeminence, second-class tribute students, annual tribute students and tribute students of excellence. This pathway was recognized as the "regular path" to enter into officialdom. Additionally, there were "precedent students" (*ligong*, 例贡) who, according to strict precedent regulations, acquired the status of tribute students through the purchase of official titles. Following successful completion of central government examinations, tribute students could be appointed "seventh-rank capital officials", district magistrates, assistant department magistrates, or educational officials.

National university students (*jiansheng*, 监生), nominally affiliated with the Directorate of Education ("Imperial Academy"), were classified into four categories: national university students by imperial grace, inheritance, excellence, and precedence. Their status was similar to that of tribute students, albeit slightly inferior, and their examination and appointment processes were also comparable. During the late Qing Dynasty, purchasing the status of a dynastic school student became imperative for those aspiring to enter official positions through donations to the government. Consequently, the term "dynastic school student" became associated with the purchased official titles, leading to an unfavorable reputation among the literati.

2. Provincial examination

The provincial examinations were conducted every three years, comprising three sessions spanning three days each. To oversee these examinations, the emperor appointed chief examiners. The examinations took place in August, thus the name "autumn examinations" (*qiuwei*, 秋闱). In exceptional circumstances, such as national celebrations, special examinations known as "grace provincial examinations" (*enke*, 恩科) might be organized. Candidates who achieved a position on the principle list were referred to as "provincial graduates" (*juren*, 举人), specifically categorized as "first-tier graduates" (*kejia chushen*, 科甲出身). The top finisher was awarded the prestigious title of "dispatched optimus" (*jieyuan*, 解元). Those who made it to the supplementary list, beyond the allocated quota, were known as "second-class tribute students" (*fugong*, 副贡). All provincial graduates were eligible to participate in the metropolitan examinations held the following year.

Candidates who failed the metropolitan examinations three times were required to submit their resumes to the Ministry of Personnel. Additionally, they needed to secure a guarantee from a capital official of the sixth rank or higher hailing from their home provinces. This procedure preceded the "grand selection" (*datiao*, 大挑), conducted once every six years. Successful participants in the grand selection, classified as first-class, became eligible candidates for county magistrate positions. Meanwhile, second-class individuals were considered for educational instructor positions within department or county schools. Both first-class and second-class individuals were required to register with the Ministry of Personnel to formalize their eligibility for these positions.

Provincial examinations took place in an examination hall, known as "examination compound" (*gongyuan*, 贡院). The layout of the examination hall possessed distinctive characteristics. It consisted of dozens rows of closely packed cells, each measuring approximately 1.33 meters in height and 1 meter in length. Every candidate was assigned an examination cell, which served as their living quarters, dining area, and examination space throughout the duration of nine consecutive days.

On the day preceding the commencement of the examinations, all candidates were required to assemble in front of the entrance gate of the examination compound early in the morning. After verifying their identities and conducting thorough inspections of their personal belongings, they were granted access to the compound. The official start date for entering the examination hall was typically on August 8th, with the examinations concluding on August 15th. Subsequently, the honors list, revealing the successful candidates, would be published approximately on September 9th (Zhao, 2007, p. 144). In his book, *Strange Tales from a Chinese Studio*, Pu Songling vividly described the sufferings of examinees in the provincial examinations as follows: entering the examination hall carrying baskets, they were like beggars; at roll-call being shouted at by officials, they were like prisoners; entering the examination cells, they were like cold bees late in autumn; upon leaving the examination hall, they were like sick birds out of cage; when anticipating the messenger, they fidgetied like a monkey in captivity; upon receiving the news of failing the examinations, they were like a poisoned fly no longer able to move.

3. Metropolitan examination

Metropolitan examinations were held after provincial examinations in March in the capital by the Ministry of Rites. The number of graduates from the metropolitan examinations was not fixed but rather determined on a temporary basis by the emperor, taking into account the number of provincial graduates. The quantity of metropolitan graduates fluctuated over time, with figures generally ranging around three hundred and reaching their peak at 406 in the 8th year of the Yongzheng period (AD 1730), and reaching their nadir at 96 in the 54th year of the Qianlong period (AD 1789). Metropolitan graduates would participate in the subsequent palace examinations, whereby the final rankings of the top finishers would be determined by the emperor. The top achiever in the metropolitan examinations was commonly referred to "principal graduate" (*huiyuan*, 会元).

4. Palace examination

The palace examination took place 11 days after the publication of the honors list of metropolitan graduates on April 15. The ranking list of palace graduates would be publicly revealed on May 1, a ceremonial event known as *chuanlu* (传胪), or the declaiming of successful candidates. Candidates were divided into three tiers. The first tier, granted the degree of "metropolitan graduate with honors", consisted of the top three performers, each conferred with the esteemed titles of *zhuangyuan* (状元, optimus), *bangyan* (榜眼, secundus), and *tanhua* (探花, tertius) respectively. The second tier was was awarded "regular metropolitan graduates", the primus of whom was also called *chuanlu*. The third tier was granted "associate metropolitan graduates". Irrespective of their tier, all graduates were designated as palace graduates and collectively known as "hanlin" (翰林).

In the Qing Dynasty, there were only two candidates who were the top finisher in provincial, metropolitan, and palace examinations.

Subsequent to the palace examination, the optimus would assume the esteemed position of "senior compiler of the Hanlin Academy", an official of the lower sixth rank. The secundus and tertius, respectively, would be appointed as "junior compilers of the Hanlin Academy", officials of the upper seventh rank. Graduates of the second and third tiers would proceed to undertake the "court examination" (*chaokao*, 朝考). Successful finishers would receive the title of "Hanlin bachelors" (*shujishi*, 庶吉士) and be granted the salary corresponding to officials of the seventh rank. They would then be admitted to the Hanlin Academy to engage in further academic pursuits at the Office of Hanlin Bachelors (*shuchangguan*, 庶常馆). For palace graduates who did not attain the status of Hanlin bachelors, various career paths awaited them. Some would be appointed as "supernumerary secretaries" in the six ministries, while others would assume roles as educational instructors and provosts at the Directorate of Education or as teachers in prefectural, departmental, or county schools. Hanlin bachelors, after three years of study, would participate in "releasing examinations" and their ranks would be decided by the emperor. Graduates from the second tier of the palace examination would be designated as "junior compilers", whereas those from the third tier would assume the position of "examining editors", officials of the lower seventh rank. Palace graduates who were not admitted to the Hanlin Academy would be appointed as secretaries at the Six Ministries, officials of the upper sixth rank, or as "district magistrates on vacancy", officials of the upper seventh rank.

iii. Regional distribution and balance of imperial examination quota

During the Han Dynasty, efforts were made to address concerns regarding regional and ethnic equality in the allocation of quotas for the recommendation of filial and incorrupt individuals. In the Eastern Han period, these quotas were distributed based on the population of each commandery. Initially, "the emperor deemed it unfair that the quotas were two for both big commanderies with a population ranging from 500-600 thousand, and small commanderies with a population around 200 thousand as well as barbarians. Therefore, the emperor passed the matter to high-ranking ministers for deliberation." Following extensive discussions, modifications were made to the quota system. "The size of a commandery or princedom's population determined the allotted quota for filial and incorrupt talents. A commandery with a population of 200,000 was entitled to recommend one individual, whereas commanderies with populations of 600,000, 800,000, 1 million, and 1.2 million were allowed to recommend two, four, five, and six individuals respectively. For commanderies with populations smaller than 200,000, a quota of one individual every two years was established. Commanderies with populations smaller than 100,000 were permitted one individual every three years" (Biography of Ding Hong, *Book of the Later Han*).

Simultaneously, special consideration was given to sparsely populated border areas with mixed populations of Han and ethnic minorities. For instance, "Provinces of Youzhou, Bingzhou, and Liangzhou were sparsely populated, but border corvée labor was substantial. Capable officials faced limited opportunities for advancement. However, the effective management and harmonious interaction with ethnic minorities relied on the appointment of suitable officials. To address this, specific quotas for virtuous and incorrupt recommendations were outlined for remote border commanderies. Commanderies with populations over 100,000 were authorized to recommend one filial and incorrupt talent per year, while those with populations smaller than 100,000 were permitted to recommend one talent every two years. In commanderies with populations smaller than 50,000, the quota was set at one talent every three years" (Annal of Emperor Xiaohe, *Book of the Later Han*).

During the Song Dynasty, a regional quota system was instituted specifically for provincial graduates. However, when it came to palace graduates, there were no regional quota restrictions and the practice of "free distribution among regions" was followed. In contrast, when imperial examinations were introduced during the Yuan Dynasty, a quota system was implemented for the metropolitan examinations. The official quota allotted places equally among Mongols, Semu (various non-Han ethnic groups), Han Chinese, and Southerners. During the Southern Song period, Southerners predominantly resided in regions such as Jiangsu, Zhejiang, Jiangxi, Hubei, and Henan. As a result, the quotas assigned to Han Chinese and Southerners, who constituted the majority of the population, were relatively small, which was a noticeable discrimination against Southerners within the examination system. While the Song Dynasty's regional quota system focused primarily on geographic considerations, the Yuan Dynasty adopted a different approach. In the Yuan Dynasty, the regional quota system was primarily based on geopolitical factors, with a particular emphasis on maintaining a balanced distribution of political power. Consequently, "the allocation of quotas was influenced more by social class or ethnicity rather than purely geographical considerations" (Lin, 2005).

During the early Ming Dynasty, there existed no explicit regulations regarding the geographical distribution of palace graduates, granting an inherent advantage to "individuals hailing from the affluent and intellectually vibrant southern and southeastern regions of the empire". This advantage was particularly pronounced in AD 1391, when all of the palace graduates hailed from these regions. This glaringly imbalanced geographical composition greatly incensed Emperor Taizu, prompting him to take drastic action. The chief examiner responsible for the biased outcome was summarily executed, and a subsequent palace examination was convened, featuring an additional ranking list reserved solely for individuals from the northern part of the empire. In AD 1425, the Ming government introduced a comprehensive system known as the "Northern and Southern Examination Papers". Under this system, 40% of the available slots for palace graduates were allotted to the North, while the remaining 60% were distributed among other regions. Subsequently, the Ming government further refined the allocation scheme, reserving 10% of the quota for the economically underdeveloped provinces of Sichuan, Yunnan, Guizhou, and Guangxi, as well as the three prefectures and three departments in the province of South Zhili. These regions received the middle examination papers. Additionally, 35% of the quota was designated for the northern regions, with candidates examined using northern examination papers, while the remaining 55% was earmarked for the southern and southeastern regions, with candidates being assessed with southern examination papers. Such an allocation scheme basically reflected the distribution of the population (Hucker, 2008, p. 39). In the 51st year of the Kangxi Emperor's reign (AD 1712) during the Qing Dynasty, the allocation of palace graduate quotas underwent further evolution, transitioning to a province-based approach, thereby introducing greater intricacy to the existing geographical distribution system.

During the Song, Ming, and Qing Dynasties, the imperial examinations by region involved not only the allocation of palace graduates but also the distribution of provincial graduates quotas. In the Qing Dynasty, for instance, the graduates quotas varied across different provinces, ranging from a minimum of 40 in Guizhou province to a maximum of 96 in Jiangxi province. Additionally, a supplementary list known as the addenda list (*fubang*, 副榜), was compiled, featuring graduates who exceeded the quota. The allocation for this addenda list amounted to one-fifth of the total number of candidates on the principle list. Candidates of the provincial examinations were selected by education commissioners through the "qualifying examinations". The number of candidates was aligned to the quota. Big provinces were allowed to select 80 candidates to competing for one slot in the principle list, middle-sized provinces, 60, and for small provinces, 50, while that of the addenda list was 20 competing for one slot.

The regional quota system, although intended as a form of "corrective justice", faced persistent scrutiny regarding its fairness and rationality. Two key issues emerged in relation to this system. Firstly, the problem of "counterfeit household registration for the examination" arose whereby candidates resorted to fraudulent practices similar to the modern phenomenon of "gaokao[17] migration". This involved individuals attempting to evade more challenging examinations by assuming false household registrations in provinces where the tests were perceived to be easier. In certain cases, candidates who had been stripped of their titles and thereby barred from taking the examinations would relocate to other provinces, assuming counterfeit household registrations, "in a bid to regain the opportunity for recognition and success". Secondly, national university students studying in the Southern and Northern capitals encountered difficulties in returning to their hometowns for the provincial examinations. Consequently, they were permitted to take the examinations in Yingtian Prefecture and Shuntian Prefecture, respectively. This arrangement inevitably encroached upon the quota allocated to local candidates. To safeguard the quota for local students from being depleted, both capitals imposed stringent restrictions on the number of national university students. The primary objective of imposing a maximum limit on the inclusion of national university students in the pool of provincial graduates was to protect the interests of local students. However, survey data reveals that the majority of national university students originated from southern provinces, such as Jiangsu, Zhejiang, and Jiangxi, where examination competition was exceptionally intense. Consequently, students from northern regions studying under the jurisdiction of the two Directorate of Education did not benefit from this policy. Consequently, the introduction of a geographically-based quota system triggered substantial controversy. Surprisingly, the Ming government's attempts at

[17] The National College Entrance Examination (NCEE), a standardized college entrance exam held annually in Chinese mainland. (Notes by translators).

reform in this regard elicited protests from national university students, resulting in the abandonment of the proposed reforms (Lin, 2005).

iv. Merits of the imperial examination system[18]

1. Fair selection

The imperial examination system during the Qing dynasty could be characterized as rigid in form and lacking in substantial content due to the confinement of question types to 700-character "eight-legged essays" and five-character-eight-rhythm regulated verses. Critics argue that "the emphasis on flashy poetry and rhythm-prose resulted in impractical knowledge acquisition, with candidates merely memorizing the Classics without true comprehension. The disparity between the learned content and its practical application was evident." Despite these criticisms, it is worth considering that the starting point of the imperial examination might not be "intentionally malicious". While it "consumed the attention of scholars for generations", it also successfully identified and selected many talented individuals.

One significant virtue of the imperial examination system was its commitment to fostering fair competition. Extensive measures were implemented to deter cheating from the outset. Candidates were thoroughly inspected for any hidden references or unauthorized materials upon entering the examination hall. Throughout the duration of the examinations, guards diligently monitored the candidates. After the conclusion of the tests, examination paper collectors meticulously removed any papers deemed inadequate or disqualified. The "sealing office" concealed the candidates' names and test numbers, whereas the original examination papers written in black ink were transcribed onto vermilion papers at the "copy office". Subsequently, these papers underwent scrutiny at the "proofreading office".

Various individuals played crucial roles in the organization of the examinations, including outer aids such as the education commissioner and presiding examiner, as well as inner examiners consisting of chief and associate examiners. All participants in the examination process, from chief examiners to gatekeepers and sweepers, were appointed on a temporary basis. Examiners found guilty of cheating faced severe repercussions, including beheading or punishment through penal military service.

2. Linking the examination to the nomination of officials

Among the three tiers of palace graduates, Hanlin bachelors, upon completing three years of study and successfully passing the releasing examinations, became eligible for nomination as junior compilers or examining editors. Upon release, Hanlin bachelors possessed the privilege of being appointed by the Ministry of Personnel with priority, earning them the revered title of *laohuban* (老虎班) or the class of tigers. For those who were not admitted to the prestigious Hanlin Academy, an alternative avenue for career advancement was available. If they were willing to accept appointments as district magistrates, they were able to register with the Ministry of Personnel. Within a relatively short span of two to three years, a substantial number of these candidates would secure official positions.

[18] Refer to Xu (1976, pp. 117–119).

For provincial graduates, a diverse array of roles was available for them through the grand selection. These positions encompassed district magistrates, department vice magistrates, assistant prefect judges, assistant county magistrates, and educational instructors.

Specifically, palace graduates from such a well-known institution as the Hanlin Academy were "provided for by the state and were assured of high official positions. They were allowed a period of time to learn everything of government in an unhurried manner." Even when they were sent to other provinces as chief examiners, they "still did not have much other official responsibility. [They travelled] to many places, learned much about local conditions and customs, and made many friends." "It was only after all these years that [they would be] appointed to an official position." "In the Ming and Qing dynasties, most great scholars and statesmen were qualified Jinshi or Hanlin scholars" (Ch'ien, 2019, p. 101).

3. Controlling examinations and sparing the need to control education

In the context of ancient China, the role of schools underwent a significant transformation alongside the evolution of the examination system, which led to the diminished significance of schools and a relatively autonomous pursuit of education within the society. Despite this apparent autonomy, the government exerted indirect control over education through its regulation and supervision of the examination process. Consequently, the government exercises a subtle influence over the educational content and direction by effectively shaping the educational pursuits of the populace. This phenomenon is often described as the form of governance known as "manipulating the simple to control the complex".

3.3 Official Rank, Qualification Evaluation and Appointment, and Performance Assessment

3.3.1 Official Rank[19]

The bureaucratic administrative system employed in ancient China was distinguished by its fundamental characteristic of hierarchical division. "This hierarchical structure entailed the subdivision of positions as well as the classification and ranking of personnel." "The system relied on two fundamental aspects: function (responsibility) and rank, both of which were integral to its functioning." The official rank system in ancient China exhibited five characteristics. "Firstly, it had reached a relatively high level of rationalization and legalization. Secondly, the official ranks were organized in a 'one-dimensional multi-sequence compound structure'. Third, a merit system was adopted for the promotion of officials, ensuring the institutionalized mobility of personnel. Additionally, apart from managing positions, the rank

[19] For the official ranks and grades in different dynasties see Lü (2015, pp. 943–991).

system also facilitated the regulation of complex identities through diverse ranks and grades. Lastly, is multifaceted approach enabled the system to serve as a vital instrument of political control and social regulation, effectively constructing a society centered around bureaucracy" (Yan, 2010, pp. 2-6). In modern rule-of-law countries, civil servant ranks typically encompass powers and responsibilities, qualifications, and salaries. However, in traditional China, two additional elements pertained to the concept of ranks: privileges and deferential treatments. Privileges encompassed various economic, legal and official election benefits, thereby comprising the concrete value associated with ranks and serving as distinct markers of identity and status (Yan, 2017, p. 12).

The development of the official rank system in China has generally gone through five stages. (1) The "title-based" (*juebenwei*, 爵本位) and "title-salary" (*jue-shi*, 爵-食) system in the pre-Qin era, where literati and clerks were distinguished and so were the noble and the mean. (2) The "title-rank" (*jue-zhi*, 爵-秩) system underlain by military titles and remuneration ranks from the Warring States Period to the Qin and Han. Different from the Western Zhou, the distinction between the noble and the mean no longer exited in military ranks and remuneration ranks and so under such an open system, commoners could also climb up the social ladder step by step, or rise to the top of the bureaucracy. (3) The official rank system and familial rank order in the Wei, Jin, Southern and Northern Dynasties. "In the Qin and Han, the remuneration rank strongly indicated the 'differentiation between positions', while in the Wei, Jin, Southern and Northern Dynasties, it shifted greatly to the 'differentiation between official ranks'". This was due to the decline of imperial power and the full development of great-family politics, whence gentry bureaucrats secured for themselves enough benefits brought by official ranks. (4) Ranks and qualifications of officials in the Tang and Song. The Sui and Tang had stepped out of the medieval great-family politics and returned to autocratic bureaucratic rule. "The nine-rank system with 18 grades and 30 levels of the Tang fused together in an orderly way the ranks of functioning officials, civil and military officials without fixed function, meritorious officials and the noble". (5) The "tripod" of rank, position and degree in the Ming and Qing. "With the center of the rank structure in the Ming and Qing shifting to 'position', the weight of 'the classification of positions' increased, while the complexity of the ranks greatly decreased." At the same time, "the prosperity of the imperial examinations made qualified degrees the most valued criterion, becoming the principal rank basis", "thus strengthening the separation of 'literati and clerks' and the separation of 'the civil and the military'" (Yan, 2010, pp. 469–483).

The lingering influence of historical factors results in the preservation of several aspects of the traditional official rank system in modern times. An illustrative example is the adoption of the 30-level "position-rank salary scale", which was officially introduced by the State Council of the People's Republic of China in 1956. This system exemplified the prevailing approach of "rank classification" and remained in effect until the implementation of structured salary reform in 1985. "This reform was geared towards transitioning to a 'position classification' system, resulting in a significant shift towards position-based remuneration" (Yan, 2017, p. 239) (Table 3.1).

Table 3.1 Classification of official ranks from the Eastern Han to Qing[20]

	Within the current of ranked officials	Informally registered officials	Approximate total levels
Eastern Han	16 remuneration levels (9 if excluding those outside the official ranks)	Personnel paid in pecks, archivists	18 (11)
Wei and Jin	16 remuneration levels, 9 official ranks		
Liang	18 grades, 9 ranks with upper and lower grades and 1st and 2nd classes, 30 levels in total	7 grades	37 34
	In the Tianjian era 125 military titles, 24 grades In the Zhongdatong era 240 military titles, 34 grades	8 grades	
Northern Wei Emperor Xiaowen	Initial classification: 9 ranks with upper & lower grades and 1st, 2nd and 3rd classes, 54 levels in total		54
	Re-classification: 9 ranks with upper and lower grades and 1st and 2nd classes, 30 levels in total	7 ranks 7 levels	37
Northern Qi	9 ranks with upper and lower grades and 1st and 2nd classes, 30 levels in total	9 ranks 9 levels	39
Northern Zhou	8 levels for military official, 9 ranks 18 levels for civil service, 36 levels for officials without fixed positions, 40 levels in total	9 ranks 9 levels	49
Sui and Tang	9 ranks with upper and lower grades and 1st and 2nd classes, 30 levels in total	9 ranks 9 levels	39
Song	30 levels for capital and court officials, 7 levels for official candidates	Subofficial functionary and servant respectively 10 levels	Over 47
	56–60 levels for military officers		56–60
Ming	9 ranks with upper and lower grades, 18 levels in total	Informally registered	19
Qing	9 ranks with upper and lower grades, 18 levels in total	Informally registered	19

[20] This table is cited from Yan (2010, p. 231).

3.3.2 *Qualification Evaluation (Appointment)*[21]

During the Han Dynasty, filial and incorrupt or wise and virtuous, and correct talents recommended from among the villages and hamlets might be appointed by the imperial court after being examined on "policy questions", or be appointed court gentlemen after being examined on "strategies to resolve problematic issues", which was called *langxuan* (郎选, literally selection of court gentlemen). There were also candidates who were appointed court gentlemen through fast-paced answering of strategic questions, inheritance, or through purchase. In the Han, chamberlain for attendants (*guanglu xun*, 光禄勋, superseding the title *langzhong ling* 郎中令 in the Qin) was one of the nine ministers, and under his command there were dozens of court gentlemen, who were reserved talents. Upon entering office for the first time, officials underwent a one-year probationary period before being officially appointed. The terms of office were not formally restricted during the Han Dynasty, and extended periods of service were highly valued. In terms of qualifications, merchants in the early Han were not allowed to be officials, and this identity-based restriction was abolished during the reign of Emperor Xiaowu of the Han. In the early Han, there was no law of avoidance for local officials. By the time of Emperor Xiaohuan, the personnel avoidance system of *sanhufa* (三互法, literally triple mutual avoidance method) was implemented, according to which a man could not assume office in three places of interests related to marital status and household registration. The early Han Dynasty, valued officials' grassroot political experience, which in the Jin Dynasty was listed as a prerequisite for the appointment of central government officials, and it was clearly decreed that "without the experience of serving as a magistrate, one would not be appointed a secretarial court gentleman".

During the Northern Wei period, notable practice was observed whereby military officers, upon retirement from service, transitioned into civil officials. However, the number of candidates far exceeded the available positions. In response to this situation, Cui Liang, the Minister of Personnel, devised a method known as *tingniange* (停年格) to establish a framework for ranking and appointing officials based on their seniority.

In the Sui Dynasty, the imperial examination replaced the recommendation system employed during the Han. Under this new system, officials below the sixth rank were selected and appointed by the Ministry of Personnel, effectively usurping the authority of local governors to appoint their own staff in provinces and commanderies. This reform aimed to centralize the administration of personnel and was characterized by the requirement that subofficials of county magistrates recruit individuals from other counties, rather than their own. "In the past, except governors and other superior officials in provinces, governors and their deputies in commanderies, and magistrates in counties, all the other staff were appointed by the governors of provinces, commanderies and counties. As a result, the number of appointees by the imperial decree in each province did not exceed dozens. By contrast, now [in the Tang Dynasty] officials of all tiers are administered by the Ministry of Personnel and

[21] Refer to Lin (1976, pp. 196–198).

their behaviors and performances are subject to assessment." This system started in the late Wei Dynasty and the Northern Qi Dynasty, passed on to and popularized in the Sui Dynasty (Chen, 2001, pp. 94–96).

The Tang Dynasty inherited the administrative system from the Sui Dynasty but implemented several modifications, notably the division between civil officials and military officials. Civil officials were placed under the jurisdiction of the Ministry of Personnel, while military officials fell under the purview of the Ministry of War. Furthermore, the selection process for palace graduates and officials was separated. Graduates were required to satisfy specific qualifications in order to embark on an official career. Only after passing the selection process conducted by the Ministry of Personnel were they appointed to their respective positions.

The selection process encompassed four primary criteria: physical appearance (body), speech (words), calligraphy (writing), and written judgment (judgment). When multiple candidates possessed equal virtue and proficiency in meeting all four criteria, the subsequent criterion considered was talent, followed by diligence. Candidates for positions below the sixth rank were appointed based on their qualifications and merits.

In contrast to the administrative system observed during the Tang Dynasty, the Song Dynasty introduced a distinctive approach that granted preferential treatment to literati. A significant aspect of this system involved the imperial examinations, which served as a means to select government officials. Within this framework, all palace graduates who met the requisite qualifications were appointed to official positions.

In the Ming Dynasty, talent selection was strict, but personnel appointment was flexible. There were three ways through which individuals could secure official positions: first, by qualifying palace graduates; second, by being selected as tribute students from provincial graduates; and third, through promotion from clerks. The administrative responsibility for of civil service affairs rested with the Ministry of Personnel, while matters pertaining to military personnel were overseen by the Ministry of War.. "Many first-time appointees, especially young metropolitan graduates, were not given regular appointments immediately, but were assigned to capital agencies as observers." "It was common for first appointments to be probationary or acting appointments for up to a year. Then, if an appointee was evaluated favorably by his superiors, his status changed into a substantive appointment. An appointee given a substantive appointment had a kind of continuing tenure for a three-year term, which, in the normal course of events, was renewed for two more such terms for a full tenure of nine years. After nine years, the appointment lapsed, and the official reported back to the Ministry of Personnel for reappointment." (Hucker, 2008, pp. 42–43)

During the Qing Dynasty, talents chosen by the emperors were not subject to qualification restrictions. For vacancies of high officials, the Ministry of Personnel (later succeeded by the Grand Council) would list qualified candidates for the emperor to make the ultimate decision. In cases concerning the appointment of local officials that fell outside the purview of the Ministry of Personnel, the respective governors or viceroys were tasked with the selection process, subsequently submitting their chosen candidates for approval to the Ministry of Personnel. In the Qing official selection system, all principal seal-holding officials, capital officials, and investigating censors necessitated adherence to selection through the prescribed regular path. Furthermore, officials at the Hanlin Academy, the Household Administration of the Heir Apparent, the Ministry of Personnel, and the Ministry of Rites were required to be qualified palace graduates. Regional administration commissioners, on the other hand, were expected to have previously served as surveillance commissioners. And following the Ming practice of appointing southern officials to the north and vice versa, local officials were often from thousands of miles away and did not know local customs or even the local language.

3.3.3 Assessment (Performance Rating)

i. The Qin and Han Dynasties[22]

The evaluation process in the Qing Dynasty encompassed both minor and terminal assessments, conducted annually and triennially, respectively. The resulting assessment records were designated as *jibu* (计簿). The responsibility of evaluating subordinates rested with the officials in charge: commandery and princedom governors alongside councilors evaluated their respective subofficials; county magistrates, in turn, evaluated their subofficial functionaries; the Prime Minister evaluated the nine ministers, governors and magistrates. The evaluation records were subsequently compiled and reported to the Office of the Prime Minister and the Office of the Censorate. The former would preside over the process of "awarding the best and punishing the worst" in accordance with the merit ratings, while the latter would "scrutinize the evaluation records, ensuring their authenticity and reliability". Following the evaluation, a system of rewards and punishments would be implemented. Meritorious individuals would receive various forms of recognition, including promotions, monetary rewards, and salary increases. Conversely, those deemed deficient may face questioning, demotion, or removal from their official positions. Remarkably outstanding individuals could even bypass the traditional hierarchical progression, while those with inferior ratings risked outright dismissal from their posts.

ii. The Sui and Tang Dynasties[23]

Following a series of annual minor assessments, the terminal assessment, commonly referred to as "ratings completed", played a pivotal role in determining the promotion or demotion of officials in the Qing Dynasty. The regulations on the frequency of terminal assessments, known as the "assessment interval" or *kaoshu* (考数), underwent various modifications over time, and in general it lengthened as the dynasty progressed.

Depending on the official's rank, the evaluation process involved different authorities. Some officials would be evaluated by the emperor himself, while others would

---

22 Refer to Sa (1975a, pp. 324–328).

23 Refer to Huang. Q (2005).

be evaluated by the Bureau of Evaluations of the Ministry of Personnel. Generally speaking, officials holding ranks below the fourth level were typically evaluated by the Ministry of Personnel, specifically by individuals such as the director, vice director, office manager, and secretary of the Bureau of Evaluations, except for regional inspectors who were assessed by imperial envoys or the emperor directly. In cases where the evaluation involved higher-ranking officials, the emperor himself would conduct the assessment. It is worth noting that a complex framework of supervision and inspection procedures governed the submission of merit ratings from various institutions across the country.

Sophisticated supervision and inspection procedures were introduced regarding the merit ratings submitted by various institutions across the country. Evaluation records were sent to the capital before the end of the year, facilitated by regional inspectors or "territorial representative". Furthermore, in response to the expanding bureaucracy and the issue of surplus candidates, promotions within the bureaucratic ranks were determined not only by merit ratings but also by seniority.

The evaluation criteria encompassed four distinct merits: *deyi* (德义), which denoted virtue and faithfulness, *qingshen* (清慎), encompassing incorruption and prudence, *gongping* (公平), representing fairness, and *keqin* (恪勤), signifying respect and diligence. A rating system was adopted to assign officials into nine tiers from "upper upper to lower lower". The pivotal point for determining awards or punishments was marked by the "average average" rating.

Four supervisors and inspectors were in charge of merit ratings: the evaluation supervisors of capital officials and non-capital officials were respectively served by supervising secretaries of the Chancellery and secretariat drafters; the evaluation inspectors of capital officials and non-capital officials were respectively served by Ministers and Vice Ministers of the Ministry of Justice and Personnel, and Censor-in-chief of the Censorate.

iii. The Song, Yuan, Ming and Qing Dynasties[24]

Performance assessment occurred on a triennial basis. The evaluation of officials stationed in the capital was known as the "capital evaluation", while the assessment of officials serving outside the capital was referred to as the "grand reckoning". During the Song Dynasty, the establishment of the Official Inspection Office (*shenguan yuan*, 审官院) and the Evaluation Office (*kaoke yuan*, 考课院) introduced a system where these positions were filled by reputable and morally upright officials. The Official Inspection Office primarily conducted evaluations of officials serving in the capital and the court, while the Evaluation Office focused on subofficials, as well as prefecture and county officials. Merit ratings were classified into three grades: upper, average, and lower.

The Yuan Dynasty implemented a seniority-based evaluation system, with the order of evaluation determined by the length of an official's service. The Ming Dynasty's assessment consisted of two categories: ratings completed and evaluation. Upon the completion of the ratings, officials would be classified into one of

[24] Refer to Lin (1976, pp. 99–101).

three grades: superior, average, and inferior. Promotion or demotion depended on the aggregated results of the three triennial evaluations within a nine-year period. There were eight variables used to determine the misconduct of officials, including avarice, cruelty, frivolity or instability, inadequacy, senility, ill health, weariness, and inattentiveness. Any of these offenses would result in one of the "four penalties", which included retirement, demotion, suspension, or dismissal.

In the case of capital evaluation, officials of the fourth rank or above submitted self-evaluations to the emperor for final decision. "In the case of the outer evaluation [of officials serving away from the capital], the heads of all local agencies sent monthly reports on all their subordinates to their prefects, and at the end of each year each prefect submitted to his provincial superiors a consolidated report on all officials in his jurisdiction. ... [A]ll provincial authorities, every third year, prepared a consolidated report on all officials in their respective jurisdictions for consideration at the capital by the Ministry of Personnel" for decisions on the merit rating and reassignment of the officials (Hucker, 2008, pp. 43-44). The Qing Dynasty inherited the framework of the Ming system, with slight modifications.

3.4 Schools[25]

3.4.1 Capital School ("Imperial Academy", "National University")

The term for educational institutions underwent changes across three dynasties. In the Xia Dynasty, it was referred to as *xiao* (校), in the Yin Dynasty as *xu* (序), and in the Zhou Dynasty as *xiang* (庠). However, the historical validity of these terms has not been conclusively established.

During the reign of Emperor Xiaowu in the Han Dynasty, a significant development in education occurred with the establishment of schools. Notably, the National University emerged, functioning under the auspices of the Chamberlain for Ceremonials and placing a strong emphasis on the study of the Classics. Building upon the framework instituted during the preceding Qin Dynasty, the position of erudite was designated by the Chamberlain for Ceremonials. Emperor Xiaowu further solidified this system by appointing erudites specifically in the Five Classics (*wujing boshi*, 五经博士), and following the suggestion of Gongsun Hong, recruited 50 disciples for the erudites. Moreover, he mandated that commanderies and princedoms and district magistrates recommend to commandery governors individuals who possessed an affinity for Confucian classics, displayed reverence towards their elders, adhered strictly to political and moral principles, demonstrated amicability towards their neighbors, and from this pool, candidates with the necessary qualifications would be

[25] Refer to Chen (1977, pp. 137–145).

selected as students to be educated under the tutelage of the Chamberlain for Ceremonials similar to the disciples of the erudites. As this institution operated under the jurisdiction of the Chamberlain for Ceremonials (*taichang*, 太常), it became known as the Imperial Academy (*taixue*, 太学).

During the reign of Emperor Zhao, the number of erudite disciples expanded to exceed one hundred, a figure that doubled during the reign of Emperor Xuan. By the end of Emperor Cheng's rule, the number of disciples reached over 3,000. Correspondingly, the number of erudites specializing in the Five Classics also increased, with all fourteen schools dedicated to the study of the New-Text Classics introduced in educational institutions. In the Eastern Han period, the Chancellor position was granted to the most knowledgeable and esteemed erudite in the Five Classics. In addition to the establishment of the National University, the construction of the Bright Hall and the Biyong Hall further contributed to the growth of scholarship. Consequently, the number of scholars continued to rise, reaching a total of 30,000 during the reign of Emperor Huan (Sa, 1975a, pp. 301-302). Although National University thrived in the Eastern Han period, education increasingly shifted towards private arrangements. While the Old-Text Classics were not taught in national schools, they held significant influence during this era. For instance, prominent Confucian scholars like Ma Rong and Zheng Xuan amassed numerous disciples, contributing to the perpetuation of Old-Text teachings.

The Imperial Academy in the Wei and Jin Dynasties garnered a reputation that was not entirely warranted. It came into existence in the fifth year of the Huangchu era of the Wei Dynasty in AD 224. The initial establishment consisted of nineteen erudites. Upon the Jin Dynasty's succession, it inherited this institution and established the School for the Sons of the State. This involved the appointment of one Chancellor and one erudite, as well as fifteen instructors, all affiliated with the Imperial Academy. The curriculum at this time prioritized the "education of the Sons of the State" (known as *guozi xue*, 国子学), referring to the training of princes and nobility. In subsequent years, the Eastern Jin reduced the number of posts and they, called Imperial Erudites (*taixue boshi*, 太学博士), were no longer confined solely to the study of the Five Classics. Notably, Taoism experienced popularity in the eastern regions of the Yangtze River. As Confucianism struggled to regain prominence, the National University, while retaining its name, ceased to effectively function as an educational institution.

The National University of the Southern Dynasties inherited the decadent characteristics from the Jin Dynasty. The School for the Sons of the State, which periodically assumed prominence, failed to establish a consistent presence, resulting in a state of desolation permeating the National University.

During the Northern Dynasties, the National University took inspiration from the educational model set forth by the Han Dynasty. A significant milestone occurred during the reign of Emperor Daowu of Wei, who founded the Imperial Academy, with erudites in the Five Classics, and 3000 licentiates. Subsequently, Emperor Xiaowen attached more importance to the Imperial Academy, and set up the University of the Sons of State, Simen schools, and Bright Hall and Biyong Hall.

During the Sui Dynasty, the organizational structure of the National University underwent significant changes. It severed its affiliation with the Chamberlain for Ceremonials and instead, came under the purview of the newly established Directorate of Education (*guozi jian*, 国子监). Simultaneously, the Court for Education (*guozi si*, 国子寺) was instituted under the supervision of the Chancellor. The Chancellor assumed responsibility for overseeing various educational institutions, including the School of the Sons of the State, the National University, Simen schools, and arithmetics schools. These establishments were staffed by erudites, educational instructors, and governmental students who typically held official rank titles during ancient times. During the reign of Emperor Yang, the Directorate of Education was established, further refining the administrative framework. The Directorate comprised offices such as the Chancellor and director of studies, among others. Notably, both the School for the Sons of the State and the National University existed concurrently. These institutions were equipped with erudites and instructors. While the enrollment capacity of the former was not fixed, the latter housed a standardized cohort of 500 students.

During the Tang Dynasty, the National University stood as the most prestigious educational institution, and its prestige was not diminished by its gentrification. Under the leadership of one Chancellor and two directors of studies, the Directorate of Education assumed responsibility for formulating national policies in Confucianism political and moral education. Additionally, it supervised the seven schools.

The School for the Sons of the State specifically admitted offspring of officials holding ranks of the third or higher, with a quota of 300 students. The National University catered to the children of officials ranked fifth or higher, with an allotted quota of 500 students. Both institutions centered their curriculum on the study of Confucian Classics, encompassing not only the New-Text but also other canonical texts. Optional subjects included chancery script (*lishu*, 隶书), *Discourses of the States* (*guoyu*, 国语, a collection of anecdotes and discourses, mostly between rulers and ministers from the Spring and Autumn period), *Explaining Simple and Analyzing compound Characters* (*shuowen*,说文, short for *Shuowen jiezi*, 说文解字, the oldest and one of the most important etymological dictionaries of ancient China), *Forest of Characters* (*zilin*, 字林, a character dictionary), the *Three Chapters* (*sancang*, 三仓, Chinese primer and a prototype for Chinese dictionaries), *Approach to Correct Expressions* (*Erya*, 尔雅, a dictionary-like glossary from the Han). These supplementary subjects were taught during students' free time.

Students whose parents were officials of the seventh rank or above attended the Four-Gates School located in the capital city. The enrollment capacity was set at 3000 students. Although the curriculum mirrored that of the National University, it held a lower status.

The Calligraphy School focused on the study of Stone Classics, *Shuowen*, and *Zilin*, with other calligraphies as sub-subjects, and the quota was 30. The Law School centered its teaching on administrative and penal codes, supplemented by rules and regulations for officials, and the quota was 50. The Arithmetics School taught different subjects at two classes, and the quota was 30. These three schools primarily catered to the offspring of officials of the eighth rank or below, as well as commoners, offering specialized skill-focused education.

Lastly, the Institute for the Extension of Literary Arts (*guangwen guan*, 广文馆) was established during the ninth year of the Tianbao era (AD 750). This institution groomed students from the National University to become palace graduates. However, it was abolished during the era of Zhide. At all the seven schools, the students were taught by erudites and instructors, and at the School for the Sons of the State and the Four-Gates School there were lecturers to assist them.

In addition to the aforementioned schools, the Chancellery also established the Institute for the Advancement of Literature (*hongwen guan*, 弘文馆), which had an enrollment capacity of 30 students. The Institute for the Veneration of Literature (*chongwen guan*, 崇文馆) was established within the Eastern Palace and admitted 20 students. These two institutions specifically catered to the offspring of the royal family and high-ranking officials, with instruction provided by academicians. Other specialized schools, such as those for mysteries and medicine, also flourished during this period.

During the Song Dynasty, the National University experienced a gradual decline, despite the introduction of a distinct educational system known as the "three-college system". Initially, only the School for the Sons of the State existed, and it wasn't until the reign of Emperor Shenzong that the school system was fully established. The School for the Sons of the State catered to the offspring of capital officials of the seventh rank or above. The Imperial Academy served the children of capital officials of the eighth rank or lower, as well as exceptionally talented commoner offspring.

Other schools such as the School of the Four Gates, the Law School, the Mathematics School and the Calligraphy School experienced periods of disuse and were no longer under the administration of the Directorate of Education. Furthermore, within the capital, there were additional educational institutions for the imperial family, including the Military Academy and the Fine Arts Academy. However, these schools also fluctuated between periods of operation and closure. Wang Anshi, a prominent politician during the Song Dynasty, introduced the "three-college system". According to this system, newly enrolled students would be initially placed in the Outer College and subsequently progress to the Inner College and Superior College in a sequential manner. Students in the Superior College were exempt from the examination conducted by the Ministry of Rites and enjoyed the privilege of being directly appointed as officials.

During the Yuan Dynasty, there was no Imperial Academy, but only the School for the Sons of the State, which was affiliated to the Academy of Scholarly Worthies. In the Yanyou era, following the suggestion of Zhao Mengfu, a distinguished calligrapher, painter, and scholar, the concept of a grade-studio, known as *jiezhai* (阶斋) in Chinese, was introduced. The implementation of the grade-studio entailed the division of students into distinct tiers: upper, middle, and lower grades. For each grade, there were corresponding left and right studios. At each season, examinations were conducted to evaluate the students' knowledge in various subjects. Those who successfully passed these examinations would progress to the next grade, mirroring the hierarchical progression system reminiscent of Wang Anshi's three-college system in the Song Dynasty. In addition to the School for the Sons of the State, the Schools for the Sons of the State for Mongols and the Hui people were established. These specialized schools provided instruction in their respective languages to accommodate the diverse linguistic backgrounds of the students belonging to these ethnic groups.

The Ming Dynasty initially held the National University in high regard. However, over time, its status underwent a transformation, and it became primarily a reservoir for nurturing talent for the imperial examination system. In the early Ming period, the School for the Sons of the State was founded, later renamed as the Directorate of Education. This institution accommodated what was commonly referred to as national university students, who were enrolled in six educational halls. Their progression to higher grades within the system was contingent upon their examination scores. Exceptionally gifted students had the privilege of direct promotion to esteemed positions within the bureaucracy.

As the imperial examinations gained increasing importance with the passage of time, the prestige associated with national university students progressively diminished. Moreover, when people could buy their way into the university, commoners could also acquire the status of licentiates and be admitted to the Directorate of Education. Consequently, the institution's prestige suffered as a result of the intricate hierarchies and grades assigned to students. In addition, another Directorate of Education was established in Nanjing. Thus, the structure of the Ming Dynasty's Imperial Academies was constituted by the North and South Directorates of Education, respectively.

During the Qing Dynasty, the National University underwent a significant decline in its functional importance. Despite its disciples and six halls, the Directorate of Education had become a mere nominal entity, devoid of substantial academic activities, merely supporting superfluous officials. In addition to the Directorate of Education, there were the School for the Imperial Family and the Banner School for the offspring of the Banners.

At the end of the Qing Dynasty, China opened up and individuals proficient in translation were in great demand. Recognizing this need, efforts were made to establish institutions dedicated to nurturing translation talents. Alongside the Guang Fangyan Guan in Shanghai, the capital saw the establishment of the School of Combined Learning during the reign of the Tongzhi Emperor, while the Guangxu Emperor's reign witnessed the inception of the Russian College.

3.4.2 Local Schools

In the Han Dynasty, local schools in commanderies and princedoms encompassed a curriculum that went beyond basic literacy and included studies on strategies and policies. The allure of recognition and material gains served as potent factors in motivating scholars. However, despite the initial establishment of these educational institutions, local government schools gradually diminished, lingering in name alone. As the Song Dynasty unfolded, private schools gradually gained prominence. Among these educational establishments, the academies rose to become particularly flourishing institutions. The Qing Dynasty witnessed notable advancements in both public and charity-based schools. While local public schools often fell short in providing comprehensive education, the Chinese system exhibited a unique framework characterized by the delineation of responsibilities and the establishment of specific offices aimed at overseeing scholars.

During the early Han Dynasty, comprehensive educational institutions were not yet established at both the central and local levels. However, an important development took place under the reign of Emperor Jing, when Wen Dang, the Governor of the Shu Commandery, took the initiative to establish a school and recruited of students from the various districts under the commandery's jurisdiction. This marked the inception of local schools in the Han Dynasty. Subsequently, Emperor Wu issued a decree mandating the establishment of schools across all commanderies and princedoms. Building upon this foundation, Emperor Ping further expanded the educational framework by stipulating the establishment of schools at various levels. Schools within princedoms were referred to as *xue*, those in districts, circuits, fiefs, and marquisates as *xiao*, while townships were to have *xiang*, and communities were to establish *xu*. The administrative staff of *xue* and *xiao* comprised one teacher specializing in the Classics, while *xu* and *xiang* were overseen by a master of the Classic of Filial Piety. With the implementation of this comprehensive system, the Han Dynasty witnessed the emergence of a well-structured school system, with educational institutions present in townships, commanderies, and the capital. "Schools of different levels seemed to be unconnected", and "students attending village schools would not be admitted to the Imperial Academy" (Sa, 1975a, p. 303).

In the tumultuous Wei, Jin and Southern Dynasties, local schools declined. But Emperor Daowu of the Northern Wei attached great importance to local schools, and each commandery was equipped with erudites and instructors tasked with the responsibility of imparting knowledge to students.

During the initial phase of the Sui Dynasty, all prefecture and district schools were abolished and thousands of students were dismissed. Though Emperor Yang restored them, the effort failed to yield desired outcome.

In the Tang, Song and Yuan Dynasties, local schools underwent a gradual decline in their effectiveness, rendering them mere symbolic entities, which were consequently replaced by the system of academies in the Song and Yuan Dynasties.

In the Tang Dynasty, schools were established in prefectures, sub-prefectures and districts, but the influence was limited.

In the Song Dynasty, after the 4th year of the Qingli era (AD 1044), all prefectures and commanderies established schools. The establishment of district schools became permissible when the number of students exceeded 200. During the Xi'ning era, the Wulu School was established. In the Yuanfeng era, fifty-three governmental schools were established in circuits and prefectures, and the three-college system of the Imperial Academy was also adopted at local schools. Local schools in the Song gradually shifted from order maintenance or pure academic learning to preparing students for the imperial examinations. Commendable scholars of the time underwent 300 days' rigorous preparation before they could take the autumn examinations. Although academies did not originate in the Song Dynasty, they flourished in the Song. Among the most prestigious ones were the four major academies, including the renowned Academy of the White Deer Cavern, whose reputation was far superior to that of local public schools. The head of teaching of academies were called *shanzhang* (山长, director of academy). The imperial court would recognize the achievements of these academies by presenting them with official tablets or granting them school fields as commendation.

Emperor Shizu of the Yuan set great store by education, and schools were established in all circuits, prefectures, sub-prefectures, and counties. Local academies also flourished. Though the Yuan ruled China as alien conquerors, the Han culture was kept, which was because education was mostly in the hands of the Han people. Confucianism teachers appointed by the imperial court at circuit, prefectures, and large and middle sub-prefectures were called instructor; those appointed by the Ministry of Rites, modern provinces, and the Pacification Commission at circuits, sub-prefectures and districts were called instructor, provost, lecturer, and academy director. In each modern province there was a Supervisorate of Confucianism, which governed the schools, evaluations, sacrifices and land tax in circuits, prefectures, sub-prefectures and districts.

During the Ming and Qing Dynasties, the educational system underwent refinements, becoming increasingly intertwined with the imperial examination system. As a result, only academies and public schools remained the real-sense educational institutions. In the Ming Dynasty, government schools were established in prefectures, subprefectures, counties, and garrisons. Each school was headed by an instructor, who received assistance from several assistant instructors. Garrison schools, catering to the children of military officials, shared similarities with prefecture schools. Prefecture schools had a quota of 40 licentiates, while the number decreased for sub-prefecture and county schools accordingly. However, during the middle of the Xuande era, the number of licentiates was increased. Students who were admitted within the regulated quota and received nourishment pay were designated as salaried students (*linshan shengyuan*, 廪膳生员), whereas those who exceeded the quota were referred to as additional students (*zengguang shengyuan*, 增广生员). Students admitted after the additional students were categorized as appended students (*fuxue shengyuan*, 附学生员). Exceptional performance in the annual licensing and qualifying examinations allowed candidates to be promoted to additional or salaried student status.

The Qing Dynasty largely retained the educational system inherited from the Ming Dynasty without major reforms. Hence, Ming and Qing local government schools, also known as "“local schools of lexicography and lesser learning”, served as the initial step for scholars to obtain qualification for officialdom, marking the commencement of the imperial examinations. Candidates who failed to gain enrollment were referred to as apprentice candidates, in the case of which “enrollment” denoted eligibility to participate in the provincial examinations rather than direct admission to an actual school.

During the early Ming Dynasty, provincial supervisors, administration commissioners, surveillance commissioners, and local officials assumed administrative responsibilities for schools. However, the administration of schools was later placed under the purview of education intendants, a position established after the Zhengtong era of the Ming Dynasty. In the Qing Dynasty, these officials were known as provincial education commissioners, who possessed considerable authority and were accountable for education administration throughout their respective provinces, independent of the provincial authorities.

Evaluation of all licentiates at schools occurred on a monthly and annual basis. In instances of minor violations of laws and regulations, local officials were not permitted to exercise discretionary punishment. Instead, they were required to notify educational commissioners and request educational officials to administer the necessary admonitions. Licentiates were exempted from corvée labor, and those with exceptional performance would receive government allowances to cover their sustenance and accommodations. Although the government's support for literati did not involve teaching, it was literally "providing for" them (Sa, 1975b, pp. 452–457).

During the Ming Dynasty, academies were categorized into public and private institutions. However, the Qing Dynasty experienced a decline in academies due to the strict cultural policies of the government, resulting in the failure to attract exceptional talents to join them.

References

Chen, G.D. (2005). Kumiao yu fen rufu: Mingmo qingchu shengyuanceng de shehui dongzuo [Weeping temples and burning Confucian uniforms: Social actions of licentiates in the Late Ming and Early Qing Dynasties]. In Y. Xing & L. Lin (Eds.), *Shehui bianqian* [Social evolution] (pp. 349–366). Encyclopedia of China Publishing House.

Chen, G.Y. (1977). *Zhongguo fazhishi* gaiyao [A brief history of Chinese legal system]. San Min Book Co., Ltd.

Chen, Y. (2001). *Suitang zhidu yuanyuan luelun gao · Tangdai zhengzhi shi shulun gao* [Draft essays on the origins of Sui and Tang institution · Draft outline of Tang political history]. SDX Joint Publishing Company.

Chen, Y. (2012). *Weijinnanbeichao shi jiangyan lu* [Lectures on the history of the Wei, Jin, Southern and Northern Dynasties]. Guizhou People's Publishing House.

Ch'ien, M. (2019). *Merits and demerits of political systems in Dynastic China* (S. Zhang, Trans.). Foreign Language Teaching and Research Press. (Original work published 2005).

Ch'ien, M. (2002). *Zhongguo wenhuashi daolun* [An introduction to Chinese cultural history] . The Commercial Press.

Ch'ü, T. (1988). *Local government in China under the Ch'ing*. Harvard University Press.

Ch'ü, T. (2003). *Local government in China under the Ch'ing* (Z. Fan et al., Trans.). Law Press. (Original work published 1988).

Fu, L. (2005). Tangxing wenhua yu songxing wenhua [Tang-type culture and Song-type culture]. In L. Kang & M. Peng (Eds), *Shixue fangfa yu lishi jieshi* [Historical methodology and historical interpretation] (pp. 354–385). Encyclopedia of China Publishing House.

Huang, J. (2005). Qingchu zhengquan yishi xingtai zhi tanjiu: Zhengzhi hua de "daotong guan" [An inquiry into the ideology of political power in the early Qing Dynasty: A politicalized view of "orthodoxy"]. In R. Chen & F. Wang (Eds.), *Sixiang yu xueshu* [Thought and academics] (pp. 245–270). Encyclopedia of China Publishing House.

Huang, Q. (2005). Tangdai de wenguan kaoke zhidu [Civil service evaluation system in Tang Dynasty]. In Q. Huang (Ed.), *Zhidu yu guojia* [Institution and the state] (pp. 206–267). Encyclopedia of China Publishing House.

Hucker, C. O. (2008). Ming government. In D. Twitchett & J. K. Fairbank (Eds.), *The Cambridge history of China: The Ming Dynasty, 1368–1644,* Part 2 (Vol. 8, pp. 9–105). Cambridge University Press.

Lin, L. (2005). Kechang jingzheng yu tianxia weigong: Mingdai keju quyu pei'e wenti de yixie kaocha [Competition in the imperial examinations and the world for all: Some investigations on the regional quotas of the imperial examinations in the Ming Dynasty]. In Y. Xing & L. Lin (Eds.), *Shehui bianqian* [Social evolution] (pp. 319–348). Encyclopedia of China Publishing House.

Legge, J. (Tran.). (1960). *The Chinese classics: Confucian Analects, the Great Learning, the Doctrine of the Mean* (Vol. 1). Hong Kong University Press.

Legge, J. (Tran.). (1970). *The works of Mencius*. Dover Publications.

Lin, Y. (1976). *Zhongguo fazhi shi* [The history of Chinese legal system] Department of Law, National Chung Hsing University. For internal circulation.

Lü, Z. (Ed.). (2015). *Zhongguo lidai guanzhi da cidian* [Dictionary of Chinese official titles] The Commercial Press.

Sa, M. (1975a). *Zhongguo shehui zhengzhi shi* [A socio-political history of China] (Vol. 1). San Min Book Co., Ltd.

Sa, M. (1975b). *Zhongguo shehui zhengzhi shi* [A socio-political history of China] (Vol. 4). San Min Book Co., Ltd.

Tian, Y. (2005). *Dongjin menfa zhengzhi* [Gentry politics in the Eastern Jin Dynasty] Peking University Press.

Wu, R. (2005). Mingqing chengshi "minbian" de jiti xingdong moshi ji qi yingxiang [The collective action model and impact of urban 'civilian uprising' in the Ming and Qing Dynasties Urban]. In Y. Xing & L. Lin (Eds.), *Shehui bianqian* [Social evolution] (pp. 367–393). Encyclopedia of China Publishing House.

Xiao, Q. (2005). Mingqing chengshi "minbian" de jiti xingdong moshi ji qi yingxiang [The collective action model and impact of urban 'civilian uprising' in the Ming and Qing Dynasties Urban]. In Y. Xing & L. Lin (Eds.), *Shehui bianqian* [Social evolution] (pp. 253–291). Encyclopedia of China Publishing House.

Xu, D. (1976). *Zhongguo fazhi shi luelun* [On the history of Chinese legal system] . Cheng Chung Book Company.

Yan, B. (1996). *Shidafu zhengzhi yansheng shigao* [Draft of the history of the evolution of the scholar-bureaucratic politics]. Peking University Press.

Yan, B. (1997). *Chaju zhidu bianqian shigao* [Draft of the history the evolution of the commandery quota system] . Liaoning University Publishing House.

Yan, B. (2001). *Yueguan yu shiguan: Chuantong zhengzhi wenhua yu zhengzhi zhidu lunji* [Music teachers and historians: A collection of traditional political culture and political institutions] SDX Joint Publishing Company.

Yan, B. (2010). *Zhongguo gudai guanjie zhidu yinlun* [An introduction to the official rank system in ancient China] . Peking University Press.

Yan, B. (2017). *Cong juebenwei dao guanbenwei: Qinhan guanliao pinwei jiegou yanjiu* [From title-oriented to official-oriented: A study on the structure of official ranks in the Qin and Han Dynasties] . SDX Joint Publishing Company.

Yu, Y. (2005). Handai xunli yu wenhua chuanbo [Benevolent officials in the Han Dynasty and cultural transmission]. In J. Wang (Ed.), *Zhengzhi yu quanli* [Politics and power] (pp. 42–111). Encyclopedia of China Publishing House.
Yang, X., & Yang, G. (Trans.) (2005). *Poetry and prose of the Han, Wei and Six Dynasties*. Foreign Languages Press.
Zhang, Y. (2003). *Zhongguo shi gang* [An outline of Chinese history] . The Commercial Press.
Zhao, X. (2007). *Da yamen [Grand Yamen]*. Law Press.

Chapter 4
Fiscal System of Ancient China

4.1 Taxation

4.1.1 Service Levy (The "Labor Tax")

In ancient China, apart from tilling their land and paying the land tax, farmers must also render labor to the state. However, farmhands were one of the most important resources of agriculture. The government often subjected the common people to too heavy and lengthy service levies, and the excessive labor and military services would impose a destructive burden on the livelihood of the farmers. The Qin Dynasty perished as a result of unbearable corvée labor. In the Han Dynasty, each farmer was subject to one month's unpaid labor to the state each year. However, one could pay a fee, called *gengfu* (更赋, rotating labor tax), to the government in lieu of one month's labor. Under the Han system, every male was supposed to serve at the frontier for three days each year, even the sons of Prime Ministers. Those who did not wish to perform the frontier service could pay 300 cash to the government to have one's service canceled. In the Han Dynasty, a man was required to enter military service at the age of 23 (or 20) and was entitled to exemption from military service upon reaching the age of 56, or if he was the single adult male of his household or disabled. In the Eastern Jin Dynasty, an adult male was subject to a labor service of not more than 20 days each year. In the Southern Dynasties, the maximum period of annual labor service was 45 days. In the Northern Wei, the age range for labor service was between 20 and 60, and a man above the age of 80 was entitled to have a son exempted from the labor service. The early Sui Dynasty pursued a policy of light corvée labor. However, Emperor Yang of the Sui reversed this policy, and the Sui empire fell apart. The Tang Dynasty continued the scheme of the Kaihuang reign of the Sui and subjected each man to 20 days (22 days for a leap year) of labor to the state each year. Those who chose not to perform the labor service should substitute each day of absence with 3 feet of silk (or 3.6 feet of cloth), and this was called the "labor tax". In case the government requested services for a longer period of time, the extra periods

X. Nie, *The History of Government and Public Law in China*,
https://doi.org/10.1007/978-981-97-6063-3_4

of service could be used to offset other taxes, 15 days of additional labor service for the textile tax, and 30 days for both the textile and the grain tax, but the total period of labor service should not exceed 50 days. Although the service levies were fairly light from the Six Dynasties to the Sui and Tang periods, aristocrats and commoners alike still sought to evade their service duties. Some aristocrats privately had their relatives and servants ordained in Buddhist or Daoist temples, only to evade service levies and preserve their farmhands. As a result, the Tang government introduced certificates for Buddhist and Daoist priests and prohibited private ordainment. Only those with certificates were entitled to tax exemption.

The Song Dynasty followed the taxation system of the late Tang in requiring the performance of labor services. Households were categorized under nine ranks, with the rank information recorded in household registration books and adjusted along with changes in the economic conditions of the households. Only households of four ranks were subject to labor services. As part of his reforms, Wang Anshi (Prime Minister of the Song Dynasty) introduced the *muyi fa* (募役法), or law on labor recruitment, so that farmers could stay focused on agriculture. Households liable for labor services would pay the recruitment fee twice a year (in spring and autumn) based on their respective household rank. Those with properties but hitherto exempted from the labor duty, such as official households and temples, should also contribute money to assist in the hiring of labor. The government was to calculate the funds for hiring labor and apportion them evenly among the people. Later the government added a premium of 20 percent called *mianyi kuansheng qian* (免役宽剩钱), i.e., surplus extension money for labor recruitment, so as to prepare for the eventuality of a crop failure in case of a flood or drought. Although this law was abused and ended up hurting the people, "if expenditure had been budgeted on the basis of revenues so that people were not over-taxed, the law could have benefited the people instead" (a remark made by Su Dongpo, a renowned poet and politician of the Song Dynasty). Sima Guang for a time abolished the *muyi fa* when he rose to power at court, but later allowed it to function in parallel with the labor service law. In the Southern Song Dynasty, there arose the practice of *yiyi* (义役, charitable labor service), in which people pooled together lands and grain as payment for those rendering the labor services. Theoretically speaking, this scheme was more convenient than the *muyi fa* and superior to the labor service law. However, although nominally organized spontaneously by the common people, it was actually manipulated by the powerful families. Consequently, it was predestined to be ineffective.

The early Ming had both unpaid labor and hired labor. In the middle Ming period, the government implemented the Single Whip Method of Taxation (to consolidate taxes and services into a single payment). According to his method, the tax and service quotas of a county were worked out by surveying the land and enumerating the *ding* (丁, adult males). Both the land tax and labor tax were paid to the government. The government provided the fund for hiring labor to perform the services. For *lichai* (力差, services that had to be performed in person), the wages for the labor involved were calculated and adjusted according to specific conditions; for *yinchai* (银差, or services paid in cash), the payable amount was computed, subject to adjustment according to specific conditions. The land tax, services and other requisitions were combined into a single item, which was levied on the land, hence the term the Single Whip Method. However, the determination of *ding* tax (a poll tax on adult males) and services was quite difficult as it relied heavily on the registration of households and compilation of household registers. To solve this problem, Emperor Yongzheng of the Qing Dynasty resolutely introduced the reform called *tanding rumu* (摊丁入亩), whereby the *ding* tax was merged into the land tax. The *ding* tax quota was frozen permanently based on *ding* returns from the population registration of the 50th year of the Kangxi reign (1711), the *ding* quota was geared to the land, and the *ding* tax was levied as part of the land tax.

Through an examination of the taxation of the Han Dynasty, a scholar has concluded that "taxes levied on people were heavy, while the tax levied on land was light". Although the land tax may have been only one-thirtieth, the total amount of taxation (including labor service) in the Han and Tang Dynasties, when converted into cash or kind, accounted for approximately one half of a farmer's total income, which was by no means a light burden. Among these, the service levy and its variants (the poll tax, textile tax) took up the largest proportion (Wang, 2012, pp. 121–123). When people could no longer bear the service burden, they resorted chiefly to desertion (protection by powerful families). This is why in Chinese history, people would from time to time run away and surrender themselves and their properties to powerful families. "The powerful families enjoyed various privileges, legitimate or otherwise, and people could evade the service levy under their protection." In order to overcome this deficiency, from the late Tang Dynasty onward, the government shifted from a taxation system that mainly targeted people to one that mainly targeted land. This shift was accomplished in a long process, from the Two-season Taxation System (*liangshui fa*, 两税法) of the Tang, via the Single Whip Method of Taxation in the Ming, to the system of *tanding rumu* in the Qing. However, each and every round of taxation reform in ancient China was carried out as an "addition", not a "subtraction". In other words, the burden of taxation was always made heavier, not lighter. "This trend persisted until the downfall of the Qing Dynasty. The difficulty of reform is made amply clear by the fact that any reform measures and remedies only led to the addition of extra taxes, and no service levies were ever truly eliminated." (Wang, 2012, pp. 123, 168)

"The service levy cannot be regarded simply as corvée labor." In the case of typical corvée labor, manpower was requisitioned for specific purposes (such as road maintenance and canal construction). Apart from manpower, the service levy covered other aspects of fiscal responsibility as well, including "a wide range of material and labor requisitions". Corvée labor arose from specific circumstances on an ad hoc basis, and "was never institutionalized". The service levy, on the other hand, was "fixed on a permanent or semi-permanent basis". Unlike the land tax, which followed the principle of uniform taxation, the service levy "was based on the concept of progressive taxation", and rich households often had to undertake greater responsibilities. (Huang. R 2008, p. 134)

4.1.2 Land Tax and Poll Tax ("The Grain Tax" and "The Textile Tax")[1]

The land tax and poll tax were regarded as the principal taxes prior to the Tang Dynasty. The land tax was the "grain tax", and the poll tax was similar to the "textile tax" (the "grain tax", "textile tax" and "labor tax" being the three types of taxes mentioned in the writings of Mencius). In the Qing Dynasty, the poll tax and labor tax were both merged into and levied as part of the land tax.

In the Han Emperor Gaozu's reign, the official tax rate was set at one-fifteenth. In Emperor Jing's reign, the tax rate was reduced to one-thirtieth. In the early Eastern Han Dynasty, the tax rate was once set at one-tenth, but in the Jianwu reign, Emperor Guangwu reverted to the old rate of one-thirtieth. The Han Dynasty levied quite light land tax from the farmers, but under the context of land acquisition by landlords, the light taxation only benefited the landlords instead of the poor people. In spite of the one-thirtieth land tax, the land owners took high rents from the tenant farmers, amounting to half of the harvest. The Han Dynasty levied a *suanfu*, similar to the poll tax of later dynasties. Each male person between the age of 15 and 56 was liable for the payment of 120 cash (called one *suan*) as poll tax. Merchants and private servants paid twice the normal amount. The revenue from *suanfu* was used for the supply of troops and the purchase and management of chariots and horses. In Emperor Wen's reign, thanks to population growth, a *suanfu* of only 40 cash was levied from an adult male above the age of 23 once every three years. This constituted a rate of only 13-odd cash for each adult male per year. Since Emperor Zhao and Emperor Xuan's reigns, the government sometimes lowered or even waived the payment of *suanfu*. In Emperor Hui's reign, a fivefold *suanfu* was imposed on unmarried girls aged between 15 and 30, but this was more of a social policy than a fiscal one. People below the minimum age for *suanfu* paid a different kind of poll tax called *koufu*. To alleviate financial pressures in Emperor Wu's reign, children reaching the age of 3 were subject to a *koufu* of 23 cash. Under this heavy burden, parents resorted to infanticide to evade this tax. Since Emperor Xuan's reign, the age limit for levying *koufu* was lifted up to 7.

When Cao Cao dominated the court in the late Eastern Han, he set the land tax at 4 *sheng* (1 sheng = 0.288 cubic meters) of grain per *mu* and the household tax at 2 bolts (*pi*) of silk and 2 catties (*jin*) of silk floss. Therefore, this was taxation calculated based on land area and the household. In the early years of Emperor Wu of the Jin, land tax was not levied so as to attract the families that had run away by granting them land. Instead, only silk and silk floss were collected from the household, with the actual amount depending on the size of the household, and this tax was called *hudiao*, or the household tax. In Emperor Cheng's reign, the farmlands were surveyed and a one-tenth tax was introduced, approximately three *sheng* of grain per *mu*. This was called the "grain tax". The Southern Dynasties did not have land to give out. The taxation had to be collected on the household since the immigrants owned no

[1] Refer to Chen (1977, pp. 319–325).

land to be taxed. In the Southern Dynasties, many common people sought protection under the gentry and wealthy families. In many cases, dozens of households were combined into a large one to evade taxation. The Northern Wei Dynasty implemented the Equal-land System and levied the household tax. A couple was supposed to pay two *dan* of grain and one bolt of silk each year. A couple's share of household tax was also levied on every four unmarried adult males (above the age of 15), or eight private servants engaged in farming and weaving, or ten plowing cattle. The Northern Qi, Northern Zhou and Sui Dynasties also adopted the household tax.

In the early Tang Dynasty, an adult male (aged between 20 and 60) paid two *dan* of millet each year, called the "grain tax". He also paid two *zhang* (cords) of silk of various qualities (*ling*, *juan* and *shi*) plus three *liang* (ounces) of silk floss in mulberry villages, or alternatively 2.4 *zhang* of fabric plus three catties of hemp in hemp villages. This was called the "textile tax". In case of a flood, drought or a locust disaster, the grain tax would be exempted if up to four tenths of the harvest were lost; both the grain tax and the textile tax would be exempted if six tenths of the harvest were lost; and the textile tax would be exempted if only the mulberry or hemp harvest was lost. A considerable number of people were exempted from taxation, including people granted such honorary titles as "filial son", "obedient grandson", "righteous man" and "chaste woman", students in the imperial capitals, imperial clansmen as well as state officials of rank 5 and higher together with their grandfather, father and brothers. In the middle Tang period, the Equal-land System became corrupted as a result of frequent transactions of land holdings. Coupled with the fact that adult males perished in large numbers and household registers were destroyed during the Rebellion of An Lushan and Shi Siming from AD 755 to 763, it became impossible to levy taxation by counting the adult males. The Two-season Taxation System arose in this context. Under this system, the grain, labor and textile taxes were converged into a single category and paid in cash. The tax was collected twice a year, in summer (not later than the sixth month) and autumn (not later than the eleventh month). Two Commissioners were designated to take comprehensive charge of the tax collection. Each year, a sub-prefecture or county would calculate its annual expenditure and taxes to be delivered to higher government levels. Then it would set its tax quota by budgeting taxation against expenditure. Residents were registered without regard to their being natives or non-natives. Taxation was based on the amount of wealth, rather than the number of adult males of a household. Merchants paid one thirtieth of their profit at the sub-prefecture or county where their commercial activities were carried out. As a measure to increase revenues of the imperial court, the Two-season Taxation System may have been effective in the short term. However, this system also had significant drawbacks. First, the Two-season Taxation System effected a change in the fundamental fiscal principle, shifting from budgeting expenditure on the basis of revenues to something like budgeting revenues on the basis of expenditure. From then on, the government could set the tax quotas according to its financial needs. "The simplified procedure of taxation could help prevent frauds on the part of officials, but did not necessarily benefit the common people." Second, the essence of the Tri-tax System of the Northern Dynasties, the Sui and the Tang lay in the equalization of land, while the Two-season Taxation System was only geared towards tax collection.

The Tri-tax System featured clearly defined categories of taxation, but under the Two-season Taxation System, all taxes were lumped under a single all-inclusive category. "Distributing farmland to people and levying the grain tax thus became levying the grain tax without distributing farmland." "The original intent of the Tang tax system, i.e., to ensure that everybody had land, was completely lost, so that polarization between the rich and the poor and takeovers of land became an unstoppable trend." Later, land acquisitions grew to such an extent that any hope of reviving the Equal-land System was irrevocably lost. Third, "payment of taxation in cash benefited the merchants but disadvantaged the farmers". Amidst price fluctuations across various localities, officials had more opportunities to practice frauds when labor and textile taxes had to be commuted into cash. Furthermore, under the Two-season Taxation System, taxation was based on the amount of land. However, information on land holdings reported by the officials was not always authentic, and rich families were more likely to profit from tampered data on land holdings (Qian, 1996a, pp. 417–421).

Taxation of the early Song Dynasty was one-twentieth or thirtieth, which was lighter than that of the Tang. Later, state revenues fell short of covering the expenditure as the Song struggled to cope with rising external threats, and Wang Anshi introduced the Equal Tax Law to survey the land and equally distribute the tax. However, Wang's massive reforms required enormous financial support as well. Consequently, the reforms were targeted at solving the financial problem of the state and became extortionate. Instead of benefiting the people, they sacrificed the interests of the people (Sa, 1975, pp. 44–45). Another factor that led to the failure of Wang Anshi's reforms was that he carried them out too hastily and neglected the inherent problems of the bureaucracy. "He stayed focused on a single goal and did not pay due attention to several key events in actual politics that were connected with his reforms." "He only valued inflexible laws, but ignored dynamic personnel affairs." (Qian, 1996b, pp. 574, 578) After failure of the reforms, the government only pursued the collection of higher taxes as its top priority.

In the early Ming Dynasty, taxation was levied on the household based on the household registers (Yellow Registers and White Registers), with the land regarded as household property. Registration of households and compilation of household registers were quite challenging tasks due to constant changes in the households. Thus, this method of taxation gradually became corrupted. In the 9th year of the Wanli reign (1581), Zhang Juzheng, the First Grand Secretary, implemented the Single Whip Method of Taxation (*yitiaobian fa*, 一条鞭法), a measure that was first introduced, and then discontinued and reinstated for several times in the Jiajing reign. This was another instrumental reform in the history of taxation (Huang. RY 1974, p. 299).[2] Under the previous system of taxation, a multitude of taxes in myriad categories were levied, including the land tax, labor services and local products,

[2] R. Y. Huang (1979, p. 428) believes that Zhang Juzheng held a comparatively cautious attitude towards the controversial Single Whip Method of Taxation and did not promote it throughout the country. "Though Ming-shih claims that general implementation of the Single Whip Reform was first decreed in 1581, within the period when Chang [Zhang] was in power, the statement is clearly erroneous. Only in 1588 did the governor of Shansi request its adoption in that province, by which time Chang Chü-cheng [Zhang Juzheng] had already been dead for six years."

imposing an unbearable burden on the common people. With the Single Whip Method of Taxation, all the taxes were consolidated into a single item levied in silver, and this made taxation slightly more convenient for the people. (Under the Two-season Taxation System of the Tang, the labor tax was merged with other taxes into a total tax, but later the labor tax arose again and was levied in parallel with the total tax. The Single Whip Method of Taxation essentially merged the labor tax a second time into the total tax.) In the Chongzhen reign of the Ming, the government introduced three extra levies (*sanxiang*, 三饷) on top of the Single Whip Method of Taxation to finance its military campaigns, which amounted to several times of the principal tax.

The early Qing Dynasty levied both the land tax and the *ding* tax. The *ding* registers were revised on a quinquennial basis, with the *ding* enumerated from household to household. Thanks to population growth, an imperial edict was issued in the Kangxi reign (1661–1722) to freeze the *ding* tax quotas based on the 1711 *ding* returns. Only since then was the *ding* tax lightened. In the Yongzheng reign (1722–1735), the *ding* tax was merged into the land tax and collected on the land in a reform called *tanding rumu*. (This reform could be easily implemented since the *ding* figures and ding tax quotas had been fixed in the Kangxi reign). After this reform, all taxation was levied from people with land holdings, while people without landed properties were not liable for any taxation. In the Guangxu reign, tribute grain was commuted into a payment in silver. A land levy called *mujuan* was imposed in addition to the land tax to pay the Boxer indemnity of 1900.

The taxation of the early Qing was apportioned between the land and taxable *ding* (adult males), and was therefore called land-*ding* tax (*didingyin*, 地丁银). The land tax was levied in cash based on the fertility of the soil. The *ding* tax resulted from failure of the late Ming Single Whip Method of Taxation to thoroughly merge the labor tax with the land tax and was essentially a combination of the poll tax and the service levy. Hence it was also called *dingyaoyin* (丁徭银) or *yaoliyin* (徭里银), i.e., labor service money. It was imposed on adult males aged between 16 and 60. In some provinces, the rates were classified into three grades and nine divisions according to the taxpayer's economic status. The tax rate varied in different provinces and also within the same province. "The tax rate ranged from 0.015 tael of silver to 1.3 or 1.4 tael, or even to eight or nine tael per *ding*." "In the north where the *ding* tax was heavy, it was generally levied by dividing *ding* into different grades based on their economic status; in the south where the ding tax was relatively light, a uniform tax rate was applied in most localities." Collection of the *ding* tax was extremely chaotic in the early Qing period. This was caused chiefly by government underlings who manipulated tax collection and landlords who shifted their tax burden to the poor. Crushed by the heavy tax burden, the poor deserted in large numbers to evade population registration. In order to meet the prescribed tax quotas, the local government had to impose a heavier *ding* tax on the remaining *ding* to compensate for the amount lost as a result of desertion. This further intensified the problem and brought about tax evasion on an even larger scale. It was under the dual pressures of intensified social contradictions and fiscal problems resulting from widespread tax evasions that reforms were carried out in the Kangxi and Yongzheng reigns. Levied along with *didingyin* was an extra charge called "meltage fee" (*huohao*, 火耗, silver lost in the process of melting). Theoretically speaking, people should pay their taxes in silver, but in reality, the government often levied the taxes in copper coins, but at a conversion rate higher than the market rate. As a result of massive flow of silver out of China in the late Qing Dynasty, deflation of silver against copper money became a grave problem and victimized the people immensely (Shi, 2019).

4.1.3 Tribute Grain and Its Transport

In the period of imperial China, a vast empire called for an enormous central government, which, in turn, gave rise to a metropolis around the central government. None of the capitals of ancient China, such as Chang'an and Beijing, was located in a food surplus area. In order to directly support the large number of officials of the central government and indirectly feed millions of inhabitants of the capital, grain had to be brought in from other regions. In the Sui and Tang periods, the Guanzhong Region (present-day central Shaanxi), though claimed to have an abundant supply of agricultural products, actually fell short of meeting the needs of the imperial palace and government officials for food. Coupled with inconvenient water and overland transport, hauling the grain to the metropolitan area was quite an arduous task. Consequently, the emperor often moved to Luoyang, which enjoyed convenient water transport, when food supply was insufficient in case of natural calamities in the Guanzhong Region. He did not return to Chang'an until a bumper harvest was secured in Guanzhong, hence the ridicule of "an emperor in pursuit of grains". Even up to the Ming and Qing Dynasties, the collection of tribute grain and its transport were still of paramount importance to the food security of the capital. In the Yuan Dynasty, the canal route was an auxiliary means of transport to shipment by sea. In the Ming and Qing, however, the Grand Canal constituted the most important route of transport between the imperial capital and Jiangnan (the region south of the lower Yangtze). It was responsible for conveying practically all supplies and could be regarded as the economic artery of the imperial court. In addition to grains which ranked at the top, the list of supplies also included fresh vegetables and fruit, poultry, textiles, timber, stationery, porcelain and lacquer. Virtually all goods produced in China were transported via the Grand Canal (Huang. RY 1964/2015, p. 16).

The early Qing Dynasty replicated the practice of the Ming in levying, in addition to the *didingyin*, tribute grain in a number of provinces (Shandong, Henan, Hunan, Hubei, Jiangxi, Jiangsu, Anhui and Zhejiang). Tribute grain was a tax in kind, collected mainly in the form of husked rice. Prior to the period of maritime transport, it was shipped through the Grand Canal to the granaries in Beijing or to Tongzhou. The tribute grain was used to meet such needs as the salaries of officials of the imperial capital and food supply for the Eight Banner troops. It was a special form of the land tax. "Any tax income could simultaneously comprise portions of transferred revenue and portions of retained revenue for the collecting district. From the retained revenue the local officials drew their salaries. The stipends due to government students and imperial clansmen were also derived from this portion, as were local relief payments authorized by the emperor. Any surplus was kept by the provincial or local official for the crown, and could not be disposed of without the emperor's approval." (Huang. RY 1974, pp. 23–24)

The amount of grain collected per *mu*, like the land tax, varied both among different provinces and among localities within the same province. Not all tribute grain was levied in kind; a portion was collected in silver in lieu of grain and was called *yongzhe* (永折, commuted permanently to cash). In some places, there was a practice called *gaizheng* (改征), whereby the grain was substituted by another product. There were also places where taxpayers handed in cash to the Magistrates, who in turn bought the grain. Tribute grain was subject to a number of surcharges. A definite allowance for wastage, called *haomi* (耗米), was collected for every *dan* of grain, in order to cover any loss in transit or in storage. In addition, taxpayers were required to pay various surtaxes to cover the cost of transport and of repairs to granaries. As a result of constantly rising surcharges and extra fees, a taxpayer often had to hand in three to four *dan* of grain for every *dan* of grain levied by the state. This made tribute grain an extremely heavy burden on the farmers. In some localities, taxpayers were required to pay cash in lieu of grain, which created an even greater burden on the farmers. Transport of tribute grain also imposed huge tasks on the local governments along the Grand Canal. The local officials along the Grand Canal must see to it that the grain boats were not obstructed by silted riverbeds and the tribute grain was not stolen or secretly sold. They must keep an eye on the boatmen so that they did not harass the local people or take illegal salt or other personal cargo along (Ch'ü, 1988, pp. 140–144).

The transport of tribute grain was an undertaking that required massive financial support. Not only was it necessary to maintain a huge transportation corps and a large number of officials for grain transport and waterway officials for treating and dredging the canal channel, but also repairs should be made regularly to the respective tools, equipment and, in particular, over one thousand grain boats. A scholar who studied the transport of tribute grain by taking the Ming Dynasty as an example has made the following observation: The operation of the tribute grain system could hardly be seen as profit-seeking. Take the tribute grain as an example. Although transported at a very high cost, the grain was from time to time sold on the market of Beijing at a price lower than its initial price. The use of corvée labor, especially for maintaining the watercourse, often did not enter the mind of officials in charge of this undertaking. At a time when the whole empire was concentrating its efforts in hauling grain to the north, merchants were busy transporting grain from the Huai River region to the south. However, considered from a broader perspective, such abuses and malpractices were only a portion of a whole set of problematic measures of management that characterized the administration of the government of that era (Huang. RY 1964/2015, p. 248).

4.1.4 Manipulation of Conversion Rates in Taxation and Abnormal Trades in Agricultural Products

From "Chapters on Light and Heavy" of *Guanzi*, it may be seen that the rulers of the Warring States period had understood how to secure financial gains by manipulating the conversion rates between various taxes in kind such as grain and textile. They compelled the ordinary people to trade textile for grain or vice versa, therefore inducing abnormal trades and bringing forth speculative merchants (including official merchants) who made profits from the price differentials. Since the founding of the Tang Dynasty, people were supposed to pay the taxation in grain. In the 25th year of the Kaiyuan reign (AD 737), it was decreed that the taxation should be paid in textile in Jiangnan prefectures. This payment of taxation in textile in lieu of grain was an old practice of the Southern Dynasties. It began to be promoted in Empress Wu Zetian's reign and became an established practice in the Kaiyuan reign. It was considered to be "a major reform in the fiscal system of the state". Then through *hedi*, literally harmonious purchase of grain, the government would buy grain from the farmers of Guanzhong at a comparatively low price with textile (as a universal equivalent). In the flourishing reign of Emperor Xuanzong when the state coffers were full and people were well off, the government was able to purchase grain from the people at a reasonable price. However, after the Rebellion of An Lushan and Shi Siming from AD 755 to 763 when the state treasury was depleted, the government naturally tended to purchase grain from the people by force at a price below the market price. For the people who were already impoverished and could barely make ends meet, *hedi* was transformed into a policy that plagued and exploited them. Up to the reigns of Emperors Dezong and Xianzong, *hedi* (和籴) became a method for seizing the farmers' staple products by force that had to be strictly enforced. (Chen, 2001, pp. 164–174)

When a portion of his taxation had to be paid to the government in cash or another universal equivalent, the farmer had to trade his agricultural products on the market for cash. Therefore, to a large extent, a farmer selling his products was not doing so to get the money for his own consumption, but to secure the cash for tax payment. "The early emergence and use of currency in China was not entirely divorced from the attempt of rulers to seek a method of taxation with the minimal cost of exchange." Out of its selfish considerations, the government constantly manipulated the conversion rates, which indirectly raised the tax rates. "Consequently, we are faced with a paradox: On the one hand, 'fake' trades between farmers and the market were on the rise; on the other hand, the purchasing power of the farmers for their own consumption exhibited a steady downward trend. Restrained by this factor, the prospects for expansion of the ancient Chinese market became quite bleak." In fact, the phenomenon that farmers were often hurt by low grain prices after a bumper harvest may to a considerable extent be attributed to tricks played by the government in manipulating the conversion rates in taxation (Wang, 2012, pp. 185–187).

4.1.5 Miscellaneous Taxes

i. Taxes on the rich. In the Han Dynasty, merchants vied with kings and marquises in personal wealth, and Emperor Gaozu disgraced them with heavy taxation. Merchants and private servants were required to pay twice the normal amount of *suanfu*, which was 120 cash for the common people. Private servants were heavily taxed because only the wealthy could afford to have servants. Emperor Wu of the Han introduced the *suanmin* tax, a levy on commerce as well as on boats and carts. People evading the tax were subject to military service at the frontier for one year and confiscation of property. The informants were awarded with one half of the confiscated property. In the late Northern Qi, the government encountered a fiscal crisis and imposed taxes on six grades of rich people. Emperor Yang of the Sui also imposed taxes on the rich based on their amount of wealth. With the collapse of the Tri-tax System in the middle Tang period, both the central government and the Military Zones levied taxes from the rich. The Song and Jurchen-led Jin governments collected labor tax from rich households. The Jurchen Jin government imposed taxation on all properties, such as land, houses, carriages and livestock, not just on the rich. This taxation was similar to the present-day capital tax, property tax or income tax. In the late Qing Dynasty, salt merchants were required to turn in money, sometimes amounting to millions of taels of silver.

ii. Local tribute. It was not until the middle Ming Dynasty when the Single Whip Method of Taxation was implemented that the land tax, labor tax and local tribute were consolidated into a single item, to be paid in silver to the government based on the amount of land. Nevertheless, Palace Attendants (*neishi*, 内史) often purchased local products by force in the name of acquisition of goods for the imperial palace.

iii. Sale of official ranks, offices, degrees, and redemption for criminal penalties. In the late Qing Dynasty, Yuan Shih-k'ai memorialized to have the malpractice of selling offices and degrees abolished.

iv. Other taxes such as business tax and title deed tax. Under the Jurchen Jin system, for trading in private servants, cattle and horses, land and houses, the traders were taxed at 4% of the value of the traded object as recorded on the official certificate (*wenquan*, 文券), 3% on the seller and 1% on the buyer respectively. For objects whose value was not officially documented, a tax of 4% was still levied on the turnover determined based on spontaneous assessment (*sangu*, 散估). The Southern Dynasties continued this arrangement, except for the fact that both the seller and the buyer were taxed. This marked the beginning of the title deed tax in ancient China. Since the middle Tang period, there was the house tax, the *chumo* (除陌) tax levied on cash transaction, and the green-shoot (*qingmiao*, 青苗) and field (*ditou*, 地头) money levied on the land. The Song Dynasty had miscellaneous taxes such as *jingzhi qian* (经制钱, a supplementary tax collected to cover regional military and administrative expenses). The Yuan Dynasty had *ewaike* (额外课), or extra levies, a generic term for all kinds of miscellaneous taxes. The Ming Dynasty had the fish tax, commercial tax and mining tax. The Qing Dynasty had the sales tax (for cotton, tobacco, liquor, etc.), title deed tax (on the sale of land and houses), shop tax, brokerage tax, pawnshop tax, tax on the sale of livestock such as cattle and horses, tea tax, fish tax, and so on. The magistrate was required to deliver to the Regional Administrative Commission the entire sum collected from the taxpayers.

v. Customs duty. The customs duty was collected by the Customs Commissioner or customs agencies established at the treaty ports.
vi. The *lijin* (厘金) tax. The *lijin* tax was an internal tariff levied on commodities in transit. Initiated in 1853, it was earmarked for supporting military forces recruited to put down the Taiping Rebellion. Since the year of 1862, the *lijin* tax was turned into a local tax.

4.2 Regulation of Prices and State Control and Monopoly: Centering on Salt Administration

4.2.1 Regulation of Prices

In Chinese history, there has always been the thought that "one should not be concerned about poverty, but rather about the uneven distribution of wealth". Although various dynasties adopted different methods, they all worked towards the goal of "promoting trade to enrich the country, ensuring sufficient food supply for the people via famine and disaster relief, dampening fluctuations in the prices of goods, and curbing monopoly by the powerful interests." In the *Rites of Zhou*, there was the official of Director of Markets (*sishi*, 司市), who had the locations of shops arranged based on the categories of their goods to ensure fair trading and prohibited the sale of impractical luxury goods to effect uniform prices. Li Kui (counsellor of the Wei in the Warring States period), pioneered the *pingtiao* (平粜) system for stabilizing grain prices. Under this system, the local government purchased grain in times of a bumper harvest as a reserve and sold the grain in times of famine. *Records of the Grand Historian* comments that "if prices are kept stable, there will not be a shortage of supply on the market and the government will have adequate tax revenues". Acting on the advice of Sang Hongyang, the Superintendent of Finance, Emperor Wu of the Han implemented the *junshu* (均输, regulating the transports) and *pingzhun* (平准, leveling the prices) system. *Junshu* officials were set up in commanderies and subordinate kingdoms, and the various regions were ordered to select local produces whose local supply was excessive and sent them to the central government as tribute. This would raise the local prices of these products. The government then transported these goods to localities where there was a shortage of supply and sold them out. *Pingzhun* officials were designated in the capital areas. "They took monopolized control over all commodities flowing into the capital from the whole country. They would buy in when goods were cheap and sell out when prices were high, hence rendering any speculative attempts by private merchants unprofitable." Emperor Wu of the Jin tried to implement the *pingdi* (平籴) policy (buying in grains when prices were low) and failed, but the policy was eventually adopted in the Northern Wei. From the Han Emperor Xuan's reign down to the Ming and Qing Dynasties, state-run granaries called *changping cang* (常平仓, ever-normal granaries) were set up across the country, chiefly to prepare for the eventuality of famine. These granaries bought in grains when prices were low and sold them out when prices were high. They were created to forestall sharp fluctuations in prices, not for the purpose of suppressing commercial activities. In Emperor Shenzong's reign of the Song, there was the *junshu* (均输) method and the *shiyi* (市易, market exchange) method. Although different methods were used in the past dynasties, they were all aimed at regulating the market prices of goods and increasing government revenues.

Junshu and *pingzhun* were both well-intentioned concepts, but out of realistic fiscal considerations, the government often sought solid benefits in their name. Coupled with the manipulation of unscrupulous officials and nimble merchants, *junshu* and *pingzhun* often ran the risk of becoming policies that plagued the populace. The policy of setting up *changping cang* was also quite questionable. For example, the policy of *hedi* (和籴, harmonious purchase of grain) was created by Emperor Xuanzong of the Tang to address the fiscal difficulties of the government. According to this policy, the Palace Administrator of Finance would buy in grains at higher than market prices when grains were too cheap and sell them out at lower than market prices when grains were too expensive. Later, harmonious purchase at fair prices was turned into enforced purchase at low prices. For another example, in the Kaihuang reign of the Sui, the government encouraged the establishment of *shecang* (社仓, local community granaries), in order to set up grain reserves against unexpected famines. However, *shecang* gradually became *yicang* (义仓, charity granaries), for which the government collected grains from the common people by force. The Tang continued the system of *yicang* of the Sui, except that "the originally voluntary charity mechanism was turned into a compulsory tax, which became a major tax revenue under the Two-season Taxation System since the middle Tang period" (Chen, 2001, pp. 164, 167).

4.2.2 State Control and Monopoly and the Salt and Iron[3] Issue

In ancient China, equal importance was accorded to state control and monopoly, not just to monopoly alone. Besides "securing profits", state control also occupied a vital

[3] Both the establishment of salt and iron officials and the debate on salt and iron policies originated in the Han Dynasty. The treatise *Discourses on salt and iron* was also completed in the Han Dynasty. Although after the Han Dynasty, salt and iron were still mentioned together, restrictions on iron were comparatively looser than those on salt. Therefore, only the administration of salt will be touched upon in the discussion of post-Han salt and iron policies later in this book.

position in the political and economic thoughts of ancient China. "China has fallen behind in virtually all aspects, but when it comes to the domain of salt administration, China is still well ahead of other countries. Indeed, back when Western countries still knew little about the administration of salt, China had formulated quite a complete system of laws for administering the salt trade." (Ou, 1935, p. 2)

i. Origin of *Discourses on salt and iron*

In the early Western Han period, the emperors followed the Daoist principle of ruling through inaction and advocated thrift. Fiscal powers were not concentrated in the central government, and a liberal attitude was adopted towards private undertakings such as salt boiling, iron smelting and coin minting. In the reign of Emperor Wu of the Han, a great strain was placed on the state treasury owing to the military campaigns against the nomadic Xiongnu Confederation. In order to raise fiscal revenues, salt and iron enterprises were nationalized and merchants were appointed as officials to administer salt and iron trades (Du, 1988, p. 227). In the Chinese history, the institutionalization of control over salt and iron started with Kong Jin and Dongguo Xianyang, two merchants-turned officials in charge of salt and iron under Emperor Wu of the Han. Then, this trend was further strengthened by Sang Hongyang, who took salt and iron as the center around which the entire undertaking to monopolize all commercial activities of the whole country hinged. Sang Hongyang turned an ad hoc fiscal measure during the wartime into a unified fiscal system of the imperial government (Xu, 2001, p. 84).[4] In the time of Kong Jin and Dongguo Xianyang, the offices in charge of salt and iron trade were under the jurisdiction of the local government. Sang Hongyang shifted this administrative power to the central government and put it in the hands of the Superintendent of Finance. Only in this way could the empire have a unified fiscal system. With respect to the *junshu* and *pingzhun* system, simply put, *junshu* was intended to regulate the transports, and *pingzhun* to stabilize the prices of goods. Under the scheme proposed by Sang Hongyang and endorsed by Emperor Wu, the Superintendent of Finance set up *junshu* officials in the commanderies and subordinate kingdoms, who took care of the levied local produces as well as their transport to the imperial capital and other localities. The Superintendent of Finance also designated *pingzhun* officials in the capital areas, who took comprehensive charge of the commodities delivered to the imperial capital by the *junshu* officials. With the exception of commodities needed by the government, the *pingzhun* officials dealt with the commodities in the capacity of official merchants, buying in when prices were low and selling out when prices were high.

State control over salt and iron (operation by the government) led to a series of problems. ("Iron tools produced by the government were of poor quality and high prices, and the farmers were forced to pay for them; when taxes were levied on boats, there were less merchants and prices went up.") These problems undermined

[4] *Guanzi* and *The Book of Lord Shang* touched upon the administration of salt and iron. Quite a number of scholars believe that salt administration started with Guan Zhong of the Qi State as *Guanzi* was in favor of state monopoly on salt. However, this is not a verifiable historical fact, and even the era in which *Guanzi* was compiled is subject to controversy.

the livelihood of the common people. The first to oppose salt and iron monopolies by the state was an official named Bu Shi.

In the 6th year of the Shiyuan reign of Emperor Zhao of the Han (81 BC), Huo Guang, the Grand Commander-General, summoned all the Confucian scholars of the empire to the imperial capital to debate the government's economic policies. The Confucian scholars all insisted that state monopolies over salt, iron and liquor as well as the *junshu* and *pingzhun* system should be abolished, and that the government should not enter into competition with the people for profit. Sang Hongyang, the Censor-in-chief argued against the Confucian scholars on the following grounds: The state monopolies over salt, iron and liquor were crucial state policies that filled up the state coffers and financed the military campaigns to defend China from barbarian incursions. Furthermore, the profits from salt and iron could be easily monopolized by local magnates and wealthy merchants, who might pose a threat to the state and exploit the common people.[5] The profits derived from state monopolies over salt and iron could be used to cover military expenses and as funds for famine relief. Thus, the state monopolies should not be abolished. The Confucian scholars maintained that a gentleman should value righteousness above material gains, and that private ventures in salt and iron were harmless to the state. Sang Hongyang pointed out that the *junshu* and *pingzhun* system ensured fair trading on the market, and once they were abolished, the market would be monopolized by the local magnates and wealthy merchants. In summary, the Confucian scholars held that state control of salt and iron was competition with the people for profit and it oppressed and exploited the common people. Sang Hongyang, on the other hand, maintained that it had a bearing on state prosperity and market stability. The two sides also discussed other issues such as whether the country should be ruled by virtue or by law. In the end, the imperial court partially adopted the view of the Confucian scholars in abolishing the monopoly on liquor, as well as the monopoly on iron trade in the Guannei Region (central Shaanxi).[6]

Viewed from a modern perspective, the debate on salt and iron policies in the reign of Emperor Zhao was a constitutional case which had a bearing on the fiscal policies of the state. It was similar to a congressional debate (hearing), and the *Discourses on Salt and Iron* compiled by Huan Kuan was a record of this debate (hearing).[7]

---

[5] *Records of the grand historian · Treatise on Pingzhun* (Sima, 1982, p. 1425) has the following account: "The state treasury was depleted. The wealthy merchants took advantage of this opportunity to stock supplies and enslave the poor. They made such large fortunes that even the aristocrats had to ask for loans humbly from them. They accumulated enormous wealth by smelting iron and boiling salt, but would not lend a helping hand to alleviate the crises plaguing the state. Consequently, the common people became even more impoverished".

[6] This paragraph is a summary of the court debate on salt and iron as recorded in *Comprehensive statutes*. For details, see Chap. 10 of "Treatise on food and commodities" in Du (1988, pp. 227–229).

[7] The court meeting on salt and iron was held in the 6th year of Emperor Zhao's reign of the Han (81 BC). In the early years of Emperor Xuan's reign of the Han, Huan Kuan edited the minutes of this meeting into a book titled *Discourses on salt and iron*. Out of the 60 chapters of this book, 59 chapters are a record of the arguments of the two sides to this debate, presented in a dialogue format, and the last chapter "Miscellaneous notes to the book" explains how this book came to be written and the author's opinions on this issue (Huan, 1990).

Salt and iron were vital resources of the state and daily necessities of the people. From an economic perspective, there was little elasticity in their demands, and the enormous profits from boiling salt and smelting iron were quite conspicuous. In the early Han Dynasty, the state imposed no legal restrictions on salt and iron, and Emperor Wen even allowed "the people to mint coins, smelt iron and boil salt". In order to cope with the fiscal difficulties of his time, Emperor Wu nationalized the production and trade of salt and iron. Urged by Sang Hongyang, the Censor-in-chief and son of a merchant of Luoyang, Emperor Wu promulgated the law calling for state control on salt and iron (operation by the government). From then on, the Han government secured a tight grip on the two pillar industries at that time: salt boiling and iron smelting. According to the "Treatise on Geography" of the *Book of Han*, there were 48 iron offices and 38 salt offices across the country at that time. Under the direction of the central government, these salt and iron offices conveyed countless revenues to the state treasury. However, the state monopoly policies on salt and iron met with adamant opposition from Confucian scholars who prioritized righteousness over profits. They believed that these policies were essentially "competition with the people for profits". This debate also entailed the conflict between the thinking of "storing wealth among the people", advocated by Confucianists, and the thinking of "storing wealth in the state", advocated by the Legalists. In the court conference about salt and iron policies held in 81 BC, the policies of state control over salt and iron came under fierce attacks from the Confucian scholars. The bureaucrats who were pragmatic Legalists, represented by the Censor-in-chief Sang Hongyang, had to make some concessions to the Confucian scholars and repealed the state monopoly on liquor, as well as state control over iron in Guannei. However, a memorial submitted by the Prime Minister contained an intriguing comment about the Confucian scholars that "they did not have a clear idea about local administration". Does it mean the scholars did not understand the local conditions, were not familiar with the art of shepherding the people and merely engaged in empty talks? Then why was their opinion accepted and a decree was issued to remove the state monopoly on liquor, as well as state control over iron in Guannei. According to Ou Zongyou, the bureaucrats believed: "The Confucian scholars are mere stay-homes who are unable to attract and subdue the barbarians from afar and thus make our borders secure from invasions. If they were able to do that, all the taxes could be removed, not just those on salt and iron." ("Ills of the State" of the *Discourses on Salt and Iron*). Therefore, the bureaucrats removed some monopoly measures only because they wanted to put an end to the debate by appeasing the Confucian scholars. Taking the advice of the Prime Minister, Emperor Zhao removed the monopoly on liquor but retained the monopoly on salt (Ou, 1935, pp. 14–21). According to *Laws and Regulations since Ancient Times* by Du You of the Tang Dynasty, in addition to the monopoly on liquor, the iron offices of Guannei were also removed. The abolition of iron offices but not the monopoly on salt may have been due to the following reasons: First, the iron monopoly may have disadvantaged the populace even more and aroused greater discontent among the people. Second, if the "appeasement theory" of Ou Zongyou was right, then it may be inferred that salt played a far more important role than iron in the fiscal revenues of the Han government. This also explains why in later times restrictions on the iron trade were gradually loosened, whereas government control of the salt trade was always reinstated after repeated abolitions.[8] In his study of the history of thoughts in the Western and Eastern Han Dynasties, Xu (2001, pp. 73–131) believes that behind the debate on salt and iron lay the battle between the Inner Court (Huo Guang) and the Outer Court (Sang Hongyang), disputes over the frontier policies as well as other political, social and cultural factors. We will not go into further details about these points here due to the limitation of space.

ii. Further debates on salt and iron (centering on salt) after the court conference

Following the court conference on salt and iron discussed above, the question of whether state control over salt and iron should be continued was picked up time and again in later times:

> In the period of Empress Xiaoyuan, the salt offices were abolished, only to be revived three years later.
>
> In Emperor Zhang's reign of the Eastern Han, Zhang Lin, Director of the Imperial Secretariat, memorialized: "As a daily necessity, salt cannot be dispensed with even if it is expensive. It is advisable for the government to control its sale."
>
> …
>
> In the 2nd year of the Tianjia reign (AD 561) of Emperor Wen of the Chen, Yu Li (Palace Cadet to the Crown Prince) and Kong Huan (Palace Aide to the Censor-in-chief) memorialized to impose a tax on boiling sea salt, and the request was approved.
>
> In Emperor Xuanwu's reign of the Northern Wei, there were salt ponds in Hedong Commandery. There used to be a government office established to levy the salt tax, but it had long been abolished. The salt ponds became monopolized by powerful and wealthy families, while the poor and meek could not derive any benefits therefrom. At the end of the Yanxing reign, the salt office was reinstated to levy the salt tax and regulate the salt price, which benefited both the government and the people … After that, the salt office was removed and re-established repeatedly until the Yongxi reign. Since the capital was moved to Ye, sea salt was produced in the coastal area of the four regions of Cang, Ying, You and Qing… All expenditures of the troops and the state could be covered by revenues from the salt taxation.
>
> …
>
> In the eleventh month of the first year of the Kaiyuan reign (AD 713) of the Tang Dynasty, … Emperor Xuanzong instructed the courtiers to discuss the feasibility [of levying the salt tax]. All the courtiers believed that the profits from salt and iron could be used to cover government expenditures … Since the Shangyuan reign, government offices were set up to levy the salt tax, and the annual revenue from the salt tax amounted to over nine million cash. (Du, 1988, pp. 229–232)

Historical records between Emperor Wu of the Han and the Tang Dynasty seemed to be in favor of state monopolies on salt and iron. In addition to raising fiscal revenues to cover expenditures of the government, the monopolies were said to be beneficial to both the state and the people. Increased state revenues could not only fund the military and government undertakings but also sponsor efforts to improve people's

[8] In fact, in the account of salt and iron in the "Treatise on food and commodities" of *Comprehensive Statutes*, although salt and iron are sometimes mentioned together, salt is mentioned alone in many more instances, and not even once is iron administration mentioned in isolation. It may be reckoned from this that iron carried by far less weight than salt in the fiscal system.

livelihood and settle refugees. "The fund can be used to purchase plowing oxen, to be provided to the returning refugees. This can encourage people to apply themselves to agriculture so as to secure bumper harvests in Guanzhong." (Du, 1988, pp. 229–230) In the Kaiyuan reign of the Tang Dynasty, when Liu Tong (Left Reminder) touched upon the subject of salt and iron in a memorial to the throne, he particularly stressed the role of state control on salt and iron in promoting agriculture and restraining commerce, and highly commended the salt and iron policies of Emperor Wu of the Han. He said that these policies, which both reinforced agriculture and enriched the country, represented sound governance and the way to supremacy and should be upheld as the model to follow. "Indeed, boiling salt from the sea, minting coins and cutting timber from the mountain, these trades are undertaken by the wealthy. Those who are hired by others or cannot afford their own clothing and food are the poor. If the government can wrest from rich industrialists and merchants the profits out of the mountains and seas, it can lighten the burden of taxation on the poor. This is the so-called "supplementing the deficient by diminishing the excessive". "Isn't this the kingly way to run a country?" (Du, 1988, p. 231) In spite of their theoretical arguments against state monopolies on salt and iron, the Confucianists were unable to impede the de facto advances of the government to further monopoly the profits of salt and iron.[9] Although salt and iron offices were repeatedly abolished and revived, it may be seen that in the course of time, there was a steady increase in the government's reliance on profits from salt and iron. The government seemed to have become so addicted to salt and iron monopolies that it could no longer extricate itself from them. When discussing this issue, Chen (1977, pp. 332–333) came to the following conclusion:

[9] When discussing revenues derived from the administration of salt, Lü (2002, p. 479) says: "Taxes should be levied from multiple sources, and then the government will have sufficient revenues and people will not be crushed under the heavy burden of taxation. However, Chinese politicians did not have a clear understanding of this point. Prior to the Sui and Tang Dynasties, the land tax and poll tax were regarded as the principal taxes. Since the middle Tang period, tax revenues of the imperial government became scanty as large amounts of land became dominated by the Military Zones. As a result, the government had to turn to miscellaneous taxes such as salt and iron taxes for revenues. Since the Song Dynasty, salt and iron taxes became indispensable revenues for the government. Up to now, the salt tax has come to account for a major proportion of the revenues of the state. In spite of its de facto rise in importance, the salt tax was never regarded as a sound source of revenue by scholars in ancient China from a theoretical perspective." Theoretically, the Chinese government had always adhered to the thinking of "promoting agriculture and restricting industries and commerce" and regarded the land tax and poll tax as the principal taxes. In reality, however, the government grew increasingly reliant on revenues from miscellaneous items such as salt and iron. With the respect to the term of "salt tax" used by Lü, the author thinks its interpretation may be expanded to mean revenues from salt in general (including both the salt tax and revenue from the monopoly on salt trade). Lü has put the salt and iron issue in the chapter titled *zheng-que* (征榷). In classical Chinese, *que* (榷) may be interpreted as either "levying of taxes by the government" or "state monopoly". ("Biography of Che Qianqiu" of the *Book of Han* records: "Believing he had helped generate revenues from state monopoly (*que*) and control, Sang Hongyang felt proud of his accomplishment." The commentary says *que* here means to monopolize the trade and secure profit for the government. When *que* is mentioned alongside with *guan* (筦, state control), it does not make sense if interpreted as "levying taxes".)

> The State of Qi imposed control on profits from mountains and seas, and the State of Qin (which later became the Qin Dynasty) had state monopolies on salt and iron. The Han Dynasty instituted salt and iron offices to control these industries, prohibited the common people from brewing liquor and put the liquor business exclusively in the hands of the government. These practices were continued all the way down to the Qing Dynasty, except for some adjustments in the scope of control and monopoly. Wang Mang imposed control on six industries, and the Jurchen-led Jin Dynasty had state monopolies on ten industries. These were historical periods with the largest number of state controls and monopolies. The Qing had the least monopolies, only on salt and tea. In ancient China, the establishment of state control and monopoly was regarded by some as competition with the people for profit, and attempts were made to abolish them to show that the government was willing to share the profits with the people. However, the consequences were not reassuring. Powerful and wealthy families would take advantage of these opportunities to seize the resources, and brutal and violent forces would rise up to acquire more properties. The common people did not become better off, and nor was the state more affluent. This is the reason why the state control and monopoly always ended up being reinstated after repeated abolitions. (Chen, 1977)

iii. Paradoxes in the salt and iron debate

Ou (1935, pp. 14–21) summed up Sang Hongyang's justifications for state monopolies on salt and iron as follows:

1. Legal justification: As a Chinese saying goes, "All the land under heaven belongs to the Monarch." According to the law, salt is owned by the emperor. Therefore, it makes perfect sense if the government imposes a monopoly on the operation of this business.
2. Fiscal justification: The government wished to conquer foreign enemies and stabilize its territory, enrich the country and strengthen its troops. Huge expenses were required for all these efforts. Profits derived from salt would be sufficient to cover these expenses without causing pain to the people. There were no other sources of such huge revenues available at that time.
3. Political justification: In case such power and wealth were seized by people from lower echelons of the political hierarchy, they could rise in power and attempt to topple the government. (For example, the King of Wu became increasingly powerful through salt production and coinage in the reign of Emperor Wen of the Han. He later revolted in the reign of Emperor Jing.)
4. Social (economic) justification: The production of salt was not possible without the investment of large capitals. Those owning vast amounts of capital were prone to engage in speculation and manipulation of prices, which would widen the gap between the rich and the poor.

At first sight, these four justifications offered by Sang Hongyang seem to be valid, but they cannot stand the test of further scrutiny. The first justification was too domineering and ran contrary to the Confucian thinking that the government should not enter into competition with the people for profit. If we proceed further along this line of thinking, private properties as well as private industries and commerce would all be stripped of their legitimacy. The rise of a group of economic bureaucrats represented by Sang Hongyang as a result of state monopolies on salt, iron and liquor (or may be called monopolies by bureaucratic capital), together with the colossal wealth and extravagance of their families (Xu, 2001, p. 93) constituted a partial negation of the fourth justification, and by the same token, of the third justification. Some people even suspected that all the theories advanced by Sang Hongyang were no more than a pretext, and went on to completely refute the legitimacy of participation and intervention by the government in commercial (economic) activities. "Policies such as state monopolies on salt, iron and liquor, *junshu* (regulation of transportation by the state), and the *suanmin* tax (a tax on commerce, boats and carts) were introduced in the name of suppressing the powerful and wealthy families, but they all ended up disadvantaging the people. The truth behind these policies might be that suppression of the powerful and wealthy families was not the original motive, but an excuse after all." (Du, 1988, p. 483) What remains now is only the fiscal justification, the most practical consideration for the government, but even this justification is not so impeccable. At least the reasoning of "not causing pain to the people" was weakened by rising salt prices as a result of monopoly by the bureaucratic capital. The fact that "iron tools produced by the government were of poor quality and high prices, and the farmers were forced to pay for them" was another counter-argument against state monopoly. Among all these arguments in favor of state monopoly, only two points can survive our scrutiny. First, profits from salt (and iron) could meet the government's fiscal needs. This point needs no explanation. Second, state control and monopolies on salt and iron served to facilitate the government's control over the economy, which could accomplish the same objectives listed in the third and fourth justifications. Control over the economy could strengthen the concentration of power on the one hand, and check the growth of merchants on the other. In ancient China, control and monopoly were often mentioned alongside with each other, not just monopoly in isolation. In addition to securing profits, control occupied a vital position in the political and economic thinking of ancient China as well.

Upholding the Confucian thinking of "placing righteousness above material gains" and "storing wealth among the people", the Confucian scholars were opposed to state intervention in the economic life of the people as well as the *junshu* and *pingzhun* system centering around state monopolies on salt and iron. However, this in effect facilitated accumulation of wealth as well as monopoly and speculation by private merchants, which contradicted the Confucian thinking of promoting agriculture and suppressing commerce. Therefore, if checked against the vital Confucian principle of prioritizing agriculture above commerce, the above view of the Confucian scholars was self-defeating. From the perspective of modern economics, we may venture to say that the scheme proposed by the Confucian scholars, at least in terms of its outcome, checked the advance of nationalization and defended a liberal market economy (commodity economy). Of course, we may deny that promoting agriculture and suppressing commerce was peculiar to the Confucian school of thought. In fact, it may have been a piece of common ground shared by Confucianism, Daoism and Legalism based on the basic understanding that China was a rural society. ("On the formulation of economic policies, there were points where Confucianism and Legalism converged. On the goal of policies, Confucianism and Daoism shared some common language." (Xu, 2001, p. 86) Nevertheless, it was after all an important thought of Confucianists after Xunzi. In the early Han Dynasty, the government used taxation as the leverage to regulate the market and attempted to restrain merchants by means of heavy taxation. However, it turned out that "the merchants, who were despised under the law, eventually grew rich, and the farmers, who were held in esteem, were made destitute and humble. What was cherished by the people was despised by the ruler; what was looked down upon by the officials was venerated under the law. With such contradictions and paradoxes, it was impossible to enrich the state and render the law firmly established." ("Treatise on food and commodities Part One" of the *Book of Han*) Emperor Wu of the Han implemented the *junshu* and *pingzhun* system to take control of the market through direct state intervention in the economy and nationalization of vital industries.

In terms of the actual well-being of the people, both sides to the debate were losers. Instead of achieving their professed goal of enriching the common people, the idealistic Confucian scholars in effect only encouraged the takeovers, exploitation and speculation of wealthy merchants and local magnates. The outcome of their proposal was also a refutation of their own principle (of promoting agriculture and suppressing commerce). The realistic Legalists (represented by Sang Hongyang) were defeated by the bureaucratic system and lost the support of the people. The dilemma of the salt and iron policies also foreshadowed the paradoxes in the reforms introduced by Wang Anshi in the Northern Song Dynasty. (Wang Anshi liked to speak of profit, but eventually failed to profit the country or the people. Those who opposed his reforms could repeal the policies that wrought havoc, but were unable to introduce their own policies to benefit the government and the people.)

The Legalists represented by Sang Hongyang, who recommended controlling the economy via nationalization, could neither convince the Confucian scholars in theory nor improve the well-being of the people in reality. Nevertheless, state control and monopoly became more and more entrenched and indisputable in the course of time. The root causes underlying this trend were the realistic fiscal needs and political philosophy of control on the part of the rulers. Realistic political considerations prevailed over Confucian doctrines and ideals of a better life for the people, with fiscal needs being the top political consideration.

State monopoly on salt was not peculiar to ancient China,[10] but such heavy reliance on salt for fiscal revenue was indeed seldom witnessed in countries other than ancient China (As a saying goes, "Profits from salt account for half of the state revenues", and even up to the early Republican period, the central government of China was still requesting loans from foreign bankers using salt tax as the security for repayment). The underdeveloped state of capitalism (private industries and commerce) in China may have played a role. In contrast, Britain in history did not have the system of state monopolies, and the salt tax was abolished and revived time and again. There was a time "when the market was filled with smuggled salt, resulting in substantial loss in revenue from the salt tax. Various measures were taken to stop salt smuggling, but they only inconvenienced the people without achieving the desired goal. Later

[10] For a comparison of the evolution and status quo (up to the time when the author wrote the book) of salt administration across different countries of the world, please see Lin (1930, pp. 7–18).

as fishing and industries flourished, … the salt tax was resolutely put to an end in 1825" (Lin, 1930, p. 9). On the other hand, in such a vast empire as China, neither the state was powerful nor the people well-off up to the late Qing Dynasty. This may have been the crux of the salt problem (and even of the fiscal problem) in ancient China.

iv. Evolution of the system of salt administration in ancient China

1. Overview of salt policies in ancient China (and comparison with salt policies of other countries of the world)

"China has fallen behind in virtually all aspects, but when it comes to the domain of salt administration, China is still well ahead of other countries. Indeed, back when Western countries still knew little about the administration of salt, China had formulated quite a complete system of laws for administering the salt trade." (Ou, 1935, p. 2) The system of salt administration in ancient China varied from dynasty to dynasty, and even within the same dynasty, it also differed from time to time and from locality to locality. Broadly speaking, the system of salt administration existed mainly in the following three types (Zeng, 1936, pp. 1–2):

(1) No salt tax.[11] This arrangement was based on the belief that salt was a daily necessity and the common people should be allowed to take and supply it free from any tax or monopoly. (This arrangement was only found prior to the three dynasties of antiquity (Xia, Shang and Zhou) as well as in the Sui and early Tang Dynasties.)
(2) Salt tax. This arrangement was based on the argument that the amount of tax needed by a person was small even though it was indispensable. Therefore, the tax burden of the people was not heavy and tax collection was fairly convenient. The salt tax, which accounted for a major proportion of the state's fiscal revenues, could be used to cover military and state expenditures. The tax was levied at the center of salt production. Once the tax was collected, salt could be transported and traded freely by private merchants without any restrictions whatsoever. (This arrangement was adopted in the three dynasties of Xia, Shang and Zhou, the Qin, the early Western Han, the Eastern Han and the Six Dynasties.)
(3) Salt monopoly. The argument for this arrangement lay in the belief that salt was too vital a business to fall into the hands of merchants and should be run by the state. This could not only prevent the exploitation and speculation by the capitalists (suppressing merchants), but also lighten the burden on the common people and increase government revenues. This arrangement had five sub-types: ① Partial monopoly/monopoly of a narrow scope: Salt production was undertaken mainly by private producers and to a limited extent by the government. Transport and sales were controlled by the government (as recorded in *Guanzi*). ② Full monopoly/monopoly of a broad scope: Production, transport and sales were all controlled by the government (the practice implemented in the

[11] In the opinion of the author of this book, it may be more appropriate to call it "the free-trade system" or "restriction-free system".

reign of Emperor Wu of the Han). ③ Turnover Monopoly/indirect monopoly: Salt was produced by private producers and then sold to the government. The government in turn released the salt to merchants, who took care of the transport and sales (the practice proposed by Liu Yan in the Tang Dynasty, implemented in the middle Song, Jurchen-led Jin, Yuan Dynasties and in the Ming Dynasty prior to the Wanli reign). ④ State and commercial monopoly/mixed monopoly: Sales areas were strictly demarcated, with the government in charge of some sales areas and merchants taking care of the others. (This scheme was adopted in the Five Dynasties, Song, Liao, Jurchen-led Jin and Yuan periods.) ⑤ Enfranchised merchant monopoly/dual monopoly: The government granted merchants the right to trade in salt and levied taxation from them. (This arrangement was found in the late Ming and Qing Dynasties.) It was possible for ③ and ④ to exist simultaneously in different localities within the same dynasty.

As for the system of salt administration in other countries of the world, there were roughly three types of arrangements: free trade, salt tax and monopoly (Ou, 1935, pp. 1–2; Lin, 1930, p. 8).[12]

(1) Free trade. No taxation was imposed on the salt trade (such as in Britain and Belgium).
(2) Salt tax. This arrangement was further divided into two types: ① Taxation was levied at the production centers (such as in Germany, France and Italy). ② Customs tariff. No taxation was collected from domestically produced salt, but taxation was imposed on salt imported from other countries (such as in the United States, Denmark, Norway, Spain, Portugal, and Russia prior to the 1917 Revolution).
(3) Monopoly. This arrangement was further divided into three types. ① Full monopoly. The production, transport and sales of salt were all operated by the government (such as in the Austro-Hungarian Empire, Switzerland and Tunisia before the First World War). ② Partial monopoly. Under this arrangement, the production of salt was open to private producers or jointly undertaken by the government and private producers, the transport and wholesale were controlled by the state, and the retail of salt was open to private traders (such as in Italy, Greece and Turkey). ③ Turnover monopoly: Salt was produced by private producers and then sold to the government. Merchants were free to engage in the transport and sales of salt (such as in Japan and India).

Through the above comparison, it can be seen that the system of salt administration was fundamentally the same between China and other countries of the world. The only practice found in foreign countries but not in China was the collection of tariffs. This was due to the fact that ancient China for a long time was secluded from the outside world and did not import salt from foreign countries. Arrangements unique to China included mixed monopoly by the state and merchants, and enfranchised merchant monopoly. In other words, by the Tang Dynasty, China had developed all

[12] The information given on salt administration of the countries of the world was current up to the times the books were written.

the arrangements for salt administration commonly adopted around the world with the sole exception of customs tariff on salt. Since the Five Dynasties period, China blazed a new trail and introduced the unique arrangement of licensed salt merchants. Salt certificates were also peculiar to ancient China. In fact, salt certificates co-existed with the participation of merchants in the salt monopoly. Whether it was mixed monopoly by the government and merchants, or enfranchised merchant monopoly in which the government withdrew to the back stage, salt certificates (or the embryonic form of salt certificates) were only the means to an end. Through the issuance of salt certificates and the division of salt distribution areas, the government assumed control of the salt business (to secure revenues), and merchants were entitled to participate in the transport and sales of salt. Enfranchised merchant monopoly may be summed up as "control by the government + distribution by merchants + taxation levied by the government". That franchised merchant monopoly was essentially a form of monopoly rather than a salt tax lay in the fact that the merchants took part in the salt trade under government control, hence the term "dual monopoly". Under the system of salt certificates, control, monopoly and taxation were fully integrated, which rendered the debate of taxation versus monopoly meaningless.

2. Evolution of China's system of salt administration and periodization of its history

> China's system of salt administration started with Guanzi, was further developed and promoted by Sang Hongyang and flourished as a result of the reform of Liu Yan. From the Han to the Sui, the administration of salt switched from state monopoly to salt tax, and then to free trade. In the course of the Tang Dynasty, the administration of salt backtracked from free trade to salt tax, and then to monopoly. Since then, salt policies became increasingly complicated. Division of the country into zones of salt administration originated in the Five Dynasties, was continued in the Song, and became a fully established institution in the Yuan. Licensed merchants first appeared in the Song, and the practice was continued in the Yuan and prevailed in the Ming and Qing Dynasties. (Lin, 1930, p. 7)

Tian (1929, pp. 1–7) divided the history of salt administration of ancient China into three periods:

(1) Period of alternation between salt tax and state monopoly (pre-Qin—the Han—the Northern and Southern Dynasties—the Sui—the Tang);
(2) Period of salt certificates in the embryonic form (the Five Dynasties—the Song);
(3) Period of formation of the system of salt certificates (the Jurchen Jin—the Yuan—the Ming—the Qing).

Zeng (1936, pp. 2–29) classified the administration of salt in ancient China into three types:

(1) Free trade in salt. (This arrangement existed prior to the three dynasties of antiquity, i.e., the Xia, Shang and Zhou Dynasties. Later, Emperor Wen of the Sui replicated this system: "In the 3rd year of the Kaihuang reign (583 AD), the government shared the use of salt pools and salt wells with the common people.")
(2) Salt tax. ("Levying of the salt tax started from the Xia Dynasty.")

(3) Salt monopoly. It may be further divided into five types: partial monopoly, full monopoly (which started in the reign of Emperor Wu of the Han), turnover monopoly (which started in the Tang Dynasty), mixed monopoly by the state and the merchants[13] (which started in the Five Dynasties), and monopoly by licensed merchants (which started in the 45th year of the Wanli reign, or 1617).

What Zeng (1936) offered is a classification of the systems of salt administration rather than a periodization of the history of salt administration, but this classification is basically presented in a chronological order (except for the reversal to free trade of salt in the Sui and Tang period). Therefore, this classification is also treated as a scheme of periodization in the present discussion.

Ou (1935) divided the history of salt administration of ancient China into the following periods along dynastic lines: salt administration of the pre-Qin period, of the Han, Jin and Six Dynasties period, of the Sui, Tang and Five Dynasties period, and of the Song, Yuan and Ming period. According to the understanding of the author of this book, this division is periodization based on institutional changes that took place in the chronological order: The relevant discussions in *Guanzi* and the *Book of Lord Shang* may be regarded as the embryonic period of thoughts on salt administration in ancient China prior to the institutionalization of salt administration; next came the period of repeated abolitions and reinstatements of state monopoly starting with the institutionalization of salt administration in the reign of Emperor Wu of the Han; this was followed by the period of development of the system of salt administration beginning with free trade in salt introduced by Emperor Wen of the Sui when he abolished the restrictions on salt trade until the budding of salt certificates in the Five Dynasties; next was the last period in the history of salt administration in ancient China, in which the system of salt certificates emerged and matured.

Tian (1929) especially highlighted the vital position that the system of salt certificates occupied in China's history of salt administration, but as the other side of the same coin, he has accorded too much importance to the system of salt certificates. Besides, it was not quite precise to characterize the pre-Tang period as a period of alternation between salt tax and state monopoly.[14] Zeng (1936)'s scheme of periodization also has deficiencies in that it does not pay attention to the issue of regression in the system of salt administration in history and the classification is too minute. Ou (1935)'s method seems to be the optimal scheme, which takes into

[13] Chen (1977, p. 335) explained: "They are essentially different methods for contracting state monopoly by merchants at certain prices." Therefore, the so-called monopoly by merchants under the salt-certificate system was no more than contracting of state monopoly by merchants.

[14] According to Lü Simian's *A history of China's institutions*, at least in the pre-Tang period, the government did not take the salt tax as an important source of fiscal revenue. Before the Han Emperor Wu's reign, the salt tax was levied primarily to suppress the salt merchants (even though this goal was not achieved). Therefore, the author of this book believes that the alternation between salt tax and state monopoly was only a superficial phenomenon, and the key lay in the existence or abolition of state monopoly rather than the presence or absence of the salt tax. Renunciation of the salt tax in the interval of 128 years in the Sui and early Tang Dynasties was also an eloquent testimony to this view.

full account and coordinates the two major factors of the historical process (dynastic changes, chronological order) and institutional changes.

Through a critical review of the periodization of China's history of salt administration, we may outline the historical trajectory of the evolution of China's system of salt administration: period prior to institutionalization of salt administration → period of repeated abolitions and reinstatements of salt (and iron) monopoly starting from the reign of Emperor Wu of the Han → period of explorations in salt administration in the Sui, Tang and Five Dynasties period (free trade, salt tax, monopoly, and burgeoning of salt certificates) → period of further development and finalization of the system of salt administration in the Song, Yuan, Ming and Qing Dynasties (State control, which was the ultimate goal of salt administration, was effected by issuing salt certificates to licensed merchants, who served as the main agents for carrying out the salt trade).

3. Predicament in the evolution of China's salt administration system and rethinking

The Sui and Tang Dynasties were the most benevolent period in salt administration ever since the three dynasties of antiquity (the Xia, Shang and Zhou). Renunciation of the salt tax in the Sui and Tang Dynasties was nothing short of a miracle in the history of salt administration. Since the time of Liu Yan, salt administration became more and more complicated and chaotic, summed up as follows:

> The practice of tax-free salt trade started in the 3rd year of the Kaihuang reign (AD 583), when restrictions on salt trade were lifted. The early Tang Dynasty continued this arrangement of the Sui and did not levy the salt tax. Therefore, no taxation on salt was collected in a period of 128 years, from the 3rd year of the Kaihuang reign to the last year of the Jingyun reign of the Tang (AD 711). This is an important period in China's history of salt administration that should be commemorated. In the early Kaiyuan reign, a court discussion was held on levying the salt tax, but blocked by opponents, this proposal was not implemented. The salt tax was not imposed until the 10th year of the Kaiyuan reign (AD 723), but the power of taxation was vested in the local governments. Restrictions on salt trade were loose and no applicable laws were enacted. When An Lushan revolted in the late Tianbao reign, the military expenditure of the Tang government soared. As the Pacification Commissioner of Hebei, Yan Zhenqing seized the salt resources of Jingcheng Prefecture and sold salt to other prefectures for a profit as an expedient. This measure generated sufficient revenues to cover his military expenses. In the Zhide and Qianyuan reigns, Diwu Qi[15] was entrusted with supervision of the Salt-and-Iron Commissioners in all Regions of the empire. He imitated and made some adaptations to the practice of Yan Zhenqing and revived the salt monopoly system ... Diwu Qi's system of salt administration, which was similar to the theory put forward in *Guanzi*, may be described as private production plus government distribution. In the Baoying reign, there emerged Liu Yan's method of salt administration, ... which may be summed up as private production, purchase and resale by the government, and transport and retail by the merchants. This arrangement was essentially the same as turnover monopoly. Liu Yan's design was possibly the best method of salt administration since Guanzi ... After Liu Yan, the system of salt administration grew increasingly chaotic. (Ou, 1935, pp. 25–26)

[15] Diwu Qi is the name of a person, who once served as a Salt-and-Iron Commissioner, Coinage Commissioner, and was later entrusted with the supervision of Salt-and-Iron Commissioners of all the Regions.

The post-Song period was the final stage in which the salt administration of ancient China assumed its definitive form. Based on the developments made in the Five Dynasties, this period produced the system of franchised merchants characterized by salt certificates. Burgeoning in the Five Dynasties, the salt certificates were called "*chao*" (钞, voucher) in the Song and "*yin*" (引, certificate) in the Yuan. The salt administration system of the Qing Dynasty featured the co-existence of salt certificates (*yin*) and salt tickets (*piao*, 票).[16] The so-called salt certificates were licenses for salt distribution issued by the government to merchants at a certain cost (for delivering grain to the frontier or making a money payment). Each certificate entitled its holder to trade a certain amount of salt. The government prescribed strict restrictions on the routes and geographical scopes for the distribution of salt by the merchants. In the Song Dynasty, two modes of salt distribution existed side by side, albeit in different localities, i.e., state monopoly (whereby both transport and sales were controlled by the government) and enfranchised merchant monopoly (whereby under the direct control of the government, the salt was released to certificated merchants, who then distributed the salt within designated areas). This arrangement was referred to as a twofold mode featuring the co-existence of government distribution and merchant distribution of salt. In the Chongning and Zhenghe reigns, the Song Emperor Huizong abolished state monopoly in favor of salt distribution by merchants. In later dynasties, there gradually emerged the system of hereditary salt merchants, who carried out salt trade under strict government control. The salt administration of the Song, Yuan and Ming Dynasties may be summarized as follows:

> In the Song Dynasty, financial power of the government was vested in the Three Divisions, with the Salt and Iron Division being one of them. Since the Zhenghe reign, each route had a Tea-Salt Affairs Managing Department to control the profits from "mountains and seas". Under this arrangement, it was the county officials who took care of sales of all the salt of the country, … and special pains were taken to fight against salt smuggling. … In Emperor Renzong's reign, Fan Xiang introduced the salt-voucher method. Under this arrangement, a merchant could buy in a frontier region a salt voucher at the price of 4,800 cash. The voucher would in turn permit the merchant to collect 200 catties of salt, which the merchant was free to distribute on the market. Revenues derived from selling salt vouchers were used to strengthen fortification of the frontiers. This marked the beginning of the salt-voucher system of the Song Dynasty, which was the precursor of the salt-certificate system of later dynasties. In the Jurchen Jin Dynasty, the government imposed taxes on ten commodities, with salt topping the list of taxed commodities. A salt certificate was required for engaging in salt trade, and the certificate was valid only within a prescribed geographical scope … In the Yuan Dynasty, the government implemented the salt-certificate system … Forgery of salt certificates involved the death penalty … Smuggling was punishable by two years of penal servitude … Sales areas were strictly demarcated, and any transgression of their boundaries was punished by a grade lighter than that for the crime of salt smuggling. Salt Distribution Commissions were set up in such regions as Lianghuai and Liangzhe, and these operating agencies were retained in both the Ming and Qing Dynasties. In the Ming Dynasty, a Salt Distribution Commission or a Salt Distribution Superintendency was set up in each salt production center (with the former controlling a major production center and

[16] "Salt certificates and tickets were used in the following manner." "Salt certificates were sold to the merchants." "In case there were not enough merchants to buy all the salt certificates, salt tickets were made and sold to the common people. The ticket entitled the bearer to trade a certain amount of salt in any area." (Lü, 2002, p. 508)

> the latter a minor one). Salt distribution was still carried out by the use of salt certificates (*yin*). Merchants were invited to deliver grain to the border garrisons, in return for which they would receive salt certificates. The salt certificates entitled the merchants to buy salt from the government. The salt revenue during the Qing Dynasty came from three sources ... The first was called the "pan tax" (*zaoke*), collected from the producers. The second was the certificate tax (*yinke*), levied on salt certificates from merchants when they purchased salt from the producers. Hence it was also called the "merchant tax". The third was miscellaneous fees (*zake*) levied in connection with the salt business, such as house rent, fines, and interests on loans for the salt works. Later new taxes were invented, such as *yanli*, a tax levied on salt in transit. The salt certificate (*yin*) was also a unit of weight, with one *yin* of salt weighing from 240 to 560 catties. Salt merchants must first obtain salt certificates before they could purchase salt from the salt producers. Upon paying the certificate tax, a merchant enjoyed monopoly of sales within his respective sales area. Salt for which the certificate tax had been paid was called official salt, and that for which the certificate tax had not been paid was called illegal salt. Salt on sale in a region other than its designated sales area or sold beyond the prescribed quota was also treated as illegal salt. In regions such as Shandong, Zhejiang and Lianghuai, both salt certificates and salt tickets were used. Salt certificates were issued the Ministry of Revenue, while salt tickets were issued by a regional agency of salt administration. Both were essentially methods of the government to sell to merchants the exclusive right of salt distribution at a set price. (Chen, 1977, pp. 333–335)

There were no more than three methods of salt administration: free trade, taxation as well as control and monopoly. Besides the period prior to the three dynasties of antiquity (the Xia, Shang and Zhou), free trade in salt was only found in the Sui and early Tang period of 128 years. This may have been made possible by the fact that the government did not rely on salt for its revenues thanks to the prosperity of the Sui and Tang Dynasties, especially the reigns of Zhenguan and Kaiyuan.[17] With an overview of the entire history of salt administration in ancient China excluding the short interval of 128 years, the following pattern would come to light: From Emperor Wu's reign of the Han to the Sui Dynasty, the system of salt administration merely oscillated between the salt tax and government monopoly. From the middle Tang Dynasty up to the Qing Dynasty, the system featured experimentation of various methods of production, transport and sales, all for the purpose of securing fiscal revenues based on government control. All these changes in salt administration may be boiled down to the substitution of one evil with another. A method was devised out of fiscal considerations, and abolished mainly because of its defects. Then another method was devised, still out of fiscal considerations. This process of devising new methods of salt administration and reforming malpractices became an endless cycle, but the defects of the system could never be truly eliminated.

In the wake of the Rebellion of An Lushan and Shi Siming from AD 755 to 763, there was a sharp drop in the taxpaying population and a drastic increase in military expenses. In an attempt to secure large-scale sources of revenue, the Tang Emperor Suzong put the financial official Diqu Qi in power, who depreciated the currency and set up state-owned enterprises. These measures "disrupted the relaxed economic atmosphere of the early Tang Dynasty and harkened back to the tradition of the

[17] Du Fu wrote in a poem: "Thinking of the past flourishing days of Kaiyuan, a small city could house ten thousand families. Rice looked greasy and corns white, public and private barns were all full."

Han Emperor Wu" (Guo, 2017, p. 168). By the end of the Tang Dynasty, China had experimented with all methods of salt administration commonly adopted in other countries of the world (with the sole exception of levying the customs tariff) and China's system of salt administration was becoming increasingly mature. "Perhaps there was no scheme of salt administration better than that devised by Liu Yan ever since the time of Guanzi." Liu Yan's method of salt administration had two important policies: The first one was to relax control and let the government withdraw partially from the market. Thus, full monopoly (the government controlling all links of the salt business, including production, distribution, transport and retail) was transformed into turnover monopoly (production by private producers, resale by the government, transport and retail by merchants). This arrangement injected the vitalities of private merchants into the salt trade and eliminated the corruption and inefficiency of official merchants. The second policy was to regulate market prices through economic means to keep salt prices at a level acceptable to the common people ("the common people no longer had to live on saltless meals"). He set up state salt reserve granaries to curb the hoarding and speculation by merchants and regulate salt prices through economic means. This measure could not only control salt prices and secure salt taxes but also curtail the influence of merchants and alleviate social contradictions. On the basis of the above policies, Liu Yan also intensified efforts to fight against salt smuggling. Liu Yan's system of salt administration was so effective that by the end of the Tang Dynasty, salt revenues had come to account for one half of the fiscal revenues of the whole country. The advantage of Liu Yan's method was that a distinction was drawn between collection of profits by the government and control by the government, and rational efforts were made to maintain a balance between these two aspects. The first policy was targeted at collection of profits, while the second was aimed at control of the market (benefiting people's livelihood through the establishment of state salt granaries). Both policies achieved their goals. However, Liu Yan was demoted as a result of intrigues of Prime Minister Yang Yan in the complex court struggles. "When Liu Yan was gone, the system of salt administration gradually became chaotic." The first indication of chaotic salt administration was soaring salt prices when the successor of Liu Yan complacently attempted to increase revenues simply by raising salt prices in an effort to highlight his merit. The second indication was rampant salt smuggling in spite of repeated prohibitions (caused actually by roaring salt prices). Incited by the mounting prices of official salt, smuggling was bound to become unstoppable. To deal with illegal salt, the government had to impose stricter control and severer penalties, resulting in a vicious cycle.[18] Since the late Tang period, salt administration grew steadily more complicated, and the system of salt certificates, a unique invention of China, was introduced. Associated with the system of salt certificates were the method of dual monopoly by the government and merchants as well as the method of enfranchised merchants (monopoly by merchants).

The Tang Dynasty was able to embrace tax-free salt trade (free trade in salt) in its early period and establish a sound system of salt administration in its middle period.

[18] For changes in the system of salt administration of the Tang Dynasty, please see Zhang (2002, pp. 79–83).

Judging from the status of the Tang Code in the Chinese legal history (Although some believe that *The Great Qing Legal Code* is a synthesis of the legal codes of ancient China, the Qing Code cannot compare with the Tang Code in terms of its status in the legal history of China and even of the world[19]), it may be safe to conclude that, in spite of the salt certificate system developed after the Five Dynasties period (a unique invention of China), the system of salt administration of the Tang Dynasty (excluding the chaotic late Tang period) has been the best one in the Chinese history.

Before switching to state monopoly, the Western Han levied a salt tax not less heavy than that of the Qin Dynasty. The heavy salt tax, instead of suppressing the merchants, only served to victimize the common people and benefit the salt merchants, because the merchants were able to shift the tax burden to the common people. Out of fiscal considerations of the government, Emperor Wu of the Han nationalized the salt and iron businesses and institutionalized control on salt and iron.[20] Subsequently, the state monopoly on salt and iron was repeatedly abolished and reinstated. As full state monopoly turned out to be infeasible, there emerged turnover monopoly and dual monopoly by both the government and merchants. Eventually, the system of salt administration evolved into a mode featuring a combination of monopoly and taxation, in which the government franchised the right of transport and sales of salt to merchants and levied taxation in between. Essentially, this was not so much a combination of monopoly and taxation as a combination of control and taxation. The government still relied on salt taxes (with salt taxes existing in diversified forms, including the pan tax, the certificate tax, miscellaneous fees as well as *lijin* on salt), and the distribution of salt was carried out under strict government control. However, the defects of salt monopoly were never eliminated since the time of Emperor Wu of the Han,[21] and salt merchants accrued wealth not to be surpassed by that of any other group of the country (see stories about salt merchants of Yangzhou in the Ming and Qing Dynasties). "Salt used to be a vital source of revenue before the Industrial Revolution and was made use of as well by other countries of the world such as France. However, in the Ming Dynasty, the salt trade was controlled completely in line with a bureaucratic spirit, which brought about more harms than benefits. Sometimes, the salt production centers were piled up with salt because the salt merchants, who had already made the payment, were unable to pay the extra fees. The salt consumption regions, on the other hand, suffered from a shortage of stock. In

---

[19] The Qing Code was based on the Ming Code. In spite of some adaptations in the overall structure and specific clauses, the Ming Code was fundamentally the same as the Tang Code in terms of the major institutions and basic thinking. In addition, some adaptations from the Tang Code to the Ming Code, which were not the result of careful thinking, often turned out to be self-defeating. See Xu (1976, pp. 95–99).

[20] At least before the Sui and Tang Dynasties, the salt tax was not regarded as an important tax. Prior to the Sui and Tang period, the salt tax presumably played a greater role in suppressing salt merchants in addition to increasing the fiscal revenue.

[21] The major problem with salt administration of the Song Dynasty lay in the official-merchants. Prime Ministers (such as Jia Sidao and Shi Songzhi), officials in charge of salt administration as well as officials of salt production and distribution centers engaged in salt smuggling one after another. Quite a number of officials smuggled salt on their official trips. Salt smuggled by officials sometimes even secured a monopoly status. For details, see Zhao (2001, pp. 137–143).

this deadlock, funds were frozen and salt was being wasted. Only a small number of speculative merchants and unscrupulous officials made a fortune, while the government, decent merchants and the common people were all victimized. This situation was never rectified up to the end of the Ming Dynasty."[22] The goal of the government was control rather than rendering services. In the entire history of evolution of salt administration, from free trade to taxation to monopoly (which had a multitude of specific forms), and eventually to a combination of taxation and monopoly[23] under government control, there were efforts to eliminate current defects, but no attempts to generate long-term benefits. Since the late Tang Dynasty, the political and economic philosophy of control prevailed. A millennium of salt administration may be boiled down to government control and collection of revenues!

The goal of state control was to suppress the influence of salt merchants and benefit the livelihood of the people, while the goal of monopoly and taxation was to secure revenues for the government. To properly address the contradiction between fiscal revenues of the government (enriching the country) and interests of the civilian population (enriching the people), strike a balance between these two poles, achieve a win–win situation and administer the salt business in a scientific manner was the key to the issue of salt administration. Liu Yan of the Tang Dynasty, who skillfully handled the relationship between enriching the state and enriching the people, worked out a scheme that truly benefited both the government and the common people. However, the tax-free (free trade) arrangement of the Sui and early Tang Dynasties, tinged with a strong hue of Confucian idealism, lasted for only a brief interval, and the sound method of salt administration of Liu Yan in the middle Tang period was put to an end as soon as Liu Yan fell from power. How come Liu Yan's benevolent policies were implemented but failed to last for a prolonged period of time? This has become the so-called "Liu Yan mystery" in the history of China's salt administration.[24] Since the late Tang period, it may be seen that the government failed to view salt revenues rationally and design a sound scheme of salt administration. Instead of achieving a win–win situation for both the state and the people, the government colluded with the merchants to make a fortune. The author of this book here ventures to make a bold assertion: The system of salt certificates and franchised merchants since the Song and Yuan Dynasties was fundamentally a failure, even though it blazed a new trail

[22] For problems with the salt administration of the Ming Dynasty, see Huang. RY (2004, pp. 67–70). Problems with the salt administration of the Qing Dynasty were similar to those of the Ming: collusion between officials and merchants and prevalent salt smuggling under the backward bureaucratic system (Lü, 2002, p. 508).

[23] "Que" (榷) hereby means both taxation and monopoly.

[24] According to the conjecture of the author of this book, the reason why Liu Yan was able to implement a sound system of salt administration was that under the influence of the tax-free legacy of the Sui and early Tang Dynasty, the government was able to exercise restraint in seeking revenues and state control was relatively loose. His benevolent policies were put to an end not long after he fell from power. This was due not only to the coincidental factor that his successor out-smarted himself, but also, more importantly, to the reality of separatist rule by Military Zones since the middle Tang period. Here lurks an interesting question: Emperor Yang of the Sui went to every extreme to extort excessive taxes and levies, but how came he did not tap the salt tax?

and was a unique Chinese invention as compared with the systems of other countries of the world.

In retrospect of the process of evolution in salt administration in ancient China, it is difficult to say that the system had been progressing. The hurriedly improvised system of salt administration for "saving the time" (raising revenues or eliminating defects) became closely intertwined with the backward bureaucratic system oriented to control rather than rendering services. This resulted in endless defects in salt administration which kept surfacing one after another. In the course of time, all parties to this issue ended up being losers except for a small number of unscrupulous officials and merchants. The Confucian scholars (who "valued righteousness above material gains" and "did not have a clear idea about local administration") lost to the practical fiscal needs of the government. Sang Hongyang and his later adherents (practical bureaucrats who liked to talk about revenues) lost to the actual operation of the system of salt administration (the bureaucratic system). Hence the debate on salt and iron was reduced to empty talks. The root cause of the dilemma of salt administration of ancient China did not lie in the underdeveloped state of capitalism (industries and commerce), but in the system itself, including institutional changes that lacked planning and progress as well as a control-oriented bureaucratic system. "When social progress was stifled by a political power that harbored a control-oriented doctrine, how could capitalism emerge in China?" (Hsu, 1998, p. 328).

4.3 Social Policies: Taking Famine Relief Policy as an Example

4.3.1 Laws and Thoughts on Social Policies

Social (welfare) policies were always entitled to a foothold in the traditional Chinese thinking on fiscal administration. In spite of variations in the effect of social policies implemented by the government of different dynasties, the social policies themselves had become an integral component of the traditional concepts for state governance, and some were even embodied explicitly in government laws and decrees. Confucius regarded elimination of poverty and realization of social justice as the premise for stability of a state: "Those who have kingdoms and possessions should not be concerned that they do not have enough possessions, but should be concerned that possessions are not equally distributed; they should not be concerned that they are poor, but should be concerned that the people are not contented. For with equal distribution, there will be no poverty; with mutual goodwill, there will be no want; and with contentment among the people, there can be no downfall and dissolution." (Chapter 16 "Ji Shi" of *The Analects of Confucius*). "The Operation of Etiquette · the Great Harmony" of the *Book of Rites*, one of the Confucian cannons, further proposes the concept of *Datong*, or Grand Unity: "The old are cared for until death, the adults are gainfully employed, and the children are nurtured. Widowers, widows, orphans, childless seniors, the disabled and diseased are all taken care of." (Li, 1999, p. 658) "Schools and granaries complemented each other ideologically. The promotion of education and economic welfare were twin commitments of the local magistrate; thus, the term *jiaoyang*, 'to instruct and nourish', was considered a basic feature of government." (Wong, 1997, p. 115) The specific social policies and practices of the Confucian school were as follows (Chen, 2015, 497–604):

(1) The Well-field System (a public land system). "The *jingtian* system [the well-field system] and socialism both aim at equality of wealth, and at allowing the producers to get all that they produce."
(2) Condemnation of monopoly. First, Confucius does not approve of monopoly imposed simply for fiscal reasons. "The state should control prices, but should not monopolize the whole market." Second, in order to restrict private monopolies, the government may control demand and supply.
(3) Government control of demand and supply. This is done so that "the state gets profit, the people constantly enjoy a reasonable price, and the distribution is nearly equal."
(4) Government control of grain. For a ruler, food supply was of paramount importance to the livelihood of his people. In the Warring States period, Li Kui, a statesman of the State of Wei, introduced the *pingdi* policy (buying in grains when prices were low) to regulate grain prices. In Emperor Xuan's reign of the Han, the government began to set up *changping cang* to regulate the market and level out grain prices, a practice that persisted all the way down to the Qing Dynasty. The system of *yicang* was introduced in the Sui Dynasty. Grain was collected from farmer families during a normal year at progressive tax rates and distributed freely to the inhabitants during a bad year. The reasoning behind this system is that "it got more taxes from the rich and gave more benefit to the poor". In addition to *yicang*, there was also a system of village granaries called *shecang*. "The difference between these two systems was that the former distributed grain freely, while the latter loaned it."
(5) Public relief. This includes, in addition to famine relief which is the focus of present section, a succession of measures adopted in various dynasties. The principle of giving special favor to the widower, widow, etc., was first put in practice by Emperor Wen of the Han. In the Song Dynasty, the government set up almshouses. "In the almshouse, food, clothes, and beds were all given; servants, cooks, and nurses were all supplied." Emperor Taizu of the Ming "decreed several times to support the widower, widow, etc." In the Qing Dynasty, every district has an almshouse. According to *The Great Qing Legal Code*, "If the officials do not support the four classes, the very sick person and the infirm and superannuated who need public support, they shall be punished with sixty blows of the long stick."

4.3.2 Policies for Famine Relief

"The undertaking of social relief was usually called charity in China. It dated back to very early historical times, but it was mostly temporary relief or famine relief. From the perspective of the government, it was listed as famine relief policies in the dynastic histories." Upon an examination, it may be found that social relief had no more than the following three motives: "(1) Benevolence, the core thinking of Confucius … Benevolence is a consistent doctrine and an ethical thinking of Confucius, and the Chinese people are deeply influenced by benevolence. (2) Righteousness, which is a component of Confucianism as well … Mencius once said when he met with King Hui of Liang: 'Why must the king speak of profit? I have only [teachings concerning] benevolence and righteousness.' This is an outlook on social morality … (3) Kindness. This was the major motive of the ordinary people in the past and was derived from the moral concepts of religion. They believed that 'if you do good deeds for others, you will reach the land of kindness', 'Heaven will bless those who harbor kind intentions', and 'to rescue one person from death is better than to build a seven-storied pagoda for the god'. They thought that if they accumulated merits in this life, they would be assured of happiness in the next life (Ke, 1942, pp. 306, 308). In order to ensure social stability, win the goodwill of the people and consolidate their power, the rulers of the past dynasties attached special importance to the undertaking of social relief centering around famine relief policies and regarded it as an important means for maintaining the legitimacy of their rule. Theoretically, it was supported by such Confucian doctrines and popular beliefs as benevolent government, putting the people first, valuing righteousness above material gains, and virtue having its reward. For famine relief as an important and urgent administrative goal and task in ancient China, although the possibility of civilians (social groups) being involved in assisting its implementation cannot be completely ruled out, power organs of the state (the government) were still the principal force that carried out this undertaking. The complete bureaucratic system of traditional China (or in other words the precocious bureaucratic country) paved the way for the high efficiency, institutionalization and standardization of the social welfare policies of the state.

It is generally believed that the twelve famine relief policies proposed in "Grand Minister of the Masses" of the *Rites of Zhou* are the fountainhead of China's famine relief system. The Han government initially granted imperial land and land belonging to the local governments to the poor as the primary form of relief. However, this way of helping the famine-stricken farmers was not sustainable as the land holdings of the government were limited. Later, the government had to turn to distribution of grain as the major means of providing help in times of famine (Hsu, 1980, p. 31). By the Qing Dynasty, the system of famine relief had become quite complete. Famine was carried out in three stages: reporting of the calamity, investigation of the calamity, and famine relief. Famine relief was a measure whereby grain and money were distributed directly to the calamity-stricken people. For famine relief, there was an emergency procedure and a regular procedure. The latter could be further divided into such relief forms as principal relief, additional relief, relief commuted to cash, work relief (providing employment as a form of relief) and loans. The grain and money of principal relief were customarily distributed on a monthly basis. The calamity-stricken people received their portion at the stations set up by the government in the county seat upon presenting their relief certificates. The relief certificate would be stamped and then returned to the bearer during each time of distribution in order to prevent the famine victim from claiming the relief a second time. The relief certificate would be taken back by the government when the relief grain and money were granted for the last time (Liu, 2016). In the case of work relief, the calamity-stricken people would be organized to work for state infrastructure projects (such as water conservation works) or deliver military provisions, and in return, the government would distribute the relief supplies and money to the people in the form of wages. The calamity-stricken people could get relief on the one hand, and the state acquired corvée labor on the other. This practice was similar to the social policy advocated by Keynesianism and widely used in Franklin Roosevelt's New Deal to create job opportunities for unemployed people through government-funded projects of public works. Since the Song Dynasty, work relief became the relief method most commonly used by the government because it benefited both the poor people and the government. The Qing Emperor Jiaqing once commented: "There are no other methods of famine relief better than work relief" (Yang, 1992, p. 1499). In the Qianlong reign, the government attached special importance to work relief, and the central government had a clear overall planning for the local public projects to be undertaken in the course of work relief. "Whether the harvest is good or bad cannot be known beforehand, but a plan should be made for the projects that are to be undertaken so that they may be commenced at any time. Within a province, no project is more massive than the construction of walled cities. The provincial authorities shall be ordered to identify which city and which part of the city should be built first. They shall establish the priorities, make the estimates and prepare a list to be submitted to the Ministry of Revenue. If work relief is to be made in case of floods or droughts in the future, it will be carried out without delay based on the list so compiled."[25] The Qing Dynasty had a comparatively complete set of laws on famine relief. In addition to provisions for investigation of calamities and crop damages, which were practically the same in the legal codes throughout the Tang, Ming and Qing Dynasties, *Regulations and precedents of Da-Qing Huidian* (*The Code of the Qing Dynasty*) and *Regulations of the Ministry of Revenue* also contained extensive information on policies of famine relief, with detailed provisions on the categories of calamities qualified for famine relief, the preconditions and procedures of relief, the specific schedule of relief, percentages of tax exemption, loan interest together with its reduction and exemption, etc.

A conspicuous feature of China's social economy lay in "its precociousness and maturity, centralization of power, and stability of the bureaucratic system, and this point can better explain the existence of those detailed and institutionalized disaster

[25] Article 137 "Ministry of Revenue: Exemption and relief–construction of civil projects", Fascicle 288 of *Imperially commissioned regulations and precedents of the grand Qing* (Guangxu reign edition).

relief procedures … Preparations against calamities and disaster relief were indeed a top priority of the bureaucratic system. This was part of the Chinese traditional paternalistic rule and reflected the Confucian teaching that supporting the people made it possible to better educate the people" (Will, 1980/2006, p. 4). In addition to simply helping the poor survive, famine relief of the government also had social policy considerations. The state hoped to retain the economic independence of small landowners by granting them relief so that they would not have to sell their land holdings or be trapped by usury and become dependents of property holders. Besides famine relief, the government also, in concerted efforts with social forces, set up *changping cang*, sold out grain and rendered loans from the local granaries to regulate market prices. The government could also effectively supervise interregional trade by controlling major docks, passes and trade routes. Researchers have found that the system of famine relief had attained a fairly developed state prior to 1750, with a relatively high level of institutionalization and standardization in the investigation of calamities and distribution of supplies. The rules formulated meticulously by the state were well applied, and "apparently the necessary capability and measures for alleviating agricultural crises of such a vast scope and across such long periods were already in place". The efficiency, flexibility and innovation of the Qing bureaucratic government "by far exceeded the extent indicated by the official laws and regulations as well as assessments of Chinese bureaucrats made by 19th century writers" (Will, 1980/2006, pp. 221–226).

"China's fiscal regime was well suited to promote the material welfare of the general population under a preindustrial set of economic possibilities. The direct consequences of low taxes and high public goods expenditures were economically positive. China's fiscal regime was well able to absorb a variety of natural and social shocks that could have challenged the material security and economic well-being of the people. The equilibrium between principles of taxation and expenditure broadly stayed in balance." (Rosenthal & Wong, 2011, p. 199) However, as the Qing Dynasty proceeded down the road of decay, the official famine relief activities grew increasingly difficult since the Jiaqing reign. Especially since the middle 1890s when internal wars and foreign invasion severely crippled the state's capability of intervention, "the state fiscal resources became increasingly strained", and "the local governments of quite a number of regions were plunged into chaos", so that "famine relief grew more and more reliant on local charity and commercial forces" (Will, 1980/2006, pp. 4–5).

References

Article 137 "Ministry of Revenue: Exemption and relief–construction of civil projects", Fascicle 288 of Qinding daqing huidian shili [Imperially commissioned regulations and precedents of the grand Qing] (Guangxu reign edition).

Chen, G. (1977). Zhongguo fazhi shi gaiyao [An overview of China's legal history]. San Min Book Co., Ltd.

Chen, H. (2015). Kongmen licai xue [The economic principles of Confucius and his school]. The Commercial Press.

Chen, Y. (2001). Sui tang zhidu yuanyuan lüelun gao: Tangdai zhengzhi shi shulun gao [Draft essays on the origins of Sui and Tang institutions: Draft outline of Tang political history]. SDX Joint Publishing.
Ch'ü, T. (1988). *Local Government in China under the Ch'ing*. Harvard University Press.
Du, Y. (1988). Tong dian [Comprehensive statutes]. Zhonghua Book Company.
Guo, J. (2017). Zhongyang diguo de caizheng mima [The fiscal code of the central empire]. Lujiang Publishing House.
Hsu, C. (1980). *Han agriculture: The formation of early Chinese agrarian economy (206 B.C–A.D. 220)*. University of Washington Press.
Hsu, C. (1998). Lishi fen'guang jing [A spectroscope on history]. Shanghai Literature and Art Publishing House.
Huan, K. (1990). Yan tie lun [Discourses on salt and iron]. Shanghai Chinese Classics Publishing House.
Huang, R. (2008). The Ming fiscal administration. In D. Twitchett & J. K. Fairbank (Eds.), *The Cambridge history of China: The Ming Dynasty 1368–1644* (Vol. 8, Part 2, pp. 106–171). Cambridge University Press.
Huang, R. Y. (1974). *Taxation and governmental finance in sixteenth-century Ming China*. Cambridge University Press.
Huang, R. Y. (2004). Da lishi buhui weisuo [Macro history will not wither]. Guangxi Normal University Press.
Huang, R. Y. (2015). Mingdai de caoyun [The Grand Canal During the Ming Dynasty, 1368-1644] (H. Zhang et al., Trans.). Lujiang Publishing House. (Original work published 1964).
Ke, X. (1942). Woguo shehui jiuji shiye zhi jiantao [Review of China's Social Relief Cause]. Xuesi [Learning and thinking], *1*(12).
Li, X. (Ed.). (1999). Liji zheng yi [Commentaries on the Book of Rites]. Peking University Press.
Lin, Z. (Ed.). (1930). Zhongguo yanzheng jiyao [A summary of China's salt administration] (Vol. 1). The Commercial Press.
Liu, X. (2016). Qingdai huangzheng de fayuan [Legal source of famine relief administration of the Qing Dynasty] (Unpublished master's thesis). [Unpublished master's thesis]. Tsinghua University.
Lü, S. (2002). Zhongguo zhidu shi [A history of China's institutions]. Shanghai Education Publishing House.
Ou, Z. (Ed.). (1935). Zhongguo yanzheng xiao shi [Short history of China's salt administration]. The Commercial Press.
Qian, M. (1996a). Guo shi dagang [Outline of the Chinese history] (Vol. 1). The Commercial Press.
Qian, M. (1996b). Guo shi dagang [Outline of the Chinese history] (Vol. 2). The Commercial Press.
Rosenthal, J. L., & Wong, R. B. (2011). *Before and beyond divergence: The politics of economic change in China and Europe*. Harvard University Press.
Sa, M. (1975). Zhongguo shehui zhengzhi shi [A socio-political history of China] (Vol. 4). San Min Book Co., Ltd.
Shi, Z. (2019, November 6). Qing qianqi caizheng gaiyao [Overview of finance of the early Qing period]. Chinese Literature and History Web. http://www.historychina.net/jj/355556.shtml
Sima, Q. (1982). Shiji [Records of the grand historian]. Zhonghua Book Company.
Tian, B. (1929). Zhongguo yanshui yu yanzheng [China's salt tax and salt administration]. Jiangsu Provincial Government Printing Bureau.
Wang, J. (2012). Zhongguo lishi tonglun [A survey of Chinese history]. SDX Joint Publishing.
Will, P. T. (2006). Shiba shiji zhongguo de guanliao zhidu yu huangzheng [Bureaucracy and famine in eighteenth-century China] (J. Xu, Trans.). Jiangsu People's Publishing House. (Original work published 1980).
Wong, R. B. (1997). *China transformed: Historical change and the limits of European experience*. Cornell University Press.
Xu, D. (1976). Zhongguo fazhi shi lunlüe [Brief discussion of China's legal system]. Cheng Chung Book Co., Ltd.

Xu, F. (2001) Lianghan sixiang shi [Intellectual history of the Western and Eastern Han Dynasties] (Vol. 3). East China Normal University Press.
Yang, J. (Ed.). (1922). Xing gong [Promoting industries]. In C. He, Y. Wei, et al. (Eds.), Qing jingshi wen bian [Collected writings on statecraft of the Qing Dynasty] (Vol. 41, pp. 1025–1027). Zhonghua Book Company.
Zeng, Y. (1936). Songdai guanshang jiqi falü tiaozheng [Official merchants and legal adjustments in the Song Dynasty]. The Commercial Press.
Zhang, Z. (2002). Tangdai jingji minshi falü shulun [On the economic and civil law in Tang Dynasty]. Law Press China.

Chapter 5
Mixed Ownership of Land

5.1 Divided Property Rights on the Premise of a Communal Ownership of Land

5.1.1 Enfeoffment and the Well-Field System

Land is considered to be the earliest and most primitive form of state-owned assets. In the primitive society, people cultivated the land collectively and distributed it equally, so that land was naturally viewed as collective property, which was the origin of the well-field system; after the country came into being, the public ownership of land continued and was transformed it into the state ownership; the state-owned land meant the king-owned land, and the two were mixed into one because the king was considered to be the representative and symbol of a country (Tao, 2000). The public ownership had been practiced before Li Kui of the Wei introduced "maximization of agricultural productivity" in the state of Wei and Shang Yang abolished the well-field system and "restructured roads and paths".[1] Under the well-field system, the land belonged nominally to the public, the king or the state, but it was essentially enfeoffed to the feudal lords who, in turn, granted the land to their ministers and grand masters. That was how feoffs came into being. The commoners did not own any land, and had to farm the given land like serfs (Chen, 1977, p. 307). Although "under the wide heaven, all was the king's land", it was not the king (the Son of Heaven) but the feudal lords and their ministers and grand masters that actually possessed the enfeoffed land the commoners cultivated. In return, tributes were paid along the bottom-up order of servicemen, ministers and grand masters, lords and the king so that the yield was shared among the parties. Therefore, it might be said that a joint ownership of land was institutionalized between the state and private owners with the establishment of the country in China.

[1] Newly unearthed historical records show that the Qin's land reform was "strict land granting instead of free trade" (Qin, 2003, p. 315).

X. Nie, *The History of Government and Public Law in China*,
https://doi.org/10.1007/978-981-97-6063-3_5

5.1.2 Remedies for Land Consolidation and Reflections on the Well-Field System

Private ownership of land was gradually recognized in the history from the introduction of "regular taxation of land" in the state of Lu in the second half of the Spring and Autumn Period to Shang Yang's reform of "abolishing the well-field system and restructuring roads and paths" in the state of Qin. When the land was being privatized, a non-coincidental campaign for written law was under way in various states in the Spring and Autumn Period and the Warring States Period from the "Cast Penal Code" that Zichan of Zheng pioneered to the first systematic statutory law, the *Book of Law* that Li Kui of Wei compiled. Although their contents are not known, those statutory laws undoubtedly provided commoners with a "guarantee of rights" by which the inferior could fight against the arbitrary superior. Academic research revealed the earliest written laws to be statutes of property (Huang & Fan, 2003). As soon as the well-field system was abolished and "the land could be privately owned, division became an established principle. However, land was again concentrated in the hands of those families who also made fortunes by way of industries and commerce, which was the regular practice in the Warring States period. Consequently, it was hopeless to restrain the violent land consolidation". To seek remedies, the Qin, Han and succeeding dynasties proposed "land laws and policies" "after the idealized initial well-field system"; in spite of being a figment of imagination by later generations, the well-field system was "considered by both supporters and opponents to be a holy system of the golden age" because Mencius' notion of it had been deeply rooted in the hearts of the people (Chen, 1977).

Mencius said, "The first thing towards a benevolent government must be to lay down the boundaries. If the boundaries be not defined correctly, the division of the land into squares will not be equal, and the produce available for salaries will not be evenly distributed. On this account, oppressive rulers and impure ministers are sure to neglect this defining of the boundaries" (Teng Wen Gong I).[2] "The rich owned vast fields connected by paths and the poor had no room to put his awl in" in the Han Dynasty, which was worse than the Qin. When Emperor Wu of Han was in power, Dong Zhongshu thought that "it was hard to immediately put the ancient well-field system into effect, but partial restoration should be made to limit the rate of field area per person". Dong proposed restrictions of the size of land owned by people, ordinary and powerful alike, but his proposal was rejected.[3] Under the rule of Emperor Ai

[2] Translations are James Legge's (Mencius, 1970, p. 243).. (Notes by translators)

[3] Dong's petition reads, "In ancient times, a title was collected and people were able to afford it; three-day corvee labour was demanded per year and people were able to provide it … It was not the case with the Qin where Shang Yang's reform was adopted to change the previous political system, abolish the well-field system, and allow free trade of land so that the rich owned vast fields connected by paths and the poor had no room to put his awl in. Benefits from rivers and lakes were monopolized and fertile hills and forests were seized. People indulged in debauchery beyond the limit and valued extravagance. The county city had people as great as the king while the township had people as wealthy as dukes and marquises. How could be the commoners rich? Military service was performed in rotation monthly … The corvee was 30 times that of the ancient times while the

of Han, ministers like Shi Dan, Kong Guang and others again counseled to "limit field area per person" so that "a maximum of 30 *qing*[4] per person was allowed, regardless of kings, lords, officials or commoners", but again it was dismissed due to oppositions from powerful ministers (Lü, 2002, p. 437).

The Han solved the imbalanced population across regions in two ways: migration, allowing or encouraging the surplus population to move from densely populated areas to areas with more arable land; land granting which means lending or leasing public land (including the royal land, such as parks and other reserves, and land owned by local governments) to the poor. The *Book of Han* recorded a total of 11 land grants.[5] However, the land resources were limited. When the government ran out of its own land, it had to plea imperial relatives and ranking officials to surrender part of their land in order to resettle the poor landless people. That marked a fundamental shift in the Han land policy "from creating more cultivated acreage toward a better distribution of landholding" (Hsu, 1980, p. 32).

After usurping the Han throne, Wang Mang "was victoriously optimistic, confident and loyal to the ancient system", but he was not as prudent as Dong Zhongshu and Shi Dan. Believing the well-field system Mencius had promoted to be "feasible", Wang "wanted to initiate a new economic system for the general welfare and social justice by following ideas of the ancient sages and the rational calling". He issued an edict ordering all land to be state-owned and all land transactions to be banned; a "well" or 900 *mu* of land to be the maximum for a family of eight men or under[6]; excess land of a family to be redistributed to fellow clan members, neighbors or others of the same village; the government to distribute land to the landless. Soon, the new economic policy hit the rocks and it was abolished three years later at the Ou Bo's proposal that said, "The well-field system, in spite of being the ancient kings' institution, has long been extinct ... Without hundreds of years' progression, it would be Sisyphean to restore the system of thousands of years ago against the people's will even if emperors like Yao and Shun were resurrected" (Zhang, 2003, pp. 223–225).

The failure of Wang Mang's reform did not discourage people from viewing the well-field system as an ideal, but those believers retreated technically to the secondary choice, the equal-field system by which "Every tiller had his lot". At

---

field tax and poll tax and the profits from salt and iron were 20 times. When the Han Dynasty was established, the rules continued. Now, it is hard to immediately put the ancient well-field system into effect, but partial restoration should be made to limit the rate of field area per person so that the needy could be relieved, the land acquisition, prevented, and the profits from salt and iron, returned to citizens. Serfs needed to be released and the authority over capital punishment should be taken back to the central government. Taxes and corvee should be reduced to ease the burden of the people. Good governance would be achieved when all of above have been done." (Treatise on Food and Commodities, *Book of Han* I). Dong meant to value agriculture over commerce, restrain land acquisition, and reduce corvee and taxes so that people could recuperate and build up strength.

[4] *Qing* is a unit of area in China, about 3.33 ha now. However, in ancient China, the size of *qing* varies in different dynasties. For example, in the Han, it is about 4.176 ha. (Notes by translators)

[5] The land was given to peasants for free in a few cases.

[6] *Mu* is a unit of area in China and a *mu* is about 667 m^2. However, in ancient China, the size of *mu* varies in different dynasties. For example, in the Han, it is about 456 m^2. (Notes by translators)

the end of the Eastern Han Dynasty, Xun Yue pioneered the idea of "farming the land without owning it", that is, the separation of the land ownership and the land use right: "The lords are forbidden to own more land than stipulated, but the rich have acquired excess fields under their name, and become wealthier than the dukes and marquises, which is arbitrary possession of land. Grand masters are forbidden to dispose of land, but people take the liberty of trading land, which is arbitrary disposal. Someone asked, 'What about restoring the well-field system?' 'No,' Xun answered, 'arbitrary possession of land does not comply with the old system as well as the old system does not suit the current situation'. 'Now what?' 'It is advisable to allow farming the land without owning it until a sound system is formulated'" (Zhao, 1984, p. 261). Concerning limitation of field area per person, Xun Yue argued that "the well-field system may work well in a vast and sparsely populated land, and improperly in a densely populated country. The policy would not go well due to complaints and chaos arising from the government's attempt to abolish the well-field system in a thinly populated land and establish it in a populous country by hastily depriving the powerful of their concentrated land … When laws are not totally ready for the well-field system, it would be better to set a limit on the field area per capita and ban land transactions so that everyone shall have land to cultivate, the poor and the weak, be supported, and land consolidation, be prevented, to make prearrangements for a perfect system." (Du, 1988, p. 13)

Under the Eastern Han government, the agricultural poverty relief dwindled from land granting to food giving: "At the beginning land was granted to the people from the imperial directly controlled estates. Then the emperors had to trust the local administrators to execute the order. Thereafter imperial grace was reduced to granting permission to collect food and other items in the imperial parks. And finally, the government could extend relief to the poor only by distributing food." (Hsu, 1980, p. 33) The first reason is that the Eastern Han did not have enormous amounts of uncultivated land like the Western Han; more importantly, the Eastern Han government usually distributed the land to the poor instead of lending it to the poor for farming as the Western Han government did. The land given away to the poor was often subject to private acquisition so that the government-controlled land kept decreasing and the aid-to-the-poor programs were not sustainable (Hsu, 1980).

5.1.3 Rise and Decline of the Equal-Field System

Based upon previous theories and lessons, the Western Jin government promulgated the *Order of Officials' Land Occupation and Their Tax-Free Client Households* and Land *Occupation Edict* which determined the land quota of officials and ordinary people to curb land consolidation. 50 *qing* was allowed to officials of Rank 1, and it decreased by 5 *qing* for every rank down the list so that an official of Rank 9 had a quota of 10 *qing*. A maximum of 70 *mu* was allowed to an ordinary man, and 10 *mu* to an ordinary woman (Du, 1988, p. 15). This heralded the equal-field system of the Northern Wei Dynasty.

In AD 485, Emperor Xiaowen of the Northern Wei initiated the equal-field system that continued for about 300 years into the Northern Qi, Northern Zhou, Sui, and Tang Dynasties. Prolonged wars had forced people to flee their homes, leaving the land desolate. The peasants who had chosen to stay had to depend on the noble families to be free from exorbitant taxes and heavy corvee. In response to the situation, the government of Northern Wei issued the *Equal Field Edict*: A man over 15 years of age was given 40 *mu* of arable land and a woman, 20 *mu*; the man was furthermore given 20 *mu* of mulberry fields, and the woman, 5 *mu*; but the man would be granted 10 *mu* of hemp fields and the woman, 5 *mu*, in the hemp production area. Serfs had the same benefits. The land was also granted 30 *mu* per ox of four years old or above, and that applied to a maximum of four oxen. The arable land, owned by the government, was given to people at the legal age of taxpaying, and must be farmed for grain crops instead of cash crops. It was strictly forbidden to leave the land untilled or trade it. The land had to be returned to the government when the peasant died or was old enough to be exempt from tax and corvee, and the same was valid for the loss of serfs and oxen. In contrast, the mulberry fields were "inheritable and would never be given back". Land giving was scheduled for January (the slack season) to avoid the normal cultivation and harvest season. "A *mu* was granted to three new settlers or five serfs for their housing", similar to the homestead today. Local officials were allotted certain quotas of public land, depending on their ranks, near their office, but they were strictly prohibited from trading the land which started the office fields for dynasties to come (Du, 1988, pp. 17–19).

The equal-field system took full account of reality under the general principles of "equal distribution of land" and state ownership (right of disposal). For example, it takes years for the perennial mulberry trees to grow up, and the farmer will incur losses if the government takes back the land and grant it to someone else when the trees start to yield returns. On that account, the *Equal Field Edict* stipulated that mulberry fields did not need to be given back and could be passed down to descendants. The fields were called "hereditary fields" in the Northern Qi. However, a family might have accumulated vast fields of mulberry trees after several generations (Du, 1988, p. 18). In this regard, the *Equal Field Edict* specified that "those who have excess mulberry fields shall neither return nor receive land, but those who have less than the stipulated quota shall be legally granted more land for mulberry planting. The former may sell the excess, and the latter may buy land to make up the shortfall". However, the seller was forbidden to sell his quota, and the buyer, to buy more than his shortfall. In addition, the uneven population distribution across different regions made it unfeasible to allot the land evenly so that the land granting quota should be greater in the sparsely populated areas to avoid abandoned land, and it should be less in the densely populated places to prevent short supply. With those scenarios in mind, the *Equal Field Edict* of the Northern Wei regularly authorized the government to double the arable land granted so that a man was usually given 80 *mu* of land and a woman, 40 *mu*, which was called "double field system". But the system was not adopted in a heavily populated region (Sa, 2007, p. 303).

The equal-field system of the Northern Wei relatively realized Xun Yue's idea of "farming the land without owning it" by the land granting and returning system by which the government recovered the ownership of vast arable land and the peasants had the right to occupy and use (cultivate) the land instead of the right to dispose of (sell or buy) it. The separation of land ownership from its use rights restricted the land trade and concentration and the dream was fulfilled that "every tiller should have his lot". However, its limitations must be noted. On the one hand, the government based the system on the enormous amounts of abandoned land at its disposal after peasants fled their homes because of the running wars. As soon as population grew, the imbalance would be bound to reemerge between a large population and limited land resources. On the other hand, the system meant even distribution of land on the part of ordinary people, but official were granted more office fields or public land which was changed later into tradable permanent property under Emperor Xuan of the Northern Wei. By relinquishing the right to dispose of the office fields, the government seriously damaged the separation of ownership and use rights established by the equal-field system and made a freehold property of the office fields, giving rise to land consolidation and concentration. What's worse, numerous bureaucrats bulk-bought or seized peasants' land under the banner of "trading office fields" so that peasants could not keep their small land holdings. "In fact, the Northern Qi government permitted land trade where the sellers were certainly the poor and the purchasers were large landowners. 'Consequently, the powerful bullied the powerless and took their land by force, the rich owned vast fields connected by paths, and the poor had no room to put his awl in'. It was difficult to keep the equal-field system working in such a situation". "The eighty plus years from the end of the Northern Wei Dynasty to the end of the Sui Dynasty witnessed several problems with the equal-field system, the major one being whether the peasants were able to keep their small landholdings ... The solution to their problem was not how to increase the arable land, but how to keep what they had been given. In the land trade, they were the sellers instead of the buyers" (Xu, 1957, pp. 445, 447, 450). The problem might be essentially reduced to whether the government had enough land to grant and retained the right to dispose of the land after it had been granted.

The early Tang Dynasty inherited the equal-field system (grain-labor-kind tax), but relaxed the restrictions on the free land trade. The granted land was divided into state fields and hereditary fields. The former given when the person was a grownup would be returned to the state upon the recipient's death whereas the latter could be passed down to descendants, but theoretically, neither of them could be traded freely because the articles relating to Household and Marriage from the *Tang Code* listed the sale of state fields as an account of crime. However, according to the *Tang Code with Commentaries* finished during the years from AD 650 to 655, hereditary fields could be sold when the family was too poor to afford a burial; the state fields could be sold, too, when the family moved from a populous region to a thinly populated place, and they might also be traded as housing, mills, and brokers' storehouses; bestowed land and the hereditary fields of officials of rank five or above could be put on the market freely (*Tang Code with Commentaries*, Section 15).[7] The free flow of land led to the prevalent land consolidation, increasingly undermining the equal-field system.

[7] For the details of the Tang codes and their commentaries, see Zhangsun (1936).

Meanwhile, the population kept expanding against the limited land resources; the population density varied visibly from place to place, and it was difficult to match the land data on record up with the actual population distribution so that "insufficient land for granting and uneven distribution" occurred frequently. During the Kaiyuan era (AD 713–741) of the Tang, "peasants were seriously under-granted, and in the capital area 'packed with families, the fields were insufficient when granted on the basis of the quota system'" (Chen, 2008, p. 14). In addition, "the household registry stayed the same too long to show the recipient's death and the change of landowners." After the Rebellion of An and Shi, "the good governance of the ancestors was swept away and the military commissioners' secessions disrupted the unity of the regime. Therefore, it was impossible to set it in order even if the government wanted to" (Xu, 1935, p. 63).

The Song Dynasty saw more concentrated land so that Emperor Renzong issued an edict to "limit the land a farmer could have", but "it was soon revoked because officials excused themselves from executing the order" (recited from Sa, 1975, p. 115). At that time, the large landlords occupied the absolute majority of the country's arable land, and small farmers declined rapidly in number (Yang, 1957).[8] What's worse, the government forced peasants to sell their land to the government, turned it into government land, and leased it back to the peasants for profit. Such government lands were not really public because they were actually government-run estates the ruling cliques owned and profited from (Cheng, 1957). Thereafter, it was no longer possible to revive the equal field system aiming to equalize land rights.

5.2 Divided Property Rights on the Premise of a Private Ownership of Land

The period from the Five Dynasties to the Song Dynasty was an important turning point in Chinese history when the "Song learning" replaced the "Han learning" academically; the land ownership underwent drastic formal and substantial changes summarized by scholars as "privatization of government land and government rent". Previously "when the Eastern (Asiatic) characteristics were at work, the land system headed toward the opposite direction: nationalization of private land and private rent by which the state was the landlord and collected taxes as rent when his land was legally granted as private land or 'hereditary property' in the name of the state. Now, the Five Dynasties and the Northern Song reversed the course, and the state delegated the land more considerably to the ordinary landlords ... so that the latter notably consolidated their land ownership without knowing it. Even though the feudal state owned some land, it would run the land exactly like an ordinary landlord and exploit peasants on it" (Zhao, 1984, pp. 387–388). It may be concluded in a sense that the national land policy was centered on "even distribution" before the Tang Dynasty, and on "consolidation" after the Song Dynasty. However, the deepening

[8] For the land consolidation data, see Yang (1957, pp. 476–478).

privatization of land from the Song to the Qing did not mean that all land rights headed from separation to union. Divided Ownership such as communal ownership and shared ownership still existed under the premise of private land ownership.

5.2.1 Communal Ownership (Collective Ownership)

In traditional China, "An individual could not be independent of groups because his or her existence depended on the latter. Of all groups, the most solid and influential were the village and the clan … Clans usually had their public property, such as ancestral temples, sacrificial fields, charity parks, clan property, and so on while villages had theirs, such as public lumber lands and pastures, common lands, public cemeteries, public temples, and temple property. The owner of the public property was an inclusive clan or village. The public property was the total composed of various functions that constituted the ownership, and it belonged to the group and its members" (Dai, 1966, p. 304). Clan property and village property were mainly land whose property rights were divided. When land was being privatized in the Five Dynasties and the Song Dynasty, the government no longer liked to move ahead with equal land rights for small farmers, but the people had to seek private relief so that they initiated mutual assistance and provided aid for the poor within the collectives, that is, the clan or the village. Accordingly, the clan organizations revived together with emergence of the sacrificial fields and charity parks in the Song Dynasty.[9] In the early and mid-twentieth century, statistically, the communal property of clans was less than 1% of the total arable land in the totally privatized northern China, about 15% in the Yangtze River Basin, such as Hunan and Hubei, and 30–80% in Guangdong, Zhejiang, and Jiangsu where traditional folk communities (clan organizations) were most active. "In many parts of those three provinces, small landlords were members of clan communes instead of traditional peasants." (Qin, 2003, pp. 312–313) It is clear that the collective ownership of rural land had a long history in a considerable part of China. Even when the land was family-owned, the patriarchal management and instruction made its property rights compositionally different from the private property rights in the West.

i. Clan property

Sacrificial fields and charity parks were typically clan property. Sacrificial fields were allocated primarily for ancestral sacrifices and secondarily for poverty relief among clansmen and education so that "they went beyond personal interest of clansmen toward a common goal". A keeper was appointed to take care of the sacrificial fields, but major decisions needed to be made by the clan assembly through collective

[9] The ancestral temple was common in the ancient times, but in the Song Dynasty, the separated clans started to jointly build their ancestral temple and joined together in the ancestral sacrifice. Prevalent in the Six Dynasties period due to the eminent families, the genealogy declined after the middle of the Tang and revived after the Song. Now politically useless, it aimed to unite the clansmen to support and defend the clan (Dai, 1966, pp. 192–193).

resolution. The charity parks were said to have originated from the Fans' Park created by Fan Zhongyan, a politician and poet of the Northern Song Dynasty. Designed to help the poor and the widowed by using the income from the parks, they were also used to offer sacrifices to ancestors and educate children. Compared with the sacrificial fields, the charity parks were more independent from the clan. They owned property under their own name as a legal entity represented by the manager entrusted to rent the fields, collect rice as rent, and distribute it. The clansmen jointly established the parks and enjoyed their yields, but they could not claim their ownership rights according to the charter (Dai, 1966, pp. 195–198).

ii. Village property

Village property was the total property of the village and the villagers, and its management and disposal were subject to the village whereas the villagers enjoyed the right to use the pasture and lumber land and share the returns. The villagers were jointly liable for the debts of the village (the village assembly and the village temple). The rights and corresponding obligations resided with the villagers who settled in the neighborhood, and terminated when they migrated (Dai, 1966, p. 305).

iii. Family property

Different from a nuclear family in the modern West, the traditional Chinese family consisted of three generations including grandparents and grandchildren, uncles and nephews, and sisters-in-law, enjoying the same property and housing. As long as the family stayed together, all family members jointly owned the family property and were entitled to a certain amount of returns the property yielded. Men of the same generation each had an equal share of the property when the family divided. However, the parents (especially the lineal parents) had the authority over the management and disposal of the property. All this clearly shows the separation of property rights.

5.2.2 *Perpetuated Tenancy and Separation of Ownership Rights from Permanent Tenancy to Two Landlords to a Field*

Permanent tenancy, which prevailed after the middle of the Ming Dynasty, was a form of tenancy in the late traditional Chinese society. A tenant who leased the land from a landlord in the form of permanent tenancy had the right to permanently farm the land without rent arrears, but he could not sublease the land to another tenant without permission. Viewed from institutional economics, the permanent tenancy provided the landlord with stable long-term rental income, reducing costs of supervision, management, and contract signing; it also brought tenants stable expectations of long-term returns on investment, encouraging them to increase investment and improve land fertility. "The landlord merely collected land rent, and the change of the landlord did not affect the tenant. That is, a change of the landownership had no impact on the tenancy. This system reflected both the tenancy's relative independence and its tendency toward perpetuation" (Chen, 2008, p. 22).

Separation of the ownership rights means the system of two landlords to a field, which, historically recorded in the Song and Yuan, prevailed in South China after the Ming Dynasty. The ownership was divided into rights of two layers: topsoil (*tianpi*, 田皮) and subsoil (*tiangu*, 田骨) of the land. Usually, the landlord had the subsoil rights and the tenant, the topsoil rights, but it was the opposite in certain regions. In Taiwan Province, the two types of rights were respectively called large and small rents. There were three reasons for the division of land ownership. The first was reclamation and improvement. The landlord leased the land in the form of permanent tenancy to the highly qualified tenant for reclamation and improvement. After a long time, the permanent tenant assumed himself as the landowner and usually got recognized as such. Consequently, the ownership was divided into two layers with the original landlord as the owner of the subsoil and the tenant as the owner of the topsoil. This case was different from the general "permanent tenancy" in that the topsoil owner (the original permanent tenant) could sublease the land to collect excess land rent and even sign a new permanent tenancy with a subtenant, and that the subsoil owner (the original landowner) should not recover the land even in case of rent arrears. Secondly, the landlord might be able to sell part of his land ownership, that is, the right to collect rent (large rent), the right to farm the land or the right to sublease (small rent). Thirdly, the landlord might be able to transfer the rent collection right gratis to temples or powerful families for charity or favor (Dai, 1966, pp. 301–303). Of the three cases above, the first one was the regular. That is, the permanent tenancy tended to turn the tenant into one of the two landlords to a field. In addition, in the Qing Dynasty, the landlords sometimes granted the tenants the topsoil rights to stimulate their enthusiasm for reclamation and production when establishing a tenancy. It was especially common in newly developed areas such as Taiwan and Rehe (Yang, 1988).

5.3 Characteristics of the Traditional Chinese Land Ownership

5.3.1 Particularity of the Land System in China

Different from the land system under the Anglo-American and the European Continental property laws, the land system was both one of the top political issues and an important social policy in dynastic China; with a dual nature of public and private law, it featured the separation of property rights, and its tradition continues into today with inconclusive disputes over relevant systems. Traditional China was a typical agricultural country with a large population so that the tension between the people and the land was acute thousands of years ago. That is the point *Comprehensive Statutes* of Du You (AD 735–812) started with: "The people live on grain; the grain lives on the land; the people are the subjects the monarch rules. The country is strong with grain, the people have sufficient food with clearly defined fields, and corvee is evenly distributed with an accurate population census. Governance is how to regulate those three factors" (Du, 1988, p. 2). The "clearly defined fields" relates to the land ownership which was one of the paramount issues in imperial China for thousands of years. Based on the "Asiatic mode of production" proposed by Karl Marx' and the family tradition advocated by Confucianism, traditional China evolved a unique idea and system of land ownership, which had a far-reaching influence. The system typically featured the separation of property rights, that is, parallel ownership rights to the same land of different classes who enjoyed the possession, use, fruits, and disposal of the land in different ways. After a century's legal modernization, Chinese features are still visible in today's land system. For example, the national (collective) ownership of rural land is separated from the individual's right to use the land and enjoy the returns. The national ownership of urban residential land is also separated from the individual's use rights.

Some scholars consider land ownership as an absolute and unlimited property right and "Chinese characteristics" merely mean an obsolete system of unclearly defined land ownership so that complete privatization of land is the best choice. However, some others believe that the land ownership is a fluid logical concept instead of a fixed one, and it changes with historical or specific events. In fact, the history of comparative legal system saw two opposite legal traditions concerning the ownership of land (real estate): the Roman and the Germanic. The land ownership (including the entire real property right) in ancient China was different from the classical Roman legal tradition in the West, and was closer to the Germanic collectivism. Firstly, the Roman legal tradition pursued individualism whereas the Germanic law and ancient Chinese law promoted collectivism, and their land ownership had features of identity laws. Secondly, the Roman land ownership was an absolute and exclusive right, but the Germanic and Ancient Chinese land ownership was a right of superficies compatible with other kinds of property rights. Thirdly, the former was a single and abstract right with certain content while the latter could be divided economically into specific ownership rights enjoyed by two or more different classes. Fourthly, the former belonged to private law, but the latter mixed the land ownership under the private law with the right to use the land under the public law (Dai, 1966).

The special political and socio-cultural situation kept ancient China hesitant upon absolute property rights (especially land property rights) despite the fact that statutory laws were created quite early in traditional China and the private ownership of land was established far earlier in China than in the European feudal countries. Zhao Lisheng, an authority on land system history, described the changes of the land property system in traditional China in terms of "softened" and "heightened" private ownerships. The softened private ownership meant that "private ownership of land encountered obstacles from the very beginning" with "the first obstacle being the ancient community (the remnants of the commune) and the second, the interference of state power in private property (including private ownership of land)" (Zhao, 2013, pp. 9–10). Conceptually, the ancient Chinese, who never failed to speak of the three earliest dynasties and value the public over the private, tended to consider the public land system (the well-field system) that represented the ancient communal tradition, as the highest ideal of the land property system. Even though the reality prevented the ideal from being attained, the land system needed to approach it by limiting the private ownership. Socio-economically, it was an important social policy of the ancient Chinese government to suppress land consolidation and help the peasants in need of land because China did not have sufficient arable land for a large population in the ancient times. The ancient governments frequently attempted to restrict private land property ownership, as can be seen from the Jin's land quota system and the Northern Wei's equal-field system. The tenacious genes of ancient communities, together with developed state power, made China's socially orientated legislation relatively mature long before the private property right was "heightened". Different from the Western classical liberalism, the state interference in the citizens' land rights was viewed not as a natural "evil" but as a necessary "good" in traditional China. However, the pursuit of a public land system could not repel the economically motivated campaign of the property owners to privatize the land so that the noble and the wealthy eventually swept aside the restrictions the equal-field system imposed on the land sale. The land ownership was highly private after the Song Dynasty. Although the state still owned a large amount of land, it managed land "just like private landowners" and "there was no big difference between them", which was a heightened private ownership of land (Zhao, 2013, pp. 327–329).

However, even when the private ownership of land was heightened after the Song (the state abandoned the land socialization), the tradition of the ancient communities still posed a major obstacle to absolute private ownership of land property. In traditional China, "an individual could not be independent of groups because his or her existence depended on the latter." (Dai, 1966, p. 304) Within the scope of families, clans and villages, the public property of small communities still coexisted with the private property of individuals. In addition, governmentally, the highest principle of handling civil property disputes was harmonious coexistence instead of absolute protection of property rights; when the enforcement of property rights threatened the right to survival, traditional laws would not defend or would even deny the legitimacy of absolute property rights: "The game would not be worth the candle if one sought to fully exercise one's rights in disregard of the neighbors' claim of their right to survival" (Hiroaki, 2012, pp. 223–225). For example, when the tenant family were forced into a corner due to the landlord's termination of the tenancy (legal reclamation of his land), they might commit suicide as the last confrontation in the weak position. The landlord might have to bear criminal responsibility in accordance with the penal article "forced suicide" although there was no direct causal relation between the landlord's exercise of his right and the tenants' death.

5.3.2 Institutional Tradition and Folk Custom Under Collectivism

In traditional China, collectivism (familism) was observed ideologically, emphasizing the national and collective interests over the personal interests. State ownership of land (king-owned land) was pursued politically as can be seen in the Minor Odes from the *Book of Songs* which regards "the whole country as the king's land". That is, land ownership was subordinate and subject to state power. In the daily economic life, the land ownership was not an absolute and exclusive right because it might be collectively owned, or coexist with other real rights, or get split up into ownership rights enjoyed by different classes. A study of the institutional history of China's land property rights enabled the author to conclude with three characteristics which were inseparable from the separation of land property rights in operation and are still practically significant today.

i. The political idea and practice of public ownership of land

In the Chinese history, the public land system was the highest ideal which kept winning supporters in spite of being inappropriate. The well-field system was theoretically a pure public land system, and the equal-field system was a public land system compatible with private ownership of land on the condition that the country had an enormous amount of grantable land. In traditional China, "any seemingly private property right would be restricted by the state and would not go totally private even after repeated struggles"; "state ownership was everyone's ownership virtually"; "ancient Chinese did not have such contractual relationships as that between kings and peers of all ranks, merchants, burghers in medieval Europe because family heads in various forms represented all relations as the sole legal representatives, and those heads formed a hierarchy of subordinate relationships topped by the king or emperor, the ultimate family head of property rights" (Wang, 1999, pp. 2, 5). Public ownership of land (state-owned or king/emperor-owned land) was also the fundamental path to curb land consolidation and fulfill the ideal of "land for every tiller". In the Western Zhou Dynasty, the land and the population were theoretically owned by the king and the system of top-down hierarchical enfeoffment and possession resulted in split land property rights, forming a special ownership of land. The equal-field system from the Northern Wei to the Tang separated the small farmers' usufruct and long-term possession of land from the state ownership, and the state restricted the right to dispose of land (free trade); the state, as a landlord, collected land rent from small farmers in the form of taxes ("combination of tax and rent"). Basically, the ideal of public ownership of land was realized through different ways of separation of land property rights in the well-field system and the equal-field system. However, as the state was debilitated in its control over the right to dispose of land, the separation of property rights broke down, followed by rampant land consolidation and destruction of public ownership of land at the cost of small farmers.

In recent years, "privatization of land" has come to be an option relished by quite a few scholars of law and economics because it is considered to be the core issue of property rights protection. However, do privatization and free flow of land really benefit the common people in the long run in such a country as China that has a large population, limited land resources and glaring issues relating to agriculture, rural areas and farmers? Historical experience and lessons should not be ignored. As for the argument that "the state's refusal to give up the state ownership of land is merely based on practical interests", it may be found from the post-Song history that the state's rejection of the public ownership of land does not mean its termination of heavy taxation, i.e., the state may raise its revenue by collecting more taxes than under the equal-field system. In that case, the common people might suffer double exploitation by the big landowners and the government as well.

ii. The folk tradition of collective land ownership

In post-Song southern China, land owned by such groups (collectives) as clans and villages accounted for a considerable proportion of all cultivated land; within the family, all the members shared the property as a small group. The property rights of these collectively owned "public lands" were a complex "aggregate ownership" because the groups and individuals all enjoyed the management, disposal, use, and returns of the land as a whole.

A study of this folk tradition may significantly help to understand the origin and changes of the current collective land ownership in the rural areas. It's advisable to realize the rationality and positive value of the collective ownership as a "long-term reality" instead of simply labeling it as "vaguely defined property rights".

iii. The customary separation of land property rights in social and economic life

Land was the basic means of production and livelihood for the traditional Chinese people. Given a large population and limited land resources, the people placed a high value on land property rights so that they would never totally give up land when there was an alternative. Consequently, the separation of the use right from the ownership was complemented by the system of two landlords to a field by which the original landlord transferred part of his land ownership and retained the remaining part. In addition, in order to retain the land ownership while obtaining the land value, the ancient Chinese designed "pawn" and "the pawnbroker's rights", which, as unique real estate property rights in traditional China, were paralleled with the land ownership; even when the land as a whole had to be sold, pawn (unregistered transfer of land ownership for a certain amount of time) was adopted over registered transfer of ownership. All these were original Chinese ways of handling land property rights. The separation of land property rights or split ownership does not agree with the "Western nomology",[10] but it was widely accepted by traditional customs, which graphically demonstrates "experience over logic".

[10] The Western nomology here means the Continental legal tradition which has a strict definition of ownership. The Anglo-American legal system is more flexible because the ownership is considered to be not a single right but a bundle of rights and the partial transfer of the rights will not lead to transfer of the ownership.

References

Chen, G. (1977). *Zhongguo fazhi shi gaiyao* [History of Chinese legal system]. San Min Book Co., Ltd.

Chen, H. (2008). *Gudai nongcun tudi zhidu sixiang de kaocha* [A study of thoughts on the rural land system in the ancient times] [Unpublished master's thesis]. Fudan University.

Cheng, S. (1957). Nansong de guantian zhidu yu nongmin [The public land system and the peasants in the Southern Song Dynasty]. In Editorial Board of Historical Research (Ed.). Zhongguo lidai tudi zhidu wenti taolunji [Essays on land systems in the dynastic China] (pp. 489–502). SDX Joint Publishing Company.

Dai, Y. (1966). *The legal history of China*. San Min Book Co., Ltd.

Du, Y. (1988). *Tongdian* [Comprehensive statutes]. Zhonghua Book Company. Hsu, C. (1980). *Han agriculture: The formation of early Chinese agrarian economy*. University of Washington Press.

Hiroaki, T. (2012). *Rights and injustice: Collected essays on Chinese legal history* (Y. Wang et al., Trans.). Tsinghua University Press. (Original work published 1953).

Hsu, C. (1980). *Han agriculture: The formation of early Chinese agrarian economy*. University of Washington Press.

Huang, D., & Fan, Z. (2003). Chunqiu zhu xingshu xingding jiujing zhaoshi le shenme [What revolutions did the Cast Penal Code and Law Tripods reveal in the Spring and Autumn Period?] Faxue [*Law Science*], (2): 53–61.

Lü, S. (2002). *Zhongguo zhidu shi* [History of Chinese systems]. Shanghai Education Press.

Mencius. (1970). *The Works of Mencious* (J. Legge Trans.). Dover Publications.

Qin, H. (2003). *Chuantong shilun—bentu shehui de zhidu wenhua jiqi biange* [Ten lectures on tradition: Native social systems, culture and reform]. Fudan University Press.

Sa, M. (1975). *Zhongguo shehui zhengzhi shi* [A socio-political history of China] (Vol. 4). San Min Book Co., Ltd.

Sa, M. (2007). *Zhongguo shehui zhengzhi shi* [A socio-political history of China] (Vol. 2). San Min Book Co., Ltd.

Tao, Y. (2000). Chanquan xuzhi de lishi zhuizong [A historical study of nominal ownership]. Xueshu yuekan [Academic Monthly], (3):52–54. https://doi.org/10.19862/j.cnki.xsyk.2000.03.009

Wang, J. (1999). Zhongguo chuantong shehui nongye chanquan bianxi [A study of agricultural property rights in traditional China]. *Shilin* [Historical Review], (4): 21–29.

Xu, D. (1957). Juntianzhi de chansheng he pohuai [The origin and ruin of the equal-field system]. In Editorial Board of *Historical Research (Ed.). Zhongguo lidai tudi zhidu wenti taolun ji* [Essays on land systems in the dynastic China], (pp. 429–455). SDX Joint Publishing Company.

Xu, S. (1935). *Zhongguo tianzhi shilue* [A short history of Chinese land system]. The Commercial Press.

Yang, G. (1988). Lun Zhongguo yongdianquan de jiben tezheng [On essential characteristics of Chinese permanent tenancy. *Zhongguo shehui jingjishi yanjiu* [Journal of Chinese Social and Economic History], (2): 10–16.

Yang, Z. (1957). Beisong de tudi jianbing wenti [Land consolidation in the Northern Song Dynasty]. In Editorial Board of *Historical Research (Ed.). Zhongguo lidai tudi zhidu wenti taolun ji* [Essays on land systems in the dynastic China], (pp. 476–478). SDX Joint Publishing Company.

Zhang, Y. (2003). *An outline of Chinese history*. The Commercial Press.

Zhangsun, W. (1936). *Gutanglu shuyi* [Tang Code with commentaries] (Vol. 12). The Commercial Press.

Zhao, L. (1984). *History of Chinese land system*. Shandong Qilu Press Co., Ltd.

Zhao, L. (2013). *History of Chinese land system*. Wuhan University Press.

Chapter 6
Judicial System in Ancient China

6.1 Judicial Organization

6.1.1 Judicial Structure of the Qin Dynasty

The Qin Dynasty established a highly centralized political system, wherein the supreme judicial power of the country was vested in the hands of the emperor. Below the imperial echelon, both central and local administrative structures had full-time or part-time judicial officials to handle a variety of specific legal issues.

i. The Chamberlains for Law Enforcement (*tingwei*, 廷尉). The title *tingwei* referred both to a specific judicial official and a judicial office. As one of the "Nine Ministers" in the central government, the head of the Chamberlain for Law Enforcement stood as the highest-ranking judicial official beneath the emperor, shouldering the responsible for nation-wide legal and judicial affairs. In addition, censors during the Qin Dynasty also undertook judicial responsibilities, including the supervision and disciplinary surveillance of officials who had offenses or neglected their duties.
ii. Commandry and county. The administrative organs at the commandry and county levels had full-time or part-time judicial officials to attend to the local judicial affairs.

6.1.2 Judicial Structure of the Han Dynasty

i. Central judicial organ

The Han Dynasty inherited the judicial system of the Qin, where the emperor holding the supreme judicial power. All serious and complex cases must be reported to the emperor for a final decision. The emperors of the Han often heard cases themselves.

X. Nie, *The History of Government and Public Law in China*,
https://doi.org/10.1007/978-981-97-6063-3_6

1. The Chamberlain for Law Enforcement. As the head of the central judiciary, the Chamberlain heard criminal cases assigned by the emperor ("imperial cases" subjected to imperial edicts for conviction), and serious and difficult cases reported by various local offices. Under the Chamberlain were several subordinate officials namely left and right aides (*zuoyouzheng*, 左右正), left and right police officers (*zuoyoujian*, 左右监), and left and right judges (*zuoyouping*, 左右平), to assist with and take charge of specific trials. For particularly pressing or substantial cases, a joint hearing consisting of the Prime Minister, Censor-in-chief and the Chamberlain for Law Enforcement would be convened, a process known academically as "mixed hearing".
2. The Censor-in-Chief (*yushi dafu*, 御史大夫). The Censorate (*yushi tai*, 御史台, lit., terrace or pavilion of imperial scribes, i.e., of censors) had a Secretarial Censor (*zhishu shiyushi*, 治书侍御史) responsible for interpreting the laws. By the time of Eastern Han Dynasty, the power of Vice Censor-in-chief (*yushi zhongcheng*, 御史中丞)[1] was further expanded, who not only took responsibility for investigating malfeasance among officials and impeaching high-ranking ministers for misconduct, but also engaged in the revision of laws and the hearings of major and difficult cases. Therefore, metaphorically speaking, the Censorate became the emperor's "ears and eyes", playing dual role in judicial trial and legal supervision.
3. Metropolitan Commandant (*silixiaowei*, 司隶校尉). The Metropolitan Commandant had the power to oversee stagnant cases, miscarriage of justice, and malpractice by judicial officials within the metropolitan area and central organs, possessing the authority to penalize minor offenders but presenting more severe cases directly to the emperor for final verdicts bypassing the Prime Minister.
4. Imperial Secretariats (*shangshu*, 尚书). Emperor Cheng of the Han Dynasty set the precedent with the establishment of the Section for the Three Dukes (*sangong cao*, 三公曹) in the Imperial Secretariat. This body had charge of hearing cases and making judgement, thus taking over partial judicial authority. In the Eastern Han, the status of the Imperial Secretariat was elevated so that "all matters shall be channeled to the Imperial Secretariat". Six sections were set up respectively below the director and vice director of the Secretariat, and Section for Commandery Governors (lit., Section for 2000-bushel officials, *erqiandan cao*, 二千石曹) "presided over judicial issues", paving the way for the subsequent formation of the Ministry of Justice in the Sui and Tang Dynasties.

ii. Local judicial organ

In the Han Dynasty, local governance had the two-tier administrative structure of commandry and county. The governor of commandry was both the executive and judicial head, assisted by full-time Judicial Section officials (*juecaoyuan*, 决曹掾) to hear specific cases. Likewise, the county magistrate served as both the executive and judicial head, with a subordinate section (*cao*, 曹) to assist with case trials. The local judiciaries in the Han were judicially powerful because the commandry

[1] Also translated into Palace Aide to the Censor-in-chief (Notes by translators).

governors and county magistrates not only wielded the power to sanction and report local cases, but also to adjudicate death penalty cases. However, cases of considerable importance and difficulties must be memorialized to the central authorities and the emperor for a final verdict.

In the early Han, each vassal state (princedom) held its own jurisdiction, with the metropolitan superintendent (*neishi*, 内史) as an assistant for the kings and marquises to hear cases. After Emperor Jing of the Han, the status of princedoms was reduced to that of commandry and county, the jurisdiction of which was shifted to the Prime Minister.

Since Emperor Ling of the Eastern Han, inspective regions, originally under the supervision of Regional Inspectors, gradually evolved into the highest local administrative unit to govern commanderies and counties. Regional Governor had the jurisdiction of that region and was responsible for hearing major cases reported by its commanderies and counties.

6.1.3 Evolution of Judicial Structures in the Wei, Jin and Southern and Northern Dynasties

i. Establishing the Court of Judicial Review (*dali si*, 大理寺)

The Northern Qi Dynasty formally established the Court of Judicial Review, headed by Chief Minister (*dali si qing*, 大理寺卿) and Vice Minister (*dali si shaoqing*, 大理寺少卿). The establishment of the Court of Judicial Review not only amplified the adjudicative functions of the central judicial organ, but also laid an important foundation for the later dynasties to improve on it. (The Empire of Cao Wei changed the Chinese character 平 in their title to 评, both pronounced as "ping", with the former implying fairness and the latter denoting reviewing, and Emperor Yang of the Sui Dynasty added 48 Case Reviewers (*pingshi*, 评事), marking the precursor to judicial officials in ensuing ages.)

ii. Strengthening the supervisory power of the Imperial Censor

During the Three Kingdoms Period, the two Jin Dynasties and the Southern and Northern Dynasties, in order to suppress the separatist forces, the supervisory power of the censors was significantly augmented. In the Jin Dynasty, the Palace Aide to the Censor-in-Chief was appointed as the head of the Censorate, who wielded a wide range of authorities, under the direct order of the emperor to censure all legal cases. Moreover, secretarial censors were placed to impeach and try law-breaking officials.

iii. Imperial Secretariats vested with judicial power

During the Three Kingdoms Period, the two Jin Dynasties and the Southern and Northern Dynasties, the status of the Imperial Secretariats was further enhanced. Under the Cao Wei regime, the role of judicial oversight and management of prisoners was transitioned to the Minister for Criminal Administration. This administrative evolution laid the foundational precedent for the Minister of Justice during the Sui and Tang Dynasties to assume responsibilities related to judicial review and adjudication.

6.1.4 Judicial Structure of the Tang Dynasty

i. Central judicial organ

1. The Court of Judicial Review

The Court of Judicial Review had a Chief Minister and Vice Minister, exercising the central judicial power and hearing cases involving central government officials and punishments more serious than penal servitude in the metropolitan area. Sentences of banishment and imprisonment should be sent to the Ministry of Justice for review and capital cases must be memorialized to the emperor for approval. Furthermore, the Court of Judicial Review had the authority to review cases of death penalty and those of doubt and difficulty transferred by the Ministry of Justice.

2. The Ministry of Justice

The Ministry of Justice was led a Minister and a Vice Minister, further divided into four courts, i.e., Bureau of Judicial Administration (*xingbu*, 刑部), Criminal Administration Bureau (*duguan*, 都官), Bureau of Review (*bibu*, 比部) and Bureau of Frontier Control (*simen*, 司门). The Ministry of Justice had the power to engage in the hearings of grave cases, to review cases submitted by central and local authorities, and to hear appeals of the remanded in custody.

3. The Censorate

The Censorate was led by the Censor-in-Chief and the Palace Aide to the Censor-in-Chief (or Vice Censor-in-Chief), consisting of three sections, namely the Headquarters Bureau (*taiyuan*, 台院), the Palace Bureau (*dianyuan*, 殿院) and the Investigation Bureau (*chayuan*, 察院). As the central supervision institution, the Censorate had the authority to oversee the trials of the Court of Judicial Review and the Ministry of Justice, participated in the hearings of difficult cases, and handled administrative litigation.

4. The Three Judicial Offices System

In the Tang Dynasty, to deal with serious cases in central or local areas, a joint supreme court would be temporarily organized comprised of the Vice Minister of the Ministry of Justice, Vice Censor-in-Chief and the Minister of the Court of Judicial Review, titled the "Three Judicial Offices" system. When a grave case occurred at locality and it was not convenient to transfer it to the central jurisdiction, the three commissioners—a case reviewer of the Court of Judicial Review, the vice director of the Ministry of Justice, an investigating censor of the Censorate would be dispatched to manage it. Furthermore, the Tang Dynasty also set up a collegial panel at the Head

Office of the central government. In the event of a serious case of death penalty, the emperor ordered the "fourth-rank and above officials of the Secretariat and the Chancellery, and the nine ministers of the Chamberlains of the Imperial Secretariat to deliberate on it" for prudent consideration of punishment.

ii. Local judicial organ

In the Tang Dynasty, the local judicial bodies remained under the purview of their corresponding chief administrative officials. Accessory clerks such as Adjutants of Law Section (*facao canjun*, 法曹参军) or judicial administrators at the prefecture level and judicial assistants or scribes at the county level, were established to assist prefecture and county governors with judicial trials. Local headmen below the county level, including *xiang* (乡, town) and *li* (里, village), took the responsibility of overseeing criminal cases. They were also vested with the power to mediate and handle minor offenses and civil disputes. However, any decisions or resolutions reached had to be reported and ratified by higher authorities.

6.1.5 Evolution of the Judicial Institution in the Song Dynasty

i. Creation and abolition of the Judicial Control Office

Emperors in the Song Dynasty intervened in the administration of justice by law. Besides the Three Judicial Offices, Emperor Taizong created within the palace the Judicial Control Office (*shenxing yuan*, 审刑院), which was staffed with multiple administrators. All lawsuits adjudicated by the Court of Judicial Review should be forwarded to the Judicial Control Office for review and presented to the emperor for the final approval via the Palace Secretariat. During the Yuanfeng Reform (a large-scale bureaucratic reform in the Yuanfeng reign period), Emperor Shenzong decided to abolish the Judicial Control Office and restored the old system of the Court of Judicial Review and the Ministry of Justice.

ii. Shifts in the jurisdiction of the Three Judicial Offices (Na, 2004a, pp. 170–174)

In the early Song Dynasty, the Ministry of Justice saw a significant diminishment in its authority due to the overarching influence of the Judicial Control Office. However, after the Yuanfeng Reform, the power of the Ministry of Justice expanded considerably. It assumed comprehensive oversight of the nation's judicial affairs. Criminal law, legal proceedings, legal records and documents, granting of amnesties, and reinstatement of demoted officials all fell within its jurisdiction. "The Judicial Control Office is responsible for reviewing death penalty cases in the capital area, selectively reexamining death penalty sentences outside of the capital area, rectifying ill-settled lawsuits by the Court of Judicial Review, the capital area of Kaifeng, and the Palace Command, and in case of appeals, exercising its discretion to either aggravate or mitigate the penalties, to grant amnesty, demote, or fully exonerate (*The History of the Song Dynasty Treatises on State Offices*—The Ministry of Justice).

Before the Yuanfeng Reform, the Court of Judicial Review did not engage in direct interrogations of the accused. Instead, its primary role was limited to reviewing written legal proceedings, and no detention facility or prison was set up therein. Cases arising in the capital region were predominantly overseen and adjudicated by the Kaifeng Prefecture and the Censorate. However, subsequent to the Yuanfeng Reform, the jurisdiction of the Court of Judicial Review expanded to encompass direct hearings of cases within the capital, accompanied by the establishment of its own detention facilities.

The Censorate in the Song, relative to its Tang Dynasty predecessor was noticeably understaffed, and its judicial authority and purview were substantially curtailed.

iii. The establishment of the office of the Superintendency of Penal Affairs

Emperor Taizong of the Song started to strengthen local judicial supervision. Above the level of prefectures and counties, the office of the Superintendency of Penal Affairs was established, serving as the central government's judicial envoy across various jurisdictions. The office regularly inspected prefectures and counties, supervised local hearings, and meticulously documenting the details of prisoners. In situations where local officials were found to have transgressed legal boundaries during trials, it could immediately intervene and render a decision in minor cases, or, in graver cases, submit it to the emperor for a final verdict.

iv. Separating trial from judgment (Xu, 1975, pp. 97–98)

The principle of separating "trial" from "judgment" entailed that the body responsible for investigation (or interrogation) was distinct from the decision-making entity in charge of legal deliberation and sentencing. This was instituted to mitigate the risks of arbitrary judgments by a single official. In the Song Dynasty, this bifurcation was practiced at the central government level, circuits (the Superintendency of Penal Affairs) and subprefectures (prefectures). The only exception was at the county level. The Court of Judicial Review expanded its personnel by appointing two more deputy ministers, the Right Bureau and the Left Bureau; within subprefectures and prefectures, judicial administrators undertook the investigative role, while administrators for public order (*sili canjun*, 司理参军) determined legal matters and appropriate sentences.

6.1.6 Judicial Structure in the Yuan Dynasty

i. Central judicial organs

During the Yuan Dynasty, the Court of Judicial Review was abolished and the Ministry of Justice assumed the primary role in adjudication, thereby consolidating the powers of judicial examination and administrative oversight. However, the

Ministry of Justice could not adjudicate cases involving Mongolian nobility, princes and dukes. Instead, these cases were under the exclusive purview of the Mongol High Court of Justice, which functioned independently without any reciprocal oversight with the Ministry of Justice. Although the Censorate held a prominent status within the bureaucratic hierarchy, it lacked the authority to supervise the judicial proceedings of the Mongol High Court of Justice. In addition, the Yuan Dynasty established several specialized institutions: Bureau of Military Affairs, which concurrently took charge of military-related trials; Commission for Buddhist and Tibetan Affairs, responsible for religious trials; Daoist Office, designated for cases related to Daoism; and Household Service for the Empress, responsible for cases originating within the imperial palace. The simultaneous exercise of judicial authority by various central, religious, military, and administrative institutions in the Yuan Dynasty resulted in a lack of uniformity in judgments and ambiguity in legal application. This fragmented system posed significant challenges to the effective governance and stability of the Yuan Dynasty.

ii. Local judicial institutions

During the Yuan Dynasty, the local judicial framework was delineated into five hierarchical levels: provincial, circuit, prefectural, subprefectural and county. This structure maintained the integration of both judicial and administrative functions.

6.1.7 Judicial Structure of the Ming Dynasty

i. Central judicial organs

The Ministry of Justice was responsible for adjudication, the Court of Judicial Review, for review, and the Chief Surveillance Bureau Censorate (*ducha yuan*, 都察院), for legal oversight and also adjudication, the three of which were collectively known as the "Three Judicial Offices". Given that the Ministry of Justice took full charge of court trials, its structure was expanded from an original four bureaus to thirteen, which attended to local appeals, cases concerning central officials and cases within the metropolitan area. Upon the completion of adjudication, the case documents, together with the convicted, should be transferred to the Court of Judicial Review for review. Regarding sentences less severe than exile, should the Court of Judicial Review affirm the judgements appropriate, the Ministry of Justice would then prepare relevant documents for imperial memorial and proceed with the punishment; otherwise, the case would be remanded for retrial. In situations involving capital punishment, after the initial deliberation by the Ministry of Justice and subsequent review by the Court of Judicial Review, the case had to be presented to the emperor for final approval before any execution could be carried out.

In the Ming Dynasty, *Yushi tai*, the Censorate was renamed as *ducha yuan* (都察院), the Chief Surveillance Bureau, marking a significant expansion in both its organizational structure and jurisdictional reach. This bureau was staffed with prominent positions such as Left Censor-in-chief, Right Censor-in-chief and investigating censors, responsible for censuring and impeaching officials throughout the country for any malfeasance or criminal transgressions, and participating in trials of grave and difficult cases and overseeing the enforcement of laws. The Chief Surveillance Bureau had their own detention facilities, specifically designated for high-profile detainees whom the emperor personally ordered to be incarcerated. From the 10th year of the Xuande reign (AD 1435) onward, the Ming divided the country into 13 administrative circuits, with a total of 110 investigating censors directly under the lead of the Chief Surveillance Bureau and spearheading local supervisory functions. As part of their mandate, these censors would routinely embark on inspection tours, ensuring adherence to judicial standards at the local level. Upon uncovering misconduct or illegal activities perpetrated by local officials, they held the authority to "report major cases to the emperor for final judgment, while promptly adjudicating lesser infractions".

ii. Local judicial institutions

In the Ming Dynasty, local judicial institutions were organized into a tripartite hierarchy, encompassing provincial, prefectural (or sub-prefectural), and county levels. The Surveillance Commissions at the provincial level possessed the authority to adjudicate cases that warranted sentences of imprisonment or lesser penalties while cases demanding punishments above penal servitude must be submitted to the Ministry of Justice for approval and execution. Prefectures and counties implemented a unified system that combined the judiciary and the executive, where prefects and magistrates took charge of local judicial matters. The Ming Dynasty also built within each subprefecture, county and township "Statement Pavilions" (*shenming ting*, 申明亭), which publicly displayed proclamations detailing local transgressions, serving not only as a record but also as a means of societal edification. Within this framework, esteemed senior citizens, distinguished for their moral standing and respect within the community, were tasked with mediating and resolving local civilian disputes. This mechanism played a crucial role in preserving and upholding the conventional social hierarchy and order.

iii. Depots and Guards interfering with judicial affairs

In the Ming Dynasty, besides the regular judicial organs, special espionage judicial agencies were set up, notably the Brocade Guards (*jinyiwei*, 锦衣卫), the Eastern Depot (*dongchang*, 东厂), the Western Depot (*xichang*, 西厂) and the Palace Depot (*neihangchang*, 内行厂). These establishments were conceived to buttress the autocratic imperial authority and to meticulously monitor both officials and commoners. The intervention of the Depots and Guards in the judiciary started in the 15th year of the Hongwu reign (AD 1382), when Emperor Taizu of the Ming ordered the Brocade Guards to have charge of penal affairs, investigative operations and detentions. The Brocade Guards administered two divisions, namely the Southern Chief Prison and the Northern Chief Prison. The latter was particularly responsible for liaising directly with the emperor on legal matters, executing imperial edicts, and also operating its distinct court and detention facility to manage felonies involving conspiracy, heresy, homicide and major theft. As a result, prisoners of grave offenses were often detained in the Brocade Guards. While the latter phase of Emperor Taizu's rule saw a brief interdiction of the Brocade Guards' activities, his successor, Emperor Chengzu, promptly reinstated them. In an expansion of the surveillance apparatus, Emperor Chengzu introduced the Eastern Depot, a secret agency manned by eunuchs and singularly focused on uncovering insurrection, treachery and other heavy crimes, holding a status surpassing even the Brocade Guards. Emperor Xianzong and Emperor Wuzong of the Ming respectively established the Western Depot and the Palace Depot, the latter of which was emerged as the preeminent entity, overshadowing the other two Depots in its jurisdiction and influence. The Depots and Guards pervasively intervened in judicial matters, causing significant disruptions. This undue influence manifested in multiple ways, which are elucidated as follows.

First, under the pretense of "executing imperial mandates", the Depots and Guards passed judgments which the Three Judicial Offices had neither the authority to revise nor challenge, and at times, were compelled to implement.

Second, the Depots and Guards practiced unlawful detentions and meted out punitive actions without any legal constraints. Their actions, rather than being grounded in concrete evidence, were often predicated merely on street rumors or a solitary accusation. Consequently, an atmosphere of palpable dread permeated the empire, where the populace was "gripped by pervasive trepidation, and robbed of the simple joys of existence". This heightened societal and political tensions, culminating in the hastened decline of the Ming Dynasty.

6.1.8 Judicial Structure of the Qing Dynasty

i. The central judiciary (Na, 2004b)

Drawing from the legacy of the Ming Dynasty, the Qing Dynasty continued to operate with the Three Judicial Offices—the Ministry of Justice, the Court of Judicial Review, and the Chief Surveillance Bureau—placing them at the center of the judicial system. In addition, a plethora of organizations collectively contributed to jurisdiction, such as the Deliberative Office, the Grand Secretariat, the Grand Council, the six Ministries of Personnel, Revenue, Rites, War and Public Works, the Department for Ethnic Affairs, the Office of Transmission, the Office of Commander-general of the Eight Banners, the Office of Commanders-general of the Infantry, the Censorate of Five Capital Wards, the Court of the Imperial Clan, the Imperial Household Department, all of which served as judicial organs in a broad sense. Inheriting the judicial system of the previous dynasty, the Qing established the Three Judicial Offices system comprised of the Ministry of Justice (hearings), the Chief Surveillance Bureau (oversight) and the Court of Judicial Review (review). "It is the Ministry of Justice that upholds justice, the Chief Surveillance Bureau that censures law enforcement, and the Court of Judicial Review that serves as the remedy for judicial wrongs." (*Da-Qing Huidian, The Code of the Qing Dynasty*[2]).

1. The Ministry of Justice

The Ministry of Justice served as the principal entity overseeing nationwide legal matters, encompassing both adjudication and judicial administration. It "was vested with the authority to dictate punitive edicts throughout the realm, aiming to support the emperor in ensuring societal order. Issues concerning the judicious application of laws, the fidelity of judgments to established statutes, considerations of leniency or rigor in sanctions, and specifics of confiscations, penalties, and redemptions were to be communicated by respective offices to the Ministry of Justice. There, senior officials, including the Imperial Secretaries, would convene and deliberate. Weighty matters were presented to the emperor, while less significant ones were promptly adjudicated by the Ministry, underscoring the reverence for national legal codes." (*The Code of the Qing Dynasty*) The actual authorities of the Ministry of Justice can be distilled into six pivotal aspects, namely: (1) reviewing cases from various provinces that pertained to sentences surpassing penal servitude; (2) Adjudicating matters within the capital that bore penalties exceeding penal servitude; (3) jointly reviewing autumn assizes cases in each province; (4) jointly reviewing court assizes cases in the metropolitan area; (5) holding administrative jurisdiction over areas like judicial analytics, prison governance, confiscation of illicit assets, and evaluation of the Ministry's personnel performance; (6) leading the endeavors to amend legal codes and precedents, routinely amassing case examples for comprehensive consolidation when when the Codification Office convened. Of the three judicial offices, the Ministry of Justice was the most powerful. According to the *Draft History of Qing*, "all provincial criminal cases shall be reviewed by the Ministry of Justice. Neither the Court of Judicial Review nor the Censorate had the prerogative to intervene in cases not rightfully within their domain. The Ministry of Justice took the lead in drafting for those cases necessitating judicious arbitration. All lawsuits in the capital area, whether memorialized to the throne or not, fell squarely within the jurisdiction of the Ministry of Justice, a testament to its unparalleled and prodigious influence."

2. The Chief Surveillance Bureau

The Chief Surveillance Bureau "was entrusted with overseeing the propriety and discipline within the bureaucracy, examining the operations of various governmental departments both within and beyond the metropolitan area, and weighed the efficacy of governance and the integrity or misconduct of officials." "For grave offenses warranting capital punishment, decisions are collaboratively made by the Ministry of Justice, the Chief Surveillance Bureau and the Court of Judicial Review. The Chief Surveillance Bureau also plays a role in autumn assizes and court assizes". (*The Code of the Qing Dynasty*) The Chief Surveillance Bureau was nicknamed as fengxian yamen, acting as the stewards of institutional norms and the conduct of the

[2] *The Code of the Qing Dynasty* is the largest judicial corpus on administrative matters compiled during the Qing period. (Notes by translators)

officialdom. While its primary responsibilities lay in surveillance, assessment, and remonstrance, its judicial purview was but one facet of its multifaceted role. It had 15 circuits (provinces) and 6 offices. The 15-circuit (provincial) censors inspected and handled judicial cases in their respective province while the Supervisor Censor of the Six Offices of Scrutiny oversaw the Ministries of Personnel, Revenue, Rites, War, Justice and Public Works respectively. In the first year of Emperor Yongzheng of the Qing (1755), these six offices were incorporated into the Chief Surveillance Bureau, culminating in a streamlined, unified entity.

The Chief Surveillance Bureau participated in judicial proceedings, where its duties were twofold. First, it engaged in judicial review, i.e., scrutinizing all cases across the nations that proposed capital punishments. According to The Qing Tongdian (The Administrative History of the Qing Dynasty)[3], "Prisoners condemned to capital sentence by the Ministry of Justice should be jointly reviewed by imperial censors, case reviewers of the two departments of the Court of Judicial Review (Right and Left Court of Review, 右寺，左寺), officials from the Ministry of Justice. This collective examination, which seeks to rigorously assess the merits of the case and ensure the propriety of the capital judgment, is termed 'the assemblage of the lesser three judicial authorities'. When these capital cases ascend to the Censor-in-Chief, the Minister of the Court of Judicial Review, Minister and Vice Ministers of the Ministry of Justice for joint hearings, each party contributes it jurisprudential perspectives to the ministerial discussion, a process designated as 'the assemblage of the greater three judicial authorities'". Second, the Chief Surveillance Bureau participated in autumn assizes and court assizes and submitted a memorial in reply to the emperor for ratification of execution.

3. The Court of Judicial Review

The Court of Judicial Review was mainly responsible for passing judgements. As a department of prudent sentencing, it also had control over judicial trials and administration. According to *The Code of the Qing Dynasty*, "[The Court of Judicial Review] passes final verdicts on criminal cases nationwide. It marshals its subordinate officials to jointly review and discuss the capital cases, to join the nine ministers to review serious cases related to state politics, participate in autumn assizes and court assizes." The judicial authority of the Court of Judicial Review was mainly fourfold, namely, to jointly review death penalty cases in each province; to jointly review death penalty cases in the capital area; to jointly review autumn assizes cases in each province; and to jointly review court assizes cases in the capital area. The judicial activities of the Court of Judicial Review resembled those of the Chief Surveillance Bureau. Specifically, the Court of Judicial Review collaborated in hearings for capital offenses within the capital and in the collective scrutiny of capital punishment cases from the provinces, in the manner of circulating for perusal the suggested adjudication prepared by the Ministry of Justice and countersigning. Central to the Court's

[3] Also called *Qingchao tongdian*, it is an administrative history compiled on imperial order between 1767 and 1786. (Notes by translators).

role in these collaborations was an emphasis on rectification—vigilantly examining and redressing instances of miscarriages of justice.

ii. The local judiciary

1. Subprefectures, counties, and detached subprefectures

Governors of subprefectures and counties were obligatory to try all cases personally within their jurisdiction. This gave rise to the adage, "All cases originate from subprefectures and counties." As courts of first instance, subprefectures and counties had the authority to mete out punishments involving bamboo strokes, but sentences graver than penal servitude must be escalated to higher judicial bodies. Amidst the myriad cases they processed, local governors had no ultimate jurisdiction over severe criminal cases punishable with penalties higher than penal servitude; such cases were mandatorily elevated for sequential scrutiny at each successive administrative tier. Cases warranting penal servitude should undergo the first instance of subprefectures and counties, and tiered reviews of prefectures, the Provincial Surveillance Commission and the provincial governors or viceroys, with the final verdict being rendered by the latter. For heinous crimes, particularly those involving capital offenses or major thefts, post the first instance at the subprefecture and county level, both the accused and the corresponding case records were dispatched to superior authorities for further examination and adjudication.

Another category of cases under the purview of subprefecture and county administrators pertained to disputes over land rights, domestic affairs, and minor physical altercations, collectively termed "self-adjudicated disputes." This category encompassed two subtypes: firstly, civil disputes arising from household registry, inheritance, marriage, lands, water source management, and debts and secondly, minor criminal offenses that warranted punishments like bamboo stroke (beating with a light or heave stick) and cangue-wearing (a shoulder-borne portable pillory) in public due to brawling, inflicting minor injuries, and theft. According to the *Draft History of Qing*, "Cases pertaining to domestic affairs, land rights, and minor offenses meriting bamboo strokes are settled conclusively by magistrates of subprefectures and counties, typically referred to as 'self-adjudication'". The laws of the Qing Dynasty unambiguously articulated the independent judicial power of subprefectures and counties over such kind of cases, as "Subprefectures and counties shall, on their own, handle all lawsuits related to households, marriages and land disputes." (*The Great Qing Legal Code · Criminal Laws · Indictment · Lawsuits Rejected*)

2. Prefecture/directly administered subprefecture/directly administrated prefectures

Prefectures (or superior prefectures) had charge of reviewing criminal cases submitted by their subprefectures and counties, formulating preliminary sentencing recommendations and reported to their respective provincial Surveillance Commission. "Cases from subprefectures and counties should be reviewed and moved up to a superior jurisdiction by their corresponding prefectures ... while cases from counties below directly administered subprefectures and prefectures, by directly administered subprefectures and prefectures." (*Da-Qing huidian, The Code of the Qing Dynasty*) When prefectures adjudicated cases from their associated subprefectures and counties, it constituted a second-instance review. Similarly, when directly administered subprefectures and prefectures presided over cases from their respective subordinate entities, they too were acting in a second-instance capacity. However, when prefectures, directly administered subprefectures, and directly administered prefectures dealt with cases arising within their immediate jurisdiction, it marked a first-instance adjudication.

3. Circuit

Circuits did not a necessarily hear cases. Per *The Code of the Qing Dynasty*, cases within the jurisdiction of the directly administered subprefectures and prefectures should be reviewed and moved up by circuits. So should cases from the regions within the direct jurisdiction of prefects." When the directly administered subprefectures and prefectures had no subordinate counties, the circuit hearing was the second instance. However, when subordinate counties were present, the circuit acted as the third tier.

4. The Provincial Surveillance Commission

The Provincial Surveillance Commission served as the central repository for all criminal matters within a certain province, reviewing cases more serious than penal servitude submitted by prefectures or circuits[4] as well as interrogating prisoners sentenced to military exile or death penalty. In scenarios where interrogations aligned with confessions, such cases would be forwarded to the provincial governors or viceroys for validation. Nonetheless, if discrepancies or oversights were detected, such cases could either be referred back for a meticulous review or redirected to an alternate subprefecture (county) or prefecture within the same province for retrial.

5. Governors-general (Provincial Governor)

In accordance with the *Great Qing Legal Code*, penal servitude cases no involving fatalities were directly subject to the conclusive approval of the Governors-General or Provincial Governors.

6.2 Judicial Procedure

6.2.1 Judicial Procedure in the Qin Dynasty

Models for Sealing and Investigating, a manuscript discovered among the bamboo slips unearthed from Qin tombs, recorded a large number of judicial case analyses, which shows that a relatively systematic and sophisticated system had been established for judicial hearing in the Qin Dynasty.

---

[4] Cases transferred by prefectures underwent the third instance of surveillance commissioners while cases transferred by circuits, the third or fourth instance.

i. On-site investigation and inspection. The *Models for Sealing and Investigating*
ii. Interrogation. Under the principle of "Presumption of Guilt", employing interrogation techniques on the accused was a standard legal procedure. According to the statutes of the Qin Dynasty, the primary method of interrogation should be through verbal questioning, carried out exhaustively. Achieving truth without resorting to physical coercion was considered the optimal outcome. However, if, after repeated attempts, the truth remained obscured, only then was the use of torturous methods sanctioned to extract a confession.
iii. Jurisdictional texts. Documents chronicling judicial activities were termed *yuanshu* (爰书, judicial document), including narratives of the case, statements from the accused, testimonies from witnesses, and accounts of interrogations. The laws of the Qin Dynasty stipulated that all trials should be recorded by this kind of document.
iv. Plea for retrial. A petition for retrial was called *qiju* (乞鞫, lit., begging for trial), which may be either initiated by the defendant directly or presented on their behalf by a proxy.

6.2.2 The Luqiu (Judicial Review) System in the Han Dynasty

The term *luqiu* (录囚, lit., prisoner transcript) referred to a system in which higher judicial organs would supervise and scrutinize the judgements passed by their subordinate counterparts, by reviewing and auditing the transcripts of prisoners' hearings. This was done with an aim to rectify miscarriages of justice and expedite lingering legal cases. Since the middle Western Han Dynasty, government officials routinely visited prisons to inspect the legal documents of inmates; after the Eastern Han, sometimes the emperor and the empress dowager also heard cases personally as a display of their "imperial benevolence". The importance of the *luqiu* system was underscored by its continual endorsement and adoption by subsequent dynasties, as it proved instrumental in accelerating the disposition of protracted legal matters and in exonerating those wrongly accused or unjustly condemned.

6.2.3 Retrial and Appellate System in the Tang Dynasty

The Tang legal codes provided that upon the conclusion of a case, the verdict should be read aloud to the convicted and their family members. If the offender raised an appeal, it should be reheard by the original judicial authorities. Rejecting an appeal resulted in a penalty of 50 blows with the light stick while rejecting death-row prisoner's petitions, 100 blows with the heavy stick. As prescribed by *The Six Statutes of the Tang Dynasty*: following an initial appeal, should the original court maintain its decision, the case could be appealed progressively up the hierarchical judicial system, even up to the emperor himself. However, any attempts to bypass the structured appellate levels, jumping directly to a higher authority, were strictly prohibited.

6.2.4 Judicial Procedure in the Song Dynasty

i. The emperor's direct involvement in judicial review and adjudication

To enhance the oversight of the judicial process, emperors of the Song Dynasty took it upon themselves to exercise judicial powers directly. Admittedly, objectively speaking, many monarchs during this era were well-acquainted with the nuances of the legal system. For example, Emperor Taizong "frequently heard trials himself and made verdicts for complex cases within the capital region"; Emperor Huizong often "handwrote imperial edicts and amended the existing legal statutes". When the emperor personally adjudicated a case, a practice termed as "Zhihui" (or "commanded"), it meant that no further appeals could be made, nor could there be any delays in executing the judgment; any contraventions were met with penalties. Moreover, in the Song Dynasty, any legal matters that were not explicitly outlined in the codified law had to be presented to the emperor for a final judgment. Those failing to adhere to this were held accountable, reinforcing the sacrosanct nature of the emperor's judicial prerogative. Emperor Taizu continued the tradition of personally reviewing prisoners' case. In the fourth year of the Qiande reign (AD 966), Emperor Taizu "heard in person the cases of inmates from the Kaifeng Prefecture, leading to several pardons". Successive Song emperors emulated this hands-on approach to the judicial system.

ii. Retrial after retracted confessions and evidence inspection

From the Tang Dynasty onwards, if a defendant retracted their confession, the protocol demanded that the case be reevaluated from the beginning. This practice, known as "re-judgment", persisted into the Song era. Under Emperor Taizu, a specialized system for dealing with such retractions was implemented. If a defendant, during the proceedings, withdrew their testimony (*fangong*, lit., flipped confession) and the matter of significant import, it should be transferred to another judge or another jurisdiction (alternative investigation) for a complete retrial by either another judge of the same judiciary or another court after verdicts overturned on two occasions (Xu, 1975, pp. 153–162).

Both the Northern and Southern Song Dynasties placed great stress on proof for trial, the burden of which lied on both the plaintiff and the defendant. The local judicial bodies of the Southern Song Dynasty prioritized on-site investigation and formulated a professional catalogue of forensic examination, giving rise to one of the earliest global texts on forensic medicine, the *Collected Records of Amending Unjust Verdicts*.

6.2.5 Judicial Procedure of the Qing and Ming Dynasties (With a Focus on the Qing Dynasty)[5]

i. Joint hearing by the Nine Ministers

The Joint Hearing by the Nine Ministers was an important retrial system in the Ming and Qing Dynasties. This institutional framework was designed to address complex and high-stakes cases that were referred from local jurisdictions. In instances where the accused remained dissatisfied with the verdict even after undergoing two levels of appeals, the case would be subjected to a comprehensive examination by a panel of nine high-ranking officials known as the "Nine Ministers" comprised of the six Ministers of the six ministries, the Chief Minister of the Court of Judicial Review, the Left Censor-in-Chief of the Censorate and Commissioner of the Office of Transmission. Ultimately, the fate of the case rested with the emperor, who held the ultimate authority to issue a final judgment.

ii. Heat assizes

Heat assizes, as a part of the judicial review system in the Ming Dynasty, applied to minor criminal cases within the metropolitan area for retrial. In the first year of the Hongzhi reign (AD 1488) of the Ming, heat assizes were formally established as a customary practice. This annual process, which took place during the summer months, involved a collaborative effort between officials of the Court of Judicial Review, censors in each province and the office in charge under the Ministry of Justice. [6]The primary objective of heat assizes was to facilitate expeditious adjudication or release of individuals serving sentences involving bamboo strokes, with a particular emphasis on demonstrating the principles of "careful application of law".

iii. The "litigation announcement on the third and eighth days" and limited litigation period

In order to mitigate the pervasive "litigious" culture among the populace and promote a cessation of legal disputes to ensure agricultural production, the laws in the Tang, Song and Yuan Dynasties all stipulated that civil matters concerning households, marriage and lands were not accepted (heard/tried) during the half-a-year span from each April to September. *The Penal Law System of the Song Dynasty · Household Code* also prescribed a special division to deal with "marriage and land complaints". The Ming Dynasty repealed such kind of regulations, but prefecture and county courts still enforced specific litigation announcement dates. Except major cases, trivial matters should not be submitted to court beyond the said dates, which were, before the Qing on the third, sixth, ninth day of the first, middle and last ten days of each month (i.e., the third, sixth, ninth, thirteenth, sixteenth, nineteenth, twenty-third, twenty-sixth, twenty-ninth in the lunar month); and after the 19th century, the

[5] This section has a focus on the Qing Dynasty. For more details, see Na (2004a, 2004b, 2004c, 2006)

[6] The Brocade Guards in the Ming Dynasty also participated in heat assizes.

third, eighth day of the first, middle and last ten days of each month (i.e., third, eighth, thirteenth, eighteenth, twenty-third, twenty-eighth in the lunar month). This shift led to the establishment of the widely recognized "litigation announcement on the third and eighth days". In the Kangxi reign of the Qing Dynasty, the practice of "suspending litigation during busy farming season" in the Tang, Song and Yuan Dynasties was restored. No lawsuits were permitted in the busy farming period from the first day of April to the thirtieth day of July in the lunar calendar. During this time frame, local governments refrained from handling "minor cases" concerning marriage, lands, etc. Failure to adhere to this directive could result in local officials being specifically named and subjected to disciplinary action by provincial viceroys in accordance with the prevailing legal provisions (Yang, 2005, p. 427).

iv. Judicial review tier by tier

In the Qing Dynasty, the judicial process moving up from local jurisdictions up to the central government comprised the following stages: (1) first instance by prefecture, county and detached prefecture; (2) review by the directly administered subprefecture and prefecture; (3) review by the circuits (provinces); (4) reconsideration by the (Provincial) Surveillance Commission; (5) reconsideration by provincial governors-general and governors; (6) consultations with the Ministry of Justice, formulations of official memorial and personal memorials to the throne; (7) review by the central judicial offices (with cases related to imprisonment, exile, penal military service under the purview of the Ministry of Justice while capital offense cases by the three judicial offices); (8) preparing the draft rescript, provisional adjudication and final verdict for death penalty sentences. Cases entailing bamboo strokes were tried and concluded by subprefecture governors and county magistrates. Routine cases of imprisonment were closed upon governors-general and governors' review and ratification, and were collected and compiled into quarterly reports by the (Provincial) Surveillance Commission to present to governors-general and governors, who in turn forwarded the records to each ministry. Regarding death penalty cases reconsidered by governors-general and governors, typical cases were communicated to the emperor through official memorials, while particularly severe cases necessitated submission through personal memorials, presented in person to the emperor.

1. Cases of imprisonment, exile, penal military service reviewed by the Ministry of Justice

The Ministry of Justice had the authority to scrutinize and reassess cases about which each province presented for consultation, that is, to examine imprisonment and exile sentences compiled on a quarterly basis and to reconsider special cases of imprisonment, exile, penal military service. Any decision made by the Ministry—whether it's an affirmation of the original verdict, an amendment, or a recommendation for retrial—required imperial endorsement to become effective.

(1) Affirmation of the Original Verdict: When the established facts were coherent and the applied legal provisions were deemed appropriate, the Ministry would formally present the case to the throne for confirmation.

(2) Amendment of the Original Verdict: If an inconsistency in the application of legal codes was identified, the Ministry would formally present the corrected judgment to the emperor for his approval.
(3) Recommendation for Retrial: In instances where either the facts were not congruent with logical inference or there was an inappropriate application of legal codes, the Ministry could advise a retrial. Following the emperor's endorsement of this advice, an official directive would be sent to the relevant provincial governor-general and governor for further action.

2. Capital cases reviewed by the Three Judicial Offices (deliberation of sentencing, collective review and memorial drafting)

Cases officially memorialized to the throne by each province were usually assigned at the emperor's order to the Three Judicial Offices, which would conduct concerted reviews, make judgement and present a personal memorial to the throne in reply; capital cases personally memorialized to the throne were usually dispatched at the emperor's order to the Ministry of Justice, which would carry out discussions, or conduct reviews and make judgements, and thereafter prepare the official or personal memorial to the throne in reply. Capital case of critical importance specially memorialized to the throne must be dealt with as soon as possible, so that the Three Judicial Offices were spared from a joint hearing and only the Ministry of Justice took charge of the hearing and presented a special memorial to the emperor afterwards. Regarding assemblage review and countersigning, according to the *Da-Qing Huidian* (*The Code of the Qing Dynasty* · Precedent Case): Whenever the Three Judicial Offices are summoned by an imperial decree to jointly review a matter, the Ministry of Justice takes the initial responsibility to clarify the case. After consolidating testimonies and determining sentences, they draft the judgment and forward it to the Chief Surveillance Bureau for a supplemental review. Subsequently, the case is dispatched to the Court of Judicial Review for another layer of scrutiny. The three judicial authorities jointly present the imperial memorials when they agree upon the same verdict, but, in instances of dissent, submit their respective memorial articulating its unique standpoint.

Following a review by the central judicial offices, the outcomes typically included: concurrence with the initial judgment; rectification or annulment of the prior verdict; mandating a retrial; attaching a slip of petition to the case presented to the emperor for discretion (primarily in cases of significant moral concern); two judgments from the Three Judicial Offices (indicating divergent and irreconcilable views held among the three judicial bodies). The *Da-Qing Huidian* (*The Code of the Qing Dynasty*) reads that: "When the Three Judicial Offices jointly review grave cases and differing opinions surface, those with dissenting views are permitted to articulate their perspectives. The final adjudication rests with the imperial decree. Nonetheless, each judicial body must refrain from adopting a stance starkly at odds with the Ministry of Justice. When the Ministry of Justice drafts the imperial memorial, As the Ministry of Justice prepares its imperial memorial, it should not proffer annotations distinguishing the merits and flaws of the dual opinions, but rather present them impartially, in anticipation of the emperor's ultimate determination".

3. Death penalty cases: draft rescripts, provisional adjudication and final verdict

(1) The Grand Secretariat drafted the endorsement response to the imperial memorial and the Grand Ministers of the State discussed together to render preliminary judgment. Capital case submitted by each province in routine memorials, after reviewed by the Three Judicial Offices, shall be written out and reported to the throne via imperial memorials, to which the Grand Secretariat shall attach their suggestions in smaller script written on a leaflet.
(2) The emperor's ruling was applicable to the following situations: First, deferred judgment. This was only applicable to cases of less severity, such as certain cases of murder, robbery or other capital crimes. Here, the sentence was provisional, meaning those condemned to death are not executed immediately. Instead, their fate was determined during the autumn assizes of the subsequent year. Secondly, immediate execution. This more drastic form of justice was wielded in particularly heinous crimes. It applied to cases such as the decapitation of chief culprits implicated in robbery, or the more gruesome dismemberment of those convicted of high treason or acts of rebellion. Once the emperor issued this judgment, the execution was to be effected without delay. Furthermore, typical capital cases involving severe instances of murder or robbery also fell under this category of prompt enforcement.

v. Judicial procedures for cases in the metropolitan region

Judicial procedures for cases in the metropolitan region of the Qing Dynasty were significantly simplified compared to those for local cases.

1. First instance by the Censorate of Five Capital Wards (Patrolling Censors) and the Office of Commanders-general of the Infantry[7]

In the early Qing period, the banner people (Manchus) resided in the inner city of the capital area, with their security and judicial matters overseen by the Infantry Brigade Commanders. Conversely, the Han civilians inhabited the outer sector, coming under the jurisdiction of the Censorate of Five Capital Wards. This clear demarcation began to blur post the mid-reign of the Kangxi Emperor, as the Manchu and Han populations intermingled, leading to an overlapped jurisdiction between the two courts over both territorial zones and their respective inhabitants. Civil litigations, pertaining to household affairs, matrimonial disputes, and land-related issues, were primarily addressed by the Censorate of Five Capital Wards, with the Patrolling Censors responsible for delivering the final verdict. Criminal proceedings, especially those warranting corporal punishments, were collaboratively adjudicated by both the Commanders-General of the Infantry and the Censorate of Five Capital Wards. Cases bearing graver implications than penal servitude or those of an exceptional nature were referred to the Ministry of Justice for further examination and judgment.

[7] Its full name is the Brigade Commanders commanding the infantry brigades of the Nine Gates and the Five Patrol Garrisons.

2. Second instance by the Ministry of Justice

Cases warranting punishment more severe than penal servitude must be sent to the Ministry of Justice for immediate trial (substantive trial or trial in person, not *ex post facto*). Cases of exile and penal military service can be tried and concluded by the Ministry of Justice; ordinary capital cases must be reviewed by the Three Judicial Offices, but still drafted by the Ministry of Justice; death penalty cases of paramount gravity specially memorialized to the throne were solely processed by the Ministry of Justice.

3. Third instance by the Three Judicial Offices

Cases jointly reviewed by the Three Judicial Offices should be drafted and memorialized to the emperor. Decapitalization and strangulation cases should be executed without delay upon the approval of imperial rescript; remand prisoners should be reconsidered by court assizes.

vi. Autumn and court assizes

The tradition of autumn assizes, judicial reviews concerning cases demanding death penalty, can trace its lineage back to the Ming Dynasty. At that time, it was termed the "court assizes" and was confined to examining the fate of those sentenced to death within the metropolitan precincts. However, the Qing Dynasty expanded this scope to encompass capital cases from the entire nation. Within this broader framework, the evaluation of capital offenses within the metropolitan domain retained the title of "court assizes", while examinations of similar cases from regions beyond the metropolitan boundaries were dubbed "autumnal assizes".

The autumn assizes, also known as the "Grand Autumn Judicial Ceremony", was annually held in the eighth lunar month in the west of Jinshui Bridge (Gold Water Bridge) at Tian'anmen (Gate of Heavenly Peace). Reprieve cases of decapitalization and strangulation across the country were sent for a joint hearing to the nine Ministers, Heir Apparent (*zhanshim*, 詹事), the Supervising Secretariats of the Censorate (*kedao*, 科道), the Grand Councilors, and the Grand Academician of the Grand Secretariat and other eminent officials. The Qing Dynasty specifically formulated *Autumn Assizes Regulations*, laying down basic guidelines for autumn trials. Court assizes in the Qing referred to the revisitation of grave verdicts passed by the Ministry of Justice, particularly those implicating beheadings and strangulations in and around the capital. The organizational approach for these court sessions mirrored, in essence, that of the autumnal assizes.

Upon undergoing review through the autumnal and court assizes, cases were typically categorized into four distinct resolutions: (1) Affirmation, where the criminal facts were verified and the determined punishment were deemed appropriate. In such instances, a request would be memorialized to the throne, seeking approval for the execution of the death penalty. (2) Deferred Execution. In instances where the facts were established, but the crime was assessed to have caused minimal harm, there were several potential outcomes. The sentence can be commuted into exile of 3000 *li* (about 1,500 km) away from the capital, or penal military service in far-away borderland or garrisons in miasmic regions (usually regions in the southwest of China), or remanded in custody for reconsideration in the coming autumn; (3) Pitiable Mitigation Cases that, upon validation, revealed elements of pity or introduced doubt, could result in leniency. Such offenders might be spared the death penalty, instead facing sentences like banishment or penal servitude; (4) Mitigation for Family Duty. In situations where the crime was confirmed and the proscribed penalty deemed just, yet the convicted individual was the sole caregiver for elderly or ailing parents, special consideration was given. The offender could petition for a reprieve from execution to continue their familial duties of care and ancestral observances. The emperor's decree determined whether this plea for clemency was granted.

vii. Adjudication of cases involving the imperial clan and the banner people

1. Cases involving the imperial clan

In the capital area, the Court of the Imperial Clan should jointly hear cases related to households, marriage and lands involving the imperial clan with the Ministry of Revenue, and those of homicide and fighting with the Ministry of Justice. In Shengjing (now the provincial capital of Shenyang in Liaoning), the ancient Manchu capital, the imperial cases shall be heard by the Ministry of Justice and Banner Generals there. When members of the imperial family committed a crime, it should be in principle reported to the emperor. However, during the later periods of the Qing Dynasty, this protocol was relaxed for lesser offenses.

2. Cases involving the banner people

(1) The banner people in the capital area

Within the jurisdiction of the *niulu* (牛录, the basic tribal living-fight group consisting of 300 people), lawsuits related to households, marriages, and lands involving the banner people were presided over by their respective Company Commander (*zuoling*, 佐领) and his higher authority. Should the company commander decline to handle such a case, the banner people could petition the Ministry of Revenue for adjudication. Criminal cases were under the purview of the Commander-general; of the Eight Banners. In the 55th year of the Kangxi reign (AD 1716), it was regulated that homicide cases should be jointly heard by banner commanders and the Ministry of Justice. In the 13th year of the Yongzheng reign (AD 1735), the Ministry of Justice took over cases entailing punishments greater than imprisonment related to the Eight Banners people, thereby ending the jurisdiction of the Commander-in-chief of the Eight Banners over such matters.

(2) The banner people in provincial Banner Garrisons

The Qing staffed banner garrisons with Judicial Assistant Prefect or Judicial Departmental Administrator, who had charge of civil lawsuits when both parties were of the banner ethnicity; if one party was Han-Chinese, the case was processed by prefectural governor or county magistrate. Criminal cases, on the other hand, were heard, verified and processed by Judicial Assistant Prefect (Judicial Departmental Administrator) or sometimes in collaboration with banner members. Cases concluded by assistant prefects in each province were mandatorily submitted to the Provincial Banner General, Commander-general or Vice Commander-general of the Eight Banners for review.

viii. Judicial Proceedings Pertaining to Official Misconduct

1. Scope

All civil and military officials of the ninth rank and above in the central and local government committing crimes were subject to judicial proceedings (with separate regulations for the nobility of the imperial family and banner people).

2. Jurisdiction

Aside from the cases brought to the central court, cases involving governmental officials in each province were, in principle, under the jurisdiction of the corresponding provincial governors or viceroys. The conventional judicial progression usually began with the first instance by circuit intendant or prefect, a review by the surveillance commissioner, and a subsequent retrial by the governors or viceroys. In the capital area, cases involving public officials were under the jurisdiction of the Ministry of Justice or the Three Judicial Offices, among which cases involving civil officials necessitated collaborative proceedings with the Ministry of Personnel, while those related to military officials, with the Ministry of War. When central administrative entities, such as various Ministries or the Chief Surveillance Bureau (Censorate), had members implicated in misdeeds, the case oversight was typically a joint effort between the Ministry of Justice or the Three Judicial Offices and the concerned Ministry or the Chief Surveillance Bureau (Censorate).

3. Impeachment through imperial memorial

In the Qing, the crimes of officials in the capital area or in the provinces were mandatorily reported to the emperor. The act of impeachment, presented through an imperial memorial, was typically undertaken by provincial authorities such as governors, viceroys, military commanders, and the Commander-in-chief in each province. At the central level, the primary responsibility often fell to the Chief Surveillance Bureau (Censorate) and its supervisory secretariats. Moreover, these central institutions, including ministries and courts, retained the prerogative to impeach any misbehavior or negligence exhibited by their affiliated officials. Significant officials in each province committing offences shall not be detained for questioning until their provincial governors or viceroys memorialized the impeachment to the throne and obtained the imperial approval. For lesser provincial officials, detention and inquiry could be initiated immediately upon the day of their impeachment by the respective provincial authority. Upon impeachment, if the veracity of the allegations raised suspicions and necessitated adjudication by the Ministry of Justice, preliminary actions such as suspensions or terminations could be effected by the Ministry of Personnel or the Ministry of War.

Conclusively, after the resolution of cases involving public officials, a comprehensive report, drafted in alignment with the prevailing legal protocols, had to be memorialized and presented to the emperor.

ix. Capital appeal (*jingkong*, 京控)[8]

1. *Yamen* (government office) in charge of capital appeal

The Ministry of Justice, the Chief Surveillance Bureau (Censorate), the Office of Commanders-general of the Infantry, Public Petitioners Drum Office (*dengwengu ting* 登闻鼓厅) took cognizance of the common people's appeals directly addressed to the superior tribunals in the capital region, the majority of which were presented to the Chief Surveillance Bureau (Censorate) in the Qing Dynasty.

2. Methods of capital appeal. The predominant mode of appeal was the submission of a formal written petition to superior courts. However, when directing grievances to the Office of Transmission, an aggrieved party was compelled to strike a drum, irrespective of whether they had tendered a written petition. This act is traditionally termed as "beating the yamen drum in appeal for justice" in ancient Chinese judicial practices.
3. Capital appellate processes by central judicial authorities

For grave offenses, the grievances should be formally memorialized to the emperor. Minor complaints were communicated to the respective provincial governor for trial, or, the appellant concerned might be temporarily handed over to the Ministry of Justice for custody without wearing shackles. During this period, the Ministry of Justice would meticulously review the case files, determining subsequent action. The Chief Surveillance Bureau and the Office of Commanders-general of the Infantry were mandated not to flatly decline petitions originating from each province. Except for severe cases that were immediately memorialized to the throne, those directed back to their originating provinces were often collated and periodically presented to the emperor in comprehensive reports, typically on a bi-monthly basis. The majority of cases from the capital appeals were redirected to the provincial governors for resolution. Only a handful were elevated to the emperor's attention, and even among those, the emperor's directives often mandated their return to the concerned province. These cases, recognized as "imperial decree cases", necessitated the direct involvement of the provincial governor. For less severe offenses under the scrutiny of the Ministry of Justice, a nuanced approach was adopted. Outcomes could vary: from dismissing the need for a retrial, requisitioning case files for a detailed examination in the capital, delegating the case back to the originating province, or even dispatching an imperial envoy for a dedicated investigation.

4. Prohibition of bypassed appeals

Article 332 of the *Great Qing Legal Code* clearly stipulated: "Individuals who bypass their local jurisdiction or superior authorities without first filing a complaint, or

[8] More details about capital appeals can be found in Ocko (2004).

those who appeal directly to the capital while their case is still under review and unresolved, shall be, upon verification by the Ministry of Justice, primarily penalized for sidestepping proper judicial procedures." Following this, the offender would be remanded to their respective province, mandating that the provincial governor or viceroy conduct a fair review and subsequently report their findings to the central tribunal.

x. Knocking at the palace door (*kouhun*, 叩阍) to voice grievances directly to the emperor

1. Methods of *kouhun*

(1) Palace gate appeals: Individuals would approach the palace gate, kneeling and voicing their grievances. While these appeals were taken into consideration, those making them were typically subjected to a penalty.
(2) Intercepting the imperial carriage. During the emperor's public processions, aggrieved parties would present their complaints by stopping the emperor's carriage. If this act did not cause a disruption to the procession, the appeal would be formally registered and considered. Otherwise, it would be dismissed. A notable instance occurred during the Kangxi Emperor's visit to West Lake in Hangzhou. "A man swam toward my boat in Hangchow with a petition tied around his neck, shouting out that he had a certain enemy who was the number-one man in the world for committing evil acts." (Spence, 1988/2011, p. 52)
(3) Submitting sealed petitions. Under the Qing regulations, only high-ranking officials, specifically including the central Nine Ministers and Censors as well as provincial leaders, had the privilege to submit sealed petitions. Any unauthorized submissions with such seals were promptly returned unopened. The violators would then be detained and punished by the Ministry of Justice.

2. Handling *kouhun* appeals

Kouhun appeals often caught the emperor's attention and were typically referred to the Ministry of Justice, various other ministries, or their respective agencies for examination. Some were dispatched to provincial governors for scrutiny, with such cases labeled as "imperial mandate cases". When directed to the Ministry of Justice, the judicial proceedings adhered to the substantive review protocols of the ministry. During the emperor's official tours, *kouhun* cases were frequently assigned to the traveling regional Ministry of Justice for adjudication. Upon concluding the hearings for cases allocated to the Ministry of Justice, or to other ministries and their subordinates, a proposed verdict would be drafted and memorialized to the emperor for final judgment. The emperor then had several options: he could accept the recommendation, request a reevaluation, convene senior ministers for a collective consultation, designate a special imperial envoy to oversee the matter, or independently decide on an alternate course of action.

6.3 From *Chunqiu jueyu* to Parent-Official-Style Individualistic Judgement

6.3.1 Chunqiu jueyu

i. *Chunqiu jueyu* and confucianization of laws

Chunqiu jueyu (春秋决狱, literally judging criminal cases on the basis of the *Spring and Autumn Annals*) refers to the practice whereby criminal cases were judged by invoking the doctrines and examples given in the *Spring and Autumn Annals* as a supplement to enacted laws, especially in solving difficult criminal cases. The *Spring and Autumn Annals* (hereafter called the *Annals*) is a chronicle of the State of Lu compiled by Confucius. It reflects the political thinking and criteria for right and wrong of the Confucian school. Since Emperor Wu of the Han Dynasty decided to dismiss the hundred schools of thought and revere Confucianism alone, traditional laws began to be confucianized, and *chunqiu jueyu* was a manifestation of this trend in the judicial realm. Under this practice, criminal cases were judged in accordance with the spirit and principles of Confucian cannons such as the *Annals* rather than in accordance with the law alone.

Chunqiu jueyu is regarded as an important step in the Confucianization of Chinese laws. The Han Dynasty replicated the legal system of the Qin, which was essentially a system of the Legalist laws. However, this harsh system of laws was modified by the Confucian school in judicial practice. It is said that the Chinese system of laws has a body created by the Legalists and a life endowed by the Confucianists. *Chunqiu jueyu* means, to be more precise, to judge criminal cases by citing the meaningful entries of the *Gongyang's Commentary on the Spring and Autumn Annals*. Among the three commentaries on the *Annals*, *Zuo's Commentary* is the most faithful to historical facts, the *Gongyang's Commentary* excels in the meaningful precedents, while *Guliang's Commentary* focuses on canonical interpretation. Among later scholars who expounded the subtle words and great meaning of the *Annals*, Dong Zhongshu (philosopher and politician of the Han Dynasty) was the most prominent one. With *chunqiu jueyu*, the classical events in the *Annals* were cited as the criteria for making legal decisions, especially when it came to difficult cases. The crime (or innocence) was established essentially by examining the intent of the accused rather than his behavior (what he actually did). When the motive of the accused accorded with the Confucian doctrines of loyalty and filial piety, his punishment could be reduced or even exempted even if he had inflicted harms on society. Conversely, punishment should be meted out when his motive ran contrary to the Confucian spirit, even if his behavior caused no serious consequences.

ii. Core ideas in *chunqiu jueyu*

In ancient China, Confucian scholars worked out a technique of judging criminal cases, i.e., *chunqiu jueyu*, to strike a balance between the norm and expediency, between common sense and inflexible legal provisions.

1. The norm and expediency

What can be done when due to various reasons, the design of the system cannot guarantee an optimal result and produces an outcome that runs contrary to common sense? The doctrine about the norm and expediency in Confucian cannons offers a way out of this predicament. In *Mengzi · Lilou I*, it is said: "For males and females not to allow their hands to touch in giving and receiving is the general rule; when a sister-in-law is drowning, to rescue her with the hand is a peculiar exigency."[9] According to traditional ritual, men and women should not touch each other in giving and receiving. A brother-in-law and a sister-in-law should especially observe such social norms. However, when the sister-in-law fell into the water, the brother-in-law should lend a helping hand instead of sticking to the rigid rules at the expense of his sister-in-law's life. Life and kinship are precious and by far outweighs the rigid rules in importance. Therefore, Zhao Qi says in his commentary: "Expediency is what deviates from the norm but in the meantime is good." As long as it is good, it does not matter if the norm is breached for the time being. Breach of the norm within a certain extent actually saves the norm itself, for a system that is rigid to the extent of often violating human nature and producing an adverse outcome would inevitably be evaded, ignored and ultimately forsaken.

2. Judgment in the light of humanity with consideration of individual circumstances

Most researchers of *chunqiu zheyu* have focused on such aspects as judgement based on the intent of the accused and incorporation of Confucian doctrines into the law. Here in this book, we are more concerned with transformation of a serious offence into a minor one by considering individual circumstances. Judgement based on the intent of the accused was often manifested as alleviation or exemption of the punishment for a crime by consideration of the individual circumstances. As the great historian Sima Qian (1974, pp. 1161, 1157) pointed out, "Rites originated with human beings", "Rituals were formulated by considering human sentiments, and ceremonies were designed based on human nature". In fact, incorporation of rites into the law under Confucianism also entails integration of the human touch into legal decision, which helps inject a humanistic element into the cold and harsh system of laws. Confucianism is gentle, while the law is rigid. *Chunqiu jueyu* in a sense seeks to soften the rigid law with Confucianism. The Confucian cannons may be regarded as the flexible unwritten law, while statutes as the rigid written law. When the rigid written law (statutes) and flexible unwritten law are combined to complement each other, it becomes possible to reconcile the rigidity and flexibility of law (Huang, 1982, p. 201).

We may also compare *chunqiu jueyu* with similar examples in the *Bible*. The Jewish Law contains provisions about the Sabbath, which were strict to the point of being over-rigid. However, Jesus said to people that the Sabbath was made for man, not man for the Sabbath. He sought to restore the true spirit of the Sabbath with human nature:

---

[9] Translations are James (Mencius, 1970, p. 307). (Notes by translators)

On the Sabbath, Jesus met a man with a withered hand and wanted to heal him right away. The Pharisees raised an objection from the legal perspective: "Is it lawful to heal on the Sabbath?" Jesus replied: "Which one of you who has a sheep, if it falls into a pit on the Sabbath, will not take hold of it and lift it out? Of how much more value is a man than a sheep! So it is lawful to do good on the Sabbath." (*English Standard Version Bible*, 2001, Matthew. 12: 8; Mark. 2: 27–28; Luke. 13: 10–16, 14: 1–6; John. 5: 16–18)[10]

iii. Cases of *chunqiu jueyu*

Case 1

B, the father of A, had a fight with C. C tried to stab B with his knife. In return, A attempted to hit C with his stick, but wounded his father instead. What should be done with A? According to some people, A was guilty of beating his father, a crime punishable by the death penalty. However, I (Dong Zhongshu) rule that the father-son kinship was the closest relationship in the world. Upon hearing that his father was in a fight, the spontaneous response of a son was to feel concerned and came to his father's aid. It was not the son's original intention to beat his father. In a similar case, when his father was ill, Xu Zhi [prince of the State of Xu] tried to nurse his father back to health. Unfortunately, the medicine he administered poisoned, rather than healed, his father. Nevertheless, the *Spring and Autumn Annals* believed that Xu Zhi's original purpose was not to poison, but to cure his father, and he was eventually exonerated from the capital punishment. By the same token, A's behavior was not beating his father as stipulated by the law and he should be exonerated as well. (Li et al., 1960, pp. 2860–2868)

According to Confucian doctrines, beating one's father is a monstrous crime, which should be punished by decapitation under the law of the Han Dynasty. In this case, expediency was resorted to by invoking the precedent of Xu Zhi administering medicine to his father and A was exempted from punishment for the crime of beating one's father.[11] In fact, this was not so much Confucianization of the law as qualification of dogmatic application of Confucian doctrines with the human touch.

Case 2

A had a son B, whom A abandoned to C. B was raised by C and grew up. One day, A got drunk and said to B: "You are my son." B was enraged and hit A twenty times with a stick. Knowing that B was indeed his son, A was furious and sued B at the county government. I (Dong Zhongshu), however, rule that even though A was the father of B, he did not raise his son and relinquished him to C. For this reason, their kinship had been broken. Consequently, B was not guilty even though he hit A with a stick. (Du, 1988, p. 1911)

This is another case of a son beating his father. Even though A did not rear B, A was nevertheless B's biological father. Ostensibly, B was exempted from punishment because the kinship had been broken. The root cause, however, was that A was unscrupulous. Here Dong Zhongshu cited the example of Shensheng's (Crown Prince of the State of Jin) suicide. Shensheng was not killed personally by Lord Xian of

[10] Translations are from ESV Online. https://esv.literalword.com/. (Notes by translators)

[11] Xu Zhi administered the medicine to cure his father, Lord Dao of Xu, who died after taking the medicine. The *Annals* uses the Chinese character "弑" (*shi*, to murder one's sovereign or parent) to denote that the Lord died as a result of Xu Zhi's unintentional fault, but the character "葬" (*zang*, to bury with a decent funeral) also implies the attitude of Confucius. The fault of Xu Zhi, who had no intention of murdering his father, should be pardoned.

the Jin, but the *Annals* used the word "杀" (*sha*, to kill), implying that Lord Xian did not have the feeling of family affection for his child and the father-son affinity was lost. In the above case, even though A was the biological father of B, he did not fulfill his duty of rearing his son. Now that he had failed to perform his duty as a father, the father-son relationship no longer existed. Therefore, when the father did not carry out his duty as a father, the son need not carry out his obligations as a son. B, who beat A without being aware that A was his biological father, should not be held guilty of beating his father.

Case 3

> Once there was a tricky case: A, who was childless, found an abandoned child named B on the roadside and raised him as his own son. When he grew up, B committed murder and told A about his crime. A hid his son. How should we judge this? I (Dong Zhongshu), however, rule as follows: "A had no child and adopted the abandoned child B as his own son. A was not B's biological father, but who could be more of a father to B? *The Book of Songs* says: 'The moth has children, but the wasp carries them away on her back.' According to the *Annals*, a father is supposed to conceal the misconduct of his son. Therefore, A should help B evade the punishment." A should not be convicted. (Du, 1988, p. 1911)

In this case, Dong Zhongshu defended concealing the wrongdoing for one's father or son by citing the *Book of Odes* and the *Annals*. He stressed that if the father disclosed the crime of his adopted son, he would forfeit his identify as a father as he had no paternal affection for his son.

Case 4

> A's husband was out captaining a boat. Unfortunately, there were great winds on the sea, causing the boat to sink and B to drown. His corpse could not be located, and thus he could not be given a proper ritual burial. After four months, A's mother remarried A to a new husband. How should we judge this? According to some people, A's husband was never buried after his death. The law [of the Han Dynasty] prohibited remarriage under such circumstances. Thus, she should be publicly executed. I (Dong Zhongshu), however, rule: "The *Annals* has the story and precedent of a wife who returned (归) to Qi", her parental state. According to the *Annals*, if a husband dies without a son, the wife is entitled to the option of a remarriage. After all, the Chinese character 归 also means "to remarry". Here in this case, A's conduct was not selfish or arbitrary. She was only obeying the instruction of her parents. She did not have a heart of lust. Nor did she remarry presumptively for selfish, personal motives. Thus, she was not guilty of any crimes and therefore should not be punished. (Li et al., 1960, pp. 2860–2868)

In this case, A should be punished with the death penalty under the law, but should be acquitted according to the tenet of Confucian cannons. Here Dong Zhongshu cited the Confucian cannons and took into consideration the predicament faced by women in ancient China ("A's conduct was not selfish or arbitrary"), reflecting his keen observation of social reality. The story cited by Dong Zhongshu from the *Annals* is as follows: Lady Jiang (a princess of the Qi State) was the principal wife of Lord Wen of the Lu. However, Lord Wen favored his concubine Jing Ying. In order to make her son Tui the successor of Lord Wen, Jing Ying conspired with Xiang Zhong to murder the two principal sons of Lady Jiang. Tui was installed as the crown prince, who later became Lord Xuan. With no foothold for her in the Lu State, Lady Jiang was compelled to go back to the Qi State, the state of her parents. It looked as if Lady Jiang had been divorced by his husband and forced to go to her mother's home (*chu*, 出). However, *chu* was a character used only when the wife was abandoned by the husband, and it was not appropriate since Lord Wen had already died by that time. Therefore, the *Annals* used the character "归" (*gui*, to return or remarry). Though outwardly, Lady Jiang returned to Qi as if she had been divorced, the true reason for her return lay in the fact that Jing Ying and Lord Xuan of the Lu denied any foothold for her in the Lu State. An analogy may be drawn between A's situation and the story in the *Annals*. Like Lady Jiang, A did not remarry of her own accord, and therefore should not be punished.

Case 5

> In the fifth year of the Shiyuan reign of Emperor Zhao (82 BC), a man … arrived at the north gate [of Chang'an] and claimed to be the former crown prince, Liu Ju. The Gate Traffic Control Office (*gongche*, 公车) summoned marquises, prominent officials and generals to identify this stranger. Tens of thousands of officials and commoners of Chang'an gathered at the scene to watch this spectacle … When Jun Buyi (Governor of the Capital) arrived, he barked out an order for his clerks to arrest the imposter. Some objected that it was not yet clear whether this man was the real prince or not, and they counseled prudence. Jun Buyi replied, "Why do you gentlemen fear the former prince? In ancient times, Kuaikui, the crown prince of the Wei, offended Lord Ling of the Wei and fled to the Jin State. When Kuaikui attempted to return to the Wei upon the death of Lord Ling, Zhe, who had succeeded to the throne, refused to admit him into the state. The *Annals* approves Zhe's decision. The former crown prince offended Emperor Wu. If he had indeed fled instead of committing suicide and is now visiting the palace here in person, he is a criminal." Jun Buyi had the man sent to prison. (Ban, 2019, p. 709)

Liu Ju, a son of Emperor Wu of the Han, used to be the crown prince. He committed suicide in the fallout of the witchcraft case, but it was rumored that he was still alive. In the reign of Emperor Zhao, a man showed up at the north gate of Chang'an and claimed to be the former crown prince Liu Ju. This created a chaos and the officials on the scene were at a loss as for what to do. If the man had indeed been the former crown prince, as the eldest son of Emperor Wu, he was in a position to undermine the legitimacy of Emperor Zhao's rule. At this point, Jun Buyi, the Governor of the Capital, arrived at the scene and had the man arrested. Jun Buyi justified his action with Kuaikui's story in the *Annals*: In the 14th year of the reign of Lord Ding of the Lu (496 BC), Kuaikui, the crown prince of the Wei, disobeyed his father's order and fled to the Song State, and later to the Jin State. Lord Ling set up his grandson Kuaizhe as the crown prince, who later ascended the throne as Lord Chu. Later, Kuaikui wished to return the Wei, but Kuaikui refused to welcome him back. The *Annals* approved of Kuaizhe's decision on the ground that Kuaikui should not have fled since Lord Ling had no intention of killing his son. Jun Buyi believed that in the present case, the alleged Liu Ju was in a situation similar to that of Kuaikui. Even if the stranger had indeed been the former crown prince, he would still have been a criminal. In this case, *chunqiu juyu* was used as a legal means to solve a tricky political problem.

iv. Drawbacks of *chunqiu juyu* (Huang, 1982, pp. 173–175)

The greatest drawback of *chunqiu jueyu* lies in its lack of universality and definiteness. In specific applications, the decision makers could make an error in their subjective judgement. Even worse, they might deliberately cite the *Annals* to cover up their political motive. They rendered a case decidable under either this law or that precedent and "executed people justifiably"[12].

1. Deviation in citing the Confucian cannons

For instance, Fan Yanshou, Chamberlain for Law Enforcement of the Han Dynasty, once came across a case, in which three men took the same woman as their wife, and they produced four children. Fan had the three males executed and gave the children to the mother on the ground that these people acted like birds and animals and "birds and animals follow their mother, but not their father". Shen (1985, p. 1523) commented on this case as follows: "The three men did not commit a crime punishable with the death sentence under the law, but all of them were executed. Besides, they were treated like birds and animals, which was a degradation of mankind. This case resulted from bad customs, but instead of reforming the customs, the official only resorted to legal punishment. This was truly a bewildering verdict that accorded with neither Confucian doctrines nor the popular belief. Officials of the Han were prone to outsmart themselves when giving verdicts on criminal cases, but these verdicts were not necessarily appropriate when laws were the only resort. Advocates say the cases were judged according to canonical teachings, but it is difficult to align these teachings with the specific provisions of the law."

2. Arbitrary decisions in the name of *chunqiu jueyu*

For instance, Lü Bushu, a disciple of Dong Zhongshu, was an Aide to the Prime Minister in the Han Dynasty. However, he did not acquire the Confucian spirit of his master, and only embellished his legal decisions with Confucian doctrines.[13] It is recorded in "Accounts of Confucian Scholars" in *the Records of the Historian*: "When presiding over the case of rebellion of the King of Huainan upon an imperial order, he decided the verdict by himself without reporting everything to the emperor. He judged the case according to tenets implied in the *Annals*, and the way he handled the case won the approval of the emperor." However, although outwardly upholding the lofty principles of the *Annals*, he was extremely cruel in handling this case of rebellion, resulting in the imprisonment or death of tens of thousands of people. His conduct by far deviated from the teachings of his master Dong Zhongshu. Contemporary cruel officials, such as Zhang Tang and Du Zhou, also cloaked their cruelty with the spirit of the *Annals*.

---

[12] This section mainly refers to Huang (1982, pp. 173–175).

[13] For example, when a fire broke out in the temple dedicated to Emperor Gaozu (the founding emperor of the Han Dynasty), Dong Zhongshu wrote an article, in which he attributed the incident to problems with the court policies. This article was presented by an official at odds with Dong Zhongshu to Emperor Wu. Emperor Wu summoned some scholars and showed them the article. Not knowing that the article had been composed by his master, Lü Bushu condemned the idea in the article as idiotic, which led to the imprisonment of Dong Zhongshu.

v. Defense of *chunqiu jueyu*

We may regard *chunqiu jueyu* as a judicial technique, which in judicial practice was a means to an end instead of the end itself. It did not necessarily lead to Confucianization of the law. Confucianists and upright officials could promote benevolent government by examining the original motive of the accused, whereas cruel officials could turn *chunqiu jueyu* into a tool for attacking their opponents and twisting the law in their own favor. We should not judge *chunqiu jueyu* too critically. "Denunciation of *chunqiu jueyu* as being aimless or random from the modern empirical legal perspective makes sense for vulgar scholars and cruel officials who had limited learning and invoked the Confucian cannons in a far-fetched manner, but runs the risk of being too harsh when it comes to learned scholars and upright officials who strove to supplement the law with the Confucian tenets." "The biggest defect of Legalists lies in their failure to understand the true origin of the legislative power." As long as laws emanated from the emperor, there could be no judicial independence. In the absence of judicial independence, we cannot find fault with Confucian officials making legal decisions by invoking Confucian cannons, for there was no rule of law in the true sense of the term under an autocratic monarchy. Confucianists could contribute in two ways when they judged criminal cases based on the doctrines implicit in Confucian cannons under an autocratic monarchy: preventing the despotism of the emperor, and curtailing the cruelty of the law. We should not treat the ancients too harshly, who had their own difficulties to deal with (Huang, 1998, p. 177).

6.3.2 The Law, the Humanity, and Parent-Official-Style Particularistic Judgements

The tradition of *chunqiu jueyu* did not perish after the Han Dynasty. Confucian scholar-turned officials did not always adhere rigidly to statutory laws. Instead, they often oscillated back and forth between the norm and expediency, between state laws and humanity.

i. Pursuing the ideal of harmony and no litigations

The Chinese rural society was never the individualistic atomized society of the West. Against the background of social solidarity, it was quite difficult for a person to assert his or her individual rights independent of others. In an acquaintance society, the distinction between right and wrong was often blurred. European and American scholars on Chinese traditional laws have joked that since the Chinese have a long memory, the judgement of a case should not be confined to a single time or incident, and nor should the judgement be based entirely on the relationship of causality. For example, A sued B in the *yamen* for not repaying a debt. B defended himself not in terms of the debt itself, but on the ground that B's father had rendered A's father a great help twenty years ago. Consequently, A's family owed B's family a favor (debt). For this reason, A had no right to force B to repay the debt irrespective of the favor he owed to B's family.

Furthermore, it was not easy to uncover the facts of a case. The judge, undertaken by a scholar-official, never had any legal training, and his private secretaries, clerks and runners were not to be trusted in terms of their moral integrity. With this judicial reality in mind, an official would find it more advisable to exhort the people to live in harmony and refrain from litigations rather than to judge the legal cases rashly. For example, a local official once put up a couplet at the gate: "You folks, in case you have any spare time, should apply yourselves to your own businesses; do not enter the gate of the *yamen* and bother the parent official with your petty affairs."

From the perspective of the common people, they would incur considerable expenses if they brought their litigation to the *yamen*. With a prolonged litigation under way, they would have no time for their farm work. They had to deal with the manipulations and exactions of the clerks and runners (illegitimate fees). The outcome of the litigation was highly uncertain. Under such circumstances, evasion of litigations was the inevitable choice upon weighing the benefits and harms of a litigation.

In spite of the government's efforts to forestall and the people's aversion (and dread) of litigations, ancient China was also a society that was to a certain extent fond of litigations. This may be attributed not only to the large quantities of disputes as a result of the relatively high mobility in political and economic status in China, but also to the problem of propensity to litigations arising out of people's love of face and their willingness to do whatever it took to protect their reputation. In addition, we should never view *songshi* (讼师, litigation masters) in ancient China in the same light as we do present-day lawyers, for the former lacked the fundamental professional ethnics of the legal occupation. Stirring up trouble, instigating disputes, and exaggerating and fabricating information were their basic means of securing material gains. Maybe "litigation villains" was a more appropriate appellation for them (Yamamoto, 2012, pp. 576–601).

ii. Pluralistic criteria for legal decisions and individualistic judgement

For a local official, enacted laws were not the sole criterion for making a legal decision. Instead, he should take a host of factors into comprehensive consideration, including heavenly principles, state laws, common sense, as well as the customs of minority ethnic groups and clan regulations.

Case: an inheritance dispute (Hiroaki, 1953/2012, pp. 273–297)

Danxin Archives, a collection of administrative and judicial archives from Tamsui Sub-prefecture, Taipei Prefecture, and Hsinchu Prefecture of Taiwan in the Qing Dynasty, contains a case of an inheritance dispute. The litigation dragged on for about eighteen months until a reconciliation was reached under the mediation of the government. The details of the case are as follows: Zheng Rugang had four sons, i.e., Shannan, Weiye, Weiyue and Yunti. Among the four sons, Weiye and Weiyue died prematurely without leaving behind any male offspring. Shannan had a son named Bangchao. Yunti also died early, but left behind two sons with his wife Mrs. Zheng,

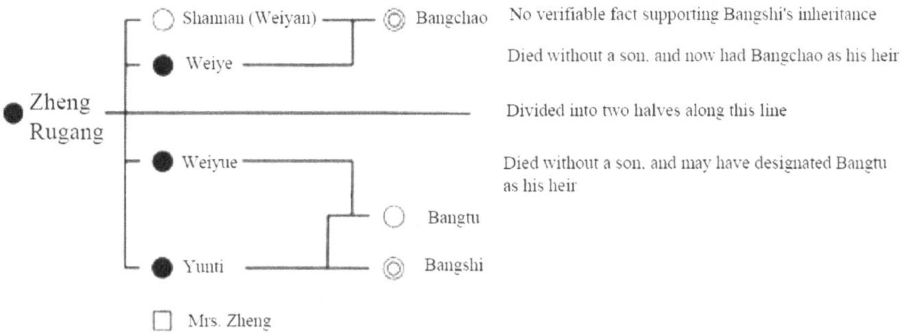

Fig. 6.1 Zheng Rugang's family relationships (cited from Hiroaki, 1953/2012, p. 280)

named Bangtu and Bangshi respectively. Bangchao, the son of Shannan, was also designated as the heir to Weiye. Bangtu, a son of Yunti, became the heir of Weiyue by adoption. The other son of Yunti, was the legal heir of Yunti. These relationships are depicted in the following diagram (Fig. 6.1).

After the death of Zheng Rugang, the Zheng people lived together as a compound family, with Shannan, the only surviving son of Zheng Rugang, as the head of the family. After the death of Shannan, Mrs. Zheng wanted to split the family and live apart. The property of the Zheng family was divided up into four equal portions, with one portion for each son of Zheng Rugang and inherited by each son's designated heir. Outwardly, this seemed to be a fair arrangement, but Shannan's son Bangchao, who was the heir to both Shannan and Weiye, inherited two portions of the family property, whereas Bangtu and Bangshi ended up with only one portion each. Dissatisfied with this scheme of inheritance, Bangshi, one of the sons of the widow Mrs. Zheng, seized the rent of the land already allocated to Bangchao. When Bangchao complained about this to Mrs. Zheng, Bangshi fled. However, Mrs. Zheng fought back and sued Bangchao at the local government. She claimed that Bangshi had been adopted by Shannan (which was not true) and thus was entitled to inherit Shannan's property. She accused Bangchao of infringing upon Bangshi's right of inheritance and injuring Bangshi in a fight. After finding out the truth, the government did not punish Mrs. Zheng for making a false accusation, but instead asked the clan chief to mediate the dispute. In the end, Bangchao, pressured by both the clan chief and local officials, was compelled to surrender part of his inherited property to the side of Mrs. Zheng and reach a compromise. "In this case, Bangchao enjoyed an overwhelming advantage under legal principles, but he was unable to resist the unanimous judgement of the people around him, who were in favor of a more equitable division of the family property. He had no choice but to accept the new scheme of property division." (Hiroaki, 1953/2012, p. 288)

iii. Parent-official-style judgement and Judge Bao-style justice

Sub-prefects and magistrates in Chinese history were called "parent officials". As "parents" of the people, they meted out penalties when their "children" committed a crime, but they might also blur the line between right and wrong for the sake of family or social harmony. A happy ending for all was preferable to a tragic one, even if it meant twisting the law to some extent.

Case: Prefecture Governor Qiao arbitrarily paired marriages (Fan et al., 2011, pp. 271–272)

Legend has it that in Emperor Renzong's reign of the Song Dynasty, Liu Pu, the son of a Liu Family, fell seriously ill. The Liu Family decided to hold the wedding for Liu Pu to marry Zhuyi, the daughter of a Sun Family and to whom Liu Pu had been betrothed, in an attempt to counteract the back luck and dispel the disease. Reluctant to marry their daughter to a dying man, the Sun Family hatched a plan and sent Zhuyi's younger brother Yulang (who had been betrothed to Xu Wenge, the daughter of a Xu Family), disguised as the bride, to the Liu's. On the wedding night, Liu Pu was too sick to enter the bridal chamber. Therefore, the Liu Family sent their daughter Huiniang (who had been engaged with Pei Zheng, the son of the Pei Family) to accompany the "sister-in-law" for the night. It turned out that Yulang and Huiniang fell in love with each other and cemented on their relationship. When Liu Pu recovered, however, this relationship was exposed. The several families fought with one another and brought their complaint to the local government. When Prefecture Governor Qiao took this case, he summoned the four parties, i.e., the Sun, Liu, Pei and Xu families, to the *yamen* and gave the following verdict to resolve this dispute:

> The bride's younger brother went through the wedding disguised as the bride, and the bridegroom's younger sister accompanied the "bride" for the night. We cannot find fault with the two families, who acted out of affection for their children, but it ended up with a young man and a young woman spending the night together. Now that Huiniang has lost her virginity to Yulang, I hereby declare that they are to be husband and wife. As Yulang has taken possession the fiancée of another man, he should also suffer his own fiancée to be possessed by another man. Therefore, (Xu) Wenge is to be married to Pei Zheng. Thus, the brides are exchanged, but how much difference does it really make? With the government acting as the matchmaker, the families should pick an auspicious date and proceed with the weddings.

In ancient China, people like Yulang and Huiniang, who engaged in a love affair without their parents' approval, were not sanctioned by the ethical code and enacted laws. However, Prefecture Governor Qiao did not adhere rigidly to these rules. Instead, he made the best of a messy situation and reshuffled the marriage arrangements as a self-appointed matchmaker, which secured a happy ending for all and left behind a widely circulated story.

Traditional Chinese folk literature on the theme of administration of justice contains not only the romanticism of literati like Governor Qiao, but also the individualistic heroism in the style of Judge Bao (an extremely honest and upright judge in Chinese popular fiction and drama, with the prototype being an official in the Song Dynasty). The stories of Judge Bao hearing cases in Chinese drama have been summed up by a modern legal professional into the following joke: "Comrade Bao was an academician of the Chinese Academy of Sciences, Mayor of Kaifeng City and concurrently chief of the municipal public security bureau, head of the people's procuratorate and chief justice of the intermediate people's court. In accordance with the principle of 'severity for those who confess and even greater severity for those who resist', he stripped all criminals of the rights of defense and appeal and sent a large number of heinous criminals to his specially designed guillotines (lever-knives)." The authenticity of Judge Bao's titles of Grand Scholar of the Longtu Pavilion and Prefect of Kaifeng Prefecture aside, the judicial power in ancient China was reasonably divided rather than highly concentrated. The Song Dynasty, in particular, championed division of the judicial power. The power to review cases involving the death penalty had always rested with the central government and the emperor, and neither were lever-knives legitimate instruments of punishments. Although inconsistent with historical facts, the stories of Judge Bao and his three lever-knives have been circulated and passed down to our time. This more or less reflects the traditional view on justice and its administration among the people.

iv. Balance between the law and specific circumstances: the judge's rigid application of the law and overstepping the legal boundary

The Ming and Qing statutes contained highly detailed provisions, but "legal provisions were limited, while specific circumstances were infinite". When the specific circumstances of a case fell beyond the coverage of statutes, the problem of "re-legislation" was bound to emerge. In the context of grand unification under an imperial autocracy, statutes must be applied faithfully down to the letter, which theoretically left no leeway for flexible interpretation and maneuvering by the judge. On the other hand, faced with diversified specific circumstances, the judge also had to strike a balance between the law and differing circumstances. If a judge exercised too much caution and refused to make any judgement outside the scope of the law, he would be reprimanded by his superior (or even the emperor) as "being too rigid". "Besides, only by paying meticulous attention to varying circumstances was he worthy of the high reputation of a scholar-official." However, if the judge gave full rein to his discretion, he ran the risk of being denounced as "overstepping the legal boundary". How to maintain the precarious equilibrium between the law and specific circumstances was a formidable challenge for a judge (Hiroaki, 1953/2012, p. 343).

The strong tendency to include a human touch in judicial practice of imperial China stemmed from the fact that, under a centralized power system, the Emperor was able to intervene in legal cases and officials of various levels only judged individual cases on behalf of the emperor: "As the emperor himself often did not possess sufficient knowledge about the law" ("judicial rationality"), "resorting to common sense and human sentiments could not only prevent judicial bureaucrats from undermining the monarchical power under the pretext of legal expertise, but also provide a solid basis for wielding the monarchical power". "Substantive justice aimed at the supreme good was both the monarch's duty and his means of winning popular support and moral legitimacy." (Wang, 2017, p. 135)

v. Judicial precedents with uncertain legal force: the leading case system

In addition to the written code, there were also the so-called "judicial precedents" in ancient China as a supplement to enacted laws. The judicial precedents were known by various names in different dynasties and were termed "leading cases" in the

Qing Dynasty. Although this practice differed considerably from case laws under the Anglo-American legal system (the Common Law), judicial officials in ancient China also engaged in judicial reasoning by drawing analogies between cases, comparing their severities and making inductions. Although on some occasions, leading cases might even challenge enacted laws, "they were never officially sanctioned by the enacted laws throughout the Qing Dynasty". The emperor held a vague attitude towards leading cases, and "neither did the judicial officials reach a consensus about them". However, "despite the different attitudes of various parties towards them, leading cases still wielded considerable influence in judicial practice. Leading cases were a necessary means of understanding statutes and increasing experience". The original intention behind the prohibition against invoking leading cases was to protect the legislative power of the central government from being eroded, but in actual judicial practice, "similar cases naturally needed to be given similar verdicts". "Not only could the balance between the law and the human touch or common sense upheld by the emperor be accomplished by invoking leading cases, but also the intuitive decisions made by the chiefs of government departments could be rationalized via leading cases." "Of course, in actual application of the leading case system, what facilitated the manipulation by superior officials was its uncertainty. Whenever the result produced by invoking a leading case was not satisfactory to the superior official, he could always reject it on the ground that the leading case had not been turned into law." "Taking advantage of this defect in legal force, an official could exercise his veto power against a leading case when it led to an unfavorable result, and was always ready to accept a leading case which could produce a favorable result. This was no doubt a highly pragmatic attitude." (Wang, 2017, pp. 137–172)

vi. The distinction between major criminal cases and trivial civil cases

In China's traditional judicial practice, a distinction was made between major criminal cases and trivial cases (such as civil cases involving family affairs, marriages, land and debts) based on their specific circumstances. The former were to be handled by the government whenever they arose, whereas the latter were only accepted by the government on several designated days of each month and would be rejected altogether in the four busy months of farming in the spring and summer. After the first instance at the sub-prefectural or county level, a major criminal case would be transferred to and heard by successive levels of government, or even submitted to the judiciary organ of the central government and the emperor for the final verdict. A trivial civil case or a minor offense punishable by beating with the light or heavy stick, on the other hand, fell under the jurisdiction of the sub-prefect or magistrate, and the case could be closed upon judgement at the sub-prefectural or county level. Sometimes, a party to the case might commit suicide for a petty dispute in order to turn a small case into a serious one and attract the attention of higher levels of the government. This would transform the case into a major criminal case, which, according to the law, must be heard by higher levels of the government and submitted to the imperial court for the final verdict. Instigated by the traditional thinking that a killer should be put to death and the social mentality of saving face and winning honor, and supported by the law punishing those who brought about the death of others by persecution, similar tragedies were not rare occurrences in society. In the eyes of foreigners, Chinese people in the late Qing Dynasty were accustomed to resorting to suicide for venting their grievance or seeking revenge:

> After carrying luggage for a customer, a porter was paid a fee which was less than the agreed amount by a small sum of ten cash ... He committed suicide to avenge himself, for he knew this would cause quite some trouble for his client. At another time, a man jumped into the river to drown himself, but was dragged by someone onto the shore. The man then sat on the shore without eating and drinking anything until he died. It turned out that the man was seeking retribution on another man who had cheated him ... One day, Mrs. Feng's sow accidentally knocked over Mrs. Wang's gate, which was slightly damaged. Mrs. Wang immediately demanded compensation for her gate, but this request was rejected by Mrs. Feng. Then there ensured an intense quarrel between the two women, until Mrs. Wang threatened to commit suicide. Upon hearing this threat from Mrs. Wang, Mrs. Feng lost no time in killing herself ahead of Mrs. Wang. This move of Mrs. Feng trapped Mrs. Wang in a very difficult situation, who, in turn, drowned herself by jumping into the river. (Wilson & Norman, 2000, p. 313)

Whoever caused the death of others were held accountable by the law, irrespective of the specific circumstances. This encouraged suicides for the purpose of venting grievances and seeking revenge and gave rise to an unwholesome or even absurd social ethos. The forgoing stories were not malicious invention by foreigners. Shen Jiaben mentioned similar cases when discussing the need to revise the article of the late Qing statute on persecuted death.

> Regarding quarrels over petty matters and fights for the sake of prevailing over others, these were merely ordinary brawls and there was nothing serious about them. In case of loss of property, the victim would inquire those who might have committed the theft, but this was also the natural course of action. In another case, a creditor might repeatedly intimidate a debtor with exaggerated threats who had failed to repay his debt, in the hope the debt could be cleared. There was nothing out of the ordinary about such cases, which could happen from time to time and constituted no ground for committing suicide. People committed suicide because they felt they had been humiliated when they got beaten in a fight, had been wrongly accused of theft, or had been dishonored for failing to raise the money in time to repay a debt. Indeed, these people had chosen death of their own accord. They could have opted to sue those who beat them up, argue with those who wrongly accused them of theft, or plead the creditor to extend the term of payment instead. Who could have foreseen that they would resort to suicide? The suicide was due to the foolishness of the dead, and their counterparts should not undertake full responsibility for their death. (Shen, 1985, p. 2091)

If people killed themselves because of humiliation for being beaten up, being wronged for a theft, or failure to repay a debt, then it was only foolishness on the part of the victims, who sought their own destruction. On the other hand, the victims chose suicide also because they lacked other channels of legal remedies. In this connection, the traditional legal provisions and the traditional judicial system were also to blame.

References

Ban, G. (2019). *Han shu* [Book of Han]. Zhonghua Book Company.
Du, Y. (1988). *Tongdian* [Laws and regulations since ancient times]. Zhonghua Book Company.
English Standard Version Bible (2001). ESV Online. https://esv.literalword.com/
Fan, Z., Zheng, D., & Zhan, X. (2011). *Qing li fa yu zhognguo ren* [The human touch, reason, law and Chinese people]. Peking University Press.
Hiroaki, T. (2012). *Rights and injustice: Collected essays on Chinese legal history* (Y. Wang et al., Trans.). Tsinghua University Press. (Original work published 1953).
Huang, Y. (1982). *Handai Chunqiu jueyu zhi yanjiu* [Study on chunqiu zheyu of the Han Dynasty] (Unpublished MA thesis). National Chung Hsing University.
Huang, Y. (1998). *Zhongguo chuantong fazhi yu sixiang* [Chinese traditional legal system and ideology]. Wu-Nan Book Inc.
Li, F., et al. (1960). *Taiping yulan* [Readings of the Taiping Era]. Zhonghua Book Company.
Mencius. (1970). The Works of Mencius (J. Legge Trans.). Dover Publications.
Na. S. (2004a). *Zhongguo shenpan zhidu shi* [History of Chinese trial system]. Zhengdian Publishing Co., Ltd.
Na, S. (2004b). *Qingdai Zhongyang sifa shenpan zhidu* [The central legal institutions in the Qing Dynasty]. Beijing University Press.
Na. S. (2004c). *Mingdai Zhongyang sifa shenpan zhidu* [The central legal institutions in the Ming Dynasty]. Peking University Press.
Na. S. (2006). *Qingdai zhou xian yamen shenpan zhidu* [The legal institutions of prefecture and county court in the Ming Dynasty]. China University of Political Science and Law Press.
Ocko, J. K. (2004). A thousand ways to the capital: Direct litigation in the Qing Dynasty. In K. Turner, H. Gao, H., & He, W. (Eds.). *Meiguo xuezhe lun zhongguo falü chuantong* [Recent American academic writings on traditional Chinese law], (pp. 512–551). Tsinghua University Press.
Shen, J. (1985). *Lidai xingfa kao* [Study of the criminal law of the successive dynasties]. Zhonghua Book Company.
Sima, Q. (1974). *Shiji · lishu* [Records of the grand historian]. Zhonghua Book Company.
Spence, J. D. (1988). *Emperor of China: Self portrait of K'ang-hsi*. Vintage.
Wang, Z. (2017). *Qingdai guojia fa: dayuan chayi yu jiquan tongyi* [State law in the Qing Dynasty: Heterogeneous plurality and power centralization]. Social Sciences Academic Press.
Wilson, J., & Norman, H. (2000). *Subjects under the Dragon Flag: Modern Chinese Society and Customs* (H. Deng et al., Trans.). Guangming Daily Publishing House.
Xu, D. (1975). *Zhongguo fazhi shi lunji* [A collection of essays on the history of the Chinese legal system]. Zhiwen Publishing House.
Yamamoto, E. (2012).Understanding and reality of the pro-litigation tendency: Taking Ji-an Prefecture of the early Qing Dynasty as an example. In Institute of Legal History of China University of Political Science and Law (Ed.). *Riben xuezhe zhongguo fa lunzhu xuanyi* [Selected translation of the essays on Chinese law of Japanese scholars]. China University of Political Science and Law Press.
Yang, Y. (Ed.). (2005). *Xianbian zhongguo fazhi shi* [A new compilation of the Chinese legal system history]. Social Sciences Academic Press.

Chapter 7
The Spread of Western Law to the East and the New Policies in the Late Qing Dynasty

7.1 Unprecedented Turn Millennia

7.1.1 From the "World" Down to the "State"—Tribute System Changed into Treaty System

Prior to the First Opium War (AD 1840–1842), China continually perceived itself as the epicenter of the world, with all areas outside its boarder deemed as barbaric states. Other civilizations were not considered as its equals and its relationships with surrounding vassal states were governed by a tribute system. During the reign of the Qianlong Emperor, the British Empire sought to establish diplomatic relations with China on equal terms, only to be arrogantly refused by the Qing Court. With the outbreak of the First Opium War, China signed a degrading treaty with Britain (*Treaty of Nanking*) in 1842, leading to the gradual disintegration of the tribute system. This treaty caused a seismic shift in China's self-perception from being a paramount and unique Celestial Empire representing the entire "world" to becoming a member of the international community as a "state."

Before the First Opium War, China's foreign trade was handled by local authorities in Guangdong. After the opening of the five treaty ports, the responsibility for domestic and international commerce shifted to the general governors of Liang-Jiang (Jiangnan and Jiangxi provinces) and Liang-Guang (Guangdong and Guangxi provinces). The Qing central government was reluctant to develop direct diplomatic relations with the Western powers, while the latter desired bilateral diplomacy with the central government rather than the regional ones. This dissonance served as one of the triggers for the Second Opium War (AD 1856–1860). Subsequent to the conclusion of *Convention of Peking*, the envoys of Britain, Russia, France, and the United States became officially stationed in Beijing, and the Qing government established a modern-sense diplomatic institution, referred to as the Foreign Office (*Zongli geguo shiwu yamen* 总理各国事务衙门, lit., office for the general management of affairs

X. Nie, *The History of Government and Public Law in China*,
https://doi.org/10.1007/978-981-97-6063-3_7

concerning various countries, for short *Zongli yamen* 总理衙门, or *Zongshu* 总署). Ranking above the six ministries, this office took over foreign affairs (including the Westernization Movement and diplomatic issues), which had been under the charge of the Ministry of Rites and the Department for Ethnic Affairs.

The nineteenth century witnessed the first wave of globalization of law sweeping across the world outside of Europe and the United States, the focus of which was international law (public international law). In the course of translating and publishing works on international law, the Chinese also began to study international law and used it as a guide for their international dealings. However, the introduction of international law did not lead to any immediate movement towards the repudiation of those unequal treaties imposed on China. "Because of their peculiar history, culture, and institutions, the Chinese of the mid-nineteenth century did not seem to consider tariff restrictions, consular jurisdiction, and the most-favored-nation treatment to be serious infringements on national rights. On the other hand, they considered such ceremonial matters as diplomatic accreditation and audience without the kowtow to be grave humiliations" (Hsü, 1968, p. 139). "Without the conception of sovereignty, the Ch'ing officials seemed to consider their concessions not so much serious reductions of their national powers as expressions of China's liberality toward the aliens" (Hsü, 1968, p. 141). "Even in the seventies and eighties, when China's knowledge of the West was far improved, there were still no concrete plans to abrogate the unequal treaties, as there were in Japan. The mandarins merely urged the use of international law to restrain the 'wild' foreign consuls, but they never strove to deprive the consuls of the basic raison d'être of their 'wildness,' namely, the right to control their own citizens" (Hsü, 1968, pp. 141–142).

7.1.2 Impact of the Taiping Rebellion

The Taiping Heavenly Kingdom (1851–1864) has been a subject of extensive debate within academic circles. One notable aspect is that alongside the Confucian ideology, the leaders of the Taiping Heavenly Kingdom incorporated and adapted elements of Western Christianity, which presented a significant challenge to the long-standing imperial Chinese traditions.

Certain documents produced by the Taiping Heavenly Kingdom government, such as the Land System of the Heavenly Dynasty and the New Treatise on Government, presented ambitious institutional reforms. However, it is noteworthy that these proposals did not materialize into actual implementations. Furthermore, it is pertinent to mention that certain documents were classified in nature, lacking formal promulgation as legally binding instruments.[1] Take *New Treatise on Government* by Hong Rengan as an example. It "was the first truly global proposal for reform in China's

[1] "*Land System of the Heavenly Dynasty* can be considered an "internal document". While it held the status of an official document that was approved for promulgation, and had been printed at least three times, only a few copies were produced during each printing. As a result, the document had

history." Hong Rengan, who regarded the Chinese Empire as one of the states in the world rather than the center of world civilization, proposed to abandon the traditional tribute model of diplomacy and implement new equal diplomacy. "Hong Rengan's treatise presented, for the very first time in a Chinese context, a vision of the country as a modern industrial power." "He even called for the founding of Western-style insurance companies that could offer policies to protect people's homes, property, and livelihoods" (Platt, 2012, pp. 140–141).

7.1.3 The Westernization Movement, the Defeat in the First Sino-Japanese War and the Hundred Days' Reform

Following two decades of strained relations and conflicts with Western powers, starting from the First Opium War in 1840 and culminating in the peace negotiations in Beijing in 1860, China undertook a significant shift in its approach to diplomatic engagement with the West. This transformation involved the establishment of the Foreign Office within the central government, signifying a proactive stance towards learning from Western nations in order to enhance its own capabilities. The renaming of the "Foreign Office of Trade" to simply the Foreign Office, as initiated by Prince Gong, reflected the recognition that foreign affairs encompassed more than just trade-related matters. The Foreign Office, under the leadership of princes and grand ministers, operated under the supervision of the Grand Councilors. Its personnel were chosen from secretaries at the Grand Secretariat, the Ministries, the Censorate, and the Grand Council, and served in a rotational manner. In essence, the Foreign Office shared many similarities with the Grand Council in many aspects. Firstly, it is important to note that "both were temporary organizations rather than official institutions". Secondly, "both entities followed a collegial organizational structure, with each having a leader who held a concurrent position. The secretaries of these organizations were often transferred from other institutions." Notably, many Grand Councilors concurrently served as Grand Ministers of the Foreign Office, resulting in a significant integration between the Foreign Office and the Grand Council. Furthermore, there was a discrepancy between their names and actual functions. Initially, the Grand Council was primarily responsible for handling military secrets, but it eventually assumed the role of overseeing all state policy-making. Similarly, the Foreign Office initially focused on matters related to Sino-foreign trade and negotiations, but later expanded its jurisdiction to encompass various foreign-related affairs, including trade, religion, and the Westernization initiatives. These initiatives encompassed the adoption of Western customs, ships, firearms, schools, railways, wires, mining operations, and the development of the navy, among others. In essence, during

limited visibility at the time and is seldom referenced in the extensive historical records pertaining to the Taiping Heavenly Kingdom (Qin, 2015, p. 121).

the Tongzhi and Daoguang eras, the success and future prospects of the national rejuvenation endeavor heavily relied upon the efforts of the Foreign Office." (Guo, 2012, pp. 133–134)

The late Qing period witnessed the emergence of the "Tongzhi Restoration", which primarily focused on the Westernization Movement. This movement aimed to bolster China's strength by adopting Western military industries and technologies, fostering the development of modern industry and commerce, and establishing modernized armed forces. To address the need for talents, various new educational institutions, such as translation schools and military schools, were established, and students were sent overseas for further studies. Notable figures like Yan Fu, a prominent translator in the modern Chinese enlightenment, graduated from the Royal Naval College in Greenwich. Tang Shaoyi, the first Premier of the Republic of China, and Zhan Tianyou, a renowned engineer, were also among those who pursued education abroad during this period. These efforts laid a solid foundation for China's subsequent modernization endeavors. However, the Westernization Movement, which heavily relied on learning from abroad, suffered a significant setback following China's defeat in the First Sino-Japanese War in 1894.

The Chinese people were motivated by the defeat in the First Sino-Japanese War, which led to the introduction of the concept of a modern constitution in China, alongside the gunboat diplomacy employed by the Great Powers. Kang Youwei and Liang Qichao were among the first proponents of "constitutionalism", viewing it as a viable solution to rejuvenate the Qing Dynasty and address the country's challenges. However, they also emphasized that "the establishment of a constitutional government necessitated the enlightenment of the populace". They advocated for the Qing court to "inform the people of China's transition to a constitutional monarchy", with the constitution to be implemented "within a span of twenty years". Although constitutionalism had emerged in China prior to the Russo-Japanese War, it remained primarily a concern of scholar-bureaucrats who harbored concerns for the nation's future. It had not yet gained widespread public support, which contributed to the failure of the Hundred Days' Reform in 1898.

7.1.4 The Central Government's Loss of Control Over the Judiciary

i. Evangelism and missionary cases

Following the opening of China by western powers, it was not only businessmen who found cause for celebration, but also missionaries. With a population of approximately 400 million non-Christians, China presented a significant opportunity for missionaries to spread the gospel. Motivated by the concept of "Christian Occupation of China", a considerable number of missionaries ventured into remote regions of inland China with the aim of establishing churches and converting the local population. However, not all converts were driven by genuine faith; some were what is commonly referred to as "rice Christians" who sought personal benefits and support from the church. "These individuals strategically aligned themselves with foreigners through their allegiance to the church in order to evade local government authority." "There existed a perception within the church that non-converted Chinese were to be disregarded." It is worth noting that the spiritual connection with God of those who had converted did not necessarily deepen, but they were brought closer to the foreigners represented by the church. As a result, unscrupulous converts "felt emboldened to engage in wrongful behavior within their communities, often asserting that their 'Christian affiliation protected them from legal consequences'" (Yang, 2014, pp. 217–218).

The cultural conflicts that arose between foreign missionaries and ordinary Chinese individuals, along with the misconduct of deceitful rice Christians, resulted in significant confrontations between the local population and the church within Chinese society. These confrontations often escalated into collective violence and bloody conflicts, commonly referred to as "missionary cases". Local officials found themselves in a delicate position when handling these missionary cases. On the one hand, they were tasked with protecting the interests of the "foreign masters" in order to prevent diplomatic disputes, which often involved indulging the church and its believers. On the other hand, they had to find ways to pacify the local population and prevent the intensification of confrontations. During the late Qing period, numerous conflicts between the Chinese government and Western powers were triggered by missionary cases.

ii. Consular jurisdiction and the system of mixed court

The misinterpretation of consular jurisdiction as extraterritoriality in modern China resulted from a lack of understanding of public international law among the Chinese populace. The interchangeability of these terms can be attributed to the lifting of the sea ban, which exposed Chinese society to foreign influences and legal concepts. Notably, the exercise of consular jurisdiction by Western powers in China was not grounded in customary practice but rather relied upon treaty provisions. Through a series of treaties, the Qing government gradually ceded its jurisdiction over foreign nationals in China. This erosion of sovereignty provided Western powers with a privileged status that they often exploited to the detriment of the Chinese population. This exploitation went unchecked, as the Qing government lacked the capacity to sanction these foreign nationals. Consequently, the abusive and unconstrained exercise of consular jurisdiction became a recurrent issue during the late Qing era, particularly evident in cases involving missionaries.

The Mixed Court (*huishen gongxie* 会审公廨, aka. *huishen gongtang* 会审公堂) was an extraterritorial judicial institution established in 1864 in the Shanghai International Settlement as stipulated in an agreement between the Qing government and the British, American, and French consuls. According to the provisions of the 1868 *Pidgin Official Joint Trial Regulation*, in all legal cases involving foreign nationals, consular officials of the defendant's nationality were required to participate in the adjudication process. For civil disputes between Chinese and foreign litigants, if the defendant was a citizen of a treaty power, the case would be adjudicated by their consul. Otherwise, the consul would serve in an advisory capacity during the proceedings. In principle, the Chinese magistrate presided over the trials with consuls formally acting as assessors. However, in practice, the "mixed court" was mixed in name only, since even lawsuits solely concerning Chinese litigants in the Settlement necessitated "observation" by foreign consuls who could influence the final verdicts. Hence, the establishment of this extraterritorial judicial mechanism represented an expansion of foreign consular jurisdiction in China, further encroaching upon Qing judicial sovereignty. Within the International Settlement, the Shanghai Municipal Council functioned as the supervisory authority, annually selecting a three-member consular court from the consular corps stationed in Shanghai to adjudicate specific cases.

The controversial "*Su Bao* Case" in 1903 represented a seminal trial heard by the Mixed Court that engendered grave concern within the Qing court. The Qing authorities deemed the contentious essays authored by Zou Rong and Zhang Binglin published in the *Su Bao* newspaper as constituting seditious rhetoric fomenting revolution and defaming the Guangxu Emperor. Pursuant to the statutory provisions outlined in the *Great Qing Code*, such acts qualified as the felony offense of "propagating heterodox and subversive texts and discourse", punishable by execution of the authors. However, the Shanghai International Settlement refused to extradite Zhang and Zou for prosecution and adjudication under Qing jurisdiction. Following approximately six months of protracted negotiations, Qing authorities and British officials reached a tenuous compromise to jointly constitute an ad hoc extraterritorial tribunal within the existing the Mixed Court in the Settlement to adjudicate the case. The resultant legal proceedings contravened conventional Mixed Court praxis, instead implementing Westernized trial procedures and jurisprudential principles.

The foreign defense counsel appointed by the Shanghai Municipal Council invoked the tenet of presumption of innocence, demanded the prosecution substantiate the allegations beyond reasonable doubt, and appealed to sacrosanct principles of freedom of expression as pillars of the defense. At the conclusion of the trial, the Chinese magistrates preemptively pronounced sentences of life imprisonment for the defendants, eliciting immediate objections from the British vice consul serving as a juridical assessor. With the accused detained under the auspices of the Municipal Council and enforcement of judicial determinations within the purview of foreign authorities, the rulings of the Chinese judges could not be imposed. Further diplomatic negotiations between Qing and British officials resulted in reduced sentences of two years incarceration for Zou and three years for Zhang, to be served in Tilanqiao West Prison in the Settlement. Indeed, in the late Qing era, numerous revolutionary organizations exploited the extraterritorial protections conferred by the International Settlement to evade prosecution under Qing law, profoundly eroding Qing judicial sovereignty (Zhao, 2007).

Even subsequent to the dissolution of the Qing Dynasty, the Western Great Powers obstinately retained the International Settlements and attendant privileges acquired in China prior to the regime change. It was not until 1927, when the National Revolutionary Army occupied the cities of Hankou and Jiujiang during the Northern Expedition, that Britain was compelled to relinquish control of concessions in those locales. The Western powers reached a tenuous compromise with the Nanjing National Government (NNG), preserving some concessions, especially the strategically vital Shanghai International Settlement. However, even in Shanghai, foreign authorities were forced to dismantle the longstanding Mixed Court. In 1930, the Mixed Court was superseded by newly constituted judicial institutions—the Shanghai Special District Court, and the Second Branch of the Jiangsu High Court, which excluded foreign intervention in judicial decision-making (Bergère, 2008, pp. 813–814).

iii. Local governors or viceroys' power of "summary execution"

In imperial China, capital punishment decisions were centralized and subject to stringent layers of bureaucratic review quite early, with execution verdicts requiring ratification by the Ministry of Justice, other judicial offices, and ultimately the emperor himself. However, after the cataclysmic Taiping Rebellion erupted, smooth communication channels between the central and local governments were disrupted. To expedite suppression of the uprising, the Qing court conferred provincial governors the emergency powers to summarily approve executions without referring cases centripetally for sanction by central authorities. However, provincial authorities refused to relinquish this power after quelling the rebellion, defying repeated edicts from central judicial offices demanding its withdrawal. Thereby, the Qing court's judicial sovereignty was encroached upon not only by assertive foreign powers but also intransigent provincial governors.

7.1.5 The Boxer Rebellion and the Launch of the New Policies in the Late Qing

During the Boxer Rebellion of 1900, Empress Dowager Cixi declared war against the Great Powers, but her forces were swiftly defeated. However, amidst this conflict, several influential provincial governors formed an agreement known as the "Mutual Protection of Southeast China", in which they pledged to keep their armies and provinces out of the war. In January 1901, in an effort to demonstrate goodwill to the Great Powers and a commitment to reform, the Qing government issued an imperial edict announcing the implementation of New Policies.

This imperial edict acknowledged the importance of upholding the three fundamental bonds and five constant virtues, which were considered "eternal principles" in Chinese society. However, it also recognized the need for governance to adapt to the changing times. The edict summarized the deep-rooted social issues in China as follows. "The weakness of China is caused by the strength of convention and the rigid network of regulations. We have many mediocre officials but few men of talent and courage. The regulations are used by the mediocre men as the means of their self-protection, and taken advantage of by the government clerks as sources of profit. The government officials exchange numerous documents but they never touch reality. The appointment of men of talent is restricted by regulations which are so rigid that even men of extraordinary talent are missed. What misleads the country can be expressed in one word, selfishness ([*si*]) and what suffocates all under heaven is precedent (*li*). The recent Westernization Movement learns only superficial words and phrases, and the manufacturing of machines, but not the fundamentals of Western political systems" (Ichiko, 2008, p. 375).[2] Zhang Zhidong, Liu Kunyi and other provincial governors submitted the *Three Joint Imperial Memorials of Jiangchu on Reform*, and took the lead in putting forward suggestions for revision of the Legal Code. On March 11, 1902, the Qing government issued a decree to revise the Qing code:

> Throughout Chinese history, laws and regulations have undergone continuous additions and modifications, particularly during the Han and Tang dynasties. The *Great Qing Legal Code*, established during our dynasty, represented a comprehensive and meticulous synthesis of legal principles. However, as governance necessitates adaptation, it is crucial to adjust the law to align with the current social reality to ensure its effective enforcement. In recent times, the geographical advantages of China have expanded, leading to increased prosperity in commerce. Consequently, it is essential to establish specific regulations and provisions within the legal framework, particularly in areas such as mining, railway, and commerce. To achieve this, ministers dispatched abroad are instructed to examine the laws and regulations of various countries and provide reports to the Ministry of Foreign Affairs for reference. Furthermore, individuals such as Yuan Shih-k'ai, Liu Kunyi, and Zhang Zhidong are entrusted with the responsibility of carefully selecting and recommending experts who possess a deep understanding of both Chinese and Western laws and regulations. These experts will form a commission tasked with drafting legal codes, which will then be subjected to review and promulgation under imperial order. The aim is to develop a modified legal code that is practical, fair, and accepted both domestically and internationally. This endeavor serves the purpose of demonstrating the government's sincerity in being flexible and amicable towards the people (*Veritable Records of Emperor Dezong*, 1987, p. 537).

7.1.6 Modernization and Pursuit of Prosperity

Liang Qichao, a prominent Chinese intellectual, identified three stages in China's modernization process: material, institutional, and ideological and cultural. The material stage began after the First Opium War when Chinese society started incorporating Western technologies and weapons. This period, known as the Westernization Movement, focused on modernizing material artifacts. Unfortunately, the achievements of the Westernization Movement suffered a tragic defeat in the First Sino-Japanese War. In contrast, Japan's Meiji Restoration was highly successful, enabling Japan to become strong enough to defeat both the Qing Empire and the Russian Empire. Consequently, China began to recognize the need to adopt Western institutions, including constitutionalism. Despite the establishment of the Republic of China, the modernization efforts in terms of material artifacts and institutions failed

[2] Translations are from Ichiko (2008, p. 375), except for the last sentence. (Notes by translators)

to yield the desired results within a short timeframe. As a result, China remained at a disadvantageous position in its competition with the Great Powers. This realization prompted the Chinese people to reflect upon their traditional culture in the hope of restoring their nation's strength and identity.

Due to its unique terrain, climate, and abundant natural resources, Chinese society prior to the late Qing Dynasty entered a stage of civilization at an early period and enjoyed a state of "glorious isolation". The loyalty of imperial bureaucrats to the emperor was unwavering, and the commoners showed remarkable tolerance towards state mismanagement. As a result, dynasties were able to maintain their rule with minimal military and economic power. However, limited income led to a government structure that was imbalanced and "top-heavy". Any hasty tax increases would only result in a further accumulation of outstanding taxes. "The history of Qing China before 1800 conforms with the expectation of low tax, high public good reputational equilibrium. The subsequent history does not" (Rosenthal & Wong, 2011, p. 198).

It was in war that Eastern and Western cultures had their first significant encounter. The old empire found itself powerless in the face of confrontations with European and American powers. After enduring multiple struggles, China had to undergo a transformation, learning from the West and establishing modern national institutions in order to achieve national prosperity. "The shift from 'barbarian affairs' (*yiwu*, 夷务) to 'Western affairs' (*yangwu*, 洋务) and eventually to 'current affairs' (*shiwu*, 时务), reflects the rising influence of the West in the Chinese consciousness. The derogatory term 'barbarian' (*yi*, 夷) was replaced with the neutral term 'Western' (*xi*, 西), and eventually with the reverent term 'Western' (*taixi*, 泰西, lit., the Far West). This progression indicates the gradual recognition of the West's growing power in the Chinese mindset." "After encountering Western invasion, the Chinese shifted their focus from reason to strength", combining the traditional legalist thought of "wealth and strength" with the Western evolutionary theory. This led to a rediscovery of "the previously suppressed legalist thought on agriculture and warfare, and further extended to the realms of commercial and academic competition" (Luo, 2014, pp. 22–23).

"A system of unequal treaties created conditions of 'constrained sovereignty' after 1842, but China escaped formal colonial rule" (Halsey, 2015, p. 20). "Domestic and foreign conflicts reshaped the dominant patterns of taxation, resource distribution, and government spending over the course of six decades. The state's extractive capacity continued to grow as the country prepared for war, and total revenues tripled in inflation-adjusted terms between 1842 and 1911" (Halsey, 2015, p. 20). In addition to the financial, diplomatic and military aspect, the late Qing era, spanning the late 19th and early twentieth centuries, also marked a significant period of bureaucratic development in modern China, including the establishment and evolution of local government structure. Although the construction of a modern military-fiscal state "did not transform China into a great power in a few decades, but [it] enhanced the country's strategic capabilities beyond the minimal threshold to retain its independence" (Halsey, 2015, p. 147).

"China's earliest modern industry was created by state power," "which was certainly abnormal in comparison with the Euro-Western model." "At that time, what belonged to the economic sphere in the Western world had to be produced in a rush with political power in China." For a country which was "vulnerable to attack due to its backwardness" and desperate to "catch up", China had no choice but to "follow the established practice of state-run handicraft industry, and the generation of people engaged in the Westernization Movement naturally resorted to the state for the development of modern industry, which was also historical path dependence" (Yang, 2014, pp. 227–228). Influenced by the thought of "commercial warfare", "officials developed a neo-mercantilist philosophy of governance and abandoned their earlier commitment to maintaining a stable agrarian order throughout the empire" (Halsey, 2015, p. 101). The Merchants Steam Navigation Company "served as an effective instrument of mercantilist policy in the late nineteenth century" (Halsey, 2015, p. 187), and it was founded to meet China's "express strategic goals" (Halsey, 2015, p. 79). High-ranking officials like Li Hongzhang associated the company with the safeguarding of national sovereignty, particularly in terms of protecting economic rights. This unique model of enterprise, which entailed the fusion of private capital and state sponsorship, diverged from the conventional Western business paradigm.

The Westernization Movement, which aimed to achieve "victory" and "prosperity" during the late Qing period, had some detrimental consequences. "Traditional Confucianism strongly discouraged profit-seeking competition, yet under the New Policies, endeavors such as 'the construction of railroads, the opening of mines, and increase of taxation' directly deprived the people of their profits. As a result, the populace experienced a loss of confidence." "The introduction of new policies necessitated substantial expenditures, which were ultimately extracted from the people. Consequently, instead of enriching the population, these policies ended up causing harm. Despite claiming to strengthen the nation, they actually weakened it." "The envisioned 'prosperity' of the country remained a distant aspiration, while the burden of taxation on the people continued to grow" (Luo, 2014, pp. 73–74). Although the perspectives of the aforementioned conservatives may have been biased, it is noteworthy that the "Railway Protection Movement", which played a significant role in triggering the Xinhai Revolution of 1911, was closely associated with the New Policies implemented during the late Qing period.

7.2 Preparatory Constitutionalism and Political Reform

7.2.1 Launch of the Preparatory Constitutionalism

Following the conclusion of the Russo-Japanese War, constitutionalism emerged as a prominent topic of interest among the Chinese population. Notably, public opinion strongly favored the adoption of constitutional principles, with even Qing court envoys stationed abroad, court officials, and frontier officials petitioning for constitutional reforms. Consequently, the constitutionalism movement gained traction throughout the country (Jing, 1984, pp. 84–87). During this period, the war between Japan and Russia was widely perceived as a clash between constitutional and autocratic regimes. The victory of Japan, a small constitutional country, over the larger autocratic power of Russia, served as a source of great inspiration and made a profound impact on the Chinese people. In 1904, Liang Qichao established the Political Information Institute in Japan with the aim of advocating for constitutionalism. Subsequently, in September of the same year, overseas Chinese jointly petitioned the Qing court, urging the adoption of constitutional reforms.

Under mounting pressure, the Qing government found itself compelled to adopt a stance of "imitating constitutionalism" in 1905. In October of the same year, the Qing court established the "Commission for Studying the Ways of Government" and dispatched ministers abroad in December to study the constitutions of major world powers. Furthermore, students were sent to various countries for educational purposes. In August 1907, the commission underwent a name change to the "Commission for Studying Constitutional Government", signifying its dedicated focus on constitutional reforms. Among its primary responsibilities were the compilation of laws and regulations, as well as the maintenance of political records.

Within the purview of drafting laws and regulations, the commission undertook several critical tasks. Firstly, it assumed "the responsibility of reviewing and responding to imperial memorials pertaining to constitutionalism, as assigned by the emperor. Additionally, the commission engaged in the compilation and investigation of relevant documents assigned by Grand Councilors." Secondly, "an examination of the constitutions of various countries was conducted, with the ultimate aim of formulating a draft constitution." Thirdly, "examination and scrutiny of the draft code by the Law Codification Committee." Fourthly, the commission undertook the examination of "special laws drafted by ministries and provinces". Lastly, the commission played a significant role in "reviewing administrative laws and regulations, including the revision of the official system and appointment regulations" (Peng, 2011, p. 18).

From the perspective of the ruling authority, the adoption of constitutionalism brought forth three significant advantages. Firstly, it ensured the stability and permanence of the throne. Secondly, it was believed that external crises would gradually diminish. Lastly, it was anticipated that domestic unrest would subside. In line with these considerations, an imperial edict on preparatory constitutionalism was promulgated in September, under the guiding principle of "essential powers residing in the imperial court and public opinion allowed in government affairs". As the domestic situation grew increasingly turbulent, the rise of the capitalistic constitutional movement, the spread of international democratic constitutionalism, and the activities by advocates of the constitutional monarchy within the ruling class exerted pressure on the Qing government from both external and internal sources. In response, the government was compelled to declare "preparatory constitutionalism" on September 1, 1906, and subsequently published the "preparatory constitutionalism" plan on August 27, 1908, known as the "List of Yearly Preparations by Imperial Order".

In addition to the implementation of preparatory constitutionalism, a significant aspect of the New Policies during the late Qing era was the abolition of the imperial examinations. "On September 2, 1905, the Qing government decisively changed the regulations that had been put in place over a year ago, which aimed to gradually reduce the number of graduates from the imperial examinations. Instead, they opted for an immediate suspension of the imperial examination system, marking the end of an over 1300-year-old tradition in Chinese history." "This move signaled the shift towards comprehensive and profound political reforms, extending beyond the realm of examinations to encompass broader polity reform and the advancement of preparatory constitutionalism. Consequently, reforms were initiated in the internal and external official systems, as well as in various other institutions, indicating the comprehensive and progressive nature of the New Policies during the late Qing period." (Guan, 2019, pp. 92, 121).

7.2.2 Reform of the Bureaucratic System

Reforming the official bureaucracy was the Qing court's first critical step in implementing preparatory constitutionalism. As stated in the imperial edict on preparatory constitutionalism, "the reform of the official system is the first step to weed out accumulated defects and clarify responsibilities" (Grand Secretariat, 1979, p. 44). Subsequently, an edict was issued to establish the Compilation Commission of Official System, with the appointment of Zaize and thirteen other members for this purpose. Provincial governors were instructed to send their respective authorities to Beijing to participate in the deliberations. Notably, Yili—Prince Qing, Sun Jianai—Grand Secretary of the Hall of Literary Profundity, and Zhai Hongji—Grand Minister of State were assigned to oversee the examination process. One of the key objectives of the official system reform was to seize the opportunity to curtail the power wielded by Han provincial governors.

i. Reform of the official system in the central government

During the initial stages of the "New Policies", preceding the implementation of preparatory constitutionalism, the Qing government introduced a series of structural reforms within its administrative framework. In March 1901, the Bureau of Government Affairs was established as the central hub for government reform initiatives. Initially affiliated with the Grand Council, the bureau later came under the jurisdiction of the Grand Secretariat. The ministers of the bureau concurrently held positions as Grand Councilors or Grand Secretaries. It was not until 1911, with the establishment of a responsible cabinet, that the bureau was abolished. In June 1901, the Qing government undertook a reorganization of the Foreign Office within the Ministry of Foreign Affairs. This was followed by the establishment of the Ministry of Trade in July 1903. Subsequently, in September 1905, the Ministry of Police and various police and gendarmerie institutions were created. The Ministry of Education was also added in 1905 to address educational matters. In March 1903, the Finance Office was established by the Qing court to oversee national finances. Furthermore, in May 1903, the positions of Ministers of Military Training and the Bureau of Military Training were established, which were later merged to form the Ministry of Army. In order to directly manage all customs services, as well as the Chinese Maritime Customs Service responsible for customs duties, the Taxation Administration was established in April 1906 (Zhang, 2008, pp. 282–290).

In August 1906, a memorial titled *Request to Revise the National Official System in Preparation for Constitutionalism* was submitted by Dai Hongci and others, highlighting the importance of Japan's experience in reforming its official system prior to the establishment of constitutionalism. The memorial emphasized the similarity of China's situation to that of Japan at the time, suggesting that Japan's experience could serve as a valuable reference. Within the memorial, eight specific measures were proposed for the reform of the official system:

(1) Partial imitation of the cabinet system to unify the central administration.

(2) Clarification of the power distribution between the central and local governments.

(3) Appointment of assistant officials at crucial internal and external institutions, with a particular emphasis on the consolidation of duties and responsibilities under a single headship for chief officials of the ministries.

(4) Flexibility in the addition, elimination, and merging of positions within the central government as deemed necessary.

(5) Modification of the local official system.

(6) Separation of judicial affairs and tax collection from the responsibilities of local officials.

(7) Replacement of sub-official functionaries with clerks in both internal and external government institutions.

(8) Updating of regulations pertaining to the appointment, promotion, punishment, salary, and reward of officials, as well as the overall system of officials.

Following the submission of the memorial, the Qing government prioritized the reform of the central government official system as the initial step in preparing for constitutionalism (Grand Secretariat, 1979, pp. 367–383).

In September 1906, the Qing government established the Compilation Commission of Official System, which formulated five basic principles for the reform of the official system in preparation for constitutionalism. These principles included:

(1) Reference to the official system of constitutional monarchies, with a focus on reforming the executive and judicial systems while leaving other aspects untouched for the time being.

(2) The goal of the reform was to ensure that "officials fulfill their duties and responsibilities, promoting a culture of dedication and accountability".

(3) The adoption of the principle of separation of powers, starting with the reform of the executive and judicial systems due to the unfeasibility of establishing a parliament at that moment.

(4) Classification of officials into different categories based on their ranks and responsibilities: imperial envoys, Grand Ministers of Grand Secretariat and provincial governors, and officials above metropolitan ministers fell in the category of *tejian guan*, i.e. officials directly appointed by the emperor. Posts of the third- and fourth-rank at the Ministries and the Censorate were termed *qingjian guan*, i.e., officials to be appointed through selection. Officials of the fifth- to the seventh-rank were *zoubu guan*, who would be appointed through the institution of recommendation, and of the eighth- and ninth-rank *weiyong guan*, the appointment of whom was the responsibility of the officials-in-charge.

(5) The establishment of the Academy of Scholary Worthies (*jixianyuan*, 集贤院) and the Political Advisory Council to accommodate redundant staff after the reform (*New code of the Qing Dynasty*, 2010, pp. 673-674).

On November 2, 1906, Yikuang (Prince Qing), Sun Jianai (a statesman in the late Qing), and others submitted the imperial memorial titled *Revision of the Official System of the Central Government*, which highlighted the importance of reforming the official system as the foundation for implementing constitutionalism in the country. Grounded in constitutionalist principles, the memorial identified flaws in the existing bureaucratic structure and proposed realigning institutions along Western lines of separation of powers. In response, the Qing court issued the *Resolution on Yikuang and Others' Revision of the Official system of the Central Government* (Grand Secretariat, 1979, pp. 367–383), accepting these proposals. This resolution affirmed the need to reform institutions as the foundation for constitutional preparations. The Grand Secretariat and the Grand Council remained unchanged, and all ministers would be deputy ministers at the Bureau of Government Affairs. The Ministry of Foreign Affairs and the Ministry of Personnel would remain, and the Ministry of Police was changed to the Ministry of Interior. The Ministry of Revenue and the Commission of Finance would be reorganized into the Bureau of General Account. The Court of Imperial Sacrifices (*taichang si*, 太常寺), Court of Imperial Entertainments (*guanglu si*, 光禄寺) and Court of State Ceremonial (*honglu si*, 鸿胪寺) would merge into the Ministry of Rites. The Ministry of Education would remain. The Ministry of War, the Commission for Army Reorganization (*lianbing chu*, 练兵处), and the Court of the Imperial Stud (*taipu si*, 太仆寺) would be combined to form the Army Ministry. Before the establishment of the Ministry of Navy and the Military Advisory Office, relevant affairs would be handled by the Ministry of Army. The Ministry of Punishments would be reorganized into the Ministry of Justice (*fabu*, 法部) and be devoted to judicial administration. The Court of Judicial Review) would be changed to the Supreme Court of Justice (*dali yuan*, 大理院), taking exclusive control of trial. The Ministry of Works and the Ministry of Trade would merge to form the Ministry of Agriculture, Industry and Commerce. The Ministry of Posts and Communications would be set as the special institution in charge of ships, railways, electric wires, and postal services. *Lifan yuan* (the Department for Ethnic Affairs) would be renamed into *lifan bu*. The senior posts at the Ministry of Foreign Affairs would remain, but those of all other ministries would be changed with one minister and two vice ministers for each ministry, whether Manchu or Han. The senior posts in the Censorate would now be one Censor-in-chief and two Vice Censors-in-chief. The post of Supervising Censor of the Six Offices of Scrutiny (*liuke jishizhong*, 六科给事中) would be changed to Supervising Censor (*jishizhong*, 给事中), and the posts, together with those of other Supervising Censors, would remain for the moment. The Political Advisory Council and the Audit Department would be created, and other *yamen* did not require any change.

In an imperial meeting, it was determined that the ongoing reform of the central government official system would adhere to the principle of excluding discussion on five specific issues, namely, the Grand Council, the Imperial Household Department, the Eight Banners, the Hanlin Academy, and eunuchs. Consequently, the official system reform, under the aforementioned principle of "five non-discussions", primarily involved the reorganization and consolidation of certain ministries and departments, as well as changes in names and titles of specific institutions and offices. The Qing government officially announced the central government official system in November 1906, which consisted of eleven ministries, while the Grand Secretariat and the Grand Council remained unchanged. Subsequently, during the Xuantong period, the Ministry of Navy was established, and the Ministry of Rites was transformed into the Ceremonial Office. It is noteworthy that the Manchu aristocrats within the Qing court utilized the reform as an opportunity to marginalize Han bureaucrats and consolidate central power.

ii. Reform of the local official system

After the formulation of the reform plan for the central official system, the Qing government proceeded with the implementation of reforms in local governments. However, conflicts arose among the ministers tasked with compiling the official system, prompting the government to seek the opinions of provincial governors through telegrams (Hou, 1993, pp. 82–83).

> In the process of preparing for constitutionalism, the reform of provincial official systems should align with the changes implemented at the central government level. As part of this reform, local governments were restructured into three administrative levels: prefectures, departments, and districts. Under the new system, prefects, holding the lower fourth rank, are solely responsible for the administration of *fuguo*, which referred to districts whose magistrates operated within the same county as the prefects, regardless of the subordinate departments and districts. The position of the principal magistrate, responsible for a provincial capital's district, will be abolished. Magistrates of independent departments and independent subprefectures are relieved of the duty of administering their subordinate districts. They, along with magistrates of normal departments, are collectively referred to as department magistrates, holding the upper fifth rank. Assistant magistrates of independent subprefectures and district magistrates are grouped together as district magistrates, holding the lower fifth rank. At each level of governance (prefectures, departments, and districts), officials ranging from the sixth to ninth ranks are assigned roles in overseeing taxation, law enforcement, education, prisons, agriculture, industry and commerce, and general affairs. Local courts will be established to handle legal disputes. Additionally, each prefecture, department, and district will have an assembly composed of elected members engaged in discussions on political matters. The promotion of this system aims to facilitate the creation of lower-level independent institutions in the future. Furthermore, the number of general surveillance circuits will be adjusted according to circumstances, and corresponding posts supporting officials within these circuits will be created.
>
> In the context of provincial capital government institutions, two approaches have been proposed for the reform of posts. The first approach involves the establishment of provincial yamen, led by provincial governors who hold positions comparable to ministers of various ministries. Regional administrative commissioners and surveillance commissioners are appointed as regional assistants, while the posts at the branch offices within the provincial yamen resemble assistant administration commissioners. This arrangement promotes collaboration between provincial governors and their subordinate officials, eliminating the

> need for information and work report transfers. Official documents from prefectures, departments, and districts can be directly transmitted to the provincial departments, and vice versa. Additionally, each province establishes a High Court to handle appeals. This approach incorporates specialized officials to manage executive and judicial functions, streamlines paperwork, and ensures effective interconnectivity among institutions, thereby resembling the official system of a constitutional state. The second approach involves provincial governors directly overseeing foreign and military affairs, as well as supervising executive and judicial organs. Regional administrative commissioners are responsible for civil affairs, agriculture, industry, and commerce. Surveillance commissioners are tasked with judicial administration and supervise the High Court. Furthermore, a Finance Office is established to oversee finance and transportation matters. All branch offices are staffed with subordinate officials to assist with administration. Provincial authorities responsible for education, salt, grain, customs, and rivers remain unchanged, operating under the guidance of provincial governors. This system modifies the existing official system and clearly defines the duties, responsibilities, and authorities of officials.

One of the four key principles established during the imperial conference on official system reform, known as the "constitutional government", was that "provincial governors in the existing system be abolished, and that the newly created position of provincial governor possesses authority comparable to that of prefectural governors in Japan, with both financial and military powers being centralized to the central government." However, this proposition faced opposition from provincial governors, resulting in its suspension. In 1907, the Qing government initiated reforms to the local government, with the following details:

> (1) The Ministry of Army directly appointed military counselors to Provincial Military Commissions (*dulian gongsuo*, 督练公所) in order to strip provincial governors of military power.
>
> (2) The Bureau of General Account dispatched officials to oversee financial affairs in the provinces, aiming to regain control over financial power from provincial governors.
>
> (3) The military and financial powers previously held by provincial governors were respectively allocated to the Ministry of Army and the Bureau of General Account.
>
> (4) The role of the surveillance commissioner was replaced by the commissioner for judicial affairs. Additionally, police intendants and industrial intendants were established. The number of sub-regional administrative commissioners and sub-regional judiciary commissioners was reduced or eliminated, while soldiers were retained to guard the circuits.
>
> (5) Judicial bureaus were established, with the addition or alteration of posts for subordinate officials.

The reform of the provincial official system was met with varying attitudes from provincial governors, leading to the decision to pilot the reforms in the Three Eastern Provinces before implementing them nationwide. The initial implementation took place in the provinces of Zhili and Jiangsu, with plans for expansion to other provinces within a 15-year timeframe. The reform of the local official system in the Three Eastern Provinces commenced in April 1907, encompassing several significant changes. The highest official in the Three Eastern Provinces was the general governor, overseeing provincial governors and the newly established provincial offices. Each provincial office consisted of a Provincial Secretariat (*chengxuan ting*, 承宣厅) and a Provincial Assembly (*ziyi ting*, 咨议厅). Additionally, seven bureaus were established in each province to handle foreign affairs, banner affairs, civil affairs, education, finance, industry, and Mongolian affairs. The Provincial Military Commissions for Army Reorganization were established to oversee military affairs in the Three Eastern Provinces, while commissioners for judicial affairs were responsible for judicial administration in all provinces. The sub-provincial government structure consisted of three levels: prefecture, department, and district, with no subordinate districts under prefectures. Subsequent to the implementation in the Three Eastern Provinces, other provinces carried out similar reforms, albeit with varying degrees of progress. To mitigate resistance from influential provincial factions, the Qing court promoted prominent Han officials Yuan Shih-k'ai, the general governor of Zhili and grand minister for foreign commerce in north China, and Zhang Zhidong, the general governor of Huguang (Hubei and Hunan provinces), to positions within the central government and bestowed them nominal titles as Grand Councilors. However, it is worth noting that "despite these reforms, the provincial official system during the late Qing period remained largely unchanged, with the exception of the establishment of education, judicial affairs, and foreign affairs bureaus, as well as police and industry circuits, and the reorganization of the Three Eastern Provinces into modern provinces" (Zhang, 2008, p. 300).

7.2.3 *From* Outline of the Imperial Constitution *to* Nineteen Articles

i. Outline of Imperial Constitution

Following extensive investigations into constitutionalism in both Eastern and Western countries, the Qing court ultimately decided to adopt the models of Japan and Germany, which featured strong monarchical traditions. In 1908, the Qing government issued the *Outline of Imperial Constitution*, which was drafted by the Commission for Studying Constitutional Government. This document marked a significant milestone as the first modern constitutional legal document in the history of the Chinese legal system. The outline, drawing inspiration from the *Constitution of the Empire of Japan* established in 1889, aimed to establish a semi-constitutional monarchy.

Comprising 23 articles, the outline encompassed two main components: the body text titled *Powers of the Monarch* and an appendix titled "Rights and Duties of Subjects". The Commission for Studying Constitutional Government and the Political Advisory Council explicitly emphasized the structure of the outline in an imperial memorial. They stated that "the initial section focused on delineating the powers of the monarch, underscoring the guiding role of the monarch over the subjects." "The subsequent section addressed the rights and duties of subjects, highlighting the essential role of the people as the foundation of the state. While both the monarch and the people were subject to the rule of law, ultimate power still resided within the imperial court."

The "Powers of the Monarch", comprising 14 articles, commenced with the opening article stipulating that "the emperor of the Qing Dynasty shall reign over and govern the Qing empire with his majesty's unbroken line of succession for ages eternal." It further emphasized the sacred and inviolable status of the emperor. This article bestowed upon the emperor a range of powers, including the authority to promulgate laws, propose motions to the parliament, convene and dissolve the parliament, establish bureaucratic systems and pay plans, and promote or demote officials. Additionally, the emperor possessed command over all military forces and held absolute power to declare wars, negotiate peace, conclude treaties with foreign nations, dispatch envoys, and, in times of emergency, proclaim martial law and restrict the rights of the populace. Furthermore, the emperor retained judicial authority, surpassing even the powers granted to the emperor under the *Meiji Constitution*. The *Rights and Duties of Subjects*, consisting of nine articles, primarily focused on the obligations of subjects to pay taxes, serve in the army, and abide by the law. The articles pertaining to rights and freedoms were relatively concise. Within the boundaries of the law, individuals enjoyed freedoms such as speech, writing, publication, assembly, and association, with the exception of restrictions specified by law. Moreover, individuals possessed the right to engage in litigation and be tried by judicial organs, among other rights.

ii. Establishment of Provincial Assembly and Political Advisory Council

1. Provincial Assembly

In anticipation of the implementation of constitutionalism, the late Qing government established Provincial Assembly (*ziyi ju*, 谘议局) in 1909 as local advisory body. The preparations for this assembly began in 1907. Subsequently, in 1908, *Charter of Provincial Assembly*, drafted by the Commission for Studying Constitutional Government, was approved for promulgation. Provincial governors were mandated to establish a Provincial Assembly within their jurisdictions within a year. According to the *Charter of Provincial Assembly*, the primary objective of the Provincial Assembly was to "gather public opinion, identify and present the strengths and weaknesses of the provinces, and formulate plans for local security." It is crucial to note that "the Provincial Assembly's responsibilities encompassed both parliamentary and advisory functions, extending beyond a mere 'provincial parliament'." "The inclusion of the terms 'advisory council' in the nomenclature was influenced by the imperial edict issued on September 13th in the twenty-ninth year of the Guangxu era (1903). This choice of terminology suggests that the Provincial Assembly served as both a decision-making body and an advisory entity."(Meng, et. al., 2015, pp. 4–5)

The eligibility criteria for candidates of the Provincial Assembly were highly rigorous. Based on relevant statistics from that period, it was found that no more than 1% of the population in each province met the qualifications. The term of office for members of the Provincial Assembly was set at three years. The Provincial

Assembly held various functions and powers, which encompassed deliberating and making decisions on matters that the provincial government needed to develop or reform. This included discussions on the province's budget, tax laws, public debts, as well as the allocation and removal of responsibilities and rights. The Provincial Assembly also had the authority to propose additions, deletions, and amendments to the province's rules and regulations. Additionally, it was responsible for the election of members to the Political Advisory Council, responding to consultations from the Political Advisory Council or the provincial governor, addressing matters brought forward by the self-government assembly or the province's inhabitants, and settling disputes within the self-government assembly. The Provincial Assembly held two types of meetings: annual meetings and temporary meetings. These meetings were convened by the provincial governor, who not only possessed supervisory and decision-making powers over the Provincial Assembly but also had the authority to suspend its activities or submit a memorial to the emperor for its dismissal.

The Provincial Assembly gathered the enlightened local gentry so that they could legally assemble to participate in politics, which laid the foundation for the constitutionalists' organization of the "Parliament Petition Movement" and the independence of the provinces after the Xinhai Revolution. By 1909, nearly all members of the Provincial Assembly had been elected. Since October 14 of the same year, provinces began to convene council meetings to discuss matters concerning the power of the Provincial Assembly, and the Provincial Assemblies of different provinces jointly initiated the petition for the immediate convocation of the Parliament and the establishment of a responsible cabinet. In the process of exercising their powers, the Provincial Assemblies underwent many a conflict with provincial governors.

2. Political Advisory Council

In 1906, the Qing court issued an edict announcing the initiation of constitutionalism and introduced the concept of "preparative constitutionalism", which emphasized the concentration of "essential powers within the imperial court while allowing for the inclusion of public opinion in governance affairs" (Grand Secretariat, 1979, pp. 43–44). Drawing inspiration from Japan's establishment of the House of Assembly, the Qing government decided to establish the Political Advisory Council as a quasi-parliamentary organ during the preparatory constitutional period (Zizhengyuan, 2010, p. 692). The name "Political Advisory Council" was not initially intended to be grand, as it was created to accommodate redundant officials resulting from the 1906 reform of the official system (Bianzuan, 2010, p. 673). In essence, the Political Advisory Council served as a central "advisory body" during the period of "preparatory constitutionalism". Similar to the Provincial Assembly, the establishment of the Political Advisory Council commenced in 1907. On August 23, 1909, in the first year of the Xuantong era, the Qing government promulgated the *Charter of the Political Advisory Council*. The first article of the Charter stated that "the mission of the Political Advisory Council was to gather public opinions and lay the groundwork for the establishment of the Upper and Lower Houses in accordance with the imperial edict." Accordingly, the *Charter* granted the Political Advisory Council the authority to deliberate and make decisions on matters such as the state's budget, tax laws, public bonds, and new codes and law amendments, excluding the constitution. Additionally, it could address other matters specified by special decrees. However, all resolutions passed by the Political Advisory Council had to be submitted, along with the opinions of the Grand Councilors or ministers, to the emperor for a final decision. Furthermore, the emperor retained the power to suspend or dissolve the Political Advisory Council through the issuance of a special decree.

The Political Advisory Council consisted of two types of members: "imperial nominees" and "representatives elected by popular vote". The former encompassed various groups, including princes, both Manchu and Han aristocracy, vassal princes (Mongolian, Tibetan, and Hui), the Manchu family of the Gioro, ministerial and court officials ranging from the fourth to the seventh rank (excluding judges, prosecutors, and patrol officers), erudite Confucians, and significant taxpayers. It is evident that a majority of the "imperial nominees" were individuals from the imperial clan or held high-ranking positions within the government. On the other hand, the "popularly elected" members were chosen from among the members of the Provincial Assemblies and were subject to the "approval" of provincial governors (Daqing, 2010, pp. 89–98).

As outlined in the *Charter of the Political Advisory Council*, the composition of the council was to consist of 100 imperial nominees and 100 popularly elected members. This structure resembled a unicameral system, where all members convened together, rather than a bicameral system with separate chambers. In comparison to the Public Council (House of Representatives) in pre-constitutional Japan, the Political Advisory Council bore more resemblance to the congress of a modern constitutional state in terms of its system, and the procedures adopted by the Qing court were notably more radical than those of Japan.[3] Consequently, the constitutionalists were able to legally convene in the Provincial Assemblies and the Political Advisory Council for political discussions, thereby exerting greater control over these assemblies.[4]

---

[3] In the second year of the Meiji era (1869), Japan established the Public Council as the central deliberative body in the central government. This council consisted of approximately 270 members who were elected by the domains. However, the government frequently rejected most of the proposals put forward by the Public Council. Recognizing the inefficiency of the council, Okubo Toshimichi and others argued that there were excessive and unproductive discussions taking place. As a result, after only four months of its establishment, the council was reorganized into the House of Assembly. The House of Assembly primarily processed proposals referred to it by the Council of State, rather than initiating proposals itself. This shift led to a diminished emphasis on public discussions and a strengthening of centralized power. In the eighth year of Meiji (1875), the Japanese government issued an edict to establish a constitutional government. This included the formation of the Chamber of Elders, composed of 13 members and functioning not as a full legislature but the upper house. The lower house was called the Council of Magistrates. However, it was not until the 22nd year of Meiji (1889) when the imperial constitution was promulgated that a genuine National Diet was established. For more information, see Akio, Y. (1996, pp. 147, 149–150, 239–240, 291).

[4] The Qing court adopted a strategy of including an equal number of imperial nominees and members elected by popular vote in the same convention venue. This approach aimed to dilute the influence of the popularly elected members and exert control over them through the imperial nominees. To pass a major motion, a 2/3 majority was required, which was intended to restrict the actions of the constitutionalists. However, the members elected by popular vote proved to be highly active and influential, even swaying some passive imperial nominees to align with their interests. As a

On September 23, 1910, the Political Advisory Council gathered its members for the inaugural meeting, marking the official commencement of its activities. Subsequently, on October 3, the council held its opening ceremony in conjunction with its first annual meeting. The annual meeting, spanning over three months, witnessed the passing of significant resolutions by the Political Advisory Council. These resolutions included the immediate convening of the Parliament, the impeachment of the Grand Councilors, and the granting of pardons to political offenders. These decisions generated significant attention and had far-reaching implications at the time. Following the Wuchang Uprising (1911), the Political Advisory Council held its second annual meeting on October 22 of the same year. During this meeting, the council passed a series of significant proposals, notably including the swift removal of restrictions on political parties.

In contrast to the National Assemblies of Britain, the United States, and France, the "Political Advisory Council" lacked the authority to effectively check the government, thereby limiting its characterization as a Parliament in the modern sense. Its primary objective was to serve as a platform for "the expression of public opinion in government affairs" and to "pave the way for the eventual establishment of a parliamentary system". Historical evidence suggests that the creation of the council may have been a mere symbolic gesture by the Qing government. However, the council's significance was substantiated through the active engagement and discussions of its members.

Since its establishment, the Political Advisory Council became a focal point for various waves of unrest, with continuous proposals, inquiries, and opposition voiced against the Qing court. Notable instances include the impeachment of the Grand Councilors, which is discussed in detail in Sect. 7.3 of this chapter, as well as the clash between rites and laws, both of which unfolded within the Political Advisory Council (Li, 2011). While the council's resolutions held limited influence over the government, the participation of its members in political discussions served as a valuable democratic exercise. This engagement provided council members with political training, enabling them to accumulate experience and enhance their prestige. Consequently, many members of the council went on to become prominent figures in the early years of the Republic (Shang, 1998).

iii. Petition movement for convening the Parliament

The release of *List of Yearly Preparations Before the Convening of the Parliament*, also known as the *Nine-year Preparation List for Constitutionalism*, accompanied that of the *Outline of Imperial Constitution*. According to this list, preparations for the establishment of Provincial Assemblies were scheduled to commence in 1908. By 1910, Provincial Assemblies would be established, and members of the Political

result, the 2/3 voting threshold failed to effectively impede the actions of the constitutionalists. This strategic decision by the Qing court proved to be a significant mistake. If the imperial nominees and popularly elected members had been assigned to separate upper and lower chambers, it could have potentially fostered a system of checks and balances between the two chambers.

Advisory Council would be elected. In 1916, the Constitution, Parliament Acts, and Election Law of the Upper and Lower Houses, all falling within the purview of the Commission for Studying Constitutional Government, would be introduced. Subsequently, the election of parliament members and the convening of the Parliament would take place, also under the oversight of the Commission for Studying Constitutional Government (Grand Secretariat, 1979, pp. 61–67). The Qing government's move towards constitutional government was viewed by some constitutionalists as "an unprecedented event", while others advocated for the adoption of a constitutional monarchy similar to that of Britain (Hou, 2011, p. 151). Although the nine-year preparation period for constitutionalism may not appear lengthy when compared to Japan's example, it was considered a luxury given the political climate and popular sentiment of the time. In 1908, constitutionalists petitioned for an expedited timeline, urging the immediate convening of the Parliament. The establishment of Provincial Assemblies in 1909 provided constitutionalists with a legitimate platform for engaging in political discussions and forming connections. The petition movement to convene the Parliament gained momentum by 1910, with the Provincial Assemblies acting as its center of activity and guided by constitutionalist leaders.

The constitutionalists made repeated petitions to shorten the preparation period and promptly call for the Parliament. Some even demanded the abolition of the autocratic monarchy in favor of a parliamentary one. The Qing court, however, consistently delayed convening the Parliament, contending that the constitution should be promulgated first. Despite these challenges, the establishment of Provincial Assemblies provided legal platforms for the discussion and propagation of constitutionalism, thereby fostering the momentum of the petition movement during this period.

The petition movement unfolded through three significant episodes. The first petition occurred during the winter of the first year of the Xuantong era (1909). It was led by Zhang Jian, Chairman of the Provincial Assembly of Jiangsu, who mobilized representatives from sixteen provinces to form the "Petition Federation of Provincial Assembly". Their delegation traveled to Beijing with the objective of demanding the immediate convening of the Parliament and the formation of a responsible cabinet. Regrettably, the Qing court overlooked this petition and sought to stall by invoking the notion of "nine years of preparation for constitutionalism". Subsequently, the Petition Federation joined forces with the "Association for the Establishment of the Parliament" in Beijing, organizing the "Comrade Petition Union for the Establishment of the Parliament" and inviting representatives from Provincial Assemblies, chambers of commerce, education associations, and overseas Chinese groups contribute to the petition. The second petition transpired in May 1910. However, the Qing government employed the same excuse to delay any concrete action. In September, the third petition was submitted. In response to public outcry, the Qing court eventually relented by shortening the preparatory period and issuing an edict to convene the Parliament in 1913. The court emphasized that the decision to shorten the preparatory period was made at the insistence of various parties but made it clear that "no further changes could be accepted". Nevertheless, despite facing significant obstacles, Tang Hualong from Hubei province and Tan Yankai from Hunan province remained steadfast in their pursuit of an expeditious convocation of the Parliament, and even devised a strategy to initiate a fourth petition in Beijing. Regrettably, their endeavors were met with suppression by the Qing court, resulting in the eventual decline and dissolution of the petition movement (Luo, 1974, pp. 157–166).

iv. The promulgation of the new cabinet system and the Imperial Cabinet

During the Qing's official system reform in 1906, prominent figures such as Yikuang and Yuan Shih-k'ai proposed the establishment of a responsible cabinet. However, their proposal was met with opposition from Cixi, resulting in its indefinite postponement. Subsequently, following the demise of Guangxu and Cixi, the political landscape of the Qing Dynasty underwent significant changes. Concurrently, the Provincial Assembly emerged as a focal point for the petition movement, gaining momentum and witnessing an upsurge in revolutionary activities. Under mounting internal and external pressures, the Qing court issued an edict aimed at expediting the implementation of constitutionalism. This edict not only emphasized the need for expeditious promulgation and trial of the official system but also led to the reduction of the original nine-year preparatory period for constitutionalism to five years in 1910. In the next March, the Qing government enacted the 19-article *Official System of the New Cabine*t and the 15-article S*ubordinate-Official System of the Cabinet*. This new official system entailed the dissolution of the former Grand Secretariat and Grand Council, and the establishment of a new cabinet comprising the Prime Minister, Deputy Prime Minister, and ministers from ten ministries. On May 8, 1911, the Qing court officially promulgated the *Official System and Provisional Charter of the Cabinet*, formally instituting the cabinet system. The cabinet was composed of Yikuang as the Prime Minister, Natong and Xu Shichang as the Deputy Prime Ministers, Liang Dunyan as the Minister of Foreign Affairs, Shanqi as the Minister of Civil Affairs, Zaize as the Minister of Finance, Tang Jingchong as the Minister of Education, Yinchang as the Minister of Army, Zaixun as the Minister of Navy, Shaochang as the Minister of Justice, Pulun as the Minister of Agriculture, Industry and Commerce, Sheng Xuanhuai as the Minister of Posts and Communications, Shouqi as the Minister of Dependencies. The cabinet consisted of thirteen members, with eight being of Manchu ethnicity, four being Han Chinese, and one being Mongolian. Given that five of the eight Manchu members hailed from the imperial clan, the cabinet was commonly referred to as the "Imperial Cabinet". Consequently, the establishment of the new cabinet led to the abolition of the previous Grand Secretariat, the Grand Council, and the Bureau of Government Affairs.

The establishment of the "Imperial Cabinet" marked a significant step forward in terms of its institutional framework. However, the composition and subsequent actions of the cabinet were met with ridicule by both contemporaries and later generations. The dissatisfaction with the Imperial Cabinet spread throughout the nation, prompting the constitutionalists, acting under the banner of the Federation of Provincial Assembly, to petition the Censorate to intervene on their behalf. They argued that the Imperial Cabinet deviated from the principles of a constitutional monarchy and called for its reformation. Nevertheless, the Qing court maintained that the appointment and dismissal of officials rested solely with the emperor as the supreme authority. They firmly believed that members of the Provincial Assembly should not be allowed to interfere in such matters. Consequently, a growing divide emerged between the Qing court and the public, which continued to widen until the outbreak of the Wuchang Uprising. It was during this period that the Qing court expressed a desire to "return the government to the people" and implement a constitutional monarchy. However, these attempts came too late to bridge the gap between the court and the public (Luo, 1974, pp. 166–168).

v. Nineteen Major Articles of Good Faith on the Constitution

The Xinhai Revolution erupted on October 10, 1911, leading to the declaration of independence by provinces across China. In response, constitutionalists and influential military leaders submitted memorials urging the emperor to promptly promulgate the constitution and convene the Parliament. Faced with mounting internal and external pressures, the Qing government tasked the Political Advisory Council with drafting the constitution. Remarkably, the council managed to formulate and pass the *Nineteen Major Articles of Good Faith on the Constitution* (referred to as the *Nineteen Articles*) within a mere three days. These articles were officially issued on November 3, 1911.

Compared with the *Outline of Imperial Constitution*, the *Nineteen Article* differed significantly in style and content. Notably, they embraced the British-style parliamentary cabinet system and imposed restrictions on imperial power while expanding the authority of the parliament. The *Nineteen Articles* outlined several key provisions, including the specification of imperial power in the constitution, the establishment of a succession order for the throne, the requirement for the Political Advisory Council to draft and the emperor to promulgate the constitution, the authority of the Parliament to amend the constitution, the election of the Prime Minister by the Parliament and their appointment by the emperor, the emperor's direct command over the army and navy, but with the stipulation that neither force could be mobilized to resolve internal matters without the approval of the Parliament, the necessity for the Parliament's approval for any treaty, and the prescription of the official system and regulations in accordance with the law. Additionally, the *Nineteen Articles* mandated that the Political Advisory Council would act as a temporary substitute for the Parliament until its establishment. Following the provisions of the *Nineteen Articles*, the Qing court reappointed Yuan Shih-k'ai as the Prime Minister. However, it is noteworthy that the *Nineteen Articles* did not address the democratic rights of the people. Ultimately, the *Nineteen Articles* proved insufficient in saving the Qing court, leading to Emperor Pu Yi's announcement of his abdication on February 12, 1912. This marked the end of the two-thousand-year imperial rule in China.

7.2.4 Debate Over Two Approaches: Constitutional Monarchy and Republican Revolution

During the late Qing period, two main factions emerged with differing visions for the future of China's political system. The "royalists", led by Kang Youwei and Liang Qichao, advocated for the reform of the existing imperial system into a constitutional monarchy. On the other hand, the "constitutionalists", represented by gentry members such as Zhang Jian in various provinces, sought to establish a constitutional monarchy within the Qing Dynasty. Concurrently, revolutionaries led by Sun Yat-sen insisted on overthrowing the Manchu Dynasty altogether and establishing a republic. The pro-constitutional monarchy forces engaged in various forms of conflict with the "anti-Qing" revolutionaries. Overseas, both groups vied for support among overseas Chinese communities. Domestically, the revolutionaries responded with revolutionary actions to counter the constitutionalists' "reformist" approach and the Qing court's proposal of preparatory constitutionalism. The revolutionaries and the reformers (constitutionalists) respectively put forward the slogans of "Expel the Tartars" and "Convene the Parliament". Debates and discussions between the revolutionaries and the reformers frequently featured in newspapers, contributing to the popularization of modern constitutionalism. "Many individuals who later became involved in republican revolution recalled how their reading experiences, particularly works by Liang Qichao, a leader of the constitutionalist movement, had inspired their 'democratic revolutionary thought'." Hu Shi, a prominent intellectual figure, even noted that "while Liang Qichao never explicitly advocated revolution, he had planted the seeds of revolution in the minds of a group of young people." "From a modern perspective, the debate between the proponents of constitutional monarchy and those advocating for republican revolution represented a significant divergence. However, for the young Chinese of that time, the distinction was not necessarily absolute." (Shen, 2019, pp. 82–83).

The political ideologies espoused by the revolutionaries and constitutionalists during this period were not easily distinguishable. Both groups called for political reform and the establishment of a democratic system. However, their main point of contention was whether to achieve these goals through peaceful or forceful means. The conservative bureaucrats of the time recognized this dichotomy clearly. They observed that "within the revolution, there were two factions: the radicals, who openly opposed the imperial court and advocated for rebellion, and the peace advocates, who sought to seize power in the name of constitutionalism." Consequently, the monarchy would be abolished through the implementation of new laws that contradicted traditional ethical norms, and the authority of the monarch would be supplanted by an authoritarian cabinet system. Previously condemned as heretical, notions of equality and freedom now held sway in political affairs. Additionally, those who had once clandestinely planned to expel the Manchus from power now served as high-ranking officials. Under the guise of maintaining an unbroken line of sovereigns, the peace advocates sought to covertly alter the trajectory of the state by seizing the monarch's power and disregarding established protocols. Their intentions were widely known, and even the imperial court recognized their treacherous designs." (Liu, 1936)

Even among the revolutionaries of the time, the criteria for a successful revolution were primarily focused on achieving a transformation in the governmental structure rather than resorting to violence. "Regardless of the country in question, whether it be a constitutional democracy or a constitutional monarchy, the attainment of constitutionalism is typically realized through revolutionary means. Revolution, in this context, signifies a significant alteration in the political system. If such a transformation does not occur, then the outcome cannot be considered a true revolution, even if the process itself involved mass killings and bloodshed. Conversely, if a substantial change is accomplished, then it can indeed be classified as a revolution. The shift from an absolute monarchy to a constitutional democracy or constitutional monarchy does not arise from the sovereign's voluntary initiation of reforms, but rather from the growing demand for popular rights within society. When democratic ideals are strong enough in a society, the result of a revolution would be contingent upon the specific adversaries encountered during the revolution." (Wang, 1906)

The distinction between the revolutionaries and the constitutionalists during this period was not primarily based on the dichotomy of revolution versus non-revolution, but rather on the distinction between a military revolution involving bloodshed and a constitutional revolution that aimed for a bloodless transition. "Liang Qichao's perspective sheds light on this differentiation, as he stated that the constitutionalists were not fighting for a change in the form of the state, but rather for a transformation in the form of government. In terms of the former, they accepted the existing situation, while in terms of the latter, they sought to realize their ideals in the future. This flexibility in their ideal was demonstrated by their willingness to accept either a monarchy or a democracy, as long as a parliamentary system was established." "The constitutionalists, who opposed the government, gradually found themselves sympathizing with the revolutionary cause, which benefited therefrom" (Zhang, 2007, pp. 181, 191). This shift in the constitutionalists' stance towards revolution can be attributed to the growing influence of Western democratic ideas in late Qing society, including the advocacy of Liang Qichao. Both the constitutionalists and the revolutionaries shared a common theoretical foundation rooted in the principles of democratic constitutionalism. The constitutionalists, initially advocating for moderate reforms, inevitably gravitated towards revolutionary ideas due to the revolutionary spirit inherent in their ideology.

7.3 Impeachment of Grand Councilors by the Political Advisory Council and the Constitutionalist Revolution

7.3.1 Roots of the Impeachment of Grand Councilors: Dispute Over the Immediate Convention of the Parliament

Following the formation of the Political Advisory Council, its members swiftly united in passing a draft memorial urging the expeditious convening of the Parliament, preferably within the upcoming year. However, the Qing government responded by issuing an edict that shortened the preparation period for the implementation of constitutionalism from nine years to a mere five years. Additionally, the government repressed the ongoing petition for the assembly's convocation. This setback led to disagreements between the constitutionalists and the Qing court. Some council members boldly predicted that, without the immediate convocation of the Parliament, the nation faced the peril of collapse before the completion of the five-year period. Tragically, their prophetic words were proven to be accurate (Li, 2011, p. 141).

Prior to the formal issuance of an edict by the Qing government regarding the immediate convocation of the Parliament, rumors began circulating, casting doubt on the assembly's prompt establishment. To address these concerns, Venerable Prince Yulang, a Grand Councilor, visited the Political Advisory Council on September 29, 1910. During their discussion, assemblymen Shao Xi and Yi Zongkui raised the issue of the countersigning responsibility of Grand Councilors, noting that "in both Eastern and Western countries, it is customary for all decrees of the monarch to be countersigned by the Ministers of State." "This practice serves two purposes: to demonstrate administrative responsibility on behalf of the monarch and to establish accountability to the Parliament. In the context of contemporary China, where the Parliament has yet to convene when the Political Advisory Council was established, questions arose regarding the purpose of these countersignatures. Were they intended to establish responsibility for the monarch and accountability to the Political Advisory Council, or did they bear no significant difference from the countersignatures of state ministers in other countries?" "After an imperial edict is issued, it will meet the people's expectations if the Parliament can be convoked the following year. However, if the assembly could not be established within the timeline expected by the people, then the Grand Councilors would be held accountable for their countersignatures. In such a scenario, further countersignatures might not be necessary" (Li, 2011, p. 110).

Following the issuance of the imperial edict, some council members expressed their concerns. They remarked that in a constitutional country, once a motion concerning the Parliament was passed, it should be approved by the emperor. "However, in practice, the emperor's approval was typically nominal, similar to the resolutions passed in the House of Representatives. The decision by the princes and grand ministers to convene the Parliament in the fourth year effectively vetoed the Political Advisory Council's resolution for the immediate convocation of the assembly the following year. This development raised doubts about the ability of the Political Advisory Council to lay the foundation for and foster the spirit of the Parliament." (Li, 2011, p. 141)

Unable to openly criticize the emperor and the regent, council members directed their criticism towards the princes and grand ministers of the Bureau of Government Affairs, who countersigned the imperial edicts, as well as the "several petty officials" of the Commission for Studying Constitutional Government. The council members accused them of disregarding public opinion, manipulating the emperor and regent, and going against the prevailing trend. They argued that the princes and grand ministers should be held accountable, as "the request for immediate convocation of the Parliament had been agreed upon by provincial governors and the people, with only a handful of princes and grand ministers opposing it." They stated that "since the preparation for constitutionalism, with the emperor still young, the regent is willing to heed public sentiment and entrusts the responsibility of legislation to the princes and grand ministers of the Commission for Studying Constitutional Government, where only a few petty officials are responsible for compiling laws." Furthermore, they emphasized that "it is imperative for the speaker of the Political Advisory Council to engage in consultation with the commission and expeditiously present drafts of the constitution, parliament acts, and election laws for the council's consideration and approval. The majority opinion should carry greater weight than that of the minority." They stressed that "while the emperor and regent hold no prejudices, special matters in the Chinese form of government required discussion with the princes and grand ministers of the Bureau of Government Affairs. Therefore, these officials should be held responsible for their countersignatures." In the view of the council members, the emperor and regent, fully aware of the rapidly-changing situation and the urgent crisis, intended to open the parliament immediately. However, the insistence of the princes and grand ministers of the bureau on the five-year arrangement made immediate convention impossible. Consequently, the princes and grand ministers who countersigned the edicts should be held responsible for all subsequent internal and external crises (Li, 2011, p. 142).

Unlike previous critiques targeting the Grand Council, the Political Advisory Council now focused its criticism on the Bureau of Government Affairs and the Commission for Studying Constitutional Government. However, the majority of Bureau ministers concurrently served as Grand Councilors, and both bodies shared responsibility for the Commission. Due to this significant overlap in membership and disputes over legislative authority, the Commission emerged as a prime target for the Advisory Council's attacks.

7.3.2 Dispute Over Legislative Power

The members of the Political Advisory Council have observed that the Commission for Studying Constitutional Government bore a resemblance to the Legislation Bureau of the central government. Its functions and powers were similar to those of the Counselors' Office established by the Council of State in the 14th year of the Japanese Meiji era (1881). As stipulated in Articles 2 and 11 of the *Charter of Commission for Studying Constitutional Government*, its duties encompassed reviewing and responding to imperial memorials pertaining to constitutionalism as directed by the emperor, as well as compiling and investigating documents assigned by Grand Councilors. Additionally, the Commission was responsible for investigating the constitutions of various countries with the aim of compiling a draft constitution, as well as examining the code drafted by the Law Codification Committee and the special laws proposed by ministries and provinces. It also conducted investigations of various countries and consolidated their laws into administrative regulations for civil service. Lastly, the Commission aimed to establish a unified national legal system (Grand Secretariat, 1979, p. 49).

However, it should be noted that the imperial edict stated that the Commission for Studying Constitutional Government would be under the temporary supervision of princes and grand ministers of the Grand Council until the establishment of the Political Advisory Council. These individuals would issue detailed instructions to the original supervisors of the Commission for conducting investigations and compiling reports (Grand Secretariat, 1979, p. 46). This raises the question of how the relationship between the Political Advisory Council and the Commission for Studying Constitutional Government should be defined. Does it imply that, following its establishment, the former would possess the authority to restrict the powers of the latter by promulgating regulatory documents? Furthermore, does it signify that the Political Advisory Council would wield greater legislative power and enjoy a higher political status, or even possess supreme legislative authority? In reality, in terms of power dynamics, the Commission for Studying Constitutional Government was subordinate to the Grand Council, which represented imperial authority. As a result, the Commission was associated with both imperial power and supreme executive power, while in opposition to the Political Advisory Council, which purported to represent "public opinion" or "popular rights". Such a situation has engendered three conflicts.

Firstly, as stipulated in Articles 2 and 11 of the *Charter of the Commission for Studying Constitutional Government*, "the process of examining and compiling documents for implementation requires submission to the princes and grand ministers of the Grand Council for review and approval, with the exception of legal codes and matters of significant importance which are to be decided by the Political Advisory Council" (Grand Secretariat, 1979, p. 51). However, the precise definition of "matters of significant importance" remains unclear, creating a vague jurisdictional area that enabled the Commission for Studying Constitutional Government and Grand Councilors to potentially usurp the authority of the Political Advisory Council. This institutional ambiguity becomes more significant considering that the Commission for Studying Constitutional Government served as both a legislative body and was attached to the supreme executive organ, namely the Grand Council, resulting in integration between legislative and executive functions. Consequently, if granted the power to formulate and interpret regulatory documents, the Commission for Studying Constitutional Government, acting as the arbiter of disputes, would inevitably display bias in favor of the government (the Grand Council and the ministries) and against the

Political Advisory Council in the event of conflicts arising in the future. "To provide further context, it is noteworthy that in the 33rd year of Guangxu's reign (1907), the Commission for Studying Constitutional Government was established as an exclusively legislative body entrusted with drafting constitutional codes. However, even after the subsequent establishment of the Political Advisory Council, the Commission continued to encroach upon the authority of the council. Accordingly, it is essential to elucidate the legislative purview attributable to the Political Advisory Council and establish a definitive delineation of authority vis-à-vis the Commission. Prior to the establishment of the Political Advisory Council, the Commission, overseen by the Grand Council, held authoritative executive power, encompassing the formulation of legal codes and the imposition of executive sanctions" (Li, 2011, p. 233).

Secondly, the Political Advisory Council and Provincial Assemblies served as key mechanisms for representing public opinion at both the central and local levels, with the aim of fostering a cohesive political community. The Political Advisory Council possessed the legal authority to mediate disputes between Provincial Assemblies and provincial governors, as stated in Articles 23 and 24 of the *Charter of Political Advisory Council.* This provision had the potential to promote the development of a political culture rooted in the principles of parliamentary governance. However, conflicts arising between Provincial Assemblies and provincial governors were routinely referred to the Commission for Studying Constitutional Government for legal interpretation and clarification, instead of being submitted to the Political Advisory Council for deliberation. This practice resembled the traditional approach and tended to result in interpretations that favor the provincial governors. "Prior to the establishment of the Political Advisory Council, the Commission wielded the power to interpret legal codes and issue authoritative directives comparable to laws. In this context, provincial governors adhered to the Commission's directives because of its authoritative interpretation of legal codes. The *Charter of Provincial Assembly* consisted of a limited number of approximately thirty articles, which underwent progressive narrowing of scope after each interpretation. These interpretations varied in leniency and strictness, leading to conflicting regulations across different provinces. As a consequence, the interpretations often clashed with one another, further exacerbating the prevailing ambiguity and inconsistency within the system." (Li, 2011, p. 234)

Thirdly, as outlined in the *Nine-year Preparation List for Constitutionalism* enacted in 1908, though the Political Advisory Council would be established in 1910, responsibility of formulating and promulgating important legal codes (including the official system, household registration act, new criminal code, civil code, commercial code, codes of criminal and civil procedures etc.) was entrusted to the Commission for Studying Constitutional Government, which functioned either independently or in collaboration with relevant government departments. Moreover, the Commission was also assigned the task of overseeing the promulgation of the constitution, the enactment of parliament acts, and the election law of the Upper and Lower Houses. It is noteworthy that the legislative authority of the Political Advisory Council primarily entailed the careful examination and endorsement of the codes prepared by the Commission for Studying Constitutional Government.

However, as stated in Paragraph 4 of Article 14 of the *Charter of Political Advisory Council* of 1909, the Council was granted the authority to make determinations on "new codes and amendments thereof, except the constitution". Additionally, Article 15 outlined the procedure for discussion of motions within the Political Advisory Council, stating that "they should be prepared in advance by the Grand Councilors or the ministers of various ministries, presented to the emperor, and deliberated upon during meetings." However, the *Charter* specified that in the case of amendments to the code outlined in Paragraph 4, "the Political Advisory Council is responsible for drafting the motions" (Daqing, 2010, p. 92). Based on the provisions stated in Articles 14 and 15, it can be deduced that the Political Advisory Council possessed the authority to vote on legal codes and their amendments, and even possessed the ability to propose bills. As the legislative body stipulated within the charter, the Council inevitably encountered conflicts with the Commission for Studying Constitutional Government, which served as the de facto legislator.

One key factor contributing to this conflict was the mismanagement of the *Charter* and the issuance of conflicting edicts by the Qing court. In contrast, the Commission adhered to previous practices established before the establishment of the Council and continued to exercise legislative power through the authority vested by the Grand Council.[5]

The identified conflicts demonstrate a fundamental antagonism between the Political Advisory Council and the Commission for Studying Constitutional Government. "The Commission for Studying Constitutional Government, designed to emulate the legislative bureaus of constitutional nations, was intended to operate under governmental control. However, it paradoxically possesses both legislative authority for creating and endorsing legal codes and executive power for issuing administrative orders. This incongruity between nomenclature and operational reality has led to confusion within the government … Frequent disagreements occur between provincial governors and Provincial Assemblies, with the Commission often favoring the former while suppressing the latter … Similarly, the Political Advisory Council holds a similar relationship to the central government as Provincial Assemblies do to provincial governors. Consequently, when conflicts of interest transpire between the Council and the central government, the Commission tends to suppress the former in defense of the latter. … The Commission's encroachment upon the Council's authority predates the Council's establishment and continues thereafter. As a consequence of this encroachment, the Council's legislative powers are curtailed, rendering

[5] We cannot simplistically conclude, on the basis of "lex posterior derogat priori", that the provisions of the *Charter of Political Advisory Council* were superior to those of the *Nine-year Preparation List for Constitutionalism*, and that the Political Advisory Council was superior to the Commission for Studying Constitutional Government in terms of legislative power. Referring to the *Essentials of the Parliament Act* presented in the *Outline of Imperial Constitution*, it is evident that "the parliament's role is limited to making suggestions, lacking administrative responsibilities." "Moreover, all resolutions necessitate the emperor's approval prior to implementation by the government" (Grand Secretariat, 1979, p. 59). It should be noted that even the parliament itself cannot function independently as a legislator, with its resolutions ultimately being subject to imperial decisions. By virtue of being commissioned by imperial order to draft the constitution, the Commission for Studying Constitutional Government clearly asserted its close association with supreme imperial authority.

it an incomplete legislative organ ... To address this issue, a comprehensive examination of all edicts issued since the establishment of the Commission becomes imperative. One must bear in mind that these edicts were formulated under the assumption that the Commission had been established prior to the Political Advisory Council, granting it the authority to draft and endorse legal codes. Given the current existence of the Council, the prerogative to determine legal codes should be reinstated to it, with the Commission retaining solely the right to draft laws." (Li, 2011, pp. 150–151).

The members of the Political Advisory Council not only expressed a demand for exclusive decision-making authority over future legislation but also sought the right to review and amend laws formulated and introduced by the Commission for Studying Constitutional Government prior to the establishment of the Council. This authority was derived from their mandate to propose legal bills and modify existing laws, as defined in the *Charter of the Political Advisory Council* (Li, 2011, p. 232). Within the organizational framework of the cabinet system, the members of the Political Advisory Council perceived the council as a deliberative body vested with equivalent powers and status to that of the Parliament, while considering the Grand Council and other bodies as purely executive in nature. "In a constitutional state, legislative and executive organs typically fulfill distinct roles.

In this context, the Grand Council and various ministries assume executive functions, while the Political Advisory Council serves as the legislative organ. As per the provisions outlined in the *Charter*, the Council possesses the authority to make determinations regarding all legal codes and subsequent amendments, except those pertaining to the constitution. Consequently, the Political Advisory Council must grant its approval before the implementation of future parliamentary acts and election laws ... The Charter explicitly delineates the hierarchical power structure between the Council and the administrative organ, positioning the former as the principal decision-making body for all matters requiring deliberation. For example, in the event of disputes, the Directors-General and the Deputy Directors-General, and the Grand Councilors or ministers of various ministries will respectively report to the emperor. On the other hand, when resolutions are reached, the Directors-General and the Deputy Directors-General will respectively join the Grand Councilors and ministers of various ministries to present a collective report to the emperor. Such an arrangement clearly establishes the preeminent role of the Directors-General and the Deputy Directors-General before the Grand Councilors or ministers from the various ministries." (Li, 2011, p. 151)

In response to the challenge presented by the Political Advisory Council regarding legislative power, the Commission for Studying Constitutional Government asserted that it could not be considered the highest legislative authority. Similarly, neither the Political Advisory Council nor the Parliament could claim this supreme status. The Commission made it explicit that it lacked supreme legislative authority, stating, "this Commission does not possess the supreme legislative power." "In accordance with the provisions outlined in the *Imperial Constitution*, the monarch holds legislative, executive, and judicial powers. Hence, it should be noted that not only the Commission, but also the newly-established Political Advisory Council, as well as the prospective Upper and Lower Houses, would function as advisory bodies with respect to legislative power" (Shen Pao, 1982, p.115).

Indeed, significant disagreements arose within the Political Advisory Council with regard to the motion aimed at "defining the legislative jurisdiction of the Council". Zhao Chunnian, a reserved assemblyman, expressed his concerns during the deliberations. He stressed that any such motion should "be grounded in the finalized constitution and should not rely on foreign constitutional models to determine the scope of Chinese legislation." Zhao further recognized that, within foreign constitutional practices, legislation encompassed both parliamentary enactments and administrative regulations. In this context, it became apparent that the Council held supremacy over the Commission for Studying Constitutional Government specifically in matters concerning parliamentary legislation, often referred to as law in its narrower sense. However, the Council lacked authority over the formulation of administrative regulations.

Zhao proposed, "The Political Advisory Council's legislative authority surpasses that of the Commission for Studying Constitutional Government. The Commission can merely draft laws subject to the Council's approval for enactment … Yet, this authority is confined to the realm of legislation. In contrast, the Commission possesses broader powers than the Council, as it assumes responsibility not only for drafting laws but also compiling them and fulfilling administrative functions… Even if the Commission is later restructured as the Cabinet Legislation Bureau and the Council as the Parliament, the Legislation Bureau retains the prerogative to draft regulations concerning official protocols and foreign affairs, which the Parliament does not have the authority to approve" (Li, 2011, pp. 235–236). However, Lei Fen, one of the esteemed members known as the "Three Talents" of the Political Advisory Council, interjected during Zhao's meticulous and cogent argument, contending that many of Zhao's "assertions concerning the Commission were beyond the purview of a specially appointed assemblyman" (Li, 2011, p. 236).

7.3.3 Dispute Over the Status of Representative Organ

Before the convening of the Parliament, the Political Advisory Council positioned itself as a representative body, purporting to embody the collective will of the populace. In a modern constitutional government, the executive authority is answerable to the legislative body. However, in the context of the Qing Dynasty, the traditional executive center, known as the Grand Council, was not held accountable to the representative body. Consequently, a confrontation ensued between the modern legislative power and the ancient executive power, leading to a misdirected struggle.

The impeachment case against the Grand Councilors was triggered by Yang Wending, the Governor of Hunan province, who circumvented the Provincial Assembly and directly presented a memorial to the imperial court, seeking authorization for the issuance of public bonds. With majority approval, the Political Advisory Council proceeded to impeach Yang Wending for his transgressions and violations of the law, acting on behalf of all council members. The impeachment was subsequently submitted to the emperor for judgment.

Regrettably, the imperial response merely acknowledged Yang's negligence without imposing any punitive measures. This provoked indignation among the council members, who contended that "even when a censor moves to impeach a provincial governor, such ineffectiveness would not be tolerated." "The futility of the entire resolution by the Council led to doubts regarding the purpose of its establishment. The council members decried the blatant infringement of laws committed by the provincial governor of Hunan, the Bureau of General Account, and the Grand Councilors, who not only hindered the immediate convocation of the Parliament but also undermined the authority of the Political Advisory Council and the Provincial Assemblies. Despite the noble intentions of the latter, as demonstrated by their varied proposals, it appeared that their endeavors would ultimately be in vain." (Li, 2011, pp. 156–159)

Following the countersigning of the edicts by the Grand Councilors, the members of the Political Advisory Council requested an explanation from them. However, despite this demand, the Grand Councilors failed to appear, resulting in a deadlock between the two sides. Subsequently, an edict, prepared and countersigned by the Grand Councilors, was issued. This edict entailed submitting the resolutions of the Council concerning the increase in salt prices in the Yunnan province and the admission of non-local individuals to the Guangxi Police Academy for review and verification by the Salt Administration and the Ministry of Civil Affairs, respectively. This decision clearly indicated that the Council was subordinate to the Salt Administration and the Ministry of Civil Affairs, which deeply angered the council members and ultimately led to the impeachment of the cabinet.

The council members argued that "In China's pursuit of a constitutional government, the Political Advisory Council was established as the cornerstone of the Upper and Lower Houses, functioning as a legislative body. Constitutional democracies universally uphold the principle of the separation of powers, distinguishing the legislative, judicial, and executive branches. The tripartite division of power implies that legislation, judiciary, and administration are all independent and inviolable. … The Grand Councilors, fully aware of the Council's independence, are encroaching upon its authority and violating the law by referring cases decided by the legislative organ to administrative institutions for review … In accordance with Article 21 of the *Charter of the Political Advisory Council*, this issue should be reported to the emperor, and the Grand Councilors should be impeached" (Li, 2011, pp. 242–243).

Lei Fen, a member of the Political Advisory Council, argued that the focus should not solely be on the Grand Councilors' violation of the law and infringement upon the authority of the Council in the Yunnan and Guangxi cases. Instead, it should emphasize their "irresponsibility to the emperor, rendering them incompetent to assist him" (Li, 2011, p. 253). The council members emphasize the term "irresponsible" used in the Grand Councilors' previous response, contending that it contradicted the spirit of a constitutional state and a parliamentary cabinet. In an attempt to appease the Council, the Qing government accepted its resolutions pertaining to the Yunnan and Guangxi cases. However, the council members refused to settle there; rather, they resolved to proceed with the impeachment, placing focus on the notion of "irresponsible". As a result, the impeachment evolved from a pursuit of individual responsibility of the Grand Councilors to an investigation of the overall responsibility of the Grand Council, ultimately calling for the abolition of the Grand Council and the establishment of a parliamentary cabinet. Initially, "irresponsible" served as a strategic pretext to impeach the Grand Councilors for their offenses. However, it now became the central issue of the impeachment, while the significance of the decisions on the Yunnan and Guangxi cases diminished. The Council's "dispute over the establishment of a parliamentary cabinet" and the previous "dispute over the immediate convocation of the Parliament" were, in fact, interconnected. The immediate convening of the Parliament aimed to hold the government accountable through the oversight, supervision, and checks and balances of a representative body of public opinion. When the immediate convening of the Parliament was not realized, the Political Advisory Council, as a self-proclaimed representative body, commenced an assault on the government's central institution, the Grand Council, demanding the establishment of a cabinet accountable to the Political Advisory Council before the opening of the parliament.

In response to the impeachment of the Political Advisory Council, the Grand Councilors submitted their resignation to the prince regent, who subsequently issued edict in person rejecting their resignations and accusing the Political Advisory Council of exceeding its jurisdiction. The prince regent emphasized that "the authority to establish the bureaucratic system, determine payment structures, and promote or demote officials rests with the imperial court, as specified in the *Outline of Imperial Constitution*. Regarding the responsibility of the Grand Councilors and the establishment of a parliamentary cabinet, the court possesses separate considerations that are beyond the purview of the Directors-General of the Political Advisory Council and others involved, and no further discussion is needed on the matter requested by the Council" (Xuantong, 1987, p. 802).

Faced with this predicament, the Council sought to avoid direct confrontation with the imperial power and continued to assert the need for clarifying the responsibilities of the Grand Councilors and expediting the establishment of a parliamentary cabinet. They lamented the lack of a platform to express their opinions owing to the absence of the Grand Councilors' signatures on the edict authored by the prince regent himself. In their opinion, "This denial of opportunity for discourse rendered the Political Advisory Council effectively ineffective, and even called into question the necessity of a future parliament. This precarious situation involved the parliament standing in opposition to the monarch, contrary to the spirit of a constitutional state where the parliament's role is to oppose the government." The Council pinpointed two potential solutions. "One is the adoption of an active autocracy that would render the Political Advisory Council, parliament, and the constitution obsolete, and the other is an extremely risky path with dire consequences, where the people would be left with no choice but to resort to violence." Accordingly, the Council considered it imperative to find a way to address this issue, while refraining from commenting on the imperial edict issued by the sovereign. Nonetheless, they believed it necessary to criticize the Grand Councilors for their role in the unfolding situation (Li, 2011, p. 386).

Following numerous exchanges, the prince regent demonstrated a steadfast reluctance to address the impeachment brought forth by the Political Advisory Council against the Grand Councilors. Furthermore, the Council itself became preoccupied with additional proposals, resulting in the gradual dissipation of the clamorous impeachment case.

7.3.4 Evaluation

Amid the discussion of the impeachment case in the Political Advisory Council, moderate member Lu Zongyu once poured cold water on the council in three aspects. First, countersignature of Grand Councilors was an established practice since the Qianlong reign, and its institutional continuity rendered them irresponsible. Second, "the Political Advisory Council differs from the Parliament of other countries" and the power of impeachment should be exercised with caution. Third, "the Political Advisory Council has many other issues of importance to discuss", so time should not be wasted on "vying with" the government on "minor issues". Council member Lei Fen refuted Lu Zongyu, "the Political Advisory Council, so far, has merely three years of life to go before it is replaced by the Parliament. Now is the right time for impeachment, which wouldn't be possible after three years. Since the cabinet has not been formed, who is responsible after all? Who can impeach the irresponsible Grand Councilors? Impeaching the Grand Councilors can facilitate the formation of the cabinet, i.e., the more the former are attacked, the greater the chance of the latter. We impeach the Grand Councilors with a vision of forming the cabinet, so there is no harm in attacking them more. Therefore, I advise you not to confine yourself to a legal perspective, but to observe the event in a political perspective." Zhongguo (1911)[6] Lu Zongyu's speech pointed out the three weaknesses of the Political Advisory Council in the impeachment of the Grand Councilors. First, the countersignature responsibility of the Grand Councilors was not established. Second, the status and authority of the Political Advisory Council were different from those of foreign parliaments. Third, entangled in the impeachment case, the Political Advisory Council neglected its duty of deliberating on bills. Lei Fen's rebuttal clearly affirmed that the purpose of the impeachment was to achieve the political goal of setting up a parliamentary cabinet, and that whether the impeachment was legally tenable was secondary.

The constitutional reforms in the late Qing were not necessarily all scams. However, the Qing government did not have a clear understanding of the will of the people and the general trend.[7] The more passive it was, the more it tried to cling to

[6] The speeches of Lu Zongyu and Lei Fen are cited from Zhongguo (1911).

[7] Half of the members in the Political Advisory Council were imperial nominees and half elected by popular vote. It is noteworthy that despite this balance, the council frequently witnessed the passage

power. Its reform policies were contradictory and anticlimactic, resulting in legislative confusions and landing the government in predicaments. After the Guangxu Emperor and Empress Dowager Cixi passed away in 1908, the prince regent and his Manchurian imperial clansmen became unconfident due to the powerful Han officials in the government. They thought that they could promote the Manchu and suppress the Han through institutional and personnel arrangements. However, this broke the balance between Manchu and Han forces in the Qing government, and the personnel changes further caused ruptures and conflicts in the political reform during the Guangxu and Xuantong periods. This cost the Qing court a good reform opportunity on the one hand, and brought about disputes between the conservatives and the constitutionalists over the contradictory imperial decrees (edicts) on the other hand. The Qing court was unable to make a decision and compromised without principle, resorting to personnel adjustments instead of systematic institutional arrangements.[8] This might be the institutional reason behind the impeachment of the Grand Councilors.

The so-called tradition of "discrimination between the Hua (Chinese) and barbarians" and "the opposition between the Han and usurpers" has always existed in the Chinese mindset. As an alien Dynasty, the Qing lost its political legitimacy no sooner than it was landed in a predicament. In the first annual meeting, the Political Advisory Council proposed to cut the queue and change the costume, and demanded the emperor to alter the ancestral system and cut the queue to set an example to the whole country; it also proposed the pardon of political offenders and the exoneration of the unjustly imprisoned during the Hundred Days' Reform (1898). These indicated the great change in public opinion at that time. By focusing on the impeachment case and examining the words and deeds of the Political Advisory Council members, we can find the difference between the constitutionalists and the revolutionaries: the former advocated constitutional revolution and the latter, violent revolution. The two camps were consistent in replacing monarchy with democracy. The constitutionalists carried out revolutions in the name of constitutionalism. They used the theories of freedom and civil rights from Europe and America as their ideological weapons, tried to remove the Confucian doctrines from the new criminal code, strove for a parliamentary cabinet in the constitutional system, and even openly proposed to cut the queue and pardon the revolutionaries. Or, it can be said that the constitutionalists and the revolutionaries in the late Qing cooperated with each other. Within one year after the impeachment of the Grand Councilors, Wuchang Uprising broke out. With the

of proposals challenging the existing government, surpassing the demanding two-thirds majority voting criterion. Remarkably, in the face of these repeated warnings, the imperial family remained oblivious to the erosion of their popular support and the precariousness of the monarchy's standing.

[8] An additional illustration of judicial reform during the late Qing era pertains to the challenges encountered in the "Ministry-Yuan Quarrel", which revolved around the delineation of authority between the judicial administrative body, namely the Ministry of Justice, and the central judiciary, represented by the Supreme Court of Justice. Notably, the Qing court did not adhere to the modern principle of the rule of law by distinctly separating jurisdictional matters from the administration of justice. Rather, their approach primarily entailed a mere rotation of leadership positions between the involved ministry and institute.

joint efforts of the two camps, it took only a few months for the provinces to declare independence and for the Qing emperor to issue an abdication edict. The Xinhai Revolution brought forth a regime change with relatively less bloodshed in modern Chinese history, partially because the Friends of the Constitution organized by the constitutionalists "adopted contingency measures during the revolution to control the political situation of each province, and the revolutionary situation was almost controlled by it. The constitutionalists started with pursuing the convocation of the Parliament and ended up with revolution, reaping what they haven't sown" (Zhang, 2007, p. 102). Though the monarchy was overthrown, the parliamentary politics of the ROC was still not on track.

The legacy of the impeachment of the Grand Councilors by the Political Advisory Council was not entirely positive. The constitutionalist members suspended the Qing court's prerequisite game rules of the preparatory constitutionalism, ignored their own constitutional status and authority, and attempted to achieve the political goal of the constitutional revolution by means of voting. Their "violation of authority and law" was even worse than that of the Grand Councilors. It is fair to say that this is because the rules of the game themselves are unfair, and that the political goals of the Political Advisory Council members are understandable, because they are the so-called "benign unconstitutionality". However, as a legislator, on the one hand, the Political Advisory Council failed to set a law-abiding example, but bent the existing rules for its own convenience, and broke the established legal order for its own political goals. On the other hand, it bragged itself as the parliament like in Britain, and claimed to be the representative of public opinion. Believing in the "omnipotent" parliamentary legislation, it intended to disrupt the actual political order and break the balance of power through voting. This is not idealism, but "utopianism". In the early years of the ROC, the bad record of "destruction and fabrication of laws" and its rough fate might not have been accidental.

This chapter concludes with an eloquent and composed speech by Political Advisory Council member Wang Rongbao: "As members of the Political Advisory Council, we must understand its duties, authorities, and status. According to the council's charter, it has the right to review and handle cases of provincial governors infringing upon the authority of Provincial Assemblies and violating laws. The word 'review and handle' can be divided into three stages of nomology: reviewing, resolution, and memorializing to the throne … However, what the imperial court chooses to do with the governors' offenses after the memorialization to the throne, whether to punish them or not, is the emperor's prerogative and not within the council's purview or intervention … Punishment is one thing; inspection is another. The emperor and his court have the power to punish, while the council has the responsibility to inspect. In fulfilling this duty, the council must have four perceptions: abiding by its charter, clarifying the scope of its authority, playing fairly, and having an unyielding resolve. Only with these qualities can the council become a true representative of public opinion and have a sound legal thinking. Otherwise, it would have no grounds to advocate for or accuse others of violating the law. Does the council fully recognize its legal status? Does it have a firm legal foundation?" (Li, 2011, p. 195).

References

Akio, Y. (1996). *Riben jindai shi* [Modern history of Japan]. (H. Lin & X. Li, Trans.). China Social Sciences Press. (Original work published 1982).

Bergère, M. (2008). The Chinese bourgeoisie, 1911–37. In J. K. Fairbank (Ed.), *The Cambridge history of China: Republican China 1929–1949, Part 1* (6th ed., Vol 12, pp. 722–826). Cambridge University Press.

Bianzuan guanzhi dachen zou liding guanzhi zongzhi zhe [Memorial by commissioners on the basic principles of compiling the official system]. (2010). In *Daqing xin faling* [New code of the Qing Dynasty] (vol. 1). The Commercial Press.

Daqing xin faling [New code of the Qing Dynasty] (vol. 6). (2010). The Commercial Press.

Dezong jing huangdi shilu [Veritable Records of Emperor Dezong]. (1987). Zhonghua Book Company.

Grand Secretariat Archives Office at the Palace Museum. (Ed.). (1979). *Qingmo choubei lixian dang'an shiliao* [Historical materials of the preparatory constitutionalism archives in the late Qing Dynasty] (Vol. 1). Zhonghua Book Company.

Guan, X. (2019). *Qingmo xinzheng zhidu biange yanjiu* [Research on the system reform in the New Policies in the late Qing Dynasty]. Zhonghua Book Company.

Guo, T. (2012). *Jindai zhongguo shigang* [Outline of modern Chinese history]. Shanghai People's Press.

Halsey, S. R. (2015). *Quest for power: European imperialism and the making of Chinese statecraft.* Harvard University Press.

Hou, Y. (1993). *Ershi shiji chu zhongguo zhengzhi gaige fengchao* [Political reform in China in early twentieth century: History of the Constitutional Movement of the late Qing Dynasty]. China Renmin University Press.

Hou, Y. (2011). *Ershi shiji chu zhongguo zhengzhi gaige fengchao: Qingmo lixian yundong shi* [Political reform in China in early twentieth century: History of the Constitutional Movement of the late Qing Dynasty]. China Renmin University Press.

Hsü, I. C. (1968). *China's Entrance into the family of nations.* Harvard University Press.

Ichiko, C. (2008). Political and institutional reform, 1901–11. In J. K. Fairbank, & K. Liu (Eds.), *The Cambridge history of China: Late Ch'ing, 1800–1911, Part 2* (6th ed., Vol 11, pp. 375–415). Cambridge University Press.

Jing, Z. (1984). *Zhongguo lixian shi* [The constitution-making history of the Republic of China]. Linking Publishing Company.

Li, Q. (Ed.). (2011). *Zizhengyuan yichang huiyi sujilu: Wanqing yubei guohui bianlun shilu* [Minutes of the meetings of the Political Advisory Council: Records of the debates on the preparation of the Parliament in the late Qing Dynasty]. Shanghai Joint Publishing.

Liu, J. (1936). Xianzheng ba [Constitutional government VIII]. In *Qingchao xu wenxian tongkao* [A general study on the continued documents of the Qing Dynasty] (Vol. 400). The Commercial Press.

Luo, Z. (2014). *Quanli zhuanyi: Jindai zhongguo de sixiang yu shehui* [Power shifts: Thought and society in modern China]. Beijing Normal University Press.

Luo, Z. (1974). *Jindai zhongguo fazhi yanbian yanjiu* [History of the legal system in modern China]. Cheng Chung Book Co., Ltd.

Meng, S., et al. (2015). *Gesheng ziyiju zhangcheng jianshi* [Annotations of the Charter of Provincial Assembly in various provinces]. The Commercial Press.

Peng, J. (2011). *Qingji xianzheng bianchaguan yanjiu* [Research on the Commission for Studying Constitutional Government in the Qing Dynasty]. Peking University Press.

Platt, S. R. (2012). Autumn in the heavenly kingdom: China, the West, and the epic story of the Taiping Civil War. Knopf.

Qin, H. (2015). *Zouchu dizhi: Cong wanqing dao minguo de lishi huiwang* [Out of the imperial system: A historical review from the late Qing Dynasty to the Republic of China]. Qunyan Press.

Rosenthal, J., & Wong, R. (2011). *Before and beyond divergence: The politics of economic change in China and Europe*. Harvard University Press.

Shen, J. (2019). *Minguo de "shichuan": Qingmo minchu zhongguo geming zai chanshi* [The "lost" of the Republic of China: Reinterpretation of the Chinese revolution in the late Qing Dynasty and the early Republic of China]. Shanghai Academy of Social Sciences Press.

Shang, X. (1998). Qingmo zizhengyuan yizheng huodong yipie [A glimpse of the political discussions of Political Advisory Council in the late Qing Dynasty]. *Beijing Shehui Kexue* [*Social Sciences of Beijing*], (2), 84–86.

Shen Pao (1982). Xianzhengguan duifu yiyuan zhiwen zhi shouxu [Procedures of the Commission for Studying Constitutional Government answering the queries of Political Advisory Council]. In *Shenbao Yingyin Ben* [*Photocopy of Shen Pao*], 109: 115. Shanghai Bookstore Publishing House. (Original work published 1910)

Wang, Z. (1906). Bo *Xinmin Congbao* zuijin zhi fei geming lun [Refutation of recent non-revolutionary theory on *The New People Miscellany*]. In *Min Pao*, (4).

Xuantong zhengji [Records of the politics of the Xuantong reign]. (1987). In *Qing shilu* [*Veritable records of the Qing Dynasty*] (vol. 60). Zhonghua Book Company.

Yang, G. (2014). *Shuaishi yu xifa: Wanqing zhongguo de jiubang xinming he shehui tuosun* [Turbulent era and Western Law: The new life of the old state and the collapse of society in the late Qing]. Zhonghua Book Company.

Zhang, D. (2008). *Qingdai guojia jiguan kaolue* [Research on state organs in Qing Dynasty]. Xueyuan Publishing House.

Zhang, P. (2007). *Lixianpai yu xinhai geming* [Constitutionalists and the Revolution of 1911]. Jilin Publishing Group Co., Ltd.

Zhao, X. (2007). *Da yamen* [Grand Yamen]. Law Press.

Zhongguo dashi ji [Chronicle of events in China]. (1911). In *Dongfang Zazhi* [*The Eastern Miscellany*], (12).

Zizhengyuan guanzhi cao'an [Draft of the official system of the Political Advisory Council]. (2010). In *Daqing xin faling* [New code of the Qing Dynasty] (vol. 1). The Commercial Press.

Chapter 8
History of Constitution-Making in Modern China

8.1 An Overview of the Constitution-Making History

Of the many legal documents enacted in modern China, if we compare them, article by article, with the codes of Germany, Switzerland and other countries, we will find that "95% of them have been either sheer copies or alterations in disguise". Does this mean that the legislative work during the ROC is worthless? As far as the jurist Wu Jingxiong is concerned, "The world's legal systems are voluminous, and the civil law and the common law of them are the most influential. The former can be further divided into four branches, the French law, the Italian law, the German law and the Swedish law. Of course, it takes quite an effort to choose among various schools before reaching a specific decision. An appropriate choice is a creation indeed, and all creations are nothing but choices." (Wu, 2015, pp. 172–173) Slightly earlier than the civil legislation in modern China, the investigation and selection of the Western constitution began in 1905, when the Qing court dispatched five ministers to visit Japan, America, France, Germany, Italy and Russia respectively and study their constitutional systems. From the *Outline of Imperial Constitution* in 1908 to the *Constitution of the Republic of China* in 1946, China became one of the countries that formulated and promulgated the largest number of constitutional documents in the world, abreast of France. Although the frequent change of constitution is not something to be proud of, the experience (lesson) in such selection and creation of constitutional system in modern China is so rich that it might make up for its relative deficiency in the science of constitution to a certain extent. As "the first Republic in Asia", modern China even surpassed the European and American models in the "creation" of constitution.

X. Nie, *The History of Government and Public Law in China*,
https://doi.org/10.1007/978-981-97-6063-3_8

8.1.1 Creation and Destruction of Constitution in the Early ROC[1]

i. Provisional Constitution of the Republic of China created amid chaos and emergency

Upon the founding of the ROC, the *Organizational Outline of the Provisional Government* was formulated, modeling the American presidential government, with the separation of powers among the President, the Senate and the Legislature. However, the Outline lacked provisions for citizens' rights and contained significant flaws in its design of governmental structure. Therefore, the temporary Advisory Council revised it and drew up the *Provisional Constitution Draft of the Republic of China*, which retained the mode of operation from the American presidential system. Shortly thereafter, peace talks between the South and the North were successful and Yuan Shih-k'ai took office as the Provisional President as agreed on before. In order to check Yuan's power, the Senate sought to implement a responsible cabinet system akin to that of France's Third Republic, transitioning from the existing presidential system to a parliamentary system, in an attempt to at least curtail, if not completely neutralize, the president's power. That's why the *Provisional Constitution of the Republic of China* came into being. However, in reality, due to internal disagreements among constitution makers and their limited knowledge of comparative constitutional law, the *Provisional Constitution* "omitted provisions beneficial for forming a responsible cabinet system, instead, favoring clauses derived from the American presidential system", which differed significantly from the true essence of a responsible government and can be described as a "curious anomaly" in the constitutional history of the ROC (Zhang, 2006).

i. Drafting and suspension of the Tiantan Draft Constitution

On April 8, 1913, the Parliament of the ROC convened for the first time in Beijing. According to the *Provisional Constitution*, the power of presidential elections and constitutional drafting were both vested in the Parliament.[2] Subsequently, the Constitution Drafting Committee was organized, tasked with formulating the draft constitution at the Temple of Heaven (Wu, 1923).[3] On October 14 of the same year, the draft was completed. However, Yuan Shih-k'ai "was dissatisfied with certain provisions that limited the presidential power, so he sent a telegram to the provincial governors of civil and military affairs on October 25 to oppose the draft constitution, claiming that the KMT representatives had interfered with the administration in pursuit of congressional despotism, urging them to make a detailed discussion on each item of the draft and to promptly reply via telegram". As most military and administrative officials were former subordinates of Yuan, they unanimously opposed the draft

[1] Xia & Hu 2004

[2] For a long time afterwards, presidential elections were often intertwined with constitution-making.

[3] This draft was historically referred to as the *Tiantan Draft Constitution*.

constitution and even deliberated on the dismissal of the KMT representatives and dissolution of the Parliament (Jing, 1984, p. 211).

iii. The Third Year Constitution of the ROC and Hongxian Monarchy

In 1913, the KMT leader Song Jiaoren was assassinated, and the Second Revolution launched by the KMT ended in failure. Yuan Shih-k'ai first changed the precedence of constitution-making over presidential election, and then coerced the Parliament into electing him as president, after which he brazenly dismissed the Parliament, leading to the abandonment of the so-called "Tiantan Draft Constitution". After dissolving the Parliament, he manipulated a purported "constitutional assembly" to craft *The Third Year Constitution of the Republic of China* (also known as "Yuan's Constitution"). The main contents were as follows: (1) the abolition of the parliamentary cabinet system and the extensive expansion of presidential power, and (2) the dismantling of the Parliament, the establishment of the Legislative Yuan as the law-making body, and a seemingly adopted unicameral system. However, it was subordinate to the president, lacking the power to impeach him, while the president retained the power to dissolve the Legislative Yuan. In addition, the Advisory Council was established as a consulting team to the president. It was stipulated that until the formation of the Legislative Yuan, the Advisory Council would act in its stead. However, throughout Yuan Shih-k'ai's reign, the Legislative Yuan never came to fruition. He further tampered with *Electoral Law of the Great President*, extending the presidential term to ten years, with no term limits, and even granting himself the power to designate his successor. Surprisingly, Article 3 of the *Electoral Law* stated that the list of successor candidates "must be penned in advance by the Great President on golden foil shaded with lush seedlings, sealed with the national seal, and covertly stored in a golden box in a specially built stone chamber in the presidential palace" (Xia & Hu, 2004, p. 464). This method was reminiscent of the confidential appointment of successors in the Qing Dynasty. Still unsatisfied, he sought to crown himself as emperor. His imperial ambitions ended in bankruptcy, followed by power misuse by the northern warlords, leading to the Parliament's dissolution for the second time.

iv. Campaigns for provincial constitutionalism and the "experimental federation of provinces"

The Xinhai Revolution of 1911 unfolded as each province declared their independence. The belief that provincial self-government would better serve China than a centralized state had widely spread since the late Qing Dynasty. "After most provinces emerged from the revolution fully autonomous, there was little disposition to surrender their accrued privileges, including command over provincial armies, the retention of tax revenues, and the selection of local and provincial officials. Moreover, local assemblies below the provincial level were increasingly influential and confident. To the minds of the provincialists, the two demands for unity and self-government could be wedded in federal structures." (Young, 1983, 2005, pp. 212–213) Drawing from the example of the US. federation, where states' constitutions preceded the national constitution, and the unstable central political situation of the early ROC, the notion of federal autonomy and provincial constitutionalism naturally surfaced. In 1920, the federal self-government movement was launched in Hunan province. Ten provinces responded affirmatively, with Hunan, Zhejiang, Sichuan, Jiangsu, Shandong and Guangdong each drafting their own provincial constitution. "Despite the fact that these provincial constitution initiatives were largely political posturing and not based on normative law, it represented a significant step forward that people considered the constitution as the foundation and rallying point for asserting regime legitimacy, in contrast to the northern warlords' blatant disregard for constitutional law." (Chen, 2001, pp. 30–31) In November 1921, Hunan's provincial constitution was ratified by a province-wide vote. It "was still, in principle, the most radical constitution that China had seen stipulating universal suffrage and provincial and county assemblies ... free education and independent judiciary, popularly elected governors and the rights of the people to make laws, vote and impeach" (Duara, 1997, p. 192). The Hunan provincial constitution, mirroring the US. constitution, even granted its citizens the right to purchase guns for self-defense (Article 13, Hunan Provincial Constitution), an unprecedented move in Chinese history. "The purpose of federal autonomy movement was twofold". The first was to promote provincial self-government, enabling them to make their own constitution, and managing their internal affairs free from interference from the central or other provinces. The second was to advocate for a federal constitution drafted by representatives elected from each province. However, in practice, these provincial constitutions were never fully implemented as planned, and the movement "was overtaken by the centralizing nationalism of the KMT, which was committed to military unification" (Duara, 1997, p. 193). Meanwhile, the Northern Expedition War, sweeping across the southern and central provinces, swept away provincial constitutions and assemblies "so as to clear the way for a centralized nation-state" (Duara, 1997, p. 203).

v. Passage and abolition of the "Bribery Constitution"

In 1923, the Parliament reconvened. Parliamentarians, bought off by Cao Kun's big checks, once again disregarded the precedence of constitution-making over presidential election and elected Cao as the president, much to the public's dismay. In order to gloss over their bribery scandal, the "prostituting parliamentarians" rushed through the second and third readings of the "Tiantan Draft Constitution" and passed the official *Third-year Constitution of the Republic of China* after electing the president. "It took only three meetings within a week to produce a constitution that had been twelve years in the making. Contentious issues that had been debated for six to seven years were settled down without further discussion." (Chen, 1947, p. 135) The *Constitution* was promulgated on Cao's inauguration day, October 10, 1923. However, a constitution borne out of such circumstances was unlikely to gain the respect or acceptance of the populace. In 1924, when Duan Qirui's government was established, this constitution was promptly abandoned. In all fairness, the content of this constitution was rather progressive, with certain provisions even leading the world at that time (Chen, 2004, pp. 32–33). However, such a sacred and solemn constitution "only remained in effect for one year and ended up with a bad name of 'bribery constitution', following an arduous eleven-year preparation from drafting to promulgation, hindered by warlords, politicians and unscrupulous opportunists." (Jing, 1984, p. 332) Thus, the decade-long constitutional history of the early Republic of China came to a disgraceful end.

8.1.2 From Sun Wen Theory to the "May Fifth Draft Constitution"[4]

The turbulent political landscape of the Beiyang Government dominated the decade following the Xinhai Revolution. This ear was marked by warlords ruling their own regions, frequent alterations of constitution, and Cao Kun's notorious "bribery constitution". The NNG, succeeding the Beiyang Government, adopted Sun Yat-sen's philosophy as its guiding principle. In 1929, the third National Congress of the KMT passed the resolution to establish "Teachings by Father of the Nation" as the highest and fundamental law during the period of political tutelage". (Five-Power Constitution Association, 1963, p. 352) Since the inception of the NNG in 1927, the KMT government cited Sun Yat-sen's national reconstruction strategy of "military rule, political tutelage and constitutional government" to justify their prolonged political tutelage, a move that met with resistance from various social sectors. The national crisis deepened following the September 18 Incident. At the Third Plenary Session of the Fourth Central Committee of the KMT, Sun Ke spearheaded "the resolution to amass national strength to rescue China from imminent imperilment", urging the prompt implementation of constitutional rule so as to galvanize national unity and strength. After taking office as the Legislative Yuan president of the National Government in January 1933, Sun Ke swiftly organized the Constitution Drafting Committee. It took the constitutional framers three years before the National Government promulgated the draft constitution on May 5, 1936. The constitution-making process was characterized by rigorous procedural adherence and sparked widespread societal dialogue, the extent of which was unprecedented.

The MFDC, to a large extent, embodies Sun Yat-sen's constitutional thoughts. It thoroughly operationalizes such concepts as the "Three People's Principles", division of powers, and "Five-power Constitution".[5] Its key features include: the adoption of the "Three Principles of the People" as the framework for the national system; the

[4] Since *Draft Constitution of the Republic of China* was promulgated on May 5th, it is known as the "May Fifth Draft Constitution" (MFDC).

[5] Sun Yat-sen's constitutional thoughts are often collectively referred to as the "Five-power Constitution" thought. This nomenclature is perhaps due to the distinctive characteristic of his ideology that emphasizes a "Five-power" government. Hence, the term seems to be a bit of an "oversimplification". Sun Yat-sen was more a statesman than an academic, and consequently, his ideas were not always coherent or consistent. Coupled with his numerous political discourses and speeches, there were inevitable discrepancies and contradictions, which made it challenging to form a comprehensive, systematic constitution from his scattered thoughts.

establishment of a central National Assembly, acting as the principal institution to exercise political power; the configuration of a five-power central government system to execute governance, with the president holding extensive powers; the introduction of an "equal division of power" model, addressing the relationship between central and local authorities.

i. An outline of Sun Yat-sen's constitutional thoughts (Five-Power Constitution Association, 1963)

"Political power, the force that controls the government, is directly exercised by the people at the county level and indirectly at the central government level; governing power, the force that serves the people, is utilized by the government through five separate Yuans (or chambers)." Well aware of the limitations of the Western tripartite system and representative politics, Sun sought to forge a new system blending Chinese traditions with Western experiences, one characterized by "popular sovereignty and strong government". He proposed a distinction between political power and governing power (division of powers), where the people had the former and the government exercised the latter. The National Assembly, a central government institution, was composed of representatives elected from each county, exercising the four powers of election, recall, initiative and referendum. According to the "separation of powers" theory, the National Assembly was a body embodying direct democracy, rather than a parliament in the representative sense. As for the government that exercised "governing power", Sun drew from Chinese historical censorial organ and "independence of examination", leading to the creation of the Control Yuan in charge of supervision and the Examination Yuan in charge of civil service examination and personnel management. These, in conjunction with the Legislative Yuan, the Executive Yuan and the Judicial Yuan, formed the five-Yuan system. The Legislative Yuan, instead of being a parliament (a representative body), was a full-time legislature made up of professionals. Since the people's "political power" undertook the supervisory function over the government, the relationship among the five Yuans was not primarily about checks and balances but functional distribution—a system where "the five powers are separate but interconnected".

Sun Yat-sen's thoughts ("thoughts of the Founding Father" or "teachings by Father of the Nation") left an enormous influence on the governmental structure and constitutional praxis of the NNG. Though distorted to some extent, Sun's idea, both ideologically and emotionally, steered the constitution-making process controlled by the KMT.

1. The conception of the "five-power" constitution

The "Five-power Constitution" is an important component of Sun Yat-sen's legal philosophy, resulting from a comprehensive study of various national constitutions, further refined and contextualized in relation to China's unique history and national circumstances. Sun consistently believed that the quality of a constitution was crucial to the governance of a country, asserting, "Only with a sound constitution can we establish a genuine republic." Besides, he considered that the doctrine of triple-power separation played a significant role in the era of Western bourgeois revolutions, yet he felt it was no longer applicable. Consequently, the ROC constitution would pioneer a novel paradigm, namely the separation of five powers to compensate for the limitations inherent in the three powers.

Sun's concept of "five powers" consisted of the traditional tripartite powers of executive, legislature and judiciary, with the addition of examination and supervisory powers. From the separation of five powers derived the five-power constitution, according to which a five-Yuan system was instituted, i.e., the Executive Yuan, the Legislative Yuan, the Judicial Yuan, the Examination Yuan and the Control Yuan. Sun contended that a government structured by the five-power constitution would be the most complete government and integrated governing entity. As per his vision, the government should be configured as follows. The central government comprised of the afore-mentioned five Yuans. After the constitution was formulated, the people of each county voted to elect the national president, who would then organize Executive Yuan, and the representatives to form the Legislative Yuan. The heads of the other three Yuans should be appointed by the ROC president upon consent from the Legislative Yuan, albeit they were not responsible to the national president or the Legislative Yuan. All five Yuans were accountable to the National Assembly. The Control Yuan should impeach personnel of dereliction of duty in each Yuan to the National Assembly, which shall impeach and remove, of its own accord, the personnel of dereliction of duty in the Control Yuan. The functions of the National Assembly shall be as follows: to amend the constitution and adjudicate public functionaries' negligence. The Examination Yuan determined the eligibility of the members of the National Assembly, the five Yuans, and all other national and local officials. That's the essence of the "Five-power Constitution".

Sun championed the independence of supervision and examination inherent in Chinese history. China, as he argued, "since the times of Emperor Yao and Shu, had *zuoshi* (左史, left scribe/historiographer), an imperial official to record the king's words and *youshi* (右史, right scribe/historiographer) to record his deeds. Later, imperial censors and Grand Masters of Remonstrance (*jianyi dafu*, 谏议大夫) were assigned across the country and they exercised the supervisory power independently. Even though they were merely petty officials of low rank, these officials wielded such influence that they could incite caution and fear among figures of all strata, from the emperor and high ministers to low-ranking officials, deterring them from transgressing the law." In light of this, Sun suggested that China should revive and uphold its tradition of independent supervision. Sun also esteemed China's dynastic examination system, arguing that it not only embodied the spirit of populism and democracy, but also outshined the modern democratic politics. This system enabled ordinary people to secure official positions through rigorous examinations, leading to a continuous flow of talents into the nation's service. Therefore, "in the future, the *Constitution of the Republic of China* shall establish an independent organ entrusted with the authority of examination and selection. All officials, high- or low- ranked, elected or appointed, must be qualified for their positions." This, as he argued, would prevent the abuse of talent selection and the practice of favoritism.

Sun's theory on the separation of five powers is a unique constitutional concept crafted from his keen observations of Chinese history and people's sentiment. It does carry certain contrived aspects, but it is primarily his subjective effort to rectify the shortcomings of the Western representative system and to address the pitfalls of the electoral process. More importantly, it paints a blueprint of "the most perfect and beneficent state in the world, a nation of the people, by the people, for the people".

His advocacy for the separation of five powers highlighted the division of responsibilities and cooperation among powers, contrasting with the Western model of separation of powers which emphasizes a system of checks and balances. The five Yuans (or chambers), corresponding to the five powers, all operated under the national president, following a model of cooperative division of labor. As stipulated in the *Fundamentals of National Reconstruction*, "The heads of the various Yuans shall be appointed, removed and overseen by the President of the State". This constitutional philosophy is intricately tied to Sun's theory of "distinction between sovereignty (*quan*, 权, which the people should have) and capability (*neng*, 能, which the government should have)".

2. The distinction between political power and governing power

The distinction between sovereign power from administrative capability embodied Sun's democratic thought to the fullest extent. Sun's "Five-power Constitution" was predicated on the doctrine that the sovereign power rests with the people while the government exercise the administrative power, thus underpinning the principle of popular sovereignty. He bifurcated political power into sovereign power and administrative power:

Politics pertains to the affairs of all people. The collective force overseeing these affairs is referred to as sovereign power or popular sovereignty. Governance is the management of the people's affairs. The collective force responsible for this management is called administrative power, synonymous with governmental power. Thus, politics includes two types of power, the power to manage the government, and the power of the government itself.

To transform China into a modern state, it is essential to separate sovereign power from administrative power. The former must be wholly entrusted to the people, enabling them to enjoy full democracy in the direct management of state affairs, and the latter, to government organs, thereby equipping them with substantial authority to administer national affairs.

China should build up a state governed by all the people, and this ideal can only be realized, in Sun's belief, on the condition that the people genuinely wield four fundamental rights, the rights to vote, legislate, veto, and recall. These rights could be grouped into two categories. The first encompasses the rights to elect and recall, allowing the populace to oversee public officials. Sun advocated "popular sovereignty characterized by people's direct participation in elections" and a system of autonomous counties nationwide, where citizens directly elect officials and representatives to form the National Assembly, the supreme authority. However, people's direct right to vote alone would not be sufficient to maintain effective control over officials, and so they must also be given the right of recall. The second category includes the legislative power, the rights to make, amend or repeal a law based on the consensus of the populace. Sun emphasized that the genuine Republic of China must safeguard the people's four rights so that they could truly exercise direct control over the government.

3. Equal division of power between the central and local government

Regarding power distribution between the central and local governments, Sun sought to transcend the binary of decentralization versus centralization and to establish a system of "balanced power", where "all administrative issues of a nationally uniform nature would fall under the purview of the central government while those requiring regional adaptations would be entrusted to the local governments". This approach aimed to achieve an equilibrium, eschewing a bias towards either centralization or decentralization.

4. The three-stage theory of "Military Government, Political Tutelage and Constitutional Government" and the practice of "Political Tutelage"

Sun's revolutionary strategy comprised three stages: the rule of military law, the rule of the provisional constitution, the rule of the constitution, that is, Military Government, Political Tutelage and Constitutional Government. This theory was put forward as early as 1906 in his *Declaration for a Military Government of the Chinese United League.*

The first stage will be governed by military law … Each county will have three years; those that are able to improve within three years will have military law lifted and shall be ruled by a provisional constitution. The second stage will be governed by a provisional constitution. Each county, upon the lifting of military law, will have their local autonomy restored to the local people by the military government. Members of local assemblies and local administrators shall be elected by the people. The rights and responsibilities of the entire military government in regard to the people as well as the rights and responsibilities of the people in regard to the military government shall be clearly delineated in the provisional constitution; the military government, local assemblies, and the people will all be bound to abide by it. Violators [of the provisional constitution] shall bear the responsibility. Within six years after the realm has been pacified, the provisional constitution shall be annulled and a constitution will be promulgated. The third stage will be governed by a constitution. After six years the implementation of a provisional constitution, a constitution shall be drafted, military and administrative authority of the military government shall be dissolved, and the people will elect a president and assembly men to organize a parliament. Political matters of the state shall be carried out in accordance with the constitution. These three stages—the first stage being a period in which the citizens are led by the military government to eliminate the old corruption, the second stage being a period in which the military government assist the people in taking local autonomy and generally sees to the matters of state, and the third stage being a period in which the military government is dissolved and the state organs shall independently manage national affairs according to the constitution—shall allow our citizens to progress in proper order and cultivate the soil for freedom and equality. It is in this where the Republic of China shall take roots.[6]

[6] Translations are Christopher C. Heselton's. (Notes by translators).

The military period was a phase of destruction, the period of political tutelage, transition, and the constitutional period, completion of reconstruction. Sun attached great importance to the transitional period of political tutelage, a step integral to the revolution but not an end in itself. Its primary aim was to train the people in exercising political power, thereby enabling them to effectively participate in democracy. However, Sun's vision of the political tutelage was later distorted and manipulated by the KMT rulers, who misrepresented it as equivalent to their one-party autocracy. Moreover, the transitional period lasted for 20 years, much longer than the originally planned 6 years. It was not until 1947 that the National Government, established in Nanjing in 1927, enacted the constitution.

In 1928, the Central Standing Committee of the KMT approved *An Outline of Political Tutelage*[7] and promulgated the *Organic Law of the National Government of the Republic of China* as the guideline of governmental organization. The full text of the *Outline* consisted of six articles, namely, (1) during the period of political tutelage of the ROC, the National Congress of the KMT, on behalf of the National Assembly, led the people to exercise the administrative power; (2) when the National Congress of the KMT was not in session, its powers were entrusted to the Central Executive Committee of the KMT; (3) the people should have the four political rights of suffrage, recall, initiative and referendum, which should be gradually promoted along with the KMT government's training of the people, so as to lay the foundation for the constitutional government; (4) the five administrative powers, i.e., the executive, legislative, judicial, examination and control powers should all be entrusted to the National Government for implementation so as to lay down the foundation for the elected government during the rule of the constitution; (5) major state affairs of the National Government should be directed and supervised by the Political Council of the Central Executive Committee of the KMT; (6) amendment and interpretation of *Organic Law of the National Government of the Republic of China* should be determined by the Political Conference of the Central Executive Committee of the KMT. In May 1931, the National Assembly passed *Provisional Constitution for the Period of Political Tutelage of the Republic of China*. Compared with *An Outline of Political Tutelage*, it introduced specific provisions safeguarding basic citizen rights. Meanwhile, it curtailed the KMT's grip over the government, consequently enhancing the government's scope of power.

The concept of "political tutelage" "ostensibly meant that the Kuomintang was to exercise 'party rule' (*dangzhi*, 党治) on behalf of the people. Party rule was expressed institutionally in the authority invested in the party organs, the Central Executive Committee and the Central Political Council. The former was the supreme organ of party power (except during the brief sessions of the National Party Congress, only three meetings were convened during the Nanking decade). It and especially its Standing Committee were charged with the formulation of the guiding principles of party rule and with the overall direction of party administration. The Central Political Council was a bridge between the party and the governmental structure. Although it

7 In 1929, *An Outline of Political Tutelage* was subsequently approved at the Third National Congress of the KMT.

was merely a subcommittee of the Central Executive Committee, it was, formally at least, the supreme authority over the National government, combining both legislative and executive functions. As a legislative body, it could initiate legislation or communicate decisions of the Central Executive Committee to the government. As an executive body, it was empowered to provide general direction to and supervision of the government. Theoretically, then, the Political Council wielded virtually unlimited powers over the civilian branch of the government. In practice, too, the Political Council was the locus of authority in the government, for the head of the council was Chiang Kai-shek … he wielded ultimate authority over the regime …with minimal concern for formal chains of command." (Eastman, 1986/2001, pp.134–136) This caused the government, a policy-making and administrative organization, to lose its vitality. By August 1937, on the cusp of the War of Resistance against Japanese Aggression, the Political Council of the Central Executive Committee was replaced by a Supreme National Defense Conference (in January 1939, it was reorganized as the Supreme National Defense Council) presided over by Chiang. Thus, Chiang was able to silence all dissenting voices within the Party and assumed control over both the administrative functions of the government and the military (Eastman, 1986/2001).

ii. The formulation of the MFDC

1. Multiple constitution drafts

The term, the May Fifth Draft Constitution, typically refers to the final draft, though occasionally it may also denote Wu Jingxiong's trial draft (or "Wu's draft"). The MFDC underwent multiple modifications from 1933 to 1936. Individual trial drafts included Wu Jingxiong's (published by Wu on his own behalf on June 8, 1933[8]) and Zhang Zhiben's (completed by Zhang on August 18, 1933[9] and published later). The official constitutional drafts included: the preliminary draft (passed after the third reading at the main drafters' meeting on November 16, 1933), the first draft (passed by the Constitution Drafting Committee on February 28, 1934), the amendment to the first draft (passed by the First Draft Reviewing Committee on July 9, 1934). The Legislative Yuan approved the draft constitution on October 16, 1934 and amended it on October 25, 1935. On May 5, 1936, the National Government formally promulgated the draft constitution (i.e., the MFDC). After the promulgation, on October 25, 1935, the Legislative Yuan passed another amendment, which was called the *Amendment to the May Fifth Draft Constitution* (Propaganda Committee of the Draft Constitution of the Legislative Yuan, 1940).

---

[8] Another saying suggests that it was published on June 8th.

[9] Zhang Zhiben resigned as vice chairman of the Constitution Drafting Committee after the preliminary draft was completed on August 18. More details about the drafting process and his main ideas can be found in Zhang (1996, pp. 77–79).

2. Numerous amendments

Given the multitude of constitutional draft versions noted above, it becomes clear that the constitution had gone through quite a few revisions during the three-year period from its preliminary formulation to the final draft.

(1) Organization of the Constitution Drafting Committee. The Constitution Drafting Committee, formed in the spring of 1933 and comprised of a chairman (Sun Ke), two vice-chairmen (Zhang Zhiben and Wu Jingxiong), and several members (Ma Yinchu, Wu Shangying, Shi Shangkuan, Huang Youchang, Chen Ruxuan and Lin Bin, et al.), had a subordinate reviewing committee consisting of (the main drafters) Zhang Zhiben (convenor), Wu Jingxiong, Jiao Yitang, Chen Zhaoying, Ma Yinchu, Wu Shangying, and Fu Bingchang. Dai Jidao, Wang Shijie, Lv Fu, et al. were employed as consultants, and JinMingsheng and Yuan Qinghui, etc. as compilers (Wu & Huang, 1937a, pp. 91–94).
(2) Formulation, review and amendment of the initial draft. This stage could be subdivided into four phases: (1) the study on the drafting principles and the publication of Wu Jingxiong's draft; (2) examining Wu's draft article by article by the main drafters of the Committee, which led to a collaborative effort by the seven Committee members to generate the preliminary draft; (3) deliberating collectively on the preliminary draft among the Constitution Drafting Committee and presenting the official initial draft in February 1934; (4) accomplishing the initial draft. When the work of the Committee came to an end, Sun Ke, the president of the Legislative Yuan, designated an additional group of 36 people, including committee member Fu Bingchang, to organize and review various perspectives, and carry out further research. This process culminated in the formulation of an amendment to the initial constitutional draft in July 1934 (Wu & Huang, 1937b, pp. 781–782).
(3) Deliberation and passage of the initial draft by the Legislative Yuan. The amendment to the initial draft constitution was submitted to the Legislative Yuan for discussion on September 14, 1934, and the legislative members met eight times successively until October 16, when it completed the third reading and submitted the bill to the National Government and forwarded it to the KMT Central Committee for verification.
(4) Discussion of the draft constitution by the Fifth Plenary Session of the Fourth Central Committee of the KMT and subsequent amendment by the Legislative Yuan. In December 1934, the Fifth Plenary Session of the Fourth Central Committee of the Kuomintang reviewed the draft constitution and raised five guiding principles. Firstly, the spirit of Sun Wen's Three Principles of the People, Fundamentals of National Reconstruction, and Provisional Constitution for the Period of Political Tutelage of the Republic of China served as the pillars of the draft constitution; secondly, the restrictions on executive power should not be rigidly prescribed; thirdly, the responsibilities of central and local institutions should be generally stipulated by the constitution and their organizational structure outlined by law ... Based on these principles, the Legislative Yuan appointed Fu Bingchang, Wu Jingxiong, Ma Yinchu, Lin Bin and three others

as members of the reviewing committee. The committee was tasked with scrutinizing the draft constitution line-by-line according to the guidelines established by the central government and then submitting the revised draft to the Legislative Yuan for the third reading (Wu & Huang, 1937b, pp. 783–784).

(5) The KMT's discussion and feedback on the amended draft. In November 1935, the Sixth Plenary session of the Fourth Central Committee and the Fifth National Congress of the KMT held discussions on the second draft of the constitution as proposed by the Legislative Yuan, and the Central Standing Committee of KMT arrived at a resolution and offered twenty review opinions (Wu & Huang, 1937b, p. 785).

(6) The "final" amendments by the Legislative Yuan in line with the KMT Central Committee's suggestions and the promulgation of the "MFDC" (Wu & Huang, 1937b, pp. 786–792).

(7) Feedback from the Central Standing Committee Meeting of the KMT on the MFDC and the amendments by the Legislative Yuan. On April 22, 1937, the Central Standing Committee of the KMT resolved to remove Article 146 of the MFDC, which stipulated, "The power of the First National Assembly shall be exercised by the National Assembly that made the constitution".[10] The Legislative Yuan was ordered to delete that article on April 30 and submitted the constitution to the National Government for promulgation on May 28 (Propaganda Committee of the Draft Constitution of the Legislative Yuan, 1940, p. 15). Hence, although the Draft Constitution of the Republic of China was generally referred to as the "May Fifth Draft Constitution", the final version wasn't identical to the original "MFDC", albeit the differences were minor.

3. The final outcome of amendments

The MFDC, originally drafted by experts, found itself constrained by several factors. The main drafters did not hold prominent political positions, and even the presiding figure, Sun Ke, could hardly be counted as a significant power broker. Consequently, the draft constitution was inevitably shaped extensively by the incumbent powers, beyond the constraints of Sun Yat-sen's constitutional ideology. In the making of the MFDC, the Japanese army was gearing up for an aggressive war, and China was grappling with a deepening national crisis. The authorities, in response, instituted an autocratic regime under the pretense of crafting a "versatile" and "omnipotent government", a move "prioritizing national survival over the pursuit of enlightenment". In a certain sense, the overall amendment process also represented an evolution in which the draft text increasingly catered to the interests and biases of those in power and gradually straying from the basic principles of modern constitutions.[11] The final draft "prolonged the term of office of the National Assembly members and the president,

[10] This indicates the difference between the Constitution-making National Assembly and Constitutional National Assembly, the former of which is responsible for making the constitution while the latter, implementing it. Once the constitution is made, it requires to reelect representatives to form the first National Assembly to carry out the constitution.

[11] Certainly, the constitution-framers' three years of painstaking efforts cannot be overlooked.

while slightly shortened that of the head of each Yuan and members of the Legislative Yuan and the Control Yuan. The president, exempt from attending the meetings of the Executive Yuan, held an increasingly elevated status. Moreover, the provision that the president could convene the heads of the five Yuans to resolve inter-Yuan disputes solidified his central role within the five branches. The presidential power to command the army, navy and air force was not confined by law. In times of necessity, he was empowered to issue emergency orders and enforce emergency sanctions without the consent of the Legislative Yuan which was, though, in session all year round. He also had the power to appoint half of the members of the Legislative Yuan and the Control Yuan during the interim period. It can be said that the governmental powers were consolidated so much as to outclass any other modern democratic state with a presidential system." (Chen, 1947, pp. 232–233)

iii. Main content of the MFDC

The MFDC stipulated that the people shall have the right to elect and dismiss county government officials, and make and repeal county government regulations. With regard to central affairs, the people shall elect representatives to form the National Assembly, which in turn exercises the right to elect the state president and vice-president, the presidents and vice-presidents of the Legislative Yuan and the Control Yuan, and the right to recall the above-mentioned officials and the presidents and vice-presidents of the Judicial Yuan and the Examination Yuan. The National Assembly shall exercise the power to enact and repeal central laws and have the exclusive power to amend the constitution. Though endowed with supreme power, the National Assembly rarely convened and had short sessions—convened by the national president every three years, lasting for one month, or two months if needed; a provisional Assembly could be convened upon the consent of more than two fifths of the representatives or under the presidential summon.

The MFDC established the position of president and five Yuans in the central government, but the relationship between them was not explicitly outlined in *Sun Wen Theory*. However, according to Sun's theory on separation of powers and omnipotent government, it can be inferred that the five branches should prioritize cooperation over checks and balances, with the president holding a position of overall leadership. The president, as the head of state and executive leader, appointed and dismissed the head of the Executive Yuan, who was directly responsible to the president. The state president also appointed the presidents and vice-presidents of the Judiciary Yuan and the Examination Yuan (Jing, 1984, p. 423). There was no rival power in the five-branch government to counterbalance the president, and the National Assembly, as the governing organ, convened infrequently with short sessions. This situation easily lends itself to the president's consolidation of power, resulting in a political system commonly referred to as super-presidentialism as established by the MFDC.

Regarding the relationship between the central and local authorities, the Constitution Drafting Committee of the Legislative Yuan at first proposed that "The central powers shall be enumerated and the local powers, implied." However, after discussion by the Legislative Yuan and the KMT Central Committee, the scope of local autonomy progressively diminished, mainly in two aspects: (1) the status of provincial autonomy was abolished, with provincial governors being appointed by the central government and the role of provincial governments restricted to executing the central government's decrees and supervising local autonomy; (2) counties became the only constitutional units for local autonomy, but the locally-governed affairs were determined by legislation, which implied that the central government might arbitrarily alter the scope of central and local powers through legislation, weakening the constitutional warrant of local autonomy.

Shortly after the promulgation of the MFDC, there was a wave of intense criticism in society, much of which centered around such core issues as the establishment of the National Assembly, the structure of the "Five-power Constitution", considerable restriction on people's basic rights and local self-governance, and the risk of a "super-president". However, the KMT Party was so overwhelmingly powerful that these criticisms had little impact on the content of the draft constitution, and the government continued to pursue its own course (Yu & Wu, 1936). Nevertheless, these critics and debates anywise laid the theoretical and popular groundwork for future constitutional amendments.

Soon after the enactment of the MFDC, the National Government proceeded with the election of representatives of the Constitutional National Assembly, and by June 1937, 950 delegates had been elected. Before long, the outbreak of the July 7 Incident and the invasion by the Japanese army forced the suspension of the election process (Jin, 1953, p. 192), which led to a delay of nine years, effectively putting the MFDC on hold. During the war of resistance against the Japanese invaders, the minority parties formed the National Political Council as a platform to assemble as a third political force outside the KMT and the Communist Party of China (CPC), launched two constitutional movements within the KTM-controlled areas, and even drew up the "Draft Constitution of the Constitutional Government Promotion Committee". This third force developed into the Chinese Democratic Political League and gradually cooperated with the CPC, which paved the way for the convocation of the Political Consultative Conference (PCC) and the establishment of the constitutional principles.

8.1.3 The PCC and PCC Constitutional Amendment[12]

i. Convening the PCC

In the wake of the War of Resistance, the National Assembly was originally scheduled to convene on October 10, 1945 for the making of constitution. However, because the CPC and other parties jointly objected to the allocation of the National Assembly seats and the content of the MFDC, it was not until January 10, 1946 that the KMT

[12] (CPC History Teaching and Research Group of Marxism-Leninism Teaching and Research Department, 1981; Research Committee of Cultural and Historical Materials of Chongqing CPC & Party School of Chongqing Municipal Committee, 1989).

re-invited the CPC, the Democratic League, the Youth Party, the Democratic Socialist Party and social elites, totaling 38, to hold the PCC in Chongqing. The PCC meeting, in addition to the plenary session, was divided into five panels that respectively focused on government reorganization, the political platform of government, military affairs, the National Assembly, and the draft constitution.

On January 19, 1946, the ninth plenary of the PCC held in the auditorium of the Chongqing National Government set out to deliberate on the constitutional draft. First, Sun Ke, on behalf of the National Government, gave a speech on the content and spirit of the MFDC, and then Huang Yanpei, Shen Junru, Fu Sinian, Hu Lin, Zeng Qi, Yang Yongjun, Zhang Shenfu, Wu Yuzhang, and Li Zhuchen delivered speeches successively (Zhu, 1989, pp. 246–247). Huang Yanpei argued for the necessity of reevaluating the draft constitution, specifically focusing on issues such as the National Assembly, the five-chamber system, the presidential system, the local government system, the people's rights, and so on. Shen Junru's speech emphasized the issue of local power. Fu Sinian pointed out the need to improve the National Assembly system, particularly arguing that the five-chamber structure could incorporate the Western congress system, with the Legislative Yuan serving as the lower house and the Control Yuan as the upper house, so that the National Assembly, though not in the name of congress, would come into de facto operation. Hu Lin noted that there was much room for discussion to improve the MFDC. While he advocated for upholding the "Three Principles of the People" and *Sun Wen Theory*, he cautioned against rigid adherence to form. Zeng Qi proposed to establish a Constitutional Draft Review Committee to scrutinize the draft constitution, to adopt the cabinet[13] and bicameral system, to preserve the spirit of the five-Yuan system without rigidity, and to establish the status of provincial autonomy. Yang Yongjun's speech highlighted the importance of local autonomy, asserting that provinces should represent the highest unit of local autonomy and that their governors should be democratically elected. Zhang Shenfu contended for necessary revisions to the draft constitution, aligning it with the nation's historical context, current conditions and global trends while keeping an eye on the future. He also endorsed expanding citizens' rights and freedoms. Wu Yuzhang's speech especially underscored the protection of people's rights and local autonomy. Li Zhuchen suggested that, of the national policy of "equalization of land ownership" and "restriction of private capital" outlined in the draft constitution, priority should be given to the former, as the development of "national capital" and "national industry" should be emphasized in China (Central Daily News, 1946; Kong, 1947, pp. 267–285; Xinhua Daily, 1946). It's fair to say that the various speeches made on the first day of the ninth plenary session of the PCC laid the foundation for the principles of constitutional revision. There were numerous aspects worth discussing in the MFDC and amendments should avoid stiff adherence to the "Three Principles of the People" and Five-power Constitution; improvement should be made to the National Assembly system; the central government should implement a cabinet system; a parliamentary system should be established with the Legislative Yuan as the lower house and the Control Yuan as the upper house; local autonomy should be

[13] Zeng, the leader of the Youth Party, strongly opposed the presidential system.

fostered; and people's basic rights should be protected rather than restricted. All these considerations were mirrored in the speeches delivered by the conference delegates.

The PCC constitutional drafting panel convoked in the afternoon of January 21 and met, in total, four times. On January 23, the panel suggested the following amendments to the five-Yuan system on the premise of acknowledging "the Five-power Constitution as the most progressive political principle in the world". First, the Legislative Yuan shall be the highest legislative body and shall be composed of representatives elected by the citizens, having the same powers as the parliaments of other democracies. Second, the Control Yuan shall act as the highest supervisory body, comprised of representatives elected by provincial, municipal, and county councils and ethnic autonomous regions. Third, the Judicial Yuan shall be the Supreme Court of the State, which held no responsibility for judicial administration. The Judicial Yuan shall be composed of a certain number of judges, nominated and, with the consent of the Control Yuan, appointed by the state President. Fourth, the Examination Yuan shall adopt a commission system, inclusive of representatives from all political factions, and focus on the examination of public officials and professional personnel. Fifth, The Executive Yuan shall be accountable to the Legislative Yuan. Furthermore, on the same day, a comprehensive committee of the PCC was formed, comprising 11 members, including Sun Ke (also the convener), Wang Shijie, Wu Tiecheng, Zeng Qi, Chen Qitian, Wang Yunwu, Fu Sinian, Zhang Bojun, Zhang Dongsun, Zhou Enlai, and Dong Biwu, (Zhu, 1989). After multiple meetings, the panel put forward twelve principles to amend the MFDC, and resolved to establish a committee to review the constitutional draft. The draft constitution deliberation committee was comprised of 25 members, with five from each of the five panels of the PCC, and 10 additional experts selected from public recommendation; the committee should be responsible for formulating amendments to the draft constitution by taking into account opinions of various parties, including the twelve principles to amend the MFDC by the PCC, "Qicheng Draft Constitution" and the discussion results of the Association for the Implementation of Constitutionalism. The committee was to complete its review of the draft constitution within a two-month period (Jiang, 1976, p. 34–35).

ii. Publication of the Twelve Principles of the PCC and further bilateral compromise

During the PCC meetings, the KMT and the CPC, as well as third-party forces (comprising other political parties and social elites), engaged in exhaustive discussions on the political, military, and constitutional issues. On January 31, 1946, the PCC concluded with five agreements on government reorganization, political platform of government, military affairs, the National Assembly, and draft constitution. Concerning the last issue, there was a unanimous belief, barring the KMT, that the MFDC, although termed the "Five-Power Constitution", was in actuality a one-power constitution, which failed to meet the basic requisites of democratic governance and hence necessitated amendment. The twelve agreements reached on the draft constitution (historically known as the "Twelve Principles of the PCC") are encapsulated as follows.

1. The National Assembly: The entirety of the electorate, exercising four powers, is termed the National Assembly.[14] Prior to the implementation of universal suffrage for the presidency, the national president shall be elected by an electoral body comprised of assemblies at the central, provincial and county levels. The exercise of the twin powers of initiative and referendum shall be regulated by separate legislations. The process of recalling the national president shall be in the same manner as that of electing the national president.
2. The Legislative Yuan: The Legislative Yuan shall be the highest legislative organ of the nation, elected directly by the people and functioning as the parliament of a democracy.
3. The Control Yuan: The Control Yuan shall be highest control organ of the State, elected by various provincial assemblies and ethnic autonomous regions and exercising the powers of consent,[15] impeachment and supervision.
4. The Judicial Yuan: The Judicial Yuan shall serve as the Supreme Court, without handling judicial administration. It should be composed of a designated number of Grand Justices, who shall be nominated and, with the consent of the Control Yuan, appointed by the national president. Judges of all levels shall be nonpartisan.
5. The Executive Yuan: The Executive Yuan shall be the highest administrative organ of the nation. The president of the Executive Yuan shall be nominated by the national president and appointed with the consent of the Legislative Yuan. The Executive Yuan is responsible to the Legislative Yuan. In instances where the Legislative Yuan expresses a vote of no confidence in the Executive Yuan as a whole, the Executive Yuan may either resign from office or request the national president to dissolve the Legislative Yuan. However, the same executive president may not request the dissolution of the Legislative Yuan twice.
6. The president: The national president, by resolution of the Executive Yuan, may issue emergency decrees in accordance with the law. Such decrees shall, within a month of their issuance, be presented to the Legislative Yuan. It is not necessary to specify in writing that the President can convene meetings with the heads of the various Yuan.
7. Local system: Provinces are established as the highest unit of local self-governance. The provincial governor shall be directly elected by its citizens. Provinces have the authority to enact their own constitutions, provided that they do not contradict the national constitution. Powers are equally divided between the central and local government.

The "Twelve Principles of PCC" made the following significant amendments to the MFDC. First, the National Assembly became incorporeal, and the Legislature Yuan was changed from a legislative organ to a parliamentary body. Second, the

[14] This is the so-called "incorporeal National Assembly", which means there is no need to set up a national congressional body.

[15] The power of consent refers to that the President, Vice President, Grand Justice of the Judicial Yuan and the President, Vice President and members of the Examination Yuan shall be nominated by the President and appointed with the consent of the Control Yuan.

super-presidential system was altered into the cabinet system, and the Executive Yuan was held responsible to the Legislative Yuan; the president was reduced to the head of state, no longer serving as the executive leader. Third, federalism was incorporated into the division of powers between central and local governments; provinces, led by democratically elected governors, were established as the highest unit of local self-government and were granted the power to enact their own provincial constitutions; the Control Yuan assumed the roles and responsibilities akin to a Senate, and its control members, elected on a local basis, exercised the consent power to the appointments of presidents, vice-presidents and important members of both the Judicial Yuan and the Examination Yuan.

After the publication of the Twelve Principles, the Second Plenary Session of the Sixth National Congress of the KMT passed a series of resolutions to amend the draft constitution. "First, the drafting of the constitution shall be fundamentally based on the *Fundamentals of National Reconstruction*. Second, the National Assembly shall be a corporeal institution, exercising its powers as stipulated in the *Fundamentals of National Construction* through regular assembly sessions. The frequency of these sessions shall be increased. Third, the Legislative Yuan shall exercise neither the power of consent nor the power of non-confidence over the Executive Yuan. The Executive Yuan shall not have the power to request the dissolution of the Legislative Yuan. Fourth, the Control Yuan shall not have the power of consent. Fifth, it is not mandatory for provinces to formulate their own constitutions". In due course, Sun Ke submitted the KMT's proposals to representatives of various political parties for further negotiations in the constitutional drafting process. Based on the panel discussions, the PCC finally reached a new agreement on the principles to amend the draft constitution as follows. First, the National Assembly shall exist as a substantial institution exercising four distinct powers; second, the Legislative Yuan's power of non-confidence and the Executive Yuan's power of dissolution would be abolished; third, the idea of provincial constitutions would be forsaken in favor of allowing "provinces to enact their own self-governance regulations" (Kong, 1946, pp. 307–308).

iii. The formulation of the PCC Constitutional Amendment

After the closing of the PCC, the remaining constitutional issues were taken over by the Draft Constitution Review Committee. The Committee members were Sun Ke (also the convener), Wang Chonghui, Wang Shijie, Shao Lizi and Chen Bulei from the KMT Party; Zhou Enlai, Wu Yuzhang, Dong Biwu, Qin Bangxian and He Sijing from the Communist Party; Zeng Qi, Chen Qitian, Yu Jiaju, Yang Yongjun and Chang Naihui from the Youth Party; Zhang Junmai, Huang Yanpei, Shen Junru, Zhang Bojun and Luo Longji from the Democratic League; independents such as Fu Sinian, Wang Yunwu, Hu Lin, Mo Dehui and Miao Jiaming; and 10 invited experts, including Wu Jingxiong, Wu Shangying, Lin Bin, Shi Shangkuan, and Qian Duangsheng, six of whom participated in the drafting of the MFDC (CPC History Teaching and Research Group of Marxism-Leninism Teaching and Research Department of Sichuan University, 1981, pp. 114–115).

On February 14, 1946, the Draft Constitution Review Committee convoked its inaugural session, during which it primarily addressed procedural issues before transitioning to a discussion on the National Assembly. This conversation continued during the Committee's second meeting held on February 15. The third meeting on February 16 focused on central political issues. Particularly contentious was the debate over whether or not to implement a Western-style parliamentary system. The fourth meeting on February 18 carried on the discussion on the central political issues. The fifth meeting on February 19 centered around the issue of local government systems; the sixth meeting deliberated on the people's rights and duties, elections, basic state policies, and the power to amend the constitution (Kong, 1946, pp. 291–307; Zhu, 1989, pp. 433–484).

The "incorporeal National Assembly" designed in the "Twelve Principles of the PCC" was explicitly opposed by Chiang Kai-shek, but encountered minimal resistance within the Draft Constitution Review Committee. Following negotiations between the involved two sides, it was adopted almost as originally planned. However, the cabinet system (where the Executive Yuan is responsible to the Legislative Yuan) provoked protracted deliberation within the Committee.[16] Because Zeng Qi, the leader of the Youth Party, strongly advocated the cabinet system, the KMT did not want to lose a "like-minded sympathizer" and so it was improper to deny it flatly. After a lengthy negotiation, an "inventively crafted" clause outlining a "limited cabinet system" was eventually adopted (Jiang, 1976, pp. 57–58).[17] The realities of existing conditions and tradition precluded the adoption of a pure cabinet or presidential system. The PCC Constitutional Amendment finally came out after a careful consideration of all parties' interests, striking a delicate balance among them." (Jiang, 1976, p. 173) Overall, the debate on the Executive Yuan were the most time-consuming in the Draft Constitution Review Committee and that on the local government system, the most heated.[18] Nonetheless, a consensus was finally reached, albeit with difficulty. To the end of April 1946, the Committee held its last meeting where the PCC Constitutional Amendment was passed with reservations.[19]

[16] Chiang Kai-shek once invoked the *Provisional Constitution* in the early republican era as an example to indicate his opposition to the cabinet system, stating that the transition from a presidential to a cabinet system was akin to "inflicting upon others that which one would not desire oneself".

[17] The so-called "modified cabinet system" incorporates elements of a presidential system into the cabinet system. Specifically, it does away with the traditional parliamentary mechanisms of a non-confidence vote leading to the dissolution of the cabinet, and the cabinet head's ability to dissolve parliament. Instead, it adopts a reconsideration system, akin to that of the U.S. presidential system, to resolve potential stalemates between the executive and legislative powers. Wang Shijie argued that given the challenging circumstances in China, holding general elections was not an easy feat. If the design of the "Twelve Principles of the PCC" were to be maintained, this could potentially lead to the frequent dissolution and re-election of the Parliament.

[18] The most controversial issue was whether provincial self-governance regulations need to be passed or approved by the central Legislature.

[19] In terms of the aforementioned "reservations", a full consensus was not reached on key issues, including the election of local judges and matters related to the Executive Yuan. Moreover, as pointed out by the KMT representative Wu Tiecheng, a draft constitution not ratified by the National Assembly could only be considered as meeting records rather than official legislation.

In the drafting of the PCC Constitutional Amendment, Zhang Junmai's personal contribution was significant, as he was the principal framer of the draft, and his draft served as the basis for discussion at the Draft Constitution Review Committee. Initially, the president's term was set for four years, with provisions for re-election and consecutive terms. However, to prevent the potential for a long-term presidential tenure, Zhang Junmai proposed extending the term to six years, but limiting re-election to a single subsequent term (Jiang, 1976, p. 190). The provision that self-governance regulations formulated by provinces should be submitted to the Judicial Yuan was called "Qin Bangxian's provision"; the conceptualization of "a modified cabinet system" was mainly credited to Wang Shiji. Furthermore, the proposal to defer the application of the right to initiate and veto legislation until half the nation's counties had enacted the legislation was put forward by Wu Tiesheng (The Central Party Department of the Democratic Socialism Party, 1976, p. 57).

8.1.4 *Final Passage of* Constitution of the Republic of China

The CPC and the Democratic League withdrew from the Constitutional National Assembly because the KMT disrupted the atmosphere of its reconciliation with the CPC.[20] In order to establish a formal legitimacy to his rule (constitutional legitimacy), Chiang Kai-shek did not want to bear the "one-party constitutionalist" reputation and sought to entice the Democratic Socialist Party and the Youth Party to participate in the National Assembly. However, the Youth Party declared its attendance on the condition of the presence of the Democratic Socialist Party, which, with Zhang Junmai as its leader, would attend only upon the premise of the KMT's compliance with the PCC agreement and the "PCC Constitutional Amendment". After the adoption of the "PCC Constitutional Amendment" in April 1946, the political and military situation worsened and in Zhang Junmai's mind, the "Constitutional Amendment" he authored was already a dead letter. In June, Zhang translated the "Constitutional Amendment" into English and presented it to the US. representative George Marshall, where it was met with considerable attention. In August, Wu Tiecheng, on behalf of the National Government, paid a visit to Zhang, claiming that the KMT would accept the "Constitutional Amendment" and submit it to the imminent National Assembly (Zhang Junmai Society of the Republic of China, 2005, p. 198). As the chief drafter, Zhang was intensely keen for the Amendment to be passed. Due to the pressure from the Democratic Socialist Party to engage in state affairs, the Democratic Socialist Party eventually agreed to attend the Constitutional

[20] The CPC and the Democratic League never acknowledged the legitimacy of the *Constitution of the Republic of China*. Nevertheless, it was the burgeoning strength of the CPC, challenging the long-standing unilateral dominance of the Kuomintang, that enabled third-party entities to strategically exert influence. This shift in power dynamics provided the momentum needed to draft and ratify this Constitution, which was notably more progressive in its contents compared to the MFDC.

National Assembly under certain conditions. This decision led to a divide between Zhang and the Democratic League and subsequently caused a schism within the Democratic Socialist Party (Jiang, 1976, pp. 169–191).

On November 9, 1946, Chiang Kai-shek, Chairman of the National Government, wrote to Sun Ke, the head of the Legislative Yuan, urging for a swift conclusion to the review process of the draft constitution. Chiang directed that the constitution should "be drawn up in accordance with the principles of amendment agreed upon at the PCC in January 1946 and the three amendments to the above principles made by the comprehensive group of the PCC in March of the same year. Efforts should be made to consider a range of perspectives, provided that they do not contravene the tenets of the Three Principles of the People." (Zhu, 1989, pp. 856–857) On November 15, the Constitutional National Assembly convened in Nanjing and by December 25, it had passed the *Constitution of the Republic of China*. This constitution was then promulgated by the National Government on the New Year's Day of 1947 and came into force on December 25 of the same year.

On November 28, the third session of the Constitutional National Assembly was convened with an open address by Chiang Kai-shek. Sun Ke proceeded to detail chapter by chapter the amendment content and its difference from the MFDC. Then, from November 29 to December 5, a conference was held, generating extensive and spirited discussions on the draft constitution. Following this, the draft was divided into eight panels for concurrent deliberation. The KMT delegates, holding an overwhelming majority, attempted to reject the "PCC Constitutional Amendment" and restore the MFDC, which presented a risk of overturning all the principles of the "PCC Constitutional Amendment". The Democratic Socialist Party and the Youth Party firmly opposed any modifications to the PCC principles and threatened to withdraw from the Constitutional National Assembly (Ruan, 1970; Wang, 1966). Chiang's pressure on the KMT delegates tempered the dispute slightly, but the Eighth Review Panel still made great changes to the "Constitutional Amendment", particularly expanding the powers of the National Assembly. On December 14, the Comprehensive Draft Constitution Review Committee was formed, with 200 members representing each panel, to collect and review the preliminary outcomes from each panel. After five days' negotiations among political parties and alleviations of various tensions, which fully demonstrated "the grace of the majority respecting the minority", the draft constitution was almost restored to the original "PCC Constitutional Amendment". The first reading was completed on December 21 and the second reading, on the 24th. After the third reading on the 25th, it was finalized. The *Constitution of the Republic of China* adopted by the National Assembly was in essence consistent with the PCC Constitutional Amendment, except for some minor wording adjustments (Chen, 1947, pp. 284–289). "Zhang Junmai, leveraging his unique position as the leader of a small opposition party, forced the dominant KMT to accept his draft constitution, a feat considered uncommon in the history of modern Chinese constitution-making." (Xue, 1993, p. 265).

It is fair to say that compromises were brokered on the issue of constitution-making, culminating in a constitution that encapsulates a balance of interests and reciprocal concessions among various parties. For example, both the CPC and the third-party forces initially opposed the use of the Three People's Principles as the state's system. However, under the KMT's insistence, Article 1 of the *Constitution* stipulated, "The Republic of China, founded on the Three People's Principles, shall be a democratic republic of the people, to be governed by the people and for the people." In this way, the Western constitutional concept of "government of the people, by the people, and for the people" somewhat replaced Sun's Three People's Principles. The *Constitution* is generally considered a significant advancement over the previous MFDC.[21]

Sun Ke played a highly important role from the inception of the MFDC to the final adoption of the *Constitution of the Republic of China*. He served as the Legislative Yuan president for a long period, chairman of the Draft Constitution Committee for the MFDC, and the convener of the Draft Constitution Review Committee for the "PCC Constitutional Amendment". Among the KTM members, he was, at the very least, regarded as progressive; as the philosophical successor of Sun Yat-sen, he vigorously rebutted the internal conservative faction of the KMT's attacks on the PCC Agreement and the Constitutional Draft, disrupting the political impasse rooted in blind adherence to the "Legacy of the Founding Father". During the deliberation on the "PCC Constitution Amendment", when the experts invited by the National Government "lambasted parliamentary politics", he countered by saying, "The teachings bequeathed by the former Prime Minister aren't necessarily infallible, and the resolutions of the PCC aren't necessarily devoid of merit." Only then was the contention quelled and the principles of the PCC were preserved as much as possible (Xue, 1992, p. 175) During the review of the "PCC Constitutional Amendment" by the Legislative Yuan, when some legislators questioned its stark divergence from the MFDC, Sun contended forthrightly that the "PCC Constitutional Amendment" excels the MFDC (Zhang Junmai Society of the Republic of China, 2005, pp. 198–199). During the Constitutional National Assembly's review of the "PCC Constitution Amendment", the KMT conservatives, represented by Zhang Zhiben, attempted to overthrow the PCC principles under the pretext of upholding the "legacy of the Founding Father" and to reinstate the division of powers envisioned in the MFDC. In immediate response, Sun rebuked, "Please do not quote the words of the Founding Father at every move in order to seal the mouth of others and make the situation worse. Even the words of the Founding Father are hardly free from mistakes. Times have changed, and the Founding Father's theory, though applicable to his era, may not necessarily be universally suited to the present. If we truly pay homage to our Founding Father, we should adhere to his accurate teachings and dismiss his erroneous ones." (Jiang, 1976, pp. 176, 179) Therefore, Zhang Junmai, reputed as the "Father of the Constitution of the Republic of China", believed that Sun Ke should "take the most credit" for the passage of the *Constitution* (Zhang Junmai Society of the Republic of China, 2005, p. 199).

---

[21] Ruan wrote in his diary, "[Chiang Kai-shek] asked for my opinion about the constitution, and I said, the constitution cannot make everyone satisfied, but it is better than the MFDC. That's for sure. The relationship between the Executive Yuan and the Legislative Yuan, and the equal division of power between the central government and the provinces and counties are the most creative masterpieces ..." (Ruan, 1970, p. 84).

The 1946 constitution altered the Legislative Yuan from a full-time centralized legislative body, as prescribed by the MFDC, into an organ exercising power on behalf of the people. This shift fundamentally deviated from Sun Wen's theory on "separation of powers", readopting a representative political system termed the "Limited Parliamentary Cabinet" (or "Reformed Cabinet System"). In terms of the relationship between executive and legislative powers, the president of the Executive Yuan was nominated by the national president and approved by the Legislative Yuan after voting, and the Executive Yuan was accountable to the Legislative Yuan, thus establishing a cabinet system for the operation of the central government; furthermore, the 1946 constitution endowed the national president with greater powers than the conventional head of state within a cabinet system, reflecting a compromise between the PCC principles and the proposals from the KMT (Zhang, 1947, pp. 70–71). As to the relationship between the national president and the Executive Yuan, the president's role was not merely symbolic, though his power was considerably constrained, precluding him from direct management of political affairs. According to Article 37 of the *Constitution*, laws proclaimed and mandates issued by the president necessitated the counter-signature of the Executive Yuan president or with the counter-signatures of both the Executive Yuan president and relevant department heads. This compromised arrangement, on one hand, preserved the essence of the cabinet system in which the executive was accountable to the legislature so as to prevent the president from fully controlling the executive and becoming a dictator. On the other hand, it stabilized the political situation, avoided frequent dissolution or collapse of the Parliament, and satisfied the ambitions of influential figures such as Chiang Kai-shek, who sought both the prestige (presidency) and the power it conferred.

Compared to the MFDC, the 1946 constitution vested substantially increased autonomy in local governments. Provinces became local self-governance units, possessing the authority to enact their own self-governance regulations. The locally elected Control Yuan had powers akin to those wielded by the Senate in federal countries. It is also worth mentioning that the provision granting the Judicial Yuan the power to interpret the constitution did not capture special attention during its making. Some people even thought that "interpreting the constitution and unifying the interpretation of laws and orders" should not constitute the primary responsibility the Grand Justices, who they believe should focus on final adjudication instead (Lei, 1957). However, in fact, the "Grand Justices of the Judicial Yuan" did not exercise the power of final adjudication, and their authority was limited to "interpreting the constitution and unifying the interpretation of laws and orders". Its power of "normative review" had far-reaching implications, influencing not only the entire system of the ROC National Government, but also on the evolution of the constitution itself (Fig. 8.1).

According to the regulations of the PCC, the National Assembly was not to convene until the end of the civil war, the reorganization of government, the termination of political tutelage and the completion of constitutional amendment. However, the KMT tore up the resolution of the PCC in order to legitimize its ruling base; then, the CPC, some non-governmental organizations, and other political parties, announced their non-recognition of the Constitutional National Assembly summoned

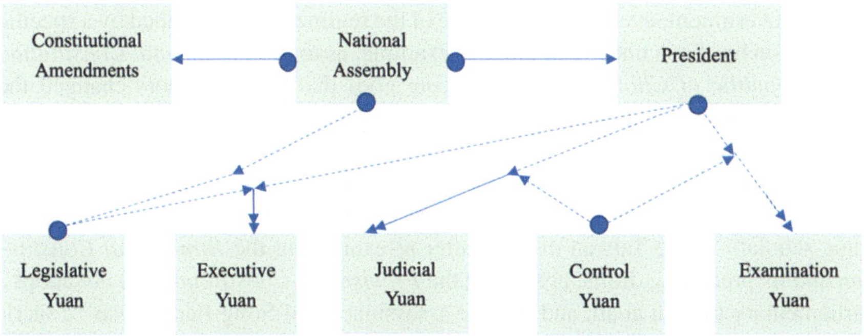

Fig. 8.1 The five-power constitution structure in the 1946 *Constitution*

by the KMT, as well as the constitution making itself (Xie, 2001, p. 37). In reality, the KMT accepted the 1946 constitution somewhat reluctantly, regarding it as a mere interim solution.[22] In an effort to present a façade of peace, the authorities expedited the constitution-making process instead of devoting serious contemplation to it. This mindset paralleled the attitude displayed during the passage of the "Cao Kun Constitution" in the 1920s, foreshadowing a tumultuous trajectory for this constitution.

8.2 Debate Over the Polity Throughout the Constitutional History

The choice between a presidential system and a parliamentary system has been one of the most critical and controversial constitutional issues in modern China. The core of the issue revolves around the relationship between executive power and legislative power: whether to adopt a parliamentary system in which the executive and legislative powers are fused and the executive power (the cabinet) is derived from and subject to the parliament, or to establish a presidential system in which the powers are separated and the executive power is highly concentrated in the presidency. When compared to a parliamentary system, the presidential system carries the twin advantages of executive flexibility and higher efficacy. However, it may run the risk of degenerating into authoritarianism on one hand and cause internal depletion and inefficiency in government operation during periods of gridlock between the executive and the legislature on the other. From the 1911 *Organizational Outline of the Provisional Government* to the constitutional bill read thrice by the ruling government in December 1925, each constitutional document laid down a different

[22] Chiang Kai-shek once provided guidance to the KMT representatives at the National Assembly, emphasizing, "The utmost priority is the completion of the Constitution, and any shortcomings could be amended by future legal amendments, so there is no necessity for rigorous contention at this juncture." (Chen, 1947, p. 282).

form of government; even the exact nature of the regime type prescribed by a specific constitution has been under dispute. For example, as to the *Provisional Constitution of the Republic of China*, a popular saying goes that the legislators changed the presidential system to a parliamentary one in order to curb the power of soon-to-be President Yuan Shih-k'ai; however, others maintain that, due to drafters' insufficient understanding of a parliamentary cabinet, many statutes appeared to emulate a presidential system (Qian et al., 2008, p. 18; Wang & Qian, 1997, p. 264); in recent years, some scholars in the Taiwan district, after re-examining the *Provisional Constitution* and its preceding drafts, argue that the *Provisional Constitution* did not adopt a parliamentary system at all, and that the assassination of Song Jiaoren was "a sacrifice to a mistakenly recognized parliamentary system" (Zhang, 2006). For another example, the 1923 *Constitution of the Republic of China*, tarnished by Cao Kun's vote buying, is generally considered to largely modeled itself after the German *Weimar Constitution* (*Weimarer Verfassung*), thus "aligning with the so-called parliamentary cabinet system" (Wang & Qian, 1997, p. 264); however, the *Weimar Constitution* is deemed as the first semi-presidential (semi-cabinet) constitution. For a long time, the dichotomy between presidential and parliamentary systems has dominated the history of constitutionalism. Yet, a comparative view of various constitutions reveals that many nations have chosen a hybrid regime. Given the political realities of the ROC, neither a purely parliamentary nor a presidential system is either practical or desirable. In fact, the 1946 constitution largely maintained the mixed form of government prescribed by the provisional constitution of the ROC.

8.2.1 Presidential System, Parliamentary System and Mixed System

When the ROC was just founded, there were three major forms of government among the European and American republics: the American presidential system, the French cabinet system, and the Swiss council system. The uniqueness of the Swiss council system, though praised by Zhang Taiyan, found little favor among politicians, and the presidential system and cabinet system were two viable options for China at that time. The presidential system is characterized by a unitary executive where political power and responsibility are consolidated in the president, which often leads to the president's sense of "solitary mental strain" and the possibility of autocracy. Thereof, many scholars believed that the cabinet system was superior to the presidential system in light of democratic checks and balances.

> Flexible checks and mechanical sanctions may be the critical distinction between the cabinet system and the presidential system. The cabinet in the parliamentary system, backed by parliamentary confidence, owns the power to make decisions in all facets. Despite its considerable powers, the system mitigates the risk of misuse of power. The president is entrusted by the electorate to preside over the administration, and his maladministration can only be corrected in the subsequent general election four years later. The congress can only be forced

> out of office by the inelegant method of impeachment. Thus, although the president's hands are often tied, it is still possible for him to abuse powers. (Zou, 1988, p. 155)

However, under a cabinet of parliamentary sovereignty, there is potential agency cost and congressional despotism.

> All the powers of government ... fall to the legislative body. Concentrating these in the same hands is precisely the definition of despotic government. It doesn't matter if these powers are exercised by many people or a single person. One hundred and seventy-three despots would surely be as oppressive as one. (Hamilton, 2010, p. 338)

The theory on "congressional despotism" in the *Federalist Papers* also finds its practical application in the early days of the ROC Congress. "Long accustomed to autocratic despotism, the Chinese people did not understand the principles of constitutional checks and balances, believing that democracy resides in the congress, unaware of that both congressional despotism and autocratic despotism runs counter to the spirit of constitutionalism." It leads to "a congress overriding the legislature" and even a "super-congress system" (Liu, 2013, p. 50). Some political scientists have drawn empirical conclusions from worldwide democratic governmental systems "experiments", suggesting that those with a cabinet system have a higher success rate (lasting longer) than those with a presidential system, as the latter is more prone to bring about "democratic breakdown"; however, others have questioned such kind of conclusion, arguing that statistical samples in different periods can lead to drastically opposing results. In the twentieth century, "... there have been two waves of breakdowns of democracy... one between World War I and World War II and the other in the 1960s. The first wave claimed mostly parliamentary regimes (and no true presidential regimes). The second claimed mostly, but not exclusively, presidential systems" (Shugart & Carey, 1992, p. 39). The relative success of these systems post-1990s remains a topic for future observation.

A few years after the establishment of the ROC, the *Weimar Constitution* in Germany was promulgated in 1919, thus creating a mixed system of government. This innovative mixture of presidential and parliamentary systems originated from the Weimar constitution-makers' wariness of the restoration of autocracy and their dislike of parliamentary hegemony that would make the executive power fall under the complete control of the congress. Nonetheless, this system, unlike the constitutional system of the French Fifth Republic instituted in 1958, could not be termed as a typical semi-presidential structure. The powers granted to the president of the Weimar Republic were not purely constitutional in nature; instead, they stemmed from the realities of German party politics, characterized by a plethora of small parties and the unique circumstances of being a defeated country. In an environment where neither a single party commanding a majority of seats nor a stable coalition was achievable in the Parliament, the president was provided the leeway to influence the cabinet's composition. Germany, facing sanctions after defeat, suffered frequent political, economic and social crises. Consequently, the presidential power to issue emergency orders, originally an exceptional power, gradually became normalized. After Hitler's Nazi Party gained the most seats in the Reichstag and Hitler seized the chancellorship, President Hindenburg's hands were tied.[23] Semi-presidentialism prevails in the world today, but was uncommon or atypical before World War II. Countries like France, Russia, Portugal, Finland, and South Korea, adopted semi-presidentialism in the 1950s or even after the 1980s.

Interestingly, modern Chinese constitution seemed to tilt towards a reconciliation between the presidential and parliamentary systems from the its inception, culminating in the 1946 *Constitution of the Republic of China*, which established a comparatively typical semi-presidential system. Although the *Weimar Constitution* of 1919 did serve as a "precedent", it could not have influenced the "Tiantan Draft Constitution", which formed the constitutional basis of the ROC Beijing government and had been fundamentally shaped by 1913. Moreover, post-World War II, during the drafting of the 1946 Constitution, the *Weimar Constitution* was certainly not seen as a favorable exemplar due to the lessons learned from the fall of the Weimar Republic.[24] For instance, six years prior to the *Weimar Constitution*, the "Titan Draft Constitution" already provided for the presidential power to issue emergency decrees, which, according to the constitutional framers, was inspired by such semi-constitutional monarchies as Austria, Prussia, and Japan (Wu, 2013, pp. 221–222). In other words, for the framers, not only could the specific provisions of republican constitutions—both parliamentary and presidential—be adopted as deemed fit, but elements from monarchic constitutions could also be emulated. This section hereby does not seek to preach that modern China was a pioneer in the establishment of mixed governmental systems, preceding the Weimar Republic or outstripping the French Fifth Republic. Rather, the author is trying to present the fact that, like both the Weimar Republic and the French Fifth Republic, modern China independently "devised" its own semi-presidential (or semi-parliamentary) mixed system—an act of constitutional creativity in its own right.

8.2.2 Mixed Government: A Master Stroke Amid the Bankruptcy of Parliamentary Confidence

The choice between a presidential system and a parliamentary system was one of the most contentious constitutional issues in the early days of the ROC. The *Organizational Outline of the Provisional Government* opted for the American presidential system, but in the milieu of peace negotiations between the North and the South, the framers changed it to a cabinet system by passing the *Provisional Constitution* within

[23] On January 30, 1933, the Hitler-led cabinet was appointed by President Hindenburg, not as a presidential cabinet, but as a cabinet that relied on the majority support of the Reichstag; the appointment was made "in a manner fully compliant with the constitution" (Shirer, 1960/1979, pp. 268–270).

[24] Naturally, there exists a divergence of views within the scholarly community as to whether a direct causal relationship can be drawn between the *Weimar Constitution* and the downfall of the Weimar Republic. Some scholars posit that the political crisis during the Weimar era held enough potency to dismantle any governing structure.

a few months in order to limit the power of the future President Yuan Shih-k'ai. Some scholars found that the articles in the *Provisional Constitution* contained traces of both parliamentarism and presidentialism. Specifically, first, the *Provisional Constitution* provided a vice president position, which seems unnecessary should the role of the president be largely symbolic; second, impeachment proceedings against cabinet members initiated by the Parliament required an absolute majority, diverging from the French model's simple majority, and the president retained the right to request reconsideration of the impeachment; third, the Parliamentarians were not permitted to concurrently serve as cabinet members (state ministers), differing from the British cabinet; fourth, in the event of conflict between the executive and legislative branches, the *Provisional Constitution* did not stipulate mechanisms for no-confidence motions or dissolution of the Parliament, but instead incorporated the American-style presidential veto over congressional legislation (Zhang, 2006). Some scholars attribute this hybrid system to the constitution makers' inadequate understanding of parliamentarism, which led to the incorporation of numerous presidential characteristics (Wang & Qian, 1997, p. 264). However, considering the notorious record of the Parliament in the early period of the ROC and the brazen history of the government illegally dissolving the Assembly twice, the framers' "intentionally or unintentionally" blending of presidential and parliamentary elements in the *Provisional Constitution* can indeed be deemed as a "masterstroke".[25]

Interestingly, despite the unwavering ideological stand of early ROC political figures in the dispute over the form of government, attempts at harmonizing the presidential and parliamentary systems were not lacking in the actual constitution-making process. For example, even the "Tiantan Draft Constitution", which championed parliamentary sovereignty, not only reserved the presidential power to veto legislation, but also empowered the president to issue emergency decrees, similar to the provisions of the 1919 *Draft Constitution of the Republic of China*; the 1923 *Constitution* revoked the president's power to issue emergency orders, but still retained his authority to veto legislation. For another example, although it was repeatedly suggested during the constitution-making process that the position of vice-president was uncalled-for because a president served largely as a figurehead under the parliamentary system; provision for the vice-president nevertheless were retained in all previous constitutional documents. In contrast, the "Third Year Constitution" which espoused super-presidentialism (akin to a dictatorship) under President Yuan Shih-k'ai's reign did not establish a vice-presidency. Furthermore, Article 55 of the "Tiantan Draft Constitution" and Article 71 of the 1923 *Constitution* read, "The executive power of the Republic of China shall be exercised by the president under the assistance of the state ministers." (Xia & Hu, 2004, pp. 445, 526) To this respect, Wu Zongci, a member of the Constitution Drafting Committee, gave an explanation from the legislative perspective: per the draft constitution, the legislative power shall be exercised by the Parliament, and the judicial power, by the courts; then in

[25] The *Provisional Constitution* refrained from adopting the general parliamentary stipulation of dissolving the legislature, an aspect that could arguably be the most profound reflection of the framers' political wisdom and foresight.

the spirit of "separation of powers", Therefore, it was necessary for the constitution to define an entity to exercise the executive power; the use of the phrase "by the President under the assistance of the state ministers", rather than simply stating the executive power should be exercised by the President, was designed to embody the spirit of a parliamentary cabinet (Wu, 2013, p. 221). Actually, the wording of "under the assistance of" does not suffice to conclude that the presidency is merely ceremonial; furthermore, the notion of "separation of powers", a defining characteristic of a presidential system, markedly differs from "parliamentary sovereignty" inherent in a parliamentary system. It might be argued that the so-called parliamentary systems of the *Provisional Constitution of the Republic of China* and *Tiantan Draft Constitution* were, in fact, modifications based upon the presidential system in the *Organizational Outline of the Provisional Government*. This adaptation inevitably carried over elements of the original system due to institutional inertia, especially considering the early constitution drafters' limited understanding of the significant theoretical difference between the concepts of "separation of powers" and "parliamentary sovereignty". Therefore, the artful integration of elements from both the presidential and parliamentary systems in the constitutional texts could be seen as a historical inevitability.

Although the *Provisional Constitution*, viewed from a modern perspective, could be identified as a modified form of a parliamentary system, the inchoate Parliament during its exercise of powers did not rigidly adhere to the constitutional provisions. The parliatarians not only endeavored to craft a new constitution ("Tiantan Draft Constitution") aimed at restricting and divesting the then sitting President Yuan Shih-k'ai of his power, but also flagrantly disregarded the presidential powers prescribed by the existing constitution (such as the power to promulgate laws and veto bills). Consequently, Yuan Shih-k'ai reproached the Parliament for its legal overreach and hypocrisy in demanding unilateral legal adherence from the government, deeming it neither fair nor beneficial for the future of Republican constitutionalism. "I humbly reckon that once this precedent is set, the current Parliament of the ROC will freely exceed the bounds set by the constitutional provisions. The Assembly one-sidedly seek to hold the government accountable for constitutional compliance, and the citizenry responsible for obedience to the constitution, which is plainly in contravention of mutual fairness and logic, and is certainly not a blessing for the Republic's future." Furthermore, the Parliament repeatedly complicated the government's attempts to form a cabinet. "The change of a cabinet depends on partisan views. No political affairs are administered properly, which almost reduced the country to a state of anarchy." (Wu, 2013, pp. 174–176) After Tang Shaoyi, the first cabinet premier, resigned, Yuan Shih-k'ai nominated Lu Zhengxiang, a professional diplomat, to form a cabinet. However, dissatisfied with Lu's parliamentary speech, the Senate unanimously rejected all six minister nominations he proposed. People of the time commented, "In all fairness, the Senators' rejection of the six state ministers is quite naive, akin to a child who, having acquired a toy knife, haphazardly flails it around, without considering the efficacy or potential harm of their actions" (Li, 2002, p. 335).

When the Parliament was reconvened in 1922, legal scholar Wang Chonghui formed a cabinet, more than half of whose members had overseas education backgrounds with high moral character and prestige in the political sphere. Figures such as Minister of Foreign Affairs Gu Weijun, Minister of Finance Luo Wengan, and Minister of Education Tang Erhe graced the cabinet, thereby earning the name of "Cabinet of Virtuous Men" ("Government of Virtuous Men"). However, under Cao Kun's secret support, Wu Jinglian and Zhang Bolie, Speaker and Vice Speaker of the House of Representatives, violated established legal procedures. They accused Luo Wengan, a figure esteemed as a "gentleman of the last days", of bribery and dereliction of duty, and had him arrested and imprisoned. Astonishingly, following Luo's exoneration and release by the prosecution, the House of Representatives passed a resolution for a re-investigation into Luo's case, even demanding the examination of the prosecutors who had previously released him. As a result, Luo was re-jailed. Although Luo was eventually acquitted by the capital's judiciary after the trial, the political turmoil led to Wang Chonghui's cabinet announcing its resignation soon after (Ding, 2012, pp. 16–28). The early Parliament's naive abuse of power and willful distortion of laws were apparent to all. With the Parliament's reputation decimated following two dissolutions and the scandal of Cao Kun's vote-buying, the faith in representative politics crumbled, casting doubts on the parliamentary system as an ideal form of government. In the meantime, Concurrently, Yuan Shih-k'ai's enactment of the *Third Year Constitution of the Republic of China*, leading to a super-presidential autocracy, imprinted a poignant image of the perilous metamorphosis of a presidential system into a dictatorial regime.

8.2.3 Modification of Parliamentary System/Presidential System and Polity Innovation

Subsequent to the *Provisional Constitution*, the 1913 "Tiantan Draft Constitution" stipulated that the Parliament shall exercise the impeachment power against the President and Vice President (Article 41) and the vote of non-confidence towards the State Council (Article 43); the President was granted the power to issue emergency orders in case of "public security" and "extraordinary calamities" (Article 65); the President shall dissolve the House of Representatives given a majority consent from the Senate (Article 75), which is also adopted by the *Constitution of the Third Republic* and the *Constitution of the German Empire.*[26] Not until Yuan's monarchy was overthrown was the First Parliament reconvened in 1917 to resume deliberation on the *Draft Constitution of the Republic of China.* The provision on the dissolution of the Parliament provoked significant controversy, and no consensus was achieved even after the

[26] As previously discussed, France provides an illustrative example. In the era of the German Empire, the Imperial Government also had the ability to dissolve the Reichstag, which was a body elected via suffrage, provided it had the consent of the Bundesrat, constituted of representatives from each individual state (Qian, 2009, pp. 8–9).

second reading of it (Wu & Huang, 1937a, 1937b, p. 65). The 1919 *Draft Constitution* (Article 63) contained a provision concerning the dissolution of parliament, thus revoking the Senate's power to consent to the President's order of dissolution, but retained the presidential power to issue emergency orders (Article 53), thus expanding the authority of the President. The 1923 *Constitution of the Republic of China* abolished the President's emergency power as stipulated in various constitutional drafts since the "Tiantan Draft Constitution", and reinstated the Senate's power of consent to the dissolution of the House of Representatives, thus trimming the power of the President. Per Article 89 of the 1923 constitution, "Upon the passing of a vote of non-confidence against a Cabinet Minister, the President shall either remove the Cabinet Minister from office or dissolve the House of Representatives; however, the dissolution of the House of Representatives necessitates the consent of the Senate." (Xia & Hu, 2004, p. 527) This article restored the Senate's check on the President's power of dissolution, while setting the prerequisite for the exercise of the dissolution power "when a vote of non-confidence has been passed against a Cabinet Minister". This prevented the President from arbitrarily dissolving the Parliament under other pretexts. The 1923 *Constitution* was promptly abandoned following the collapse of Cao Kun's regime, without having the opportunity to be put into actual effect.

The establishment of the NNG in 1927 did not quell the debate over the structure of governance, which continued to pose a significant challenge for constitutional drafting. During the 1930s, under the monopoly of the Kuomintang (KMT) in the constitution-making process, the "Temporary Provisions against the Communist Rebellion" was introduced. This instrument propagated a "super-presidential" system, wherein the President held power that was virtually unchecked. Following the triumph of the War of Resistance against Japan, the PCC set up the Constitutional Deliberation Committee in 1946 to rewrite the constitution, and the framers' first task was to rectify the "super-presidential system" (presidential dictatorship) in the MFDC. History repeats itself—the selection of the President had already been predetermined, destined to be political and military heavyweights—Yuan Shih-k'ai in the early Republic and Chiang Kai-shek in 1946; however, the framers had learned their lessons from the failures in the previous constitution-making and abandoned the strategy of "tailoring the system to a particular person"—neither did they cater to the "leader's" insatiable lust for power, nor did they count on a paper constitution to whittle down his power to nil. Zhang Junmai, often celebrated as the "Father of the ROC Constitution", proposed the establishment of an accountable government that upheld the spirit of a parliamentary cabinet to prevent the President or the cabinet from acting arbitrarily. He believed that the specifics of this parliamentary cabinet system could be flexibly adapted and even substantially revised.

In response to the KMT government's concern that the introduction of a cabinet system would give rise to government instability (frequent no-confidence votes of the parliament caused "repeated resignations of cabinets"). Zhang, together with others, proposed to separate the responsible government from the vote of non-confidence and institute a "modified parliamentary system". Specifically, the head of the Executive Yuan was accountable to the legislature similar to those in British and French cabinet systems, the manner in which these responsibilities were enacted could vary;

besides the major adjustment to the motion of non-confidence (dissolution of parliament), the constitution also discards the feature of collective responsibility of cabinet members, typical of standard parliamentary systems; regarding personnel placement, the appointment of cabinet members other than the executive head did not require legislative approval, which gave the state president (and the head of the executive) considerable power over personnel appointments[27]; the constitution further stipulated that parliamentarians shall not concurrently serve as government officials (typical of the presidentialism), which implied that cabinet members need not be elected from among parliamentarians, thereby widening the scope for cabinet selection. The constitution delineated Presidential powers somewhere between those of the United States and France's Third Republic. "We do not support a presidential system because we are unwilling to place the executive power entirely in the hands of the President as is done in the United States. Nor do we favor the French model of absolving the President of any responsibility. The President, elected by the National Assembly, served as the head of state, in command of the army, navy and air forces, and could appoint civil and military officials. Therefore, not only is he a political head of state for show, but also a person bearing substantial national responsibility. However, for sake of the President's security and for him to enjoy love and esteem by the whole nation, someone must countersign his orders and measures and accordingly bear the responsibility for the countersignature. To this connection, a responsible government is called for besides the President." (Zhang, 1947, pp. 65–68) In terms of the relationship between the President and the Executive Yuan, the President nominated the president of the Executive Yuan, and the heads of various ministries and commissions were recommended by the Executive Yuan to the President for appointment; on the surface, the President and the Executive Yuan share the power to form the cabinet (jointly deciding on the appointment of cabinet members), but in reality the framers were aware of and acknowledged the possibility of a strongman President having full authority over cabinet formation. "The day Chiang Kai-shek assumed presidency, the choice of ministers would naturally have to first meet his approval." (Zhang, 1947, p. 149).

Concerning potential collisions between executive and legislative powers, the "PCC Constitutional Amendment" adopted neither the design of collapse of the cabinet and dissolution of parliament inherent in a parliamentary system, nor the review procedure from a presidential system.[28] Instead, it adopted a hybrid model of review and cabinet dissolution (motion of non-confidence). This institutional innovation was largely absorbed into Article 57 of the 1946 *Constitution*. "The Executive Yuan shall be responsible to the Legislative Yuan in accordance with the following

[27] This regulation is related to the history of the ROC Beijing government when cabinet formation often failed due to boycotts from the Parliament.

[28] A pertinent example can be found in Article 70 of the MFDC, which states, "Prior to official announcement, the President is entitled to submit any legislation to the Legislative Yuan for reconsideration. If the original resolution is upheld by the Legislative Yuan, through a decision passed by no less than two-thirds of the committee members present, the President is obliged to immediately promulgate or enforce it. However, in the case of legislative proposals or treaty agreements, they should be submitted to the National Assembly for review" (Xia & Hu, 2004, p. 987).

provisions (1) … (2) If the Legislative Yuan disagrees with important policy of the Executive Yuan, it may, by resolution, request the Executive Yuan to make changes. The Executive Yuan may, with the approval of the president of the Republic, transfer the resolution back to and request the Legislative Yuan for reconsideration. If, after reconsideration, two-thirds of the members of the Legislative Yuan present at the meeting maintain the original resolution, the Executive Yuan president must either accept it or resign from office. (3) If the Executive Yuan deems a resolution on a statutory, budgetary, or treaty bill passed by the Legislative Yuan difficult to implement, it may, with the approval of the president of the Republic and within ten days after its transmission to the Executive Yuan, request the Legislative Yuan to reconsider. If two-thirds of the members of the Legislative Yuan present at the meeting uphold the original resolution after reconsideration, the President of the Executive Yuan must either accept the bill or resign from office." (Xia & Hu, 2004, p. 1108).

The framers knew well that should a confrontation arose between the Executive Yuan and the Legislative Yuan, the essential conflict would not rest with the executive leader but the state president, who exerted a considerable influence over the Executive Yuan's personnel administration and policies. However, through mechanisms such as counter-signing and the resignation system for the head of the Executive Yuan, they assigned responsibility to the Executive Yuan leader. This arrangement could be encapsulated by the notion, "The president holds power, while the cabinet bears responsibility." Sun Ke, President of the Legislative Yuan and convener of the Draft Constitution Review Committee, made the following explanation at the National Assembly, "This regulation is to avoid direct conflicts between the naitonal president and the Legislature … The presidential responsibility is shouldered by the leader of the Executive Yuan, who can immediately step down when the Legislative Yuan fails to pass a resolution, and then the national president can nominate a new executive head. In this way, it can lessen the presidential burden and save him from being affected by the political fluctuations." This, however, does not mean that "the Executive Yuan has turned into a responsible cabinet, nor the Legislative Yuan into a British or French parliament". The Executive Yuan president is only, according to the constitutional articles, "conditionally accountable to the Legislative Yuan, and thus it cannot be called a responsible cabinet system". In addition, the constitution does not provide for collective cabinet responsibility or non-confidence vote. Furthermore, the roles of the president of the Executive Yuan and the ministers and chairmen of commissions are not to be concurrently held by legislative members. This markedly differentiates the system from typical parliamentary systems. More importantly, "the Executive Yuan remains under the presidential command", which suggests that it can best be characterized as a "modified presidential system" (Secretariat of the National Assembly, 1946, pp. 395–396).

The 1946 *Constitution* harmonizes elements of the presidential and cabinet systems, establishing a dual-responsibility framework for the Executive Yuan towards both the President and the legislative bodies. In theory, this does give rise to a "dilemma of dual loyalty" for the executive head, putting him in an awkward position. However, on one hand, it mitigates the risk of a lopsided "parliamentary despotism" under the cabinet system; on the other, it averts the constitutional impasses inherent in pure presidential systems (where the president cannot be removed from office by the Parliament, nor can the Parliament be dissolved by the President) in cases of deadlock between the president and the legislature. By assigning the responsibility to the head of the Executive Yuan, governmental operations can continue unhindered by constitutional deadlock. Under the credo of "the president commands, the cabinet answers," the dual-accountability mechanism of the Executive Yuan serves as a buffer between the president and the legislative entities, which, though unfair to the executive head, suits well to the uncompromising political culture of the ROC. The hybrid political structure established by the 1946 *Constitution* was referred to as a "modified presidential system" by Sun Ke, a representative from the KMT, and a "modified cabinet system" by Zhang Junmai, representing third-party forces. Despite their divergent stances, both agreed that, in adopting Western constitutional models, the Chinese are capable of making modifications and innovations based on the realities of China, as evidenced in their respective speeches. "We have made use of the strengths of the stable executive branch under the American presidential system, without neglecting the due spirit of a responsive government in a democracy. Having studied Western democracies for decades, we are not content to mimic their every step childishly, but instead seek to inject a degree of creative spirit into the process." (Zhang, 1947, pp. 71–72).

8.2.4 Summary

From the *Provisional Constitution* of 1912 to the 1946 *Constitution*, the constitutional history of the ROC seems to have come full circle on the issue of political structure. Aside from the institutional features of the five-Yuan system and National Assembly stemming from Sun Yat-sen's idea Five-power Constitution, the *Provisional Constitution* and the *Constitution* share many similarities. For instance, both stipulate that the executive head is to be nominated and, upon the consent of the legislature, appointed by the president; they abandon the provision for dissolution of the cabinet or parliament, replacing them with the presidential veto power over legislative bills; cabinet responsibility is not collective or joint and cabinet members need not be parliamentarians, etc. Compared to the *Provisional Constitution*, the 1946 *Constitution* endows the president with greater authority, providing an independent popular base (with the president and vice president elected by the National Assembly, rather than by the legislature); however, the executive branch, led by the Executive Yuan president, is not a part of the presidential aids and staff, but derives its power from and is accountable to the legislature. Both the head of state and the head of government retain distinct powers, each having their own sources of power or popular base. The hybrid design of Western presidential and parliamentary systems seems to subtly coincide with China's enduring political culture of a "monarch-minister balance".[29] It is neither a genius stroke drawn by Zhang Junmai or other constitution makers, nor a "dragon's constitution" (quotes from Li Hongxi, who considered the Five-power Constitution redundant, just like painting a footed snake), but rather an original *modus vivendi* born from the Chinese political reality.

According to Steven B. Smith, what makes Plato, Aristotle, Machiavelli, Hobbes, Locke, and Tocqueville great as political philosophers, or what distinguishes them from those contemporary academics ensconced in ivory towers was "the practical dimension of political philosophy" that "The great political philosophers were all engaged in the politics of their times and provide us with models of how to think about ours." (Smith, 2012, pp. 7–8) The political figures and thinkers (scholars) mentioned in this chapter, such as Sun Yat-sen, Zhang Junmai, and Wu Jingxiong, were prolific writers with extensive knowledge of both Chinese and Western thought, and were recognized by foreigner as Doctors, indicative of their vast learning.[30] All of them were also deeply involved in the practical politics and constitution-making endeavors of modern China. While their constitutional theories' breadth and originality may be subject to scrutiny, it is indisputable that these "constitutional forebears" made significant constitutional choices and innovations, transcending Western models in response to the perceived needs of their era.

References

Central Daily News (Chongqing). (1946, January 20).

Chen, R. (1947). *Zhongguo Xianfa shi* [The constitutional history of the Republic of China]. Wenhai Press.

Chen, X. (2001). *Zhonghua minguo xianfa shilun* [Explanation of the Constitution of the Republic of China]. For internal circulation.

Chen, C. (2004). *Xianfa xue* [Constitutional jurisprudence]. Angle Publishing Co., Ltd.

Ding, Z. (2012). *Beiyang junfa shihua* [Historical stories of the Northern Warlord] (Vol. 4). The Commercial Press.

Duara, P. (1997). *Rescuing history from the nation: Questioning narratives of modern China*. University Of Chicago Press.

Eastman, L. E. (1986/2001). Nationalist China during the Nanking decade 1927–1937. In J. K. Fairbank & A. Feuerwerker (Eds.), *The Cambridge history of China* (3rd print, Vol. 12, Part 1, pp. 116–167). Cambridge University Press.

[29] In the Confucianist ideal, the throne is passed on by the emperor to his son while the position of prime minister claims the able and virtuous. The monarch, though largely passive, remains the ultimate arbiter, while the prime minister oversees the daily governance. The monarch's legitimacy is founded on lineage, and the Prime Minister's on virtuous character, talent, and public support (Qian, 2001).

[30] Wu Jingxiong's Juris Doctor degree (JD) was a genuine one; Sun Yat-sen was titled as Dr. probably because of his modern medical educational background; Zhang Junmai, after obtaining a diploma in political science and economics from Waseda University, came back to China to take the examination held by the Qing court for returned students, and was awarded the scholastic title of *shujish* (庶吉士, Hanlin bachelor) of the Hanlin Academy, that is, the so-called *yanghanlin*, i.e., returnees taking the official position of Hanlin Academy in the late Qing Dynasty.

Five-Power Constitution Association. (Ed.). (1963). *Wuquan xianfa wenxian jiyao* [A digest of five-power constitution literature]. Pamir Press.
Hamilton, A., Madison, J., & Jay, J. (2010). Federalist papers (X. Yin, Trans.). Yilin Press. (Original work published in 1787)
Jiang, Y. (1976). *Zhongguo jindai shi zhuanzhe dian* [Turning points in the modern history of China]. Union Book.
Jin, T. (1953). *Guomin dahui zhi lilun yu shiji* [Theory and practice of the National Assembly]. Central Cultural Relics Supply Press.
Jing, Z. (1984). *Zhongguo lixian shi* [The constitution-making history of the Republic of China]. Linking Publishing Company.
Kong, F. (Ed.). (1946). *Wuwuxiancao zhi pingyi* [Commentary on the May Fifth Draft Constitution]. Times Press.
Lei, Z. (1957). *Zhixian shuyao* [A synopsis of constitution-making]. Union Book.
Li, J. (2002). *Zhongguo jin bainian zhengzhi shi* [A centurial history of Chinese politics]. Fudan University Press.
Liu, Z. (2013). *Minguo jishi benmo* [The chronicle of the Republic of China]. Guangxi Normal University Press.
Propaganda Committee of the Draft Constitution of the Legislative Yuan. (Ed.). (1940). *Zhonghua minguo xianfa cao'an shuoming shu* [The instructions for the draft constitution of the Republic of China]. Zhengzhong Press.
Qian, M. (2001). *Zhongguo lidai zhengzhi deshi* [Merits and demerits of political systems in dynastic China]. Joint Publishing.
Qian, D., Sa, S., Yang, H., et al. (2008). *Minguo Zhengzhi shi* [History of the political system of the Republic of China]. Shanghai People's Publishing House.
Qian, D. (2009). *Deguo d zhengfu* [The government of Germany]. Peking University Press.
Research Committee of Cultural and Historical Materials of Chongqing PCC & Party School of Chongqing Municipal Committee. (Eds.). (1989). *Zhengzhi xieshang huiyi jishi* [Chronicle of the Political Consultative Conference] (Vol. 2). Chongqing Publishing House.
Ruan, Y. (1970). *Zhixian riji* [A diary on the constitution-making]. The Commercial Press.
Shen, Y., Xie, W., & Hu, Y. (Eds.). (1996). *Zhang Zhiben xiansehng fangwen jilu* [The interview record of Zhang Zhiben]. The Institute of Modern History of the Academia Sinica.
Shirer, W. (1979). *The rise and fall of the Third Reich: A history of Nazi Germany* (Vol. 1) (L. Dong et al., Trans). World Affairs Press. (Originally published 1960)
Shugart, M.S., & Carey, J. M. (1992). Presidents and assemblies: Constitutional design and electoral dynamics. Cambridge University Press.
Smith, S. B. (2012). *Political philosophy.* Yale University Press.
The Secretariat of the (Constitutional) National Assembly. (Ed.). (1946). *Guomin dahui shilu* [The National Assembly memoir]. For internal circulation.
The Central Party Department of the Democratic Socialist Party. (Ed.). (1976). *Zhang Junmai xiansehng nianpu chugao* [A draft of Zhang Junmai's life chronology]. For internal circulation.
The CPC History Teaching and Research Group of Marxism-Leninism Teaching and Research Department, Sichuan University. (Ed.). (1981). *Zhengzhi xieshang huiyi ziliao* [Documents of the Political Consultative Conference]. Sichuan People's Publishing House.
The Society of Zhang Junmai of the Republic of China. (Ed. & Trans.). (2005). *Zhongguo disan shili* [The third force in China]. Daoxiang Press.
Wang, Y. (1966). *Guomin dahui gongli ji* [Personal experiences at the Constitutional National Assembly]. The Commercial Press.
Wang, S., & Qian, D. (1997). *Bijiao xianfa* [Comparative constitution]. China University of Political Science and Law Press.
Wu, Z. (1923). *Zhonghua minguo xianfa shi* [The history of the constitution of the Republic of China] (Vol. 1, 2). For internal circulation.
Wu, J., & Huang, G. (1937a). *Zhongguo zhixian shi* [The history of constitution making in the Republic of China] (Vol. 1). The Commercial Press.

Wu, J., & Huang, G. (1937b). *Zhongguo zhixian shi* [The history of constitution making in the Republic of China] (Vol. 2). Commercial Press.

Wu, Z. (2013). *Zhonghua minguo xianfa shi* [The history of the constitution of the Republic of China] (pr. by M. Yu, et al.). Law Press.

Wu, J. (2015). *Falv zhexue yanjiu* [Study on legal philosophy]. Tsinghua University Press.

Xia, X., & Hu, X. (Eds.). (2004). *Jindai zhongguo xianzheng lichen: shiliao huicui* [The constitutional course in modern China: A collection of historical materials]. China University of Political Science and Law Press.

Xie, Z. (2001). *Zhonghua minguo xiuxian shi* [History of constitutional amendments of the Republic of China]. Yang-Chih Book, Co. Ltd.

Xinhua Daily (Chongqing). (1946, January 20).

Xue, H. (1993). Zhang Junmai and the formation of the constitutional system of the Republic of China. In Institute of Modern History of Academia Sinica. (Ed.), *Jindai Zhongguo lishi renwu lunwen ji* [A collection of essays on the historical figures in modern China]. Academia Sinica.

Young, E. P. (1983/2005). Politics in the aftermath of revolution: The era of Yuan Shih-k'ai, 1912–16. In J. K. Fairbank (Ed.), *The Cambridge history of China: Republican China 1929–1949* (6th printing., Part 1, pp. 208–255). Cambridge University Press.

Yu, Z., (Ed.), & Wu, J. (Pr.). (1936). *Xianfa wenxuan* [Selected essays on constitution]. Shanghai Law Editing and Translating Press.

Zhang, J. (1947). *Zhonghua minguo minzhu xianfa shijiang* [Ten lectures on the constitution of the Republic of China]. The Commercial Press.

Zhang, M. (2006). A mistaken reception of the parliamentary system—A re-examination of the 1912 legislation of the Provisional Constitution of the Republic of China. *Fazhi shi yanjiu [Legal History Research], 9*, 133–174.

Zhu, H. (Ed.). (1989). *Zhonghua minguo shishi jiyao (chugao)* [A summary of the history of the Republic of China (a preliminary draft)], January–March 1946. Academic Historica.

Zou, W. (1988). *Daiyi zhengzhi* [Representative government]. Pamir Press.

Chapter 9
Basic Rights and Social Rights in Modern China

9.1 Constitutional Basic Rights and Their Legal Restrictions

Typically, modern countries constitutionally affirm the existence and value of basic rights yet the exercise of these rights is not without restrictions. Since the twentieth century, constitutions around the world have commonly provided legal restrictions on basic rights, reflecting the intricate nature of rights and their interrelationship with socio-economic developments. An essential question in constitutional law arises. "How, under the influence of the constitution's supreme principles and binding force, can the 'realization' and 'restriction' of basic rights operate optimally within the legal system?" (Chen, 2002, p. 182) To achieve a balance between the two is one of the major issues in the study of constitutional law. Throughout the constitution-making history of China in the first half of the twentieth century, the issue of legal restrictions (also known as legal reservations) on basic rights by constitutional provisions aroused much controversy. This problem, impacted by Chinese tradition and contemporary global trend, posed complexities even beyond those faced in the West.

During the constitutional history of China spanning nearly half a century since the end of the Qing Dynasty, generally speaking, the conventional trend was to prioritize the structural organization of the government, often relegating basic rights of the people to secondary importance. Moreover, each constitutional draft typically incorporated legal restrictions upon these basic rights, implying that, in the constitutional history of China, citizens' fundamental rights were never deemed as "sacred and inviolable" absolute rights. The "Matthew Effect" also seemed to be confirmed on the issue of the constitutional basic rights, which were initially considered secondary in the constitution-making process by the ruling and opposition parties and subsequently curtailed upon their inclusion in the constitution. Post the warlord rule of the Beiyang Government, men of insight and foresight began emphasizing more on constitutional protections for people's rights. However, under the influence of Chinese tradition, the impact of Western "societal-oriented" theories, and the realistic limitation of the

X. Nie, *The History of Government and Public Law in China*,
https://doi.org/10.1007/978-981-97-6063-3_9

political climate, China failed to cultivate a philosophy of individual freedom and limited government ("limits of power"). It ended up almost unconditionally accepting a constitution endorsing the principle of "legal restrictions" on fundamental rights.

The key question is not about quarrel between legal restriction and constitutional protection, but about the fact that constitution framers either took legal restrictions on basic rights for granted, or used the global trend and Chinese socio-political reality as pretexts to suppress individual liberties with unbridled restrictions. The act of acknowledging basic rights and imposing "exceptions" and "necessities" on them deviates greatly in both theory and practice from "denying individual freedoms and rights" and constraining them "without any premise", "without contemplation" and "freely".

9.1.1 From the Late Qing Dynasty to the Beijing National Government Era

The 1908 *Outline of Imperial Constitution*'s attached "Rights and Obligations of Subjects" followed the doctrine of legal restriction, using such wording as "within the scope of the law, freedom is granted" or "unless in accordance with the law, it is prohibited", etc. Concerning subjects' property and residence, it merely prescribed, "no disturbance without cause", thus conferring upon the government a significant degree of authority, without any legal limits (legal reservations). The *Nineteen Significant Provisions of the Constitution* of 1911 did not provide for the people's rights. Article 6 of the *Provisional Constitution of the Republic of China* of 1912 enumerated seven basic rights of citizens, two of which were restricted by "except in accordance with the law, it is prohibited", though these two may be interpreted as offering special protection to people's physical existence and domiciles (residences). However, Article 15 of the *Provisional Constitution* ("The rights of citizens as provided in the present chapter shall be limited or modified out of necessity for the promotion of public welfare, for the maintenance of public order or on account of extraordinary exigency") gave general authorization to legislators and was a classic example of legal restriction. The 1913 "Tiantan Draft Constitution", acclaimed for its progressive nature, provided for a rather complete list of basic civil rights from Article 5 to Article 11, which enumerated the rights of bodily integrity, residential security, private correspondence, freedoms regarding domicile (migration) and profession, freedom of assembly and of association, freedom of speech, authorship and publication, and religious freedom. Each of these was accompanied by the phrase "unless in accordance with the law, ... shall not ..." Article 12 stipulated that "disposal" of property ownership "necessitated by public interest shall be done in accordance with the law". The second chapter of the *Third Year Constitution of the Republic of China* ("Yuan's Constitution") of 1914, titled "Citizens", teemed with phrasing like "except in accordance with the law, ... shall not ...", "within the scope of the law, ...shall ..." or "in accordance with the law, ... shall ...". The *Constitution of the Republic of China* of 1923 ("Cao Kun's Bribery Constitution") based on the "Tiantan Draft Constitution", reportedly influenced by the German *Weimar Constitution* to a certain extent, earned its place among "good constitutions". However, it continued to adopt the doctrine of legal restrictions concerning citizens' rights.

Reflecting on the constitution-making history from the late Qing Dynasty to the era of Beijing National Government of the ROC (Beiyang Government), it becomes apparent that almost all rights and obligations of the people were defined by a doctrine of legal restrictions. Putting aside the "constitutional monarchy" of the Qing Dynasty and *Provisional Constitution of the Republic of China* of the early ROC, does the "Tiantan Draft Constitution" known as "a model of democracy" stand out as a different case? During the drafting of the "Tiantan Draft Constitution", one of the major constitutional issues in the outline was "whether the people's rights and obligations should be enumerated" (Wu & Huang, 1937, p. 46), with no mention of the doctrine of constitutional guarantee or legal restriction. In the review of the draft, some drafters suggested deleting the legal restriction worded in individual articles. For instance, Qin Guangli proposed to remove the words of "... not violable unless in accordance with the law" regarding citizen's privacy of correspondence, and Liao Zongbei suggested altering the original "Property ownership of the people of the Republic of China is not to be violated. But its disposal necessitated by public benefit should be done according to law" simply into "Property ownership of the people of the Republic of China is not to be violated". However, these proposals were in the minority. In fact, provisions on civil rights phrased with legal reservation were adopted by an absolute majority in the second reading (Wu, 1923, pp. 167–171). Evidently, the constitution makers then did not pay much attention to the question of whether the basic rights of the people should be protected by constitutional guarantee or legal restriction. More accurately, they hardly questioned legal reservation at that time.

We may infer from the constitutional texts and background of that period that both the ruling and the public were generally unaware of the improperness of restricting citizen's basic rights by law. This obliviousness extended even to Zhang Junmai, who would later be dubbed "Father of the Constitution of the ROC". When drafting the constitution for the National Affairs Conference in 1922, Zhang implemented the doctrine of legal restriction in the chapter entitled "Rights and Duties of the People", filling it with phrases such as "shall not ... except in accordance with the law".

9.1.2 The Period of the Nanjing National Government

i. Legal restriction on people's basic rights during the KMT's Political Tutelage

After the establishment of the NNG, constitutional texts featured an unprecedented degree of legal restriction on the fundamental rights of the people due to the following three reasons. First, the ruling KMT was originally a political party that flaunted the ideology of "Three Principles of the People". Second, the concepts of liberalism and limited government ("power control") were absent from traditional Chinese culture. Third, traditional Chinese culture coincided with a broader shift in Western thinking, transitioning from an "individual-centered" to a "society-centered" perspective (Wu, 2004, p. 83–85). In the *Provisional Constitution for the Period of Political Tutelage of the Republic of China* of 1931, the basic law of the Nanjing National Government, all provisions on people's rights of freedom (Articles 9–17) in the second chapter titled "Rights and Duties of the People" were formulated as "... shall not be denied or restricted except in accordance with law" in line with the nature of basic rights, and those on social rights (Articles 21–24) were rendered as "shall have the right ... in accordance with the law"; in addition, in the fourth chapter of "People's Livelihood" and the fifth chapter of "Education of the Citizens" (28 articles in total), all articles concerning social rights ("People's Livelihood"), freedom to make contracts and choose professions (e.g. Articles 37, 38 and 45) all contained explicit legal reservation. The *MFDC* of 1936 essentially maintained the doctrine of legal reservation found in the *Provisional Constitution for the Period of Political Tutelage of the Republic of China.*

ii. Debate over the MFDC

The *Provisional Constitution for the Period of Political Tutelage of the Republic of China* was an utter product of the KMT's dictatorship (and also a constitutional document for its implementation of "political tutelage"). Under this system, dissenting voices were effectively silenced. The making of the MFDC took three years, during which the draft underwent multiple revisions. The main drafters, Wu Jingxiong and Zhang Zhiben, even published trial drafts under their personal names for public scrutiny, sparking an unprecedented social debate. As soon as the first draft of the MFDC was published, many personages questioned why the articles on civil rights and freedom still contained such statement as "... shall not be denied or restricted except in accordance with law." "If freedom granted by the constitution can be stripped away by ordinary laws, isn't constitutional protection tantamount to a farce?" (Wang, 1934, recited from Yin, 2003, p. 11) Among these critics, Zhang Youjiang specifically authored an essay criticizing the provisions about people's rights (Zhang, 1936). This piece began by clearly outlining its purpose and theme.

The primary function of a constitution is to define the people's rights, the powers, duties, and interrelations of the principal government organs ... Since the publication of Mr. Wu Jingxiong's initial draft constitution, many people have voiced their criticism on it, most of which, nonetheless, has revolved around the provisions about the authorities, functions and interconnections of the government's key organs, with scant attention paid to the specifications of people's rights. This is a very strange phenomenon. Learning from the past history, we can firmly assert that constitution originated from people's demand for codified recognition of their rights. The incorporation of the major government organs in the constitution is due to the direct impact their powers and functions have on the safeguarding of people's rights, highlighting the critical importance of these rights within the constitutional framework. Moreover, the rights of the Chinese people have been severely undermined. Not only have they not been adequately protected by law, but they have been trampled upon by warlords, politicians and imperialists. Against such a background, the Chinese nationals should pay more attention to how the draft constitution prescribed the people's rights.

Wu's draft, in striving for conciseness or due to some other insurmountable obstacles, enumerated the rights and duties of the people through such wording as "... shall not be denied or restricted except in accordance with the law", which is no different from asserting "... shall be denied or restricted in accordance with the law". This constitutes another major flaw in his draft. Under such kind of provisions, the people's rights as stipulated in the constitution are neither final nor supreme, but require further legal interpretation to become truly meaningful. Consequently, the entire constitutional text is made up of merely empty words, which not only undermines the constitution's dignity, but also lead to numerous malpractices. Yuan Shih-k'ai once took advantage of the ineffective articles regarding civil rights in the *Provisional Constitution*, issuing two decrees to suppress freedom of speech. The first was the *Newspaper Regulation* enacted on April 2, 1945, followed by the *Publication Act* of December 4, 1945 and the *Public Security and Police Act* of 1945, which restrained liberty of assembly. This serves as a historical lesson. Article 18 of the draft asserts that "Laws placing restrictions on people's freedoms and rights delineated in the preceding articles of the present chapter shall not been enacted except by such as may be necessary to maintain public welfare or avert an imminent crisis. Nor shall they be enacted if the restriction goes beyond a reasonable extent." Although this article sets a degree of limitation for future supplementary laws (or standalone laws), expressions like "public welfare" and "to avert an imminent crisis" are so "broad and indefinite" that "in reality, there is no limitation at all". Article 15 of the (*Provisional*) *Constitution*, misinterpreted by Yuan shih-k'ai, still contains such abstract terms as "to advance public welfare", "to maintain public order" or "whenever it is very exigent and indispensable".

Therefore, in my view, while drafting provisions pertaining to the rights of the citizenry, it is more advantageous to avoid the verbiage of "in accordance with the law" or "except in accordance with the law", opting instead for an approach of absolute protection. This robust form of protections means that constitutional provisions concerning civil rights should be regarded as final or supreme, curbing any undue interference from both the executive power and the legislative power. For example, per Amendment I of the Constitution of the United States, "Congress shall make no law respecting an establishment of religion, or prohibiting the free exercise thereof". If applying such absolute protection proves challenging in practice, the provisions should, at least, demarcate a clear scope of the right or freedom, to elucidate the specific grounds (comparatively speaking) for interference, to outline the methods of interference, and to specify measures for redress in the event of an infringement (such as compensation).

Zhang Youjiang then critically commented on, in great detail, the draft constitution's provisions concerning people's rights, offering relevant suggestions for revision. The author's extensive reference to Zhang's work aims at elucidating the following points. Firstly, enlightened individuals at that time had already recognized the inherent bias making process that unduly prioritized governmental structure over safeguarding citizens' rights—a bias, unfortunately, that was still prevalent. Secondly, the newfound emphasis on the constitutional protection of citizens' basic rights emerged from the long-standing abuse suffered by the populace who had been "trampled upon by warlords, politicians and imperialism" to the fullest extent since the founding of the ROC. Thirdly, Yuan Shih-k'ai leveraged constitutional clauses—those legally limiting citizens' basic rights—to promulgate deleterious laws that infringed upon these rights, thereby instigating vigilance against the potential peril of legal reservation. Fourthly, people back then possessed a remarkably lucid understanding of absolute protection (constitutional protection) and relative protection (legal restriction) in terms of nomology through comparative analysis of foreign constitutional systems.

In response to these critical voices, Sun Ke, the dual-officeholder of President of the Legislative Yuan and Chairman of the Constitution Drafting Committee of the Legislative Yuan, remarked as follows:

First, "the common practice of the rule of law does not confer upon the people absolute freedom". (Sun, 1936, p. 1089)

Secondly, unlike the previous warlord rule, upon the promulgation of the constitution, all legislative decisions will be made by representative organs, so there is no need to worry about the protection of people's rights. (Sun, 1936, p. 1089)

Thirdly, the rights of individuals should not supersede collective national interests and the welfare of the state as a whole, especially during times of crisis and adversity.

The constitution should not only safeguard the rights of individuals, but also, or more importantly, protect the interests of the whole in order to guarantee the rights of the majority, particularly emphasizing the collective interests of the nation nowadays. If individual freedoms are allowed to proliferate unchecked, I am afraid, it will impede national freedom and even jeopardize the liberty of the entire populace. It is impractical to sacrifice the country and the nation for the individual. Furthermore, the current urgency lies in charting a path forward for the nation, not in concentrating solely on personal interests—a task that reality does not permit us to undertake. Even if possible, it cannot be universally applied. In instances where a conflict emerges between personal liberties and the state, the prudent course of action would be to relinquish personal freedoms and fiercely safeguard national liberty. In conformity to this principle, the draft constitution therefore only granted the people "freedom of residence", "freedom of speech" and "freedom of assembly and association". However, it also contains a provision stating that "... shall not be restricted except in accordance with law", which means the same the other way round, that is, the state can restrict the people's freedom in accordance with law. (Sun, 1936, p. 1122)

Wu Jingxiong responded to the criticism as follows.

First, he rejected the concept of "natural rights", contending that the origin of rights and duties lies within the contours of prevailing societal and historical currents. As such, rights and duties must operate within the scope defined and permitted by these societal and historical forces, (quoting Sun Yat-sen, "Civil rights are not naturally occurring, but borne out of social and historical trends.") (Wu, 1936, p. 1133–1136)

Secondly, only restricted by law can freedom and rights be honed into a societal benefit. (Wu drew an analogy: freedom and right can be likened to a piece of raw jade; the law, to a jade carver; the constitution, to the jade's owner. The owner merely instructs the carver on the fundamental principles of shaping the jade.) (Wu, 1936, p. 1139)

Thirdly, "our current constitutional movement is an endeavor to marshal the collective strength of the country towards its salvation... We are championing freedom, but our starting point is from a communal perspective. The freedom we are striving for pertains to the country and the nation... If our aim is to rescue the nation, then it becomes imperative to call upon the individual to sacrifice their personal freedoms in pursuit of collective liberty." (Wu, 2012, p. 122)

Both Sun Ke and Wu Jingxiong denied the doctrine of "natural rights" and absolute protection of human rights (i.e., constitutional protectionism). It may have a bearing on the Chinese tradition which has often been seen as lacking an inherent concept of individual rights. Western socio-centric legal philosophies and legislative trends have, in turn, appeared to dovetail with this particular cultural orientation.

The MFDC was initiated in the wake of the "January 28th Incident" amidst the imminent threat posed by the advancing Japanese invaders. The formulation of the MFDC, referred to by the KMT as the "end of political tutelage and implementation of constitutional government", was a reaction to the national strategy of "amassing national strength, resisting foreign aggression and saving the nation from peril" "in the face of national crisis" (Xie, 2000, p. 251). The legal constraints on the fundamental rights of the citizenry as outlined in the MFDC epitomize the ethos of "National salvation taking precedence over enlightenment".

The criticism of the MFDC, though vehement, did not alter the content of the constitution since there was no force to compete with the KMT.[1] The leading drafters' responses to these critiques seemingly held reason and, as such, the constitution

[1] Zhang Zhiben and Wu Jingxiong, the two main drafters and vice chairmen of the "Constitution Drafting Committee of the Legislative Yuan", both published trial drafts. Wu's manuscript applied a sheer legal restriction to the protection of people's basic rights. Zhang's draft, by contrast, modified legal restriction by concretizing the restrictions, which helped restrain the power of the government and secure the rights of the people. For example, Article 20 stipulated, "All persons shall have the liberty of speech, writing, and publication: such liberty shall not be denied or restricted except in accordance with criminal law." For another example, Article 23 read, "All persons shall have the freedom of assembly and formation of associations without prior notification to the authorities. However, an assembly to bear arms or an association to disturb public order for the purpose of committing a crime may be prohibited or dissolved." However, Zhang resigned from his post as Vice-Chairman of the Constitutional Drafting Committee on August 18, 1933 following the completion of his trial draft. In contrast, Wu remained involved and, with the support of Sun Ke, assumed a significant leadership role throughout the entire process of drafting the MFDC. Wu even actively participated in the formulation of the *Constitution of the Republic of China* in 1946 (as an expert on behalf of the National Government). Zhang's resignation and the establishment of Wu's leading position are probably not accidental in history.

makers proceeded in an unswerving manner.[2] As a result, the final draft passed by the Legislative Yuan still subjected the people's rights to various legal restrictions. However, these criticisms and ensuing discussions did lay a theoretical and popular foundation for future amendments to the constitution. It was only in 1946, when the Political Consultative Conference revised the MFDC, that a shift occurred. At this point, the Chinese Communist Party (CPC) had gained sufficient strength to challenge the KMT, allowing the so-called "third forces", represented by intellectuals and democratic figures in society, to leverage their influence (Liu, 2005). Eventually, the legal restrictions attached to the provisions concerning the basic rights of the people were removed. This revision was generally incorporated into the subsequently enacted Constitution of the Republic of China.

iii. From the PCC's adjustment of legal restrictions to provisions of the 1946 *Constitution of the Republic of China*

On January 31, 1946, the PCC approved the twelve principles for amending the draft constitution. Among them, the ninth principle pertaining to "Rights and Duties of the People" read "People shall enjoy all the rights and freedom inherent in a democratic state. Laws should be formulated with the intention to protect, not restrict". After the adoption of the twelve principles, the PCC resolved to organize a committee to review the draft constitution. This led to the formulation of "Amendment to the MFDC" (known as the PCC Constitutional Amendment), with Zhang Junmai as the principal drafter.[3] The *Constitution of the Republic of China*, passed by the National Assembly in 1946, did not introduce substantial modifications to the "Amendment to the MFDC" as conceived by the PCC.

Compared to its predecessors, the 1946 *Constitution* took a more proactive approach towards the protection of basic human rights by eliminating article by article phrases such as "shall not be restricted except in accordance with law" and similar expressions. This was aimed at preventing potential governmental abuses of legislative power to deprive the people of their rights, marking a clear departure from previous constitutional texts. However, Article 23 of the *Constitution* provided, "The enumerated freedoms and rights shall not be restricted by law except by such as may be necessary to prevent infringement upon the freedoms of other persons, to avert an imminent crisis, to maintain social order or to advance public welfare". This exception clause effectively left a loophole for legal restrictions on people's fundamental rights. In fact, there were two differing views on the specific wording of this article (Article 24 of Amendment to the MFDC). Zhang Junmai, a principal drafter and the leader of the Democratic Socialist Party, proposed a version identical to the finally enacted version. Meanwhile, one of the Amendment compilers,[4] Wu

[2] The issue of legal restrictions on the basic rights of the people, in the drafting process of the constitution (including the review meeting and the discussion of the first draft by the main draftsmen of the Constitution Drafting Committee, and the deliberation on the draft by the Legislative Yuan), was either neglected or completely ignored.

[3] For more details about Zhang's constitutional thought, see Zhang (1947, pp. 70–71).

[4] Another compiler was Wang Chonghui.

Jingxiong suggested: "The law shall be aimed at safeguarding the people's rights and freedoms; all articles concerning the people's freedoms and rights shall not be restricted by law except by such as may be necessary to ensure national security, to avert an imminent crisis, to maintain social order or to advance public welfare." This was the only article in the amendment draft where both viewpoints were preserved for further consideration. The critical divergence between these two perspectives lied in Wu's inclusion of "ensuring national security" as a precondition for curtailing freedoms and rights, which carries considerable political implications. The 1946 *Constitution* adopted Zhang's view. However, this does not mean that the 1946 *Constitution* endorsed constitutional protection over legal restriction, as it incorporated the wording of legal restrictions on civil rights from the MFDC into its Article 23. "Thus, despite its ostensible espousal of direct protection, in practice, there was little distinction between the two approaches—both adhered to the principle of legal reservation. It's not surprising that Professor Sa Mengwu criticized it as 'It is just like there is no difference between morning star and evening star?'" (between "playing fast and loose" and "playing loose and fast") (Wu, 2004, p. 84) A more moderate and eclectic evaluation was made by Xiao Gongquan, who argued the 1946 *Constitution*'s provisions on human rights struck a balance between "between the MFDC and the PCC principles" (Xiao, 1982, p. 158).

In reality, the method of safeguarding the basic rights of citizens did not provoke severe contention in the course of constitution making. The KMT was more concerned with and stubbornly defended issues such as whether the National Assembly should be corporeal or incorporeal, the choice between a presidential or parliamentary system, provincial constitutions, and even the purely ideological question of whether constitutionalizing the Three Principles of the People.[5] The author ventures to speculate that if Zhang Junmai or other influential figures had staunchly advocated for the constitutional protection of basic human rights, such a principle could have feasibly been included in the constitution. However, it seems that they may not have intended to pursue this course of action.[6] The KMT opposed the

[5] For more details about the KMT's stance, see Jing (1984, pp. 443–444).

[6] As mentioned above, when drafting the constitution for the State Affairs Conference in 1922, Zhang Junmai also employed legal restrictionism in the chapter "Rights and Duties of the People", characterized by such wording as "shall not … unless in accordance with law. In his essay "The Background of Modern Constitutionalism" published in *Oriental Magazine* in January 1944, he also indiscriminately adopted legal restrictions on personal freedom, speech, publication, and assembly and association in the MFDC, voicing no objections (Zhang, 2006, pp. 392–393). His monograph of "Ten Lectures on the Constitution of the Republic of China", completed in August 1946 (on the eve of the passage of the *Constitution of the Republic of China*) and published in 1947 (after the publication of the *Constitution of the Republic of China*), was claimed by himself to distill the "essence" of the 1946 *Constitution*. In the lecture titled "Human Rights as the Fundamental of Constitutionalism", he cited a number of constitutional provisions containing legal restrictions from various countries. These were compared with similar provisions in the MFDC, with no discernible critique of the principle of legal restrictionism. He even added, "Regarding the people's rights, one can refer to the chapter on the rights of the people in the MFDC to gain clarity." (Zhang, 1947, pp. 32–38) It is plausible that due to the constraints of his time, Zhang did not emphasize the distinction between direct or indirect protection of the basic rights of the people in the Constitution.

amendment to the MFDC by the PCC both politically and ideologically. Nevertheless, Chiang Kai-shek had to accept Zhang's amendments in order to gain the support of the Democratic Socialist Party and the Youth Party for the National Assembly, to pass the constitution and establish a form of legitimate governance.[7] Shortly after the enactment of the constitution, the National Government passed the *Temporary Measures for the Maintenance of Social Order*, *Mobilization Order during the Period of Rebellion*, *Regulations on the Organization of Special Criminal Courts*, *Regulations on the Trial of Special Criminal Courts*, and *Implementation Outline of Mobilization during the Period of Rebellion*, etc. The National Assembly also formulated the *Temporary Provisions Effective During the Period of Rebellion* attached to the *Constitution.* These "temporary" acts expanded the government's powers, especially those of the president, and limited the people's rights and freedoms.

9.1.3 Summary

Examining the evolution of basic rights provisions in different constitutional texts in modern Chinese history reveals an increasingly nuanced understanding of the issue of legal restrictions on these constitutional basic rights: from a popular cognition of taking legal restriction as it ought to be during the period of the Beiyang Government, to different voices (albeit unheeded by the constitution-makers) in the making of the MFDC, to the constitution-making principles (i.e., "Twelve Principles of the PCC") during the formulation of the 1946 *Constitution* which articulated that "The law shall protect rather than restrict" people's freedom and right, and ultimately to the finalized provisions in the *Constitution* which imposed certain restrictions on legal restrictions. However, neither the Beiyang Government nor the NNG embraced the concept of individual freedoms and a limited government ("power control"), rendering it impossible for them to genuinely respect the fundamental rights and freedoms of the people during the constitution-making process. Further compounding this, the absence of constitutional practice at the time, including the practical application of the constitution and the exercise of power to interpret it, along with a lack of in-depth academic discourse, left the constitutional provisions regarding fundamental rights as nothing more than nominal declarations. Nevertheless, the deepening consciousness of rights since the Xinhai Revolution and the progressive evolution of the constitutional texts should not be undervalued. The enhanced awareness of rights reflects a collective learning from historical lessons, while the advancements in the constitutional text represent the fruits of political struggle. These historical lessons should not be forgotten, and the accomplishments should not be dismissed.

It is also worth noting that although Zhang was well-versed in Western constitutional theory, he was not a bona fide legal expert.

[7] Zhang served as the leader of the Democratic Socialist Party, on the premise of whose attendance the Youth Party attended the National Assembly.

9.2 Balancing Severity with Leniency: Social Rights in the Constitution of Modern China

Constitutional provisions on human rights have always faced a twofold conundrum. On one hand, the rigid constitutional code, being superior to ordinary statutes, affords more robust protections for people's rights; on the other hand, as mentioned in the preceding section, these constitutionally safeguarded rights are inevitably restricted by the legislative, executive, and judicial powers of the state. The realization of positive constitutional social rights is often even more compromised than the fulfillment of negative liberties. The constitution-making history of modern China offers us a unique perspective on whether the framers could incorporate the relatively "flexible" social rights provisions into a "rigid" constitutional code, thereby blending the ideal of social justice with the reality of the rule of law.

9.2.1 The Principle of People's Livelihood and Ideal of Great Harmony

The early endeavors in modern China to include social welfare rights into constitution can be traced back to the 1922 *Draft Constitution of the State Affairs Conference.* Both "Draft A" by Zhang Junmai and "Draft B" by Zhang Taiyan, in spite of their divergent political architectures, provided for a separate chapter on "Education and Livelihood of the People", stipulating the dedication of special funds to promote educational and cultural development, redistributing social wealth through taxation, and limiting land ownership to secure the livelihood of ordinary people (Xia & Hu, 2004, pp. 749–769). The detailed enumeration of social rights in the constitution seemed to have been influenced by contemporary European intellectual currents and the *Weimar Constitution* promulgated in 1919. At the time of the promulgation of the German constitution, Zhang Junmai was studying in Germany and after reading the constitutional text, quickly translated it into Chinese and published it in China in April 1920. He clearly pointed out that the *Weimar Constitution* stood for the latest constitutional paradigm of the twentieth century contrasting with the eighteenth century *Constitution of the United States* and the nineteenth century *Constitution of the First French Republic*, reflecting the zeitgeist of the social revolution of that ear (Zhang, 2006, p. 254).

In the aftermath of the First World War, Chinese scholars, represented by Liang Qichao and Zhang Junmai, reevaluated the individualistic philosophy of Anglo-American tradition. They started to combine European philosophy with traditional Chinese Confucianism (the "New Confucianism of the Song Dynasty"), accentuating the value of human beings and the priority of people's happiness through reappraisal of the Western materialism. This perspective was mirrored in their advocacy of constitutional social rights initiated by the *Weimar Constitution* (Xue, 1993, pp. 38–39). Serving as an advisor to the Chinese delegation to the Paris Peace Conference appointed by the BNG, Liang accomplished his book *The Records of Travels in Europe* after his European sojourn. This book devoted a whole chapter to introducing the League of Nations and the International Labor Pact in the *Versailles Contract*, and criticized that the Chinese people at that time were "not yet enlightened" on the subject of social rights, thereby showing Liang's keen interest in the issues of labor protection and social security prevalent in Europe at that time (Guo, 2011, pp. 670–671). Zhang, who accompanied Liang on his trip to Europe, further extrapolated Liang's conceptualization of social rights into the domain of constitutional theory. In his memorandum "National Constitutional Proposal" for the "Draft Constitution of State Affairs Conference", Zhang integrated the traditional Chinese ideal of Great Harmony with the modern Western ideological trend of socialism, zealously preaching the constitutional provisions of socialism. He wrote:

> I venture to inform my compatriots. The discourse on Great Harmony in *The Conveyance of Rites* and the saying of "worrying over unequal distribution of wealth instead of poverty" in the *Analects of Confucius* embody the quintessence of our civilization and serve as the bedrock of nation-building. In Europe and the U. S., people and states own private property, which inevitably leads to class struggle at home and world wars with foreign countries. That's not the path we should follow"; "The so-called individualism or liberalism... the guiding ethos of Western culture in the past century, eventually precipitated the European wars. This is the inevitable outcome of a society built on industry and commerce"; "The development of industry and commerce is a natural trend. Yet, this development must harmonize with social ethics"; "The organization of a nation's livelihood must fundamentally depend on justice"; "The chapter on Livelihood in this constitution generally uses the German constitution as a blueprint. The original version contained an article concerning large industries owned by the state, provinces and localities, but it was abolished because of unanimous opposition from all the conferees. (Zhang, 2006, pp. 85–92)

Indeed, long before the Xinhai Revolution and the First World War, Sun Yat-sen had placed "equalization of land rights" and "restriction of private capital" at the core of people's livelihood, which, together with nationalism and democracy, constituted his ideology of the Three Principles of the People. The so-called "equalization of land rights and restriction of private capital" were not only connected to the Western theories propounded by social theorists such as Henry George,[8] but also resonated deeply with tradition Chinese thought. In terms of "equal land distribution" and "land to the tiller", the public field system was perceived as the supreme ideal of Confucianism, and the "equal-field system" was implemented for hundreds of years spanning from the Northern Wei Dynasty to the Tang Dynasty. Although the traditional Chinese industry and commerce were not well developed, the conception of restraining private capital had already been in place since ancient times, as illustrated by the historical example of the salt monopoly system. Tracing back to the Western Han Dynasty, in *Discussions on Salt and Iron*, Sang Hongyang, the then Censor-in-Chief, put forward the idea of and reason for capital regulation. Producing salt required colossal capital, and those large-capital-owners tended to hoard and

[8] It is said that Sun Yat-sen's idea of "Value Increment Belonging to the Public" originated from Henry George's *Progress and Poverty*, among other works (Tang, 2015, pp. 378–379).

corner for speculation, and manipulate market prices, inevitably leading to a significant wealth disparity; on the contrary, nationalizing salt industry can dramatically increase state revenue without further burdening the people. This strategy would also undermine the power of the wealthy and aggressive class, fostering social equality and stability (Ou, 1935, pp. 14–21). In practice, the central fiscal revenue accrued from the state-owned salt industry could be used not only for military and national construction, but also for resettling displaced people, supporting people's livelihood, and achieving social welfare objectives.[9]

It is commonly believed that Sun Yat-sen's espousal of nationalism (embodied in his call to "to expel the Tartars and restore China") struck at the heart of acute national contradiction in the late Qing Dynasty and therefore had a strong appeal[10]; however, in terms of the sociopolitical base of the KMT, Sun's idea on the people's livelihood was perceived as overambitious, radical and unrealistic. Yet, after the establishment of the NNG in 1927, the authorities still upheld the Three Principles of the People as their guiding ideology including the people's livelihood. The constitution and laws promulgated also embraced many elements reflective of the people's welfare, such as the *Land Act* of 1930 and the chapter on "Fundamental State Policies" in the *Constitution of the Republic of China* of 1946. Redistributing land property asserted in the *Land Act* shows that the legislators were earnest in their pursuit of equal land rights. Even though this legislative revolution on paper did not fully materialize into a substantive social revolution, it cannot wholly negate the National Government's initial intention to actualize the principle of people's livelihood. In fact, the *Weimar Constitution*, often considered a model constitution for social revolutions, outlined social rights that were not legally enforceable and ended up as empty rhetoric; however, the ideals and principles of "social state" were later embraced and carried out by the Basic Law of the Federal Republic of Germany post the Second World War. The lyrics of the ROC national anthem was literally interpreted as "The Three Principles of the People, the foundation of our Party; Using this, we establish the Republic; Using this, we advance into a state of total peace" (San Min Chu-in, Our aim shall be: To found a free land, World peace, be our stand). This indicates that after the establishment of the ROC, the social revolution to promote the people's livelihood and achieve the great harmony should be envisioned as progressive endeavors.

---

9 According to historical records, the government of the Three Kingdoms Period ever "used its direct profits to purchase plows and oxen, which were then distributed to the populace, and promoted agricultural activities and grain storage, aiming to foster prosperity in the Guanzhong region" (Du, 1988, pp. 229–230).

10 In that period, the slogan of "Revolution to expel the Manchus" "almost became an unquestionable religion". (Hou, 2011, p. 128)

9.2.2 Constitutionalizing Social Rights and People's Livelihood in Modern China: Controversies and Debates

As the civil society organization was preparing the *Draft Constitution of the State Affairs Conference*, concurrently, the Parliament, the legal constitution-making body of the BNG, reconvened in August 1922 to contemplate incorporating provisions or even a dedicated chapter on social rights into the constitution. The rationale behind this consideration was derived from three primary sources: the age-old Chinese tradition emphasizing the importance of people's livelihood and equality; the recent experiences gained from the Weimar Constitution of Germany; and the harsh socio-economic realities faced by the Republic of China. "The provisions of this chapter are mostly adapted from those of the new German constitution on economic life. Thus, it would not be incorrect to say that this section draws extensively from the German constitution"; "However, the livelihood of the people has always been central to our nation's longstanding political ideologies. As Confucius has said, 'The heads of states or noble families worry not over poverty but over unequal distribution of wealth; they fret not over underpopulation, but over insecurity. Now, if there is equality in distribution there will be no poverty; if there is harmony in society there will be no underpopulation, and if there is security, there will be no subversion'.[11] This shares the same ideal with modern socialism"; "Although the constitutional law provides for the citizens' rights to freedom and equality, there are local cases where lands have been passed from one owner to another several times while the tenants themselves and their descendants remain tenants, a situation analogous to serfdom … The Chinese people today endure severe socio-economic pressures, and their living conditions can be described as far worse than anything experienced in Europe or America." (Wu, 2013, pp. 1021, 1074) Interestingly, even though the BNG in the inchoate ROC did not adopt the Three Principles of the People as its guiding ideology, some members of the Constitution Drafting Committee still suggested that the chapter on social rights be named "People's Livelihood". "The chapter is titled 'People's Livelihood' for its comprehensive and lucid connotation. While some have suggested the heading of 'Financial Planning' or 'National Means of Life', neither can capture the broad connotations of livelihood. The term 'Economic System' seems more appropriate, but the Chinese characters "经济" for 'economy' are derived from Japanese, which deviates considerably from the original meaning of "经济" in Chinese. Moreover, the term 'livelihood' does not only cover food and clothing, but also occupation and freedom. Therefore, Chapter Two of the German constitution, which deals with freedom of marriage, assembly, association, and voting, is entitled 'Community Life'. Modelled after the German constitution, the third chapter of our constitution is captioned as 'Means' of Life, which is also not encompassed by the word "经济", as it underscores not only on economic aspects but also on the freedom and support for

[11] Translations are A. Charles Muller's. http://www.acmuller.net/con-dao/analects.html(Notes by translators).

those unemployed and incapacitated… Therefore, the committee chair still decides on the term 'People's Livelihood' after weighing these considerations" (Wu, 2013, pp. 1076–1077).

Wu Zongci, one of the incumbent constitution-makers then, considered the two chapters on livelihood and education extremely important and even more significant than the issue of the separation of powers between central and local governments. "The entire constitution rests upon the local system, with its overall spirit embodied in the twin chapters on livelihood and education." (Wu, 2013, p. 1019) However, despite the fact that quite a few constitutional drafters vigorously advocated for a dedicated chapter on social rights and proposed various versions of text, these provisions were ultimately absent from the *Constitution of the Republic of China* passed in 1923. Some scholars explained that the representatives, under increasing pressure from Cao Kun's scandal of election bribery, were so eager to pass the constitution to "conceal the disgrace" that they had no time deliberating on the chapters on education and livelihood (Wang & Qian, 1933, p. 388). However, if one simply concludes that "The chapter on social rights of the constitution was discarded due to 'no time for deliberation'", doesn't it mean that the social rights clauses were not indispensable in the view of the majority of the constitutional delegates? In contrast, the chapter on local governance (i.e., the relationship between central and local governments), the most disputable issue that had caused a big fight in the legislature, was ultimately negotiated and written into the constitution. Why were the chapters on livelihood and education, perceived as more consequential by Wu, sacrificed? Does it mean that the framers still held divergent views over the inclusion of social rights in the constitution and could not possibly split their differences in a short term so that they shelved it up? Considering that the legitimacy of incorporating social rights into constitutions continues to provoke worldwide debate to this day, this query is far from being an academic conjecture. As a matter of fact, some framers then did raise objections for the sake of, firstly, economic considerations, arguing that capitalism was underdeveloped in modern China and "restraining private capital" would hinder the survival and development of industry and commerce, and secondly, the concern for the protection of fundamental rights, claiming that the government's proactive implementation of constitutional social rights would inevitably infringe upon the people's negative freedoms. "Our country's industry is not well-developed, necessitating the promotion of capital, not its suppression"; "There are no instances of capitalist oppression of labor in our nation, so addressing livelihood issues in the constitution would amount to 'moaning and groaning about imaginary illnesses"; "The so-called public interest is undefined and all-encompassing. If this is the basis for legislation, the promulgation of the constitution could potentially undermine the people's land ownership rights. The dangers of such a situation cannot be overstated." (Du, 2014, pp. 131, 136)

In the making of the *Draft Constitution of the Republic of China* in the 1930s, under the background of the KMT's one-party control adhering to the "Teachings by the Founding Father", constitutional social rights were consistently delineated as a distinct section across various iterations from initial to final draft. In the texts drafted by Wu Jingxiong and Zhang Zhiben, this part was flatly captioned as "People's

Livelihood", specifically comprising two sections: national livelihood and national education; in the final draft of the MFDC, it was divided into "National Economy" and "Education", taking up 23 out of a total of 148 articles. Evidently, this portion was far from negligible. The draft constitution covered a wide range of social domains such as land reform, state-operated economy, labor security, special protections for women and children, social relief, free and compulsory education, and the safeguard of a preordained percentage for educational budget allocation (Xia & Hu, 2004, pp. 990–991). In response to China's underdeveloped capitalism and the over-progressive concept of Sun Yatsen's "restricting private capital", Wu Jingxiong, the then vice chairman of the Constitution Drafting Committee, refuted that "China is backward in industry. At the outset of revolutionary transformation, instead of pursing a capitalist trajectory and provoking potential tragedies caused by class struggle, it would be better to be prudent at the very beginning and avoid an unnecessary path." That explained why Sun "supported the principle of people's livelihood and the restraint of capital in order to prevent private capital from becoming too developed and thus controlling people's livelihood. Meanwhile, the equalization of land rights was supposed to forestall large-scale private landownership. This stance is akin to the *Weimar Constitution*'s declaration that "organization of economic life should conform to the principles of justice, with the goal of achieving a dignified life for all and securing the economic freedom of individuals". What the MFDC safeguarded is "the equalization and adequacy of people's livelihood" (Article 116), that is, "a fair and adequate life for the general population" (Wu, 2005, pp. 133–135).

When proclaiming the MFDC, the Legislative Yuan particularly underlined the importance of the principle of people's livelihood. "In the inaugural year of the ROC in 1912, the Founding Father Sun Yat-sen gave speeches around the country with a distinct focus on the principle of people's livelihood. At that time, some short-sighted people claimed that it sufficed to overthrow the Qing Dynasty, establish a parliament and a responsible cabinet, rendering the Principle of People's Livelihood redundant. However, Sun excoriated this argument and said: 'Without fighting for the people's livelihood, I would quit from the revolution'. It is evident how determined he was to carry out the principle of people's livelihood. The constitution our country needs now is a constitution of the Three Principles of the People, and so a constitution involving national economy falls into place naturally. Any assertions that the national economy does not form an essential functionality of the constitution and thus need not be provided for are fundamentally misconstrued ... The implementation of the Principle of People's Livelihood aims at equitable land distribution and capital restriction so as to bring the nationals' productivity into full play, and gradually to reform the economic structure to avert future social revolutions. Therefore, an economic system grounded on the principle of people's livelihood seeks to curtail private capital and develop state capital in order to realize popular ownership. The manifesto of the United League states: '[We aim] To establish equality of citizens to enjoy the happiness and prosperity of a civilization with equal property rights ... All must be allowed to live in plenty and that none within the four seas are unable to obtain what is needed.' That is the true meaning of the livelihood of the people." (Propaganda Committee of the Draft Constitution of the Legislative Yuan, 1940, pp. 97–98).

9.2.3 *Fundamental National Policy: A Reconciliation Between Rigid Constitutional Mandates and Flexible Rights*

Now, "the boot is on the other foot." Apart from Sun Yat-sen who proposed the principle of people's livelihood, Zhang Junmai was a pioneer in advocating for constitutional social rights, drawing on Chinese Confucian traditions and the experiences of the German Weimar Republic. However, he renounced the primacy of social rights when engaged in the drafting of the "PCC Draft Constitution" in 1946, largely due to the *status quo* of human rights at that time (Xue, 1993, pp. 99–101). Ultimately, the upholding of constitutional social rights necessitated some compromises on basic rights (freedoms), and intellectuals of the time arrived at a common understanding of safeguarding citizen's liberties and limiting the government's infringement upon these basic rights through constitutional means (Nie, 2007). Notwithstanding this consensus, Article 23 of the *Constitution* still provided that "advancing public welfare" shall be one of the legal grounds for restricting people's freedoms and rights. In addition, in Section 3 "National Economy", Section 4 "Social Security", Section 5 "Education and Culture", and Section 6 "Frontier Regions" of the chapter on "Fundamental National Policy", there were 28 articles in total related to constitutional social rights. Originally, Zhang Junmai's "PCC Draft Constitution" simplified the chapter on "National Economy" of the MFDC to a great extent, merging it "National Defense and Foreign Policy" into a single chapter titled "Fundamental National Policy", thereby diluting the distinct emphasis on the national economy within the constitution; however, during the National Assembly's deliberation of the "PCC Draft Constitution", due to the majority of the assembly delegates being from the Kuomintang (KMT), who staunchly upheld Sun's principle of people' livelihood, the final constitution text reverted from a "relative value neutrality" on social rights issues back to the "value-rich" stance embodied by the MFDC (The Secretariat of the (Constitutional) National Assembly, 1946, pp. 448—450, 91—497). Section 3 "Economic Life" of Chap. 13 "Fundamental National Policy" clearly stated that "the basic rationale of the state's economic development relies on the principle of people's livelihood. This implies that the state is duty-bound to intervene in ensuring equitable land ownership and restraining private capital, thereby guaranteeing a plenty and fair distribution of means of life; Section 4 on "Social Security" then directly introduces advanced social welfare systems in European industrial democracies after the Second World War, such as Germany and Sweden's full employment and social insurance policies, Britain and Sweden's national health services, family policies in France, Belgium, and Austria, as well as the worker protection policies established in these aforementioned nations since the advent of the Industrial Revolution." (Su, 2006, p. 280)

In general, the paramount controversy during the constitution-making in 1946 centered on the issue of governmental structure, while issues related to the legal limitations on constitutional freedoms also elicited considerable attention. However, the revisions and adoption of constitutional social rights provisions unfolded relatively uneventfully, possibly linked to the ambivalent attitudes of constitution makers, such as Zhang Junmai, towards the inclusion of social rights in the constitution. It should be particularly noted that unlike the *Weimar Constitution*, which put social rights into the section "Basic Rights and Duties of the Germans", the modern Chinese constitution, be it the *State Affairs Conference Draft Constitution*, or the MFDC, or the *Constitution of the Republic of China* of 1946, all placed social rights in a separate chapter instead of the chapter on "Rights and Duties of the People", To this connection, scholars usually distinguish these social rights provisions (called "national means of life", "people's livelihood", or "basic state policies") from the constitutional provisions on people's basic rights (freedoms). From a semantic interpretation, social rights are not "fundamental" rights. Economically (according to a purposive interpretation), social rights are deemed costly rights; systemically (regarding textual arrangement), the chapter on "Rights and Duties of the People" of the 1946 *Constitution* is placed immediately after the first chapter "General Provisions", and prior to the chapters on governmental organizations. Conversely, "Fundamental National Policy", numerated as Chap. 13, is the penultimate chapter, preceding only the final chapter "Enforcement and Amendment of the Constitution". Does this allude to the awkward constitutional status and practical effect of "Fundamental National Policy"? As per prevailing academic discourse, the 1946 Constitution's inclusion of social rights within the "Fundamental National Policy" chapter aimed to provide a blueprint for the government's "basic policy". "This chapter, named as Fundamental National Policy, only articulates the legislative and executive objectives, devoid of enforceable nature. If, under certain conditions, the objectives cannot be achieved temporarily, it cannot be called unconstitutional." Although social rights provided in the constitution are only "declarative clauses" and cannot be fully enforced, it does not mean that these provisions are hypocritical or meaningless additions. The inclusion of social rights in the constitution can be viewed as "a reflection of welfare state demands and a demonstration of modern rule-of-law principles, which is of uttermost significance. The constitution itself, by incorporating this section, takes on an entirely new spirit and appearance, radically different from the past when its exclusive task was passive protection of individual rights and prevention of governmental tyranny. It now bears a proactive mandate to foster societal progress and development and to urge the government to work tirelessly towards improving citizen welfare". (Lin, 1993, pp. 245–248)

Compared with the *Weimar Constitution*, modern China has exhibited a unique acumen in the systematic arrangement of social rights within its constitution. This approach distinguishes social rights from freedoms both semantically and structurally, thereby circumventing the uncomfortable reality of incomplete implementation due to financial constraints, whilst preserving the constitution's dignity and authority. Meanwhile, it incorporates the ideological projection of social rights within the constitution, vesting the government with the political (rather than legal) responsibility to uphold social rights. This approach effectively integrates the lofty ideal of "the Great Harmony" into social reality. In tandem with the passage of the *Constitution of the Republic of China* in 1946, a number of countries endeavored to integrate flexible social rights provisions into their otherwise rigid constitutions, thereby grappling with this juxtaposition of rigidity and flexibility. In contrast to the Irish 1937 constitution and the German basic law, the 1946 *Constitution of the Republic of China* arguably outstrips its Western contemporaries in legislative technique. It adeptly negotiates the tension between constitutional social rights and civil liberties, as well as the dichotomy between a rigid constitution and flexible rights. Through balancing ideals with reality in both the constitutional text and its systemic application, it charts a distinctive, idiosyncratic path, diverging from foreign precedents.

9.3 Social Legislation and the Construction of a Welfare State

The issue of social welfare rights is not about a matter of intricate constitutional theory, but rather a social policy that requires concrete implementation across various domains. It is rooted in social needs, a responsibility imposed on the state to take care of the socially and economically vulnerable, in order to meet the basic socio-economic needs across all social strata for a peaceful community of life" (Chen, 2004, p. 236). The pioneering work of writing social rights into constitution was undoubtedly indebted to the *Weimar Constitution*, as it was the first to elevate the state's legal obligation of safeguarding people's welfare rights to a constitutional level; however, from another perspective, the constitutionalization of social rights can also be seen as an outcome of well-developed social legislation, a phenomenon evident as in both Germany and modern China.

9.3.1 Revival and Reconstruction of Traditional Thoughts on Social Welfare

As China embarked on its transition towards modernity in the latter half of the nineteenth century, the state's relief system began to falter. The traditional model of familial aid proved insufficient in accommodating the shifts in social structure. Compounding these systemic challenges were the frequent occurrence of natural disasters, such as floods and droughts, coupled with the unceasing onslaught of warfare. In order to maintain social stability, the National Government had no choice but reassume the relief responsibilities of the imperial government. Furthermore, the reach of the welfare state was expanded to encompass realms of social welfare beyond just emergency relief.

Contrary to the Anglo-Saxon tradition that venerates individualism and free competition, the traditional Chinese culture has historically embodied the philosophy of "concern not for scarcity, but for unequal distribution" and the utopian aspiration towards the "Great Harmony". In the modern era, Chinese scholars introduced the concept of Confucian "equalization" to the West. For example, in 1911, Chen Huanzhang completed his doctoral dissertation at Columbia University on the topic of Confucian economic thoughts, which inspired both economist Johan Maynard Keynes and Henry Wallace, the Secretary of Agriculture during Roosevelt's New Deal era, who later became Vice President. The ancient Chinese system of "Ever-normal Granaries" (*changpingcang*, 常平仓) even became one of the core theoretical foundations of the *Agricultural Adjustment Act* during the American New Deal period (Chen, 2010). Zhang Taiyan, a scholar of the late Qing Dynasty, commented that the traditional Chinese institutions enjoyed a "special merit, i.e., the socialistic equal-field system, which stood unparalleled by their European and American counterparts"; "it was implemented in China from the Wei and Jin Dynasties to the Tang Dynasty,, so that the wealth gap was small and local administration operated well"; apart from the land system, "all other Chinese legal statutes show the characteristics of socialism"; "now, when admiring the traditional Chinese institutions, we actually identify with socialism" (Luo, 2014, p. 244).

In the 1930s, Wu Jingxiong, a legislator and vice chairman of the Constitution Drafting Committee, wrote an article extolling the society-oriented legislation pursued by the National Government. He argued, "There is a saying: nothing happens without reason. It happens so that the latest legal thought and legislative trends in the West dovetail seamlessly with China's intrinsic national psyche! This is serendipity at its finest!" Wu summarized the Western legal socialization trend represented by Germany, maintaining that "the Western legal thought has transitioned from a mean and ungrateful individualism to a collectivism ethos featured by mutual aid and interlinked destiny". This happened to be consistent with the Chinese tradition of "benevolent governance", which integrated law and morality, thus providing a "local environment" for the transplantation of modern Western social legislation into China (Wu, 2005). Moreover, the progression of modern social legislation further enriched social rights theory, effecting a conceptual shift in social welfare from a government's unilateral "grant" or "favor" to a legal "right" of the populace and a statutory "duty" of the state.

9.3.2 Land Reform: "Social Revolution" of Property Rights and Its Setbacks

The appalling poverty in modern China's countryside, as many Chinese and foreign observers of the time believed, was rooted in the uneven distribution of land, where landlords exploited the peasants by charging high rents and leaving the latter in desperate straits. "Of the economic and social factors [contributing to the rural crisis], perhaps the system of tenancy is the most disquieting." (Eastman, 1986, 2001, p. 151) Sun Yat-sen placed "equal land rights and restraining private capital" as the bedrock of people's livelihood, and together with nationalism and democracy, they constituted the ideology of the Three Principles of the People. The nationalism endorsed by Sun

("Expel the Tartars, Restore China") effectively targeted the sharp ethnic tensions of late Qing Dynasty. However, relative to the political and social foundation of the KMT, Sun's principle of livelihood was viewed as avant-garde and ambitious. After the founding of the Chinese Revolutionary League (*Tongmeng hui*, 同盟会), Sun's revised land policy was milder than before, changed from state ownership of land and "no tilling, no land" to "appraising and fixing land prices and value increment belonging to the public". By March 1912, the Chinese Revolutionary League integrated other gentry elites, including the famous statesman Tang Shaoyi, and morphed from a revolutionary society into a public political party with a new name, the Kuomintang. This restructuring resulted in a major shift in the KMT's policy. In a bid to reach a compromise, the KMT relinquished the Chinese Revolutionary League's relatively radical social revolutionary policies and eliminated the advocacy for "gender equality" and Sun's principles related to land taxation and land "ownership" from its party platform. Although Sun's land policies had become moderate, less radical than before, they still upset those from "socially elite backgrounds" (Young, 1983, 2005, p. 219).

Although the KMT, in order to earn the support of the gentry elites, reached a compromise with them on the issue of land rent and land rights upon the founding of the ROC, Sun Yat-sen reorganized the KMT in 1924 and enforced the New Three Principles of the People, i.e., "alliance with Russia, cooperation with the Communist Party of China, and assistance to the peasants and workers", and then reintroduced the ideal that "every tiller should have his lot". After the establishment of the NNG in 1927, Sun's ideology was adopted as the supreme guiding principle. The head of the legislative branch, Hu Hanmin, led the Legislative Yuan to pass the *Land Acquisition Act* and the *Land Act* in 1928 and 1930 respectively in order to address the land problem in the rural areas (*Land Act of the Republic of China of the National Government*). As the "most socially oriented code", the *Land Act* set a ceiling for the tenancy rate (not to exceed 37.5% of the staple produce); additionally, it provided for a progressive tax on unwarranted land value increments (value increments returned to the public), functioning both as a mechanism for re-distributing land gains back to society and as an incentive for landowners to relinquish their ownership to the state or tenants. The *Act* also envisaged the eventual abolition of landlordism. For example, if tenants, on behalf of an absentee landlord, had farmed the land for over 10 years,[12] they might request the government to purchase the farmlands (still entrusting cultivation to the tenants). The state could also expropriate any land tenanted beyond the legal limit. The legal state expropriation primarily aimed to carry out national economic policies and maintain a balance in agricultural land distribution. The land reform was positively received by the intellectual community of the time. The nine principles proposed by the China Society of Land Economics on "how to stipulate the land matters in the Chinese constitution" essentially echoed the land policy of the National Government. For instance, "The use of land is the duty of all people to society and subject to state supervision and restriction"; "The state should oversee

[12] The 1946 amendment to the *Land Act* reduced the tenancy term from over 10 years to over 8 years.

land distribution, and the allocation of agricultural land shall be based on the principle of supporting yeomen"; "Any increment in land value not resulting from the owner's labor or capital investment shall revert to the public", so on and so forth (Hu, 1936).

"Equal land rights", as one of the "Teachings by the Founding Father", served as the "supreme guiding principle" of the National Government. This principle, according with the Western trend of legal socialization in the twentieth century, received extensive support from the intellectual community and was firmly enshrined in the constitution and relevant laws. The land reform should have been carried out smoothly, but "... the 1930 *Land Act* remained nothing more than an admirable expression of intent, for it was never implemented by the Nanking [Nanjing] authorities" (Young, 1983, 2005, p. 151), because the KMT, being a party closely associated with the conservative gentry class, was hesitant to estrange or dispossess landlords through land redistribution. "... They feared that an attack on the system of tenancy would provoke a social revolution, the outcome of which they could neither control nor predict" (Young, 1983, 2005, p. 152). Constrained by these class considerations, the National Government was simply incapable of putting into the effect the land reform policies in its party program and state law. It was not until 1948, when the KMT army suffered one defeat after another that "... many in the Nationalist camp suddenly realized that the livelihood of ignorant and unwashed peasants was in some fundamental way related to the debility of their own government and to the dynamism of the Communists"; "In September of 1948, 86 members of the [Legislative] Yuan finally presented a bill that would abolish the system of tenancy and make every farmer an owner of his land"; however, "As the whole Nationalist regime began caving in during late 1948, the Legislative Yuan continued fruitlessly and endlessly to debate the problem." (Eastman, 2002, pp. 83–84).

9.3.3 Residential Rent Control: Balancing Social Rights with Property Rights

"Home for all" is a basic necessity of life to citizens, as "land for each tiller" is to farmers. Given limited financial resources and an undersupply of public housing projects, many countries (including Germany and the U.S.) have regulated private residential tenancies since the twentieth century. These measures curtail landlords' property rights to guarantee tenants' right to secure and peaceful habitation. This approach has also been adopted as a key institutional choice in contemporary China.

With regards to the NNG's protective policy on residential house, the *Land Act* of 1930 had already set up a special section for "housing relief". To safeguard tenants' peaceful and comfortable occupancy, it was stipulated that landlords shall not terminate leases without legal justification; to ensure an adequate supply of housing, it was stipulated that 2% of the total urban housing stock should be allotted as reserve housing (readily available for lease). If the proportion of reserve housing fell below

1% of the total housing stock for a consecutive six months, municipalities shall: (1) standardize housing rent (not exceeding 12% of the annual interest rate on the assessed value of the land and its buildings), (2) reduce or waive the tax on new housing, and (3) construct new residences, the rent for which shall not exceed 8% of the annual interest on the assessed value of the land and its buildings.

During the War of Resistance, the population amassed in the rear lines due to warfare, which led to a glaring imbalance between housing supply and demand. Some homeowners seized the opportunity to demand exorbitant rents and security deposits while shortening lease terms as much as possible to their advantage. In order to protect tenants' interests, the National Government promulgated the *Wartime Regulations on Housing Tenancy* in December 1943, which imposed stricter restrictions on the rates of rent and security deposits that landlords could charge and established more stringent criteria for lease termination. Additionally, it mandated that tenants could extend their lease beyond the originally agreed tenancy period.[13]

Following the conclusion of the War of Resistance, the *Wartime Regulations on Residential Tenancy* reached its expiration, but the government did not diminish its regulation on rental housing. The revised provisions in the *Land Act* in 1946 were more stringent than those of the *Land Act* in 1930[14]; the temporary legislative measure, the *Wartime Regulations on Residential Tenancy*, was "upgraded" to the *Regulations on Residential Tenancy* in 1947, which can be deemed as one of the "most stringent" laws on tenancy control in history. Several key provisions of this law included the authorization for local governments to compel property owners to rent out any surplus housing not in use; the government was also empowered to order homeowners to rent out "their private housing which exceeded their actual needs" "within a specified timeframe". Non-compliance with these provisions could result in a fine up to 5000 yuan, alongside a compulsory rental order by the government. The ceiling rate of rent should be determined by local governments upon the consent of representative organs based on local economic condition. Any rent agreed upon above this threshold would be deemed unlawful gain, and the tenant could request its return within six months of payment. Furthermore, when a property owner regained possession for personal use, if the property remained unoccupied for three months, or if it was sublet within a year, the original tenant held the right to request the continuation of their lease and could demand compensation from the property owner. The law also restricted subletting to prevent any profit-seeking by secondary landlords.[15] The *Regulations on Residential Tenancy* was enacted when the CPC and the KMT were locked in a fierce civil war, and the National Government completely "lost popular support". However, "upon its introduction, the *Regulations* were universally

[13] For the terms of *Wartime Regulations on Housing Tenancy*, see National Government Gazette (1943).

[14] For example, regarding rent control, the 1946 amendment to the *Land Law* further reduced the maximum annual interest rate on the assessed value of land and its buildings from 12 to 10% (National Government Gazette, 1943).

[15] For the terms of the *Regulations on Housing Tenancy*, see National Government Gazette (1947).

lauded by both industry and academic sectors, being recognized as a prime example of legislative action under the guidance of the theory of property socialization."

9.3.4 Social Relief Act *and the Conceptual Innovation of Social Welfare*

When the ROC was just founded, the social security systems of Germany and other Western countries were translated and introduced into China. Social welfare legislation began to show effect during the period of the BNG, which, for example, in 1915, formulated the *Rules for Workhouses*, modeled after the European and American "Poor Laws". A more robust example of social welfare legislation was brought into effect during the period of the NNG with the promulgation of the *Social Relief Act* in 1943. Due to limited financial capacity and administrative resources at that time, the social legislation agenda had to give priority to the disadvantaged groups in dire poverty and the disaster-stricken population; therefore, the NNG put social relief at the center of social welfare legislation while social insurance, at a relatively subsidiary position. On September 29, 1943, the National Government promulgated the *Social Relief Act*. From the initial draft of the bill submitted by the Ministry of Social Affairs to the Executive Yuan for review, to its passage by the Legislative Yuan, and eventually, its announcement by the National Government, the process took approximately seven and a half months. This represents a rare high efficiency of legislation, which also reflects the urgency and importance of social relief amidst the wartime period. The *Act* consists of a total of 53 articles, divided into five chapters, namely relief coverage, relief facilities, relief methods, relief expenses and supplemental articles. From the perspective of the modern welfare state construct, the *Act* embodies the following three characteristics. It could be asserted that, at the very least, on a normative level, it conforms to the fundamental spirit of social legislation of modern welfare states.

i. From reactive to proactive: normalization and institutionalization of social welfare

Traditional social relief measures implemented by the Chinese government are mainly disaster relief, generally a reactive and transient coping strategy after the occurrence of a disaster. The government's purpose was merely to provide temporary relief to disaster-stricken areas and affected populations, epitomizing the principle of "providing immediate relief without addressing systemic poverty" and "palliating symptoms without addressing root causes". As for the routine relief for the society's prevalent vulnerable groups, although the ideal of regular state relief can be found in the chapter "The Operation of Etiquette · The Great Harmony" of the *Book of Rites* by Confucius, which posits that "Elderly widowers, widows, orphans, childless elderly people, the handicapped, the ill – all are provided for",[16] yet, in reality,

[16] Translations are James Legge's. (Notes by translators).

ancient governments did not proactively assume that responsibility, but predominantly relied on self-support within familial, clan, and local communities. The *Social Relief Act*, on the other hand, focused on consistent assistance to marginal groups, supplemented by temporary disaster relief. Through legislation, the state actively undertook the responsibility of regular social relief, thereby institutionalizing that obligation. As per the *Social Relief Act*, the state took the lead in planning and establishing permanent relief agencies to provide regular care for the socially disadvantaged, including, among others, homes for the aged, foundling homes, nurseries for children, workhouses for able-bodied paupers, workhouses for the disabled, workhouses for women, institutions for maternity assistance, and medical aid institutions (Article 6). Methods of relief varied, including in-facility accommodations, cash or necessities like food and clothing, free medical care, free childbirth assistance, low-priced or free housing, low- or zero-interest loans, low- or zero-interest loans for grain, land tax exemption, reformatory education and civic training, vocational training, and job placement (Article 14). It can be said that the *Social Relief Act* represents a qualitative leap in both concept and mode of relief in comparison with the "disaster relief" approach of the imperial eras.

ii. From philanthropy to obligation: state responsibility and government leadership in social welfare

The legislative principle laid down by the National Government for the *Social Relief Act*, along with the specific provisions, indicate that providing social assistance became a basic administrative function and legal obligation of the government at that time. As previously mentioned, conceptually, the undertaking of social welfare has transformed from a predominantly privately-managed and laissez-faire sector characterized by passive relief modes, to a proactive administrative responsibility led and driven by the state. Government offices in charge of social relief were established by law, and they were "the Ministry of Social Affairs at the central level, the provincial government at the provincial level, the municipal government at the municipal level, and the county government at the county level". Government office in charge of medical assistance was the Department of Health at the central level, and "in case of temporary and emergency relief, the Relief Committee shall take that charge" (Article 50). In addition to relief management, the government also had charge of the collection of relief funds, which was clearly stipulated as "relief funds shall be included in the central and local budgets (Article 44), and "relief funds shall not be solicited by apportionment or other compulsory collection methods" (Article 47). "Where relief facilities are managed by counties and municipalities, their expenses shall be covered by those counties and cities; accordingly, when the central or provincial governments organize relief facilities, the expenses should be borne by the central or provincial governments" (Article 42). If non-governmental organizations and private entities run successful relief facilities, "subsidies may be provided at the discretion of government offices in charge" (Article 43); in addition, the central government shall subsidize relief efforts undertaken by counties and cities (Article 45). The emphasis on the state's obligation to provide social welfare is a major advancement in the legalization of social rights in the ROC as well as a prominent feature of the *Act*. Similar to the traditional regulatory approaches towards private charitable activities in German-speaking countries, the *Act* provided that "groups or individuals may establish relief facilities, but they must acquire permission from the supervisory government offices" (Article 8), and that "the concerned government offices shall have the right to inspect and supervise the relief facilities of the preceding article" (Article 9). This fully reflects the *Act*'s the paternalistic control over welfare operations.

iii. Universal and compressive aid: maximizing the coverage of social welfare

The focal point of the traditional "disaster relief" has centered on victims of disasters and people displaced by natural calamities. The *Social Relief Act* expanded this scope to cover as extensively as possible, a broader range of socially disadvantaged groups (including the so-called "old, young, sick, disabled, and pregnant" in modern sense, the homeless, and the jobless and unemployed) (Article 1). The *Act* even provided rehabilitation and assistance to those disdained by traditional Chinese society, individuals engaged in improper occupations or the "habitually lazy or unemployed vagrants" (Articles 31, 32). This fully embodies the concept of modern welfare state philosophy of benefiting all citizens. In order to help multiple-children families, the *Act* even stipulated that "Families with more than five children, if unable to raise them due to financial hardship, may request government offices in charge to grant an allowance or send their children to orphanages or nurseries". (Article 20) The Ministry of Social Affairs, in its interpretative memorial of the *Social Assistance Act* draft and its principles submitted to the Executive Yuan for review, expounded explicitly the idea of maximizing the coverage of social assistance: "In addition to relief for the poor, the elderly, the sick, and the disabled, the protection of the pregnant and infants, the upbringing of young children, the assistance for the physically handicapped, the assistance for laborers, and even house renting, economic cooperation, household consumption and any aspect of people's daily needs, shall be taken into account. In the past, relief was limited to relief in kind and money, but now it has been expanded to medical, educational, and vocational relief. Contemporary countries' relief efforts towards their citizens cover the entire span of a person's life—from birth to death—and encapsulate all aspects of their living needs; the target demographic for relief has thus extended from a minority to the entire population and its coverage, from partial to full." (The Legislative Yuan Bulletin, 126)

9.3.5 Summary

The construction of a modern welfare state hinges on several pivotal factors: a country's actual financial conditions, its political and cultural traditions, and the bureaucratic system's capacity to mobilize resources. Modern China has cultivated a welfare state predicated on government leadership, leveraging Western social legislation in synergy with its indigenous Confucian principles of "Great Harmony" and

"Benevolent Governance". This approach harmonizes seminal Western ideologies of social rights with China's time-honored philosophies. Hong Lanyou, Undersecretary of the Ministry of Social Affairs, particularly wrote an article explaining the spirit of social legislation. Drawing inspiration from "The Operation of Etiquette · The Great Harmony" of *Book of Rites* by Confucius—"This ensures that the elderly enjoy a dignified final phase of life, those in their prime have suitable occupations, and the young are nurtured for growth and development. Elderly men without spouses, widows, orphans, elderly individuals without children or grandchildren, the physically challenged, and the ill – all are catered for"—he underscored the societal responsibility of caring for its members: to look after the elderly, bring up the young, care for the disabled and the sick, help the destitute and needy, learn from the virtuous people and show compassion for those who are suffering, so that no one is without a foothold or succumbs to malpractice. Hence, the cornerstone of social legislation shifted from a philanthropic perspective to a more duty-bound approach, while the implementation, from a passive stance to an active engagement, with the ultimate goal of carrying out the social policies of the Three Principles of the People and to fulfilling the durable ideal envisioned in Confucius' "The Operation of Etiquette · The Great Harmony". (Hong, 1944, pp. 6–7)

In historical discourse, there exist two polarized perspectives on the development of the legal system and the overall construction of the modern state in China. One perspective tends to romanticize the status quo of the era by attributing progress to a small cadre of elites and a sophisticated superstructure. Conversely, the other perspective employs the stark realities of setbacks as a tool to negate the concerted efforts and achievements made in the process of modernization. Besides the two schools of thought, a contingent of scholars perceive the modernization of Chinese state institutions as a protracted, continuous, and accumulative process. Irrespective of whether it is the late Qing government, the BNG, the NNG, or the government of the People's Republic of China, all administrations face roughly the same "fundamental agenda" during the course of modern state building (Kuhn, 2003). China, in its quest for affluence and national strength, has incrementally constructed a modern civilization of apparatuses and institutional systems brick by brick, a process that is far from being the so-called "fragmented and futile attempts at modernization". Instead, it represents a century-long transformation of modern statecraft guided by a novel philosophy of governance (Halsey, 2015). Within this broader context, the social legislation in modern China stands as a tangible and granular representation of this century-long journey towards a modern state.

References

Chen, C. (2004). *Xianfa xue* [Constitutional jurisprudence]. Angle Publishing Co., Ltd.

Chen, H. (2010). *Kongmen licai xue* [The economic principles of Confucius and his school] (H. Han, Trans.). Zhonghua Book Company. (Original work published 1911)

Chen, X. (2002). *Lun xiafa renmin jiben quanli de xianzhi* [Basic theories on constitutional basic rights]. (Vol. 1). Angel Publishing Co., Ltd.

Du, Q. (2014). *Minsheng yu xianfa* [People's livelihood and the constitution: The origins of social rights in the Chinese constitutional history]. In L. Xie (Ed.), Zhongde xianfa luntan 2014 [China-German constitutional forum] (pp. 122–143). Beijing: Social Science Literature Press.

Du, Y. (1988). *Tongdian shihuo* [Comprehensive statutes · Treatise on food and commodities] (Vol. 10). Zhonghua Book Company.)

Eastman, L. E. (1986/2001). Nationalist China during the Nanking decade 1927–1937. In J. K. Fairbank & A. Feuerwerker (Eds.), *The Cambridge history of China* (3rd print, Vol. 12, Part 1, pp. 116–167). Cambridge University Press.

Eastman, L. E. (2002). *Seeds of destruction: Nationalist China in war and revolution, 1937–1949*. Stanford University Press.

Guo, M. (2011). *Shehui fuli yu shehui baoxian* [Social welfare and social insurance]. In Y. Zhao et al. (Eds.), Zhonghua minguo fazhanshi: zhengzhi yu fazhi [History of the development of the Republic of China: Politics and the legal system] (Vol. 2). Linking Publishing Company.

Halsey, S. R. (2015). *Quest for power: European imperialism and the making of Chinese statecraft*. Harvard University Press.

Hong, L. (1944). Shehui jiujifa de lifa jingsheng [The legislative spirit of social relief law] *Shehui gongzuo tongxun* [Social Work Newsletter] (inaugural issue), pp. 6–7.

Hu, C. (1936). *Woguo xianfa zhong guanyu tudi shixiang yingyou zhi guiding* [Provisions due in the constitution on land matters]. In Z. Yu (Ed.) & J. Wu (Pr.). (1936). Xianfa wenxuan [Selected essays on constitution] (pp.627–634). Shanghai Law Editing and Translating Press.

Jing, Z. (1984). *Zhongguo lixian shi* [The constitution-making history of the Republic of China]. Linking Publishing Company.

Kuhn, P. A. (2003). *Origins of the modern Chinese state*. Stanford University Press.

Guomin zhengfu zhonghua minguo tudi fa [Land Act of the Republic of China of the National Government]. (1931). Shanghai Law Compilation Press.

Lifayuan gongbao [The Legislative Yuan Bulletin], No. 126, Public Documents.

Lin, J. (1993). *Zhongfa minguo xianfa zhutiao shiyi* [Article-by-article interpretation of the Constitution of the Republic of China] (Vol.4). San Min Book.

Liu, S. (2005). *Zhongguo de xianzheng xuanze: 1945 nian qianhou* [China's constitutional choice around 1945]. Peking University Press.

Luo, Z. (2014). *Quanshi zhuanyi: jindai zhongguo de sixiang yu shehui* [Power shift: Ideology and society in modern China] (revised ed.). Beijing Normal University Press.

Guomin zhengfu gongbao [National Government Gazette], (Chongqing), No. 631, December 15, 1943.

Guomin zhengfu gongbao [National Government Gazette], (Chongqing), No. 1046, April 29, 1946.

Guomin zhengfu gongbao [National Government Gazette], (Chongqing), No. 2993, December 1, 1947.

Guomin zhengfu gongbao [National Government Gazette], (Chongqing), No. 631, Regulations, pp. 1–5.

Nie, X. (2007). Xianfa jiben quanli de falu xianzhi wenti: yi zhongguo jindai zhixian wei zhongxin [The problem of legal restrictions on constitutional fundamental rights—On the history of modern Chinese constitution-making]. *Zhongwai faxue* [Peking University Law Journal], *19*(1), 51–70.

Propaganda Committee of the Draft Constitution of the Legislative Yuan. (Ed.). (1940). *Zhonghua minguo xianfa caoan shuoming shu* [The instructions for the draft constitution of the Republic of China]. Zhengzhong Press.

Su, Y. (Ed.). (2006). *Bumen xianfa* [Departmental constitution]. Angle Publishing Co., Ltd.

Sun, K. (1936). *Zhongguo xianfa de jige wenti* [Several issues of the Chinese constitution]. In Yu, Z. (Ed.) & J. Wu (pr.). In Z. Yu (Ed.) & J. Wu (Pr.). Xianfa wenxuan [Selected essays on constitution] (pp. 1117–1132). Shanghai Law Editing and Translating Press.

The Secretariat of the (Constitutional) National Assembly. (Ed.). (1946). *Guomin dahui shilu* [The National Assembly memoir]. For internal circulation.

Wang, S., & Qian, D. (1997). *Bijiao xianfa* [Comparative constitution]. China University of Political Science and Law Press.

Wu, G. (2004). *Xianfa de jieshi yu shiyong* [Interpretation and application of the constitution]. For internal circulation.

Wu, J. (1936). Xianfa zhong renmin zhi quanli yu yiwu [The rights and duties of the people in the constitution]. In Yu, Z. (Ed.) & J. Wu (pr.). In Z. Yu (Ed.) & J. Wu (Pr.). *Xianfa wenxuan* [Selected essays on constitution] (pp. 1132–1141).

Wu, J. (2005). *Falu zhexue yanjiu* [Study on legal philosophy]. Beijing: Tsinghua University Press.

Wu, J., & Huang, G. (1937a). *Zhongguo zhixian shi* [The history of constitution making in the Republic of China] (Vol. 1). The Commercial Press.

Wu, Z. (1923). *Zhonghua minguo xianfa shi* [The history of the constitution of the Republic of China] (Vol. 1). For internal circulation.

Xiao, G. (1982). *Xianzheng yu minzhu* [Constitutionalism and democracy]. Linking Publishing Company.

Xie, Z. (Ed.) & Zhang, Z. (Pr.). (2000). *Zhonghua minguo lifa shi* [A legislative history of the Republic of China] (Vol. 1). China University of Political Science and Law Press.

Xue, H. (1993). *Minzhu xianzheng yu minzu zhuyi de bianzheng fazhan: Zhan Junmai sixiang yanjiu* [Dialectical development of democratic constitutionalism and nationalism: Research on Zhang Junmai's thought]. Daoxiang Press.

Yin, W. (2003). Wuwu xiancao gongbu hou zhishijie de piping [Intellectual criticism on the May Fifth Draft Constitution]. *Zhejiang shangxue yuan xuebao* [Journal of Hangzhou Business College], (1), 9–14. Wang, Y. (1934, April 10). *Discussion on the draft constitution.* Ta Kung Pao.

Young, E. P. (1983/2005). Politics in the aftermath of revolution: The era of Yuan Shih-k'ai, 1912–16. In J. K. Fairbank (Ed.), *The Cambridge history of China: Republican China 1929–1949* (6th printing, Part 1, pp. 208–255). Cambridge University Press.

Yu, J. (2003). *Jindai zhongguo minfaxue zhong de siquan lilun* [Private rights theory in modern Chinese civil law]. Peking University Press.

Zhang, J. (1947). *Zhonghua minguo xianfa shijiang* [Ten lectures on the constitution of the Republic of China]. The Commercial Press.

Zhang J. (2006). *Xianzheng zhi dao* [The way to constitutional government]. Tsinghua University Press.

Zhang, Q. (2008). Minguo chuqi fangzu guanzhi lifa kaolue: cong zhuzhai quan de jiaodu [An examination of the legislation on houserent control in the Republic of China—From the perspective of residential rights]. *Zhengfa luntan* [Political and Legal Forum], *26*(2), 39–53.

Zhang, Y. (1936). Dui xianfa caoan chugao guanyu renmin quanli guiding zhi pipan [Criticism of the provisions on people's rights in the first draft of the constitution]. In Z. Yu (Ed.) & J. Wu (Pr.). *Xianfa wenxuan* [Selected essays on constitution] (pp. 480–508). Shanghai Law Editing and Translating Press.

Chapter 10
History of the National Assembly in Modern China

10.1 The Parliament of the Beijing National Government

The Parliament of the Beijing-based Government of the ROC was defective in conception and incapable in practice. Suppressed by such warlords as Yuan Shih-k'ai and Duan Qirui, it was dissolved and reconvened several times, barely having room for its full operation. A close examination of the Parliament indicated that it was constituted of factions instead of political parties, and its election was also laden with many disadvantages. The people in power played the game of "defending legitimacy" while the parliamentarians' performance was under expectation, which eventually tarnished the reputation of "defending legitimacy" and finally led to the ruin of the Parliament.

10.1.1 The Precarious Parliament in the Early Republican Era

i. Establishment and first dissolution of the Parliament

Though having spent many years preparing for a constitutional monarchy, the imperial government of the late Qing Dynasty had never convened a parliament till its downfall and only set up a quasi-parliament organ, named the Political Advisory Council. Not until the Xinhai Revolution did China establish its first parliament in the modern sense. According to *The Organizational Outline of the Provisional Government*, an Advisory Council, comprised of provincially elected representatives, was set up as the representative body, which later made the *Provisional Constitution of the Republic of China* to replace *The Organizational Outline*. Article 28 of the *Provisional Constitution of the Republic of China* provided that "The Advisory Council shall be dissolved on the day of the convocation of the Parliament and its powers

X. Nie, *The History of Government and Public Law in China*,
https://doi.org/10.1007/978-981-97-6063-3_10

shall be exercised by the latter." Evidently, to the constitution-makers, the Advisory Council was just a stopgap, an interim institution, rather than a true parliament.

April 8, 1913 saw the bicameral Parliament officially convened in Beijing, marking the start of a formal parliament in China. The *Provisional Constitution* stipulated that the Parliament was also a constitutional convention.[1] Song Jiaoren led the KMT to a victory in parliamentary election so that Song tried to form a cabinet to check the power of Yuan Shih-k'ai the Provisional President. However, the Beiyang warlords headed by Yuan Shih-k'ai were unwilling to stay on the track of constitutionalism. Shortly afterwards, Song Jiaoren was assassinated. An anti-Yuan force was immediately marshalled by the KMT but utterly defeated by Yuan's army upon engagement. The Second Revolution ended in failure. "When the anti-Yuan war was waged, the radical and progressive faction of the KMT adamantly believed that the Members of Parliament in Beijing had no room to exercise their power freely, and they proposed that the members should leave Beijing and relocate to the south… However, the majority turned it down. For this reason, rumors had it that the KMT radicals conspired to detonate the Parliament. Although this was also what Yuan Shih-k'ai had planned to do, he was quite convinced that the Parliament should remain in place because the presidency was not secured yet and he needed the votes from the Parliament." (Li, 2002, pp. 357–358) The constitution-making had been initially intended to precede the presidential election. However, under Yuan's pressure, the Parliament conceded to hold the presidential election first. On the day of election, the convention venue was besieged by thousands of members of the "League of Citizens", claiming "no exit for the representatives unless a worthy president gets elected today". "Those poor members of the Parliament had to go hungry. They started casting ballots at 8:00 in the morning, but not until 10 p.m. did they call it a day… After three rounds of voting, Yuan finally won the election by the number of votes stipulated in the proviso clauses. Upon hearing the result, the League of Citizens shouted loudly 'Long Live the Great President' before they were dismissed and the voters exited. Yuan took a grip on presidency and the doom of the Parliament loomed." (Li, 2002, p. 359) At that time, the Parliament was drafting the constitution—Tiantan[2] Draft Constitution, which entrusted an overriding power to the parliamentary cabinet system but limited the presidential power in many ways. On January 10, 1914, Yuan issued a decree to deprive the KMT of their seats, thus paralyzing the Parliament, and Tiantan Draft Constitution was soon discarded. This was the first dissolution of the Parliament in the early days of the ROC (Nie, 2013). "After the dissolution, Yuan resorted to numerous illegal means to forge some of his political toys, such as renaming the Administrative Conference, drafted by Xiong Xiling's cabinet, as Political Assembly to create a constitutional assembly where a new constitution was made… Prescribed by the new constitution, the Advisory Council functioned as a legislature, which nevertheless ended up as his exclusive

[1] According to Article 12 of *The National Assembly Election Law* in the first year of the ROC, constitution should be adopted by the convocation of both Houses.

[2] Tiantan is the Chinese *pinyin* of the characters of天坛, which means Temple of Heaven. (Notes by translators).

consulting team." (Luo, 1974, p. 318) Not until the day of August 1, 1916 when Yuan's monarchy was overthrown was the Parliament reconvened.

ii. The second dissolution of the Parliament and the rivalry Between the northern and southern (new and old) parliaments

In 1917, a clash between the Parliament and the warlord Duan Qirui broke out over the motion to wage a war against Germany. It ended with the second dissolution of Parliament, followed immediately by Zhang Xun's Restoration (restoring the imperial monarchy). Duan Qirui smashed Zhang's restoration attempt and reseized power in Beijing. However, Duan refused to reconvene the old Parliament with which he had a bitter feud. In February 1918, he promulgated the new Parliament organization act and the election law and manipulated the election in collusion with the Anfu Clique. In August, a new Parliament was established and was known as the Anfu Parliament. Quite a few members of the old Parliament had thus to head south to Guangzhou. At the beginning, given the absence of a quorum, an extraordinary session was held in August 1917 by the members of both Houses. In June 1918, more parliamentarians were elected by invoking the articles for emergency use, since the attendance still accounted for less than half of the quorum. When the quorum was finally met in September 1918, a constitutional assembly was reconvened to continue deliberation on Tiantan Draft Constitution (Chen, 1947, pp. 98–107). Thereupon, a confrontation came into being between the old Parliament in the north and the new one in the south.

In the South, Cen Chunxuan, the administrative chief of the military government, attempted to seek peace with the North, to which the majority of the south Parliament objected. The military government thus stopped paying the maintenance fee to the Assembly on the pretext of fiscal hardship. Cen ordered to keep a close watch on the parliamentarians and raided the Office of Secretary of the two Houses. Subsequently, the Speaker and the Vice Speaker of both Houses left Guangdong, and the Members of Parliament drifted across Yunnan and Sichuan provinces. Pestered by the local warlords, they were unable to convoke another meeting. Many a parliamentarian returned to Guangzhou and reconvened the extraordinary session to elect Sun Yat-sen as the Extraordinary President. Soon afterwards, because Sun Yat-sen broke with Chen Jiongming, a warlord, the parliamentarians had to move out of Guangdong once again. In the North, after the war between Zhi and Wan warlords, the Faction of Zhi seized the ruling power while the Anfu Parliament, under the protection of the Faction of Wan, fell apart correspondingly.

10.1.2 Harmful Factionalism and Defective Election

The success of modern parliamentary politics hinges on well-established party politics and well-developed regulations for election. It is needless to recapitulate the importance of the regulations for parliamentarian election to sustain the parliament itself. Actually, the modern political party is an indispensable tool and a prerequisite for parliamentary democracy. However, in the early days of the ROC, there existed no full-fledged political parties within the Parliament, which instead spawned political factions detrimental to democracy. Moreover, the assembly election regulations were flawed and corrupt practice was all-pervasive in the election process. Warring factions exacerbated corruption and literally poisoned the political atmosphere of the Parliament.

i. Faction instead of party and calculation instead of principles

The modern political party differs from the ancient Chinese political parties, such as "Pengdang" in the East Han Dynasty, "Niu-Li dang" in the Tang Dynasty, "Xin-Jiu dang" in the Song Dynasty and "Donglin dang" in the Ming Dynasty,[3] which are no more than a form of faction, fundamentally diverging from modern political parties in terms of organization and function. Modern political parties tend to be closely-knit with a deep-rooted tradition. They bear the mission to analyze and influence public opinions, to formulate the platform of parties, to recommend candidates and act as a liaison with different sections of a government (Zou, 1988, pp. 37–45). In an election, compared to independent candidates, those endorsed by political parties would stand a better chance of winning public trust because parties have more stable platforms and organizations to honor their candidates' political promise. Political parties entice voters with their platform and candidates need to fulfill the promise after they are elected. In turn, the ruling political party will be collectively held accountable for running a government, and the next election will reveal its credits and failures, gains and losses, and people's satisfaction index. Therefore, the spirit of democracy in parliamentary politics shows itself "not in the system of politics, but in the operation of party politics." (Zou, 1988, p. 46)

Factions, instead of political parties, constituted the Parliament of the Beijing National Government. In one of his monographs, Andrew J. Nathan, a sinologist from Columbia University, believed factionalism was a critical cause of the failure of constitutional government in the early period of the ROC. A faction is a small political clique, organized and consolidated by such different types of connections for benefits, as those built upon blood ties, bonds between teachers and students, classmates, fellow countrymen, old friendship between families, hierarchical bonds from the same institution, colleague relationship, and ties between two families after marriage. "*Guanxi*" (connection and networking) was an important political resource in Beiyang Government and laid the foundation for alliances and negotiations (Nathan, 1976, pp. 50–57). The main factions included the Zhi Clique, the Wan

[3] "Dang", with its Chinese character as 党, means a clique. Pengdang (朋党) literally means a clique consisting of friends for the same political interests. Niu-Li dang (牛李党) refers to the two factions in an ongoing contention during the middle to late Tang Dynasty. Niu and Li are respectively the surnames of Niu Sengru and Li Deyu, both serving as Chancellor. Niu dang or the Niu Faction (牛党) are viewed as a group of officials from humble origins who passed the imperial examinations to assume government positions, while Li dang or the Li Faction (李党) refers to a group of officials of aristocratic origins. Xin-Jiu dang (新旧党) in the Song Dynasty literally means New-Old Party. The new party was supported by the socioeconomic reforms known as the New Policies proposed by Chancellor Wang Anshi, while the old party opposed it. Donglin dang (东林党) refers to a Confucian political clique named after Donglin Academy in the Ming Dynasty. (Notes by Translators).

Clique centered around Duan Qirui and the Anfu Clique he fostered, the Research Clique, the Communications Clique, and the New Communications Clique, etc. (Nathan, 1976, pp. 225–261) These factions did not have a stable set of platforms, lacked ideological consensus, and were grounded on a weak basis so that instability was very common within a faction and the ties were quite volatile between various factions. These factions established the so-called "parties" which were merely loosely disciplined. In some cases, a party member was affiliated with multiple parties and some of them even broke away or defected from their party under temptations of wealth and office. For example, the Anfu Clique was the most powerful faction but by no means a stable political organization. "It appeared neither a stable political party nor a scholarly society. The faction headed by Duan Qirui had neither organization nor political aspirations. He thought that everything would be under his control given the support from some Beiyang warlords. Running a modern political party never occurred to him as a political investment. Neither did his resourceful assistant Xu Shuzheng develop such an idea as ideology. Both of them believed in the firm grip on political and military power to form a formidable influence. The accidentally founded the Anfu Clique was reduced to a tool to further their manipulation … Ill-organized, the club had neither credos nor party platforms except some liaison institutions. It was created only for networking." (Zhang, 2008, pp. 128–129) In the late Qing Dynasty, the Revolutionists and the Constitutionalists differentiated themselves into radical and conservative camps, which nevertheless merged after the Xinhai Revolution. An examination of the political parties in the early Republican era showed that the principles of each party were quite similar and all parties were dedicated to the fight over the Parliament seats. "Everyone was eager to flaunt their talent. They targeted at the end without caring about the means and, in so doing, lost their party's distinctive character. Except a few foresighted political figures, most politicians in the Republican era did not take party development as their mission." Thus, the political parties were "just nominal and essentially factious." (Zhang, 2008, pp. 90–91).

The factional politics of the Beiyang Government rested on a compromise among different factions in order to sustain the stability of the Parliament and the overall political situation. However, due to the fragile foundation for cooperation and built-in instability of each faction, the consensus achieved in such context would fail inevitably, and political unrest would ensue. There was no charismatic leader to serve as the locus to stabilize the fragmented military, political and financial powers, leading to discursive battles rivaling for power. Politics based on factions would surely bring about inevitable chaos (Nathan, 1976, pp. 222–224). Given the precarious Parliament, the government also changed its flags every other minute and the members of the Parliament traveled north and south across China, attaching themselves to regional power lords. This period, however, merely witnessed the ups and downs of factions rather than a mature party and the dawn of democracy.

ii. Absence of regulations on the parliamentary election and rampant corruption in election

Joseph Schumperter once noted that "Democracy comes with ballots and dies without." Were there ballots in the parliamentary election in the early days of the ROC? How did the electoral system work? What was the proportion between voters and the general population? How many people ever cast a sacred ballot? ... To the foregoing chain of questions, the answers would always go negative (Zhang, 2008, p. 2).

The first step of election was to determine the total number of voters. Nevertheless, not until 1953 did China conduct its first national census. Thus, no complete census data was in place for the election of the Parliament in the early days of the ROC. "The voter survey was made in a perfunctory manner, or even fabricated." The voters accounted for a very small portion of the overall population, roughly between 10 and 15% (Zhang, 2008, p. 212). Most people, with poor knowledge of election, "would rather give up their right without taking the trouble to understand voting and cast a sacred ballot. 'Indifference was prevalent'", and "those who really cast their ballots were only a tiny minority" (Zhang, 2008, p. 213).

The two elections of the Parliament (parliamentarians) in the early period of the ROC adopted a mixed system instead of a direct one. Voters cast ballots directly in the first round to elect candidates who would then decide a fixed number of parliamentarians in the second round. The mixed system of election is not only complicated in procedure but always susceptible to manipulation. In the second round of mutual election, for example, "Corruption was rampant. Those successful candidates were predominantly plutocrats while people of integrity had to stand aside and give up without financial support." (Zhang, 2008, pp. 210–211) The two elections of the Parliament went from bad to worse in terms of both the electoral system and its operation.

Bribes were used not only to win votes, but also to beat competitors amid factious strife. Take the second Parliament (the Anfu Parliament) as an example. Xu Shuzheng wielded money to crush the Research Clique. The Shanghai-based newspaper *Times* reported that "most parliamentarians of the Anfu Clique elected by Hubei province were those who had betrayed the Research Clique." "Jiangsu province was intially under the controlof the Research Clique, but most elected members were bought off by the Anfu Clique thereafter." (Zhang, 2008, p. 153) Many resorted to bribery from the very beginning. Ten or twenty cents were enough to buy one vote. In Yangzhou of Jiangsu province, it was found that people crammed a substantial number of purchased ballots into a ballot box. During the second round, the price for one vote could rocket up to 200 Yuan due to scarcity. When election went very competitive, even seven or eight hundred Yuan could not secure a vote. When the situation went the opposite, however, the price for a vote might depreciate to twenty or thirty Yuan at which still nobody would trouble to buy because those who bribed for votes spread rumors such that traders could not work off their ballots. In some other cases, election could become commercialized and some companies were even established to purchase votes. For example, throughout the election for the two Houses in Jiangxi province, the Anfu Clique ran a company to buy votes at a lower price. "With a unified price, people working in group can bring down the price, instead of driving it up." In the meantime, others organized the voters to "sell only at a certain price". The Anfu Clique held a firm grip on the politics. As organizers, they manipulated the elections from both directions. "On the one hand, they used money to bribe and buy off votes; on the other hand, they also took charge of the ballot boxes. Working in both ways, they first dominated the election with money, which made the control over ballot boxes afterwards less challenging." (Zhang, 2008, pp. 155–156) "Before the emergence of party politics, vying for election was a matter between individuals. However, with political parties, such rivalry became more organized." It was rampant among power holders to rig elections and crush dissidents. "During the period of the Anfu Assembly, political parties competed and nomination by party was adopted. Xu Shuzheng pulled the string of election and designated parliamentarians via telegram, as a way of nomination." Thus, it went under such ridicule as "nominal election as nomination was decided by officeholders" and "all signs showed this (election) to be nearly a designation". (Zhang, 2008, p. 213)

Bribery took place not only in electing the members of the Parliament, but also in parliamentarian's electing and approving of government officials. The Parliament of the Beiyang Government made little contribution to legislation, only reserving the important power to make constitution and to approve the appointment of personnel. Compared to administrative officials, parliamentarians indulged in even more severe and pronounced corruption. Without solid power in hands, they held votes which decided who could become President and whose nomination could be approved for powerful positions in government. Thus, vote buying characterized the ties between the legislative and administrative organs (Nathan, , p. 72).

10.1.3 Defending Legitimacy and Abandoning Legitimacy

The first section of this chapter has presented the tumultuous confrontation between the northern and the southern National Assemblies, both of which did not necessarily pursue the goal of "rule of law". "Both sides fought only for power in the name of 'law'." (Qian et al., 2008, p. 125) Against the political backdrop at that time, "legitimacy" was flagged just as an excuse. It served for those parliamentarians as a slogan for survival and a drapery to cover up their real purpose of seeking private interests. The authorities resorted to "legitimacy" to justify their rule and consolidate their power. Basking in "symbols of legitimacy", the Members of Parliament were also happy to connive and share benefits. In the end, the signboard of "legitimacy" was smashed to bits and the Parliament was ruined.

i. For survival or for legitimacy

After the wars between the Zhi and Feng warlords, the winning Zhi warlords, Cao Kun and Wu Peifu, upheld the banner of "restoring legitimacy" and some Members of Parliament who either stayed in or left Guangdong province moved northward in droves at Cao and Wu's invitation. The old Parliament was thus reconvened in Beijing on August 1, 1922 (Luo, 1974, p. 323).Normally, these members would not have much dissent over "restoring legitimacy", but since the second dissolution of the Parliament in 1917, the problems within the old Parliament turned more complicated. "The old Parliament in Guangzhou which convened on its own was called the Parliament in Emergency because it only had half of the Assembly. Emergency procedures were adopted to fill the vacancies in the eighth year of the ROC (1919) and this half Assembly continued to dwindle with the collapse of the military government in the ninth year (1920). What was left, however, mainly consisted of the new add-ins in the eighth year (1919). That's why this Assembly was called 'the Eighth Year Assembly'". This very attempt to restore the old Parliament was a product of the collusion between the Zhi warlords and the old members who refrained from moving south and those who withdrew from the Assembly after moving to Guangzhou. The restored Assembly was intended to be a copy of the 1917 Parliament before its dissolution so that it was known as the Sixth Year Assembly. The Sixth Year Assembly was reinstated to undermine the Eighth Year Assembly so that the "Sixth" and "Eighth" Year Assembly members put up a fight for survival known as "a tale of two camps" on the political stage. The Sixth Year Assembly members narrowly made the quorum and reconvened in Beijing on August 1, 1922. The Eighth Year Assembly members organized a "Legitimacy Sustaining Committee" in Shanghai and a "Society of Legitimacy" in Beijing. Both institutions promoted the idea that the Eighth Year Assembly was the only legitimate one, echoing each other from afar, while the members of the Sixth Year Assembly ridiculed such an assertion. The Eighth Year Assembly members flocked northward to Beijing, dashing into the avenue of the House of Representatives on August 30, requesting a fight with the Speaker. The members of "Eighth" and "Sixth" Year Assembly reached a stalemate, which paralyzed the Assembly. The Sixth Year Assembly closed on September 18, "making a nonviolent resistance". The government set up a Government Commission for those poor jobless Eighth Year Assembly members so that most of them softened, which was far away from a final solution (Li, 2002, pp. 517–518). Back then, however, those who started rivaling against the Sixth Year Assembly members were not those from the Eighth Year, but another group who were identified with those "new members of the new Parliament". In 1920 when the Anfu Parliament was dissolved, Xu Shichang followed the President's directive to elect new members for the Parliament according to the election and organization law in 1912. However, only eleven provinces followed this directive so that a quorum was not met and the Assembly failed to reconvene. The "new members", self-assumed representatives of new trends among people, advanced attacks on the restoration of the Sixth Year Assembly and retreated hurriedly when the authorities dismissed their objections

(Chen, 1947, pp. 126–127). Regarding the fight over legitimacy, Li Jiannong made the following comments:

> "Legitimacy", ... positively speaking, served as a flag under which the revolutionists justified their revolt against Beiyang warlords; negatively speaking, it was merely an excuse for hundreds of parliamentarians to keep their jobs. Parliamentarians elected in the second year of the ROC (1913) had a legal term of 3 years (6 years for Senators), but they demanded shamelessly to reconvene the Assembly in the eleventh year of the ROC (1922) when voters all over the country were neither dead nor unable to vote... Nothing would be worth mentioning concerning such a philosophy of legitimacy when its political covering was downright stripped off. However, legitimacy seemed to be a serious matter when promoted by those law-manipulating politicians and militant warlords. The general public, who were desperate for peace, took for granted that the north and the south were fighting essentially for legitimacy. Once legitimacy got defended, the unification would no longer be a problem and peace would ensue. Nevertheless, they didn't know that defending legitimacy turned out to be a mere pretext, and the chaos remained unchanged! (Li, 2002, p. 513)

ii. The final days of the Parliament in the early Republican Era

Having been resumed, the old Parliament announced that it would continue the work left by the Sixth Year Assembly and the top priority would be making a constitution. However, when the Parliament reconvened in 1922, the constitutional assembly frequently failed to convene due to insufficient attendees. In order to get the constitution drafted as quickly as possible, the Parliament lowered the quorum for presence and vote. To entice the members to a meeting, they even offered a subsidy of 20 *yuan* for attendance which was an extra sum of money the parliamentarians earned on top of the annual bonus and travel expenses. "This prevalent avarice had been rarely seen in history. It was quite reasonable that the Assembly was not well received by the public."(Chen, 1947, 129)

At that time, the members of the Parliament had divergent opinions. Those receiving stipends from Cao Kun in the Zhi Clique advocated that the Assembly should prioritize the term issue of President Li Yuanhong who just resumed the office, so as to restart the presidential election as soon as possible. However, the other camp argued that the Assembly should focus on the grand constitution-making project (Jing, 1984, p. 328). The presidential election could wait till the constitution was promulgated. The Cao clique resorted to violence to force Li Yuanhong to step down not long after he assumed the office, which incurred dissatisfaction from some parliamentarians. In August 1923, the number of parliamentarians who left Beijing to the south went up to 385. "The majority of those who relocated to the south chased after interests, hardly holding any clear political principles." On August 24, the members in Beijing convened a meeting and decided to offer an allowance of 100 Yuan for attendance to entice those who had moved to the south to return to Beijing. Given that the tenure of each member was about to terminate on October 10, they further proposed to extend their term of office till new members were elected. Thus, the Assembly members coming to the south flocked back to Beijing. The two Houses reconvened and passed the bill to lengthen the term of all members (Chen, 1947, p. 132).

To conceal their ambition for the highest position, the Cao clique proclaimed the precedence of constitution-making over presidential election. However, because the constitutional assembly did not convene on time, the clique rushed to mobilize those prostituted members of the Parliament to table a motion to start the presidential election. Having bribed the parliamentarians each with 500 *yuan* to attend the meeting for presidential election, the Cao clique still found attendance insufficient to constitute a quorum and had to send them some bigger checks to secure their votes, ranging from 5000 to 10,000 *yuan* for each. Finally, Cao Kun was "legitimately" elected as President (Chen, 1947, p. 133).

The reason for Cao Kun's successful bribery for election was that those southward relocated parliamentarians were unable to resist the pecuniary temptation. However, they returned to the north under the constitution-making flag. "Having exchanged votes with checks, they must have an explanation for making the constitution, regardless of purpose, either for fulfilling their promise, or covering up their bribery." Thus, following the presidential election, the Parliament only spent three days going through the second and third reading of the draft constitution before its promulgation on October 10, 1923, the same day when Cao Kun took office. The constitution made against such a backdrop would not be expected to earn the respect and approval from the people. In 1924, when Duan Qirui's government was established, this constitution was abolished. Fairly speaking, the constitution was progressive by content, and some parts of it even pioneered constitutions around the world. However, such a sacred and solemn piece of constitution "only existed for one year and ended up with a bad name of 'bribery constitution', despite the bumpy eleven-year preparation from drafting to promulgation, which was thwarted and damaged by warlords, politicians and those unscrupulous careerists." (Jing, 1984, p. 332)

"The political dispute in China before 1924 appeared to revolve around the mere issue of legitimacy. Upon restoring legitimacy, the prostituted parliamentarians flaunted the flag of defending legitimacy and staged a show to fabricate a 'drapery' constitution so as to cover up their real scheme. From then on, no one cared about legitimacy itself." "Since the Parliament was ruined, the constitution was abandoned, and the banner of defending legitimacy was discarded for good." (Li, 2002, pp. 536–537) With the constitution gone, what would constitute the legitimacy of the Parliament itself? On November 24, 1924, Duan Qirui built up a ruling government in Beijing, fundamentally abolishing the so-called "defending legitimacy", and the Parliament perished with it.

10.1.4 Parliamentary Politics on the Verge of Bankruptcy

Looking back on the decade-odd history of the Parliament in the early days of the ROC, we have found the following points. The Parliament was frequently dissolved and its function was little pronounced. The election in the Parliament was in disorder with prevalent bribery for election. A forest of factions existed in the Parliament while no modern political parties took shape. Many parliamentarians demonstrated poor personal qualities, and some even prostituted themselves by working for power-holders, which ruined the Assembly in the end. This was a history of making and ruining laws. Not only did warlords and politicians show no respect for the constitution and law, but those who participated as constitution makers and legislators also perpetuated the same blunder to reap their own benefits. For example, the Parliament in the south invoked the *Act of Parliament* in the second year of the ROC (1913), "those who fail to show up in a month after the Assembly convenes should be dismissed" to fire the absent members and replaced them with those bench warmers (Chen, 1947, pp. 105–106). For another example, in 1922 when the Parliament reconvened, to avoid failure, it modified *The Parliament Organization Law* and lowered the requirement of quorum for presence and vote, so as to pass the Constitution as quickly as possible (Chen, 1947, pp. 128–129). All these showed the Parliament to be just a game.

Parliamentary politics was by no means impeccable, but the early Republican era revealed its dark side to the fullest. "How can one tolerate other people snoring at his bedside?" Those who held the supreme power were inherently uncomfortable with a bunch of vociferous crowds assuming themselves as "representatives of public opinion", pointing intervening fingers to their business. In the meantime, the representatives failed to fulfill their duties. Such a parliamentary establishment was simply an import from foreign countries. Thus, it had a lower position before getting a firm foothold, and even faced the risk of being banished from the country. The two political experiments in the early republic—liberal government and dictatorship—failed and seemed to have "contributed to each other's destruction" (Young, 2008, p. 255). "Yuan Shih-k'ai found parliament and self- governed provinces debilitating to the nation-state, which, he believed, had to be centralized and strong in the age of imperialism. At his first opportunity he did away with both, as well as such auxilliary institutions as competing political parties and an uncensored press." Yuan's stand for over-centralized power inspired no enthusiasm and as a result "The dictatorship collapsed with the monarchy". Though "a liberal consensus could re-emerge and gain an institutional edge", what prevailed in politics was a decentralized military hegemony. Under the rule of warlords, soldiers became "the only voters of the warlords" and "the political struggle in China was further militarized" (Young, 2005, p. 255). There was no more parliamentary politics by its true definition.

10.2 The National Assembly of the Nanjing National Government

When the Nanjing-based National Government was in power, a parliament in the typical Western sense was replaced by a "power organ" (the National Assembly)[4] and a full-time legislature (the Legislative Yuan).[5] After the *Constitution of the Republic of China* came into effect in 1947, the Legislative Yuan served not only as a legislature, but also as a kind of European and American parliament to oversee the government; and the full-time investigative and auditory branch (the Control Yuan) was similar to the U.S. Senate in terms of election and powers. It has been claimed, therefore, that the National Assembly, the Legislative Yuan, and the Control Yuan working together were equivalent to the European and American parliaments.[6]

10.2.1 Sun Yat-Sen's Idea on the National Assembly

i. Division of powers modeled on the parliamentary system in *Sun Wen Theory*

The parliamentary system (representative government) was widely criticized for such problems as incompetent members and legislations without much consideration. What was worse, the political party manipulated representative government so much that members of the parliament were no longer mouthpieces for the people, but hired thugs of the party, further away from the ideals of democracy (Zou, 1988, pp. 164–167). A political comparison between the ROC and other nations in the same period found all the parliaments particularly problematic with a tyrannical parliament over a weak administration or the other way around. The French Third Republic, mired in the civil strife of political parties, witnessed repeated collapse of cabinets and long-term political instability so that the government could not work properly. In the German Weimar Republic, the parliament was weak and divided, and the administrative power was as arbitrary as in the Bismarck era for most of the time. Therefore, authoritarianism had been under way in Germany long before

---

[4] In the transitional period to a constitutional government, *An Outline of Political Tutelage* entrusted the governing power to the KMT National Congress on behalf of the National Assembly, and, when the KMT National Congress was not in session, to the Central Executive Committee of the Chinese KMT whose branch, the Central Political Conference, also exercised legislative powers.

[5] When the Guangzhou-based National Government was controlled by military forces, the KMT generally took the place of government in legislature: in the early days of one-party rule, most of the laws were formulated by the KMT Central Executive Committee or Political Committee. The Central Political Conference was cancelled in 1927 and the National Government exercised full legislative power; in February 1928, the Central Political Conference decided that all laws should be passed by the Central Political Conference which was, in every way, a legislature under the party. "The National Government didn't have a formal, permanent and independent legislature until the establishment of the five-chamber system and the formation of the Legislative Yuan," (Committee for the Compilation of the History of the Republic of China Law, 1994, pp. 26–27).

[6] A separate chapter is devoted to the Control Yuan in this book.

Hitler came to power (Zou, 1961, pp. 447–448, 519). Various countries adopted many remedies for the weaknesses of parliamentary politics. However, Sun Yat-sen blazed a new track and proposed a more fundamental reform to distinguish political power from governing power (division of powers) where the people had the former and the government exercised the latter. He believed that the division of powers could help both democracy and efficiency. "Popular sovereignty" and "strong government" would work together to empower the people and capacitate the government to the maximum degree. This is the core of Sun's constitutional thought upon which he developed his "Five-power Constitution".

Sun Yat-sen rejected "representative government" as the final goal of democratic politics and advocated "popular sovereignty" characterized by direct participation of the people in election, autonomous counties nationwide, directly elected officials, and directly elected representatives to constitute the National Assembly and form the supreme authority. With direct election alone, people could not oversee office-holders, so they must have the power to recall. In addition, the people would also have the legislative power, that is, to make, amend or repeal a law as needed by a universal consent. Sun emphasized that the true Republic of China must guarantee these four rights by which the people could enjoy full democracy, manage the government directly, balance with the "strong government" with five powers of administration, legislation, judiciary, examination, and control, thus promoting democracy and efficiency together to the maximum degree (Sun, 1988). China had a vast territory and a large population. How could the people exercise their power through direct participation? Sun Wen's *Fundamentals of National Reconstruction* laid out a blueprint where citizens would exercise the local power and the National Assembly, the national (central) power. "In a fully autonomous county, citizens would have the right to elect and recall officials directly, and make, amend and repeal laws directly". "After the promulgation of the constitution, the central authority would be vested in the National Assembly which would have the right to elect and recall the central government officials, and make, amend and repeal the national laws." (Five-power Constitution Association, 1963)

ii. Sun Wen's division of powers and Mill's political philosophy (Li, 1988; Zhang, 1986)

Scholars found in their research that Sun Wen's division of powers were closely related to or quite similar to John Stuart Mill's ideas.

Mill advocated elite politics, but he also believed that sovereignty must remain in the hands of the people. Therefore, in designing a democratic government, he emphasized the balance between "participation" and "competence", which was very close to Sun's division of powers. Mill proposed a distinction between the power of overseeing the government and the governing competence. The parliament should oversee the government and "review and even facilitate" good laws whereas legislation needed to be entrusted to experts like the administration and the judiciary. He said, "A numerous assembly is little fitted for the direct business of legislation, but for causing it to be done... Any government... would have as one of its fundamental elements a small body ... who should act as a Commission of legislation... chosen minds trained to the task through long and laborious study. Either House might exercise its initiative, by referring any subject to the Commission, with directions to prepare a law. Parliament should have no power to alter the measure, but solely to pass or reject it; or, if partially disapproved of, remit it to the Commission for reconsideration." In another article, Mill believed that the parliament should be composed of two houses with one representing the people and the other consisting of experts (in the U.K., members of the legislative commission, senior judges, former senior officials, professors, etc.). However, the Popular House was the supreme political decision maker of the two.

Sun's division of powers resembles Mill's political philosophy in a number of ways. First, theoretically based on a synthesis of elite democracy and participatory democracy, Sun's balance of powers and Mill's balance of participation and competence happened to work the same way. Second, as for system design, Mill's Legislative Commission was comparable to Sun's Legislative Yuan in his "Five-power Constitution" in terms of personnel composition and responsibilities; Sun's National Assembly was institutionally similar to Mill's Popular House. However, the differences between the two are also conspicuous. First of all, Sun Yat-sen was a revolutionary leader and did not have time for systematical and theoretical elaboration on his work so that his practical political approach might not agree with his division of powers. Mill was a scholar, striving for systematic and consistent thoughts. Their difference on a deeper level might be attributed to their diametrically different political milieu. Mill was trying carefully to fix the flaws on the basis of British tradition of representative government whereas Sun Wen was calling for a new paradigm as a bold revolutionary in front of an incompetent and unethical parliament in the early days of the ROC.

iii. The function of the National Assembly in *Sun Wen Theory*

1. The nature of the National Assembly

In nature, the National Assembly was directly related to its composition which determined whether it was a representative political assembly or a direct democratic congress. In *Sun Wen Theory,* the National Assembly exercised direct democracy ("government"), but it was clearly stated in *Fundamentals of National Reconstruction* that the National Assembly was composed of members elected with one member for each autonomous county. It was questionable if such an assembly comprised of thousands of people could be viewed as a direct democratic institution. "Representatives elected by the counties constitute the National Assembly exercising the four powers of direct democracy, but their number is merely 2000 plus. In Switzerland, a bill has to be signed by 30,000 people before being put to referendum where the ballots would approximate twenty or thirty thousand. Doesn't it go against direct democracy if direct democracy enjoyed by the people is entrusted to 2000 representatives?" (Zhang, 1947, p. 51).

It was generally believed that, in spite of his aspiration for direct democracy, Sun Yat-sen had to compromise facing the realities in China: a vast territory with a large population, low literacy and poor transportation, lack of democratic tradition.

However, his ideas of direct democracy were inconsistent in his works. Therefore, it was often thought that the National Assembly, to Sun Wen, was just a stopgap, a bridge measure for then. Once universal education and developed transportation were achieved, the governing power, temporarily vested in the National Assembly, would be handed over to the people to exercise directly (Five-power Constitution Association, 1963, pp. 335–336). However, the more radical camp, such as Zhang Junmai, proposed to "entrust the four powers to the people nationwide" and "turn the four hundred million Chinese into an enormous National Assembly" (thus incorporeal National Assembly). Direct democracy, if rendered impossible by unfavorable conditions, could at least "be extended to all town and county assemblies nationwide", and a relatively large National Assembly could be convened consisting of local assembly members across the country (Zhang, 1947, pp. 49, 52). The idea of an incorporeal National Assembly can be confirmed in *Sun Wen Theory*. "When introducing the newest and fully autonomous institution in Cleveland of America in the part of Democracy, Sun said, 'the National Assembly can be convened if approved of and signed by 70,000 out of 700,000 while a law can be passed if over half a population give the consent'". It's no doubt that the National Assembly here was comprised of all citizens of the county. Sun's repeated citations of Switzerland and the U.S. revealed that he yearned for a true direct democracy instead of a representative democracy (Su, 1994, p. 102). Some believed that Sun's design for the National Assembly derived from the American electoral college system and constitution amendment procedure, in which the former was originally indirect but achieved de facto direct democracy through political vicissitudes and so did the latter. Therefore "America has a National Assembly but does not have a name for it." Sun Yat-sen expanded the American democracy and "named it as National Assembly" (He, 2002, p. 409).

It was literally difficult for counties, let alone the central government, to practice direct democracy because China was an underdeveloped country with a vast territory and a large population. The idea of division of powers and the National Assembly originally grew out of the criticism on parliamentary representation. When the National Assembly was brought into being, it turned out to be a representative one which was naturally hard for people to accept. In face of that awkward situation, some reached a compromise: the National Assembly thus designed was "representative to the minimum degree" and functioned as a liaison between the people and the government (Jin, 1936, p. 34); it was "the engine of government", and "its duty was to assist rather than to replace the people in exercising power" (Chen, 1998, pp. 252–253).

2. The National Assembly and the Legislative Yuan

In *Sun Wen Theory,* the National Assembly was the supreme authority while the Legislative Yuan, in charge of making laws, was a full-time legislature and an executive branch instead of a representative institution. The National Assembly was empowered not only to create legislation principles which the Legislative Yuan had to observe in law-making practice but also to amend and repeal the laws passed by the latter. The former had the power to make, amend and repeal the national laws, by which it oversaw the latter in exercising its legislation power. *Fundamentals of National Reconstruction* entrusted the National Assembly with the power of appointing and removing the Legislative Yuan personnel.

Inconsistency recurred in *Sun Wen Theory*. Sun always designated the Legislative Yuan as an executive office, thus fundamentally different from the European and American parliaments, but he frequently treated them as the same. In *Five-power Constitution* of 1921, he noted that legislators were equivalent to the European and American parliamentarians; in *History of Chinese Revolution* of 1923, he also said that the people nationwide voted to elect representatives to constitute the Legislative Yuan, and that the heads of the Legislative Yuan, Examination Yuan and Control Yuan should be appointed by the ROC President upon consent from the Legislative Yuan. However, all the five branches (Yuan, 院, chamber or house) took responsibility for the National Assembly, while the Judicial, Examination and Control Yuan were not responsible for the ROC President and the Legislative Yuan. In *Fundamentals of National Reconstruction* of 1924, Sun enunciated his complete and final thought on constitution, to which the KMT usually resorted when views diverged in interpreting the founding father's teachings. It was proposed in the book that the National Assembly had the power to elect and remove the central government officials (including members of the five branches). Accordingly, legislators of the Legislative Yuan, elected by the National Assembly instead of a direct participation of the people, did not represent the will of people like parliamentarians, and neither did the Legislative Yuan represent a full-fledged parliament.

"It's one of the ideals of representative politics to have representative institutions oversee the government. However, the representative institution, when vested with the legislative power, might bring about many problems in both theory and practice. Theoretically, legislation, as one of the governing powers, was naturally subjected to the supervision of a representative institution. Nevertheless, the representative institution serving as the legislature might fall into an autocratic legislature without proper supervision, for which France was a case in point." In America, the judicial power checked the legislature power, but the legitimacy was questionable when the judicial branch exercised supervisory power over the representative institution. In practice, different governing powers should work together, or the government would not work efficiently. However, in the U.K. where cabinet collective responsibility was practiced with fusion of executive and legislative powers, the government's power is not actually checked and balanced, so that "the so-called supervision of the government by a representative institution is inevitably a hypocritical proposition." (Zou, 1988, p. 179) For democracy to be achieved, it would be an ingenious institutional design to cede the legislative power away from the representative institution to a full-time department composed of legislative experts with the National Assembly exercising governing power and overseeing the government and the Legislative Yuan holding its legislative power. The problem lied in whether the reigning power was completely separable from the executive power, and whether the non-standing yet overstaffed National Assembly was competent enough to oversee the government.

10.2.2 *Deliberations on the National Assembly in "May Fifth Draft Constitution" and "Political Consultative Conference Constitutional Amendments" (1933–1946)*[7]

i. Provisions on the National Assembly in the May Fifth Draft Constitution and critical responses

The Nanjing National Government, a successor to the Beiyang Government, regarded "Teachings by Father of the Nation" as the highest and fundamental law.[8] Its guiding principles of constitution making always revolved around Sun Wen's constitutional thought. Naturally, the issue of the National Assembly became pivotal to its constitution making.

The May Fifth Draft Constitution (MFDC) was greatly influenced by Sun Yat-sen's constitutional idea in his later years, and its third section was "the National Assembly". In accordance with the blueprint laid out by Sun Wen in his *Fundamentals of National Reconstruction*, Article 32 of the draft invested such great powers in the National Assembly that the assembly, despite being an indirect democratic institution, replaced people's execution of direct democracy. More seriously, Article 31 of the draft set strict restrictions on the convening of the National Assembly.[9] The assembly indeed would not be able to shoulder the responsibility of a supreme authority unless its session was considerably extended and operated after the fashion of a European or American parliament. Consequently, the intended purpose of division of powers would not be met, neither would the real political authority (namely, the people) maintain its dominance over state affairs (Hu et al, 2000, pp. 521–524). Along with its device of extraordinary presidency, this constitutional draft would bring forth a dictatorship in the name of a five-power government under popular sovereignty. Therefore, shortly after the promulgation of the MFDC, Sa (1978) pointed out in his article that its enactment would inevitably lead to presidential dictatorship. The composition of the National Assembly also basically followed Sun Wen's design. Each county was entitled to one representative. Counties with a larger population would have more representatives accordingly. The quotas for Inner Mongolia, Tibet, and overseas Chinese would be decided by law.

There had been arguments within the Constitution Drafting Committee about the problems of the National Assembly, including its short sessions and inability to exercise political power effectively. It was suggested that a standing agency of the National Assembly should exercise political power when the assembly was in recess. Zhang Zhiben, the Vice-Chairman of the Constitution Drafting Committee, supported

---

[7] Xia & Hu, 2004

[8] In 1929, the KMT passed the decision to set "Teachings by Father of the Nation" as the highest and fundamental law in its third National Congress.

[9] The draft constitution stipulated the National Assembly should be convened by the President every three years and last for one month, or even two months if needed; a provisional Assembly could be convened upon the consent of two fifths representatives or under the President's summon.

such an idea (Zhang, 1966, p. 98). This proposal was inspired by the system of the Central Political Committee of the National Government for Article 55 of the first constitutional draft provided that "A National Council shall be in operation during the closure of the National Assembly". As the standing agency of the Assembly, the National Council "shall have 21 members and 10 alternate members that are elected by the National Assembly". However, this standing agency was removed from the MFDC that was eventually passed, for the following reasons: (i) political power did not need to be exercised constantly and thus it was not interrupted when it was not exercised; (ii) the National Council whose members were elected by representatives in the National Assembly was "the indirect of the indirect" and was composed of "the representatives of the representatives", resulting from poor popular support and inability to exercise political power (Sun, 1937, pp. 787–788); (iii) the standing agency amounted to "a supreme government" over the five-power government, which would limit the administrative capacity of the government. The third reason may be pivotal to the rejection of the proposal for the standing agency.

The MFDC, in the making, drew strong criticisms, many of which were directed at Sun Wen's theory on division of powers and design of the National Assembly. "The framers of the 'May Fifth Draft Constitution' formulated direct democracy in such a clumsy way that it ceased to express the will of the people." (Zhang Junmai Society of the Republic of China, 2005, p. 202) For want of a force strong enough to check the KMT at that time, these criticisms had little impact on the contents of the draft constitution and the framers went their own way with it (Yu, 1936). Nevertheless, criticisms and discussions of this kind made theoretical preparations and stimulated popular demand for subsequent amendment of the constitution.

ii. The agreement of the Political Consultative Conference and important amendments regarding the National Assembly

At the conclusion of War of Resistance against Japanese Aggression, a National Assembly had been scheduled to be convened on October 10, 1945 to draw up a constitution. Since the Chinese Communist Party and the other parties jointly opposed the apportionment of assembly representatives[10] and the MFDC, it was not until January 10, 1946 that the KMT reinvited a group of 38 people, including members of the Communist Party of China, China Democratic League, China Youth Party, China Democratic Socialist Party and public personages, to the Political Consultative Conference (PCC hereinafter) in Chongqing. Twelve agreements were reached at this conference and were referred to as Twelve Principles of the PCC. The "Twelve Principles" made important amendments to the MFDC, according to the first of which the National Assembly would be incorporeal and the Legislature should be changed from the law-making body as previously stipulated to a parliament. "The system as

[10] The Communist Party of China and other democratic parties believed the National Assembly representatives could not represent the people's will because they were elected under KMT's reign of white-terror, and thus advocated reelection (Jiang, 1976).

arranged in the 'May Fifth Constitutional Draft'—with the National Assembly exercising real power and a strong presidency—has been radically altered in the constitution amending principles of the PCC. Consequently, the National Assembly was weakened, the Legislative Yuan functioned like a parliament, and the Control Yuan resembled a senate, which exhibited characteristics of a cabinet system of government. In addition, the amended division of powers went far to the opposite". (Hu et al., 2000, pp. 525–526) Both sides finally reached an agreement on the apportionment of the constitution-making convention and on the proceedings of drawing up the constitution. Besides the representatives of the National Assembly elected according to the preceding *Election Law*, those newly added included 150 representatives of Taiwan province, the Northeast Region of China, professionals and 700 representatives of different political parties and public personages. The assembly representatives totaled 2050. Meanwhile, to deter the KMT representatives from passing the constitution with their numerical superiority, both sides specifically agreed that "The Constitution shall be passed by three fourths of the National Assembly" (Jiang, 1976, pp. 31–34, 48–49).

Concerning the "Twelve Principles of the PCC", the following resolutions on the principles of constitutional draft amendment were passed at the Second Plenary Session of the Sixth Central Committee of KMT: "(1) Constitution making shall be based on the *Fundamentals* of *National Construction*; (2) The National Assembly shall be a physical institution and shall exercise its power as specified in the *Fundamentals of National Construction* by way of convening its sessions. The increase of the frequency of its sessions shall be considered..." In due course, Sun Ke presented the KMT's suggestions to representatives from different parties for more deliberations in drafting the constitution. A new agreement was achieved in amending the constitution draft principle, where the first article goes "The National Assembly shall be a substantial institution exercising four powers."

The PCC organized the Draft Constitution Deliberation Committee to draw up the MFDC Amendment (i.e., the PCC Constitutional Amendment) in line with the "Twelve Principles of the PCC". Zhang Junmai played an important role in the work. Compared with the MFDC, the amendment significantly weakened the power of the National Assembly if not stripping it away. In the meantime, the Legislative Yuan, originally a full-time central legislature, was turned into an organ to represent the people to exercise power (Lei, 1957, pp. 24–25), and the Control Yuan was designed as an organ resembling the American Senate in terms of function and composition.[11] In this way, Sun Wen's thought on division of power was completely abandoned and the representative institution was re-adopted.

[11] The Control Yuan members were provincially elected and exercised the power of personnel appointment of Grand Justices of the Judicial and members of the Examination Yuan.

10.2.3 The National Assembly from Constitution-Making to Constitution-Enforcement (1946–1948)

i. Convoking the Constitutional National Assembly and restricting the powers of the National Assembly

On November 15, 1946, the Constitutional National Assembly was convened in Nanjing and passed the *Constitution of the Republic of China* on December 25. At the convention, the KMT representatives, who accounted for an overwhelming majority of the total number of deputies, attempted to fully restore the powers of the National Assembly stipulated in the MFDC, to empower the National Assembly to elect and recall legislators and supervisory commissioners and to change the assembly to a biennial convention. The Civil Society and Youth Party resolutely opposed altering the PCC principles. Under Chiang Kai-shek's pressure upon the KMT representatives, the National Assembly passed a constitution textually consistent with PCC Constitutional Amendment (Secretariat of the National Assembly, 1946). The constitution makers artfully and significantly reduced the power of the National Assembly in two ways: cutting down the frequency of meetings (the plenary meeting was held only every 6 years) and delaying (suspending) its power to make, amend or repeal a law (Sa, 1993, p. 536). The National Assembly became a general assembly similar to the electoral college of the U.S. presidential campaign, meeting 90 days before the expiration of the presidency; at the same time, it also assumed the responsibility of constitutional amendment. The two powers to make, amend or repeal a law were not exercised for then. According to Item 2 Article 27 of the Constitution, only when more than half of the counties and cities across the country have exercised the two powers to make, amend or repeal a law shall the National Assembly adopt measures to exercise them,[12] which in fact prevented the National Assembly from exercising the two powers in the long run.

ii. Constitution-enforcement National Assembly and *Temporary Provisions Effective During the Period of Rebellion*

The newly passed constitution stipulated that the National Assembly should comprise representatives from all counties and cities, Inner Mongolia and Tibet, overseas Chinese, professional communities, and women's associations. In 1947, the National Government promulgated *The National Assembly Organization Law*, the *Law on the Election and Recall of the National Assembly Members*, and the *Enforcement Regulations for the Election and Recall of the National Assembly Members*, and then carried out the election of the National Assembly representatives. On March 29, 1948, the first Constitution-enforcement National Assembly was convened in the Nanjing National Assembly Hall. The electoral law prescribed the total number of representatives as 3045, whereas in fact 2908 were legally elected. 1679 representatives were present on that day where the quorum was met (Xie, 2001, p. 199).

---

[12] As Zhang Junmai recalled, this restriction was proposed by Wu Tiecheng the KMT General Secretary (Central Party Department of the Democratic Socialist Party, 1976).

The National Assembly formulated the *Temporary Provisions Effective During the Period of Rebellion* and elected Chiang Kai-shek as President. At that time, China was caught in a fierce civil war. In the early days of the convention, some representatives proposed to revise the *Constitution*, mainly because the KMT representatives attempted a comeback to restore the MFDC by amending the *Constitution*. 689 representatives headed by Zhang Zhiben proposed to amend *The Constitution*, expand the power of the National Assembly and to convene biennially, to which the representatives from both the Youth Party and Democratic Socialist Party strongly objected, and heated debates occurred at the venue. Finally, a compromise was reached to make certain amendments to The *Constitution* in the form of the *Temporary Provisions Effective During the Period of Rebellion*. Wang Shijie explained the nature of *Temporary Provisions* as follows: first, the *Temporary Provisions* were constitutional amendments; second, the *Constitution* itself was not changed, because the *Temporary Provisions* was effective in a limited span and differed from the *Constitution*'s provisions (Xie, 2001, pp. 45–46).

The main contents of the *Temporary Provisions* were as follows. First, the President was empowered to take "emergency measures"; second, an extraordinary session of the National Assembly should be convoked no later than December 25, 1950 to discuss the issue of constitutional amendment. At this stage, the KMT conservatives never forgot to urge Chiang Kai-shek to fulfill the promise of constitutional amendment in *Temporary Provisions* in order to restore the MFDC (Zhang, 1966, p. 127).[13] After the KMT government fled to Taiwan province, the illegal National Assembly altered the legal procedures due to insufficient quorum and misinterpreted the original purpose of The *Constitution* in order to reconvene the assembly and maintain its legitimacy. Upon resumption, the Assembly negotiated a deal with the President to expand its powers. It even went so far as to amend the constitution to fatten itself up, by raising the attendance allowance, setting up standing organs, and even extending its own term of office. What was worse, it took the advantage of the constitutional amendment power to suppress the Legislative Yuan and retaliate against the Grand Justice. The National Assembly resorted to every conceivable means for its own sake, and finally deserved to eat its own bitter fruit. The constitutional amendments paved the way for the utter ruin of the National Assembly system.

10.2.4 Paradoxes of the National Assembly

i. The number of representatives

Generally speaking, the National Assembly seemed more representative than the earlier Parliament of the Republic of China because it was composed of about two or three thousand members in total with each one representing a single county. However, "in terms of population, each member of the British House of Commons represents

[13] "A creditable check will be cashed sooner or later" (Zhang, 1966).

43,000 people, while each representative of our national assembly has to represent 150,000 people. Which of the two is direct democracy? … It seems unbelievable to say that this national assembly can be free from malpractice of the ordinary parliamentary representation" (Cheng, 1936, p. 1031). How could the National Assembly work with 3000 representatives in it? The representatives were too few to make direct democracy, but too many to function properly as a permanent organ. Therefore, the National Assembly thus formed fell short of both direct democracy and efficiency in political affairs. Zhang Junmai suggested an incorporeal national assembly by which the people of the whole country directly exercised political power (the first was the suffrage), or a non-permanent national assembly built upon the US presidential electoral college, but his suggestion was never accepted because it differed considerably from Sun Wen's *Fundamentals of National Reconstruction*. The paradox about the number of members composing the National Assembly was never solved. Merely a bigger body with more members without full function and power, the National Assembly was far from a symbol of direct democracy.

ii. The dilemma of power

Different from the parliaments in Western countries, the National Assembly did not have legislative, budgetary, or supervisory powers or any other tool to check the government on behalf of the people. "Constitutional amendment is not regular. Concerning political power other than suffrage, recall is considered as a 'big stick behind the door', and the powers to make and repeal laws, 'two guns behind the door'. That is, they are powers 'semper paratus, but never regularly exercised'. It is highly questionable if the National Assembly designed in this way can put an effective check on the government". (Li, 1988, pp. 162–174) Although unable to curb the government, the National Assembly never failed to get everything on the wrong track by "amending the Constitution and causing chaos". "In the power structure, the National Assembly contains contradictions. It had short sessions and few functions while the representatives served fixed terms of office without specific tasks. When those incumbent representatives, eager to cut a figure, highlighted the National Assembly as an important constitutional organ, and even attempted to amend the constitution to expand their power and interests, they tended to disturb the existing power structure, clash particularly with the Legislative Yuan which was essentially parliamentary, and subject other constitutional institutions to unexpected risks". (Zhong, 2006, pp. 232–233) As a loosely organized body with a large number of members and a few sessions, the National Assembly, despite holding great power, could not work well and posed no serious threat; however, when it worked as a permanent institution, its arbitrary expansion of power would be highly likely to occur.

"Power tends to corrupt, and absolute power corrupts absolutely." Power not only breeds corruption, but also increases its own value. Therefore, it can also be said that power tends to expand on its own, and absolute power expands absolutely. The National Assembly had the sole power to amend the Constitution, and it would be unlikely for the representatives to exercise the power without making underhand deals, peddling influence, or advancing its own power. It might be said that this

National Assembly did worse than that scandal-ridden Parliament in the early years of the ROC.

iii. The myth of political legitimac

"Political legitimacy" is a key concept in the study of the ROC constitutional history. It was self-delusional of the KMT to pin its political legitimacy on members of the National Assembly (shortened as MNAs). Those deluded MNAs began to assume the symbol of political legitimacy, greedily demanding money and power, which corrupted the Assembly. As in the early ROC, those in power flaunted formal political legitimacy, but manipulated democracy and the rule of law while the "representatives" were also happy to collude and share interests. Eventually, the signboard of political legitimacy was smashed and the National Assembly itself was ruined.

iv. Alienation of the National Assembly

The National Assembly deceased, but its fundamental significance cannot be denied, and its paradoxes cannot be entirely attributed to Sun Yat-sen's thought of national assembly (separation of powers); its institutional design was an important exploration toward democracy in a vast country with a large population. The National Assembly, designed to be different from the Western parliaments, was the sovereignty (exercising supreme power), and the Legislative Yuan was the full-time legislature. Compared with the parliament composed of three to five hundred members, the National Assembly comprised of thousands of representatives was indeed less corruptible and controllable, and more representative of the people. In 1946, the framers of the constitution (such as Zhang Junmai) designed the National Assembly upon the American electoral college, which was a better option. However, the National Assembly developed into a parliament with its members turning into full-time parliamentarians, and began to compete with the Legislative Yuan for parliamentary political resources, which was the root of all turmoil.

10.3 Parliament or Legislative Committee: The Status and Power of the Legislative Yuan

On October 8, 1928, the National Government promulgated the *Organic Law of the National Government of the Republic of China* to try out the five-chamber system Sun Yat-sen had formulated; The third chapter entitled "The Legislative Yuan" stipulated that the Legislative Yuan was the supreme legislative organ of the National Government and had the power to decide upon legislation, budgets, amnesties, declaration of war, negotiation for peace, conclusion of treaties and other important international affairs (Article 25) (Xia & Hu, 2004, p. 787). On October 20, The National Government (1928, October 26) promulgated the *Organic Law of the Legislative Yuan* (The National Government Gazette, 1928). Since the establishment of the Legislative Yuan, there was a constant debate over its status and power in the political and academic circles, and modifications were frequently made to the principles. In 1946, more than half of the twelve principles reached on the draft constitution at the PCC were related to the Legislative Yuan. However, the "twelve principles of the PCC" and even the *Constitution of the ROC* implemented since December 1947 could not end the debate over the status of the Legislative Yuan. The debate was focused on whether the Legislative Yuan, as the central legislature, was similar to the representative organ (Congress) in Europe and America, and whether it should have the same powers as a typical Euro-American Congress.

10.3.1 Representativeness of the Legislative Yuan

As discussed earlier, Sun Yat-sen was closely related or similar to J. S. Mill in terms of the relationship between the Legislative Yuan and the National Assembly he discoursed upon in his late constitutional thoughts. Mill proposed that the power of supervising the government should be distinguished from the governing competence, and the parliament was supposed to oversee the government, "review and even facilitate" good laws whereas legislation needed to be entrusted to experts like the administration and the judiciary. As a faithful follower of Sun Yat-sen's thought, Hu Hanmin, founder of the Legislative Yuan, discussed the representativeness of the chamber in nearly the same way as Mill. Hu deemed it to be different from the European and American parliaments because the Legislative Yuan was neither a supervisory organ in terms of power nor a representative institution in terms of status; the selection of legislators should be based upon their expertise and political integrity instead of their representativeness. However, since the establishment of the Legislative Yuan, Hu's idea of non-representational legislators (a non-representational Legislative Yuan) was challenged both inside and outside the KMT. Consequently, the Legislative Yuan kept certain traces of a representative organ.

i. Hard quota for underrepresented regions and ethnic minorities

Regional representation of legislators began with the establishment of the Legislative Yuan, and was focused on whether quotas should be guaranteed in regions of ethnic groups such as Mongolians, Hui and Tibetans. Certain Mongolians and Tibetans repeatedly requested hard quotas of legislators, and even submitted petitions to the KMT Central Committee; the Central Political Conference did not immediately reject the petitions, but suspended it until the creation of the Legislative Yuan. In 1929, the Legislative Yuan officially rejected the petitions because Hu Hanmin considered the Legislative Yuan to be "a legislature representing the Party instead of regions or professions" (Hung, 1999, pp. 16–18).

Hu denied the regional representation of legislators conceptually and institutionally, which does not mean that provincial and ethnic identities were not considered in apportionment of legislators. Some scholars examined the geographical distribution of legislators in the first and second Legislative Yuan chaired by Hu. The results showed that most of the 49 legislators came from Guangdong, Hubei, Hunan and

Zhejiang where the KMT had a long tradition, but, with a couple of exceptions,[14] at least one member hailed from a single province including such border provinces of ethnic minorities as Xinjiang, Inner Mongolia and Tibet (Chen & Luo, 2000, pp. 65–70). In fact, the regional distribution of legislators was roughly based upon certain rules: a naturally higher proportion of legislators came from the old National Revolutionary base areas (such as Guangdong and Hubei) and from culturally developed regions (such as Jiangsu and Zhejiang), but nearly every province was guaranteed a member. In the selection of legislators, Hu would consider recommendations or nominations from senior KMT Central Committee members and senior KMT members because the provinces did not have the power to nominate. When selecting legislators from the recommended candidates to be submitted to the National Government for appointment, he would also consider candidates' qualifications and provincial origins.

Hu's rejection of the regional apportionment of legislators stemmed chiefly from his worries not only over conflicts of regional interests and political cliques inside the Legislative Yuan but also over work efficiency of the office as a result of those conflicts. He worried the least by a manipulated balance of nominations between different provinces which did not have the power to nominate. During the KMT Tutelage Period, the Legislative Yuan featured both high efficiency and regional representation of legislators.

ii. Representation: legislators' qualifications and appointment

1. Expertise (elite) targeted appointment of early legislators

Early on October 24, 1928 when the preparation of the Legislative Yuan was under way, the appointment criteria for legislators, proposed by Hu and passed by the Central Political Council, "focused on loyal services to the party-state in the history of the KMT, freedom of any speech and action against the Party in the revolution, and considerable expertise and experience in law, politics and economy" (Xu, 1992, p. 258). The criteria can be said to include both "revolutionary" and "professional" parts. The former required the candidates not to have been a "reactionary in personal history". For example, whoever had opposed the Prime Minister would not be selected. It was not an absolutely necessity for the candidate to have been an "old revolutionary" or actively participated in the revolution; neither was it necessary for them to have been Kuomintang Party members, and unaffiliated experts (including young experts having returned from overseas studies) could also be considered (Peng, 1986, pp. 56–57). Of the legislators, many were political elites "well-connected with the party-state", but others were apolitical elites with a strong professional background. For example, Ma Yinchu, an economist, Wei Tingsheng, a financial expert, Huang Youchang, a professor of law, and Shi Shangkuan, a legal expert, all sat as legislators for four consecutive terms.[15] Dr. Wu Jingxiong sat in the third and fourth

[14] Some legislators' provincial identities hadn't been identified so that it was uncertain if the couple of provinces had a legislator at all.

[15] Shi Shangkuan returned to China in 1927, and was thirty when appointed in 1928.

Legislative Yuan.[16] Of the 49 members composing the first Legislative Yuan,, about half were well-educated in law, economics and politics, and 40% to 50% had received overseas education (political elites and professional elites included); In terms of age distribution, about half of them were under forty years old, and four were under thirty (Chen & Luo, 2000; Hung, 1999, pp. 46–7, 179).

The number of the legislators also speaks of "elitism". The 1928 *Organic Law of the National Government* stipulated that number to be between 49 and 99 (Article 27), and it was kept to the minimum of 49 when Hu Hanmin was president, rose to 60 when Shao Yuanchong and Qin Zhenxian were vice presidents, and spiraled to 90 or so and even to the maximum of 99 when Sun Ke was in office. However, the size looked "oddly small" compared to parliaments of other countries (Xie, 2000, p. 220).

2. The key to representation: appointment or election

From 1928 through 1930, the tutelage came under fire soon after its implementation, and legislators' representation was one of the targets. It is legally and politically possible to consider an independent legislature a prototype of a parliament routinely elected by the people in modern countries; even in his teachings, Sun Yat-sen repeatedly stated that legislators were elected "representatives". In society, the intellectual elite demanded the enactment of the Constitution to protect the rights of the people and the popular election of legislators to ensure their legitimacy and authority. "The Hu Hanmin-led Legislative Yuan consists of neither representatives nor experts … They do not have, and should not have legislative power which the people have not entrusted them with. Not long ago, the Nanjing Legislative Yuan went so far as to impeach the foreign minister for signing treaties without authorization when the national representative body has the sole power to ratify treaties. That attempt shows that the Legislative Yuan was arrogating legislative power to itself" (Luo, 1930, p. 22).

After Hu's resignation in 1931, the selection of legislators showed signs of transition from appointment to election with the promulgation of the *Provisional Constitution for the Period of Political Tutelage of the Republic of China* (*the Provisional Constitution* hereinafter), and enhanced representativeness helped the Legislative Yuan to establish its parliamentary status. In December 1931, the *Organic Law of the National Government of the Republic of China* (1931 *Organic Law* hereinafter), amended in accordance with the *Provisional Constitution*, increased the representativeness of the legislators by stipulating that "The Legislative Yuan shall be composed of 50–100 Legislative Members, who shall be appointed, according to law, by the chairman of the National Government at the instance of the President of the Legislative Yuan. Half of the members shall be elected by legal civil associations" (Article 30) (Xia & Hu, 2004, p. 796). The adjustment of an odd number (49–99) to an even number (50–100) made it possible to evenly distribute the appointed legislative

[16] Having received his Juris Doctor degree in America, Wu Jingxiong was recommended by Sun Ke to serve both as a legislator and as vice president of the Constitution Drafting Committee, and published a trial version of the draft constitution in his name, exerting a great influence on constitution drafting, before he joined the KMT.

members and the elected ones, the latter of whom came not from regional representation but from occupational representation the National Assembly had practiced. The amended *Organic Law* also stipulated that half of supervisory members of the Control Yuan should be elected like the legislative members (Article 48). Therefore, both of those ruling organs tended to be parliamentary when they shared powers of a Western parliament (the Legislative Yuan had legislative power and the Control Yuan had the power of impeachment).

However, the Second Plenary Session of the Fourth Central Executive Committee of the KMT resolved in March 1932 that the National Government should amend the 1931 *Organic Law* and revert to the old law by abolishing the article of even distribution of appointed and elected legislators when the January 28 incident Japan provoked in 1932 put China in grave peril. The Declaration of the Session responded to representative institution that "it takes time and procedures to establish Constitutionalism, and the immediate priority is to form a representative institution to lay a foundation for popular sovereignty during the Period of Political Tutelage" (Rong, 1985, p. 145) Yet, the "representative institution" here was not the Legislative Yuan; in December of the same year, the Third Plenary Session passed a plan to establish a representative institution, resolving to create a National Political Council as a central representative institution in addition to the five chambers of the National Government (Rong, 1985, p. 179–180). Nevertheless, the authorities soon questioned the necessity of summoning the Council after the National Assembly convened so that the Council never met since 1933 and the *Organic Law of the National Political Council* was revoked. Not until 1938 when a national war was waged again Japanese invaders did the National Government set up the National Political Council which, far from the one having been proposed in 1932, was neither a parliament nor a legislature, but a quasi-representative institution (Ma, 1987, pp. 593–594, 611–614).

It was perhaps due to the suspension of the National Political Council Program in 1933 that legislators did not deny the representativeness of the Legislative Yuan when preparing the MFDC from 1933 through 1936, and the representativeness of the Legislative Yuan was greatly boosted. The National Assembly had the power to elect legislative members, but the provinces had the power to nominate, and seats were assigned on a regional basis. "All provinces including Mongolia, Tibet, and expatriates shall nominate candidates to participate in the primary election and submit them to the National Assembly for re-election based on certain apportionment. The legislators shall not be restricted to members of the National Assembly and distributed in accordance with the following provisions: (1) Four members shall be elected for a province with a population of less than five million … 16 for a province with a population of above 30 million. (2) Eight shall be elected for Mongolia and Tibet respectively. (3) Eight shall be elected for expatriates." (Article 67 of the MFDC) (Xia & Hu, 2004, p. 987)

Significant amendments were made to the MFDC at the PCC held after the War of Resistance against Japanese Aggression, but the articles about the Legislative Yuan are essentially the same in spite of differences in quantity when a comparison is made between the MFDC and the *Constitution of the Republic of China* promulgated in 1947. The government is similar to the presidential system in the former and to the parliamentary system in the latter. Legislative members are indirectly elected in the former and directly elected in the latter which gives greater power to the Legislative Yuan. And yet, both recognize the parliamentary status of the Legislative Yuan.

iii. Representation in the Legislative Yuan: organization and rules of procedure

Whether the Legislative Yuan was a parliament depends not only on the way legislators are elected, but also on its internal representativeness. Regardless of the number of members and the way of election, a parliament has distinctive organizations and working procedures, and in those two aspects, there were no fundamental differences between the Legislative Yuan and a Western parliament during the political tutelage period. Here are a few similarities.

1. Standing committees

According to the 1928 *Organic Law of the Legislative Yuan*, the Legislative Yuan exercised its power and established the Legislative Affairs Committee, the Foreign Affairs Committee, the Finance Committee, and the Economy Committee (Article 1); Legislative members sat on different committees according to their professional expertise (Article 3). The Law also provided that the Legislative Yuan could create or abolish committees (Article 2), and accordingly, the first session of the First Legislative Yuan set up the Military Committee (The Legislative Yuan, 1929). The above five committees were permanent or specialized. During the period of political tutelage, the heavy legislative workload compelled the Legislative Yuan to form such task-based committees responsible for drafting important laws as the Civil Law Committee, the Penal Code Committee, the Constitution Drafting Committee and so on, which were called special or ad hoc committees, similar to those established by the Euro-American parliaments. The committees played a critical role in the Legislative Yuan as they examined or drafted bills according to division of labor. In order to regulate the organization and procedures of the committees, the National Government promulgated the *Organic Law of the Committees of the Legislative Yuan* in 1928.

2. Rules of procedure

a. Quorums

"The Legislative Yuan shall not convene unless a quorum of one-third of its membership is present. A resolution is passed with a simple majority of the members present, and is decided upon by the President when votes are equally divided" (Articles 18 and 19 of the 1928 *Organic Law of the Legislative Yuan*) (The National Government Gazette, 1928). When deliberating on a bill, parliaments of Western countries usually adopt a simple majority. However, Hu Hanming, the first president, set the quorum of the Legislative Yuan meeting attendance at one-third instead of the usual one-half, in order to avoid a failed session due to insufficient attendance, and to improve the efficiency of the Legislative Yuan's proceedings (The Second Historical Archives of China, 1994, p. 259). A low quorum may weaken democratic representation in legislation and increase the chance of manipulation by the President of the Legislative Yuan. However, what legally constitutes a quorum vary greatly from country to country, and the variations do not necessarily relate to democracy of the parliament.

b. Three readings

Promulgated by the National Government in 1928 and amended in 1935, the *Rules of Procedure of the Legislative Yuan* stipulated that "all bills shall go through three readings before being put to vote" (Article 10); and the third section, consisting of 11 articles (The Second Historical Archives of China, 1994, pp. 265, 267–268), specified the procedure of the three readings which, a regular practice in the legislative process of Western parliaments, aimed to reach a final resolution through repeated deliberations, phased voting, careful consideration and debates.

10.3.2 Powers and Limitations of the Legislative Yuan

Whether the Legislative Yuan was parliamentary or not depends both on its representativeness and on its powers and functions. The legislators "were not elected, but appointed by the National Government upon the advice of the President of the Legislative Yuan, and the power of impeachment had been transferred to the Control Yuan, so that the Legislative Yuan differed from a regular parliament. However, it retained powers to decide on laws, budgets, pardons, declarations of war, peace negotiation, ratification of treaties, etc. so as to be fundamentally different from the previous Legislative Bureau" (Chen, 1947, pp. 179–180). Compared with the European and American parliaments, the Legislative Yuan was not complete or unique because of considerable limitations on its powers. However, the Legislative Yuan, as an independent executive body, retained the core powers of the National Assembly. In June 1929, the Second Plenary Session of the Third National Congress of the KMT passed the *Laws on the Exercise of the Executive Powers*, Article 1 of which laid down the powers of the Legislative Yuan: "All bills relating to law (including regulations and organic bills), all financial bills relating to the tax burden on the people, treaties relating to national sovereignty, and other international agreements, shall not become law without a resolution by the Legislative Yuan on the condition that they fall within the scope of legislation. The Legislative Yuan shall raise questions when a bill is promulgated and put into effect without its approval, and failure to do so shall mean dereliction of duty. The promulgation and implementation shall be deemed ultra vires." (Rong, 1985, p. 761) During the period of political tutelage, the Legislative Yuan maintained its relative institutional and operational independence under the constraints of the institutional and political environment.

i. The legislative power

1. The *Regulation Standards Act* and the exclusive legislative power of the Legislative Yuan

Before the Legislative Yuan was founded, the *Legislative Procedures Act* of February 1928 had set it down that "The Central Political Conference has the power to decide on all statutes, which shall be submitted by the Central Executive Committee to the National Government for promulgation. All statutes made hereby are generally referred to as 'acts'" (Article 1) (The Second Historical Archives of China, 1994, p. 254). After the establishment of the Legislative Yuan, the highest legislative body of the National Government, in December 1928, the Central Political Conference adjusted its role to determine only the principles of legislation. A comparison of the first articles from the two acts, the *Regulation Standards Act* promulgated in May 1929 and the *Legislative Procedures Act*, may confirm the institutional replacement of the Central Political Conference by the Legislative Yuan as a legislative body: "All bills, passed through three readings in the Legislative Yuan and promulgated by the National Government, shall be named as 'act'". Article 2 of the *Regulation Standards Act* specified the objects that should be stipulated by a statute: "amendment or discarding of existing laws, objects required to stipulate as a statute expressly stipulated, and other objects concerning the organization of a national government agency or the rights or obligations of the people that the Legislative Yuan deems necessary to be stipulated by law." Meanwhile, the *Legislative Procedures Act* also required other national organs to make their acts, regulations and rules based on and "consistent with the laws" enacted by the Legislative Yuan, and forbid them to circumvent the Legislative Yuan by "creating their own regulations, statutes, and rules in place of necessary legislation" (The Second Historical Archives of China, 1994, pp. 255–256). Therefore, the Legislative Yuan was the supreme branch in the entire legislative system of the National Government.

2. Restrictions on the legislative power of the Legislative Yuan under the *Legislative Procedures Program*

Shortly before the establishment of the Legislative Yuan, the Central Committee of the KMT resolved in November 1928, "The Political Conference shall first lay down the legislative principles by which the Legislative Yuan will draft and formulate statutes and regulations" (Xu, 1992, p. 256). That means that, during the period of political tutelage, the Political Conference took over the power of the National Assembly to create legislative principles, limiting the legislative power of the Legislative Yuan. That resolution was elaborated and institutionalized into the *Legislative Procedures Program* adopted by the Central Executive Committee of the KMT in June 1932.[17] The *Program* focused on restrictions of the Political Conference on the

[17] The *Legislative Procedures Program* was finalized in April 1933. See more details in Xia & Hu (2004, pp. 802–803).

Legislative Yuan's legislative power chiefly by requiring the former to make laws in accordance with the legislative principles agreed upon by the Political Conference, significantly curbing the legislative discretion of the Legislative Yuan.

However, it is not to be taken for granted that the Legislative Yuan was subservient to the Political Conference. In fact, the Legislative Yuan had a strong influence at the Political Conference as could be seen from the personnel arrangement: some of the former's presidents, vice presidents and members were also members of the latter's Central Committee, even holding 1/5 of the latter's total seats; the former gained more influence when the latter was divided into groups, for three of the eight group leaders came from the Legislative Yuan in 1929; in addition, several legislators often attended Political Conference and voiced their opinions as non-voting members due to their expertise or well-established party membership, and the chairmen of the five standing committees of the Legislative Yuan sat in on the Political Conference on a regular basis after President Sun Ke's efforts (Hung, 1999, pp. 74–88).

ii. The power to approve the draft constitution

It was stipulated in the 1931 *Provisional Constitution* that the draft constitution be agreed upon by the Legislative Yuan (Article 86) and passed by the National Assembly (Article 87) (Xia & Hu, 2004, p. 835). Therefore, institutionally, the Legislative Yuan had the exclusive power to deliberate on and finalize the draft constitution, showing its unique role in shaping the constitutional system of the Republic. Since 1933 when the Legislative Yuan established the Constitution Drafting Committee, Sun Ke, President of the Legislative Yuan, worked as the chairman of the Committee for a long time. When the KMT Party, the Communist Party of China and other parties deliberated on the PCC Constitutional Amendment after the Second Sino-Japanese War, Sun was the chief representative of the KMT Party and the convener of the Draft Constitution Deliberation Committee, and most experts (such as Lin Bin, Wu Jingxiong, Shi Shangkuan, Lou Tongsun and Huang Youchang) invited to the Committee came from the Legislative Yuan (Lei, 2010, p. 101). It is true that the Legislative Yuan was constrained by the Political Conference in formulating the MFDC, and that the "Twelve Principles of the PCC" was amended by the KMT Central Committee and tested by the Constitutional National Assembly. However, the formulation of the MFDC and the PCC Constitutional Amendment unquestionably expanded both representation and power of the Legislative Yuan constitutionally.

iii. Budgetary power (fiscal power)

A parliament scrutinizes and passes bills, but it has another core function: budget review for which the parliament is figuratively compared to a treasurer holding the "money bag" of a country. The *Budget Act* the National Government promulgated in

September 1932 provided clear legal guidelines for the Executive Yuan to check the budget, and was partially amended in 1937. The *Act* specified the time limit for the Executive Yuan to submit and the central government to release the general budget. Article 15 of the 1938 *Enforcement Rules of the Budget Act* defined October 10th as the deadline by which the Executive Yuan should submit the general budget and related documents to the Legislative Yuan for review each year, and the Legislative Yuan would have to check and submit the budget to the National Government for release by December 1 of the same year (Lin, 1940, pp. 10–11, 26). In reality, the Central Political Conference had approved the general budget before it was presented to the Legislative Yuan for review[18] and technical refinement of specific entries, but it doesn't mean that the review was "merely ceremonial" and the Legislative Yuan, "having no power to appeal for reconsideration, amend and reject" (Chen & Chen, 2008), appeared unable to do anything in fiscal matters. However, Article 47 of the aforementioned Budget Law specifically stipulated solutions in case of the failure of certain parts of the general budget to pass, which at least institutionally provided a legal basis for the Legislative Yuan to reject the budget and for the corresponding remedy.

In fact, the Legislative Yuan was so much concerned about financial matters during the period of political tutelage that it monitored the national financial plans by reviewing the budget, oversaw and influenced the national financial policies by examining financial bills. It even clashed with the Minister of Finance over the *Penalty Act for Offences against the Silver Standard* and the *Regulations of the 1931 Public Bonds for Disaster Relief*, forcing the National Government (and the Central Political Conference) to compromise. Moreover, finance was the key place where the Legislative Yuan would raise questions because hard-earned money of the people mattered (Hung, 1999, pp. 142–146, 152–159).

iv. Interpellation (oversight)

In addition to the legislative and budgetary powers, a parliament also has the powers to oversee (raising questions about government policy) and to sanction (impeachment). Article 14 of the *Organic Law of the Legislative Yuan* stipulated that "The Legislative Yuan may interpellate all Yuans and all Committees and Ministries of the Executive Yuan on the execution of the resolutions passed here in this Yuan. The foregoing interpellation shall be approved and conducted by this Yuan." That is a permissive provision that authorized the Legislative Yuan to exercise the right of interpellation. The features of interpellation during the period of political tutelage may be summed up here: (1) It was the Legislative Yuan instead of individual legislative members that could interpellate so that interpellation must be approved by the Legislative Yuan; (2) Those to be interpellated in a written form included the Judicial, the examination, and the Control Yuan as well as the executive branch; (3) The reply usually took a written form and the heads of the chambers, ministries, and committees did not have

[18] The Supreme National Defense Committee, which took the place of the Central Political Conference during the war against the Japanese Aggression, had even greater restrictions on the Legislative Yuan's power to review the budget.

to appear before the Legislative Yuan for more queries; (4) Interpellation would be conducted only in two circumstances: other organs' infringement of the Legislative Yuan's power to make resolutions or failure to carry out the Legislative Yuan's resolutions; (5) Most notably, the organs did not take political responsibility for the interpellation and the Legislative Yuan had no power to force them to reply. When dissatisfied with the replies of the various organs, the Legislative Yuan could not pursue interpellation, but could refer them to the KMT Central Political Conference for accountability (Cai & Yu, 1993, p. 18).

During the period of political tutelage, the National Political Council, a provisional representative institution, had the power of interpellation like the British parliament. In March 1938, the Provisional National Congress of the KMT adopted the *Guidelines on Fighting the War of Resistance and National Reconstruction*, resolving to establish the National Political Council during the extraordinary period. In July of the same year, the first National Political Council convened in Hankou with over 30 of the 156 members coming from the opposition parties. The National Political Council, not a strictly representative institution, had no legislative power, but it had the right to advise, inquire, and hear government reports. The Councilors were usually incisive enough to overwhelm the responding officials so that, in certain cases, some ministers collapsed out of physical exhaustion when answering questions on the floor of the legislature. Improper written replies of any department might cause serious consequences so that the department head had to apologize on the floor and withdraw their replies for revision (Ma, 1987, pp. 608–609). It is not to be assumed by the remarkable political interpellation that the National Political Council was essentially as powerful as a parliament, for it did not have the legislative power, the core power of a parliament, and its motions did not relate to law. The interpellation might put pressure of public opinion on the executive branch, but a parliament could put a real check on it by exercising its supreme power (in legislation, budget, and so on) instead of interpellation. The early Parliament was politically inquisitorial and legislatively apathetic such that Sun Yat-sen amended its system later on. In addition, the National Political Council, meeting only every three months for a short session (10 days),[19] was not a permanent representative institution, preventing itself from challenging the parliamentary status of the Legislative Yuan. As a provisional representative organ, it came to an end when the *Constitution of the Republic of China* was made, a mixed polity of presidential and parliamentary systems was established, and interpellation was transferred to the Legislative Yuan after China's victory in the War of Resistance.

v. Power of consent over major concerns

The 1928 *Organic Law of the National Government of the Republic of China* decreed that, the Legislative Yuan had the power to decide not only on legislation, budgets and amnesties, but also on declaration of war, negotiation for peace and other important international affairs. "The so-called 'other important international affairs' follow 'declaration of war' and 'negotiation for peace' which are indeed important, but

[19] The Council met every six months after the *Organic Rules of the National Political Council* was amended in 1939.

it remains undefined when 'other' international matters are significant enough for the Legislative Yuan to decide on … All formal treaties may be said to constitute 'important international affairs' specified in the *Organic Law of the National Government*. The Political Committee (or the supreme National Defense Committee) should decide whether other international matters are important enough to be referred to the Legislative Yuan for consideration." (Wang & Qian, 1997, pp. 450–451) During the period of political tutelage, the Legislative Yuan had the power to examine and approve formal treaties and declaration of war and peace negotiations, and also set up a standing committee to examine foreign affairs. The power of the Legislative Yuan over declarations of war, negotiation for peace, treaties, and other important international matters (including amnesties) was "what scholars called the power of consent" which, "only vested in the parliament of a country with three powers under a constitution, was exercised by the parliamentary body, the Legislative Yuan under the experimental government of five powers … The Legislative Yuan, having the power over those matters and exercising the power of consent, was not much different from the parliament of a constitutional state" (Xie, 2000, pp. 223–224).

10.3.3 Summary

Generally speaking, although having made significant amendments to the Western representative system, Sun Yat-sen's constitutional thought could not fundamentally eradicate the parliamentary nature of the Legislative Yuan. During the period of political tutelage, the Legislative Yuan was not only seriously flawed in representation of public opinion, but also functionally subject to the KMT Central Committee acting as the National Assembly, but no other political body could replace it to assume the role of a real parliament. It is clear that the Legislative Yuan tended to enhance its representation, functions and powers from the 1932 *Provisional Constitution for the Period of Political Tutelage of the Republic of China* to the 1936 MFDC. The Legislative Yuan and its members learned to build up experience and authority during the period of political tutelage. The MFDC was not passed due to the Japanese invasion and the failure to punctually convene the Constitutional National Assembly. As a provisional quasi-central representative body in wartime, the National Political Council did not have legislative power, and could not propose bills relating to law (Ma, 1987, pp. 603–614), nor could it be considered more similar to a parliament than the Legislative Yuan.

After their trial and training during the period of political tutelage, the Legislative Yuan grew eventually into the primary (though not the only) parliament with the enactment of the *Constitution of the Republic of China* in 1947, which Hu Hanmin, the chief architect of the tutelage system and the first President of the Legislative Yuan, had not expected. To sum up, the Legislative Yuan moved in due course beyond its founding father's teachings to become a nearly full-fledged parliament institutionally, operationally, and theoretically, chiefly because its organization and powers compared with those of a regular Western parliament. Hu attempted to distinguish the Legislative Yuan from a representative body (de-parliamentarization), but he was unable to deny the underlying parliamentary paradigm when designing the Legislative Yuan during the period of political tutelage.

References

Cai, D., & Yu, Y. (1993). *Minguo yilai lifa jiguan zhixun zhidu zhi yanbian* [Development of Interpellation of the Legislative Yuan]. *Lifayuan yuanwen* [The Legislative Yuan Monthly], (12), 16–25.

Cheng, J. (1936). *Zai lun xianfa chugao xianzheng'an zhong zhi zhongyang zhengzhi yu guomin dahui* [A reexamination of the central political system and the National Assembly in the amendment to the first draft constitution]. In Z. Yu (Ed.) & J. Wu (Pr.), *Xianfa wenxuan* [Selected essays on constitution] (pp. 1029–1035). Shanghai Law Editing and Translating Press.

Chen, C. (1998). *Zhonghua minguo xianfa yuanli* [Principles of constitution of the Republic of China]. Mingwen Book Company.

Chen, H., & Luo, J. (2000). *Guomin zhengfu yi er jie lifayuan zucheng fenxi* [Analysis on the formation of the first and second Legislative Yuan under the National Government]. *Minguo dang'an* [Republican Archives], (2), 65–70.

Chen, H., & Chen, S. 2008. *Kangzhan shiqi lifayuan de tiaozheng* [The adjustment of the Legislative Yuan during the War of Resistance against the Japanese Aggression]. *Jiangsu xingzheng xueyuan xuebao* [Journal of Jiangsu Administrative Institute], (3), 130–136.

Chen, R. (1947). *Zhongguo xianfa shi* [The constitution history of the Republic of China]. Wenhai Press.

Committee for the Compilation of the History of the Republic of China Law (Ed.). (1994). *Zhonghua minguo shi falü zhi* [History of the Republic of China: Records of law] (1st draft). Academia Historica.

Central Party Department of Democratic Socialist Party. (Ed.). (1976). *Zhang Junmai xiansehng nianpu chugao* [A chronicle draft of Zhang Junmai]. (For internal circulation).

Five-power Constitution Association (Ed). (1963). *Wuquan xianfa wenxian jiyao* [A digest of five-power constitution literature]. Pamir Press.

He, H. (2002). Lun Sun Zhongshan xiansheng guanyu Zhongyang zhengzhi zhidu zhi sheji [On Sun Yat-sen's design of the central political system]. In Q. He & X. Li (Eds.), *Minguo faxue lunwen jingcui* [Collected essays on the study of law in the Republic of China] (Vol. 2). Law Press.

Hou, Y. (2011). *Ershi shiji chu zhongguo zhengzhi gaige fengchao—qingmo lixian yundong shi* [A wave of Chinese political reform in the early 20th century: History of the constitutional movement in the late Qing Dynasty]. Renmin University Press.

Hu, F., Shen, Q., Shi Z., & Zhou, Y. (2000). *Zhonghua minguo xianfa yu liguo jingshen* [Constitution of the Republic of China and the spirit of nation founding]. San Min Book.

Hung, S. (1999). *Dangquan yu minquan zhijian: xunzheng shiqi lifayuan zhi shixing (1928–1937)* [Party rights vs. people's rights: The probation of Legislative Yuan during the Kuomintang Tutelage Period (1928–1937)] [Unpublished master's thesis]. National Taiwan Normal University.

Jiang, Y. (1976). *Zhongguo jindai shi zhuanzhe dian* [Turning points in modern Chinese history]. Union Book.

Jin, M. (1936). *Wuquan xianfa lun ji* [Collected papers on five-power institution]. Zhonghua Book Company.

Jing, Z. (1984). *Zhongguo lixian shi* [The history of constitution-making in the Republic of China]. Linking Publishing Co., Ltd.

Lei, Z. (1957). *Zhixian shuyao* [Synopsis of constitution-making]. Union Book.
Lei, Z. (2010). *Zhonghua minguo zhixian shi* [Constitutional history of the Republic of China]. Daoxiang Press.
Li, J. (2002). *Zhongguo jin bainian zhengzhi shi* [A centurial history of Chinese politics]. Fudan University Press.
Lin, H. (Ed.). (1940). *Ji zheng fagui* [Collected rules and regulations of accounting and statistics]. Guocui Press.
Li, Y. (1988). Yuehan minle yu zhonshan xiansheng quanneng qufen lilun zhi bijiao yanjiu [A comparison of John Mill's theory and Sun Yat-sen's division of powers]. *Zhongshan shehui kexue yicui* [Sun Yat-sen Social Sciences Translations], 3(3), 162–174.
Luo, L. (1930). Women yao shenmeyang de zhengzhi zhidu [What political system do we need]. *Xinyue* [New Moon], 2(12).
Luo, Z. (Ed.). (1974). *Jindai zhongguo fazhi yanbian yanjiu* [Research on the evolution of modern Chinese legal system]. Zhengzhong Press.
Ma, Q. (1987). Guomin canzhenghui—zhanshi Zhongyang minyi jigou [The National Political Council: A central representative institution in the wartime]. In G. Meng (Ed.), *Guomin canzhenghui jishi (xubian)* [A sequel to historical records of the National Political Council] (pp. 603–614). Chongqing Press.
Nathan, A. J. (1976). *Peking politics 1918–1923: Factionalism and the failure of constitutionalism*. University of California Press.
Nie, X. (2013). Minchu zhixianquan wenti de zai shenshi [Rethinking the constitution-making power in the early days of the ROC—from the perspective of comparative constitution]. *Huadong zhengfa daxue xuebao* [East China University of Political Science and Law Journal], (05): 33–39.
Ou, Z. (Ed.) (1935). *Zhongguo yanzheng xiao shi* [A short history of Chinese salt administration]. The Commercial Press.
Peng, S. (Ed.). (1986). *Zhonghua minguo xingxian yilai zhi lifayuan* [The Legislative Yuan since the implementation of the Constitution of the Republic of China]. Cheng-wen Publishing Co.
Qian, D., Sa, S., Yang, H., et al. (2008). *Minguo zhengzhi shi* [History of the political system of the Republic of China]. Shanghai People's Publishing House.
Rong, M. (Ed.). (1985). *Zhongguo guomindang lici daibiao dahui ji Zhongyang quanhui ziliao* [Documents respecting Kumingtang's National Congresses and Plenary Sessions of the Central Committee] (Vol. 2). Guangming Daily Press.
Sa, M. (1978). Zhonghua minguo xianfa cao'an de tezhi [The characteristics of draft constitution of the Republic of China]. In C. Hu (Ed.), *Minguo xianzheng yundong* [Constitutionalism in the Republic of China] (pp. 859–864). Zhongzheng Book Company.
Sa, M. (1993). *Zhongguo xianfa xianlun* [A new theory on the constitution of the Republic of China]. San Min Book.
Secretariat of the National Assembly. (Ed.). (1946). *Guomin dahui shilu* [The National Assembly memoir] (For internal circulation).
Su, Y. (1994). *Zouxiang xianzheng zhuyi* [Marching towards constitutionalism]. Linking Publishing Co., Ltd.
Sun Y. -S. (1988). *Sanmin zhuyi* [Three Principles of the People]. San Min Book.
Tang, D. (2015). *Cong wanqing dao minguo* [From the late Qing Dynasty to the Republic of China]. China Literature and History Press.
The Legislative Yuan. (1929, January). *Lifayuan gongbao* [The Legislative Yuan gazette] (1). The Legislative Yuan.
The National Government. (1928, October 26). *Guomin zhengfu gongbao* [The National Government gazette] (1). The National Government.
The Second Historical Archives of China. (1994). *Guomindang zhengfu zhengzhi zhidu dang'an shiliao xuanbain* [Selected archival materials of the government and system of the Kuomintang Party] (Vol. 1). Anhui Education Press.
Wang, S., & Qian, D. (1997). *Bijiao xianfa* [Comparative constitution]. China University of Political Science and Law Press.

Wu, Z. (2013). *Zhonghua minguo xianfa shi* [A history of the constitution of the Republic of China] (Pr. by Yu, M., et al). Law Press.

Xia, X., & Hu, X. (Eds.). (2004). *Jindai zhongguo xianzheng lichen: shiliao huicui* [The constitutional course in modern China: A collection of historical materials]. China University of Political Science and Law Press.

Xie, Z. (2001). *Zhonghua minguo xiuxian shi* [History of constitutional amendments of the Republic of China]. Yang-Chih Book, Co. Ltd.

Xie, Z. (Ed.), & Zhang, Z. (Pr.). (2000). *Zhonghua minguo lifa shi* [A legislative history of the Republic of China] (Vol. 1). China University of Political Science and Law Press.

Xu, M. (1992). *Zhonghua minguo zhengzhi zhidu shi* [History of the political system of the Republic of China]. Shanghai People's Press.

Young, E. P. (2005). Politics in the aftermath of revolution: The era of Yuan Shih-k'ai, 1912–16. In J. K. Fairbank (Ed.), *The Cambridge history of China: Republican China 1929–1949* (6th printing, Vol. 12, Part 1, pp. 208–255). Cambridge University Press.

Yu, Z. (Ed.). (1936). *Xianfa wenxuan* [Selected essays on constitution]. Shanghai Law Editing and Translating Press.

Zhang, J. (1947). *Zhonghua minguo minzhu xianfa shi jiang* [Ten lectures on the constitution of the Republic of China]. The Commercial Press.

Zhang Junmai Society of the Republic of China. (Ed. & Trans.). (2005). *Zhongguo disan shili* [The third force in China]. Daoxiang Press.

Zhang, M. (Trans.). (1986). *Yuehan mier* [John Mill]. Grand East Book.

Zhang, P. (2008). *Zhongguo minzhu zhengzhi de kunjing 1909–1949—wanqing yilai lijie guohui xuanju shulun* [The plight of China's democratic politics 1909–1949: Parliamentary elections since the late Qing Dynasty]. Jilin Publishing Corporation Ltd.

Zhang, Z. (1966). *Zhongguo lixian gushi* [The tale of Chinese constitutionalism]. (Recorded by Chen, X.). Dazhong Book Company.

Zhong, G. (2006). *Xianzheng tizhi zhi jian'gou yu fazhan* [On the framing and development of the constitutional government]. Hanlu Book and Publishing Company.

Zou, W. (1961). *Geguo zhengfu ji zhengzhi* [Governments and politics across the world]. Zhengzhong Press.

Zou, W. (1988). *Daiyi zhengzhi* [Representative government]. Pamir Bookstore.

Chapter 11
The Supervisory System in Modern China

11.1 The Supervisory System of the Beijing National Government

Unlike the Western tradition of parliamentary supervision,[1] the Chinese supervisory system has a long and self-contained history. The traditional imperial censorial and admonitory system took root in the Xia, Shang, and Zhou Dynasties, solidified in the Qin Dynasty, thrived in the Han Dynasty, and persisted throughout subsequent generations. In the testing ground of modern China's political systems, an independent supervisory structure based on Chinese tradition competed with the parliamentary supervisory system from the West. The 1912 *Provisional Constitution of the Republic of China* was modeled after the parliamentary oversight system in Europe and the United States. After ascending to power, Yuan Shih-k'ai reintroduced the Suzheng Division (肃政厅), a traditional Chinese prosecutorial system. Yet, during a turbulent era marked by military rule, warring warlords, and political instability, the efficacy of the supervisory systems left much to be desired.

11.1.1 Parliamentary Oversight

During the early years of the Republic of China, under the provisional constitution, the Parliament was vested with three forms of supervisory powers: the power of

[1] The concept of congressional oversight refers to the process through which "a central representative body supervises the personnel, financial affairs, administration and other statutory matters of government agencies, including approval, impeachment, admonition, rectification, auditing and monitoring. It also necessitates questioning, inspecting and investigating needed to accomplish the foregoing tasks, aiming to prevent and penalize any legal violations of law or derelictions of duty." (Tao, 1978: 45).

X. Nie, *The History of Government and Public Law in China*,
https://doi.org/10.1007/978-981-97-6063-3_11

interpellation, the power of investigation, and the power of impeachment (Chang, 1978, pp. 81–93).

i. The power of interpellation

The power of interpellation was exercised against the Prime Minister and heads of all ministries. Interpellation could either be put forward in a writing, co-signed by members of the Assembly, or verbally by an individual member. This form of supervision over the executive branch was relatively less authoritative, and its impact was limited to the exchange of question and answer. If the interpellator was dissatisfied with the responses, they could do little more than raise further questions.

ii. The power of investigation

The system of investigation, which was created by the 1912 *Provisional Constitution*, was unprecedented in both ancient China and the Western world. According to Clause 10 of Article 19 in that constitution, "The Senate shall have the power to propose to the interim government to investigate any cases of bribery or illegal behavior of officials". However, the Senate only had the power to make proposals rather than conduct investigations. Thus, it's more accurate to describe it as the power to request an investigation. All civil and military officials were potential subjects of these investigations, but in practice, most of those investigated were governors of each province. After the formal establishment of the Parliament in 1913, the *Act of the Parliament* was promulgated in the same year, prescribing that both Houses of the Parliament shall exercise the power to propose investigations, but countersignatures of more than ten representatives are needed to propose a motion of investigation, which shall be filed to the government after approved by voting in the parliament; the government shall report back upon the closing of the investigation. In 1914 when "The Third Year Constitution of the Republic of China" (Yuan Shih-k'ai's Constitution) was promulgated, the short-lived power of investigation was no longer included in the constitutional framework.

iii. The power of impeachment

According to Clause 11 and 12 of Article 19 of the 1912 *Provisional Constitution*, the Parliament's impeachment power shall be confined to the president and members of the cabinet (i.e., the premier and heads of each ministry), respectively for treason and for offences or dereliction of duty, which differed from the prevailing practices in other countries then where ministerial officials were impeached for infringement of law instead of dereliction of duty. Impeachments were motioned through cosignatories by parliamentarians and required an absolute majority vote in the Assembly for acceptance. In accordance with the *Act of Parliament* of 1913, once an impeachment bill against the president was passed by the Assembly, the entire case would be promptly notified to the Supreme Court on the same day. Within five days, the Supreme Court would convene a special court to conduct the trial. As for impeachment cases against cabinet members, once approved by the Assembly, there was no requirement for a trial process. Instead, the case would be directly submitted to the president for dismissal. However, the president had the discretion to refer the impeachment case to the Senate for a second review.

11.1.2 (Pingzheng Yuan) Suzheng Division

In May 1914, the Yuan Shih-k'ai, through presidential decrees, issued a series of regulations including the *Organic Act of the Pingzheng Yuan, the Order on Impeachment, the Administrative Rules of the Pingzheng Yuan* and *the Regulations on the Administrative Proceedings*, leading to the establishment of the Pingzheng Yuan (平政院, Supreme Administrative Court, replacing the ancient Censorate) (Luo, 1974, pp. 409–412). The Pingzheng Yuan was not a pure administrative court. In addition to the president and case reviewers responsible for conducting hearings, it had the Suzheng Division, which dealt with disciplinary matters in politics. The division was headed by a general administrative supervisor (*dushuzhengshi*, 都肃政史) and comprised 16 full-time administrative supervisors (*suzhengshi*, 肃政史) for the impeachment of officials. These supervisors addressed cases of unlawful conduct and dereliction of duty, filed administrative lawsuits on behalf of the people, and oversaw the judgments made by the Pingzheng Yuan. Though affiliated to the Pingzheng Yuan, the Suzheng Division was not subject to the former's supervision and command, but exercised its powers independently and was directly responsible to the country's president who issued all of its administrative rules and seals. The Suzheng Division enjoyed the autonomy to issue documents, written instructions and orders. Its correspondences with the Pingzheng Yuan were in the form of "letters" or "consultations", which were customary among governmental organs of equal rank, rather than "submissions" or "orders" used between hierarchical organs. Impeachment cases proposed by the supervisors should be sent for trial to a collegial court composed of five case reviewers from the Pingzheng Yuan. When considered necessary for punishment or judicial proceedings, the case should be reported to the country's president and duly transferred to the appropriate offices in charge (Chang, 1979). In 1917, when the Suzheng Division was abolished and the *Act of Impeachment* was repealed, the Pingzheng Yuan lost its powers of investigation and impeachment and became a pure administrative adjudication body (Huang, 2000). The supervisory power of the Suzheng Division was then returned to the Parliament.

11.2 Independent Supervisory Organ in Sun Yat-Sen's Constitutional Thoughts

The Control Yuan of the Nanjing National Government was created based on Sun Yat-sen's constitutional thoughts. Were it not Sun's advocacy and persistence, it would have been difficult for the traditional Chinese censorial system (including the examination system) to revive in modern China. An important idea in Sun's five-power constitutional theory was the transformation of the old Chinese supervisory system into the modern Control Yuan, which stood alongside the three traditional Western powers (legislative, executive, and judiciary).

i. The independent supervisory organ

Sun advocated for the independence of the supervisory organ for two reasons. "First, it was an original idea derived from a comparative study of foreign democratic political systems; second, it represented an affirmation of the value and idealism of the ancient censorial system." (Chen, 2001, p. 713) As early as six years before the Xinhai Revolution in 1911, Sun, in his speech titled "The Three People's Principles and the Future of the Chinese Nation" at the anniversary meeting of *People's Report (Min Bao)* in Tokyo, put forward the idea of Five-power Constitution that would establish a supervisory power (and examination power) independent from the Parliament. He believed that supervisory organs were indispensable in all countries and should be stipulated as independent entities in *Constitution of the Republic of China.*

> From ancient times, China has had a supervisory institution known as the Censorate (*yushi tai* 御史台). However, this entity was essentially a slave of the monarch, making its continued use unreasonable. In contemporary constitutional countries, it is universal for legislative bodies to concurrently hold supervisory power, which, strong or weak, finds no way to be independent, giving rising to myriad ills. For example, in the United States, the power of impeachment is vested in the Congress, which nevertheless tends to abuse that power to manipulate the executive branch, resulting frequently in congressional despotism ... Moreover, it is psychologically untenable and theoretically indefensible that the institution adjudicating over the people achieves independence while the one overseeing officials does not. Therefore, it is imperative that the supervisory institution be independent. (Five-power Constitution Association, 1963, p. 3)

In his speech, Sun criticized the ancient Chinese imperial censors as merely the tools of emperors, asserting their poor supervisory capabilities, and meanwhile he lambasted the "parliamentary despotism" inherent within the supervision system of Europe and America. Hence, Sun considered it necessary for the supervisory power (supervisory organs) to be independent. However, his argument is not infallible. Will the Congress misuse the supervisory power to manipulate the administrative organ, resulting in a tyrannical parliament? Using the United States as an example, the Congress has rarely used the power of impeachment, but this does not exclude the possibility of congressional despotism. France (the French Third Republic) is a case in point where a tyrannical parliament and an ineffective executive led to repeated collapse of cabinets and chronic political instability so that the government, trapped in the civil strife of political parties, could not function properly.

11.2.1 *The Control Yuan in the Five-Power Constitution*

In the afore-mentioned speech, Sun held some reservations towards the traditional Chinese censorial system, characterizing the Censorate as nothing more than "a slave of the monarch". However, in the sixth lecture "The Principle of Democracy" of *The Three Principles of the People*, the old tradition was more than glorified, because the supervisory power (along with the examination power) had existed independently of the imperial power in China for thousands of years. He argued that the supervisory power (i.e., the control power), the examination power and the imperial power represented the Chinese tradition of tripartite power structure, the first two of which should be integrated into the American tripartite division, thereby transforming it into a quintet of powers unique to China.

> After winning independence, the United States adopted a tripartite division of powers and achieved remarkable results, leading other countries to follow the American approach. However, while western countries employed a three-power structure, why do we need five powers and where do the additional powers come from? The other two powers have actually rooted in China for a long time. In ancient times, China realized significant achievements through the establishment of independent systems for examinations and supervision ... The old Chinese autocratic government could also be said to have operated under a tripartite division of powers ... During the era of autocracy, the powers of examination and supervision were not vested in the emperor, resulting in a decentralization of supreme governmental authority. In this sense, China paralleled Western nations with its own form of tripartite power division. If we aim to gather the cream of the Chinese and Western political traditions to forestall any and all kinds of abuses, we must incorporate the unique Chinese powers of examination and supervision into the Western powers of executive, legislative, and judiciary. By doing so, we would form an ideally balanced five-power division, creating what could arguably be the most virtuous government in the world. (Sun, 1988, pp. 173–174)

In Sun's vision, the five powers of legislative, executive, judiciary, examination, and supervision, unlike the three powers of checks and balances, divided up the work in a collaborative way ("the five powers are separate and mutually supportive"). The five-power government, an "almighty government", was designed to circumvent the strife and sloppiness intrinsic to the *trias politica* model, but it would be subject to the National Assembly which represented the popular sovereignty. It was Sun's aspiration to establish an optimal government in which "the people are in the power and the government is capable" in order to maximize the balance between democracy and efficiency. Despite Sun's emphasis on the cooperative, rather than competitive, nature of the five powers, it is undeniable that the supervisory power itself serves as a form of checks and balances on the other four.

11.2.2 *Organization of the Supervisory Organ*

According to Sun's design, the supervisory organ should be comprised of scholar-officials. He called those who exercised the supervisory power "control officials", who were also ranked as senior or junior officials and were required to pass unified national examinations. The censorial bureaucracy in ancient China bore similarities to other administrative bureaucracies in that imperial censors and remonstrance officials were typically selected through imperial examination. This historical precedent probably influenced Sun's idea (Chen, 2001).

In the wake of the Xinhai Revolution, Sun's constitutional thoughts were not widely embraced. The early constitution makers looked to the American presidential system, European parliamentary systems, or even constitutional monarchies as their ideal models, with only a few being drawn to Sun's fusion of Chinese and Western principles in the Five-power Constitution (Chen, 2001). In 1912, as the Provisional President, Sun proposed *the Amendment to the Organizational Outline of the Provisional Government*, subtly advocating the independence of examination and control powers. "The Provisional President shall establish civil and military service systems, in addition to his responsibilities for positions, examinations, disciplinary penalty of the Examination Yuan, the Control Yuan, the Audit Yuan and the Pingzheng Yuan" (Chang, 1979, p. 410). However, the proposal was rejected by the Senate. Under the Beiyang Government, except for the short-lived Suzheng Division, the supervisory power never wrung its independence from the Parliament. It was not until 1927, after the establishment of the NNG, that Sun's ideal of Five-power Constitution began to take form from an idea to an institutional reality, with the Control Yuan firmly established within the central government.[2]

11.3 The Control Yuan of the Nanjing National Government

After the Suzheng Division and Pingzheng Yuan in the early ROC and the Control Yuan in the period of political tutelage of the NNG, the 1946 *Constitution of the Republic of China* fused the American congressional system with the traditional Chinese censorial system, rendering the Control Yuan a de facto parliamentary body. The fusion incurred enormous criticism, mainly because the Control Yuan was no more an independent organ. However, under no circumstance should its shortcomings become the very reason for abolishing the independent supervisory mechanism, which, originating from the Chinese tradition, still holds significant value to this day.

[2] On August 1, 1925, in accordance with Sun Yat-sen's idea, the Guangzhou National Government instituted the Control Yuan during its military governance period. However, the Control Yuan then had extensive powers, including the supervisory power. For more information regarding the organization and powers of the Control Yuan in the military period, see Editorial Committee of the Fact Record of the Control Yuan (1981, pp. 30–31). The Guangzhou National Government did not implement the five-yuan system, and more importantly, the government itself was not a national regime (the Beiyang Government still held legitimate power), so that this chapter leaves out the Control Yuan of this particular period.

11.3.1 The Control Yuan During the Political Tutelage Period

On October 3, 1928, the NNG promulgated the *(Amended) Organic Law of the National Government of the Republic of China*,[3] which established the central government system based on the Five-power Constitution. In November of the same year, the amended the *Organic Law of the Control Yuan* was accordingly promulgated, stipulating that the Control Yuan had the powers of impeachment and auditing, with the latter being entrusted to its affiliated Ministry of Audit. The party-state NNG set "Teachings by Father of the Nation" as the supreme guiding principle and kept to Sun's *Fundamentals of National Reconstruction* to institute the five-Yuan structure of administration, legislation, judiciary, examination and control,[4] because of Sun's irreplaceable authority in the KMT on one hand, and more importantly Chiang Kai-shek's craving for the banner of "the Premier's teachings" to ensure his "legitimate" status in the party's power struggle on the other. Against this backdrop was the Control Yuan translated from theory into practice.

Preparations for the establishment of the Control Yuan were underway from late 1928 to early 1931, during which its main responsibilities included researching the supervisory system and drafting corresponding laws and regulations. In this phase, the Secretariat of the Control Yuan received civil complaints by, and, depending on their nature, forwarded them to relevant authorities or l or set them aside to be addressed upon the formal establishment of the Control Yuan. After several years of efforts, the Control Yuan was finally put in position on February 2, 1931, with Yu Youren serving as its first president.[5] That same month, the National Government changed the existing Court of Audit into the Ministry of Audit, placing it under the jurisdiction of the Control Yuan. According to the 1928 *Organic Law of the National Government of the Republic of China*, the Control Yuan was to be led by a president and a vice-president, with the latter stepping in should the president be unable to fulfill his duties (Article 42); the Control Yuan was to consist of nineteen to twenty-nine

---

[3] For nearly 20 years before the promulgation and implementation of the *Constitution of the Republic of China* in 1947, the *Organic Law of the National Government of the Republic of China* served as the primary constitutional document guiding the governmental organization of the NNG. In contrast, the 1931 *Provisional Constitution for the Period of Political Tutelage of the Republic of China* didn't specifically prescribe governmental organization.

[4] In January 1924, the *Declaration of the First National Congress of the Kuomintang* proclaimed that the central government of the Republic should be "founded upon the principle of the separation of powers created by Sun". Later in April of the same year, Sun personally drafted the *Fundamentals of National Reconstruction of the Nationalist Government*, a document composed of 25 articles that clearly outlined the Three Principles of the People, Five-Power Constitution and other foundational national strategies. In 1929, the Third National Congress of the KMT passed the resolution to establish "Teachings by Father of the Nation" as the supreme and fundamental law in the tutelage period. Article 28 of the 1931 *Provisional Constitution for the Period of Political Tutelage of the Republic of China* stipulated, "The political agenda during the period of political tutelage and its apparatus shall conform to the provisions laid out in the Fundamentals of National Reconstruction.".

[5] The National Government had nominated Cai Yuanpei and Zhao Daiwen as the president of the Control Yuan in 1928 and 1929 respectively. However, both of them refused to take office, which postponed the formal establishment of the Control Yuan.

members, all appointed by the National Government at the instance of the president of the Control Yuan (Article 43); the Control Yuan's meetings were comprised of its members and chaired by the president of the Control Yuan (Article 44) (Xia, 2004, p. 788). After the establishment of the Control Yuan, the National Government found itself repeatedly amending the *Organic Law of the National Government of the Republic of China* to increase the number of its members because of a urge in the number of cases and a shortage of personnel.

During the political tutelage period, the members of the Control Yuan were not elected as envisaged by Sun Yat-sen in his concept of the Five-Power Constitution. There were no explicit laws outlining the qualifications for these roles, but in practice, those appointed were often esteemed scholars with considerable social standing and reputation. The position of a Control Yuan member was equivalent to a minister in the National Government, a status unprecedented for typical censorial officials in Chinese history, who used to be "petty officials vested with much power". The National Government also enacted *the Security Act of the Control Members*, offering robust protections for their position, freedom of speech, personal safety.[6] In the political tutelage period, their terms of office were not explicitly provided by law, but most of them held lifelong tenures. The incumbents of the Control Yuan were expected to be strictly self-disciplined and take no more public office concurrently. Nor should the members write letters of introduction for others to seek private benefits as resolved at the 18th meeting of the Control Yuan on January 22, 1922. Based on a quantitative analysis of their age, educational background, expertise, experience, place of origin, etc., research showed that they "could be called the political and cultural elite of the National Government, which, to a certain extent, guaranteed their qualification for the supervisory work". Specifically, the members were well-educated (with 41% having studied abroad and only 1% not having received a college education) with rich experience and high personal standards. There was a balanced distribution of age and academic disciplines among the members, and their geographical diversity lent a degree of representativeness to the group (Liu & Li, 2006).

The Control Yuan operated on a commissioner system, and all supervisory procedures were carried out independently by its members. Its president and vice president only oversaw administrative matters, and never directly participate in or interfered with specific impeachment cases. According to Article 44 of the *Organic Law of the National Government of the Republic of China*, the Control Committee, a collegial body consisting of the president, vice president and all the other members, was tasked with deliberating over various legal cases or amendments. The Control Yuan was responsible for determining its meeting procedures and regulations (Article 13, *Organic Law of the Control Yuan*).

---

[6] *The Security Act of the Control Members* stipulated: Members of the Control Yuan shall not be held accountable for statements made in the exercise of their powers; they shall not be reassigned without their personal consent; they shall not be removed from office, suspended or fined unless they are expelled from the Party (all control officials during the political tutelage period were KMT party members) or subjected to criminal punishment; they, except in cases of *flagrante delicto*, shall not be arrested or detained without the consent of the Control Yuan.

According to Article 6 of the *Organic Law of the Control Yuan*, amended and promulgated by the National Government in 1933, the central government instituted regional supervisory organs (Control Commissioners' Office) for inspection tours during the period of political tutelage, and the chief carried the title of Control Commissioner, with the Control Yuan deciding "the regions to be inspected and the rules for these inspections" (Xia, 2004, p. 860). Initially, the Control Yuan divided the country into fourteen inspection zones, which were later expanded to sixteen. In June 1935, the Control Commissioners' Offices were established successively in seven zones of Southern Jiangxi, Anhui-Jiangxi, Hunan-Hubei, Hebei, Henan-Shangdong, and Gansu-Ningxia-Qinghai. By April 1936, the National Government released *the Organic Regulations of Control Commissioners' Offices* and approved the Control Yuan's petition to set up control offices in each inspection zone. Under the directive of the president of the Control Yuan, the commissioners oversaw all matters of their office, supervised local affairs and exercised the power of impeachment in the designated zones. A Control Commissioner's role should be assumed by a member of the Control Yuan for a term of two years. After their term, they could be reassigned by the Control Yuan to other regions for inspection tours. If an inspection zone spanned more than two provinces, the Control Commissioner's Office should set up local branches in appropriate locations within each province. The primary responsibilities of these offices were touring, inspecting, and investigating. This touring inspection system drew from China's traditional practices of sending out inspectors (e.g., Investigating Censor in the Qin Dynasty, Regional Inspector in the Western Han Dynasty, Surveillance Commissioner in the Tang Dynasty, and Circuit (provincial) Censor in the Ming and Qing Dynasties). This system was characterized by the division of the country into various inspection zones (e.g., regions or provinces in the Western Han Dynasty and circuits in the Ming and Qing Dynasties), each overseen by a centrally-appointed Control Commissioner responsible for supervising local administration.

11.3.2 Evolution of the Control Yuan System and Its Parliamentarization

i. The conceptualization of the Control Yuan in the MFDC

In the early stages of political tutelage, the KMT held full control over the system of the Control Yuan (as well as the other four Yuans). Sun Yat-sen's idea of Five-power Constitution was gradually deified as the supreme ideology of the KMT. It wasn't until the drafting of *the Draft Constitution of the Republic of China* (i.e., the MFDC) that individuals outside of the KMT were given an opportunity to participate in the discussion of national affairs. There were two opposite views at that time. One group, carrying forward the legacy of the early ROC constitution-makers, argued that Sun's Five-power Constitution was not in conformity with the conventional rules of the European or American constitutionalism They asserted that the impeachment power should be vested in public representatives, namely, the parliamentarians. By contrast, the other group considered the establishment of the Control Yuan as a grand innovation. They believed the issue was not about reducing the five powers to three, but rather about the limited scope of the Control Yuan's authority. They argued that the Control Yuan should not only have the power to impeach but should also be granted the judicial power over impeachments (Gao, 1936, pp. 48–55). The Control Yuan, as prescribed by the MFDC, marked a major alternation to the supervisory system of the tutelage period. It reached a compromise between the two contrasting viewpoints by making the control members parliamentarians on one hand while granting the Control Yuan broaders powers on the other.

Firstly, the most significant change involved the election process and the term of office for the members of the Control Yuan. "Each province, Mongolia, Tibet, and overseas Chinese nationals shall respectively nominate two members from the primary election and submit them to the National Assembly for re-election, with the candidates not necessarily being national representatives" (Article 90, MFDC). The rationale behind this change was that "The Control Yuan holds the responsibility to supervise civil servants across the country, and the distribution of Control members should consider geographic representation." "Control members shall serve a term of three years and may be re-elected" (Article 91, MFDC), because "After a three-year term, the performance of the control members shall be assessed, and those who are capable can be appointed via re-election while those found lacking can be removed thereby. The National Assembly convenes every three years, which facilitates a convenient re-election process." (Draft Constitution Propaganda Committee of the Legislative Yuan, 1940, p. 59) The indirect election of control members (each province, regional and overseas Chinese nationals nominating two representatives for the National Assembly's final decision) clearly mirrors the U.S. Senate's system of electing two senators from each state. The introduction of a specific term of office also paralleled the functions of parliamentary members. This marked the onset of the Control Yuan's transformation into a more parliamentary or senatorial body.

Secondly, during the deliberations on the draft constitution, some proposed that the Control Yuan should have the power of interpellation, similar to that of Western parliaments. The Constitution Review Committee flatly paralleled the interpellation of the Control Yuan with that of the Legislative Yuan and defined the scope of the former's power. "Prior to any impeachment, the Control Yuan may present interpellations to various ministries. If the responses are deemed satisfactory, impeachment may not be necessary. Hence, the Control Yuan's power to interpellate is a supportive measure in the exercise of impeachment." Ultimately, a new article was added to the draft constitution: "In exercising its supervisory power, the Control Yuan may, in accordance with the law, submit interpellations to other Yuans, ministries, and committees." (Article 88, MFDC) (Wu & Huang, 1937, pp. 545–546) As a result, the Control Yuan took on an increasingly parliamentary-like role.

Thirdly, apart from the power of impeachment and auditing, the Control Yuan was further entrusted with the power of rectification over civil servants, which had belonged to the Judicial Yuan (the impeachment of the president of the National Government and heads of the other four chambers were still handled by the National

Assembly). In other words, the Control Yuan consolidated the powers of impeaching, investigating, and disciplining public officials, because "Rectification and impeachment are complementary, akin to the relationship between prosecution and trial in a court. Therefore, the power of rectification should be vested in the Control Yuan" (Draft Constitution Propaganda Committee of the Legislative Yuan, 1940, p. 58). Indeed, although the NNG implemented a joint system of prosecution and trial, abolished all local prosecution offices, staffed all levels of courts with prosecutors, and set up a prosecutor's office in the Supreme Court, the powers of prosecution and trial remained independent as prosecutors and judges were affiliated to different institutions. This greatly contrasted with the collegial system of the Control Yuan vested with both impeachment and rectification powers. Empowered with the ability to impeach and rectify, the Control Yuan acquired unconstrained powers, whose downsides were impossible to be proved as the MFDC, fortunately, was never put into effect.

ii. The Control Yuan defined by the Agreement of the PCC and the PCC Constitutional Amendment

During the War of Resistance against the Japanese Invasion, the two constitutional movements did not place any special attention to the Control Yuan as stipulated in the MFDC. It was not until the Agreement of the PCC that the Control Yuan was redefined. In terms of organization and powers, it resembled a Senate and still held the supervisory power. According to the third item of the Twelve Principles agreed upon by the 1946 PCC for the draft constitution: "The Control Yuan shall be the highest supervisory organ of the whole nation, elected by the assemblies of each province and national autonomous region, and shall exercise the powers of consent, impeachment and supervision." (Xia, 2004, p. 1092) Based on this, the corresponding Agreement of the PCC stipulated: "The Control Yuan shall be the highest supervisory organ of the nation, exercising the powers of consent, impeachment, and supervision." (Article 96) "The Control Yuan shall be elected by each provincial and municipal assembly and the assembly of each autonomous region." (Article 97) "The Control Yuan shall have a president and a vice-president, who shall be elected by its members." (Article 98)

The control members, locally elected, exercised the consent power over the appointment of the president, the vice president and the Grand Justice of the Judicial Yuan as well as the president, vice president and members of the Examination Yuan,[7] and elected the president and vice president of the Control Yuan, which altogether followed in the American Senate's footstep. Hitherto, the Control Yuan ceased to be a mere supervisory body, and instead became effectively senate-like (parliamentarized). The PCC Constitutional Amendment only briefly mentioned the supervisory function of the Control Yuan, stipulating that the Control Yuan exercised the powers of consent, impeachment and supervision, but impeachment was not considered part of the supervisory duties. It could be duly inferred that the PCC Constitutional Amendment did not remove the Control Yuan's power (jurisdiction) to punish and

[7] The Legislative Yuan exercised the power of consent to the president of the Executive Yuan.

adjudicate as stipulated in the MFDC. (The judiciary chapter of the PCC Constitutional Amendment didn't grant the Judicial Yuan the authority to discipline civil servants.)

11.3.3 Disadvantages of the "Parliamentarization of the Control Yuan" and Its Adjustment

In the grouped review of the draft constitution by the Constitutional National Assembly (the Fourth Review Committee) in 1946, two major controversies arose regarding the Control Yuan. The first was whether the Control Yuan should exercise the power of consent. Not a few committee members believed that the power of consent should be exercised by one organ (the Legislative Yuan) instead of two (the Legislative Yuan and the Control Yuan), which would also help tone down the political nature of the Control Yuan and preserve its impartial status. The second focused on whether the power of rectification should be entrusted to the Control Yuan or the Judicial Yuan (Secretariat of the National Assembly, 1961, p. 47). The second controversy can be seen as a technical issue while the first was a political one. In fact, the KMT wanted to sustain a centralized unitary system while other parties sought to disrupt the monopoly of one-party government and to implement the federalist local autonomy. If locally elected control members were to exercise consent power over central officials, it would represent local intervention in the central government's rule, a circumstance the KMT found it hard to swallow while the other parties strived hard to attain. Both sides were highly concerned about, not the control power itself, whether the Control Yuan could wield influence on the central personnel decisions on behalf of local governments. Therein, the Control Yuan operated primarily, as a Senate-like body and secondarily, as a supervisory organ, and its organization and functions served the first role instead of the second.

The KMT eventually made concessions to other political parties for the smooth passage of the constitution. After revisions by the Comprehensive Review Committee of the Constitutional National Assembly, the Control Yuan was allowed to retain its consent power, but the power of rectification was delegated to the Judicial Yuan (Secretariat of the National Assembly, 1961, pp. 96–101). Under the terms of the 1946 *Constitution of the Republic of China*, "The Control Yuan shall be the highest supervisory organ of the country and shall exercise the powers of consent, impeachment, censure and auditing" (Article 90).[8] "Members of the Control Yuan shall be elected by provincial and municipal councils, local councils of Mongolia and Tibet, and associations of overseas Chinese." Their seats shall be allocated as follows: five for each province, two for each municipality directly under the jurisdiction of the Executive Yuan, and eight respectively for Mongolia, Tibet, and overseas Chinese

[8] In addition to the powers prescribed by the constitutional provisions, the Control Yuan also had the power to supervise examinations for public functionaries and the power to conduct touring inspections within the designated regions throughout the country.

(Article 91). "Members of the Control Yuan shall serve a term of six years and shall be re-eligible." (Article 93)[9] Regarding the election of control members and the regulation on their exercising consent power, the Control Yuan was similar to a senate.

However, the enactment of the 1946 *Constitution* did not quell relevant controversies. As the KMT government fled to Taiwan province in 1949, dispute over the system of the "Control Yuan" continued there and still revolved around the election and appointment of control members and the exercise of the consent power, i.e., whether the Control Yuan as a supervisory organ should be part of the Senate. Opinions opposing the senate-like transformation of the Control Yuan include:

First, the fusion of the supervisory and consent powers could compromise the supremacy of the Control Yuan, because the Control Yuan would appear capricious if it exercised the power of consent over officials and then impeached them.

> Granting the power of consent to the Control Yuan not only fails to enhance its authority, but also risks tarnishing its prestige … Those officials, whose appointment is approved by the Control Yuan, may not necessarily abide by the law and act in the public interest. It is impossible for the Control Yuan to impeach and rectify the very personnel that are approved by itself. If that is the case, it indicates a bias. If the Control Yuan wielded dual powers, that is, to granting approval first and then moving to impeach later, it would display capriciousness. Sun Yat-sen wouldn't have anticipated the esteemed Control Yuan becoming reduced to an organ of inconsistency and bias. (Lin, 1993, pp. 196–197)

Second, when the "members of the Control Yuan" hold divergent views about a certain official, a contradictory situation may arise: a majority might agree to his appointment while a minority simultaneously seeks to impeach him.

> The notion of consent does not necessarily ensure unanimity. Article 94 of the *Constitution of the Republic of China* stipulates, "When the Control Yuan exercises the power of consent in accordance with this Constitution, it shall do so by resolution of a majority of the members present at the meeting." What is desired is merely a simple majority. Although the majority of the control members can exercise their consent power to support an appointment, they cannot prohibit the minority from bringing impeachment against the appointed, which then breeds internal discord, and the Control Yuan itself would become a whirlpool of political disputes. (Lin, 1993, pp. 196–197)

In short, it was impossible to merge the power of supervision with the power of consent, and the 1946 *Constitution* made the Control Yuan a clumsy and defective copycat of a senate.

> The inherent nature of supervisory power fundamentally conflicts with the power of consent. As law enforcement officers, members of the Control Yuan should maintain an independent and unbiased stance. Their role is to oversee government personnel, not to approve their appointment. The combining of these two roles in a single entity – likening a Chinese censorial department to a foreign parliament – is an awkward and ill-conceived move. Giving the consent power to the Control Yuan is fraught with peril and devoid of benefits. No other motive could be fathomed except that the constitution-framers intended to mimic the

[9] The *Constitution* also provided for a three-year term of office for the legislators in the Legislative Yuan (Article 65), contrasting with the longer term of office for control members, which obviously followed the U.S. model of short terms for House representatives and long terms for Senators.

> American system and shaped the Control Yuan as a senate, which, however, ended up an inept imitation. (Lin, 1993, pp. 196–197)

With the expansion of its powers, the Control Yuan not only exercised the passive power of impeachment, but actively shouldered the responsibility of overseeing general governmental policies. The acquisition of the consent power further toned up its political nature, making it no longer a purely neutral supervisory organ (Lei, 1953, pp. 94, 105, 112). Although constitutional supporters could find various reasons to justify it, "due to members of the Control Yuan manipulating the power to rectify and impeach executive officials, vote buying emerged in the election of control members, a 'disease' reminiscent of foreign parliaments' abuse of the impeachment power to suppress the executive power, a practice that Sun Yat-sen had initially rejected." (Chen, 2001, p. 717) This outcome ran contrary to Sun's ideals. In 1992, the Control Yuan was deprived of its power of approving personnel appointment, and the appointment became subject to nomination by the head of the Taiwan region and confirmation by the representative organ. The Control Yuan finally shed its parliamentary tone, resumed its core supervisory role and downsized substantially to a fixed number of 29 members.

In the Taiwan province today, some people believe that the Control Yuan (together with the Examination Yuan) should be completely abolished, transforming the five-power government, substituted into a tripartite system. Such kind of belief is largely ideologically driven and partially due to power overlaps and conflicts between the Control Yuan and the other Yuans (mainly the Legislative Yuan) and its own lack-luster performance. Nevertheless, a closer examination shows that the Control Yuan has its own *raison d'etre*. Firstly, the tradition of an independent supervisory system and the Control Yuan's role are deeply-rooted in the Chinese political culture, too integral to be simply discarded. "If the Control Yuan carried out effective reforms, it would be much more cost-effective to rebuild its credibility based on the traditional image than to create a new entity trying to earn the public's trust." Secondly, the functions of the Control Yuan, including investigation, impeachment, and auditing, actually need to be executed independently of the legislative and executive branches. The essence of auditing power, for example, lies in its "independence, and its capability to effectively assist the legislative power, rather than its formal subordination to any specific power or any chamber". An independent exercise of these powers by the Control Yuan and its subordinate Ministry of Audit is indeed a better institutional arrangement. Thirdly, the unsatisfactory performance of the Control Yuan does not warrant its abolition, as "the efficacy of an institution is closely related to the resources and tools it possesses". The Control Yuan's limited effectiveness is "largely due to its inadequate manpower, financial resources, and extremely broad range of responsibilities, coupled with severely restricted policy tools". "If adjustments can be made to the relevant system and authority, and due resources and tools are made available to the Control Yuan, there is a possibility to enhance its effectiveness." "Abolition is a policy issue while effectiveness is a technical one. They are different matters and should not be conflated." Fourthly, the global trend shows that an independent supervisory system remains necessary. Currently, legislative and judicial institutions still have many blind spots in providing relief against public power infringements on citizens' rights, and a supervisory system, aiming to protect the common people, could fill these gaps (Chen et al., 2006, pp. 156–160). In addition, the Control Yuan, by exercising its power independently, can avert excessive growth of legislative authority, conducive to easing the conflict between the executive and legislative authorities and contributing to political stability (The Control Yuan, 2007).

11.3.4 Supervisory Functions of the Control Yuan[10] and Its Effects

i. Exercising the supervisory powers

The Control Yuan has three types of supervisory power: impeachment, censure, and investigation. The power of investigation is a prerequisite for the Control Yuan to impeach and censure. Article 3 of the *Organic Law of the Control Yuan* stipulates that: "In exercising its powers, the Control Yuan shall inquire into or investigate the records and documents of various public offices and other organs. Shall any uncertainties arise, the official in charge shall be accountable for providing a comprehensive explanation." The powers of censure and impeachment are similar in effect, with the former often seen as a simplified form of the latter. When the Control Yuan was newly instituted during the tutelage period, there was no system of censure. However, during the War of Resistance, in response to the extraordinary circumstances and expedite the supervision process, the Control Yuan created the power of censure via *the Interim Measures for the Exercise of Control Power in Extraordinary Times*. The 1946 *Constitution* then formalized the censure power, aligning it with impeachment as one of the constitutional authorities. The censure mechanism is typically triggered by urgent cases, with a focus on inspection, punishment, and remedy. A censure can be proposed by a single control member or local control commissioners, with no need for joint signatures or submission for review, thus "giving a full play to the independent spirit of ancient imperial censors" (Chang, 1979, p. 166).

The impeachment process by the Control Yuan is divided into four stages: initiation, review, referral, and publication. A case of impeachment shall be motioned by members of the Control Yuan, and each control member or local control commissioner can initiate an impeachment. The president of the Control Yuan shall not influence or interfere with any impeachment proceedings; once an impeachment is proposed, it shall not be revoked (Articles 4, 8, 9, and 11, *Act of Impeachment*). An impeachment shall be raised, based on civil complaints (Article 13, *Act of Impeachment*), requests for investigation from ministries or regional administrative chiefs (Article 11, *Act of Discipline of Public Functionaries*), allegations by the Ministry of Audit (Article 15, *Act of Audit*), revelations in newspapers and magazines (like

[10] The consent power and the auditing power of the Ministry of Audit are not discussed here.

"wind and rumors" heard by the ancient imperial censors), or independent investigations by control members. According to Article 5 of the *Act of Impeachment*, upon initiation, an impeachment case is reviewed by three members of the Control Yuan excluding the initiator. If the majority agrees that disciplinary action is necessary, the impeachment case shall be established. If not, but the initiator demurs, the case is passed to five other members for a final decision. The review members were initially appointed by the president of the Control Yuan, but later, cases in need of review are handled by all control members in rotation, except that those involved in an impeachment case shall be removed. Once an impeachment case is confirmed, it is turned over to the relevant disciplinary organ for further action.[11] Judicial proceedings for impeachment cases shall follow the provisions in *the Act of Discipline against Public Functionaries*, except for impeachment against political appointees and military officials. If the disciplinary body finds an impeachment case valid, it can impose penalties ranging from dismissal and demotion, to salary reduction, recording a demerit, or a formal reprimand. In cases involving criminal offenses, the case is forwarded to the court for trial. Impeachment cases should be kept confidential before being transferred to the disciplinary organ. There's debate, however, regarding whether the Control Yuan can disclose impeachment cases once they've been transferred. In June 1931, during the eleventh meeting the Control Yuan, Tian Jiongjin proposed that after an impeachment case was forwarded, the Secretariat should publicize the case at the request of the initiator. Tian's proposal was accepted. Thereafter, initiators and the Control Yuan, in order to draw national attention and steer public opinion against the impeached, often publicized impeachment documents in newspapers as soon as cases were referred to disciplinary organs, which put grave pubic pressure on the KMT authorities. At a meeting of the Political Bureau of the Central Committee of the KMT in 1934, a resolution was adopted to restrict the Control Yuan from publicizing impeachment cases, for which Yu Youren, the president of the Control Yuan, resigned in anger and returned home in protest. Shortly afterwards, the above-mentioned restriction was rescinded (Chang, 1979, pp. 159–160).

As for the censure procedure, according to Article 2 of *the Interim Measures for the Exercise of Supervisory Power in Extraordinary Times*, "a member of the Control Yuan or a Control Commissioner may file a written censure when he considers a public functionary to be in violation of law or dereliction of duty, warranting immediate removal or other swift disciplinary measures." The censure case must be submitted to the president of the Control Yuan for review before being forwarded to the accused's supervisor or managing official. Should a Control Commissioner exercise their power of censure within their jurisdiction, they must submit the case to the Control Yuan and simultaneously present it directly to the supervisor or superior official of the censured. Upon receiving a written censure, the concerned superior officials must immediately decide whether to dismiss or otherwise discipline the

[11] For the disciplinary organ in the impeachment case, see "List of Disciplinary Authorities" and "Rules of Procedure of the Military Governors' Disciplinary Committee" in the 21st issue of the *Control Yuan Gazette*.

accused, or promptly provide justification to the Control Yuan if no action should be taken. If the relevant officials in charge fail to act on a censure case within one month after receiving it, do not provide any explanation, or their response lacks sufficient justification, the Control Yuan may bypass the standard impeachment review process and convert the censure case directly into an impeachment case to be handed over to the disciplinary body. The superior officials shall be held responsible in due course for dereliction of duty if the censured is impeached and disciplined.

ii. Effect of the Control Yuan

Upon the establishment of the Control Yuan, public opinion regarding its effectiveness of exercising supervisory power was split into two camps, one of which believed that under the oppressive rule of the National Government, the Control Yuan merely served as a political embellishment, incapable of truly exerting its power, and its control members could only take down some petty corrupt officials in a piecemeal manner, not daring to confront those in power. This camp was represented by Cai Yuanpei, a senior figure within the KMT, who resolutely declined his appointment as the first president of the Control Yuan. To quote him, "The supervisory system has played a critical role in democratic countries, but what can it accomplish under a regime where the wolfish high-ranking officials are at large, and the pilfering petty officials get punished?" (Xu, 1994) The other camp was represented by Yu Youren. As the first president of the Control Yuan, Yu embraced the spirit of persevering even in the face of insurmountable obstacles and worked diligently to make meaningful strides, despite the stifling pressures from the dictatorship. He assumed his position after two previously appointed presidents (Cai Yuanpei and Zhao Daiwen) declined their nominations, which had significantly delayed the formation of the Control Yuan. Yu served two terms until the collapse of the National Government in 1949. Once in office, Yu was proactive in establishing supervisory institutions, formulating oversight systems, and clearing years of accumulated cases. He also nominated a number of upright and outspoken individuals to serve as Control Yuan members, effectively exercising their impeachment powers and monitoring officials at all levels. No sooner was the Control Yuan established than two county governors were impeached, which, though acknowledged by the public, incurred such criticism as that the Control Yuan targeted low-ranking officials while turning a blind eye to more prominent figures, symbolized by the phrase, "The Control Yuan swats flies but doesn't hunt tigers". In response, Yu stated, "Either a fly or a tiger, as long as it is harmful to our people, is equally treated at the Control Yuan", which demonstrated his strong commitment to supervise officials of all ranks (Xu, 1994). True to his word, in 1933, the Control Yuan indeed struck down a number of high-ranking officials, of whom six were provincial chairmen and received penalties ranging from reprimands, dismissals or referrals for criminal investigation. The Control Yuan also successfully filed impeachments against many influential figures throughout its history. For instance, in 1932, when Wang Jingwei, the president of the Executive Yuan, brokered the treasonous *Shanghai Ceasefire Agreement* with Japan without adhering to legal procedures and submitting it to the Legislative Yuan for consideration, the Control Yuan initiated impeachment proceedings against him. The Control Yuan also impeached Ju Zheng, the president of the Judicial Yuan, for abuse of power, corruption, and dereliction, and Sun Ke, the president of the Legislative Yuan, for malfeasance (Sun, 2005). In February 1947, the nation-shaking gold scandal erupted due to the misuse of gold policy by then Executive President Song Ziwen and Central Bank Governor Bei Zuyi misused the gold policy, The Control Yuan quickly moved to impeach them. Song resigned one day prior to the impeachment, while Bei received suitable punishment (Xu, 1994). Over the years, the Control Yuan took action against various high-profile officials such as Wang Zhengting the Foreign Minister, Gu Mengyu the Railway Minister, and Zhang Xueliang the Northeast Border Commander, along with a multitude of sub-chiefs, provincial chairmen and commissioners, corps commanders, army commanders, and other key figures.

Looking at the historical data, from its establishment in 1931 until June 1936, prior to the War of Resistance Against Japan, the Control Yuan initiated 727 impeachment cases, implicating a total of 1337 officials. This number included 27 military personnel, a top-ranking officer, and 15 first-rank officials[12] (Qian et al., 2008). Between 1937 and December 25, 1947, just before the *Constitution of the Republic of China* came into effect, the Control Yuan brought forth impeachments against 1524 individuals, including 110 military officers, a top-ranking official, nine first-rank officials, and 18 generals (Chang, 1979, p. 144). From 1948 to 1949, it established 71 impeachment cases targeting 115 officials, including Wei Lihuang, the Commander-in-Chief of the "Campaign of Bandit Suppression in Northeastern China" who faced impeachment for dereliction of duty (Tao, 1978). The wealth of data indicates that the Control Yuan of the NNG was highly active and initiated numerous impeachments. Notably, many key figures were involved, including two executive presidents Wang Jingwei and Song Ziwen, along with various ministers, provincial chairmen, and military generals. Statistically speaking, it's fair to say that the Control Yuan effectively lived up to Yu Youren's promise of "swatting both tigers and flies".

Certainly, an impeachment brought up by the Control Yuan does not necessarily equate to actual punishment for the impeached party because punitive power resides in disciplinary organs, not the Control Yuan. In fact, in the milieu of Chiang Kai-shek's dictatorship and pervasive corruption within the government, many impeachment cases often fizzled out, especially those cases against high-ranking "tigers". For instance, in 1932, the Control Yuan impeached Wang Jingwei for high treason, who instead threatened to resign. The case was eventually abandoned under Chiang Kai-shek's interference. In 1933, the Control Yuan motioned an impeachment case against Gu Mengyu the Railways Minister and close ally of Wang, for alleged malpractice in purchasing railroad equipment from foreign countries at the cost of national sovereignty. However, Gu faced no retribution despite the public exposure of the case, and in retaliation, a supplementary resolution to the *Act of Impeachment* was passed under Wang's maneuver by the regular meeting of Political Bureau of the KMT Central Committee, forbidding the Control Yuan from publicizing impeachment cases. In both instances, President Yu of the Control Yuan attempted to resign

[12] In the Republic of China, the President of the five Yuans and the President of the state are elected officials and ministers are specially appointed officials.

in protest, but to no avail. Although the restriction on the Control Yuan's freedom of publication was later lifted, both Wang and Gu evaded punishment, rendering the impeachment unsuccessful (Xu, 1994). On that account, people, both in the NNG and Taiwan province today, contended that the Control Yuan could not play its role to the full if only vested with the power of impeachment and without the capacity to enforce disciplinary action. Hence, some believe that it should be granted punitive powers as well. (Gao, 1936; Zhang, 2002). As mentioned above, the MFDC had attempted at making such kind of power adjustment, but the 1946 *Constitution of the Republic* maintained the original power separation. In the author's view, there are two reasons for it. First, in line with the principle of division of powers in modern justice, the power to prosecute and the power to adjudicate must remain separated to avoid potential tyranny. As the control power is a form of judicial authority, this separation principle applies, thus dividing impeachment power from the disciplinary power. This helps prevent the Control Yuan from becoming autocratic. Proponents of merging these powers tend to focus on the possibility of impeachment cases going unresolved while overlooking the risks of potential wrongful convictions from a too powerful Control Yuan. After all, the supervisory officials are not saints. They may be biased, misjudge, or even become partisan. Secondly, no matter when or where, supervisory officials are not the ultimate authority. The final arbiter was the emperor in ancient China, and the people (or the authorities elected by the people) in modern democracies. Even if the Control Yuan were to hold both impeachment and punitive powers, it would still be subject to higher authorities, as it neither holds military nor financial power. Under the National Government, if the Control Yuan (wielding punitive power) ruled against the supreme authority on an impeachment case, the ruling would probably go unenforced, and the Control Yuan would even expose itself to risk of reprisals from those in power, as seen in the case of Wang Jingwei's response to Gu Mengyu's impeachment.

In fact, just like a Western parliament, the performance of an independent supervisory body depends on not only the robustness of its own institutional design and the caliber of its personnel, but also the broader political and cultural milieu of the nation. Under the backdrop of Chiang Kai-shek's dictatorial rule and poor bureaucratic governance within the NNG, the effectiveness of the Control Yuan was inevitably undermined. However, we can neither overlook the achievements it scored (it did, after all, managed to impeach a large number of officials and caused many of them to be disciplined, thereby creating a certain societal impact), nor deny the inherent validity or "raison d'etre" of an independent supervisory organ.

11.3.5 Summary

Since Sun Yat-sen first introduced the concept of Five-power Constitution, voices opposing the establishment of the Control Yuan (and, in the same vein, the idea of Five-power Constitution) have never fully quieted. Objectives were that Chinese and Western political traditions were fundamentally divergent, making an independent supervisory organ incompatible with a parliamentary system. They claim that grafting the Chinese censorial organs onto the Western tripartite system of government had neither rhyme nor reason. Hence, some people assert that "Three powers are adequate, five powers are overkill" (quoted from Tang Degang), while others have termed the "Five-power Constitution" as "the dragon's constitution" with unique Chinese characteristics.

At its core, the debate surrounding the Control Yuan fundamentally concerns how China should approach its own traditional institutions in the process of modernization, vis-à-vis Western ones. Advocates for the abolishment of the Control Yuan (an independent supervisory body) believe that Chinese and Western political and cultural traditions are entirely incompatible. They view the independent supervisory body as a vestige of backward, autocratic imperial politics that ought to be discarded. However, the traditional Chinese censorial institution has its own merits. After the overthrow of the Qing monarchy, the Control Yuan, as a fresh growth on an old tree, could potentially be reformed to eliminate its shortcomings that have allowed it to be susceptible to dictatorial control. This would allow it to more effectively carry out its traditional function of independent supervision. Furthermore, the Western parliamentary system and the independent supervisory system are not inherently contradictory, which is also corroborated by the success of the widespread Swedish ombudsman system around the world.[13] Moreover, the conception of independent supervision has deeply ingrained in the Chinese political culture and has a historical momentum within the Chinese political system. Historically, with the exception of the short-lived Beiyang Government, the institution of an independent supervisory body (or system) has consistently demonstrated resilience and vitality.

---

[13] The Swedish Ombudsman system, originating in the early nineteenth century, was later adopted by Nordic countries such as Finland, Denmark and Norway in the first half of the twentieth century, and has since developed into a kind of Nordic "export". In 1978, the International Ombudsman Institute (IOI) was established. More than 110 countries and territories are now members of the organization, all of which implement independent supervisory systems. Although the names, structures and roles of the ombudsmen may vary from one country to another, they all share a foundational characteristic - their powers are independently exercised, providing a bulwark against abuses of power and corruption. "The prime prerequisite for the robust exercise of oversight powers is their independence; over the years, countries around the world, have endeavored to ensure this independence, fervently seeking to remove oversight from the influence of legislative bodies. Although the legislature may have a moderate role in the selection of the ombudsman, every effort is exerted to ensure that the exercise of oversight powers remains free from legislative interference. In Nordic countries, the operation of supervisory powers is designed to be independent of executive, judiciary, and legislative influences, thus preventing any potential constraints on their use." (The Control Yuan, 2007, pp. 9–10).

The punishment and deterrence of official corruption, as well as the establishment of a transparent political system, were issues of significant importance to ancient Chinese governments. Correspondingly, an independent supervisory system with a history spanning thousands of years was developed. After the Xinhai Revolution, the modern Chinese government introduced the Western concept of parliamentary oversight, but the memory of China's traditional supervisory system remained vivid in people's minds. Whether it was the Suzheng Division (also known as the Ping Zhengyuan) of the Beiyang Government period, or the Control Yuan—a body founded on Sun Yat-sen's concept of Five-power Constitution, both represented a return to China's traditional independent supervisory system. A central challenge throughout the history of the ROC's supervisory system has been striking a balance between the traditional Chinese supervisory mechanism and the Western parliamentary oversight system. Essentially, this revolves around resolving the institutional setting and power conflicts between the supervisory authority and the Parliament.

The modern Chinese supervisory system has undergone a shift from an absolute East–West dichotomy to a state of East–West eclecticism or integration. Whether through westernization or East–West integration, one must beware of the pitfalls of excess. The political and cultural traditions between China and the West differ to a great extent, as do the origins of their respective supervisory mechanisms. Hence, melding old with new, or East with West, is no simple task. The ROC founded in the wake of the Xinhai Revolution adopted wholesale the modern political systems of the West, establishing new legislative, executive, and judicial organs. Initially, supervisory powers were vested in the Parliament in line with Western tradition. This practice, in effect, abolished the traditional Chinese independent censorial system. However, during the era of the Beiyang Government, the Parliament underperformed, ineffective in supervision. Given the far-reaching influence of China's independent supervisory system, a revival of the traditional imperial censorate system, the Suzheng Division, took place under Yuan Shih-kai's rule. The Beiyang Government's attempt to copy the Western model of parliamentary democracy and constitutional government was ill-fated. In contrast, the subsequent National Government in Nanjing adopted Sun Yat-sen's idea of Five-power Constitution, adding two traditional Chinese powers (supervision and examination) to the Western triad of powers. This formed a co-existing system of five powers (the five Yuans), in which the Control Yuan and the Legislative Yuan each exercised their distinct powers, representing a harmonious co-existence of independent supervisory institutions and modern legislative organs within a Sino-Western government framework. The Control Yuan, as defined in the 1946 *Constitution of the Republic of China*, represented a blending of Chinese and Western supervisory systems. In addition to exercising supervisory functions, it also assumed the roles similar to those of the U.S. Senate in its organization and jurisdiction, representing a bold institutional grafting attempt. However, questions remain. Is the Control Yuan a seamless integration of Chinese and Western supervisory systems, or is it merely an ill-fitting amalgamation? Are there inherent obstacles to its successful operation? Can it achieve optimal supervisory efficacy? Is there a risk of it losing the advantages associated with both parliamentary oversight and professional supervisory bodies?

Indeed, the 1946 *Constitution*'s transformation of the Control Yuan into a quasi-parliamentary organ has been widely criticized. However, this criticism does not undermine the value of an independent supervisory organ, but instead, underscores its importance. The Control Yuan functioning as a parliament does not incorporate parliamentary powers, while a parliament (senate) overpowering the Control Yuan, jeopardizes the independence of the supervisory body. The Control Yuan is tasked with exercising two potentially conflicting powers (the power of consent and the power of impeachment) and play contradictory roles (that of an approver and an impeacher). Moreover, its independent functioning may be compromised due to pressure from local political factions and electoral politics. Though not bearing the name of a parliament, the Control Yuan operates much like one (being elected and exercising the power of consent) and, as such, bears its own disadvantages. "The merit of a supervisory system lies not in its democratic façade, but in the fact that the supervisory officials are able to exercise their powers independently." (Chang, 1979, p. 419) Otherwise, it would suffice to assign supervisory powers directly to the parliament without the need for a distinct, full-time supervisory body. Paradoxically, the infusion of democratic elements threatened the Control Yuan's ability to function independently, reinforcing the contemporaneous critique of it being an ill-fitting amalgamation. After the political and parliamentary transformation of the Control Yuan in accordance with the 1947 *Constitution*, impeachment cases turned "few and far between" when compared to earlier periods (the average number of impeachment cases per year was about one-third of those during the tutelage period),[14] and the focus shifted towards political issues (such as proposing corrective measures and exercising the power of consent). This transition served as solid evidence for the diminishing supervisory function (Lei, 1953, pp. 111–112).

The deficiencies and operational ineffectiveness of the Control Yuan should not be seen as reasons to abolish the independent supervisory system. The system's drawbacks can be eradicated through institutional reform,[15] while its supervisory function can be enhanced by technical methods. Furthermore, the effectiveness of an oversight function, whether executed by an independent body or parliament, is shaped by the broader socio-political climate. Transparency and integrity in politics cannot be guaranteed solely by the presence of a supervisory authority, and it is crucial to have a robust democratic legal system in place. There is no need for us to overestimate the capabilities of supervisory organs. Neither should we attribute the success or failure of administering government officials only to the supervisory system (or organ) itself.

[14] The comparison of the number of impeachment cases can be found in the above cited data. The number of the impeached officials from 1931 to 1947, spanning a period of 17 years, was approximately 3,000, with an annual average of around 180; in contrast, the number of the impeached in 1948 and 1949 was 115, with an annual average of less than 60. This evidence clearly indicates a significant decrease in the exercise of impeachment power by the Control Yuan following its transition to a parliamentary system.

[15] The specific system includes the selection and appointment of the control members, the authority and internal structure of the supervisory organs, the local touring inspection system, etc.

The Control Yuan, created on the basis of Sun Yat-sen's idea of Five-power Constitution, marks a distinctively Chinese institutional innovation in the quest of a modern government in China after the downfall of imperial system. Its theoretical and pragmatic value should not be underestimated. The detailed institutional arrangements and the evolution of the Control Yuan during the Republic of China period, including aspects such as the selection, appointment, and job security of control members, internal operation of the supervisory organ, regional touring inspection systems, and the strengths and weaknesses of various institutional reforms, can still provide valuable insights for improving our current supervisory system.

References

Chang, Z. (1979). *Zhongguo xiandai jiancha zhidu* [*The supervisory system in modern China*]. The Commercial Press.

Chen, X. (2001). *Zhonghua minguo xianfa shilun* [Explanation of Constitution of the Republic of China]. For internal circulation.

Chen, C. (2006). *Xiangai fangxiangpan* [On the reform direction of the Control Yuan]. In J. Ye, et al. (Eds.), *The steering wheel of constitutional reform* (pp. 156–160). Wu-Nan Book Inc.

Draft Constitution Propaganda Committee of the Legislative Yuan. (Ed). (1940). *Zhonghua minguo xianfa caoan shuoming shu* [*The instructions for the draft constitution of the Republic of China*]. Zhengzhong Press.

Editorial Committee of the Veritable Record of the Control Yuan. (1981). *Guomin zhengfu jiancha yuan shilu* [A Veritable record of the Control Yuan of the Nationalist Government] (Vol. 1). Secretariat of the Control Yuan.

Gao, Y. (1936). Issues on the constitutional power of supervision. In Z. Yu (Ed.), & J. Wu (Pr.), *Xianfa wenxuan* [Selected essays on constitution] (pp. 48–55). Shanghai Law Editing and Translating Press.

Huang, S. (2000). *Minchu falv bianqian yu caipan* [Legal changes and judgments in the early Republic of China]. National Political Science University.

Lei, Z. (1953). *Jiancha yuan zhi jianglai* [*The future of the Control Yuan*]. For internal circulation.

Lin, J. (1993). *Zhonghua minguo xianfa zhutiao shiyi* [Article-by-article interpretation of the Constitution of the Republic of China] (Vol. 3). San Min Book.

Liu, Y., & Li, Q. (2006). Political elites and supervision to power—An analysis of the supervisors of Nanjing National Government (931–1949). *Dongnan daxue xuebao* [*Journal of Southeast University*] (Philosophy and Social Science), (3): 45–51+126–127.

Luo, Z. (Ed.) (1974). *Jindai zhongguo fazhi yanbian yanjiu* [Research on the evolution of modern Chinese legal institution]. Zhengzhong Press.

Qian, D., Sa, S., Yang, H., et al. (2008). *Minguo zhengzhi shi* [History of the political system of the Republic of China]. Shanghai People's Publishing House.

Secretariat of the National Assembly. (1961). *Zhonghua minguo xianfa zhi zhiding* [*Making the Constitution of the Republic of China*]. For internal circulation.

Sun, Y. (1988). *Sanmin zhuyi* [The Three Principles of the People]. SanMin Book.

Sun, X. (2005). Comment and analysis of the supervisory system of Nanjing Government. *Liaoning daxue xuebao* [Journal of Liaoning University] (Philosophy and Social Science), 33(6), 89–94.

Tao, B. (1978). *Bijiao jiancha zhidu* [*A comparison of supervisory system*]. Zhonghua Book Company.

The Five-power Constitution Association. (Ed). (1963). *Wuquan xianfa wenxian jiyao* [A digest of five-power constitution literature]. Palmier Press.

The Control Yuan. (2007). *Jiancha yuan baogao shu* [The Control Yuan report]. For internal circulation.

Wu, J., & Huang, G. (1937). *Zhongguo zhixian shi* [The history of constitution making in the Republic of China]. The Commercial Press.

Xia, X. (Ed.) (2004). *Jindai zhongguo xianzheng lichen: shiliao huicui* [*History of constitutionalism in modern China: A collection of historical materials*]. China University of Political Science and Law Press.

Xu, M. (1994). Yu Youren and the Control Yuan—A summary of the five Yuans in the National Government (Vol. 2). *Minguo chunqiu* [Republican Spring and Autumn], (2), 3–6.

Zhang, B. (2002). Tentative analyses of the causes about the low efficiency of Nanking Government's supervisory power under the system of tutelage. *Kaifeng daxue xuebao* [*Kaifeng University Journal*], (2), 36–40.

Chapter 12
Inheritance and Innovation of Talent Selection System: The Examination Yuan

"The fundamental work in running a country is merely 'talent selection' and 'administration'. With the latter resting on the former, there is no better choice than a fair examination system to select talents." (Shen, 1995, p.1) Therefore, ancient China created the world-famous imperial examination system. The selection mechanism of public officials has taken the lead for thousands of years, and even become the origin of the modern civil service examination system represented by Britain. Quite a few people even consider the imperial examination system as China's "Fifth Invention" besides the Four Great Inventions and as the greatest contribution to the whole world in the field of spiritual civilization (Guangming Daily, 2011). At the beginning of the twentieth century, the Western tide of thoughts made the imperial examinations a target of public criticism for their rigid form and empty content and were thus abolished by the late Qing government; however, the *keju* (科举) tradition featuring open and fair selection of public functionaries did not die away afterwards. Compared with the European and American constitutional paradigms, one of the main spirits of the Five-power Constitution created by Sun Yat-sen was to "attach great importance to the human factor"; "the main function of the examination power is to select competent people" while "the main function of the supervision power is to remove the incompetent ones", so that "the virtuous are well placed" and "the capable are at their posts" (Lin, 1993, p. 139). With the establishment of the National Government in 1927, the concept of a five-power government was introduced based on "Teachings by Father of the Nation". As part of this framework, the Examination Yuan was transformed into a tangible institution, drawing from *Sun Wen Theory*. Presently, as China demonstrates a committed approach to its legal system and emphasizes the rediscovery and preservation of the core principles of Chinese legal culture, there is a renewed importance in exploring the legacy and evolution of the traditional imperial examinations and civil service system in modern China.

When examining constitutional institutions of national significance like the Examination Yuan and the Control Yuan, "it becomes evident that relying on foreign constitutional principles as a research basis is inherently inadequate" (Chen, 2001,

X. Nie, *The History of Government and Public Law in China*,
https://doi.org/10.1007/978-981-97-6063-3_12

p. 687). The evaluation of such systems should be conducted in consideration of their practical implementation and operation, emphasizing the need to assess their effectiveness in achieving their intended objectives.

12.1 From the Traditional Imperial Examination System to the Independence of Examination Power

In the speech commemorating the founding anniversary of *People's Report* (*Min Bao*) in 1906, Sun Yat-sen introduced his concept of Five-power Constitution for the first time. Firstly, he first provided an overview of American history prior to the implementation of a modern civil service examination system. He argued that relying solely on elections could not guarantee the selection of genuinely capable individuals as appointments were purely a matter of sharing the spoils among political parties. In his speech, Sun said,

> In the United States, some officials were elected and some, appointed. Without a historical examination system in place, both election and appointment processes were susceptible to corruption. In electoral campaigns, candidates often relied on their eloquence and engaged in extensive pandering to the public. Unfortunately, this resulted in the neglect of learned and virtuous individuals who may have lacked in speech but possessed valuable knowledge and integrity. As a consequence, the U.S. House of Representatives has had a regrettable history, frequently plagued by the presence of unintelligent and ill-informed individuals. Turning to appointments, all appointed officials followed the president's lead, with power alternating between the Republican Party and the Democratic Party. Whenever a new president assumed office, a significant turnover of officials—ranging from the Cabinet to the Postmaster General—would take place, amounting to no less than 60,000 to 70,000 replacements. This cyclic pattern has contributed to an unprecedented level of corruption and slackness within U.S. politics, which can ultimately be traced back to the underdeveloped examination and election system. (Sun's speech, cited from Zhang & Wang, 1963, p. 541)

Sun continued to express that a revised version of the traditional Chinese examination system gained prominence in Britain and the United States, but there were two flies in the ointment. On one hand, the examination system was only applicable to junior officials (administrative officials) and did not extend to senior ones and representatives of public opinion; on the other, the examination power remained subordinate to the executive power and lacked independence. The ROC should strive for further improvements in its examination system in the future.

> The examination system was originally developed in China, but unfortunately, it had its own shortcomings. However, foreign countries borrowed and modified it, and it eventually became established in the West. The United Kingdom was the first to imitate the Chinese examination and selection system, and the U. S. followed suit—most junior officials had to pass examinations before being appointed. The implementation of this system brought improvements to the political landscape in the United States. However, it was only utilized for the selection of lower-level officials, and the power of examination remained under the jurisdiction of the Ministry of Administration. Although some remedies were implemented, they were not comprehensive. Therefore, in the future, the *Constitution of the Republic* of China must establish an independent organ dedicated to conducting examinations and

> selections. Officials at all levels should be required to pass examinations to demonstrate their qualifications. Whether elected or appointed, only individuals who meet the necessary criteria should be selected. This approach will help eliminate the drawbacks of blind and indiscriminate appointments as well as the prevalence of nepotism and favoritism. (Sun's speech, cited from Zhang & Wang, 1963, pp. 541–542)

In the aforementioned 1906 speech, Sun also addressed the issue of an independent civil service system alongside the independent examining power. He stated,

> Throughout history, China has always attached great importance to the qualification-based selection of individual, which is a commendable intention. However, in monarchies, the demotion and promotion of talented men solely relied on the whims of the monarch, rendering the notion of qualification screening meaningless. In the republics, the concept of qualification screening become highly relevant because civil servants are meant to serve the people rather than the monarch, and their appointment should be based on utmost competence. But if the examining power is retained by the Ministry of Administration, it would wield excessively broad authority, leading to various issues, and so an independent examination body should be established. (Sun's speech, cited from Zhang & Wang, 1963, p. 542)

In ancient China, the system of examination and appointment was distinct, with the Ministry of Rites overseeing the examination of civil servant (examining and selecting individuals for official appointment) and the Ministry of Personnel responsible for the appointment of scholar-officials (assigning official titles and positions) since the Tang Dynasty. The Ministry of Personnel consistently held a prominent position among the six ministries, highlighting the significant importance of personnel administration in the government organization of ancient China.[1] What is *quanxu* (铨叙)? "The Chinese character 铨 is connected to the homophonic character 权, which means "to weigh" and signifies evaluating the qualifications of personnel. On the other hand, 叙 and 序 also sound the same, indicating the order of sequence. Therefore, the combination of 铨 and 叙 implies a meticulous assessment of individuals' rank, grade, and placement after careful consideration. In modern terms, it means to calibrate and verify the actual qualifications of each civil servant with the standards set up by personnel law so as to determine the compliance with the legal requirements as well as the ranking of those eligible. Those who meet the criteria are granted suitable appointive positions, along with a designated rank, grade, and salary scale, while those who do not are not." (Xu, 1996, p. 67) Sun's mention of the independence of examination and appointment effectively integrated the examining power of the Ministry of Rites and the administrative power of civil service of the Ministry of Personnel (personnel administration power). Thus, it represents the broader concept of examining power, which should not be underestimated in its significance.

In his book *Sun Wen Theory* published in 1919, Sun proposed the establishment of five chambers (the five-Yuan structure), including the Examination Yuan and

[1] The Ministries of Rites and Personnel, as executive agencies, were both led by the Department of State Affairs in the Tang Dynasty. Since the Song and Ming Dynasties, the emperor gradually consolidated power and the system of three departments was undermined. The heads of the six ministries became the highest executives directly subordinate to the emperor, Son of Heaven, each exercising their powers independently and responsible only to the emperor.

the National Assembly, and that "the qualifications of the members of the National Assembly and the five chambers, as well as all the other officials of any rank, shall be determined by the Examination Yuan" (Five-Power Constitution Association, 1963, p. 6). According to Sun's vision, the Examination Yuan should exercise the power of examination over both central and local officials, and that the central authorities would be responsible for managing the appointment of civil servants nationwide, reflecting a consolidated system (centralized personnel administration) rather than a federal system (decentralized personnel administration). This arrangement aligns with the Chinese tradition after the Sui and Tang Dynasties. Since the Sui Dynasty when *biju* (辟举), elevation or appointment by the emperor in the Han Dynasty, was replaced by keju, the imperial examination, all officials below the sixth rank were selected and appointed by the Ministry of Personnel,[2]which took over local governors' power to appoint their own staff in provinces and commanderies. The reform included a policy requiring magistrates to employ people from other counties instead of their own, a critical step towards centralizing personnel administration. "In the past, except governors and other senior officials in prefectures, governors and their deputies in commanderies, and magistrates in counties, the remaining staff were appointed by local governors. As a result, the number of appointees by imperial decree in each province did not exceed 10. By contrast, now [in the Tang Dynasty] officials of all tiers are administered by the Ministry of Personnel and their conduct and performance are subject to evaluation." This system started in the late Wei Dynasty and the Northern Qi Dynasty, inherited by and popularized in the Sui Dynasty (Chen, 2001a, 2001b).

In his 1921 speech on the Five-power Constitution, Sun reemphasized the use of the traditional Chinese examination system as a remedy for the flaws of "general election" system derived from Europe and the United States. He used diagrams to illustrate that, while the legislative, executive, and judicial powers were subservient to monarchial authority in ancient China, the examination and censorial powers maintained a relative independence, which demonstrated that in ancient times "China also possessed a three-power constitution". In foreign countries following the *trias politica* model, the examination power was affiliated to the executive branch while the supervisory power, to the legislative branch. However, in China's future Five-power Constitution, the examination power and supervisory power should be separated from the executive and legislative organs (Five-Power Constitution Association, 1963). In April 1924, Article 15 of Sun's handwritten *Fundamentals of National Reconstruction* stated, "All candidates for and appointees to positions, whether at the central or local level, must undergo central examinations, and can only [assume office] when they are conferred with the necessary qualifications." (The Five-Power Constitution Association, 1963, p. 38)

Except the aforementioned 1906 speech, Sun did not elaborate on the responsibilities of the Examination Yuan in his speeches and writings. One of the most

---

[2] The appointment of officials above the fifth-rank should be reported to and decided by the emperor after proposed by the Department of State Affairs (*shangshu sheng* 尚书省) and considered by the Palace Secretariat (*Zhongshu sheng* 中书省) and the Chancellery (*menxia sheng* 门下省).

contentious issues is whether Sun's concept of the independent examination power in his Five-power Constitution theory pertained only to the examination and selection of officials or included the administration of the civil service personnel system. Scholars often inferred from Sun's design of examination system during the military period that the independent examination power he advocated was only in a narrow sense. Upon the establishment of the ROC, the Nanjing Provisional Government created Bureau of Civil Service, which directly reported to the provisional president and was in charge of appointments, removals, promotions and other human resource management matters. Shortly assuming the position of the provisional president, Sun ordered Bureau of Legal Affairs to draw up *Draft of Order on Civil Service Examination Commissioner Posts*, according to which chairpersons and commissioners for higher and ordinary civil service examinations were appointed to oversee the examination process (Guiding Committee of Series Books on Examination and Civil Service Administration of the Examination Yuan, 1981). In August 1924, the Guangzhou Military Government ratified and released Organic Regulations of the Examination Yuan, which stipulated that the Examination Yuan was an independent organ directly under the Generalissimo's authority to manage the national examination system and related affairs; each province was required to set up a division under the unified command and supervision of the Examination Yuan; the statutory function of the Examination Yuan shall be restricted to "examining and selecting" talents, while the registration and appointment of qualified officials and other personnel management issues shall be outside its jurisdiction (Jiang, 1997, pp. 70–71).

12.2 From the Examination Organ to the Personnel Department

12.2.1 Establishment of the Examination Yuan System

i. The Examination Yuan and its organization

In July 1925, with the establishment of the Guangzhou National Government, what was set up was not the Examination Yuan in accordance with Organic Regulations of the Examination Yuan, but rather Civil Service Division, similar to Civil Service Bureau in the early period of the ROC. Following the successful Northern Expedition, the Central Committee of the KMT Party decided to adopt the five-Yuan (five-chamber) system. On October 8, 1928, the National Government amended and promulgated *Organic Law of the National Government of the Republic of China*, which included Chap. 5 titled "The Examination Yuan". It stipulated that "the Examination Yuan shall be the highest examination organ of the National Government, responsible for conducting examinations and determining the qualifications for public service. All public functionaries must pass the examination and have their qualifications for public service determined by the Examination Yuan in accordance with the law before they can be appointed" (Article 37); "The Examination Yuan shall have a president and a vice-president" (Article 38) (Xia & Hu, 2004, p. 788). Dai Jitao, a founding member of the KMT and a close confidant of Chiang Kai-shek, served as the inaugural president of the Examination Yuan. His leadership spanned twenty years, leaving a tremendous influence on the establishment and development of the Examination Yuan system.

After taking office, Dai's primary task was to establish the Examination Yuan. Apart from recruiting talented individuals for it, institutionalization became the top priority. However, the *Organic Law of the National Government of the Republic of China* did not provide any specific information about the organization of the Examination Yuan, only stating that "The organization of the Examination Yuan shall be determined by law" (Article 40), and that "The Examination Yuan may introduce bills to the Legislative Yuan on matters within its own competence" (Article 39). On October 20, 1928, the National Government promulgated the *Organic Act of the Examination Yuan*, which established the Examination Committee and Ministry of Civil Service under the Examination Yuan (Article 1). The Examination Committee took charge of the following matters: the examination and selection of officials, judges, diplomats, and other civil servants, the examination and selection of specialized professionals, the organization of examination boards, candidate registration, holding examinations, and other related matters (Article 2). The Ministry of Civil Service had charge of civil servant registration, classification of qualified candidates, performance evaluation, verification of appointments, removals, promotions, demotions, and transfers of civil servants, screening of credentials, as well as the verification and registration of emoluments, awards, and pensions (Article 3). The Examination Committee consisted of a chairman, vice-chairman and commissioners, while the Ministry of Personnel had a minister and vice-minister, all appointed by the National Government based on the recommendation of the president of the Examination Yuan (Article 4). This article clearly shows that the president of the Examination Yuan held full responsibility during the period of political tutelage. The Examination Yuan should set up examining boards in each province by law (Article 12), which is in line with Sun Yat-sen's idea that the examination of both central and local officials should fall under the control of the Examination Yuan. Civil servants appointed by the Examination Yuan shall be dismissed without disciplinary procedures if they are found to be unqualified, unless otherwise provided by law (Article 15), which serves as a supplementary provision for the exercise of personnel administration power of the Examination Yuan (National Government Gazette, Oct. 26, 1928). It is said that initially, President Dai only valued the narrow-sense examination power, focusing solely on the examination of officials rather than the administration of human resources. At first, the Ministry of Personnel was not included as part of the Examination Yuan in the making of the *Organic Act of the Examination Yuan*. Due to the persistence of Niu Yongjian, a legislator, the *Organic Act of the Legislative Yuan* prescribed that the Examination Yuan should be responsible for both examination and civil service management. Therefore, Dai said, "Since Mr. Niu insists on instituting the Ministry of Civil Service, let's ask him to be the minister of it" (Xiao, 2008, p. 79), and Niu was indeed appointed as the Minister of the Ministry of Civil

Service in December 1930. In addition, the National Government promulgated the *Organic Act of the Ministry of Civil Service and the Organic Act of the Examination Committee respectively* in December 1928 and August 1929. These acts respectively outlined the responsibilities of the Ministry of Civil Service for the administration of civil servants, judges, diplomats, other public functionaries and qualified examinees while the Examination Committee was responsible for nationwide examination matters. On January 6, 1930, the Examination Committee and the Ministry of Civil Service were formally in place, and Dai Jitao, the president of the Examination Yuan also served as the chairman of the Examination Committee (The Guiding Committee of Series Books on Examination and Civil Service of the Examination (Yuan, 1981).

ii. Establishing the examination and civil service system

In August 1929, the National Government promulgated *the Examination Law* and *the Organic Act of the Board of Examiners*, which provided regulations on the types, timing, locations, and organizational structure of examinations, as well as examinees' qualification and test subjects. The Board of Examiners was established as the highest authority responsible for holding examinations. Between November 1930 and December 1930, the National Government promulgated the *Examination Invigilation Act*, the Enforcement Rules of the Examination Law and the Regulations for the Conduction of Examinations. From November 1930 to April 1931, the Examination Yuan also released examination ordinances for various positions, including administrative staff, accountants, statisticians, diplomats, law-enforcement officials, lawyers, prison officers, western medicine practitioners, pharmacists, etc. In March 1931, the National Government further enacted the *Special Examinations Act*, marking the completion of the establishment of the overall examination system (Editing Office of the Examination Yuan, 2012). The Examination Yuan held the first higher and ordinary examinations in 1931. According to the E*xamination Affairs Act* issued in July 1935, various examination affairs were not directly handled by the Examination Yuan, but by the Board of Examiners composed of temporarily appointed examiners; the Board of Examiners operated independently, and had the authority to schedule examinations, determine test content and grading standards, allocate tasks for test creation and grading, review the scores of test-takers, establish admission and qualification standards, and publish the names of successful candidates. Its exercise of authority was not subject to the command and supervision of the Examination Yuan, but only maintained a business-related connection with the Examination Yuan and its subordinate administrative organs (the Examination Committee) (National Government Gazette, Aug 1 1935).

According to the *Organic Act of the Ministry of Civil Service*, the Ministry of Civil Service was comprised of such departments as Registration, Screening, Performance Evaluation, Commendation and Pensions alongside the Civil Service Review Committee; its purview included screening, registration, employment, job assignment, salary review, service rating (rewards and punishments), training and education, award and pecuniary aid in the event of death; the Civil Service Review Committee was responsible for reviewing the work of each department (Qian et al., 2008). In October 1929, the National Government promulgated the R*egulations on* *the Appointment of Public Functionaries and the Regulations on the Screening and Examination of Incumbent Public Functionaries*, which delineated the appointive qualifications for various officials and established the procedures and criteria for screening and examining all incumbent public functionaries across the country. The Ministry of Civil Service served as the statutory body that exercised the power of appointment and screening. In March 1933, the National Government announced the Law of the Appointment of Public Functionaries, replacing the previous regulations. Under this law, senior, intermediate, and junior civil servants were required to be reviewed and approved by the Ministry of Civil Service, upon recommendation by the National Government or the supervising officials, prior to their appointment (Article 7); additionally, prior to formal appointment, agency chiefs may, if necessary, assign a person of equivalent standing to an interim position, but the interim period shall not exceed three months (Article 8) (National Government Gazette, Mar. 13, 1935). It means that the qualifications for all civil servants must be evaluated by the Ministry of Civil Service, aside from political appointees (including the presidents and vice-presidents of the five Yuans, heads of ministries and commissions, and members of the Legislative Yuan and the Control Yuan) who must be appointed upon resolution of the Political Conference of the KMT Central Committee or other designated authorities[3].

Apart from examining and appointing civil servants at both central and local levels, the Examination Yuan also exercised the power to conduct examinations and review qualifications of representatives at the local level. In December 1940, the National Government promulgated the *Provisional Regulations on the Examination of Candidates for County Senators and Township Representatives*, which stipulated that candidates for county senator and township representative must pass an examination to obtain their qualifications, and the examination process was divided into two parts: a written examination and a qualification examination; soon in 1941 some of these candidates' qualifications for the said offices were processed and verified (The Editing Office of the Examination Yuan, 2012). In 1943, the National Government announced the *Examination Act of Candidates for Provincial and County Public Office* to replace the 1940 Regulations, in comparison with which, the 1943 Act was widely applicable to candidates for provincial senators and municipal offices. The Act prescribed that the testing subjects and verification methods for all local public servants (representatives) should be determined by the Examination Yuan (Article 4); candidates who passed the examination would be issued a certificate of passing by the Examination Yuan, and this achievement would be publicly announced (Article 10) (The Second Historical Archives of China, 1994). On October 1, 1943, the Examination Yuan released the *Enforcement Rules for the Examination Act of Candidates for Provincial and County Public Office and Inspection and Verification Measures for Provincial and County Public Office Candidates*. These regulations stated that the

[3] Against Sun Yat-sen's plan, candidates for high-ranking government officials in the National Government (including central representatives of public opinions) were not subject to the requirement of passing examinations and qualification approval of the Examination Yuan.

Examination Committee should establish a Screening Board to handle the examination and verification of public office candidates; county governments and Provincial Department of Civil Affairs should each set up Public Office Candidate Qualification Screening Board to deal with the initial screening, follow-up screening and transfer of qualification for candidates within their respective counties (The Editing Office of the Examination Yuan, 2012).

12.2.2 Exercising the Power of Personnel Selection: Encountered Challenges and Coping Strategies

Dai Jitao strove to ensure the independence of examination power, mainly in order to counteract the prevailing spoil system of the warlord era. Statistics shows that, between 1931 to 1947, over 10,000 candidates were selected through higher and ordinary examinations while approximately 150,000, through special examinations. "Although the civil service examinations, especially the higher (upper) examination and ordinary examination in the capital, were held with much pomp and circumstance, usually following the ancient rites, and garnered nationwide attention from all sectors of society, their practical applicability remained extremely limited in terms of implementing a 'test-employment integration' merit system. Thus, these examinations bore more symbolic than substantive value." (Jiang, 1994, p. 72) Compared to the Examination Committee, the Ministry of Civil Service encountered numerous obstacles in its exercise of authority and institutional development, which stemmed less from the theoretical assumption that personnel management should be entrusted to the Examination Yuan and separated from the executive branch, and more from the real-world control exerted by hiring agencies' control over personnel affairs. Although the NNG established a unified regime in name, it failed to eradicate the divisive forces of the warlord era. Chiefs of various governmental agencies, out of both political interests and cultural psyche, often practiced favoritism in personnel appointments "arbitrarily", which ran contrary to the fundamental spirit of merit-based civil service administration, i.e., appointments, dismissals, promotions, and demotions of officials should be based on legally defined qualifications. As a result, the authority of the Ministry of Civil Service was not effectively pronounced, which in turn made the national civil service examination somewhat a façade because those qualified were not hired. Take the assigning power of the Ministry of Civil Service as an example. Dai Jitao, the president of the Examination Yuan, championed "the integration of examination with employment". As per *Regulations on Assigning Qualified Examinees of the First Higher Examination*, those who passed should register with the Ministry of Civil Service, which would then formulate a list of hiring offices and submit it to the National Government requesting the central government or provincial and regional organs to accept those recruits. Nonetheless, despite almost all successful candidates being assigned posts, they were often underutilized, or not granted official titles, resulting in a waste and loss of talent (Xiao, 2008). Both Dai

Jitao and Chiang Kai-shek gradually recognized the critical need for enhancing the civil service system (personnel administration system), a recognition which helped pave the way for the central government's endeavors to quell local separatism and centralize power.

i. The Examination Yuan's attempt to unify local personnel power: enacting and amending *the Act on the Appointment of County Magistrates*

Since the founding of the ROC, the Qing Dynasty's administrative hierarchy of "province-circuit-prefecture-county" (*sheng-dao-fu-xian*, 省—道—府—县) was disrupted. The administrative structure between provinces and counties was still forming, cities were rarely established, and therefore, the county became the basic administrative unit under province. During this period, the appointment of county magistrates was predominantly controlled by the provincial governments, with these positions serving as critical resources for provincial chairmen to appoint their own confidants and build their power base. In terms of personnel appointment and dismissal, the central government's control over counties was not as effective as it was during the Qing Dynasty. Since the implementation of *keju* in the imperial era, county magistrates were typically required to obtain qualifications through examination, after which they would be uniformly appointed and dispatched by the central Ministry of Personnel. In July 1932, the National Government promulgated the *Act on the Appointment of County Governors* (Bulletin of the Legislative Yuan, Sep., 1932), requiring candidates to be at least 30 years old and fulfill one of the following conditions: (1) passing the examination for county governors; (2) graduating from an independent college or special school studying political, legal, economic and social subjects for at least three years, passing the higher examination for civil servants, and serving as a recommended civil servant for at least one year; (3) possessing a diploma from the said schools and serving as a recommended civil servant for at least three years; (4) not passing the national examination but being examined and selected as county governors by provinces and verified by the Examination Yuan (Article 1). The appointive process was broken down into three stages: probation, acting, and official conferral (Article 3); each of the probation and acting stages lasted for one year (Articles 4 and 5); with successful completion of each stage being a prerequisite for progression to the next stage (Articles 5 and 6); the tenure of county magistrates was set at three years, during which they shall not be suspended or removed from office unless found guilty of misconduct or dereliction of duty and thus subject to disciplinary or criminal proceedings (Articles 6 and 7); the appointment of county governors required consultation with the Ministry of Civil Affairs, followed by for verification and qualification from the Ministry of Civil Service, after which it shall be submitted to the Executive Yuan to present to the National Government for approval (Article 11); acting county governor shall not take office for over three months without the preceding procedures (Article 9). The Act on the Appointment of County Governors set forth stringent requirements for qualification and employment procedure, considerably curbing the provincial chairmen's power over the appointment and dismissal of county heads and facilitating centralization. However, the overall competence of county governors in all provinces was relatively dismaying, falling short of the legal requirements. Consequently, provinces called on the central government to relax the appointment restrictions (Xiao, 2008). Under this pressure, the National Government thereof amended the Act on the *Appointment of County Governors* in June 1933, lowering the appointment threshold, simplifying the appointive procedures, and rearranging the order of the articles. In spite of these changes, the spirit of the *Act* remained the same as the appointment, removal, and transfer of county governors was still subject to strict restriction from the Ministry of Civil Service of the Examination Yuan. The "County Magistrate Qualification Examination Form and Instructions" attached to the amendment further added that appointment of acting county governors by provincial governments, in accordance with the formal appointive procedures for county governors, must, within one month from the issuance of the appointment decree, be submitted to the Ministry of Civil Affairs who would forward it to the Ministry of Civil Service for review and recommendation (The Second Historical Archives of China, 1994).

The requirements stipulated in the revised Act were still deemed excessive by the provincial governments. Thus, these regulations were often circumvented or even ignored by local governments, with only one-tenth of the total number of county governors nationwide submitted for review in 1933. The central government had no other option but to have the Executive Yuan issue additional "measures" to further reduce the qualification criteria, but the Ministry of Civil Service, in charge of qualification verification, was profoundly discontented with this approach of adopting "unwritten ordinances", and the competence of the county governors was, indeed, a matter of concern. Thereupon, the Examination Yuan, together with the Executive Yuan, submitted a proposal to the Central Political Conference, arguing that, given the county governors' direct relationship and responsibility to the populace, the selection of suitable candidates was of paramount importance and warranted substantial rectification of the status quo. In May 1937, the National Government enacted the *Principles for the Amendment to the Act of the Appointment of County Governors*, which mandated that any legally qualified candidates must undergo a review by the Ministry of Civil Service, and then transferred to the Ministry of Civil Affairs for training, before being officially appointed by the Ministry of Civil Service (Xiao, 2008). Despite the gap between these regulations and the actual circumstances, the central government remained committed to Sun Yat-sen's principle that the Examination Yuan shall unify the examination and personnel administration of central and local officials.

ii. Establishment of the Single-whip System of personnel administration

From the mid-1930s, the Examination Yuan gradually gained control over the personnel management departments and personnel in government agencies at both the central and local governments, aiming to centralize the state's personnel power. In February 1936, the Examination Yuan issued *Entrustment Measures for the Inspection of Delegated Civil Servants in Each Province*, which allowed the appointment, evaluation, and registration of delegated civil servants to be entrusted to inspection boards organized by each provincial government before the establishment of provincial civil service units. In June of the same year, the National Government promulgated Regulations on the Organization of the Civil Service Division, which prescribed that the Ministry of Civil Service should set up civil service divisions in each province to handle relevant matters of delegated public functionaries within that province as well as neighboring provinces and cities. Delegated appointees ranked the lowest among the three tiers of civil servants—the elementary (delegated), junior (recommended) and senior ranks (selected)—in the National Government (excluding specially appointed officials). It means that the Ministry of Civil Service of the Examination Yuan, operating through its provincial offices, exerted control over the personnel administration of all civil servants nationwide[4].

In 1939, Chiang Kai-shek, Chairman of the Supreme National Defense Council, proposed that "Personnel staff in various government organs should be trained in a unified manner, assigned and appointed by the Ministry of Civil Service, so as to promote the examination and civil service system and strengthen personnel management" (Ye, 1993). In March 1940, the Examination Yuan held the Central Personnel Administration Conference to discuss the issue of unified personnel administration power. In December of the same year, the Examination Yuan drew up the *Provisional Measures for Personnel Administration of Various Organs* and submitted it to the National Government for implementation. *The Provisional Measures* clearly outlined the establishment of dedicated personnel management positions in each organ, defined their responsibilities, and empowered the Ministry of Civil Service to provide guidance and oversight in the formulation, revision, and implementation of personnel administration regulations for each government branch. In July 1941, the Chairman's Council of the Military Commission and the Secretariat of the Ministry of Civil Service developed specific methods for "unified management". They formulated the *Outline of Unified Management of Personnel Agencies of the Party, Government, and Forces*, which was adopted by the Supreme National Defense Council in December 1947 and implemented through a decree issued by the National Government. The *Outline* provided that except for separate personnel establishments within the Party and military organs, all personnel administration in government organs shall be managed by the Ministry of Civil Service of the Examination Yuan; each organ was required to establish its own personnel management agency, and those without such agencies should set up one promptly; personnel agencies and officials in each government organ shall be under the command and supervision of the Ministry of Civil Service; personnel staff of each government organ shall be evaluated, appointed and removed by the Ministry of Civil Service; incumbent personnel staff should be evaluated by their supervisory authorities to determine their retention or removal; personnel staff of each government organ shall be subject to the supervision of the Ministry of Civil Service; the training of personnel staff shall be under the charge of the Examination Yuan and completed within a three-year timeframe (The Second Historical Archives of China, 1994). To provide a legal basis for unified management

[4] In February 1946, the National Government promulgated Organic Regulations on the Examination and Civil Service, replacing the Civil Service Division with the Examination and Civil Service Division, which took charge of the examination and civil service matters within each province and its operations were under the command and supervision of the Examination Committee of the Examination Yuan and the Ministry of Civil Service.

of personnel agencies and staff, the Ministry of Civil Service drafted the *Regulations on Personnel Administration* in 1942, which was subsequently promulgated by the National Government in September of the same year. The *Regulations* encompassed three main aspects. First, each government organ shall define the types of personnel management agencies and their duties; second, the personnel staff of each organ shall be directed and supervised by the Ministry of Civil Service, and appointment and removal of personnel supervisors shall be handled by the Ministry of Civil Service by law; third, the *Regulations* shall apply to personnel administration in national secondary and higher schools and state-owned organizations. On October 2, 1942, the National Government issued a decree stipulating that the *Regulations* would come into effect on the coming November 1 and the initial implementation would begin with the departments and bureaus of the National Government, the five Yuans and their direct ministries, commissions and agencies, and organs directly under the ministries, commissions and agencies. On June 11, 1943, the National Government further decreed that the Regulations would take effect on July 1 of that year in local government organs, including provincial governments, municipal governments under the jurisdiction of the five Yuans, and various organizations under them, prefecture administrative offices (provincial government organs dispatched to local areas), and county and municipal governments (The Second Historical Archives of China, 1994).

To this end, the personnel administration within both central and local governments was streamlined under the Ministry of Civil Service of the Examination Yuan, and the so-called Single-whip System of personnel administration was hence established. The Examination Yuan expanded its power from the narrow-sense examination to registration and verification, and to the independent personnel administration, and ultimately became the principal governing body in charge of the national civil service system.

12.2.3 Debate on the Position of the Examination Yuan during the Formulation of the **Constitution of ROC**

The system of the Examination Yuan during the period of political tutelage was mainly based on Sun Yat-sen's idea of Five-power Constitution and shaped through political decisions and efforts, drawing upon the traditional imperial examination and civil service system. Although the Examination Yuan faced various difficulties in exercising the power of examination and personnel administration, these difficulties were primarily rooted in practical political obstacles rather than theoretical doubts. However, during the formulation of the *Constitution of the Republic of China*, the feasibility and legitimacy of the organization and powers of the Examination Yuan were questioned by Western constitutional theory and political institutional paradigms. It is worth noting that, in comparison to the major dispute over the National Assembly, the Executive Yuan, and the Legislative Yuan, the Examination

Yuan did not receive as much attention and the debates regarding its system were not as intense as those concerning the Control Yuan. The public skepticism towards the Examination Yuan originated from criticisms of the Western three-power constitution in relation to the five-power constitution itself. Nevertheless, the entrenched nature of the Five-power Constitution, which derived from the "Teachings by Father of the Nation", made it difficult to challenge its form, and consequently constitution drafters (such as Zhang Junmai) attempted to infuse the spirit of the Western three-power constitution into the framework of Five-power Constitution. But this compromise in the system resulted in a blend of the two constitutional systems and a blurring of theoretical concepts. Although the *Constitution* explicitly provided for the Examination Yuan and its powers, it failed to resolve the disputes over the abolition of the Examination Yuan and the extent of its authorities.

In the making of the MFDC in 1930, the KMT's monopolistic control over constitution-making led to the inclusion of the Examination Yuan's authority and duties as defined in the period of political tutelage. As the Legislative Yuan deliberated on the draft constitution, debates primarily centered around textual and technical issues, such as whether the term of the Examination Yuan president should be extended to ensure independence, the necessity of establishing Examination Committee and its relationship with Board of Examiners, and the requirement for delegates to the National Assembly to pass examinations, among others (Wu & Huang, 1937). According to the final version of the MFDC passed by the Legislative Yuan in 1936, "The Examination Yuan shall be the highest examination organ of the National Government to exercise the powers of examination and determine qualifications for public service." (Article 83), and the Legislative Yuan particularly emphasized that the determination of qualifications for public service "shall be complementary to the examination and selection processes. The purpose of examinations is to select competent and virtuous talents. Only when appointment, salary scale, performance appraisal, demotion and dismissal and other civil service matters are all entrusted to the Examination Yuan will the effectiveness of the examination power be brough into full play so as to uphold the spirit of the separation of powers, as highlighted by Sun Yat-sen's frequent mention of examinations alongside civil service administration in his teachings. Therefore, this article stipulates that the power to determine qualifications for public service should also be vested in the Examination Yuan". The MFDC also stipulated that individuals who shall be examined and qualified by the Examination Yuan included public officials, candidates for public office, and professionals and technicians (Article 85). The original idea that representatives (candidates for public office) were required to pass examinations was credited to Sun Yat-sen. The administration of licensing examinations for specialized professions and technical personnel, typically overseen by professional associations in Europe and the United States, was undertaken by the Examination Yuan from its inception. This practice was also constitutionalized. The Legislative Yuan explained, "The work of these professionals is closely intertwined with the public interest of society. Failing to constitutionalize the professional and technical examinations would demonstrate a lack of caution and could lead to potential abuse." (Propaganda Committee of the Draft Constitution of the Legislative Yuan, 1940, pp. 56–57) Subsequently, the

Examination Yuan expanded its authority to include personnel administration and the examination of professionals and technicians, which may not have been Sun's original intention with the Five-power Constitution. Nonetheless, after over a decade of political practice following the establishment of the Examination Yuan in 1928, the system essentially took shape through the collective efforts of Dai Jitao and others.

During the period of the War of Resistance against Japanese Aggression, the "Constitutional Government Promotion Committee of the National Political Council", mainly comprised of non-KMT members, formulated the "CGPC Draft Constitution", which made significant revisions to the MFDC. The new draft constitution stipulated that the authority of the Examination Yuan was limited to "administering examinations", without including "personnel administration". Moreover, the provision about the scope of candidates subject to examination and appointment by Article 85 of the MFDC was deleted (Xia & Hu, 2004, p. 1037). In 1944, the Association for the Implementation of Constitutionalism put forward "Various Issues for Discussion on the Draft Constitution of the ROC", which included three topics concerning the Examination Yuan, i.e., "the appointment and term of office of the president of the Examination Yuan"; "whether all candidates should be examined first"; and "whether all public officials, professionals and technicians should be examined first" (Xia& Hu, 2008, p. 1090). Although the amendments proposed by the "CGPC Draft Constitution" and the Association for the Implementation of Constitutionalism were not accepted by the National Government, they were retained as suggestions and were partially adopted at the PCC in January 1946.The issue of draft constitution was central to the discussion at the PCC. Through the rallying efforts of the Chinese Communist Party and other parties, the PCC agreed on the Twelve Principles of the PCC, amending the MFDC to a significant extent, the fifth of which was specifically addressed at the Examination Yuan — "The Examination Yuan shall adopt the committee system, with its members nominated by the President and appointed upon the consent of the Control Yuan. Its main duty shall be the examination of public officials and professionals. The committee shall be above partisanship." (Xia & Hu, 2008, p. 1092) Regarding the authority of the Examination Yuan, the "Principles" recognized that the Examination Yuan shall be a provider of qualifying examinations for professionals (specialists and technicians), but rejected its power to examine and select representatives of public opinion. Furthermore, it highlighted that the Examination Yuan's primary responsibility should be examinations rather than personnel administration. As for the organization of the Examination Yuan, the "Principles" altered the then one-head leadership of the Examination Yuan into a committee system, and especially underscored the need for non-partisan examination members, aiming to break the ruling KMT's monopoly on personnel appointments. The KMT Central Committee raised many a suggestion on the "Twelve Principles of the PCC", but the five amendments it proposed did not encompass the issue of the Examination Yuan. The PCC formed a constitution drafting committee to draw up the "May Fifth Draft Constitution Amendment" (Political Consultative Conference Constitutional Amendment).

The drafters of this amendment were well aware of the rampant practice of personnel appointment during the National Government era. To name a few examples, Chiang Kai-shek appointed people from his hometown in the military sector and relatives in the political circle; and even Dai Jitao, President of the Examination Yuan, arranged his daughter's son as Chief Secretary of the Ministry of Civil Service. What the superiors do, everyone else copies. A Chinese idiom—When a man achieves the Dao, his poultry and dogs rise to Heaven—can vividly depict the corrupt officialdom by the prevalent culture of favoritism that far exceeded what Sun Yat-sen referred to as the U.S. political pork barrel system (Spoil System) (Lei, 2010). In addition, the amendment changed the single-head leadership of the Examination Yuan during the tutelage period to a committee system. It even stipulated that the president of the Examination Yuan shall be mutually elected among the members (Article 90, PCC Constitutional Amendment), and a special article was added to emphasize that "An open and competitive examination system shall be implemented for the selection of public officials, and no one shall be appointed without passing the examination" (Article 90, PCC Constitutional Amendment). All of these adjustments aimed to break the monopoly of the Examination Yuan president and other chiefs at all levels over personnel employment, and to seek the independence of the examination power, so as to wipe out the underhand nepotism among government heads. In drafting the chapter on the Examination Yuan in the PCC Constitutional Amendment, the most contentious issue pivoted around whether candidates for public office should be subject to examination or qualification screening. The idea of qualifying candidates for public office (representatives of public opinion) by the Examination Yuan was ideologically the legacy of the Founding Father and included in the MFDC. However, in terms of practical implementation, the National Government did not have central representatives of public opinion during the political tutelage period.[5]As previously mentioned, there were specific laws in place for the qualification screening of local representatives at various levels, and the Examination Yuan did its job conscientiously to handle relevant examination matters. Nonetheless, the drafters of the PCC Constitutional Amendment considered Sun's proposal that candidates for public office must be qualified by examination as "extremely unreasonable and lacking political common sense" in theory, and not in line with the social reality of the "democratic era". In terms of political reality, the ruling party may use the examination and qualification screening process to crowd out strong candidates from opposition parties. Therefore, the Communist Party and other democrats attending the PCC agreed to modify the relevant provisions in the MFDC. Despite repeated objections from the KMT experts, the provision regarding the Examination Yuan's power to examine candidates' qualification for public office in the MFDC was removed, no longer stipulated in Article 92 of the PCC Constitutional Amendment. Furthermore, the proposal that "the Examination Yuan shall be non-partisan" in the

[5] The legislators and control members were not elected during the period of political tutelage, and the National Political Council could not be considered a formal and complete representative organ (Nie, 2014).

Twelve Principles of the PCC was also finalized as an article in the constitutional amendment (Article 94) (Xia & Hu, 2004, p. 1099).

In December 1946, the *Constitution of the Republic of China* was passed by the Constitution-making National Assembly, and it closely resembled the PCC Constitutional Amendment. Only a few modifications were made, including two related to the Examination Yuan. First, the quota system for examinations based on different provinces and areas[6] was added to the article on fair selection in the PCC Constitutional Amendment (Article 85, *Constitution of the Republic of China*). Secondly, a more important amendment was made to the selection process of the president of the Examination Yuan. Instead of being elected by examination commissioners as proposed in the PCC Constitutional Amendment, the President, Vice President, and examination commissioners would now be nominated by the President and appointed with the consent of the Control Yuan (Article 84, *Constitution of the Republic of China*). The 1946 Constitution combined the single-head leadership during the tutelage period with the commission system designed by the PCC Constitutional Amendment, in which, besides the president and vice-president, the Examination Yuan was also staffed with examination commissioners who would exercise their powers independently by law. However, the president and vice-president of the Examination Yuan would not be elected by its members and would have relative independence in the administration of the Yuan. In fact, in reviewing the draft constitution by the Constitution-making National Assembly, various groups of the constitution reviewing committee controlled by KMT representatives attempted to overturn the PCC draft constitution and reinstate the MFDC. In the fourth reviewing, there was a proposal to reintroduce the determination of eligibility for candidates for public office, which had been excluded from Article 92 of the PCC Constitutional Amendment, into the Constitution. However, under Chiang Kai-shek's personal pressure, the Comprehensive Constitutional Reviewing Committee of the National Assembly restored the constitution to its original state, and the issue of candidacy for public office was excluded from the 1946 *Constitution* (Secretariat of the National Assembly, 1946, pp. 458–479). It is worth emphasizing that the constitutional statutes regarding the Examination Yuan are very brief. Article 89 of the *Constitution* explicitly prescribes that the organization of the Examination Yuan (including the *modus operandi* to exercise its powers) shall be regulated by law, providing legislators with significant flexibility in shaping its structure and functioning.

[6] The tradition of conducting civil service examinations with quotas specified according to different provinces and areas finds its roots in China's ancient imperial examination system. In ancient China, a unitary state where educational and cultural levels significantly varied across regions, there was a necessity to ensure regional fairness in the allocation of imperial examination quotas. The National Government's initiation of a quota system for provincial and regional examinations began in December 1930, with the implementation of the Examination Law Enforcement Rules. From 1935 onwards, the Examination Yuan introduced more lenient admission policies for candidates from provinces with fewer educational resources in the higher and ordinary civil service examinations. For additional details, see Jiang (1997, pp. 218-219). The inclusion of the provincial and regional quota system in the constitution by the Constitution-making National Assembly could be seen as a nod to the traditional imperial examination system. This, in a certain sense, represented a return to the customs of the past.

In March 1947, the National Government promulgated the *Organic Act of the Examination Yuan*. Considering that the Examination Yuan was already manned with a number of examiners, the original commission-based Examination Committee was abolished and replaced with the Examination Division. However, due to concerns that the Examination Division might be perceived as inferior to the Ministry of Civil Service, the Examination Yuan proposed an amendment to the *Organic Act of the Examination Yuan* in December 1947. As a result, the Examination Division was elevated to the Ministry of Examination and placed before the Ministry of Civil Service in the order of precedence. According to the amended *Act*, the Examination Yuan shall institute the Ministry of Examination and the Ministry of Civil Service (Article 5); the Ministry of Examination shall have charge of conducting examinations for public officials, professionals and technicians, organizing the Board of Examination, registering qualified examinees, and other related affairs (Article 6); the Ministry of Civil Service shall be responsible for the registration of civil servants, performance evaluation, personnel appointment and removal, promotions and transfers, qualification screening, examination and registration of salaries and rewards, security of pecuniary aid in case of death, retirement and old age pensions, classified registration of qualified examinees and management of various personnel units in each organization (Article 7) (Xia & Hu, 2004, pp. 1151–1152).

12.3 Major Controversies Over the Examination Yuan

12.3.1 Legitimacy of the Examination Yuan's Authority in Personnel Administration

"Among the five powers there is an examination power, and thus the Examination Yuan is established. A close look at the duties of the Examination Yuan shows that its scope extends beyond examinations and encompasses general personnel administration. In this light, instead of being named the Examination Yuan, it would be more appropriate to follow Japan's National Public Service Law and rename it the Personnel Yuan, aligning its name with its actual functions." (Sa, 1993, p. 426) As previously mentioned, under the leadership of the founding President of the Examination Yuan, Dai Jitao, the authority of the Examination Yuan gradually expanded. "Practitioners of the time over-interpreted the independence of the examination power as the independence of personnel power from the executive power, effectively equating the Examination Yuan with the highest personnel administrative body in the country." (Ye et al., 2006, p. 183) The fifth item of the Twelve Principles of the PCC attempted to significantly limit the authority of the Examination Yuan. However, this ran counter to the institutional development and political practice of the Examination Yuan, which had been steadily gaining power during the period of political tutelage. As a result, neither the PCC Constitutional Amendment nor the 1946 Constitution adhered to the Twelve Principles of the PCC. Instead, they granted the Examination

Yuan broad examination powers: "The Examination Yuan shall be the highest examination organ of the State and shall have charge of matters relating to examination, employment, registration, service rating, salaries scales, promotions and transfers, tenure security, commendations, pecuniary aid in case of death, retirement and old age pensions." (Article 83, *Constitution of the Republic of China*) (Xia & Hu, 2004, p. 1110).

The idea of having an independent body or committee to administer civil service examinations not only represents a continuance of the traditional Chinese imperial examination system, but also does not run contradictory to the common practice worldwide. Thus, it did not arouse much controversy over the Examination Yuan's exercising the narrow-sense examination power. However, once the authority of the Examination Yuan expanded to include personnel administration, it met with opposition in both academic discourse and political practice. Scholars often resorted to "executive neutrality" in the modern Western administrative theory of to emphasize the significance of having relatively independent personnel management agencies. This is believed to ensure the detachedness and autonomy of the civil service system particularly during political transitions and to guarantee continuity and stability in governance. However, when comparing civil service systems in various countries, different approaches can be observed. Some countries adopt a relatively independent system (either an extra-ministerial system or compromise system) where the personnel power stays relatively separate from executive power, such as the Civil Service Commission in the United States and the National Personnel Authority in Japan, and examination and appointment powers are exercised by independent agencies, the executive power by each ministry and commission, and the personnel system power either by independent agencies or by each ministry and commission. On the other hand, certain countries employ a bureaucratic system (an intra-ministerial system) in which personnel authority is completely integrated into the executive power, such as in Germany and France, where the various said powers in the preceding part are exercised by each ministry and commission. The Examination Yuan system in the ROC, thoroughly independent from the three powers, served as a special case, characterized by the launching of separate personnel management entities (the Examination Yuan and its subordinate the Ministry of Civil Service) independent of the executive branch. Additionally, it exercised unified command and management over various central and local personnel agencies and workers; the sing-whip personnel system, encompassing the aforementioned powers, is vested in an independent body.

As mentioned before, there has been significant controversy throughout constitutional history regarding the Examination Yuan's authority over personnel administration. Many scholars and political figures insisted that the personnel authority should be returned to the Executive Yuan since personnel power is a core function of the executive branch and should not be completely separated from executive power. Although the separation of personnel authority from executive power can prevent favoritism and ensure impartiality, it hindered administrative efficiency and risked encroaching on the executive branch's jurisdiction. Even the 1946 Constitution granting the power of personnel qualification and appointment to the Examination Yuan did not put an end to the related controversy. In practice, the implementation of personnel policies by the Examination Yuan often encountered difficulties due to active resistance or passive response from the executive authorities. In reality, the Ministry of Civil Service did not encroach on the personnel power of the executive organs. The personnel power was entrusted to various government organs while the power of personnel qualification was vested in the Examination Yuan. Each government organ retained the power to appoint public officials, determine performance evaluations and promotions, while the Examination Yuan's role was to conduct screening and inspections according to the law to prevent arbitrary personnel decisions by executive leaders (Xu, 1996). In addition, in the Five-power Constitution, the president was not a ceremonial position, but held substantial influence on the organization and administration of the Examination Yuan. Per the 1946 *Constitution*, the president had the power to nominate vice president and members of the Examination Yuan (Article 84); the president also had the power to convoke meetings to resolve disputes between different Yuans (including conflicts between the Executive Yuan and the Examination Yuan) (Article 44) (Xia & Hu, 2004, pp. 1107, 1110). Since the 1946 Constitution established a hybrid presidential and cabinet system, the state president (rather than the president of the Executive Yuan) served as the highest executive authority. The Examination Yuan, independent from the Executive Yuan though, was subordinated to the state president. In this connection, the Examination Yuan can be said to be relatively independent rather than entirely independent. Changing the authority of the Examination Yuan, which has been established for decades and supported by the constitution and laws, was not an easy task. Furthermore, the opposition from the executive branch regarding the autonomy of personnel authority can be seen as solid evidence of the Examination Yuan's effective checks and balances on executive power.

12.3.2 Organization of the Examination Yuan: One-Head Leadership or Committee System (Collegiality System)

During the period of political tutelage, the Examination Yuan operated under a system of single-head leadership, with Dai Jitao, a senior KMT member, served as the president of the Examination Yuan from its establishment preparation to the implementation of the *Constitution* in 1947. "Although an independent and detached 'Examination Committee' (during the military period) and 'Examination and Selection Committee' (during the tutelage period) were ever set up under the Examination Yuan, they were temporary organizations, and their nature was no different from the subsequent Board of Examiners established under the constitutional system. The sole decision-making authority on public officials' policies rested with the president of the Examination Yuan." (Jiang, 1997, p. 74) As mentioned earlier, in order to check the all-powerful president of the Examination Yuan associated with the ruling party, the Twelve Principles of the PCC particularly emphasized the adoption of a committee system in the Examination Yuan. According to this system, the members of the Examination Yuan must include non-KMT individuals, and the head of the Examination Yuan should be mutually elected from these members. However, the constitution finalized in 1946 changed the mutual election of the president of the Examination Yuan into political appointment (nominated by the country's president and consented by the Control Yuan).

The 1946 *Constitution* prescribed that the four Yuans of Legislative, Judicial, Examination, and Control shall exercise their powers through assembly meetings. The *Constitution*, in a certain sense, positioned the Control Yuan as a supervisory parliament, whereby it functioned as an independent supervisory body with the consent power similar to that of the U.S. Senate. The power of constitutional and legal interpretation was also granted to the Grand Justices of the Judiciary Yuan through the Council of Grand Justices; similarly, the members of the Examination Yuan, in effect, formed an independent "personnel council" and cannot exercise their authority alone but via the Examination Yuan Council Meeting, much like the Grand Justices. According to *Organic Act of the Examination Yuan*, the Examination Yuan Council Meeting, comprised of the Yuan's president, vice president and members, was responsible for coordinating examination-related matters. The Council Meeting was chaired by the president of the Examination Yuan (Article 4); however, the Act also stipulated that the president of the Examination Yuan, in addition to being the chair of the Council, had the authority to oversee the general affairs of the Yuan and its subordinate organs (Article 9) (Xia & Hu, 2004, pp. 1151–1152). In September 1948, the Examination Yuan formulated and published Rules of the Examination Yuan Council Meeting in the form of the Yuan decree. Various issues shall be deliberated on and resolved at the Council Meeting, including the work plan for examination and personnel administration policy and budget allocation, proposing examination and personnel administration bills to the Legislative Yuan, issuing normative documents in the form of orders by the Examination Yuan and its subordinate Ministry of Examination and Ministry of Civil Service and approving normative documents by the Examination Yuan, determining the schedule of various examinations and regional examinations, and addressing common issues between the Ministry of Examination and Ministry of Civil Service, etc. (Article 6). A quorum of at least half of the Council Meeting members shall be required for resolutions, although the meeting could proceed if three-fourths of the quorum were present (Article 3); resolutions shall be made by a majority vote, and the chairperson of the session has the power to cast the deciding vote in the event of a tie (Article 9) (President Office Gazette, Sept. 14, 1928).

The aforementioned Article 4 of the *Organic Act of the Examination Yuan* and the corresponding provisions in the Rules of the Examination Yuan Council Meeting together made the Examination Yuan appear to be a commission (collegial) body. However, Article 9 in the *Organic Act of the Examination Yuan* granted the president of the Examination Yuan the power to manage the overall affairs of the Examination Yuan and supervise its subordinate organs. Furthermore, the appointment of the president (vice president) of the Examination Yuan was not determined through the election by council members but rather through political appointment, introducing elements of a unitary leadership system. More notably, the actual affairs of the Examination Yuan were administered by the Ministry of Examination and the Ministry of Civil Service, but the appointment of their respective heads did not require the council members' consent. Somewhat oddly, there was no explicit provision in the law regarding the method for selecting the heads of these two ministries. Their appointments were made at the sole discretion of the country's president, even without the nomination or consent of the president of the Examination Yuan or the Examination Yuan Council Meeting. In practice, the national president may seek the advice of the president of the Examination Yuan, but the council members and the Examination Yuan Council Meeting were not involved in the appointment process, both institutionally and practically. In this sense, the actual operation of the Examination Yuan leaned towards a unitary leadership system, wherein the head might not necessarily be the president of the Examination Yuan, but rather the president of the country. The form of government prescribed in the 1946 Constitution was a mixture of the parliamentary and the presidential systems while the specific design of the Examination Yuan, a compromise between the unitary leadership during the political tutelage period and the commission system proposed by the "Twelve Principles of the PCC". Consequently, the Examination Yuan exhibited a dual leadership structure with the president (vice president) of the Examination Yuan and the council members, as well as a separate administration of the Examination Yuan Council Meeting and the two ministries. Theoretically and practically, it could give rise to serious conflicts between the Council Meeting and the two subordinate ministries regarding the examination and personnel administration policies. It can be even argued that the two ministries were in fact not purely subordinate organs of the Examination Yuan due to the direct appointment power exercised by the president of the country.

The conflict between the Examination Yuan Council Meeting and the two ministries of the Examination Yuan arose from not only the institutional complexities but also the improper personnel arrangements. There was a significant misunderstanding in the selection of council members. Despite being the main deliberative body responsible for shaping major policies and regulations in civil service examinations and personnel administration, most of the members were not experts in the field of law and politics. Instead, they were individuals from various professions, excelling in fields such as science, technology, agriculture, and medicine. The elevated status of the members, who "did not eat the food of common mortals", and their tendency to, though as laymen, instruct professionals in their decision-making, inevitably led to conflicts with the two ministries. The misunderstanding stemmed from the qualification requirements for members, which followed the earlier practice of selecting commissioners and examiners based on their "outstanding reputation" and "specialized works". This approach overlooked the fact that the duty of the examination council members ("examination" in the broad sense) was to formulate examination and personnel administration policies, rather than conduct actual examinations. "During the tutelage period, the examination commissioners were only responsible for conducting fair examinations, and with the separate organization of a temporary Board of Examiners, the operation of the examination system was free of problems. However, after the implementation of the *Constitution*, the examination commissioner acted as the council members (still in charge of legal matters related to civil service administration). This emphasis on political legitimacy took precedence over fulfilling their actual responsibilities." (Jiang, 1997, pp. 81, 311) While most of the examination members were learned scholars, "their knowledge mostly pertained to various disciplines unrelated to examination policies and personnel administration. This misconception likely arose from the government's belief that the examination members' role was nothing but handling examinations. Given the diverse range of examination subjects, it was deemed necessary to recruit talents from different fields to meet the specific demands of each examination … This is a major and fatal view. The duties of the Examination Yuan were prescribed in the constitution, which should be fulfilled jointly by the examination members. The Examination Yuan was not a long-term examination machine. Neither were the members full-time examiners. Their main responsibilities should include participating examination meetings, jointly deciding national examination and personnel administration policies, reviewing examination and civil service regulations as well as important cases submitted by the two ministries of examination and civil service ... Therefore, the selection of examination members should have prioritized scholars well-versed in personnel management or public administration, as well as individuals with substantial experience in government affairs." (Xu, 1996, pp. 60–61) On the other hand, experts and scholars in specific fields should have been assigned roles as examiners, question drafters, and graders, rather than serving as examination members throughout the process.

In fact, even if the internal organization of the Examination Yuan were unified and all examination commissioners were experts in personnel administration, the collegial system of the Examination Yuan would still present efficiency issues as a decision-making body for personnel policies and legal systems. The number of examiners was up to 19 in addition to the president and vice president of the Examination Yuan, mandated by the *Organic Act of the Examination Yuan* in 1947. As a result, reaching unanimous resolutions during examination meetings became challenging, and more obstacles emerged in arriving at resolutions that could fully accommodate the opinions of the executive branch and be accepted by the executive organs at all levels. From this perspective, the practice that the president of the country nominated or appointed the president, vice president, the examination commissioners, and the ministers of the Ministry of Examination and the Ministry of Civil Service might have been implemented to ensure mutual checks and balances within the Examination Yuan, thereby avoiding undue constraints on the executive branch. In this regard, the organization of the Examination Yuan also served to address the concerns of the executive department.

12.3.3 *Other Disputes*

i. Conflict between the single-whip system of personnel administration and local autonomy

The Examination Yuan gradually centralized personnel administration power across the country in the period of the NNG. This move primarily sought to break down the existing divide between regional and departmental factions, in order to attain power consolidation. However, this centralization also presented the potential risk of the KMT dictatorship, and so at the PCC, the Communist Party of China, alongside democratic personages, expressed the desire for the forthcoming constitution to incorporate elements of federalism. The *Constitution* finally adopted in 1946 actually did contain some federalist elements. For instance, it allowed provinces to develop their own self-governance laws. Additionally, it dictated that the central Control Yuan would be elected by the provinces and would exercise approval rights over appointments to the Judicial Yuan and Examination Yuan, which is strikingly similar to the US Senate's role. However, the 1947 Organic Act of the Examination Yuan perpetuated the spirit of centralized personnel management, sometimes referred to as the "one-whip system". The *Act* stipulated that "The Examination Yuan shall establish examination and personnel administration divisions within each province" (Article 17). These divisions, as a continuation from the tutelage period, also took charge of examination matters of each province. The Act further asserted that "The Examination Yuan shall, unless otherwise provided by law, dismiss any civil servant found to be unqualified without the need for disciplinary procedures." (Article 19) (Xia & Hu, 2004, p. 1152) The centralized appointment, management, and command of personnel administration by the Examination Yuan of the Central Government, which unified the examination and qualification of all civil servants across various provincial, municipal, and county governments nationwide, inevitably conflicted with the principle of local autonomy.

ii. The quota system of examinations according to provinces and areas

As previously noted, in order to ensure regional balance in the selection of public functionaries, the 1946 *Constitution* stipulated that "… examinations shall be held in different regions, with a specified number of positions apportioned according to various provinces and areas" (Article 85). In practice, even the nomination of examination members and Grand Justices of the Judicial Yuan was limited to a maximum of one representative per province. Historically, ancient China implemented quota allocation for imperial examinations within each province due to the absence of a parliamentary system. Hence, regional representation in the government was achieved through a quota-based examination system. After the promulgation of *Constitution of the Republic of China* in 1947, representatives of the National Assembly, the Legislative Yuan, and the Control Yuan were all elected at the local level and in particular the members of the Control Yuan were elected with an equal number of seats allocated per province, similar to the U.S. Senate, which fully ensured geographical representation within the central government. Given this background, it is worth investigating whether it is still necessary to adhere to the "ancient method" of allocating civil servant positions based on provincial and regional quotas.

iii. Dispute over the scope of the examination power: examination for civil officials or for representatives and political appointees

In both its structural design and practical application, the Examination Yuan's purview over examinations and appointments did not align entirely with the original plans of Sun Yat-sen. For instance, the licensing examination for specialized professionals and technicians, a feature absent from Sun's theories, deviated from common practice in Europe and America. Instead, it was a construct introduced solely by the Examination Yuan during the period of political tutelage. Despite these departures from the original design, this innovation persisted effectively over time without presenting significant drawbacks or challenges. With the evolution of society towards increased specialization and the emergence of what has come to be known as the "era of certifications", the relevance and reach of such examinations have steadily grown. Consequently, they have become one of the central functions of the Examination Yuan.

Originally, based on idea Sun Yat-sen's concept of Five-power Constitution and the political practice during the political tutelage period, public representatives were also expected to have their qualifications verified by the Examination Yuan. Critics, however, labelled this as elitist and "anti-democratic" by the claiming that "Anyone with a basic education and common-sense knowledge should be eligible to run representative ... The most crucial aspect for a representative is their ability to genuinely represent public opinions, which cannot be determined by examinations, but by the discerning eye and judgement of voters" (Lei, 2010, p. 287). The 1946 Constitution accepted this viewpoint, removing "qualification of candidates for public office" from the Examination Yuan's responsibilities. However, it must be noted that the quality (including moral standards) of modern Chinese assemblymen was a matter of concern. This was analogous to the scenario faced by early congressmen in Europe and America. The question of whether China should rely on improving its democratic system to elevate the caliber of assemblymen, or use an independent examination and qualification body to filter out unfit candidates, while adopting the Western congress system, is not a mere academic debate, but a practical matter of governance[7].

Another issue overlooked by the constitution framers was whether the qualifications of political appointees should be determined through examinations. Sun Yat-sen's original plan proposed that all public officials, regardless of rank, should be subject to examinations. However, both institutionally and practically, political appointees for the National Government of the ROC (including the president, the presidents of the five Yuans, and heads of ministries and commissions) were either directly appointed or nominated for election with no need for examinations. Unlike the dispute over whether representatives should be examined, a unanimous agreement

[7] In some post-developed countries and regions, consortia and mob forces often legally infiltrated parliaments through elections and thereof exerted influence on the political landscape.

seemed to be reached that political appointees need not be examined and qualified by the Examination Yuan. This practice followed the norms in Europe and America. Additionally, the high-ranking nature of political appointee positions likely exceeded the jurisdiction of the Examination Yuan. On the other hand, it may have been tied to the prevalent political culture of elitism during that period[8].

12.3.4 Summary

Since its inception, the Examination Yuan of the National Government (including the entire five-power constitutional system) has been confronted with theoretical scrutiny and political oppositions. Opponents often resorted to the Western tripartite model to attack the five-power constitution, advocating for the abolition of the Control Yuan and the Examination Yuan and, leaving only the Executive Yuan, the Legislative Yuan, and the Judicial Yuan. However, the subtracting two from the five-power structure does not equate to a tripartite separation of powers. Among the Western regimes, there is the separation of powers in the American presidential system, fusion of powers in the British cabinet system, a mixed system (semi-presidentialism) in the French Fifth Republic, and the Swiss collegial system. Each nation has chosen its own path based on its unique cultural traditions and political realities. The five-power constitution, being an original Chinese concept, should not be invalidated purely for its uniqueness. To do so would betray a lack of national self-confidence.

The legitimacy and rationality of the Examination Yuan's system are neither predicated solely on Sun Yat-sen's fervent advocacy nor the National government's firm persistence. Instead, they stem from China's millennium-long tradition of impartial, open recruitment of scholar-officials through imperial examinations, and an age-old tradition of an independent ministry (the Ministry of Personnel) handling the appointment and assessment of officials at all levels. The purview of the Examination Yuan is not confined to the narrow-sense interpretation of examination powers (the power to examine and select). It also includes recruitment power, or the authority over personnel administration; the Examination Yuan is not only the premier examination body, but also the highest human resources agency. Viewed from this perspective, the Examination Yuan is a fusion of the ancient Ministry of Rites and the Ministry of Personnel, claiming a substantial third of the total six ministries—an authority that cannot be undermined. Having the Examination Yuan take charge of personnel matters not only preserves the ancient traditions of the Ministry of Personnel, but also responds to modern China's practical needs to dismantle local and departmental separatism, and to root out the culture of nepotism rampant in the officialdom. The

---

[8] Political appointees for the National Government of the ROC usually had higher academic degrees (often from overseas institutions), making their qualifications rarely disputed. However, their practical political abilities and ethical character were another matter altogether, aspects which were technically beyond the scope of examination-based evaluation.

system of the Examination Yuan has also progressively matured with the development and refinement of the National Government's constitutional and legal systems. Opposing the Examination Yuan's exercise of personnel power on the basis that it contradicts Western constitutional theory and personnel administration science overlooks a significant reality. The examination system was "implemented according to relevant statutory provisions". "An operational system is a concrete reality—not a viewpoint, a doctrine, or a theory". (Xu, 2007, p. 5)

The primary debate surrounding the Examination Yuan's structure concerns whether personnel authority should be separated from the Executive Yuan and placed under its control. On one hand, such a system is rooted in both Chinese tradition and the practical political necessities of the country. On the other, the Examination Yuan does not infringe on the personnel decision-making powers of heads of various administrative organs; it merely exercises a verification power over personnel matters. The power vested in the Examination Yuan is fundamentally a reactive, anti-corruption mechanism, rather than a proactive human resources authority. Moreover, since the 1946 *Constitution* established a mixed form of government where the national president (not the president of the Executive Yuan) served as the ultimate executive leader and held the key power to nominate personnel for the Examination Yuan. In this sense, the Examination Yuan, though as the supreme personnel organ, is not completely but only relatively independent from the executive branch. Thus, having the Examination Yuan to have charge of the highest personnel (verification) power shouldn't pose significant hurdles.

During the period of political tutelage, the Examination Yuan operated under a single-head system, and all of its affairs were largely presided over by President Dai Jitao alone. The 1946 PCC attempted to restructure it to a commission system in order to break the KMT's one-party control over personnel administration. The *Constitution of the Republic of China*, enacted in December 1946, mixed the two systems, and this, together with the unique provisions of relevant supporting legislation, gave rise to a dynamic within the Examination Yuan where the three bodies, the president (vice-president), examination members (of the Examination Yuan Council Meeting), and the two ministries of examination and civil service, derived their powers from different sources, creating a balance of power. This situation originated from constitutional compromises, systemic mismatches, and the individual will of political figures. Yet, it's worth noting that the internal balance within the Examination Yuan somewhat counteracts its excessive restrictions on executive bodies, and instead promotes harmonization and compromise between the Examination Yuan and the executive power, thus fostering smooth governance.

There are many areas of the Examination Yuan's ideology and system that warrant further review. For instance, the "single-whip" personnel system, the regional quota examination system, and the scope of examination and selection powers are all compelling topics that blend historical and contemporary considerations, as well as Eastern and Western influences. The importance of studying the Examination Yuan today is not to doggedly replicate its model, but rather to examine this fusion of Eastern and Western institutional exploration. In doing so, we provide a more locally relevant reference point for the development of China's examination and personnel system and for the refinement of its political system, beyond simply following Western examples.

References

Lifa yuan gonggao [Bulletin of the Legislative Yuan]. No. 41, Sept 1932.
Chen, Y. (2001). *Zhonghua minguo xianfa shilun* [Explanation of the Constitution of the Republic of China]. For internal circulation.
Chen, X. (2001). *Sui tang zhidu yuanyuan lvelun gao* [A brief history of the origin of the Sui and Tang System: Political history of the Tang Dynasty]. Joint Publishing.
Guangming Daily. (2011). *Guanyu zhongguo keju zhi* [About keju in ancient China]. Oct., 24th 2011, p. 15.
Guiding Committee of Series Books on Examination and Civil Service of the Examination Yuan. (Ed.). (1981). *Jianguo qishi nian zhi kaoquan xingzheng* [Examination and civil service administration during the 70 Years after the founding of Republic of China]. Zhengzhong Press.
Jiang, D. (1997). *Woguo wenguan zhengce zhi xingcheng yu bianqian: Yige lishi/jiegou de fenxi tujing* [The policy development and change of civil servants in Republic of China: An approach of historical/structural analysis] [Unpublished doctor's thesis]. Taiwan University.
Lei, Z. (2010). *Zhonghua minguo zhixian shi: Zhengzhi xieshang huiyi xianfa caoan* [The constitution-making history of the Republic of China: The draft constitution of the Political Consultative Conference]. Daoxiang Press.
Lin, J. (1993). *Zhongguo minguo xianfa zhutiao shiyi* [Article-by-article interpretation of the Constitution of the Republic of China]. San Min Book Co., Ltd.
Guomin zhengfu gongbao [National Government Gazette]. No. 1, Oct., 26 1928.
Guomin zhengfu gongbao [National Government Gazette]. No. 1077, Mar., 13 1935.
Guomin zhengfu gongbao [National Government Gazette], No. 1808, Aug., 1 1935.
Nie, X. (2013). Neigezhi, zongtongzhi haishi ban zongtongzhi—minguo xianfa shi shang de zhengti zhi zheng [Cabinet system, presidential system or semi-presidential system—The debate over the form of government in the constitutional history of the Republic of China]. *Faxue* [Jurisprudence], *10*, 111–117.
Nie, X. (2014). *Minguo zhengfu shiqi lifa yuan de diwei yu quanxian* [The status and competence of the Legislative Yuan in the National Government of the ROC]. *Lishi yanjiu* [Historical Studies], *6*, 147–164.
Zongtong fu gongbao [President Office Gazette]. No. 100, Sept., 14 1928.
Propaganda Committee of the Draft Constitution of the Legislative Yuan. (Ed.). (1940). *Zhonghua minguo xianfa caoan shuoming shu* [The instructions for the draft constitution of the Republic of China]. Zhengzhong Press.
Qian, D., Sa, S., Yang, H., et al. (2008). *Minguo zhengzhi shi* [History of the political system of the Republic of China] (Vol. 2). Shanghai People's Publishing House.
Sa, M. (1993). *Zhongguo xianfa xin lun* [A new theory on the Constitution of Republic of China]. San Min Book.
Secretariat of the National Assembly. (Ed.). (1946). *Guomin dahui shilu* [The National Assembly memoir]. For internal circulation.
Shen, J. (1995). *Zhongguo kaoshi zhidu shi* [History of the Chinese examination system]. The Commercial Press.
The Five-Power Constitution Association. (Ed). (1963). *Wuquan xianfa wenxian jiyao* [A digest of five-power constitution literature].
The Second Historical Archives of China. (1994). *Guomindang zhengfu zhengzhi zhidu dang'an shiliao xuanbain* [Selected historical materials from the archives of the political system of the Kuomintang government]. Anhui Education Press.

The Editing Office of the Examination Yuan. (Ed.). (2012). *Guojia kaoshi ji wenguan zhidu* [State system of examination and civil service]. For internal circulation.

Wu, J., & Huang, G. (1937). *Zhongguo zhixian shi* [The history of constitution making in the Republic of China]. The Commercial Press.

Xia, X., & Hu, X. (Eds.). (2004). *Jindai zhongguo xianzheng lichen: shiliao huicui* [The constitutional course in modern China: A collection of historical material]. China University of Political Science and Law Press.

Xiao, R. (2008). *Guomin zhengfu kaoshiyuan yanjiu* [Research on the Examination Yuan of the National Government]. Social Sciences Academic Press.

Xu, Y. (1996). *Kaoquan xin lun* [New theories on examination and civil service]. The Commercial Press.

Xu, Y. (2007). *Kaoquan zhidu* [The system of examination and civil service]. The Commercial Press.

Ye, S. (1953). *Woguo suo xuyao de renshi xingzheng zhidu—jianshu zongtong dui renshi zhidu de xunshi* [The personnel administration system needed in our country—On the President's exhortation on the personnel system]. *Renshi xingzheng jikan* [Personnel Administration Quarterly], (3).

Ye, J., et al. (Eds.) (2006). *Xiangai fangxiangpan* [The steering wheel of constitutional reform]. Wu-Nan Book Inc.

Zhang, Z., & Wang, R. (Eds.). (1963). *Xinhai geming qian shinian jian shilun xuanji* [Selected essays on current events in the decade before the 1911 Revolution] (Vol. 2). Sanlian Press.

Chapter 13
The Judicial System in Modern China

13.1 The Central Judicial Institution: From the Three Judicial Offices to the Judicial Yuan

13.1.1 Review: The Three Judicial Offices in Ancient China

In ancient China, the government did not have the idea of separation of powers, but there was a division of functions. The central judicial office was called *dali* (大理) in the Xia Dynasty, *sikou* (司寇) in the Shang and Zhou Dynasties, and *tingwei* (廷尉) in the Qin and Jin states, *dali* (大理) in the Qi state and *tingli* (廷理) in the Chu state during the Warring States Period. The office evolved into a full-fledged central judicial system with improved Ministry of Justice, Court of Judicial Review and Chief Surveillance Bureau (or Censorate before the Ming Dynasty) from the Qin and Han Dynasties all the way through the Qing Dynasty. The system of Three Judicial Offices lasted for two thousand years from its inception to its end with "dramatic variations resulting from changes of dynasties and political systems". In short, "that ancient Chinese system was not monolithic through history, but kept being updated and took on a newer look" (Na, 2004a, p. 35).

i. The formation of the Three Judicial Offices System

The ancient Chinese judicial system went through "One Judicial Office" to "Two Judicial Offices" and then to "Three Judicial Offices".

The pre-Qin period featured "One Judicial Office": a single office was vested with the supreme judicial power in the central government and vassal states, and it was called *dali* in the Xia Dynasty, *sikou* in the Shang and Zhou Dynasties, and *tingwei* in the Qin and Jin states, *dali* in the Qi state and *tingli* in the Chu state during the Warring States Period.

During the Spring and Autumn Period, the Qin state created the Censorate in charge of keeping records and disciplinary surveillance. After China was unified,

X. Nie, *The History of Government and Public Law in China*,
https://doi.org/10.1007/978-981-97-6063-3_13

the Qin imperial government appointed the Censor-in-Chief as head of all censors, responsible for judicial matters as well as disciplinary surveillance, having the power to hear special cases (crimes committed mainly by nobles and officials). That marked the beginning of "Two Judicial Offices" when the special judicial organ, the Censorate, ran together with the regular judicial body, the Chamberlains for Law Enforcement. The Han Dynasty was different in that, on the one hand, the oversight authority or the Censorate developed into three oversight offices (the Censorate, Director of Uprightness under the Councilor-in-Chief, and Metropolitan Commandant), which exercised their powers independently and oversaw each other; on the other, the oversight offices were somewhat separated from the judicial offices with the former being responsible for disciplinary offences and impeachment, and any offence against law going to the latter (Sa, 1998, pp. 323–324).[1]

Before Emperor Cheng of the Western Han Dynasty came to power, the central judiciary had consisted merely of Chamberlains for Law Enforcement and the Censorate, the former being a regular judiciary and the latter, a special one. The Secretary for the Three Dukes since Emperor Cheng and the Secretary for the 2000-bushel Officials since Emperor Guangwu in the Eastern Han Dynasty were successively set up as a judicial institution. The judicial power was transferred to the Secretary of the Personnel Section of the Imperial Secretariats in the Western Jin Dynasty, to the Secretary of Justice in the Northern Wei, Northern Qi and Sui Dynasties, and to (the Secretary of) the Ministry of Justice in the Tang Dynasty so that and the system of three judicial offices was finally established (Na, 2004a, p. 43). (*Tingwei* or the Chamberlain for Law Enforcement was renamed *dali si* or the Court of Judicial Review in the Northern Qi Dynasty, and that name remained through the Qing Dynasty).

ii. The development of the Three Judicial Offices System

The third judicial office within the imperial secretariats originated largely from the opposition between the inner court (secretaries) and the outer court (three dukes and six ministers), i.e., the power struggle between the emperor and the ministers, since the emperor always attempted to directly participate in or instruct the trials. The emperor tended to favor his close underlings and distance himself from the ministers because he "worried about being suspended from the imperial power and ministers' usurpation. He sought to deprive the ministers of their power by frequently using close underlings against them. In due course, the close underlings ended up ministers themselves by taking the former ministers' power and place,[2] pushing them

---

[1] Sa Mengwu made such a conclusion based on "Life of Gai Kuanrao" from the *Book of Han* (Vol. 77): "As a metropolitan commandant, Gai impeached any official, enemy and friends alike, for any offence, serious or minor, so that his submitted impeachments piled up. After examination, the Chamberlain for Law Enforcement adopted half of his decisions." It's clear that the adjudicative power and the power to impeach were separated since only half of Gai's impeachments were adopted after the Chamberlain's reviewing.

[2] Close underlings, originally the emperor's intimate attendants, were called officials in the inner court.

to marginal positions, so that the emperor would have to do the same to those former close underlings by relying on his current close underlings. The vicious cycle from close underlings to ministers went endless," resulting in an increasingly complicated central bureaucracy (including the judiciary) in China (Sa, 1998, p. 107).

The emperor was the master of the state and head of the government, but there was an inherent contradiction between him and the state (government), because of the fundamental conflict between the emperor's disposition toward absolute power, and the government's working tendency toward institutionalization (rationalization). When the emperor was expanding his power, his close underling ministers tended to become institutionalized ministers of the state rather than his intimate attendants, and the "ambitious" emperor constantly challenged the windmill-like institution by appointing his new close underlings to important positions. The Censors began as recordkeeping personnel attending the emperor, later served as the emperor's eyes and ears spying on officials, and ended up Investigating Censors, seizing part of the judicial power long held by the Chamberlains for Law Enforcement, one of the nine ministries. When the Censor-in-Chief was institutionalized to be among the Three Dukes, the emperor shifted his trust to the Imperial Secretaries around him to such an extent that "all matters were submitted to the Imperial Secretariats" which began to assume the judicial power. In the Tang Dynasty, the Imperial Secretariats evolved into six ministries, increasingly institutionalized. In order to prevent the Ministry of Justice and the Court of Judicial Review from corruption, Emperor Taizong of the Song Dynasty created the Judicial Control Office in the palace to review the cases submitted by the two departments. The Office conducted the second trial at the central level and turned itself into the supreme court by depriving the Ministry of Justice of its power and making it an idle government agency (Na, 2004a, pp. 47–48). But the emperor could not fight for long against the increasingly complex and sophisticated bureaucracy so that Emperor Shen of the Song Dynasty abolished the Judicial Control Office and transferred its powers to the Ministry of Justice. The Yuan Dynasty had only two judicial offices, the Ministry of Justice and the Censorate without the Court of Judicial Review. The Court of Judicial Review was restored since the Ming Dynasty, but the Ministry of Justice tended to be more powerful judicially than both the Chief Surveillance Bureau (Censorate) and the Court of Judicial Review due to the reason that Emperor Zhu Yuanzhang headed the six ministries after the abolition of the Grand Councilor in the early Ming Dynasty, and the Ministry of Justice, as one of those ministries, expanded its power naturally and rapidly under the auspices of the emperor.

In the history of the Three Judicial Offices, the Imperial Secretaries turned out to be the primary judicial organ with both administrative and judicial functions; the Censorate (renamed Chief Surveillance Bureau after the Ming Dynasty) came to lose its independent judicial power; the Court of Judicial Review, the oldest of the three offices, was corrupted into the Office of Palace Justice.

13.1.2 Judicial Reform in the Late Qing Dynasty

At the end of the Qing Dynasty, the Ministry of Justice played a leading role the Three Judicial Offices because it reviewed appeals from lower courts, heard cases of offences committed by central government officials, and presided over judicial administration and amendments to laws. As a department of prudent sentencing, the Court of Judicial Review exercised the power to review cases and would return them to the Ministry of Justice for retrial if the decisions were found improper. The Censorate exercised the supervisory function and would impeach the Ministry of Justice and the Court of Judicial Review for abuse of power, but the three offices would have a joint hearing if the cases were of critical importance (Na, 2004b, 2004c).

The Western tides of thoughts forced the Qing Dynasty to revise its laws and statutes in 1902 with the judicial reform at the center and as one of the prerequisites for the abolition of consular jurisdiction because the old court system was particularly objectionable to the Western powers. In 1906, the Qing Imperial Court issued an edict to reform bureaucracy: "The Ministry of Justice, renamed *fabu* (法部), leads judicial administration; *dali si* (the Court of Judicial Review), renamed *dali yuan* (大理院, the Supreme Court of Justice), leads the court" (*Veritable Records of Emperor Dezong*, 1987, p. 468). The judicial reform went well until 1907 when contention, historically known as "the Ministry-Yuan Quarrel" (Li, 2000, pp. 234–241; Zhang, 2007), occurred between the Ministry of Justice and the Dali Yuan over judicial power and personnel appointments. In 1910, the Qing Imperial Court promulgated the *Organic Law of the Judiciary* and issued an edict: "The *Organic Law* decreed herein vests the Ministry of Justice with judicial administration, and the Dali Yuan and the lower courts with adjudication in accordance with national laws. All previously undefined powers shall be referred to the different sections of the *Organic Law* adopted herein for definition" (*Appended Political Records in the Xuantong Period*, 1987, p. 518). Consequently, the Dali Yuan was vested with the adjudicative power, and as the central judiciary, it was strictly distinguished from the Ministry of Justice as a judicial administrative organ in terms of powers. Although the judicial reform (including the entire legal reform) was beginning to take shape in the late Qing Dynasty, most of the drafted systems were either suspended or implemented perfunctorily. For example, the Dali Yuan "tended to be more modern, but it revealed a dark streak of traditional judiciary since it hailed from the traditional political system, born into an absolute monarchy, bred by traditional administration, and seizing judicial powers from a variety of central executive branches, chiefly from the Ministry of Justice which had reviewed all cases in the conservative society" (Han, 2012, p. 354).

13.1.3 The Central Judiciary Under the Beiyang Government

The *Provisional Constitution of the Republic of China*, a constitutional document promulgated after the 1911 Revolution, stipulated public and independent trials as well as protection of judges, and designed a dual system of regular and administrative litigation, but the organization of courts would be determined by law. In March 1912, Yuan Shih-k'ai, inaugurated as Provisional President in Beijing, ordered that the laws of the Qing Dynasty (except those that contradicted the ROC constitution) be adopted before the ROC laws came out (Huang, 2000, pp. 22–23). In 1910, the Qing's *Organic Law of the Judiciary* was also adopted,[3] and the Beiyang Government established the Dali Yuan (Supreme Court of Justice) with the supreme power over civil and criminal cases and unified interpretations of all laws; the judicial administration fell under the Ministry of Justice. As for administrative litigation, the 1914 *Organic Act of the Pingzheng Yuan* (Supreme Administrative Court) granted the Pingzheng Yuan the power over administrative litigations and censure and impeachments of officials (Luo, 1974, pp. 409–412).

i. The Dali Yuan

The Dali Yuan had a president responsible for the Yuan's work and supervision of its administrative affairs. According to the separation of civil and criminal affairs and the workload of cases, the Yuan established a number of civil courts and criminal courts. Each court comprised a few justices one of whom was Chief Justice. Civil and criminal divisions were also set up, comprising departments headed by a chief justice to supervise the departmental affairs and decide on the distribution of cases.

The Beiyang Government promulgated neither the penal code nor the civil and commercial laws so that the provisional and procrustean adoption of the Qing's legal system was certain to give rise to questions. By exercising the supreme power over adjudication and the unified interpretation of laws, the Dali Yuan made judicial precedents and statutory interpretations wherein crude principles of each law resided (Guo, 1931a, 1931b), which was actual legislation. Even after the National Government settled in Nanjing in 1927, the courts continued to invoke those precedents and interpretations except for those clearly inconsistent with the statute laws. As the highest judicial organ in the early Republic of China, the Dali Yuan gained unprecedented independent judicial power, normative control and administrative autonomy; the president, chief justices and justices were well-educated and relatively upright. In the era of belligerent warlords and political turmoil, the Dali Yuan left a page of innocence in the history of Chinese justice.

1. The supreme judicial authority

The Dali Yuan was the court of last resort for general civil and criminal cases, and its first ruling was ultimate for special cases that fell under its jurisdiction. Collegiate panels of five justices were adopted to hear cases. Article 37 of the *Organic Law of the Dali Yuan* decreed that the president would convene the civil or criminal departments or both, depending on the nature of the case, to make a final decision when the judicial

[3] The only change was that the imperial official titles of *zhengqing* (正卿, Director) and *shaoqing* (少卿, Deputy Director) of the *Dali Yuan* was abolished, and a president was established in their place to oversee the affairs of the Yuan.

interpretation of the Dali Yuan hearing an appeal conflicted with precedents of its own or other courts.

The precedents of the Dali Yuan were different from those of the UK, the United States, and Europe. First of all, not all its rulings could serve as precedents since precedents needed to be "either innovative, supplementary, illustrative, or normative". Secondly, the precedents were compiled in a unified format which, ignoring the factual part of the decisions, recorded the universally normative and most essential part or resume of the decision in a few words; the selection of the resume did not depend on the distinction between the main text and the appended opinion under the case law because "any key sentences that can turn into abstract principles may be extracted as resume of the ruling". Therefore, the precedents of the Dali Yuan were "abstract conclusions", formally close to statutes and judicial interpretations (Huang, 2011, pp. 114, 173–174).

The precedents made by the Dali Yuan were so influential that they compared to case law in nature and effect. From 1912 through 1921, nearly every decision became a precedent; precedents decreased significantly after 1921 mainly because the legislation relatively completed so far and existing precedents made it unnecessary to establish new ones (Huang, 2000, p. 74; Lu, 2004; Zhang, 1998; Zhou, 2006).

2. Norm controller

Article 35 of the *Organic Law of the Dali Yuan* granted the president of the Yuan the power over unified interpretations of laws and regulations; Article 203 of the Operational Regulations of the Dali Yuan even vested the Dali Yuan's judicial interpretations with a universal binding force ("binding on matters of the same nature"), a power to review abstract norms that no other Supreme Court in the world had at that time. However, when exercising the power of unified judicial interpretation, the president was "forbidden" by article 35 of the *Organic Law of the Dali Yuan* to "instruct justices in the trial of cases".

The Dali Yuan exercised its power of judicial interpretation usually at the request of the central and local government agencies, but it might also take the initiative to correct misunderstandings of law on the part of those offices and their personnel. In case of a request for judicial interpretation, Articles 206 and 207 of the *Operational Regulations of the Dali Yuan* required the president to designate, depending on civil or criminal cases, a chief justice for review and a draft reply. The request and reply, after reviewed by concerned justices or, if necessary, by a meeting of all civil or criminal court justices, would be submitted to the president for a final decision. The Dali Yuan exercised this power over unified interpretation for 16 years as if "the justices were legislating from the bench".

3. Autonomy of the Dali Yuan

The Dali Yuan was parallel to the Ministry of Justice of the Cabinet for historical and legal reasons because "the administrative regulations issued by the Ministry of Justice do not apply to the Dali Yuan" where "the president determines all rules regarding judicial administrative matters and oversees their implementation" (Huang, 2000,

p. 34). A plenary meeting of all justices had agreed upon and enacted all procedures applied to the Dali Yuan before the promulgation of the civil and criminal procedure laws in 1921. The Minister of Justice remitted personnel appointments and removals, disciplinary punishments, and budgetary bills submitted by the Dali Yuan, but had no power to reject or revise them.

ii. The Pingzheng Yuan (Suzheng Division)

The Pingzheng Yuan (Supreme Administrative Court), a product of Eastern and Western culture, combined special adjudication exercised by the oversight authority in ancient China with the distinction between administrative courts and regular ones in the West. Not a purely judicial institution under the ROC president, it had "a vague relationship with the executive power" (Huang, 2000, p. 144; Luo, 1974, pp. 409–412). The Pingzheng Yuan was staffed by a president directing and supervising the whole court, 15 justices hearing administrative proceedings, censures and impeachments, and the Suzheng Division, an administrative supervisory institution of 16 administrative supervisors headed by a supervisor-in-chief. In spite of being a subdivision under the Pingzheng Yuan, the Suzheng Division exercised its power independently.[4] The Pingzheng Yuan organized panels of five justices to hear administrative cases or censures and impeachments whereas the Suzheng Division filed administrative lawsuits against, censured or impeached officials for offences, and oversaw the decisions made by the former (Zhao, 2006, p. 430). In administrative proceedings, they seemed to be a court and a prosecutor, and in cases of censure and impeachment, they looked like a Control Yuan and a Public Functionary Disciplinary Sanction Commission of the Judicial Yuan under the five-chamber system. In 1916 when Yuan Shih-k'ai's imperial system failed, Li Yuanhong took over as President and explicitly ordered the restoration of the 1911 ROC constitution. On June 29th of the same year, the Suzheng Division, labeled as Yuan's legacy, was abolished and the *Act of Censure and Impeachment* was repealed so that the power of supervision was returned to the Parliament and the Pingzheng Yuan became a court of purely administrative adjudication after the power to censure and impeach was taken away (The Records Compilation Board of the Control Yuan, 1981, p. 27).

In 1914 and 1915, the central government set up the Disciplinary Commission for Senior Civil Servants, and Disciplinary Commission for Judicial Officers whose chiefs the ROC president would appoint the president of the Dali Yuan and that of the Pingzheng Yuan respectively, initiating the Public Functionary Disciplinary Sanction Commission of the Judicial Yuan under the NNG (Young, 2008).

iii. The Ministry of Justice

Dating back to the *Fabu* of the late Qing Dynasty and functionally similar to the Ministry of Justice in continental Europe, the Ministry of Justice was responsible for the judicial administration and supervision of prosecutorial organs at all levels.

[4] "Suzheng" (肃政) may date back to the Censorate in the later Zhou Dynasty.

First of all, it should be noted that the Ministry of Justice compared unfavorably with the Dali Yuan and the Pingzheng Yuan in terms of the judicial administrative power. In addition, the judicial reform since the late Qing Dynasty separated judicial proceedings both from judicial administration and from the prosecution so that, corresponding to different levels of the courts, the General Prosecutor's Office and the prosecutorial offices at all levels were established under the Ministry of Justice to exercise prosecutorial authority since the Dali Yuan.

13.1.4 The Central Judiciary Under the NNG

i. The Judicial Yuan under the early NNG

The Nanjing National Government, established in 1927, transformed the Dali Yuan of the Beiyang Government into the Supreme Court, the highest judicial organ in the country, with both ultimate appellate jurisdiction over civil and criminal cases and the power to interpret laws. The Ministry of Justice was also established to take charge of the judicial administration of the country (The Records Compilation Board of the Judicial Yuan, 1982, p. 3). In October 1928, the National Government promulgated the thrice-amended *Organic Law of the National Government* and set up the five Yuans (five chambers), the Executive, Legislative, Judicial, Examination, and Control Yuan in accordance with Sun Wen's theory of five-power constitution.[5] The *Organic Law* provided that "The Judicial Yuan shall be the highest judicial organ of the National Government and shall take charge of the court system, judicial administration, disciplinary punishment of officials, and administrative courts" (Xia & Hu, 2004, p. 788) The Judicial Yuan was instituted according to the *Orgainic Act of the Judicial Yuan* which the National Government published in October 1928 and republished it in November of the same year after amendment. Article 1 of the *Act* provided that "The Judicial Yuan shall be composed of the Judicial Administrative Department, the Supreme Court, the Administrative Court, and the Public Functionary Disciplinary Sanction Commission" (Xia & Hu, 2004, p. 857). In other words, the above four organs were all part and subdivisions of the Judicial Yuan. The Supreme Court took charge of ultimate appellate jurisdiction over civil and criminal cases; the Administrative Court, administrative proceedings (on a one-level and one-instance basis); and the Public Functionary Disciplinary Sanction Commission, civil service disciplinary cases. In a certain sense, the early Pingzheng Yuan was functionally divided into three institutions: the Administrative Court took over administrative litigation; the Control Yuan replaced the Suzheng Division over censure and impeachment of public functionaries; the Public Functionary Disciplinary Sanction

[5] Before the *Constitution of the Republic of China* was published, the *Organic Law of the National Government of the Republic of China* had served as the highest guiding principle in organizing the central government because the *Provisional Constitution for the Period of Political Tutelage of the Republic of China* did not specify the government organization.

Commission investigated the official for offences and dereliction of duty. The President of the Judicial Yuan took responsibility for the general affairs of the Yuan, led the judicial administrative staff, and convened the president of the Supreme Court and chief justices of the concerned courts to unify the interpretations of laws and decrees (The Records Compilation Board of the Judicial Yuan, 1982, pp. 2, 1181–1182).[6]

The previous Ministry of Justice was subordinate to the Judicial Yuan when the latter was established, and was reorganized into the Department of Judicial Administration directing and overseeing local chief executives within its jurisdiction. The department head took charge of general affairs of the department, supervising prosecutorial offices of all levels throughout the country as well as courts of all levels except the Supreme Court. The Department of Judicial Administration exercised its oversight authority, but did not interfere with the independent trial (The Records Compilation Board of the Judicial Yuan, 1982, p. 7). In terms of jurisdiction, the Department of Judicial Administration compared unfavorably with the Supreme Court, the Administrative Court, and the Public Functionary Disciplinary Sanction Commission even though they were four counterparts affiliated with the Judicial Yuan. Consequently, the four heads handled their own internal affairs respectively whereas the President of the Judicial Yuan dealt with major administrative concerns.[7]

During the period from the establishment of the Judicial Yuan to 1947 when the *Constitution of the Republic of China* and the amended *Organic Act of the Judicial Yuan* were promulgated, three major controversies were protracted over the authority of the Judicial Yuan. The first was where the judicial administrative power should reside. It fell under the Judicial Yuan when the latter was created in 1928, was transferred to the Executive Yuan in 1932, went back to the Judicial Yuan in 1934, and finally settled down with the Executive Yuan in 1943. The second was concerned with the Public Functionary Disciplinary Sanction Commission. When the *Draft Constitution of the Republic of China* (the MFDC) was in the making, it was thought that the Control Yuan should have "full supervisory authority" including both the power to impeach and the power to try cases of that nature, implying the transfer of the Commission from the Judicial Yuan to the Control Yuan (Gao, 1936, pp. 48–55). Accordingly, the Legislative Yuan amended and adopted the MFDC in 1936, excluding disciplinary power over public functionaries from the Judicial Yuan and

---

[6] The President of the Judicial Yuan was invested with the power to organize and adjudicate over unified interpretations of laws and decrees, which had been granted to the Supreme Court (the Dali Yuan) of the inchoate Nanjing National Government. He presided over the meetings of judicial interpretations and alteration of legal precedents, and published the resolutions in the name of the Judicial Yuan. Article 3 of the *Organic Act of the Judicial Yuan* authorized "the President of the Judicial Yuan to exercise power over unified interpretation of laws and decrees and alteration of legal precedents after the President of the Supreme Court and concerned chief justices reached a resolution at a meeting chaired by the President of the Judicial Yuan" (The Records Compilation Board of the Judicial Yuan 1982).

[7] The autonomy (such as independent personnel arrangement and budgetary power) that the Dali Yuan had acquired by virtue of its status as the highest judicial body was also transferred to the President of the Judicial Yuan who took charge of general matters, including transfer of judicial officers, the formulation of quasi-legislative rules, initiation of bills, and budget compilation.

transferring it to the Control Yuan (Articles 76 and 87) (Xia & Hu, 2004, pp. 987–988). The third controversy related to whether it was reasonable to adopt the unitary judicial system of the U.S. Supreme Court where regular civil and criminal trials are not distinguished from administrative trials (disciplinary sanction of functionaries) so that it was not necessary to set up the Supreme Court, the Administrative Court and the Public Functionary Disciplinary Sanction Commission within the Judicial Yuan (Weng, 1994, p. 414).[8]

ii. The Judicial Yuan after 1947

In terms of judiciary, a major innovation of the *Constitution of the Republic of China* promulgated in 1947 was the creation of Grand Justices with power over constitutional interpretation and unified judicial interpretation so that the Judicial Yuan extended its power over interpretation of abstract norms (norm control) to constitutional interpretation (Articles 78 and 79, *Constitution of the Republic of China*). The *Organic Act of the Judicial Yuan* amended and published in December of the same year granted the power of judicial interpretation to the Council of Grand Justices chaired by the President of the Judicial Yuan (Article 3, *Organic Act of the Judicial Yuan*). The disciplinary sanction of public functionaries, a long-standing controversy, still resided with the Judicial Yuan.

The 1947 *Constitution* did not explicitly state if the judicial administrative power should go to the Judicial Yuan. Since the *Organic Law of the National Government* was amended in 1943, that power of prosecutorial departments at all levels and courts at all levels below the Supreme Court resided long with the Judicial Administration under the Executive Yuan. As a result of the *Constitution*'s failure to clearly assign the judicial administrative power to the Judicial Yuan, the Judicial Administration (along with the prosecutorial departments at all levels) was never reinstated since 1943 when it was transferred to the Executive Yuan. Therefore, Although the Judicial Yuan was constitutionally the supreme judicial organ, it did not have a full judicial administrative power, and could merely control its subordinates: the Supreme

[8] A comparison of judicial systems in the world would reveal the difference between unitary and multiple courts systems. The US adopts a unitary courts system over all legal proceedings, civil, criminal or Constitutional, with the Supreme Court having the ultimate appellate jurisdiction. The Continental Europe has its tradition of a multiple courts system where regular civil and criminal lawsuits, administrative proceedings and other complaints go to different courts. Germany is a case in point where civil and criminal cases come under regular courts with the Supreme Court as the court of last resort whereas administrative proceedings go to the administrative courts; fiscal complaints, to the fiscal courts; labor proceedings, to the labor courts; social welfare lawsuits, to the social courts, with all specialized courts having their own supreme court. The different systems specializing in different fields are not subordinate to each other. Modern China's judicial system hailed from Japan, and indirectly from Germany, adopting a multiple-court system which happened to coincide with traditional Chinese three-office system. However, China's allies practiced the Anglo-American law whereas the adversaries adopted the Continental law in WWII so that some argued for a change from the Continental law to the Anglo-American law in China and the unitary courts system of the U.S. Supreme Court tended to be somewhat favorable (Weng, 1994, p. 414).

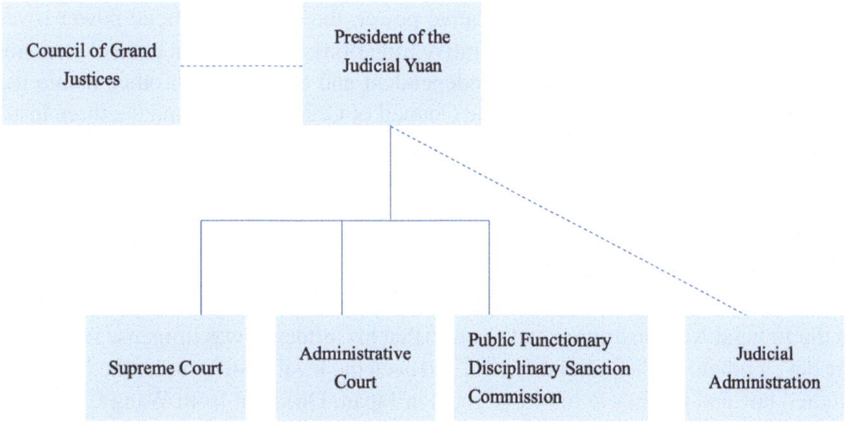

Fig. 13.1 Organization of the Judicial Yuan[10]

Court, the Administrative Court, and the Public Functionary Disciplinary Sanction Commission.[9]

The *Organic Act of the Judicial Yuan* promulgated in March 1947 was intended to partially incorporate the Anglo-American unitary courts system and seek innovation by providing that courts would be divided within the Judicial Yuan with abolishment of the Supreme Court, the Administrative Court, and the Public Functionary Disciplinary Sanction Commission (Article 4, *Organic Act of the Judicial Yuan*). However, immediately after publication, the *Act* was openly resisted by the well-established president and justices of the Supreme Court (Li, 1998, p. 713). The National Government had to amend the *Act* in December of that year to maintain the old system of three institutions within the Judicial Yuan: the Supreme Court, the Administrative Court, and the Public Functionary Disciplinary Sanction Commission (Article 5, *Organic Act of the Judicial Yuan*) (Fig. 13.1).

Sa Mengwu, a well-known scholar, made a brilliant conclusion about the nature of the Judicial Yuan: "The Chinese people did well in incorporation so that they incorporated diverse independent adjudicative organs into the Judicial Yuan" (Sa, 1993, p. 263). The Judicial Yuan may be said to be a basket into which the National Government put all the judicial and quasi-judicial organs, eventually creating a "supreme judiciary" based on the five-power constitution. However, within the all-inclusive

[9] Later on, pursuant to Article 77 of the *Constitution* granting the Judicial Yuan the power over civil and criminal cases, the Judicial Yuan demanded the judicial administrative power attached to civil and criminal trials of courts at all levels, but was long ignored by the Executive Yuan and the Judicial Administration.

[10] The Judicial Administration was subject sometimes to the Judicial Yuan and at other times to the Executive Yuan so that it's connected with the president by a dashed line. The Council of Grand Justices was created after the *Constitution of the Republic of China* and the *Organic Act of the Judicial Yuan* came out in 1947 so that a dashed line is also drawn here to indicate its relationship to the president. Solid lines are used otherwise.

Judicial Yuan, the judicial administrative power, the supreme judicial power (over civil and criminal cases and administrative litigation), and the norm control were not well-integrated so that they stayed independent and checked each other within the Yuan (Su, 2002, p. 393). Although the Council of Grand Justices and the three institutions under the Judicial Yuan were "responsible to and supervised by the President of the Judicial Yuan" (Sa, 1993, p. 262), they remained independent in terms of their powers.

Ju Zheng, a veteran KMT member, served as President of the Judicial Yuan for sixteen and a half years from 1932 through 1948, during which time he also held other important judicial positions such as President of the Supreme Court, Director of the Judicial Administration and so on so that his influence was immense in shaping the development of the judicial system and even the legal system under the NNG. He studied law and politics in his early years in Japan. Different from Wang Chonghui, another veteran party member who ever served as the president of the Judicial Yuan and received his education and doctorate in the United States, Ju Zheng was first and foremost a KMT Party member and a nationalist. In response to the "a non-partisan judiciary" accepted by the legal academia under the Beiyang Government, the NNG proposed "a judiciary of party doctrines". However, what Ju Zheng called "a judiciary of party doctrines" aimed for "a nationalized judiciary by downplaying the political implication of the term" (Jiang, 2010, pp. 74–75).

13.1.5 The Continuity and Discontinuity in the History of Modern China's Central Judicial System

Believers in modern separation of powers would find the distribution of power across the three judicial offices in ancient China to be quite vague. The Ministry of Justice in the Qing Dynasty was the foremost in the judicial system, taking charge of courts, judicial administration and law revision; The Censorate had the power to censure officials for offenses or misconduct and participate in their trials; The Court of Judicial Review, as an organ of "prudent sentencing", had a relatively small power. When the cases were of critical importance, the three judicial departments, or even the nine ministers, would hold a joint hearing with the emperor having the final decision. The Ministry of Justice, renamed *Fabu* in 1906, was vested with the administrative power (consecutively renamed the Ministry of Justice and the Judicial Administration in the Republic of China). The Court of Judicial Review was changed into the Dali Yuan exercising the ultimate appellate jurisdiction (renamed the Supreme Court under the NNG). The Pingzheng Yuan functionally replaced the Censorate after the ROC was founded, but part of it evolved into an independent office called the Suzheng Division as a prosecutorial office against public authority, separating the courts from the prosecutors. Separation of powers was more specific under the NNG. The Pingzheng Yuan's power over the administrative lawsuits was transferred to the Administrative Court, and its jurisdiction over civil servants' violation of law and misconduct went to the Public Functionary Disciplinary Sanction Commission. The Control Yuan took over the Suzheng Division and enjoyed a higher political position. Under the NNG, a dispute occurred over whether the Public Functionary Disciplinary Sanction Commission should reside with the Judicial Yuan or with the Control Yuan, and the former was the final winner, which was also consistent with the principle of rationality: separation of jurisdiction from prosecution.

A historical review of the central judicial system from "one judicial office", "two judicial offices" to "three judicial offices" in ancient China may reveal that modern China reversed the course. The judicial administrative organs and the supervisory organs gradually lost their judicial power, and the jurisdiction eventually came under a single judicial organ. In the late Qing Dynasty, the Ministry of Justice, the Court of Judicial Review, and the Censorate shared the judicial power even though they had different responsibilities. The late Qing's judicial reform ushered in the era of two judicial divisions which continued into the Beiyang Government so that the judicial administrative organ (the Ministry of Justice in the late Qing Dynasty, the Ministry of Justice under the Beiyang Government, and the Judicial Administration under the NNG) no longer had adjudicative power. The Dali Yuan was a regular judicial organ; the Pingzheng Yuan was a special one directly under the president with a trace of ancient Chinese supervisory organs, having within it the Suzheng Division responsible of censure and impeachment. The NNG had a single judicial department called the Judicial Yuan where three subdivisions took charge of regular civil and criminal cases, administrative litigations, and disciplinary sanction against public functionaries respectively whereas the Control Yuan had no more power to adjudicate. (See Fig. 13.2 for the historical changes)

The evolution from the Three Judicial Offices to the Judicial Yuan meant a transition from "sovereignty of the monarch to "sovereignty of the people". Since the Qin and Han Dynasties, the increasingly consolidated absolute monarchy pushed the judicial change from one division to three divisions where the institutions, as mentioned earlier, grew sophisticated chiefly because the emperor always attempted to bypass the established system to control, supervise, and even directly instruct the judiciary. The emperor participated in and supervised the trials through the supervisory organs, and then encroached on the adjudicative power of the Court of Judicial Review through the administrative system (Secretariat) under his direct command, and even sought to keep the judicial power to himself by setting up the Judicial Control Office in the palace. Under the Beiyang Government, Yuan Shih-k'ai, eager to be crowned, planted the *Suzheng* Division directly under his command in the *Pingzheng Yuan* to restore the ancient Censorate so that he could interfere with justice. However, the mighty tide of history made it impossible to restore monarchy and obstruct the rational progress from three judicial divisions to one judicial division.

Generally speaking, decades of development westernized and rationalized the traditional system of three judicial divisions, but the Chinese features in it cannot be ignored.

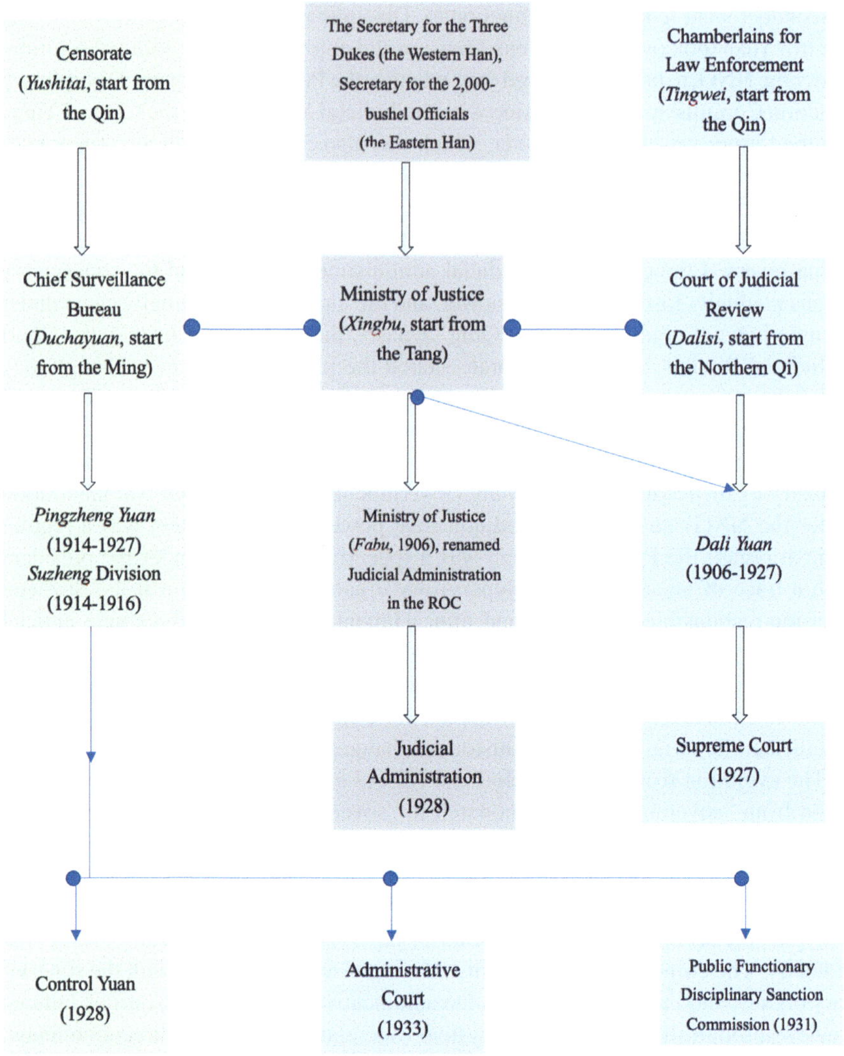

Fig. 13.2 History of the Central Judiciary since the Qin and Han Dynasties[11]

Feature 1: The unique structure of judicial administrative power

Both the adjudicative power and the judicial administrative power used to reside with the Ministry of Justice, but the latter was vested in the *Dali Yuan* after the late Qing's judicial reform; Under the Beiyang Government, the *Dali Yuan* kept its autonomy;

[11] The three judicial divisions evolved into three independent systems: adjudication, judicial administration and supervision in modern China.

Under the NNG, the Judicial Yuan was granted more powers including adjudication, quasi-adjudication, norm review and judicial administration which, however, stayed independent within the Judicial Yuan. That not only reflected rationality in modernizing the legal system, but also kept the features rooted in Chinese politics and culture in the progress.[12]

Feature 2: The abstract review of the Judiciary

Law revision was an important function of the Ministry of Justice in the Qing Dynasty. The special political environment helped the *Dali Yuan* obtain the abstract judicial review to unify interpretation of laws, which was another way of legislation. The Judicial Yuan (the Council of Grand Justices) extended its judicial review to constitutional interpretation. Therefore, the institutions may be said to have followed the same traditions in the historical development.

Feature 3: Separation of regular judicial institutions from special ones (a pluralistic judicial model).

Early in the Qin Dynasty, the Censorate was a special judicial body hearing cases of offenses committed by nobles and officials, and it was separated from the regular courts, the Chamberlains for Law Enforcement. Under the Beiyang Government, the *Pingzheng Yuan*, separated from the *Dali Yuan*, took charge of administrative proceedings, censure and impeachment of officials. Under the NNG, the Judicial Yuan was composed of the Supreme Court, the Administrative Court, and the Public Functionary Disciplinary Sanction Commission which had different responsibilities and stayed independent. That development came from both the Chinese tradition and the pluralistic European judicial model.

Institutional change is one of the research focuses of legal history, and the so-called "change" means no more than thoughts on "continuity" and "discontinuity". Generally speaking, tradition and modernity are viewed as opposites, but there is visible continuity instead of a clear-cut demarcation line between them. It is true when a scholar said that "modern legal thought or system, though having its own characteristics, still contains the legacy of previous eras; and the characteristics of the legal system or thought in a certain age is both a reaction and a supplement to the previous age" (Huang, 1993, pp. 22–23). Tradition may be a basis and reference for change as well as a burden. Figure 13.2, "History of the Central Judiciary since the Qin and Han Dynasties", illustrates the ties of the twentieth century judicial

[12] A unique Chinese understanding of power has innovatively modified the Western mechanical theory of separation of powers. Traditional Western separation of powers means the separation of adjudication and judicial administration with the former being judicial and the latter, executive. However, the judicial power is likely to be unduly influenced by the administrative power. For example, the German Federal Constitutional Court, established in 1950, openly issued a memorandum in 1952, demanding its freedom from the control of the Ministry of Justice over its personnel arrangement and budget, and expecting its President o to be a top-ranking official like the Speakers of both houses of Parliament and the Chancellor. Those requests were met until 1960 after a long-drawn struggle (Jackson & Tushnet, 2006, p. 532). In contrast, the *Dali Yuan* had a full power over its personnel arrangement and budget under the Beiyang Government, and the Judicial Yuan had a superior political position throughout its history.

reforms (including the modernization of the legal system as a whole) with the Chinese tradition. The reorganization of three Chinese traditional judicial divisions based on the Western principle of separation of powers agrees with Max Weber's inevitable institutional rationalization.

However, the entire judicial and supervisory body simply rearranged its structure of molecules and kept its atoms of Chinese tradition intact in modernization ("Westernization"). The Chinese system is even more different from the Western model if viewed from a functional perspective rather than a structural one. The author had many discussions (arguments) over this issue with Professor Duncan Kennedy at Harvard Law School. He argued for the globalization of law as an invasion of Western institutions and culture whereas the author contended that China retained its features without being swayed by the aggressive Western institutions and culture because the Western invasion since the Opium War merely catalyzed China's legal reform which would have been hard without external stimuli.

13.2 Local Judicial Authorities and the Tiered Court System

A sound tiered court system helps ensure justice and national judicial unity. To build such a system, two questions need to be answered: How many levels of courts should there be from the central to the local? And how many judicial reviews? Generally speaking, more levels of courts and more judicial reviews would mean more prudent judicial decisions and greater potential for achieving justice; more judicial reviews would increase the probability that a higher court (especially the Supreme Court) would be involved in the (final) review, which would further help judicial unity. However, as the proverb goes, "Justice delayed is justice denied". A tiered system, when excessively sophisticated, may not only lead to an inefficient judiciary, but also obstruct justice. In reality, the arrangement of courts at different levels and judicial reviews must suit the country's existing territory and vertical governmental structure on the one hand,[13] and be constrained by human resources, funding and transportation on the other. That may be seen in the evolution of China's judicial system from the late Qing Dynasty to 1949. In learning the West or specifically the European Continental judicial system, modern China geared its tiered system to the West, but the reform of the tiers (and the judicial reform as a whole) could not materialize as a result of political and social limitations. When the theory and reality were diametrically opposed, exceptions to the system or laws had to be made to accommodate reality. However, with judicial reform in mind, the government created various flexible systems and institutions as remedies. In the ROC, although

[13] "The vertical governmental structure" refers to the institution and distribution of power across the different levels of government (provincial, municipal and county). The court system varies depending on a unitary or federal system a country has adopted, and the tier system is usually influenced by local institutions.

the court of third instance as the final review was adopted in principle, the sub-provincial courts never got into gear. Consequently, "dilemma and struggle" haunted the judicial reform of modern China.

13.2.1 The Judicial Reform in the Late Qing Dynasty[14]

Contrary to the commonly held belief (e.g., "The ancient Chinese judiciary was indifferent to both procedures and lives"), the ancient Chinese tiered system was designed chiefly for "prudent consideration of punishment". In the Qing Dynasty, for example, a capital case would not be decided until it moved up through six levels and six instances from the county, the prefecture, (the circuit),[15] the provincial surveillance commission, the governor or viceroy, all the way to the Ministry of Justice or the Three Judicial Offices,[16] and was finally checked by the emperor, which means seven levels and seven instances. Cases involving punishments above imprisonment, whether the defendant pleaded guilty or not, must be submitted to a superior court for review, and the more serious ones (except minor crimes unrelated to death) had to be reviewed and decided by the Ministry of Justice because even the governors or viceroys could not adjudicate on them.[17] That is probably the most prudent review system ever in the world. But the multi-tiered system delayed the final decision, and did not help find out the truth or achieve justice. The so-called six levels and six instances are mostly formalities like staged plays. That might be attributed to not only external factors (such as the officialdom) but also the judicial officials at all levels (except the Ministry of Justice) who, mostly both administrative and judicial, were not experts and had to be dependent on secretaries and clerks alike. Those secretaries and clerks colluded and were set in their way, resulting in a rigid and malfunctioning judicial system for which Yang Naiwu and Mrs. Ge (known as Little Cabbage) were a case in point. The case was not complicated, but the county magistrate's bias and error could not be discovered by the tiers of reviews because the officials were deceitful and rigid so that those reviews were merely slavish copies. When the Yang family appealed it to Beijing, the central government remanded it to the governor of Zhejiang and the provincial surveillance commission for retrial. Zhejiang province transferred the case to a prefect and a county magistrate in a

[14] The tiered court system in ancient China is different from the modern one in that cases would not be decided but reviewed as they moved up tier by tier (Zheng, 1988).

[15] Cases occasionally went to the Circuit Court for review.

[16] Ordinary capital cases were usually reviewed by the Three Judicial Offices, but grave capital cases were submitted to the Ministry of Justice for review because it was easy and normal to mete out a capital sentence in the latter whereas it was necessary for the three institutions to consider criminals between life and death in the former, which shows prudent consideration of punishment.

[17] For more details about the relevant judicial system in the Qing, see Na (2004a, 2004b, 2004c). Civil cases might be decided by the county magistrate in the county court of first instance, but might also be appealed all along the prefecture, the Circuit and the provincial administration commission, and even to the Ministry of Revenue.

different place for re-examination, but injustice had yet to be redressed, resulting in a celebrated case known in China and abroad (Alford, 1984).

A scholar concluded that, "China used to mix up the judicial with the administrative, the civil with the criminal, and the prosecution with the court. The so-called judicial system was no more than the ranked executive system. ... It was praiseworthy because it showed deep concern for human lives, and defective because decisions might be reversed anytime, a huge backlog of cases waited to be heard, and only the emperor could make a ruling, which does not agree with the modern collegial institution" (Wang, 1936, pp. 8–9).

Under the impact of the Western tide, the Qing government began to reform and revise laws in 1902, and one of the major motives was to abolish the consular jurisdiction. It was believed then that the Western powers insisted on consular jurisdiction in China because the Qing Dynasty had unsound laws, harsh penalties, mix-up of justice and administration, disregard for procedures in justice, confusion of civil and criminal cases, and torture, etc. Accordingly, it was thought that those Western nations would automatically give up consular jurisdiction after the revision of laws and improvement of justice. They had promised to do so,[18] and had done the same to Japan after the Meiji Restoration.

To reform the official system after a constitutional government, the Qing Dynasty issued an edict in 1906: "The Ministry of Justice shall be renamed *Fabu* responsible for judicial administration while the Court of Judicial Review shall be changed to the *Dali Yuan* in charge of judicial review" (Veritable Records of Emperor Dezong, 1987, p. 468). In the same year, the *Dali Yuan* submitted the memorial *Method of Determining Jurisdiction*, proposing to adopt a four-level and three-instance system, a "foreign practice" represented by Japan. The proposal for the Japanese or the Continental judicial system was made for several reasons. Firstly, the judicial reform was part of the late Qing's constitutional movement, and it was in the best interests of the Qing royal family to learn from Japan and Germany practicing a dual monarchy where the monarch retained great power, different from the powerless British king in the parliamentary monarchy. Secondly, the political and social traditions determined that China need to follow Japan and Germany both of which had had a long history of authoritarian government, different again from the British tradition of "big society and small government". Thirdly, it was natural to learn from Japan because Japan and China are neighboring countries and their languages are similar. Moreover, The Chinese were shocked that the little Japan overpowered the great Russia after the Meiji Restoration. It is usually thought that China modernized its legal system by borrowing directly from Japan and indirectly from Germany.

[18] The U.K. was the first to seize the consular jurisdiction and the first to make such a commitment. Article 12 of the *Mackay Treaty* signed in the 28th year of Emperor Guangxu of the Qing Dynasty provided that "China is eager to reform its legal system to be consistent with those of Western countries. The United Kingdom is willing to assist in this endeavor to the best of its ability. When China has settled its legal system, adjudication, and all related matters, Britain will agree to relinquish its extraterritorial jurisdiction" (Zhu, 1958). In the next year, a similar article was also included in the treaties between China and the US, Japan, Portugal and other countries.

In November 1907, the Ministry of Justice issued the *Regulations for a Pilot Court System at All Levels*, attempting to establish the *Dali Yuan*-led courts at every level separated from the corresponding executive branch. In 1910, the Qing royal court formally promulgated the *Organic Law of the Judiciary* to establish a four-level and three-instance judicial system after the manner of Japan and Germany (Li, 2004, pp. 66–81). The law stipulated creation of the *Dali Yuan* at the central level, high courts at the provincial level, superior courts at the prefectural level (or subprefectural level if the subprefecture was directly under the central government), and trial courts at the county level to hear civil and criminal cases; accordingly, the Prosecutor General's Office and the prosecutor's offices at each level were set up to exercise prosecutorial powers. That split up the judiciary and the executive that had been combined for thousands of years. Under the four-level and three-instance court system, minor civil and criminal cases were heard in the trial courts and might be appealed to superior courts for rehearing and to high courts of last resort whereas relatively serious cases were heard in the trial courts and might be appealed along to the high courts and the *Dali Yuan*.

"Compared with the six-level and six-instance system, the four-level and three-instance had one third fewer levels and half as many hearings", which "relatively suited the national circumstances of late Qing Dynasty" (Li, 2004, pp. 66–81). More importantly, the local judicial organs at all levels became independent, which changed the tradition of the "principal seal-holding official" holding both administrative and the judicial office and greatly promoted the specialization of the judiciary. The prosecutorial organs were also separated from the judiciary to ensure the relative neutrality of the judges in the proceedings.

In the few years before the Xinhai Revolution, the Qing royal court established different tiers of courts in provincial capitals and trade ports. However, at the very beginning of its implementation, the new four-level and three-instance system fell into dire straits due to shortage of funds and qualified judicial personnel. With a stringent budget, the late Qing government could not pay for construction (of court buildings) and normal operation (such as the salaries of judges) of courts at all levels, and the judicial budget compiled by the Ministry of Justice was a mere formality. Although the abolition of the imperial examination made the study of law and politics a shortcut to fame and wealth, competent legal talents were still in short supply in the society. The personnel from the traditional judicial system filled up the new judicial organs at all levels, making it difficult for the legal newcomers to join in (Li, 2004, pp. 185–192). The four-level and three-instance system stipulated in the *Organic Law* was not practiced because most of the prefectures, subprefectures and counties across the country did not establish new judicial institutions, and the few newly established courts agonized over two major problems: funding and human resources.

13.2.2 The Nominal Four-Level and Three-Instance System Under the Beijing Government of the ROC

After the Xinhai Revolution in 1911, the Nanjing Provisional Government theoretically continued with the Qing's *Organic Act of the Judiciary*, but there were no unified regulations on tiers of courts so that practices varied from place to place. Sun Yat-sen advocated the four-level and three-instance system which, he thought, should not be readily abandoned even though it was the Qing's institution. He specifically refuted the view that a two-tier system might apply to minor cases, thinking that "it is not a prudent way of handling people's lives and property to base the tiers of courts on the quality of cases, and the right to appeal is one of the civil rights. Decisions should not be made hastily in terms of abolition of a right" (cited from Zhang & Li, 2004, p. 122). Soon after the Beijing Government (Beiyang Government) of the ROC was founded, the four-level and three-instance system was amended so that the trial courts were replaced by county magistrates concurrently in charge of judicial affairs, and various flexible courts were established under the provincial high courts. That amendment was attributed to the political and social circumstances, and chiefly to shortage of funding and human resources. Statistics shows that, by 1926, only 66 superior courts and 23 superior court branches had been established nationwide in addition to the *Dali Yuan*, 23 high courts located in provincial capitals, and 26 high court branches in major trading ports. However, there were as many as 1,800 county judicial institutions where the magistrates administered justice (Na, 2004a, pp. 342–343).

i. Reform of the local official system and abolition of trial courts

In order to centralize power in the central government, President Yuan Shih-k'ai ordered to revise the local official system in 1914, relegating the late Qing's administrative regions such as prefectures, subprefectures, detached subprefectures, and counties all to counties so that the five-tier administrative system from the central to the provinces, the circuits, the prefecture and finally down to the detached subprefectures or counties was transformed into a four-tier system without the prefectures (Na, 2004a, pp. 342–343). The circuits were basically dispatched institutions that did not necessarily hear cases in the Qing Dynasty, and the correspondence was disrupted between those regional administrations and their judicial courts stipulated in the *Organic Law of the Judiciary* when the prefectures were abolished. In April of the same year, the Political Conference abolished the trial courts on account of the administrative and military governors' proposals and shortage of judicial personnel and financial resources.[19] The *Organic Law* was amended accordingly for summary

[19] Jiang Guiti, Commander-in-Chief of Jehol, together with commissioners-in-chief and governors of all other provinces, proposed to the central government to abolish and create some judicial institutions because of funding and human resources. "It is advisable to suspend trial courts, prosecutor's offices of the same level, and reviewing clerks. All judicial affairs will go to the county magistrates to save expenditure. But high courts and prosecutor's offices need to be maintained at the provincial level and in trading posts. Talents shall be recruited to fill up their posts to be ready

divisions to be set up within superior courts to handle cases that had been heard in the trial courts. That actually divided the same court into two tiers in order to practice four-level and three-instance system which, therefore, came to be nominal (Wang, 1936, p. 9).

ii. Branch courts external to the four levels of courts

In addition to the *Dali Yuan*, high courts, superior courts and trial courts, the Beiyang Government established various branch courts, flexible enough to meet diverse needs. Those branches, instituted within or under the different levels of courts, could solve real problems arising out of a vast territory, inconvenient transportation as well as an enormous backlog of cases due to limited manpower of the *Dali Yuan*, high courts and trial courts.

1. The *Dali* Branch Court

Remote provinces with inconvenient transportation each might set up a *Dali* Branch Court within its High Court (Article 40, *Organic Law of the Judiciary*). The *Dali* Branch Court had one court for civil cases and one for criminal litigations (Article 41). The justices might be appointed by the *Dali Yuan* or might be those concurrently serving as justices in the high court of the province where the branch was located, but only two dual office-holders were allowed in either court (Article 42). The *Dali Yuan* would be requested to hear the case if the Branch Court's interpretation of laws differed from precedents of its own or other courts (Article 44) (The Beijing Government of the Republic of China, 1922, pp. 61–61). Articles 42 and 44 regulated the *Dali* Branch Courts in a certain way: firstly, the maximum number of dual office-holders could not surpass half of the bench[20]; secondly, the *Dali* Branch Court must either follow precedents in making decisions, and in time of inconsistency, cases would have to be submitted to the *Dali Yuan* in Beijing for a final decision.

2. High court branches

The high court was the highest judicial authority in a province. The *Organic Law of the Judiciary* allowed "provinces with a vast area or other inconveniences to set up high court branches within the superior courts" (Article 28), but the high court and its branches had the same jurisdiction. Each branch might have one civil court and one criminal court (Article 29). The justices might be appointed by the high court or those concurrently holding an office in the superior court from the region where the

for the abolishment of consular jurisdiction." The Political Conference compromised two plans and made a resolution: "It's necessary the keep the provincial high courts and prosecutor's offices and established superior courts and parallel prosecutor's offices in the capital cities. Superior courts and parallel prosecutor's offices in trading posts will be decided after prudent consideration. The two departments at the county level shall be both abolished due to shortage of funds and talents and their responsibilities shall be transferred to the county administration" (Li, 2005, pp. 190–191).

[20] The *Dali Yuan* and its branch courts adopted collegial panels of five justices.

branch was located or from a neighboring region, but only one dual office-holder was allowed in a collegial panel of three justices, and a maximum of two was allowed when the panel consisted of five (Article 30). Article 30 revealed that justices were in such short supply at that time that the justices of a high court or even a neighboring high court had to concurrently hear cases in the branches. However, the *Organic Law of the Judiciary* still attempted to limit this flexible approach by stipulating the dual office-holders to be the minority in collegial panels.

The judicial talent shortage required the justices of superior courts or high courts to work concurrently in the high court branches. A problem might arise when the same justice attended two levels of hearing of the same case, and it became more serious when the superior court was the second instance because that justice might hear the same case in the high court of last resort, de facto depriving the defendant of the right to a fair trial through appeal, so that the three-instance system might fall into a two-instance system. At that time, Hubei, Jiangxi, Henan, Shaanxi and other provinces all raised that issue, and then the Beijing Government ordered that the ultimate jurisdiction go to the high court in every province when the high court branches took the responsibilities of the superior courts to hear appeal cases as courts of second instance (The Beijing Government of the Republic of China, 1922, pp. 475–478). The gesture shows that the Beijing Government endeavored to practice modern justice despite limitations of reality.

3. The high court divisions and the affiliated judicial officers in the circuit governments

A "circuit" (general administration circuit) used to be an administrative tier in the Qing Dynasty, and there were 90 plus circuits after the ROC was founded. In January 1913, the Beijing Government promulgated the *Decree on Unifying the Administrative Organization of the Circuits*, stipulating the intendant of a circuit to be surveillance commissioner (*guancha shi*, 观察使); in May 1914, the government issued the circuits' bureaucratic system by which the circuit administrative office was set up with a governor (*daoyin*,道尹) as its head (Qian et al., 2008, pp. 480–482). The circuit government was the only administrative tier between the provincial government and the counties under the Beijing government of the ROC so that it was natural to set up a judicial branch affiliated with the circuit government, given the vexing appeals resulting from considerable distances between the counties and the provincial capital.

The *Organic Law of the Judiciary* stipulated the establishment of high court branches, and on September 24, 1914, the Beijing government published the *Provisional Regulations of the High Court Divisions*, providing that, in those remote regions from the provincial capital, provisional high court divisions might be established at the location of the circuit administration. A division comprising three justices adopted a collegial mechanism in hearing cases, having less jurisdiction than a high court and its branches so that any civil case involving objects above a certain sum and any criminal case involving punishment above a certain degree would be transferred directly to the high court. However, in case of inconvenient transfer, the high court might entrust the case to the division, but the ruling would not be pronounced until the high court reviewed it; the parties might file a challenge if they did not want the division to hear their case on behalf of the high court (Qian et al., 2008, pp. 457–460).

The judicial officers affiliated with the circuit administrative office were "a remedy for remedies". Due to constraints of financial and human resources, high court branches and divisions were uncommon in the vast areas between provincial capitals and counties, and the superior courts were rare, too. In order to remedy the inconvenient appeals, the central government ordered the provincial high court to designate a number of county trial courts in the province to hear appeals from the neighboring counties (The Beijing Government of the Republic of China, 1922, pp. 501–502).[21] However, since counties were of the same tier, misgivings would be natural in hearing a case when county A was county B's appellate authority. As a result, there was a growing demand for establishment of courts of appeals. To meet the demand, some judicial officers were instituted in the circuit administration office to hear appeals within a certain area. Located in those remote regions without courts of appeals, the institution had limited jurisdiction and would be abolished when high court divisions were set up (Qian et al., 2008, pp. 460–461).

4. Superior court divisions (Qin, 1942, p. 123; The Beijing Government of the Republic of China, 1922, pp. 76–78)

The superior court divisions began in 1914 when abolition of trial courts dramatically increased caseload in the superior courts now as courts of first instance, resulting in an enormous backlog and all second appeals going vexingly to the Dali Yuan. Therefore, on March 13 of the same year, the Ministry of Justice ordered the superior court in the capital to establish a division taking over both the office and responsibility of the abolished trial court, and ordered all provinces on May 7 of the next year to set up similar superior court divisions. On April 22, 1917, the Ministry of Justice formulated the *Provisional Organic Act of the Superior Court Divisions* composed of 14 articles, requiring all provinces to practice the law in all counties under their respective jurisdiction. Consequently, divisions were instituted in all the county governments under jurisdiction of each superior court and had jurisdiction over the counties respectively with the name "X County Division of X Superior Court" (Article 1 and 2). All civil and criminal cases in the county went to the superior court division of first instance (Article 3) and appeals against its decisions would be filed to the superior court. However, when the superior court was the first instance, appeals would go up to the high court or its branch (Article 5).

iii. County judicial organs external to the trial courts

1. Judicial station (Qian, 2008, p. 614)

Not all counties had trial courts in the early years of the ROC so that judicial stations were established in those counties without trial courts in March 1912. Affiliated with the county government, a judicial station consisted of the county magistrate and one

[21] *Temporary Regulations for System of Appeals of Neighboring Counties* was formulated then.

to three judges. The judges took charge of civil and criminal cases at first instance and appeals from neighboring counties, but could not handle any administrative affairs whereas the magistrate played the part of a prosecutor. The appeal against the judges' ruling might go to the superior court, and might also go to the judicial station in the neighboring county if the superior court was far away while the appeal against the decision by the superior court as the first instance must be taken to the high court or its branch. In April 1914 when the magistrate took over the judicial matters, the judicial station was abandoned.

2. County magistrates as judicial officers

In April 1914, the Political Conference abolished the trial court, and in the same month, the Beiyang Government promulgated the *Provisional Regulations on the Administration of Judicial Affairs by County Magistrates* and the *Provisional Regulations on the Trial of Lawsuits by County Magistrates*, stipulating that the magistrate hear all civil and criminal lawsuits that fell under the jurisdiction of the trial courts in counties without a trial court or under the superior courts (Article 1). Since the county magistrates were too busy to focus on judicial trials, one to three trial examiners were appointed in the county government to assist the magistrate in hearing cases. Their institution needed to be submitted by the magistrate to the high court for approval, and might be suspended where the caseload was light (Article 4). In each county with trial examiners, the examiners would be solely responsible for cases that fell under the jurisdiction of a trial court even though they heard the cases in the name of the county government. The magistrate and examiners would be jointly responsible for cases that fell under the jurisdiction of Superior Court even though the former might assign them to the latter (Qin, 1942, p. 120).

As head of both the executive and judicial branch, the magistrate might find it hard to balance, and there was also a suspicion that his position meat the restoration of the Qing judicial system by which the intendant was invested with the administrative, judicial and prosecutorial powers. When hearing litigations, the trial examiners or the magistrate's assistants might make unfair or even wrong decisions due to their dismaying quality and independence.[22] In September 1914, that is, less than six months after the magistrate's dual office-holding, the Beiyang Government promulgated the *Regulations on Judicial Review* to remedy the loopholes of that system, stipulating that criminal cases the county magistrate had heard must be presented within a prescribed period to the high court or its branches for review whether the defendant appealed or not (Li, 2005, pp. 187–203).

[22] Ruan Yicheng worked at the Ministry of Justice for a long time since the beginning of the ROC. He summarized the problems with the dual office-holding in administration and judiciary at the county level. Firstly, it was impossible for one or two trial examiners to handle cases properly and promptly because of the heavy workload of civil and criminal hearings, crime scene investigation, autopsy, and execution of decisions. Secondly, the trial examiners are ill-paid without a judge's standing so that common talents would not take the position. Thirdly, the country magistrate frequently interfered with the judiciary to flaunt his authority. Fourthly, the trial examiners' fair decisions might be compromised by the magistrate who might have established connections with the landed gentry to meet his administrative purpose (Han, 2003, pp. 283–284).

3. County judicial office (Qin, 1942, pp. 121–123; The Beijing Government of the Republic of China, 1922, pp. 78–79).

To further eliminate the problem with the executive county magistrate holding the judicial office, the Beijing Government promulgated the *Regulations on the Organization of County Judicial Offices* in May 1917,[23] requiring every county without a trial court to set up a county judicial office "in principal" taking charge of all civil and criminal cases at first instance regardless of their seriousness (Articles 1 and 4).[24] Instituted in the county government, the judicial office consisted of one or two judges who, before taking office, had to pass the qualifying examination that the chief justice of the high court presided over according to the *Regulations of Examination and Appointment for Judges*, and to be submitted to the Ministry of Justice for approval (Article 2, 4, and 5). The magistrate took full charge of prosecution, arrest, investigation, penal transportation, law enforcement, and other prosecutorial matters, but was forbidden to interfere in the judicial matters the judges were fully responsible for (Article 7). The *Regulations*, criticized then for its "principle" in Article 1 made abuse of "exceptions" possible,[25] stayed on the shelf until 1922 when counties began to have judicial offices, which continued into the ROC under the NNG (Qian et al., 2008, p. 615).

13.2.3 The Three-Level and Three-Instance System Under the NNG

When the NNG was founded in 1927, the four-level and three-instance system did not change immediately except that the *Dali Yuan* was renamed the Supreme Court, and all levels of Judicial offices were changed into courts. On October 28, 1932, the NNG

[23] In his *History of Political Institution in the Republic of China,* Ch'ien Tuan-sheng (2008, pp. 614–615) considered the county judicial office to begin in 1914 when the judicial station was abolished and the dual office-holding magistrate was instituted. Institutionally, the judicial office was the rule while the dual office-holding was an exception. However, Wang Yongbin (1936), Qin zhusang (1942) and other scholars thought that the county judicial office, resulting from the loopholes of the magistrate's dual office-holding, was established in 1917. Given that the *Regulations on the Organization of County Judicial Offices* was published in 1917, this book adopted the latter idea that the county judicial office was instituted after the magistrate's dual office-holding.

[24] Article 1 of the *Regulations* reads, "Any county without a trial court shall have a judicial office. In case of unusual circumstances that prevent the establishment of a judicial office, the chief justice of the high court, the director of the high public prosecutor's office, or the director of the judicial Preparatory office, or the director of the Judicial Office of the provincial government shall submit a report stating the reasons to the Ministry of Justice. When approved, the institution would be suspended and the magistrate would concurrently hold the judicial office".

[25] "Article 1 of the *Regulations* clearly allows suspension in case of unusual circumstances, opening the door for many provinces to finding excuses for not setting up such an office. Those provinces which had been ready for it terminated the work immediately without being investigated. Therefore, under the Beijing Government, 90 percent of the county magistrate held both the executive and judicial office" (Wang, 1936, p. 16).

promulgated the *Organic Act of the Court*, substituting the previous system with a three-level and three-instance system by which the Supreme Court, high courts, and district courts were set up from the central to local levels with three instances as the regular practice and two instances as the exceptional (Zheng, 1936, pp. 58–59). In principle, a single judge would hear cases in the district courts with a collegial panel of three justices in the high courts and a collegial panel of five in the Supreme Court (Article 3). The *Act* was not put into effect after publication mainly because district courts could not be established nationwide. By the end of 1934, no progress had been made with the implementation of the new *Act* so that the power of the district courts had to be weakened with establishment of high court branches to change the jurisdiction. On June 11, 1935, the government ordered the law to take effect on July 1 of the same year, and the Ministry of Justice issued decrees on the 18th of the same month, granting a one-year suspension of the law to nine provinces including Guangdong (Qian et al., 2008, pp. 251, 306). By 1947, 37 high courts and 119 branches of high courts were instituted together with new district courts in only 748 counties, and most of counties stayed the same as before (Xie, 1948, Chap. 2, p. 1). An examination of the tiered court system under the NNG reveals that it was not a significant change in itself, except for the limited remedy for the previous system under the Beijing Government, and its replacement of the inoperative four-level and three-instance system with a three-level and three-instance system. Here are some of the main problems with the then system.

i. The county magistrate as chief of both the executive and judicial department

Obviously, there are at least three problems with the county magistrate holding both the executive and judicial office that dates back to the Beiyang Government. First, the judiciary and the prosecution were mixed up; second, the humble and ill-paid trial examiners, having dismayingly poor judicial education, were subject to the influence of the administration; third, the bar system was not applicable (Zheng, 1936, pp. 303–305). The Beiyang Government attempted to remedy the problems by creating a county judicial office, but made so little progress that 1436 counties still had dual office-holding magistrates until 1936 (Wang, 1936, p. 19). In 1929, the Judicial Administration compiled the *Yearly Agenda during the Period of Political Tutelage* which contained a six-year plan for establishment of district courts nationwide with county courts as transitional courts. However, the plan was different from the facts because the six-year plan fell through when the 1935 deadline came; Article 9 of the 1932 *Organic Act of the Court* requiring every county or city to set up a district court remained on paper and in theory (Wang, 1936, pp. 16–17).

However, the government did do something to improve the situation. In 1933, the Examination Yuan of the National Government published the *Provisional Regulations on the Examination of Trial Examiners*, defining the qualifications of trial examiners (assisting county magistrates in hearing cases) through examinations. It was clearly impossible to institute district courts at one stroke nationwide in China where dual office-holding magistrates were prevalent. To find a transitional measure, the Ministry of Justice drafted the *Provisional Regulations on the Organization of*

County Judicial Departments, which was passed by the Legislative Yuan on March 27, 1936 and promulgated on July 1 of that year. "In terms of creation and intent, the law was similar to the *Regulations on the Organization of County Judicial Offices* published in May 1917" (Zheng, 1936, p. 309). The 1936 *Regulations* expected any county without a district court to set up a judicial department affiliated with the county government to take charge of all judicial affairs (Article 1). Judges of the department, exercising their powers independently (Article 2), were selected by the chief justice of the high court from among candidates with certain legal qualifications and submitted to the Judicial Administration for approval. Compared with the previous dual office-holding system by which trial examiners were submitted by magistrate to the chief justice of the high court for appointment, this law was more demanding in terms of qualification and procedures. The judges enjoyed the salary of assistant grade, the rank of a county magistrate in accordance with the civil service system of the National Government (Article 5). The magistrate assumed responsibility for the prosecutorial duties in the judicial department (Article 4). The Legislative Yuan passed the law with an amendment that the law would be in effect within a period of three years (Article 13). Wu Jingxiong a member of the Legislative Yuan's Legislative Affairs Committee submitted a review report of the Regulations, saying that:

> It was abnormal and long criticized that the county magistrate should take charge of the judicial affairs. The *Organic Act of the Court* was expected to sweep away the abnormality, but scarcity of funds and talents prevented most of the counties from starting a district court so that the dual office-holding institution stayed on. Meanwhile, provisional judicial departments were established in counties without courts to institute the principle of independent trial, laying a preliminary foundation for the prospective courts. It is understood that this transitional method is not the true spirit of the *Organic Act of the Courts*, but an improvement over dual office-holding magistrate, providing for a three-year effective period when the Judicial and Executive Yuan could raise sufficient funds for a sound organization of the courts. (Zheng, 1936, pp. 309–310)

After the promulgation of the *Provisional Regulations on the Organization of County Judicial Departments*, the Judicial Administration granted every provincial high court a three-year limit to set up judicial departments in counties managed by dual office-holding magistrates in phases of six months from July 1, 1936 to the end of December 1937, and transform the judicial departments into district courts in phases of six months again from January 1, 1938 to the end of June, 1939 (Wang, 1936, p. 18). The summary table of the first phase shows that a total of 384 counties had set up judicial departments with Shandong, Gansu and Shaanxi provinces having completed the institution in all of their counties by July 1, 1936; Jiangsu Province, where the central government was located, was exempted from the first phase and got down directly to district courts in phases; However, seven provinces did not take any action or submit the data to the Judicial Administration (Wang, 1936, pp. 21–23). Soon, the Japanese invasion disrupted the agenda. It's not certain if the three-year plan could have been fulfilled without the war, but it might be inferred that the second stage of setting up district courts nationwide would be much more demanding than the first stage of setting up county judicial departments.

By 1946, the magistrate's dual office-holding function had been abolished in all provinces except Xinjiang (Xie, 1948, Chap. 2, p. 1) and the then statistics showed that 992 of all counties had judicial departments affiliated with the county governments take charge of judicial affairs (Ch'ien, 1950, p. 254). In 1947, the National Judicial Administration Review Conference proposed to the Judicial Administration that all county judicial departments, as a transitional organ, should be converted into formal courts within a prescribed period (Xie, 1948, Chap. 2, p. 1). However, it was easier said than done. Little progress was made with district courts by the NNG during the last two years of the ROC.

ii. Branch courts

Similar to the Beijing Government of the ROC, the NNG set up a variety of branch courts by the same reason of "a vast territory" and with similar statutes such as superior court branches (Article 9, *Organic Act of the Court*) and high court branches (Article 16). When the *Organic Act* was in the making, a dispute arose over whether the supreme judicial organ (the Supreme Court) could have branches. On the one hand, "China has a vast area and numerous legal proceedings. If all final judgments went up to the Supreme Court at the seat of the central government, delayed delivery and a huge backlog would be the likely consequence. In civil cases, things might have changed in due course and disputes would likely turn more bitter; in criminal lawsuits, it might be even more likely and dismaying for the defendants to stay long in jail and die pending judgment. Therefore, the Supreme Court branch needed to be established on the part of the people" (Xie, 2000, p. 1043). It can be viewed as a judicial convenience, but construction of over 20 years improved transportation and postal service under the NNG so that the establishment of the Supreme Court branches would be theoretically and practically harmful to the unification of the legal system. In April 1930, the Judicial Yuan drew up the *Draft Organic Act of the Court* on the basis of which the Central Political Conference laid down some legislative principles, the sixth being that "In case of poor transportation, it's necessary to establish branches of the Supreme Court in regions remote from the seat of the central government, but there should be restrictions on unified judicial interpretations" to avoid confusing judicial practices resulting from disparate judicial interpretations (Nie, 2007; Xie, 2000, p. 104). In July 1932, Luo Wengan, Minister of the Judicial Administration, drafted the *Amendment to the Legislative Principles of the Organic Act of the Court* with the reasons for the amendment. One of the proposals in it was that the Supreme Court should not have branches. The *Amendment* was remitted by the Executive Yuan to the Central Political Conference which then included "only one Supreme Court" into the principles for the *Organic Act of the Court*. Eventually, the *Organic Act*, published in October, 1932, did not allow branches of the Supreme Court to be instituted (Xie, 2000, pp. 1045–1049).

iii. Disputes over the second instance or the third instance as the last resort

It was mentioned above that more tiers of courts are not necessarily the better because they may demand more manpower and financial resources and result in delayed final decision and wait-and-see mentality of the people[26] in spite of their benefits for division of jurisdiction across the courts and protection of the right to appeal.[27] In 1927, the Wuhan National Government adopted a two-level and two-instance system by which the court of second instance would be the last resort for regular cases and the court of third instance would be ultimate for capital cases. The system was abandoned when the Nanjing and Wuhan governments joined to form a coalition, but the call to reduce the tiers did not fade away. Ju Zheng, the first president of the Judicial Yuan under the NNG, considered the clumsy court system to be a feudal residue by which "The cunning man uses his financial resources to appeal repeatedly, resulting in years of delay for minor cases and unattained goal of legally protecting people. Eventually, the people would see justice as undesirable and lose faith in the government". Soon, the four-level and three-instance system implemented since the late Qing Dynasty was replaced by the three-level and three-instance system with the exceptional rule of the second instance court as the final to alleviate sufferings from litigations. The increasing backlog of cases in the courts prompted quite a few scholars to propose a universal adoption of the second instance court as the final whereas others stood firm on the third instance as the final with the primary reason that, in spite of risk of increasing litigation by the three-instance system, it was vital for the Supreme Court to retain its ultimate jurisdiction at the third instance to guarantee the right to appeal and unified judicial interpretation when the courts of first instance and second instance were not well-instituted, and numerous county magistrates were concurrently in charge of judicial affairs (Zhang & Li, 2004, pp. 122–124).

iv. The creation and abolition of circuit courts

The creation of circuit courts by the NNG began in August 1928 when the Ministry of Justice[28] drafted the *Provisional Organic Act of the Court*, aiming to replace big-budget regular courts with circuit courts in inaccessible vast regions (Xie, 2000, p. 1039).[29] When the *Organic Act of the Court* was in the making, the establishment of circuit courts was proposed and rejected because of two inconveniences. "(1) It is appropriate to handle litigation at the time when it happens, and substantial delays might occur when the circuit court is not in place; (2) The circuit court is no more itinerant when it has to stay in one place for a case because investigation cannot be completed at one stroke" (Zheng, 1936, p. 243). The citation is quite insightful even from hindsight. The Anglo-American circuit courts were a judicial system of long ago when it was hard to file complaints to courts because of poor transportation and

[26] "Minor cases have little impact on human rights, merely building up wait-and-see mentality of the people if there is another tier of court, which is the first problem; The judicial principles are characterized by prudent decisions and swift executions, and executions might be delayed when tiers of courts increase, which is the second problem." (Zheng, 1936, pp. 77–78).

[27] Cases went to different tiers of courts according to their seriousness.

[28] The Ministry of Justice was changed into the Judicial Administration after the publication of the *Organic Act of the Judicial Yuan* in November 1928.

[29] The Guangzhou National Government piloted circuit courts in 1925 and the NNG approved of the request of Gansu province to adopt circuit courts to hear appeals.

only a short time was required for the trial. However, the circuit courts do not fit in modern society with improved transportation where courts are easily accessible and a year may be needed to hear a case. In 1932 when resolving the principles for amending the *Organic Act of the Court*, the Central Political Conference considered a slight borrowing of the foreign circuit courts. When necessary, the high court or district court might dispatch judges to hear cases in the makeshift court formed of the government office of those regions distant from a court where it was not worthwhile to institute a branch court for a small caseload there (Xie, 2000, p. 1047). Consequently, Article 64 of the 1932 *Organic Act of the Court* required the high court or district court to hold temporary sessions in areas without branch courts under its jurisdiction if need be; the judges might hail from their courts, the branch or subordinate courts of the high courts, or the branches of the district courts. However, both the high court and the local court could set up branches which might function as circuit courts to some extent so that the scenario stipulated in Article 64 of the *Organic Act of the* Court was merely an exception and supplement to the branch court system instead of a truly institutionalized circuit court system.

The circuit courts were put into use under NNG during the War of Resistance when "Transportation was disrupted in the war zone, creating an obstruction to appeals. For cases at the second instance, it was better for the judges to go to the parties rather the other way around". The government had sent letters to its ambassadors to the U.K. and the U.S., requesting information about the circuit courts there before the Judicial Yuan published the *Regulations on Circuit Court Trials in the War Zone*, and the *Provisional Regulations on Civil and Criminal Proceedings in the War Zone Circuit Courts* consecutively in 1938. Article 1 of the first law expected "The high court or its branch court to dispatch justices to hear civil and criminal cases under its jurisdiction for the convenience of litigants in the war zone" and specified circuit courts as the second instance in the war zone. "The circuit court shall sit in the judicial office, county government office or other suitable place under its jurisdiction" (Article 5). "The local judicial organs or county governments shall supply clerks, registrars, bailiffs, examiners, judicial police, court officers, and servants, but the circuit judge may take court personnel with them when necessary" (Article 7). In 1944, the Judicial Administration proposed to promote the circuit courts in the inaccessible areas of the non-war zones in the rear provinces and drew up the *Draft Regulations on the High Circuit Courts* on the grounds that "circuit courts were valuable for both its justice and its contribution to the legal literacy of the public". Soon after, the War of Resistance ended. So did the two laws in December 1945, and with them went the circuit courts (Xie, 1948, Chap. 5, pp. 1–2).

13.2.4 The Failure of Modern Judicial Reform and Its Causes

An historical examination of modern Chinese tiered court system reveals that the tiered system based on modern legal philosophy from foreign countries (mainly civil law countries) could not work perfectly well. Due to the political, social, and financial factors and shortage of human resources, the government had to make exceptions and modify general laws by special laws without discarding the general principles of the modern legal philosophy. Exceptions that accommodated the reality ended up the rule, and the so-called "principles" (concepts) in the system turned out "unprincipled" so that special laws (such as regulations, provisional regulations, etc.) were in full force in reality whereas general laws (the *Organic Law of the Judiciary* and the *Organic Act of the Court*) merely blueprinted a distant beautiful vision (ideal) of a four-level or three-level and three-instance system which barely made a part of the Six Codes.

The dual office-holding was a case in point where the county magistrate and his subordinates also administered justice as an expedient, stipulated as a provisional judicial institution when the litigation could not wait until creation of the new courts and the government did not have sufficient funds or legal talents. However, the stopgap came to perpetuate. In fact, new courts were not established in the vast majority of China's counties until 1949, creating a divided judicial system: new courts and procedures were adopted in provincial capitals and major cities whereas only slight progress was made in most of other cities and villages in terms of law enforcement and the settlement, compared with the Qing Dynasty (Na, 2004a, p. 345).

> At the same time, the public did not identify culturally with the instituted new courts:
>
> China's judiciary, still in its infancy, has not had a consolidated foundation. An unusual beginning is usually terrifying so that both talents and mediocre people indulge in their self-assumed fair assertions, and both major cities and remote regions are agitated with baseless claims. It is no wonder that the legally ill-educated public would panic at first mention of constitutional provisions and truths about a republic. And the court of law is even more widely unknown. (cited from Han, 2003, p. 233)

The institution of new courts did not necessarily bring justice with it because "In connection with the issue of cost-effectiveness, the formalization agenda also raised the issue of procedural/formal justice versus substantive justice" (Xu, 2008, p. 11); "... as late as 1937 that the civil and criminal procedural laws were not entirely suitable to China's societal needs, and that overelaborate procedural formalities burdened both the system and the people. Not only did ordinary people fail to understand the formalities, but judges considered them restrictive, unnecessary, and conducive to case backlogs" (Xu, 2008, p. 12). Unqualified judges might be worse than the parental officials of the Qing Dynasty because "judicial independence" protected judges who made decisions by bending laws and practicing favoritism.

> Judicial independence is intended to enable the judge to make rulings by following the law and his conscience, leaving no room for interference and solicitation ... Since the founding of the ROC, hundreds of new political institutions were being created day and night, and new and old laws were under revision such that regulations, incompatible with etiquette and customs, rewarded evil deeds, or the procedures, inconsistent with the facts, merely proliferated confusion. Public confusion had been bred before the foundation was laid down. Moreover, the trained judges were in short supply whereas the selected ones were not proficient. The government spending fell short, but encouragement of integrity was insufficient. Incompetent men filled up the positions and corrupt officials were rampant. Worse still, lawyers colluded and distorted the law more than clerks of the court. Fellow townsmen

> and neighbors tended more to be partial, and police officers were abnormally brutal. Long-delayed cases were building up with resentments running wild. Widespread rumors were terrifying … Nowadays, there are many well-educated and dedicated judges outside the capital, but there are as many fatuous judges feeding at the public trough without integrity. They tend to go clearly against the public sentiment and ignore civilian suffering while enjoying undeserved protection by assuming themselves to be inviolable, so that the institutions intended to protect the people are hurting the people. Is that the original intention of the state to enforce judicial independence? (cited from Li, 2005, p. 189)

In that social and cultural context, the public psyche was not ready for the modern judicial philosophy, and unworthy judges and judicial corruption intensified the public dissatisfaction with modern courts and judges so that the construction of a modern tiered court system and even the entire judicial reform were bound to be on rocks. A review of judicial history of the ROC shows that "a series of judicial reform bills failed to take effect, and judicial corruption was one of the prime targets of criticism in the national political life", which was also one of the main reasons the public was disappointed with the National Government (Zhang, 2005, p. 6).

Viewed from another perspective, the ROC government adopted regulations and provisional regulations to modify the judicial reform, set up various branch courts in addition to the statutory tiers of courts, and created a dual office-holding institution, but the principle of four-levels or three-level and three-instance system was always maintained in the provisions of the general judicial laws (*Organic Law of the Judiciary* and *Organic Act of the Court*). Although that might seem hypocritical, the government's refusal to abandon its ideals deserves much attention. In accommodating the reality, the government made numerous exceptions, but it also tried to regulate them. When the judges affiliated with the county government was not proficient enough for independent trials, the qualification examination was introduced to put it right and judges' salary grade was raised to achieve their independence. To eliminate the problematic dual office-holding magistrates, the county judicial offices and judicial stations were created in their place. The branches of the high courts and the superior courts, short of staff, had to share judges between themselves, and then it was stipulated that the dual office-holding justices should be the minority in the collegial panels, and that jurisdiction would be returned from the branch court to the mother court at the second instance when a justice had to hear the same case at first and second instance. The branch courts of the Supreme Court were rejected eventually in the *Organic Act of the Court* adopted by the NNG because they were harmful to the judicial unity. Although there was an ongoing appeal for the second instance rather than the third one to be the final, the government held fast to three-instance system because the courts of first and second instance had not been well-established and their hearings had not been satisfactory. "…centralization and uniformity were institutional prerequisites for an impartial and fair judiciary … Centralization was therefore vigorously and persistently pursued in the judicial field throughout the Republican era" (Xu, 2008, p. 6).

13.3 Public Law Litigation

13.3.1 Legislating from the Bench in Election Litigation[30]

i. Introduction

The introduction of the Western parliamentary system (including election of parliamentary members and election litigation) into China began with the establishment of the provincial advisory bureaus and the Central Political Advisory Council in the late Qing Dynasty. It took merely two years from first election of members of advisory bureaus in 1909 to the Xinhai Revolution so that there was little experience in parliamentary election when the ROC was founded. What's more, the "first republic of the Far East" adopted an election law that, fully featuring "radical republicanism", even compared with that of developed Euro-American countries in terms of universal suffrage. Compared with the late Qing Dynasty, the eligibility to exercise active and passive suffrage was significantly lowered in terms of age, property, education, and citizenship, substantially increasing the electorate. However, the election technology and the democratic political awareness among the public did not improve much so that it was common to see the central and local government officials collude and manipulate election, and those candidates buy votes, control ballot boxes, threaten voters by force, and fight due to electoral fraud (Zhang, 2008, pp. 77–81, 127–165). It was certainly demanding to fit the rigid laws and regulations to the infinite variety of occurrences in election when a great leap was taken in the context without basic democratic electoral experience and culture.

In order to maintain a fair election of assemblymen and a legitimate assembly, a neutral body was needed to handle election disputes impartially and effectively. The *Dali Yuan* played a different role in election litigation from what it did in civil and criminal cases. Election was something new that had been unknown for thousands of years, so that it could not be regulated merely by a grafted election law. Consequently, the defective system of election litigation frequently went wrong when dealing with specific cases. For example, litigants were unable to distinguish between election complaints and election crimes, and habitually filed electoral disputes to the prosecutor's office, resulting in "disagreements" and "delays". Again, "the election law only stipulates the priority of election lawsuits over all the other types of lawsuits, but no deadline is specified so that the litigation drags on at different levels of judiciary and eventually escalates into a raging storm" (Ye, 2015, pp. 190–191). On the one hand, the *Dali Yuan* needed to resolve electoral disputes to ensure fair elections; on the other, as the Supreme Court, it should not only interpret the law strictly, but also remedy the loopholes in laws and initiate new norms for normal operation of democratic elections.

The author's rough statistics shows that, from 1912 through 1927, the *Dali Yuan* made 2012 interpretations, at least 50 or nearly 2.5% of which relating directly to

[30] Refer to Nie (2018)

election issues with a few being painstakingly repeated interpretations and clarifications of the same issue; of the approximately 3900 resumes of decisions published by *Dali Yuan*, a minimum of 72 or 1.8% (deriving from 32 decisions by the Dali Yuan) involved elections. Those interpretations and decisions concerned such laws as *Act on the Election of Senators*, *Act on the Election of Representatives*, *Act on the Election of Members of the Provincial Assembly*, *Regulations on the Election of Members of the County Assembly*, and *Enforcement Rules* of each law. When making rulings or judicial interpretations, the *Dali Yuan* regularly invoked precedents or previous interpretations and also required the lower courts to do so in order to repeatedly affirm and strengthen its authority as "a supplementary legislature". Of the 32 decisions involving election litigation by the *Dali Yuan* on, 10 had "multiple precedents", i.e., multiple resumes abstracted from a single decision as election rules for all levels of courts to follow thereafter. The most notable of all is Decision No. 889 of 1918 from which 19 resumes were taken. That shows that the *Dali Yuan* made active contributions to legislation in election law and that the election legislation was so sloppy that numerous problems arose in electoral affairs. The *Dali Yuan* had to constantly clarify if the same rule could apply to electoral disputes of different representatives (senators, representatives, provincial assemblymen, county assemblymen) because their election rules were not entirely consistent with the proceedings for electoral disputes.

ii. Breakdown analysis

1. Election litigation: jurisdiction and procedures

The jurisdiction over electoral disputes was vested in judicial or quasi-judicial organs called regular courts, administrative courts, constitutional courts, ad hoc election courts or electoral commissions so that a professional organ relatively independent of the political branches (the legislature and the executive) could resolve those disputes. Given the reality in the early ROC, only the courts at all levels below the *Dali Yuan* could take on the challenging task. In the context of a weak central government and divisive warlords, judges at all levels were still appointed by the central government, and the entire judicial system was in principle free from local interference so that election lawsuits over applicable law might be appealed and reviewed all the way up to the top of the court system, the central *Dali Yuan* which contributed to legislation by way of ultimate appellate jurisdiction and judicial interpretation. That was nearly the only feasible way to achieve consistency in the interpretation and application of national election laws.

The Senate was initially granted the power to interpret the election laws, but it was too occupied to punctually resolve innumerable questions of law arising from crude election laws. In September 1912, at the President's request, the Senate replied that it was agreed "for administrative convenience" that "the interpretation of the provisions of the election laws" "should go to the Bureau of Preparatory Parliament Affairs" (BPNAA hereinafter) (Yang, 2014, pp. 18–19). However, as an electoral organ, the BPNAA was a non-permanent institution subordinate to the executive branch so that it could not compare naturally with regular courts in terms of professionalism and independence. The *Dali Yuan* acquired the power to interpret election laws and regulations by exercising final adjudication of election lawsuits and abstract judicial interpretation. Interestingly, the BPNAA sometimes requested of its own accord the *Dali Yuan* to interpret the election laws.[31] Instead of "returning the favor", the *Dali Yuan* declared that "the bulletin on election supervision and the BPNAA's interpretation to be void" in its decision (Decision No. 890 of 1918) (Guo, 2013, p. 193).

Although the election litigation was public in nature, it had to follow the civil procedure and be heard by regular courts such as the Dali Yuan and lower courts so that it was called "formal civil litigation". Given that "public law began to develop of late, it was natural that the substantive law or procedural law was not yet completed. Before public law was instituted, the application of private law in place of public law was inevitable in spite of some opposition as long as the nature of public law was not tampered. In addition, since all laws were based on common principles, civil procedures could be applied understandably to election and removal proceedings as long as the purpose of public law was not hampered" (Liu, 1990, p. 130). It might be viewed as a miracle that the *Dali Yuan* approved the application of civil procedures to public law litigation and boldly shaped the election system relating to key political issues in its final adjudication and replies to questions of law the lower courts had raised.

In approving application of civil procedure to election lawsuits, the *Dali Yuan* even went to extremes to declare that, since election lawsuits were governed by civil procedure, the court should stay out and allow the concerned parties to settle between themselves by following the principle of autonomy of will, and even that "the contract shall be honored without enforcing the decision when the decision goes against the contract" (Interpretation No. 1009, 1863) (Guo, 2014, pp. 881, 1313). It was highly controversial in theory if the non-interference policy in civil litigation could be adopted in election lawsuits because the latter involved public power. In this issue, the *Dali Yuan* was suspected of being obsessed with the form of civil litigation and ignoring the substance of public law litigation, showing the sheer power of the *Dali Yuan*'s judicial interpretation. However, the *Dali Yuan* did not take over all the election affairs, and reiterated by way of several interpretations that, after the all levels of assemblies were established, the disputes over the election of speakers and vice speakers would be the internal affairs of the assemblies beyond election litigation (Interpretations No. 881, 905, 975, 1187, and 1632). Furthermore, it decriminalized the fraudulent elections of the speakers and vice speakers, stating that obstruction of election under the criminal law was only applicable to the election of national and regional assemblymen, which prevented the prosecutors (and the judiciary) from intervening in the election of speakers.[32]

---

[31] For example, Interpretations No. 944 and 1517 by the *Dali Yuan* are directly addressed to the BPNAA.

[32] "Whether the election of speakers is valid or not shall be referred to Article 36 of the *Provisional Regulations on the Provincial Assembly*: Criminal prosecution does not relate to validity of the

2. Litigation and legislating electoral rules from the bench

Election litigation was a typically judicialized political issue. Highly competitive election put candidates constantly at the edge of the law, circumstances the legislature had not expected occurred occasionally, and the rulings were made largely under the influence of policy selection and political balance. On the grounds of statutory regulations with ambiguity and limited provisions, the *Dali Yuan* granted itself and lower courts universal jurisdiction over election litigation by way of decisions and judicial interpretations, regulating election litigation and supplementing election rules which specifically included the distinction between election complaints and obstruction of election, the eligibility and right to sue, statute of limitations, tiers of courts and the appeal system, eligibility of candidates and voters, regulation and recusal of election personnel, punishment for voter impersonation and proxy voting. That may be said to be comprehensive legislating from the bench.

The *Dali Yuan* was also challenged and obstructed by the government branches due to its jurisdiction over the election litigation. The Parliament and the President even passed bills to limit the tiers of courts hearing election complaints, thereby depriving the *Dali Yuan* of its final jurisdiction over the election proceedings of senators and representatives. However, the *Dali Yuan* withstood the political pressure, overcome practical difficulties, and continued to judicially shape laws and regulations on election of assemblymen at the central, provincial and county levels by decisions and interpretations. In fact, it replaced the central election agency (the BPNAA) as the authority to interpret the election rules, somewhat monopolizing judicial, legislative and administrative powers. In the awkward predicament where there was no independent and complete legal procedure for election lawsuits and the intendants generally supervised courts of first instance, the *Dali Yuan* settled for the civil lawsuits, clarified the electoral rules, and regulated litigation by publishing resumes of its decisions of specific cases and abstract judicial interpretation. In order to achieve recusal of the county magistrates, the *Dali Yuan* adopted cross-regional jurisdiction and designated jurisdiction. Under the political pressure to conclude a case rapidly, it initiated procedures for appeal and retrial to ensure the rights of the parties and fair and valid elections so that the national electoral system could be unified.

Two examples here show that the *Dali Yuan* legislated from the bench in election lawsuits.

(1) Literacy qualification of voters and candidates

Although the electorate expanded notably in the national and local assembly elections in the early ROC, there were property or literacy restrictions on voters and candidates. For example, Article 6 of *Act on the Election of Representatives* and Article 5 of *Act on the Election of Members of the Provincial Assembly*, both enacted in 1912, forbid "the illiterate to vote and stand for election" (Jiangsu Civic Election Watchdog, 1921,

election and its resolution because obstruction of election in the *Criminal Law* is limited to the election of national and regional assemblymen (speakers' fraudulent election is not obstruction of election in the criminal law). This interpretation is binding except the exception stipulated in Article 35 of the *Organic Law of the Judiciary*" (Guo, 2014, p. 790).

pp. 26–27, 74).[33] However, a controversy arose over who the "illiterate" meant so that the *Dali Yuan* further defined the word through its ruling: "The illiterate refer not to those who do not know B from a battledore, but to those who do not understand commonly used written language. Therefore, the legally stipulated illiterate mean those who can merely write their names and household information and read petitions and terms without being able to understand the regularly used text. They shall not have the right to vote and run for the provincial assembly" (Decision No. 1212 of 1918) (Guo, 2013, p. 202).

(2) Legal consequences of voter impersonation

In the real election, voter impersonations occurred from time to time, and the election watchdogs were unable to identify all of them one by one. However, a lawsuit would be lodged over validity of the election when the fraud was discovered. The *Dali Yuan* ruled that the election would be void only when the illegal ballots were numerous enough to overturn the results or the election had proved to be manipulated. Firstly, the legal ballots and the election won with sufficient votes could not be ruled invalid when the illegal ballots and abstentions had no effect on the results: "When the illegal votes are removed, and the winner's votes and abstentions cannot undermine the outcome, the legally cast ballots and the election won with enough votes shall not be nullified because of a single illegal vote or abstention" (Decision No. 61 of 1922) (Guo, 2013, p. 204). Secondly, "in case of voter impersonation, the election shall be valid when the winner's verified votes minus the invalid ones add up to the stipulated number" (Interpretation No. 1570) (Guo, 2014, p. 1150). "The election shall not be undermined if the election officials have not connived in the voter impersonation before the impersonator's detention" (Decision No. 889 of 1918) (Guo, 2013, p. 198). Thirdly, "impersonation verified by the signatures on the register, voting, ballots in the name of the absent voters" should not lead to a simple assumption that the fraudulent election nullified the results because "the validity depends on whether the watchdogs are aware of and have suppressed the impersonation" (Interpretation No. 1767) (Guo, 2014, p. 1256).

3. Legislating peak from the bench: decision No. 889 of 1918 comprising multiple precedents

So many questions arose in election events that the *Dali Yuan* had to institute multiple abstract rules (resumes) from its decision on a specific case, making a spectacle of "one decision with multiple precedents". As mentioned earlier, it abstracted 72 resumes from its 32 decisions on election lawsuits, and 10 of them contributed 40 resumes in total. The *Dali Yuan*'s legislating from the bench peaked in Decision No. 889 of 1918 which was generalized into 19 resumes supplementing the *Act on the Election of Senators*, the *Act on the Election of Representatives*, and other laws, and specifically involving identification of the defendants in lawsuits over an election's validity, limitation of actions relating to the primary election, whether the election

[33] Article 5 of *Act on the Election of Representatives* even required candidates for representatives in Mongolia, Tibet, and Qinghai to be "fluent in Chinese" in addition to other stipulated qualifications.

watchdogs could get elected, omissions on the transcribed electoral roll, legality of multiple ballot boxes, various criteria for invalidity of various elections, and many other aspects. In addition to those quoted before, this decision included criteria for illegitimate elections: "The election shall be illegitimate when fraudulent practices result from the election official's initiative or indifference"; "Improper decisions on voter eligibility cannot be viewed as fraud"; "voters' ineligibility shall not invalidate election as long as it does not undermine the outcome"; "Decisions on voter eligibility unpublished in newspaper shall not make elections illegitimate"; "Rare presence of election watchdogs shall not nullify elections" (Guo, 2013, pp. 191–192, 197–199).

The *Dali Yuan* made such a remarkable contribution to election litigation as to be viewed as an exception in the early ROC under the Beijing Government characterized by frequent dissolution of the Parliament, constant cabinet reshuffles, seriously defective election laws, severe shortage of election experience, and recurrent vote-buying scandals.

13.3.2 Administrative Trials and Judicial Practices of the Civil Service Protection System Nie (2017)

i. Overview

The early ROC adopted the Western system protecting the independence and position of the civil servants, but their professionalism and stability were severely threatened by political turmoil, crude legislation, naive party politics and tyrannical warlords. Built on a fragile jurisprudential foundation, the *Pingzheng Yuan* surprisingly located itself at the center of the political storm by proactively accepting administrative lawsuits involving civil service protection, resolutely declaring the major reshuffles of the Ministry of Internal Affairs and the Ministry of Communications illegal, and amending or revoking their penalties. Therefore, the *Pingzheng Yuan* established its jurisdiction politically and legally through the precedents (instead of legislation) and eliminated the potential risks of the spoils system in the first place.

In judicial practice, the *Pingzheng Yuan* heard administrative disputes both within the executive organs and between the executive and its counterparts, including major sanctions against civil servants (such as demotion, suspension, removal, etc.) as well as disputes over authority among administrative institutions (the *Pingzheng Yuan* did not usually hear disputes over minor disciplinary sanctions, such as salary reductions and reprimands). In the disciplinary actions against civil servants, the majority of cases were decided by the Disciplinary Commission for Senior Civil Servants and the Disciplinary Commission for General Civil Servants,[34] but a few particularly controversial cases would be remitted to and heard by the *Pingzheng Yuan*.

[34] Statistics made from 1914 through 1916 show that the Disciplinary Commission for Senior Civil Servants alone made decisions on 100–200 cases, half of them relating to removal or demotion, with merely 5% free from any sanction or punishments (Chen, 2009, p. 38).

The statistics compiled by scholars shows that the *Pingzheng Yuan* made decisions on 187 administrative lawsuits during the 14 years from 1915 to 1928 with 22 or 12% of the total relating to qualifications, which was not a small percentage.[35] The author's careful examination of the 22 qualification lawsuits reveals that 13 concerned protection of public officials' positions (the rest were disputes of students and monks), 3 had their original punishments amended, 7 had their original sanctions lifted (including the Ministry of Justice's sanction against a Chief Justice), and 3 upheld the decision (including the sanction against a vice speaker of a county assembly, a county commissioner appointed by a provincial Bureau of Opium Prohibition, and a speaker at a county literacy center) (Huang, 2007, pp. 901–1001). Considering that none of the parties who had their decisions upheld were civil servants (or they had been removed from office), 10 cases in total concerned protection of positions of civil servants (including one judge), 7 or 70% of them had the original punishment, and 3 or 30% had their punishments amended so that not a single case relating to civil servants had its decision upheld. Of the 187 cases, 54% had their decision upheld; 24%, cancelled; and 22%, amended (Huang, 2011, pp. 384–85). Therefore, the *Pingzheng Yuan* was very aggressive in its rulings on lawsuits over civil servants' qualifications.

Generally speaking, the *Pingzheng Yuan* heard and decided on merely a few cases with less than one case annually involving protection of civil servants, but by examining the substantive and procedural justice of typical civil servant disciplinary sanctions, it safeguarded the legitimate rights and interests of civil servants and established the standards of civil service protection through its decisions, closing the loopholes in legislation. Compared with the quasi-judicial body, the Disciplinary Commissions for Civil Servants that made numerous disciplinary decisions, the *Pingzheng Yuan* made just a few critical rulings, providing a role model for administrative hearings in a certain sense and playing an incomparable role in the enforcement of the entire civil service protection system.

ii. Cases

1. The reshuffle of the Ministry of Internal Affairs (MIA) and the institution of the *Pingzheng Yuan*'s jurisdiction

In 1916, Yuan Shih-k'ai failed to restore the monarchy and died. After "the Republic was rebuilt", Sun Hongyi, who had proactively opposed Yuan's restoration, was appointed Minister of the MIA. Believing the MIA officials to have been particularly keen on Yuan's Restoration Ceremony under the then MIA minister of Zhu Qiqian (who had also headed the Preparatory Office of Yuan Shih-k'ai's coronation ceremony), Sun decided to rectify the MIA and clean up those "royalists". On September 8th, 1916, Sun issued a ministerial order to suspend 64 officials who had participated in the Restoration of the monarchy, which was called the MIA Reshuffle.

Despite the pressure from both the assemblymen's questioning and the Pingzheng Yuan's decision to hear the case, Sun Hongyi mounted a robust defense, challenging

[35] The statistics here are merely those cases the *Pingzheng Yuan* heard and decided upon, and do not include the majority of cases the *Pingzheng Yuan* rejected (Huang, 2011, pp. 382–383).

the jurisdiction of the *Pingzheng Yuan*. First, "the *Pingzheng Yuan* shall only accept lawsuits between civilians and officials instead of those between staff members and their leaders in the government" so that the removed officials were not qualified entities in the administrative litigation. Secondly, the *Pingzheng Yuan*, a political institution Yuan Shih-k'ai left, "would not be constitutionally necessary, and the litigation of the kind would naturally perish with the fundamentally shaken court". It was noteworthy that Sun Hongyi did not even submit a formal defense at the request of the *Pingzheng Yuan*. Instead, he "replied in the inter-departmental communications", which showed Sun's challenge to the jurisdiction of the Pingzheng Yuan (Zhang, 2014).

After a plenary session, the *Pingzheng Yuan* agreed that the administrative lawsuit should protect the rights of not only civilians but also officials except for the explicitly stipulated exceptions, and therefore, the suspended officials had the right to appeal to the *Pingzheng Yuan*. In its decision, the *Pingzheng Yuan* pounced upon the procedural defect, the MIA's refusal to file a response, to state that "the defendant has not filed a formal answer so far to the plaintiff's complaint sent by this court, and shall be deemed to have relinquished the right to reply therein". It determined that the MIA had violated the law and exceeded its authority ("Contempt of the President") and its disciplinary measures should be cancelled. The *Pingzheng Yuan* declared that "the general administrative jurisprudence invests the minister with the supervisory power over his staff members for capability assessment, which is not prohibited. However, definite and legitimate reasons need to be given when it is considered necessary to dismiss a member. Removal of the senior officials needs to be submitted to the President for approval; even the dismissal of junior officials shall not take effect without legitimate reasons" (Huang, 2007, p. 920).

Sun Hongyi refused to comply with the decision of the *Pingzheng Yuan*. President Li Yuanhong, Premier Duan Qirui, and several members of the Parliament were involved in this political dilemma, which ended up with the removal of the MIA Minister Sun Hongyi, along with the resignation of Secretary General of the State Council Xu Shizheng and Secretary General of the President's Office Ding Shiyi (of the same faction as Sun Hongyi) (Ding, 2013, pp. 319–322). Objectively speaking, the final result of the political struggle established the Pingzheng Yuan's authority and jurisdiction so that no one challenged the court's jurisdiction since then.

2. Xu's removal from office and the substantive review of the improper disciplinary sanction

The plaintiff, Xu, a middle-ranking official at the Ministry of Transport, was "removed from his post by order of the Ministry" without any reason and told to "await another appointment". After investigation, the *Pingzheng Yuan* determined that "the dismissal was legally groundless and unfair", and that "no offer was made a year after the removal, and the Ministry's 'another appointment' was merely a false promise". Therefore, the punishment "should be cancelled" (Huang, 2007, pp. 991–994). The decision showed that the *Pingzheng Yuan* not only reviewed substantive issues, but also stressed procedural justice in handing down sanctions.

3. Zhou Shuren's complaint against the Ministry of Education (MOE) and the judicial guarantee of fair disciplinary procedures

The complaint Zhou Shuren (Lu Xun) lodged against the Ministry of Education was sensational in 1926 when he was Deputy Director of an MOE department, and concurrently instructor at the National Women's Normal University. As an MOE official, Lu was alleged to "have colluded with the students" "against the MOE order" so that Zhang Shizhao, the MOE Minister, submitted immediately for his removal from his office. Concurrently minister of the Ministry of Justice, Zhang was defended by Premier Duan Qirui. Lu, as an MOE official openly challenging the MOE administrative order, violated the principle of civil service neutrality and should be punished according to law. However, Lu seized on the inconsistency of his dismissal with the legal procedures, and eventually won the administrative lawsuit (Huang, 2011, p. 385). The *Pingzheng Yuan* ruled that "The defendant failed to provide evidence for the plaintiff's defiance against the MOE order to shut down the National Women's Normal University where the plaintiff concurrently held a teaching post. Even if the charge had been true, it was legal for him to have been delivered to the Disciplinary Commission for Civil Servants for sanction according to the civil service code. The defendant's hasty request for his removal proves inconsistent with the current statutory procedures." The defendant argued that "it had intended to follow legal procedures to have the plaintiff punished, but the case was so gross as to inspire numerous copycats if no administrative penalty was imposed". However, the *Pingzheng Yuan* believed that "it would have been an adequate warning if the plaintiff, suspected of defiance against the MOE order, had been suspended from office or taken legally to the commission for disciplinary sanction. It's unnecessary to worry about potential copycats and impose unusual sanctions so swiftly". Therefore, it was ruled that "the plaintiff's removal the defendant requested is illegal and should be cancelled" (Huang, 2007, pp. 995–998).

When reviewing such typical cases, the *Pingzheng Yuan* focused on the procedural flaws of the sanctioning authority, ignoring whether the sanction was substantively justified. Objectively speaking, the adherence to the due disciplinary procedures in trials helped to put government agencies on the legal track in disciplining civil servants and to establish the authority of the Disciplinary Commission for Civil Servants.

References

Alford, W. P. (1984). Of arsenic and old laws: Looking anew at criminal justice in late imperial China. *California Law Review, 72*(6), 1180–1256.

Chen, G. (2009). *Yuanshikai zhengfu shiqi de wenguan chengjie zhidu yanjiu (1912—1916)* [A study of the disciplinary system for civil servants under the Yuan Shih-k'ai-led government, 1914–1916] [Unpublished master's thesis]. Henan University.

Ch'ien, T. (1950). *The government and politics of China.* Harvard University Press.

Ding, Z. (2013). *Beiyang junfa shihua* [A story of the warlords under the Beiyang Government] (Vol. 2). The Commercial Press.
Dezong jinghuangdi shilu [Veritable Records of Emperor Dezong] (8). (1987). In *Qing shilu* [Veritable records of the Qing Dynasty] (Vol. 59). Zhonghua Book Company.
Fu xuantong zhengji [Appended Political Records in the Xuantong Period] (28). (1987). In *Qing shilu* [Veritable Records of the Qing Dynasty] (Vol. 60). Zhonghua Book Company.
Gao, Y. (1936). Xianfa shang jianchaquan de wenti [Issues on the constitutional power of supervision]. In Z. Yu (Ed.) & J. Wu (Pr.), *Xianfa wenxuan* [Selected essays on constitution] (pp. 48–55). Shanghai Law Editing and Translating Press.
Guo, W. (Ed.). (1931a). *Daliyuan panjueli quanshu* [Full text of rulings of the Supreme Court]. Huiwentang Xinji Books.
Guo, W. (Ed.). (1931b). *Daliyuan jieshili quanwen* [Full text of interpretations of the Supreme Court]. Huiwentang Xinji Books.
Guo, W. (Ed.). (2013). *Daliyuan panjueli quanshu* [Complete decisions of the Dali Yuan]. China University of Political Science and Law Press.
Guo, W. (Ed.). (2014). *Minguo daliyuan jieshili quanwen* [Full text of interpretations of the Dali Yuan in the Republic of China]. China University of Political Science and Law Press.
Han, T. (2012). *Wanqing daliyuan: zhongguo zuizao de zuigao fayuan* [The court of judicial review: The Supreme Court in the late Qing Dynasty]. Law Press.
Han, X. (2003). *Sifa duli yu jindai zhongguo* [Judicial independence and modern China]. Tsinghua University Press.
Huang, Y. (1993). Zhongguo fazhishi kecheng jiegou de huigu ji xiankuang [A review of the course of Chinese legal history]. In Y. Huang, et al. (Eds.). *Zhongguo fazhishi kecheng jiaoxue yantaohui lunwenji* [Collected essays on the course of Chinese legal history] (pp. 1–34). Chengchi University Press.
Huang, Y. (2007). *Pingzhengyuan caipan lucun* [Records of the administrative judgments of the Pingzheng Yuan]. Wu-Nan Book Inc.
Huang, Y. (2000). *Mingchu falü bianqian yu caipan* [Judgment and change in law of the early Republic of China]. Chengchi University Press.
Huang, Y. (2011). *Mingchu daliyuan yu caipan* [The Supreme Court and its judgments in the early Republic of China]. Angle Publishing Co. Ltd.
Jackson, V. C., & Tushnet, M. V. (2006). *Comparative constitutional law* (2nd ed.). Foundation Press.
Jiang, Z. (2010). *Zhongguo falv kanbujian zhongguo: juzheng sifa shiqi (1932–1948) yanjiu* [China law "can't see China": Ju Zheng as President of the Judicial Yuan (1932–1948)]. Tsinghua University Press.
Jiangsu Civic Election Watchdog. (Ed.). (1921). *Xuanju fagui* [Electoral regulations]. Zhonghua Book Company.
Li, G. (2000). *Shen Jiaben zhuan* [Life of Shen Jiaben]. Law Press.
Li, Q. (2004). *Wanqing geji shenpanting yanjiu* [Research on courts at all levels in the late Qing Dynasty]. Peking University Press.
Li, Q. (2005). Minchun fupan wenti kaocha [An examination of the trial of capital cases]. *Qinghua faxue* [Tsinghua University Law Journal], (5), 187–203.
Li, X. (1998). Shixian jiyao [Minutes of constitutional interpretation]. In the Judicial Yuan (Ed.), *Sifayuan dafaguan shixian wushi zhounian jinian wenji* [Essays in honor of the fiftieth anniversary of the Supreme Court Grand Justices' constitutional interpretation] (pp. 707–714). The Judicial Yuan. For internal circulation.
Liu, H. (1990). *Woguo xuanju bamian susong zhidu* [Election and removal litigation in the Republic of China]. Wu-Nan Book Inc.
Lu, J. (2004). *Minchu lisi wenti de falv yu caipan: yi daliyuan minshi caipan wei zhongxin* [Law and adjudication over inheritance in the early Republic of China: A study of the civil rulings of the Dali Yuan]. Peking University Press.

Luo, Z. (1974). *Jindai zhongguo fazhi yanbian yanjiu* [History of the legal system in modern China]. Cheng Chung Book Co., Ltd.
Na. S. (2004a). *Zhongguo shenpan zhidu shi* [History of Chinese trial system]. Zhengdian Publishing Co., Ltd.
Na, S. (2004b). *Mingdai zhongyang sifa shenpan zhidu* [The central legal institutions in the Ming Dynasty].
Na, S. (2004c). *Qingdai zhongyang sifa shenpan zhidu* [The central legal institutions in the Qing Dynasty]. Beijing University Press.
Nie, X. (2007). Minguo sifayuan: jindai zuigao sifa jiguan de xin fanshi [The Judicial Yuan in the Republic of China: A new model of the supreme judicial organ in modern China]. *Zhongguo shehui kexue* [China Social Sciences], (6), 143–157.
Nie, X. (2017). Pingzhengyuan caipan yu jindai zhongguo wenguan baozhang zhidu de sifa shijian [The decisions of the *Pingzheng Yuan* and the judicial practices of the civil service protection system]. *Huadong zhengfa daxue xuebao* [Journal of East China University of Political Science and Law], (2), 174–181.
Nie, X. (2018). Minchu xuanju susong zhong de faguan zaofa [The judicial lawmaking in the election litigation in the early years of the Republic of China]. *Zhongwai faxue* [Peking University Law Journal], (3), 744–762.
Qian, D., Sa, S., Yang, H., et al. (2008). *Minguo zhengzhishi* [History of the political system of the Republic of China] (Vol. 2). Shanghai People's Publishing House.
Qin, Z. (1942). *Fayuan zuzhifa* [The Organic Law of the Court]. China University Lectures.
Sa, M. (1993). *Zhongguo xianfa xinlun* [A new theory on the Constitution of the Republic of China]. San Min Book Co., Ltd.
Sa, M. (1998). *Zhongguo shehui zhengzhishi* [A socio-political history of China] (Vol. 1). San Min Book Co., Ltd.
Su, Y. (2002). *Zouru xinshiji de xianzheng zhuyi* [Constitutionalism: Towards the new century]. Angle Publishing Co. Ltd.
The Beijing Government of the Republic of China. (1922). *Xiuding sifa ligui* [Amended judicial regulations]. The Ministry of Justice.
The Records Compilation Board of the Control Yuan. (1981). *Guomin zhengfu jianchayuan shilu* [Veritable records of the Control Yuan of the National Government]. The Control Yuan. For internal circulation.
The Records Compilation Board of the Judicial Yuan. (1982). *Sifayuan shishi jiyao* [Veritable records of the Judicial Yuan of the National Government]. The Judicial Yuan.
Wang, Y. (1936). *Ershiwu nian lai zhi sifa xingzheng* [Judicial administration in the last twenty-five years]. The Judicial Administration.
Weng, Y. (1994). *Fazhi guojia zhi xingzheng yu sifa* [The administration and the judiciary in rule-of-law countries]. Angle Publishing Co. Ltd.
Xia, X., & Hu, X. (Eds.). (2004). *Jindai zhongguo xianzheng lichen: shiliao huicui* [The constitutional course in modern China: A collection of historical materials]. China University of Political Science and Law Press.
Xie, G. (1948). *Zhanshi sifa jiyao* [Records of the wartime judicature]. The Judicial Administration.
Xie, Z. (2000). *Zhonghua minguo lifa shi* [The legislative history of the Republic of China] (Vol. 2). China University of Political Science and Law Press.
Xu, X. (2008). *Xiandaixing de monan: ershi shiji chuqi zhongguo sifa gaige (1901–1937)* [Trial of modernity: Judicial reform in early-twentieth-century China, 1901–1937]. Stanford University Press.
Yang, H. (2014). *Minguo choubei guohui shiwuju yanjiu* [A study of the Bureau of Preparatory Parliament Affairs] [Unpublished master's thesis]. Shaanxi Normal University.
Ye, L. (2015). *Hunan jindai xuanjushi, 1908–1948* [Modern history of elections in Hunan province, 1908–1948]. Hunan People's Publishing House.

Young, E. P. (2008). Politics in the aftermath of revolution: The era of Yuan Shih-k'ai, 1912–16. In J. K. Fairbank (Ed.), *The Cambridge history of China: Republican China 1929–1949* (6th ed., Part 1, pp. 209–255). Cambridge University Press.

Zhang, C. (2007). *Buyuan zhi zheng: wanqing sifa gaige de jiaocha lukou* [The Ministry-Court Quarrel: Judicial reform at a crossroads in the late Qing Dynasty]. Peking University Press.

Zhang, C. (2014). Zhengzhi yu falv de hudong: sunhongyi yu 1916 nian pingzhengyuan shouli de neiwubu tingzhi an [Interaction between politics and law: On the case of the Ministry of Internal Affairs' suspension accepted by the *Pingzheng Yuan* in 1916]. Beijing shehui kexue [Social Sciences of Beijing], (8), 118–128.

Zhang, P. (2008). *Zhongguo minzhu zhengzhi de kunjing 1909–1949: wanqing yilai lijie guohui xuanju shulun* [The dilemma of Chinese democracy, 1909–1949: Legislatures and elections since the late Qing Dynasty]. Jilin Publishing Group Co., Ltd.

Zhang, R. (2005). *Sifa fubai yu shehui shikong* [Judicial corruption and social control, 1928–1949]. Social Sciences Academic Press.

Zhang. S. (1998). Minguo chuqi de daliyuan: zuigao sifa jiguan jianxing minshi lifa zhineng [The *Dali Yuan* in the early Republic of China: The supreme judicial organ with civil legislative functions]. *Zhengfa luntan* [Tribune of Political Science and Law], (6), 118–123.

Zhang, S., & Li, Q. (2004). Zhongguo jindai sifa gaige: cong siji sanshen dao sanji sanshen [Judicial reform of modern China: From the four-level and three-instance system to the three-level and three-instance system]. *Zhengfa luntan* [Tribune of Political Science and Law], (5), 120–126.

The Nanjing Provisional Government. (2004). *The Nanjing Provisional Government Gazette* (34).

Zhao, X. (Ed.). (2006). *Zhongguo fazhi shi yuanli yu anli jiaocheng* [History of Chinese legal institutions: Principles and cases]. China Renmin University Press.

Zheng, B. (1936). *Fayuan zuzhifa shiyi* [An interpretation of the Organic Act of the Court]. Huiwentang Xinji Books.

Zheng, Q. (1988). *Qingdai sifa shenpan zhidu yanjiu* [A study of the judicial system in the Qing Dynasty]. Hunan Education Publishing House.

Zhou, B. (2006). *Minguo chunian qiyue ziyou gainian de dansheng: yi daliyuan de yanshuo shijian wei zhongxin* [The birth of freedom of contract in the early Republic of China: Theory and practice of the Dali Yuan]. Peking University Press.

Zhu, S. (1958). *Guangxuchao donghua lu* [Official documents of the reign of Guangxu] (August 1902). Zhonghua Book Company.

Glossary

English Chinese (pinyin)

Academy of Scholarly Worthies 集贤院 jixian yuan
Accessory Clerk 佐史 zuoshi
Adjutants of Law Section 法曹参军 facao canjun
Administration Hall 政事堂 zhengshi tang
Administrative Consultant 参知机务 canzhi jiwu
Administrator for Public Order 司理参军 sili canjun
Administrator of the Judicial Control Office 知院事 zhiyuanshi
Advisory Council 参政院 canzheng yuan
Aide in the Prime Minister's Office 长史 zhangshi
Annual Tribute Student 岁贡 suigong
Apprentice Examination (District Examination) 县试 xianshi
Assessment Department 考课院 kaoke yuan
Assistant County Magistrate 县丞 xian cheng
Assistant Department Magistrate (Qing) 州判 (清) zhoupan (Qing)
Assistant Director 佥都御史 qiandu yushi
Assistant Director of Studies 训导 xundao
Assistant Examiner 同考 tongkao
Assistant Magistrate 抚民通判 fumin tongpan
Assistant Prefect 理事厅员 lishiting yuan
Attendant Gentlemen 尚书郎 shangshulang
Auditing Department 审官院 shenguan yuan
Autumn Examinations 秋闱 qiuwei
Bachelor 庶吉士 shujishi
Benevolent Official 循吏 xunli
Branch Ministry of Military Affairs 行枢密院 xingshumi yuan
Branch Ministry of Supervision 行御史台 xingyushi tai
Brocade Guards 锦衣卫 jinyiwei
Bureau of Evaluations 考功司 (考功清吏司) kaogong si (kaogong qingli si)
Bureau of Frontier Control 司门 simen

X. Nie, *The History of Government and Public Law in China*,
https://doi.org/10.1007/978-981-97-6063-3

Bureau of General Account 度支司/部 duzhi si/bu
Bureau of Military Affairs 枢密院 shumi yuan
Bureau of Supervision 察院 chayuan
Case Reviewer 评事 pingshi
Case Reviewer of the Two Departments of the Court of Judicial Review 大理寺左右寺官 dalisi zuoyou siguan
Cavalier Attendants-in-Ordinary 散骑常侍 sanji changshi
Censorate/the Imperial Censorate 御史台 yushi tai
Censorate of Five Capital Wards 五城察院 wucheng chayuan
Censor-General 都肃政史 du shuzhengshi
Censor-in-Chief 都御史 duyushi/御史丞 yushicheng/ 御史大夫 yushi daifu
Censors/Imperial Censor 御史 yushi
Central Commissioner 节度使 jiedushi
Centralized Administration 郡县制 junxianzhi
Ceremonial Office 典礼院 dianli yuan
Chamberlain for Attendants 郎中令 langzhongling/光禄勋 guanglu xun
Chamberlain for Law Enforcement 廷尉 (汉) tingwei (Han Dynasty)
Chancellery 门下省 menxia sheng
Chief Minister of the Court of Judicial Review 大理寺卿 (正卿) dalisi qing (zhengqing)
Chief Receptionist 谒者令 yezhe ling
Chief Surveillance Bureau (Censorate) 都察院 ducha yuan
Circuit (Province) 道 dao
Circuit (Provincial) Censor 道御史 daoyushi
Circuit Administrative Office 道署 daoshu
Circuit Intendant 道员 daoyuan
Clerk of the Prime Minister 丞相史 chengxiangshi
Clerks 令吏 lingli/书吏 shuli
Commander of a Remote Area 校尉 jiaowei
Commander of Bodyguard 卫尉 weiwei
Commander of Waterways 水衡都尉 shuiheng duwei
Commander-General 都统 dutong
Commanderies and Counties 郡县 junxian
Commanderies and Princedoms 郡国 junguo
Commander-in-Chief 都督 dudu/ 总兵 zongbing
Commander-in-ordinary 中尉 zhongwei
Commandery 郡 jun
Commandery Governor 郡国守相 junguo shouxiang/郡守 junshou
Elevation on recommendation/ commandery quota system 察举 chaju
Commission Examination 院试 yuanshi
Commission for Army Reorganization 练兵处 lianbingchu
Commission for Buddhist and Tibetan Affairs/Supreme Control Commission 宣政院 (元) xuanzheng yuan (Yuan Dynasty)
Commission for Studying Constitutional Government 宪政编查馆 xiangzheng biancha guan

Commissioner for Judicial Affairs 提法使 tifa shi
Commissioner for Salt and Iron 盐铁使 yantie shi
Commissioner of the Office of Transmission 通政使 tongzheng shi
Commissioner of Waterways 都水使 dushui shi
Company Commander 佐领 zuoling
Compilation Commission of Official System 编制馆 bianzhi guan
Confucian Apprentice 童生 tongsheng
Controllers-General 通判 tongpan
Cooption Commission 招讨使 zhaotao shi
County Commander 县尉 xianwei
County Magistrate 县令 xianling
Courier Superintendent 提塘官 titang guan
Court Architect 将作大匠 jiangzuo dajiang
Court Gentlemen 郎官 langguan
Court of Imperial Entertainments 光禄寺 guanglu si
Court of Imperial Sacrifices 太常寺 taichang si
Court of Judicial Review 大理寺 dali si
Court of Review 比部 bibu
Court of State Ceremonial 鸿胪寺 honglu si
Court of the Imperial Clan 宗人府 zongren fu
Court of the Imperial Stud 太仆寺 taipu si
Criminal Administration Bureau 都官(司) duguan(si)
Cultivated Talent 秀才 xiucai
Deliberative Council 议政王大臣会议 yizhengwang dachen huiyi
Deliberative Office 议政衙门 yizheng yamen
Department for Ethnic Affairs 理藩院 lifan yuan
Department Magistrate/Prefect 知州 zhizhou
Department of State Affairs 尚书省 shangshu sheng
Department of the Grand Astrologer 太史寮 taishi liao
Depots and Guards 厂卫 changwei
Deputy Chief Secretary 中书侍郎 zhongshu shilang
Deputy Director 仆射 puye
Deputy Minister of Review 给事黄门侍郎 jishi huangmen shilang
Detached Subprefecture 厅 ting
Directly Administered Subprefecture 直隶厅 zhiliting
Director for Compilation of the National History 监修国史 jianxiu guoshi
Director of Markets 司市 sishi
Director of Studies/Instructor 学正 xuezheng/教谕 jiaoyu
Director of the Academy 山长 shanzhang
Director of the Archives Secretariat 秘书令 mishu ling
Director of the Central Secretariat 中书令 zhongshu ling
Director of Uprightness 司直 sizhi
Directorate of Astronomy 司天监 sitian jian
Directorate of Education 国子监 guozi jian/ 国子寺 guozi si
Director-General of Grain Transport 漕运总督 caoyun zongdu

Director-General of Waterworks 河道总督 hedao zongdu
District Magistrate 知县 zhixian
Divination 卜筮 bushi
Drafters in the Secretariat 舍人 sheren
Eastern Depot 东厂 dongchang
Education Commissioner 学政 xuezheng
Enlistment and Recommendation 辟举 biju
Equal Tax Law 方田均税法 fangtian jushui fa
Equal-land System 均田制 juntian zhi
Essay Examiner 房师 fangshi
Evaluation Office 考课院 kaoke yuan
Examination about Strategy 策试 ceshi
Examination Overseer 监试 jiangshi
Examinations Held on Imperial Order 制举 zhiju
Examiner 座师 zuoshi
Examining Editor 检讨 jiantao
Exhorter 正言 zhengyan
Final Court Examination 朝考 chaokao
Financial Supervisor 转运使 zhuanyun shi
Fourth-rank officials and above of the Palace Secretariat and the Chancellery 中书、门下四品以上 zhongshu menxia sipin yishang
Full-time Subordinate Judicial Officials 决曹掾 juecaoyuan
Functioning Official 职事官 zhishi guan
General Governor 总督 zongdu
Gentry Politics 门阀政治 menfa zhengzhi
Government Office 衙门 yamen
Government Student 生员 shengyuan
Governor of a Circuit 道尹 daoyin
Governor of a Commandery 郡守 junshou
Governor of Subprefectures and Counties 州县官 zhouxian guan
Governors and Magistrates 守令 shouling
Governors-General and Governors 督抚 dufu
Grain Intendant 督粮道 duliang dao
Grand Astrologer 太史 taishi
Grand Commander 大司马 dasima
Grand Council 军机处 junjichu
Grand Councilor 军机大臣 junji dachen
Grand Guardian 太保 taibao
Grand Master 大夫 dafu
Grand Master of Remonstrance 谏议大夫 jianyi dafu
Grand Minister of the Deliberative Council 议政王大臣 yizhengwang dachen
Grand Preceptor 太师 taishi
Grand Scholar of the Jixian Hall 集贤殿大学士 jixiantian daxueshi
Grand Scholar of the Longtu Pavilion 龙图阁大学士 longtuge daxueshi
Grand Scholar of the Zhaowen Pavilion 昭文馆大学士 zhaowenguan daxueshi

Grand Scholar 大学士 daxueshi
Grand Secretariat 内阁 neige
Grand Secretary 内阁大学士 neige daxueshi
Grand Secretary of the Hall of Literary Profundity 文渊阁大学士 wenyuange daxueshi
Grand Steward 太宰 taizai
Guanglu Grand Master 光禄大夫 guanglu dafu
Hanlin Scholar 翰林学士 hanlin xueshi
Head of Hanlin Academy 翰林(明朝) hanlin (Ming Dynasty)
Headman of a town or a village 乡官/里正 xiangguan/lizheng
Headquarters Bureau 台院 Taiyuan/台 tai
Heir Apparent 詹事 zhanshi
High Officials in Charge of Military Finance 办理军需大臣 banli junxu dachen
High Officials Regularly Reporting to the Emperor 朝觐官 chaojin guan
High-Ranking Minister 公卿 gongqing
Household Administration of the Heir Apparent 詹事府 zhanshi fu
Household Service for the Empress 中政院 zhongzheng yuan
Imperial Academy 翰林院 hanlin yuan
Imperial Charioteer 太仆 taipu
Imperial Commissioner 钦差大臣 qingchai dachen
Imperial Gateman 郎中 langzhong
Imperial Household Department 内务府 neiwu fu
Imperial Recruitment 征辟 zhengbi
Imperial Secretariat 尚书台 shangshu tai
Independent Departments/Independent Sub-prefecture/Directly Administrated Prefecture 直隶州 zhili zhou
Industrial Intendant 劝业道 quanye dao
Infantry Brigade Commander 步军统领 bujun tongling
Inner Settlement/Metropolitan Revision (Evaluation of Metropolitan Officials) 内计/京察 neiji/jingcha
Intendant of the Imperial Secretariat 录尚书事 lushangshu shi
Interim Council 总理事务王大臣 zongli shiwuwang dachen
Investigating Censor 监察御史 jiancha yushi
Investigation Commission 廉访司 lianfang shi
Joint Hearing by the Nine Ministers 九卿圆审 jiuqing yuanshen
Judicial Assistant Prefect 理事同知 lishi tongzhi
Judicial Assistant or Archivist 司法佐/史 sifa zuo/shi
Judicial Control Office 审刑院 shenxing yuan
Judicial Departmental Administrator 理事通判 lishi tongpan
Judicial Section 决曹 juecao
Judicial Supervisor 提点刑狱佥事 tidian xingyu qianshi/提刑按察使 tixing ancha shi
Junior Clerk of the Prime Minister 丞相少史 chengxiang shaoshi
Junior Compiler of the Hanlin Academy 翰林院编修 hanlinyuan bianxiu
Junior Guardian 少保 shaobao

Junior Mentor 少傅 shaofu
Junior Preceptor 少师 shaoshi
Junior Steward 小宰 xiaozai
Jurisdictional Texts 爰书 yuanshu
Land System of the Heavenly Dynasty 天朝田亩制度 tianchao tianmu zhidu
Law on Labor Recruitment 募役法 muyifa
Lecturer 教谕 jiaoyu
Left and Right Aides 左右正 zuoyou zheng
Left and Right Judges 左右平 zuoyou ping
Left and Right Police Officers 左右监 zuoyou jian
Left Bureau of the Court of Judicial Review 左断刑 zuoduanxing
Left Censor-in-Chief of the Censorate 左都御史 zuo duyushi
Left or Right Censor-in-Chief 左右都御史 zuoyou duyushi
Left Scribe/Historiographer 左史 zuoshi
Local Supervisor 巡察使 xuncha shi
Magistrate 县知事 xian zhishi
Magistrate of an Independent Subprefecture 直隶厅抚民同知 zhiliting fumin tongzhi
Managers of Governmental Affairs 平章政事 pingzhang zhengshi
Managing Prefect 知府事 zhifu shi/知州事 zhizhou shi
Merit Land System 名田制 mingtian zhi
Metropolitan Commandant 司隶校尉 sili jiaowei
Metropolitan Superintendent 内史 neishi
Military Supervisor 安抚使 anfu shi/经略安抚使 jinglue anfu shi
Military Zones 方镇 fangzhen
Minister 卿 qing
Minister/Imperial Secretaries/Department Directors 尚书 shangshu
Minister of Defense 太尉 taiwei
Minister of Justice 刑部尚书 xingbu shangshu
Minister of Personnel 吏部尚书 libu shangshu
Minister of State 冢宰 zhongzai
Minister of the Court of Judicial Review 大理卿 dali qing
Ministerial Department 卿事寮 qingshi liao
Ministers of Criminal Administration 都官尚书 duguan shangshu
Ministries and the Censorate 部院 buyuan
Ministry of Education 学部 xuebu
Ministry of Justice 法部 fabu
Ministry of Justice 刑部 xingbu
Ministry of Personnel (Personnel Department) 吏部 libu
Ministry of Police 巡警部 xunjing bu
Ministry of Public Works 工部 gongbu
Ministry of Revenue 户部 hubu
Ministry of Rites 礼部 libu
Ministry of War 兵部 bingbu
Mixed Court 会审公廨 huishen gongxie

Mongol High Court of Justice 大宗正府 dazong zhengfu
Mounted Courier 走马承受 zouma chengshou
National University 太学 taixue
National University Student 监生 jiansheng
New Treatise on Government 资政新篇 zizheng xinpian
Nine Ministers 九卿 jiuqing
Nine Ministers of the Chamberlains of the Imperial Secretariat 尚书九卿 shangshu jiuqing
Nine-Rank Selection Method 九品中正 jiupin zhongzheng
Northern Chief Prison 北镇抚司 bei zhenfusi
Observer 观政 (进士任官前) guanzheng (jinshi renguan qian)
Office Manager (Supervisor of an Agency's Internal Clerical Work) 都事 dushi
Office of Commanders-General of the Infantry 步军统领衙门 bujun tongling yamen
Office of Commanders-in-Chief of the Eight Banners 八旗都统衙门 baqi dutong yamen
Office of Hanlin Bachelors 庶常馆 shuchang guan
Office of the Censorate 御史府 yushi fu
Office of the Superintendency of Penal Affairs 提点刑狱司 tidian xingyu si
Office of Transmission 通政使司 tongzhengshi si
Officers Inside/Outside the Curtain 内帘官 neilian guan/外帘官 wailian guan
Official Inspection Office 审官院 shenguan yuan
Optimus (Metropolitan Graduate with Honors) 状元 zhuangyuan
Ordinary Grand Master 中大夫 zhong dafu
Outline of Imperial Constitution 钦定宪法大纲 qingding xianfa dagang
Overseer of Bandits 司寇 sikou
Overseer of Lord Lineages 公族 gongzu
Overseer of Mounts 司马 sima
Overseer of Ritual Affairs 宗伯 zongbo
Overseer of the Masses/Minister of Education 司徒 situ
Pacification Commission 宣慰司 xuanwei si
Pacification Commissioner 宣抚使 xuanfu shi
Palace Administrator of Finance 少府 shaofu
Palace Aide to the Censor-in-Chief (Vice Censor-in-Chief) 御史中丞 yushi zhongcheng
Palace Attendant 侍中 shizhong
Palace Bureau 殿院 dianyuan
Palace Censor/Attendant Supervisor 侍御史 shiyushi
Palace Command 殿前马步司狱 dianqian mabu siyu
Palace Depot 内行厂 neixingchang
Palace Examination 御试 yushi/廷试 (元) tingshi (Yuan Dynasty)
Palace Memorial 密折 mizhe
Palace Secretariat 中书省 zhongshu sheng
Palace Supervisor 殿中侍御史 dianzhong shiyushi
Pan Tax 灶课 zhaoke

Para-Secretary-Reviewer 同中书门下平章事 tongzhongshu menxia pingzhangshi
Para-Third-Ranking Official 同中书门下三品 tongzhongshu menxia sanpin
Patrolling Censor 巡城御史 xuncheng yushi
Pingzheng Yuan (Supreme Administrative Court) 平政院 pingzheng yuan
Placation Commission 安抚司 anfu si
Police Intendant 巡警道 xunjing dao
Policy Questions 策问 cewen
Posts of the Third- and Fourth-Rank at the Ministries and the Censorate, Appointed through Selection 请简官 qingjian guan
Precedent Student 例贡 ligong
Prefectural Examination 解试 jieshi
Prefecture 府 fu
Prefecture Commander 都尉 duwei
Prime Minister 丞相 chengxiang
Princes and Grand Ministers 王大臣 wang dachen
Principal Seal-Holding Official 正印官 zheng yinguan
Principle List of Graduates 正榜 (乡试) zhengbang (xiangshi)
Private Secretaries 幕友 muyou
Provincial Commissions for Army Reorganization 督练处 dulianchu
Provincial Education Commissioner 提督学政 tidu xuezheng
Provincial Graduate 举人 juren
Provincial Military Commission 督练公所 dulian gongsuo
Provincial Nominee 乡贡 xianggong
Provincial Secretariat 承宣厅 chengxuan ting
Provincial Surveillance Commission 省按察司 shengancha si
Provost 学录 xuelu
Public Functionaries 职官 zhiguan
Public Petitioners Drum Office 登闻鼓厅 dengwengu ting
Quality Evaluation by the Ministry of Personnel 铨选 quanxuan
Receptionist 通事 tongshi
Receptionist-Secretary 通事舍人 tongshi sheren
Recruitment and Appointment on Imperial Order/Invitation 征辟 zhengbi
Rectifier 补阙 buque, 中正 zhongzheng
Red scripts 朱卷 zhujuan
Region/Prefecture/Sub-prefecture/Department 州 zhou
Regional Administrative Commission 布政司 buzheng si
Regional Administrative Commissioner 布政使 buzheng shi
Regional Administrative Commissioner and Surveillance Commissioner 蕃臬两司 fannie liangsi
Regional Assistant 部丞 bucheng
Regional General 将军开府 jiangju kaifu
Regional Governor 州牧 zhoumu
Regional Inspector 刺史 cishi
Regional Ruler 方伯 fangbo

Regional Supervisor/Provincial Governor/Grand Coordinator 巡抚 xunfu
Registrar 主簿 zhubu
Relief Supervisor 提举常平司 tiju changping si
Remonstrance Official 谏官 jianguan
Remonstrator 司谏 sijian
Restricted Regional Inspector 单车刺史 danche cishi
Revenue Section/Ministry of Section 度支曹 duzhi cao/司 si
Right Bureau of the Court of Judicial Review 右治狱 you zhiyu
Right Scribe/Historiographer 右史 youshi
Rituals Supervisor 司礼监 sili jian
Royal Scribe 御史(周朝) yushi (Zhou Dynasty)
Runners 衙役 yayi
Salt Administrator 盐政 yanzheng
Salt Controller 盐运使 yanyun shi
Salt Distribution Commission 盐转运使 yanzhuanyun shi
Salt Distribution Superintendency 盐课提举yanke tiju
Salt Intendant 盐法道 yanfa dao
Salt Taxes Supervisor 盐课提举司 yanke tiju si
Scholar Class 士阶层 si jieceng
Scholar-Gentry (Local Elite) 士绅 shishen
Scholar-Official/Scholar-Bureaucrat 士大夫 shidafu
School for the Sons of the State 国子学 guozi xue
Secretarial Censor 治书侍御史 zhishu shiyushi
Secretarial Court Gentleman 台郎 tailang
Secretariat Drafters 中书舍人 zhongshu sheren
Secretariat-Chancellery 中书门下 zhongshu menxia
Secretary 主事 zhushi
Secretary for the Three Dukes 三公曹 sangong cao
Section Clerk 曹缘 caoyuan
Section for Commandery Governors (2000-Bushel Officials) 二千石曹 liangqiandan cao
Section for General Administration 中都官曹 zhongduguan cao
Section for Receptions 客曹 kecao
Section for Regular Attendants 常侍曹changshi cao
Section for the Civil Population 民曹 mincao
Section of Personnel 吏曹 licao
Section, a generic term for specialized units among which the clerical or administrative staffs of larger agencies were distributed, found at all levels 曹 cao
Secundus (Metropolitan Graduate with Honors) 榜眼 bangyan
Senior Compilers of the Hanlin Academy 翰林院修撰 hanlinyuan xiuzhuan
Senior Rectifier 大中正 dazhongzheng
Servicemen/Elite 士 shi
Services that have to be performed in person 力差 lichai
Single Whip Method of Taxation 一条鞭法 yitiaobian fa

Six Ministers of the Six Ministries 六部尚书 liubu shangshu
Six Ministries 六部 liubu
Six Offices of Scrutiny 六科给事中 liuke jishizhong
Soldiers Guarding Numbered Cells 号军 haojun
South Studio 南书房 nan shufang
Southern Chief Prison 南镇抚司 nan zhenfusi
Special Aides of the South Studio 南书房行走 nanshufang xingzou
Subofficial Functionary 吏 li, 文吏 wenli, 胥吏 xuli
Subofficial of County Magistrate 县佐 xianzuo
Sub-regional Administrative Commissioner 分守道 fenshou dao
Sub-regional Judiciary Commissioner 分巡道 fenxun dao
Substitute Audience 聘 (周) pin (Zhou Dynasty)
Superintendent of Finance 治粟内史 zhisu neishi
Superintendent of Palace Buildings 大匠卿 dajiang qing
Superintendent of Protocols 典客 dianke
Superintendent of Rituals 奉常 fengchang
Superintendent of the Imperial Clan 宗正 zongzheng
Superintendent of the Imperial Treasury 大府卿 taifu qing
Superintendent of Waterways 都水卿 dushui qing
Superior Grand Master of the Palace 太中大夫 tai zhong dafu
Superior Lord 上公 shanggong
Supervising Censor of the Six Offices of Scrutiny 六科给事中 liuke jishizhong
Supervising Officials 提调 tidiao
Supervising Secretariats of the Censorate 科道 kedao
Supervising Secretary/Supervising Censor 给事中 jishizhong
Supervisor 中书监 zhongshujian
Supervisor of Confucian Schools 儒学提举司 ruxue tiju si
Supervisor of Constructions 司工 sigong
Supervisor 判部事 panbushi
Supervisory Bureau of Government Affairs 督办政务处 duban zhengwu shi
Supervisory Commissioner 制置使 zhizhi shi
Supervisory Imperial Clerk 监御史 jianyushi
Supreme Court of Justice (Qing) 大理院 (清) dali yuan (Qing Dynasty)
Surveillance Commission 按察司 ancha si,提刑按察司 tixiang ancha si
Surveillance Commissioner 按察使 ancha shi, 观察使 guancha shi/巡按使 xunan shi
Temple of Distant Ancestors 祧庙 tiaomiao
Territorial Representative 朝集使 chaoji shi
Tertius (Metropolitan Graduate with Honors) 探花 tanhua
Three Commissioners 三司使 sansi shi
Three Commissions 三司 sansi
Three Dukes 三公 sangong
Three Dukes and Six ministers 三公六卿 sangong liuqing
Three Guardians 三辅 sanfu
Three Judicial Offices 三法司 sanfa si

Three Judicial Offices System 三司推事 sansi tuishi
Tribute Student 举贡 jugong
Tribute Student of Excellence 优贡 yougong
Tribute Students for Preeminence 拔贡 (生) bagong(sheng)
Tri-tax System 租庸调制 zuyong tiaozhi
Two-Season Taxation System 两税法 liangshui fa
Vice Censor-in-Chief 副都御史 fu duyushi
Vice Commander-General 副都统 fu dutong
Vice Director 员外郎 yuanwai lang
Vice Magistrate 州同 zhoutong
Vice Minister of Justice 刑部员外郎 xingbu yuanwai lang
Vice Minister of the Court of Judicial Review 大理寺少卿 dalisi shaoqing
Well-Field System 井田制 jingtianzhi
Western Depot 西厂 xichang

The manufacturer's authorised representative in the EU is Springer Nature Customer Service Centre GmbH, Europaplatz 3, 69115 Heidelberg, Germany. If you have any concerns regarding our products, please contact ProductSafety@springernature.com

Printed and bound by CPI Group (UK) Ltd, Croydon, CR0 4YY
01/10/2026
02225929-0017